Korean
Filmography

Korean War Filmography

91 English Language
Features through 2000

ROBERT J. LENTZ

McFarland & Company, Inc., Publishers
Jefferson, North Carolina, and London

The present work is a reprint of the illustrated case bound edition of Korean War Filmography: 91 English Language Features through 2000, *first published in 2003 by McFarland*.

LIBRARY OF CONGRESS CATALOGUING-IN-PUBLICATION DATA

Lentz, Robert J., 1960–
Korean war filmography : 91 English
language features through 2000 /
Robert J. Lentz.
p.   cm.
Includes bibliographical references and index.

ISBN 978-0-7864-3876-1
softcover : 50# alkaline paper ∞

1. Korean War, 1950–1953 — Motion pictures and the
war.   2. Motion pictures — United States — History.   3. Korean
War, 1950–1953 — Motion pictures and the war — Film catalogs.
4. War films — United States — History and criticism.   I. Title.
DS918.16.L46   2003   016.79143'658 — dc21   2002015084

British Library cataloguing data are available

Cover photograph: *M*A*S*H*, 1970
(20th Century–Fox Film Corporation)

Manufactured in the United States of America

*McFarland & Company, Inc., Publishers
Box 611, Jefferson, North Carolina 28640
www.mcfarlandpub.com*

For those who served,

and for my father,
James R. Lentz,
a World War II veteran
who always enjoyed
a good war movie

ACKNOWLEDGMENTS

I would like to thank everyone who helped make this book a reality. Madeline F. Matz and the staff of the Library of Congress, and Kristine Krueger and the staff of the Margaret Herrick Library were very helpful with furthering my research.

Many thanks to Sheryl Aumack, Jim Berrien, Eddie Brandt's Saturday Matinee, John Buckley, James Buffington, Barbara and Jerry Douglass, E. Hagen, the late Alan Henwood, George Johnson, the Library of Congress, Robert Manerchia, R. D. Mitchell, the UCLA Film and Television Archive and others who provided many obscure Korean War titles so that this book could be written.

Jerry Ohlinger and the staff of Jerry Ohlinger's Movie Material Store (New York), Jim Shepard of Collectors Book Store and the staff of Eddie Brandt's Saturday Matinee (Hollywood), Tom Boyle and the staff of Yesterday (Chicago) and Art Harvey (New Jersey) were especially helpful in procuring stills and movie artwork.

Studios and production companies represented by photographs and artwork include Aaron Spelling Productions, All Girl Productions, Allied Artists, the American Broadcasting Company, American International Pictures, Aspen Productions, Associated Producers Inc., Bernhard Productions, Border Productions, Breakston-McGowan Productions, Breakston-Stahl Productions, British Lion Films, Camera Eye Pictures, the Cannon Group, Carl Krueger Productions, Cinema-Video International, Columbia Pictures Corporation, Cy Roth Productions, David L. Wolper Productions, Deputy Corporation Productions, Eagle-Lion, Eastern Film Productions, Fernwood-Reynard Productions, Heath Productions, Hemdale Film Corporation, Home Box Office Pictures, Ishihara International Productions, Ivan Tors Productions, Jack Schwarz Productions, Jaguar Productions, Ken Kennedy Productions, Lippert Pictures, M. C. Productions, Manson Distributing Corporation, Melville Productions, Metro-Goldwyn-Mayer, One Way Productions, Oranda Films, Pacemaker Productions, Paramount Pictures, Paul Mart Productions, Perlberg-Scaton Productions, Rainbow Productions, Realart, Republic Pictures Corporation, RKO Radio Pictures, Rockingham Productions, Roncom Films, Rysher Entertainment, Samuel Goldwyn Productions, Savoy Pictures, Security Pictures, Spartan Productions, Spring Creek Productions, Springfield Productions, T-D Enterprises, Tiger Productions, Toluca Productions, 20th Century-Fox, Underwater Productions, United Artists, United States Pictures Productions, Universal, Warner Bros., Wessex Film Productions, William Goetz Productions and Wray Davis Productions. Photographs and advertising illustrations are used only to present their properties which, due to their Korean War content, are discussed and reviewed in this book.

Michael Ferguson listened patiently and offered suggestions on how to improve the book, while my wife Barbara served as muse and proofreader, correcting my grammatical mistakes. Any mistakes that appear in this book are my own.

— R.J.L., October, 2002

CONTENTS

INTRODUCTION

The Korean War has been called — and is still widely considered — the Forgotten War. Though it lasted three years at a cost of more than fifty-four thousand American lives (not to mention the fourteen thousand personnel of the twenty-two other countries under the United Nations banner, or the forty-six thousand personnel from South Korea's army killed in action), the Korean War was never a popular cause for the American public and was never widely supported.

President Truman's "police action" became the bridge between World War II's fight for global freedom and the confused jungle fighting in Vietnam. It was America's first war of limited scope, designed to stop the Communist aggression in South Korea without leading to global warfare against the Soviet Union or Red China. Events during the war led directly to the humiliating public retirement of General Douglas MacArthur and greatly fanned the fires of the Communist-hunting blacklistings in the United States. The Korean War ended America's relatively happy post-war years and reminded the world that even the threat of atomic destruction would not prevent armed aggression.

One of many ways to gauge the social impact of the Korean War is to examine Hollywood's various depictions of the conflict. Cinema can be seen as a mirror in which we are able to witness ourselves, our actions and our beliefs. Because films usually reflect the social attitudes of the times, they are invaluable in looking back at our history, even when that history is distorted or misrepresented, as often occurs. This book will examine the films of the Korean War and attempt to place those films in the proper historical context, assess the essential truthfulness of each film in regard to the war and judge each film's intrinsic entertainment value.

Films about the Forgotten War reflect that war's anonymity. It is undeniable that the majority of Korean War films are of minor status. Most people would be hard-pressed to name five Korean War films; to name ten would be most impressive. Nevertheless, study of these films as a genre can provide a valuable view of the time and the pervasive social attitudes of that time, especially when compared to World War II and Vietnam War dramas. Just as this particular war provokes differing responses in people than the previous and later international conflicts, so do the films about the war.

The fact that there are few classic films about the Korean War accurately reflects the confusion, ambivalence and lack of understanding about the war by filmmakers as well as the public. During the conflict, American film studios saw the war as an excuse to make (and make money with) war pictures and as a result some Korean War films are indistinguishable from World War II films. These movies are filled with stereotypes, clichés, gun battles and fiery explosions, and are meant to be nothing more than an exciting (though all too often not) way to pass eighty minutes. Films such as *Air Strike, Hell's Horizon, Sky Commando* and *Iron Angel* are neither instructive nor incisive, although they do fit within the normal parameters of the Hollywood war film.

The best Korean War films are the ones which pass beyond those familiar parameters into uncharted territory. Of course, this is true for most genres. The classic films which define various genres usually attempt to do more than their imitators, which tend to scale back character and plot to their basic elements.

It is often said that Hollywood is five years behind the times; that is, a topic of great interest today will be one or more major motion pictures five years down the road. While this development time is often necessary, it should be noted that films regarding the fighting began to appear in 1951, during the war's second year. During the actual fighting from 1950 to 1953, some twenty films which examined specific aspects of the international situation were released by Hollywood.

Most of these (excepting Samuel Fuller's two treatises on war — *Fixed Bayonets!* and *The Steel Helmet*) were strictly minor movies. All of the film studios saw the timeliness inherent in Korean War films and quickly manufactured a few of them to take advantage of what popular interest there was. The small studios — Allied Artists, Realart, Republic, RKO, etc. — focused on battle stories which they could produce cheaply with Department of Defense aid and stock battle footage from Korea or World War II. The larger studios — 20th Century–Fox, Columbia, Paramount, MGM, etc. — leaned more toward specific angles (intensive military training in *Take the High Ground!*, a MASH unit in *Battle Circus*, G.I. integration with Greek soldiers in *The Glory Brigade*, prison camps in *Prisoner of War* and *The Bamboo Prison*, etc.) than the generic battle stories favored by the smaller studios.

After the war ended, however, Holly-

wood's big studios finally began to make truly major motion pictures about the war. Between 1954 and 1959 the biggest and most popular films about the war — *The Bridges at Toko-Ri, The McConnell Story, Men in War, Battle Hymn, The Hunters, Time Limit, The Eternal Sea, Men of the Fighting Lady, Pork Chop Hill* — were made and released. Thus, the five-year truism was largely accurate, at least in terms of major Hollywood product.

Soon after the war's conclusion, Hollywood scriptwriters had assessed the war, chosen general subjects (the air war, P.O.W.s, racism, etc.), specific settings and incidents (the inner workings of an aircraft carrier or the helicopter rescue service; the battle for Pork Chop Hill or the prosecution of soldiers who were accused of collaborating with the enemy) and people (the lives and military careers of fighter ace Joseph D. McConnell, Jr., one-legged Admiral John Hoskins, fighter pilot and minister Dean Hess, etc.) to pinpoint in high profile movies. For further analysis of themes and subjects of these war movies, refer to the element listings of Appendix D.

The cycle of high profile Korean War films continued at a slower pace after 1958, with only one or two major releases per year — *Pork Chop Hill, All the Young Men, The Great Impostor, War Hunt* — and reached its pinnacle in 1962 with the nightmare vision of *The Manchurian Candidate.* After that, the Korean War would appear sporadically in big films (*MASH, MacArthur, Inchon*) but was largely forgotten. With the fiftieth anniversary of the Korean War just past, it is an opportune time to take a look back at the last half-century of cinema and examine just how filmmakers have explored various facets and experiences of the Korean War.

This book references ninety-one English language films, most of them from Hollywood, which dramatize some aspect of the Korean War. Some are fictional representations of the war; others are historically authentic. Some take place solely on the faraway, bloody battleground of Korea; others occur right here in the States, as young men of draft age face a frightening future. Some are intensely dramatic, a few horrific and some are surprisingly funny. Many are dull; a few are nerve-wracking. All are movies about a period in our history with which most people are relatively unfamiliar.

To qualify for inclusion and commentary in this book, each film had to fulfill at least one of two criteria (and preferably both): at least some of the film's story and action must be set in Korea during the war, or the war must be important enough to the film's story that character action is affected by the war. Thus, *Love is a Many-Splendored Thing* qualifies because William Holden's war correspondent character visits U.N. troops and sees enemy action firsthand (though only briefly near the movie's end), *I Want You* because of the war's pervasive effect on the rural American life of its characters, and *Back at the Front* and *Geisha Girl* because the war profoundly affects the films' action six hundred miles away in Japan. Others, such as *The Rack, Japanese War Bride, Top Secret Affair* and *Chattahoochee* refer to specific (fictional) incidents which occurred during the war which are crucial to their storylines. Thus, they are included as well.

There are three films which are only generally included, however, because copies could not be found for viewing. *Marine Battleground* (1966), *No Man's Land* (1964) and *War Is Hell* (1964) are definitely Korean War films, and should be noted as such, but they simply, and unfortunately, could not be fully covered here. There are a few others which may also qualify as Korean War films, but they also could not be located. These titles are *Here Come the Jets* (1959), *Mission Inferno* (1984), *Ride the High Iron* (1956) and *A Yank in Indo-China* (1952). Reader help in locating these obscure titles would be appreciated.

Approximately half of the included films are set exclusively during the war and feature fairly extensive battle action. A much smaller number follow a character from World War II to Korea while others have characters who interact with the war for a short time or only peripherally. Still others feature people's memories of the war through flashbacks or are genre films which happen to earmark the war in some fashion. All are linked to the war strongly enough to warrant inclusion and commentary.

As a whole, these films form a general impression of the war from the American frame of reference. For additional perspectives, four further sections are included. The first is a concise history of the actual war, with sidebars which describe various cinematic efforts to dramatize historical events. This is included as a chapter, "The Korean Conflict 1950–1953," before the main text, and can be used for familiarization with significant events during the war. Second is a listing of films with "incidental" references to the war. This section, which appears as Appendix E, briefly discusses a sampling of films with tangential relationships to the war. Third, Appendix F, is a non-comprehensive listing of non-fiction documentary and compilation films spotlighting various aspects of the war; almost all of these films are also English-language. These are listed in alphabetical order and are provided for further reference.

The fourth listing, Appendix G, illuminates films about the war which were made and released in South Korea. Compiled and written by Darcy Paquet of the Institute of Foreign Language Studies of Korea University in Seoul, this section introduces some of the more famous cinematic chronicles of the war from the country which suffered the most because of it. The addition of such a listing is a happy one, and adds an extra layer of depth to this work. For further information, visit Darcy's website, www.Koreanfilm.org on the internet.

Completing the book are four additional appendices which collate the films in four ways: chronologically (Appendix A); by production company and distributor (Appendix B); by levels of historical accuracy and patriotic propaganda, as judged by the author (Appendix C); and by subject and thematic elements, which are defined and discussed (Appendix D). A detailed bibliography of critical references for each film is included, as is a comprehensive index. It is hoped that these elements and the commentary of the text will reveal a seldom seen side of modern cinema — films of the Korean War.

This book is intended to provide the fullest picture possible of Korean War films. Each plot is discussed in detail — meaning that story secrets and surprises are unavoidably revealed and often deliberated. It is recommended that readers view the films before consulting the text, or at least be aware that "spoilers" are scattered throughout.

—*R.J.L.*

THE KOREAN CONFLICT
1950–1953

There are many histories of the Korean War which delve deeply into the military, socio-economic, political and human aspects of the conflict; for a thorough understanding of "The Forgotten War," such books are definitely recommended reading. Please consult this chapter's bibliography for a listing of such sources. This chapter is intended to provide a basic overview of the so-called "police action," and to indicate which important incidents, trends and personalities were later dramatized in films about the Korean War. Commentary regarding films is italicized and follows the historical information on which such films are based.

Korea is a large peninsula roughly the size of the state of Kansas which protrudes southward from the southeast region of China. Korea, with the Yellow Sea to its west and the Sea of Japan to its east, separates the islands of Japan from China. Almost all of Korea's land boundary borders China; a mere eleven miles at the northeastern tip borders Russia. Its location between three powerful countries has always made Korea an important strategic point, and has ensured that Korea has had to endure a bloody history.

The whole of Korea had been invaded and occupied by Japan during the brief Sino-Japanese War of 1894–95, became a Japanese protectorate after the Russo-Japanese War of 1905 and was formally annexed by Japan in 1910. Korea remained under Japanese control until the end of World War II, when it was finally provided with long-promised independence. At least, that was the international plan.

At the end of World War II, Russian forces occupied the northern half of the peninsula and American forces occupied the area south of the 38th parallel. A provisional agreement was made that these forces would remain until a unified Korean government could be established. Three years later, after much political wrangling and discussion, efforts to unify the country were abandoned. Separate governments were established in each half of the country, with each claiming ultimate authority for the entire peninsula. The result was a political stalemate which divided the country across the middle, with the Communist Soviet Union supporting the North and the democratic United States supporting the South.

Russia formally withdrew its troops in 1948 and America followed suit in 1949, theoretically leaving the two halves of a divided nation to negotiate their own destiny. Although Russia had withdrawn its troops, it had not abandoned the idea of forcing Communism upon all of Korea. Russia secretly (or at least discreetly) provided tanks, artillery, aircraft, other weapons and military training to the North Korean forces, the army of the deceptively named Democratic People's Republic of Korea. Meanwhile, the army of South Korea — the Republic of Korea — was undermanned, largely untrained and unprepared for the imminent danger from the north.

On a rainy Sunday morning at 4 a.m. — July 25, 1950 — seven assault divisions of the North Korean infantry, supported by one hundred fifty Russian-made T-34 tanks, swept across the 38th parallel and invaded South Korea. Approximately 89,000 soldiers marched twenty-five miles to Seoul, the South Korean capital, and captured it in just four days. The South Korean army numbered just 38,000 soldiers and had no tanks or artillery, and many of its soldiers were on leave when the well-planned invasion took place. The first phase of the war began, and there was little resistance.

Curiously, few Korean War films deal directly with the invasion. **Inchon** *does dramatize the situation, but does so inaccurately and with an unfortunate American slant, as lovely Jacqueline Bisset is imperiled by the Communist advance while anonymous South Koreans suffer and die.* **Korea Patrol** *takes place on the first two days of the invasion but is not an authentic view of the situation.* **One Minute to Zero** *offers an intriguing glimpse of that fateful morning, but it is very brief and curiously underplayed. The invasion is rarely dramatized because the Americans simply weren't there. The invasion took everyone by surprise, actual film footage of the attack is extremely rare and American lives were not yet involved. When the invasion is dramatized on film, it's usually done with a big explosion, the year "1950" superimposed on the screen and stock footage of tanks rumbling across rural countryside.*

News of the invasion is included in many Korean War films, but most often, it is simply reported over the radio in scenes designed to show American soldiers' feelings when asked to travel overseas and fight. Typical is Mark Stevens' caustic dialogue in **Torpedo Alley** *when told the news: "How about that. Every time I join the Navy, somebody starts a war."*

As the North Korean army moved closer, Seoul was evacuated. Civilian refugees jammed the roads heading south, mingling with soldiers moving south to the new ROK army headquarters established at Taejon. South Korean soldiers had abandoned much of their equipment as they fled south in panic. The state of panic reached its peak when the South Korean army chief of staff destroyed a strategic bridge over the Han River immediately after crossing it himself. North Korean soldiers were still six to eight hours away, but General Chae Pyong Duk ordered the bridge demolished though it was packed with soldiers and civilians also heading for safety. Estimates are that five hundred to eight hundred South Koreans died on the bridge because their general couldn't wait and didn't care. General Duk was killed in action several weeks later.

Perhaps the most tragic and senseless act of the war is the demolition of the Han River bridge, crowded as it was with civilian refugees and ROK soldiers. Only **Inchon** *recreates this sad moment, but it again distorts history. In the movie, an enemy tank attacks the bridge and the refugees are provided time to jump into the river. And lovely Jacqueline Bisset, in a car with five young Korean children, miraculously escapes the explosion.*

In the United States, word of the invasion reached President Harry S Truman at his home in Independence, Missouri. The U.S. ambassador to Korea contacted the State Department with the news of "an all out offensive against ROK," and John Foster Dulles, a special advisor to Secretary of State Dean Acheson, cabled that "[I] believe that if it appears the South Koreans cannot themselves contain or repulse the attack, United States forces should be used even though this risks Russian counter moves. To sit by while Korea is overrun by unprovoked armed attack would start [a] disastrous chain of events leading most probably to world war."

President Truman's reaction to the invasion news is dramatized in the excellent biographical and historical film **Collision Course: Truman vs. MacArthur** and in **Truman**. Both films examine the Truman administration's response to the threat of international Communist aggression and the president's determination to halt it in its initial stage. Both films, coming more than two decades after the actual events, are shaped by retrospection and historical perspective, but they do convey the president's shock and fervent determination to prevent another world war.

Truman immediately called an emergency session of the United Nations, giving the young international organization its first important test. A resolution was passed which condemned the North Korean aggression and called for an "immediate cessation of hostilities" and withdrawal. The United Nations resolution was passed unanimously because Russia had been boycotting meetings for the previous five months in protest over the exclusion of Communist China from the organization. Because Russia was absent once again, the U.N. was able to pass the resolution with little difficulty. In Korea, the U.N. resolution was resolutely ignored.

Two days after the hostilities began, the U.N. Security Council took a further step, resolving that "the members of the United Nations furnish such assistance to the Republic of Korea as may be necessary to repel the armed attack and to restore international peace and security in the area." Because Russia was again absent from the vote, the call for action was passed unanimously and without dissension. Twenty-two countries answered the call and sent men and women to the world's hottest spot; sixteen of those countries provided ground forces to fight the Communist aggression.

Various movies do spotlight United Nations actions and contributions made during the war. Two of the first three Hollywood films about the war, **Korea Patrol** and **A Yank in Korea**, feature actual footage of the United Nations first resolution being adopted before beginning their stories, which take place at the commencement of the war. Later, **The Glory Brigade** shows how American and Greek soldiers (sometimes uneasily) combine their skills to fight the Red menace, while the British-made **A Hill in Korea** (aka **Hell in Korea**) depicts the battle action of a British platoon. The Royal Canadian Navy is featured in **The Great Impostor**, though its focus is on chameleon Ferdinand Demara, Jr. **Field of Honor**, made in the Netherlands, features a Dutch platoon that encounters enemy action. And of course, quite a few movies also feature token British, Australian or European soldiers involved in the fight.

The American military response to the Korean invasion was placed in the hands of General Douglas MacArthur, who was quickly appointed supreme commander of the United Nations forces. MacArthur was in Tokyo, just six hundred miles from Seoul, in charge of the Japanese reconstruction effort after World War II. He was confident that the North Koreans could be stopped, but he first had to organize and facilitate a resistance utilizing the meager forces present at the scene. Air and sea forces were given permission to attack the invaders, and the first air encounter between the U.S. and North Korea occurred on June 27, the day of Truman's authorization of force against North Korean troops. This battle resulted in three Russian-built Yak fighter planes being downed by U.S. F-82 fighter planes. Four more Yaks were destroyed in other battles the same day, which lessened the North Korean air force by a percentage of one-sixth.

Relatively few films cover this early aspect of the air war, although **Battle Hymn** and **Dragonfly Squadron** do make the attempt. Both of these films were based on experiences by Colonel Dean Hess, who was entrusted with the job of training Republic of Korea pilots to fly American fighters. It would be months later, as Russian-made MiG fighter jets entered the scene and the air war intensified, that filmmakers began to take closer notice of Korea's air war.

After Seoul was captured, MacArthur received Truman's permission to use ground forces and on June 30th, five days after the initial invasion, American Eighth Army troops landed at Pusan and headed north to join the fight to save South Korea. The initial U.S. ground forces engaged the North Koreans at Suwon, retreating six hours later with more than 20 percent casualties. They had not been able to stop the advance of North Korean tanks and had been enveloped by the North Koreans, who attacked the flanks of the American force rather than the front. The North Koreans did not use radios; they deployed their men by the signals of bugles and whistles.

*The North Korean (and later, Chinese) sounding of bugles to direct military maneuvers was a distinctive note of the war, one which was used many times, but is, strangely, included in relatively few Korean War films. **Pork Chop Hill** is the most effective to present this practice, depicting the fear and confusion of American soldiers having to face the audible signal of enemy advancement. In **Fixed Bayonets!**, an enemy bugle is captured and played by an American soldier, causing much confusion for Chinese commanders.*

Over the first few days of July, American forces landed at Pusan, were motored to points north of Pusan and told to hold back the North Korean army. Time was the ultimate goal: time to locate, organize and deliver heavy weapons and ammunition to the front; time to move experienced troops into position with an effective battle plan. Each division sent north of Pusan was a stopgap measure to give MacArthur and his generals time to prepare for what had become a serious shooting war. Time and time again, however, the North Koreans drove their tanks through American lines, enveloped American positions and watched as the American and South Korean troops turned and ran after being surrounded, often leaving their weapons, supplies and radios behind.

Back in the states, President Truman decided not to ask for a congressional declaration of war. He wanted to avoid angering or threatening the Soviets or Chinese and hoped to contain the fighting quickly enough to avoid a larger confrontation. William F. Knowland, a Republican Senator from Cali-

fornia, coined the term "police action," which Truman promptly appropriated for his own use. At a June 27 news conference, Truman attempted to clarify the issue for the media:

Q: Mr. President, everybody is asking in this country, are we or are we not at war?

A: We are not at war.... The members of the United Nations are going to the relief of the Korean Republic to suppress a bandit raid on the Republic of Korea.

Q: Mr. President, would it be correct under your explanation to call this a police action under the United Nations?

A: Yes, that is exactly what it amounts to.

The distinction between a "police action" and a congressional definition of war is an important one. Since Truman's precedent, Congress has not been asked to declare war in Vietnam, Grenada, Panama or the Persian Gulf. Such avoidance of the congressional declaration process leaves control of any aggressive military action firmly in the hands of the president. If the president does not seek political approval, he does not have to listen to their wishes or instructions regarding his actions. For "limited" conflicts, which is how the Korean situation was viewed, the president wanted his hands free and untied by political constraints, but he also wished for the absence of a national declaration, which would have been sure to threaten the Communist empires of China and Russia.

Politically the distinction is an important one, but the fighting men and regular Joes in Korean War movies regard the term "police action" disdainfully. In almost every case, the term is muttered with contempt, either because a "police action" isn't viewed as being as important or exciting as a real war, or because of its limitations. Fighting forces fight to win, but one cannot win a "police action." The films which recognize that the war is not being fought to be won contain a mistrust of the political process which has designated American soldiers as policemen and in some cases a disdain for the military for being used for that purpose.

The key difference between World War II films and Korean War films is that, generally speaking, World War II protagonists fight for a cause which is easy to understand and support. Although the cause of our involvement in the Korean War was clear, its objectives were not. Thus, the Korean War film protagonists face complex moral, political and military dilemmas with no easy answers. The men and women in these movies often openly question their orders, their futures and the reasons for being in Korea at all. And most of them are unhappy about being there.

The North Korean army continued to push south throughout July, and the American forces suffered heavy casualties in battles at Chonan and Taejon. Throughout the steaming 105° days of August, General Walton "Bulldog" Walker rallied American and South Korean troops behind the Naktong River, on the southeastern corner of the Korean peninsula, backed against the Sea of Japan. This second phase of the war was dubbed the "Pusan Perimeter" and was ordered to be held at all costs while MacArthur pieced together a fighting force from military units arriving in the area from the United States and several other U.N. members. Reinforcements and replacements were sent to Pusan and put into place by General Walker, who moved the military units like chess pieces to the areas where they were most needed. Despite fierce attacks by the North Koreans in a desperate attempt to push the U.N. forces into the sea, the Pusan Perimeter held into September.

The weeks that the United Nations forces held the Pusan Perimeter were perhaps the most crucial of the war, yet few Korean War films acknowledge the importance of this "holding" strategy. It is probable that Hollywood producers could not see the heroic possibilities of an ongoing battle where victory was measured by holding the status quo. **Flight Nurse**, **Inchon**, **MacArthur** and **One Minute to Zero** refer in passing to the Pusan Perimeter, but in these films it is simply a respite between battle action.

Most Korean War films do, however, make note of the sweltering heat of South Korea. Films downplay the horrible smell of the open fields (where human excrement was used as fertilizer), but a large number of films make a point of verbally or visually describing the heat and humidity that rusted weapons and turned roads into bogs of mud. One reason is that films shot in southern California could easily pass for South Korea during its summer. There are also films which depict the winter fighting in North Korea, but their quantity is much smaller.

Meanwhile, General MacArthur prepared a plan designed to ease the burden on the Pusan Perimeter and to change the course of the war with one decisive, offensive strike. His plan was titled "Operation Chromite" and involved an amphibious landing at the port of Inchon.

While U.N. military leaders in Japan, Korea and Washington D.C. recognized the need for such an operation, they were unanimously against invading Inchon. With its tidal swings of more than thirty feet, the Inchon harbor was considered difficult to navigate, and the severe tidal swings meant that ships could only approach the shoreline — and its fifteen-foot seawall — during the three hours of high tide. There would be a twelve-hour wait between high tides, forcing any troops that landed to stay on shore for that period of time, no matter what they encountered. Other factors were also unfavorable, leading to the consensus against MacArthur's chosen target. But MacArthur argued that its very difficulties made Inchon the perfect spot to strike, that this particular location was one sure to surprise and stun the North Koreans. The general pressed his case and, with only six days' advance notice, won final approval for his plan.

"Operation Chromite" was a smashing success and initiated the third phase of the war. On September 15, fifty thousand Marines and Army soldiers were safely transported to the shores of Inchon and pressed inland toward Seoul. Within two weeks, MacArthur's gamble had liberated the capital of Seoul, completely cut the North Korean supply lines heading south and sent the North Korean army scurrying back the way it had come. MacArthur had, with one swift and punishing blow, utterly disrupted the Communist advance and saved a country from total ruin. Inchon was a military master stroke and the crowning achievement of General Douglas MacArthur's illustrious career.

The amphibious landing at Inchon and the liberation of Seoul are dramatized in **MacArthur**, **Inchon** *and* **Retreat, Hell!** *and referenced in several other films. Actual footage of the invasion is briefly included in* **Collision Course: Truman vs. MacArthur**. *In every case, and for the best of reasons, the Inchon landing is viewed as America's brightest shining moment during the war. Its setting is perfect for Hollywood heroics: incredibly difficult and dangerous physical obstacles, the perceptive vision of one leader, the right timing to change the course of history. Most of the movies treat "Operation Chromite" with respect and awe; it is sad and unfortunate that the one film designed to sanctify the event itself,* **Inchon**, *trivializes the situation through ridiculous casting, historical distortion and the layering of a silly and illogical love story into its fabric.*

The role of the Navy in the Korean War was largely limited to support, patrol and use of aircraft carriers as launch platforms. Aircraft carriers are the central characters of **Men of the Fighting Lady**, **Air Strike**, **The Eternal Sea** *and* **The Bridges at Toko-Ri**. *Submarines were used during the war, but as depicted in the few Korean War submarine dramas like* **Submarine Command**, **Torpedo Alley** *and* **Underwater Warrior**, *they were mainly utilized for specialized raids on the Korean coast.* **Return From the Sea** *is about the only Korean War film that takes place on a regular Navy ship.*

As the North Koreans in South Korea realized that they were now trapped between two armies in hostile territory, many of them made a pragmatic choice, threw away their weapons, stripped off their uniforms and pretended to be civilian refugees. Indeed, one of the major difficulties for the U.N. troops was distinguishing between North and South Koreans. For many North Koreans who had been forcibly conscripted, it was the only avenue toward survival. They fended for food with the real refugees and took their chances. Others were South Koreans to begin with who

had been conscripted into North Korean service as the Communists swept southward. At the first opportunity, these people rejoined their own countrymen. Still others pretended to be refugees but continued to carry weapons under their loose clothing and disrupted U.N. policing whenever the opportunity arose.

The North Koreans took great advantage of their civilian anonymity. It became standard practice for North Korean soldiers to infiltrate battle lines dressed as civilians, and then attack the U.N. forces from the rear. During the early weeks of the war, U.N. forces were attacked from both front and rear simultaneously on several occasions after letting columns of refugees past their defensive positions. This, of course, raised the ire of the soldiers, but General William Dean forbade them from killing indiscriminately. "We won't kill civilians to kill the enemy." It was this situation which led to one of the most controversial incidents during the course of the war.

In September of 1999, the Associated Press reported statements from American veterans and South Korean civilians which referred to an incident where U.S. soldiers allegedly killed up to four hundred civilians beneath a railroad bridge at the town of No Gun Ri during the first month of the war. The story won the Pulitzer Prize for investigative journalism and sparked a governmental investigation that concluded in January of 2001, as President Clinton expressed regret for the loss of lives, which local Korean sources tabulated at 248. While stopping short of an official apology, Clinton did announce the establishment of a memorial and a scholarship fund in the memory of "these and all other innocent Korean civilians" killed during the war. Other such incidents are also being investigated, but they also seem to fall into the category of "tragedies of war."

Several movies reference this problem, but one in particular describes this very situation. **One Minute to Zero** *features a sequence when Robert Mitchum, as the general in charge, must decide how to control a parade of refugees, many of whom are believed to be Communist guerillas. His answer is to bomb the column, killing* *many people, including innocent refugees. The decision to include this episode intact caused the U.S. Department of Defense to withdraw its support from the production, but the film had already been completed. Yet the movie and this key sequence—which today seems tragically ridiculous, not to mention politically incorrect—drew scant attention from audiences or critics. Most people simply didn't care, as the victims were anonymous.*

MacArthur drove the U.N. troops northward after the retreating North Korean army. On October 9th, the Eighth Army crossed the 38th parallel and continued into North Korea on two separate fronts. MacArthur was determined "to clear out all North Korea, to unify it and liberalize it." South Korean President Syngman Rhee had long wished for a unified country to rule; now he urged his ROK army north, stating "We will not allow ourselves to stop!" The politicians in Washington were caught off-guard by the turn of events; they were stunned at the incredible success of the Inchon landing and were unable to finalize plans for the region ahead of MacArthur's northward rush. The intoxicating elixir of victory caused everyone in power to assess the situation with overconfidence, and too little regard was given to a warning from China not to cross the 38th parallel.

Throughout October 1950, U.N. troops marched northward into the mountains, meeting with reduced opposition from enemy troops. MacArthur broadcast two appeals for the North Koreans to surrender, which were totally ignored. Air Force and Navy fighter-bombers inflicted heavy damage on North Korean men and equipment, and the U.N. troops began to relax. Rumors flowed that the war "would be over by Christmas," once the fleeing North Koreans were pushed completely out of the country. The North Korean capital of Pyongyang was captured on October 19th, four days after a historic meeting occurred between President Truman and General MacArthur on Wake Island, during which MacArthur insisted that China would stay out of the war.

Many Korean War films show the ground-based U.N. forces calmly pushing northward, convinced that the war will be over within weeks. Almost all present this period as a time for relaxation for the troops. They talk about girls, food and what they will do when they get back home. They minimize the increasingly cold conditions and characterize the coming weeks as "a mop-up operation." Then comes news that the Chinese have entered the war en masse. The frivolity stops; the men realize that the fight will be tougher than ever, and that many of them will not be returning home.

*Infantrymen and Marines are the heart and soul of most Korean War movies, from **The Steel Helmet** to **Retreat, Hell!** They view Air Force pilots as "glamour boys" who watch from above while they do the real work on the ground. The wide majority of Korean War films focus on the plight of the foot soldier, whether he be facing death on the battlefield or "whooping it up" on leave in Japan. These films run the gamut of quality from inept to superb, and they, more than any other subgenre, are most representative of the actual fighting in Korea.*

Chinese "volunteers" began crossing the Yalu River southward into North Korea during October under cover of darkness. One hundred and fifty thousand Chinese troops, armed with Chinese and Russian weapons, moved at night and kept their presence concealed until October 25, just after General MacArthur issued orders "to secure all of North Korea." They struck at the northernmost U.N. troops, which were within forty miles of the Yalu River, and slaughtered hundreds of South Korean advance troops. The first reports of Chinese interdiction were not believed by the U.S. commanders, but within a few days it became apparent that not only had the Chinese joined the fight, but that they completely outnumbered the U.N. forces, which were spread across North Korea in a ragged line from coast to coast. The fourth, and most catastrophic, phase of the war began in earnest.

The Chinese specialized in pincer movements that enveloped the enemy. They would feign a frontal assault, then attack the flanks, probing for weaknesses of which they might take advantage. The Chinese, even more than the North Koreans, used bugles and whistles as signals, and when they attacked, the din of bugles, yelling voices and gun, mortar and artillery fire would be deafening. And the Chinese, perhaps because of their numerical superiority, did not seem concerned with a high percentage of casualties. Time and time again, they mobilized and attacked, running into concentrated fire from defensive positions. If they met with strong resistance, they would eventually withdraw; if resistance was weak, they would pour men into the area until the U.N. forces were overrun.

General MacArthur assessed the updated situation and decided that the Chinese were protecting the North Koreans, but would not continue to fight. He ordered a "final offensive" to the war to begin November 15th, but it was delayed until November 25th to better resupply the front-line units. As the offensive began, MacArthur could be heard on public radio detailing his battle plans, a fact that distressed officers who had been trying to keep them secret. With advance warning, the Chinese were ready and they pounced on the ROK and U.N. forces with incredible swiftness and power. Intense fighting for three days proved that the Chinese held superior numbers and were gaining ground. General Walton Walker called for a general withdrawal on November 29, 1950.

Thousands of U.S. Marines and Army soldiers were stationed near the Chosin (Changjin) Reservoir. They began the "final offensive" on November 25th and found that they were encircled by Chinese forces. The temperatures dipped to 30° below zero at night, freezing humans and their equipment alike. As many men died from exposure and frostbite as from Communist-fired bullets. A withdrawal was finally ordered on November 30th, and the next day, a long stream of men and equipment began the trek south, under fire, to the Sea of Japan, seventy-eight miles away. The trip took two weeks, with soldiers under sporadic fire all of the way, but almost twenty thousand troops returned to safety. War correspondents reported the retreat as a rare defeat for the U.S. Marine Corps, but General Oliver Smith of the corps defined the maneuver differently, saying "We are not retreating. We are merely attacking in another direction."

Under sporadic Communist fire, the Marines and soldiers tramped southward, carrying their wounded and dead with them on trucks or on stretchers. Two long weeks later, they arrived in Hungnam, a port city on the eastern coast of Korea, where hundreds of ships were evacuating men and materiel from the battle area. One fourth of the soldiers involved in the Chosin Reservoir campaign were killed, wounded or captured. Another quarter suffered from frostbite. But the rest made it back, with equipment largely intact, to be rested and redeployed in the ongoing fight against Communist aggression.

Several movies commemorate the Marines' historic "attack in another direction," most notably **Retreat, Hell!**, **Hold Back the Night** *and* **Battle Flame**. *Each of these movies depicts the physical hardships of the climate and terrain and the omnipresent danger from the pursuing Chinese forces, but they emphasize the grit and character of the Marines who were trying to survive under dire circumstances. These films are undeniably jingoistic, but they do not cross over into propaganda because their stories are true, harrowing and inspiring.*

The Hungnam evacuation was one of the largest in military history. One hundred and five thousand troops and ninety thousand refugees were rescued and delivered safely to South Korean and Japanese ports. Hundreds of ships also transported more than seventeen thousand vehicles and three hundred fifty thousand tons of supplies away, to be redistributed as the U.N. forces regrouped in South Korea. General Walton Walker was killed in an automobile accident and General Matthew Ridgway became commander of the Eighth Army, assuming command on Christmas Day, the date by which MacArthur had promised that his soldiers would be home.

While troops battled for every foot of ground in North Korea, American airpower and naval power had quickly eliminated opposition in the early days of the war, and for a long time, American airplanes and warships patrolled without much danger. American naval superiority continued throughout the war but the introduction of Russian-made MiG fighter jets in late 1950, paralleling the entry of the Chinese into the war, signaled an equalization in the skies above Korea. America's old World War II fighter planes were quickly replaced with new F-86 Sabre jets, F-80 Shooting Stars and F9F-2 Panther jets to duel with the new Russian technology. The Russian MiGs were more maneuverable and could fly at a higher altitude than American jets, but they were also less stable at high speeds and contained inferior gunsights. Sabre jets were faster than their Russian counterparts and American pilots seemed to be better trained in combat tactics. MiGs were shot down at a rate of 8 to 1 early in the war, and that rate increased to 17 to 1 during the final months of the war.

As jets entered the fray, the air war became sexy enough to lure filmmakers to its subject. Fighter pilots became a standardized group, heroic but often flawed. Visually, the air war opened the wide blue yonder to audiences, providing thrilling dogfights and exciting bombing missions to enhance a decidedly unpopular war. Studios secured the support of the Air Force and Navy often, with the result that most air war adventures are far more patriotic and jingoistic than those of other Korean War film subgenres.

Sabre Jet, An Annapolis Story, The Bridges at Toko-Ri, Air Strike, Men of the Fighting Lady, The Hunters, The McConnell Story *and* ***Battle Hymn*** *all explore the mystique of fighter pilots during the war and soon afterward, with the comedy* ***Not With My Wife, You Don't!*** *following suit fifteen years later. The air war films are visually exciting, though once on the ground they generally seem stilted. Nevertheless, they remain the most popular celluloid aspect of the Korean War.*

Chinese and North Korean forces organized and made a push into South Korea on the final day of 1950. Some 350,000 Communist troops began their second attempt to force South Korean and U.N. troops past the southern port of Pusan and into the sea. Under heavy attack, the South Korean army fled and yet again abandoned equipment and weaponry to lighten their load. Within one week, Seoul was again in the hands of the North Koreans, accompanied this time by Chinese colleagues. U.N. troops had withdrawn nearly two hundred eighty miles within six weeks and found themselves in the northern half of South Korea before the Communist advance finally stalled.

Allied commanders were gradually beginning to recognize the pattern of enemy attacks. The North Korean and Chinese troops would attack with speed, power and overwhelming numbers, usually forcing the U.N. troops to withdraw before the enemy onslaught. For two or three days the Communists would push forward at great speed, but inevitably the attack would stall four or five days after the initial push for lack of supplies. Communist supply lines simply could not maintain the same pace as their attack troops, and rations and ammunition would decrease rapidly during combat. It was discovered that their food supplies usually ended on the third or fourth day of the attack, and that the Reds preferred to move back to meet their own supply lines rather than wait for supplies to reach them.

As might be expected, few Hollywood films address this portion of the war. The overwhelming Chinese advance is mentioned in ***MacArthur*** *and* ***Collision Course: Truman vs. MacArthur*** *and is intimated in others but no Korean War film focuses on this disorderly retreat.*

General Ridgway learned to save lives by keeping his troops moving during sudden Communist attacks, and to counterattack four and five days later, when the Reds were scrambling for food, ammunition and replacement gear. In mid–January of 1951, the U.N. troops were as far southward as they would go, and they began to march back north. Realizing that morale was very low following the debacle at the Chosin Reservoir and the long flight south, General Ridgway on January 21st released a statement titled "Why Are We Here?"

What Are We Fighting For?" to be read by all Eighth Army personnel. The last section of Ridgway's mission statement was directly aimed at bolstering troop morale:

"The issue now joined right here in Korea is whether communism or individual freedom shall prevail; whether the fight of fear-driven people we have witnessed here shall be checked, or shall at some future time, however distant, engulf our own loved ones in all its misery and despair. You will have my utmost. I shall expect yours."

In late January, Ridgway began his counterattacks, codenamed "Operation Thunderbolt," "Operation Roundup," "Operation Killer" and "Operation Ripper," beginning the fifth phase of the war. These carefully orchestrated battle movements advanced the U.N. soldiers through the capital city of Seoul for the second time in six months and slightly past the 38th parallel. By March, 1951, the dividing line between the two sides was approximately where it had been before the North Korean invasion, just nine months previously. With Seoul back under South Korean control and the Communists chased back into North Korea, President Truman began to make overtures to settle the war. In Truman's view, the interdiction of U.S. and U.N. troops had prevented the Communists achieving their stated objective, which was to unify Korea under communist rule, and had successfully proven to North Korea, Russia and China that such naked aggression would not be tolerated.

General Douglas MacArthur did not view the situation as Truman did. MacArthur was convinced that Communism must be totally defeated and was unwilling to accept any solution other than unconditional surrender. While Truman and his political staff sought a negotiated truce, MacArthur announced that he was "ready at any time to confer in the field with the commander in chief of the enemy forces in an earnest effort to find any military means whereby the realizations of the political objectives of the United Nations in Korea, to which no nation may justly take exception, might be accomplished without further bloodshed." President Truman considered MacArthur's demand for the enemy's surrender to be an attempt to formulate and execute foreign policy, and the commander in chief decided to relieve his most popular general of duty.

On April 10, Truman sent MacArthur a cable informing him of the decision, but public news of the firing reached MacArthur before the cable did. The general returned home to a hero's welcome and the largest ticker-tape parade ever held in New York City. He addressed a joint session of Congress and explained his desire to halt the spread of Communism, and made several other public appearances wherein he advocated "total victory" over the "prolonged indecision" which he could not understand. But even high-ranking military officers agreed that MacArthur needed to be removed, noting that his own philosophies were not in synchronization with that of the elected government. MacArthur's firing invited powerful criticism of President Truman, but Truman held his ground. "In the simplest terms, what we are doing in Korea is this: we are trying to prevent a third world war," he stated in a national address regarding his decision.

The removal of General Douglas MacArthur from command was a historic decision that is recounted in the biographies MacArthur and Truman, and is the sole subject of Collision Course: Truman vs. MacArthur. The latter telefilm, which is remarkably faithful to actual history, is an even-handed account of the situation and goes to great pains to include relevant political detail and ramifications. Interestingly, while MacArthur's dismissal was among the biggest news stories of the war, it is rarely even referred to in other Korean War films, perhaps because the move was so controversial and publicly contentious.

General Ridgway was named to replace MacArthur as Supreme Commander of United Nations forces, and General James Van Fleet assumed command of the Eighth Army. They were ready when the Chinese began the sixth phase of the war, launching a spring offensive on April 22, 1951, with the stated purpose of destroying the U.N. command. The Chinese advanced to within a few miles of Seoul in bitter fighting over the period of a week, but never entered the city. For two months, the Chinese persistently attacked without gaining much ground. A key battle was fought by the British 29th Brigade. One battalion of the Gloucestershire Regiment, surrounded on all sides, attacked the Chinese rather than waiting to be overrun. Many of its men were captured; only thirty-nine returned, singly and in small groups, to the U.N. lines. Over one thousand Gloucestershire men were lost, but Seoul was saved from yet another invasion and General Van Fleet called their heroism "the most outstanding example of unit bravery in modern warfare."

*Although the Gloucestershire Regiment's fate has not been dramatized on film, **A Hill in Korea** (aka **Hell in Korea**) does honor a fictional British platoon, spotlighting sacrifice by National Servicemen, young men who never dreamed that they would be fighting a war thousands of miles from home when they were drafted. British involvement in the war is noted in other films, but this is the only one that focuses entirely on their unique perspective.*

With the Communists stopped, U.N. forces dug in along what became known as the "No Name Line," since it was in between preestablished battle lines. On May 15th the Communists attacked again. They gained twenty miles of ground before running out of supplies on May 20th. By the end of the month, U.N. forces had pushed the Communists completely out of South Korea again and were marching north. The front lines stabilized in mid–June, cutting Korea in half on a northeasterly plane from Panmunjom near the west coast to just south of Kosong on the east coast. This military stalemate began the seventh and longest phase of the war. Ultimately, this dividing line — after many more battles and human deaths — would become the demilitarized zone once the armistice was signed, some two years later.

Once the military situation had stabilized, leaders on both sides began to seriously discuss peace. The first obstacle was South Korean President Syngman Rhee, whom the United States had returned to power when they liberated Seoul for the first time after the battle of Inchon. A staunch anti-Communist, Rhee refused to accept the idea of truce. "Our goal is unification. If we seek an armistice now, we accede to national division. I categorically oppose a truce," he stated. Nevertheless, the initial armistice meeting took place on July 10, 1951, in Kaesong, attended by officials from the United States, the United Nations, North Korea, South Korea and China.

*South Korean President Syngman Rhee was a very intriguing person who is not well represented in Korean War films. Rhee appears in **Inchon**, but he is relatively unimportant to its story, and he is barely even mentioned in other films which are otherwise historically accurate. Perhaps because of his virulent stance on Korean unification — which extended to public refusal to agree with decisions made by American politicians — Rhee, at least on film, has been treated as an insignificant character.*

Setting a pattern which was to be repeated many times over, peace negotiations were hindered by argument over detail and protocol, while substantive issues were rarely discussed. Both sides argued over the agenda for the meeting, where delegates would be positioned, what media members could report and other relatively minor matters. The agenda was finalized on July 26 and negotiations lasted until August 10. At that time, the North Korean negotiator insisted on using the 38th Parallel to divide the two countries. The U.N. negotiator replied "We will not discuss further the 38th Parallel as a military demarcation line. Don't try to recover at this table what you lost on the battlefield."

Talks continued into the fall at a new location, Panmunjom, while the military commanders of both sides made efforts to strengthen their positions. Battles were fought over specific territory across Korea, at such locations as Bloody Ridge, Heartbreak Ridge, the Punchbowl, Capital Hill, J Ridge, Lightning Hill, Jane Russell Hill, Triangle Hill, Jackson Heights, T-Bone, Pork Chop Hill,

Old Baldy, White Horse Hill, Big and Little Horn, The Hook, Nevada Cities and Anchor Hill. Over the next two years, enemy soldiers within a few miles of each other battled fiercely for possession of these desolate rises of earth while negotiators in Panmunjom argued over minute details of wording or phrasing in various peace documents that were inevitably rejected by one or both sides.

The peace process, included as an important element of some Korean War films, has in itself never been targeted for serious cinematic exploration. Ultimately, two years of frustrating, sometimes bitter argument and gamesmanship were enacted at Kaesong and Panmunjom before an agreement was reached. Creating an interesting movie from such a non-visual, dialogue-driven situation fraught with a considerable and often deliberate lack of communication has proven more of a challenge than any Hollywood filmmaker has yet been willing to take.

By the end of 1951, a basic agreement had been forged. Then the issue of prisoners of war was raised. The Communists wanted all prisoners of war held by U.N. forces to be returned to North Korea, whether they wanted to return or not. America's position was that those people who did not want to return to a Communist state should not be forced to, and could remain free in South Korea. The North Koreans and Chinese rejected this concept immediately. They also stated that they held only a few thousand U.N. prisoners, a number which the Americans felt was entirely too low. Neither side budged on the issue, and the war dragged on while the peace talks dragged on.

Uprisings occurred at a U.N. prison camp at Koje Island, where more than one hundred thirty thousand North Korean and Chinese prisoners were being held. It was reported that only seventy thousand of the prisoners wished to return to North Korea or China when they were to be repatriated. Eventually, the Koje Island prisoners were transferred to smaller, more manageable prison camps, because conditions at Koje had deteriorated to the point where armed guards used force on several occasions to quell violent uprisings between prisoners who argued for democracy and those who followed Communism. Two separate generals who were given command of the camp were later removed and demoted to colonels following questionable actions.

As bad as Koje Island became, conditions for U.N. soldiers in North Korean prison camps were much worse. Thousands of American soldiers, as well as those of other nationalities, lost their lives in prison camps due to starvation, exposure, torture and execution. As the number of prisoners increased, men were marched from one camp to another without rest, food or water. Those who fell by the sides of the road were left to die. Medical care was minimal, and soldiers were subjected to intense Communist indoctrination methods which occasionally included physical torture. As the peace talks continued, the Communists actively searched for soldiers who would publicly betray the American way of life, and they found some through torture, blackmail and brainwashing.

Every few weeks the Reds would produce an audio confession or a filmed press conference where an American soldier would confess to participating in bacteriological or germ warfare, or simply refute capitalism in favor of the socialist political system. Most of these confessions and broadcasts were forced, but a few were made by people who had genuinely switched sides. At the end of the war, some twenty-one American soldiers refused repatriation to America, choosing to remain in North Korea as Communist sympathizers. This phenomenon was new to the American public and distressed a great many people. Some returning soldiers indicated the amount of indoctrination and torture used by the Communists, but the public at large found it hard to believe that any patriotic young American male would accept collaboration with the enemy before death.

*Prisoner of war films comprise a major subgenre of the Korean War film. Titles such as **The Bamboo Prison**, **Prisoner of War**, **The Fearmakers**, **Strange Intruder** and **Time Limit** vividly depict atrocious conditions and brutality* that was common for United Nations prisoners held by the North Koreans and Chinese, while *The Rack*, *Flight Nurse* and *Toward the Unknown* cover the same ground without physical depictions of the violence. Prisoners of war are also important to the films *Three Wishes* and *The Manchurian Candidate*. However, the subject of enemy prisoners in U.N. camps, particularly those at Koje Island, has been ignored by filmmakers.

Brainwashing and resulting collaboration with the enemy are investigated in *The Bamboo Prison*, *Prisoner of War*, *Time Limit* and *The Rack*. These movies try to offer some explanation as to how the Communists were able to "turn" Americans against their home country and honestly depict the cruel and barbarous physical and psychological conditions to which prisoners were subjected. *The Manchurian Candidate* takes the situation to its zenith, contending that American soldiers might be turned into secret weapons under Communist control. At the time of its release in 1962, critics felt the film was fantasy; it does not seem so far-fetched today.

In early 1952, American air raids against the city of Pyongyang and eleven hydroelectric plants along the Yalu River were undertaken to force the Communists to reconsider their objections to the peace plans and generally accelerate the peace process. Military offensives for individual hills took place all summer but succeeded in gaining little ground. Casualties for both sides climbed as commanders searched for public victories which their sides could use for propaganda at the peace table. People died for a few yards of dirt, territory which would be fought over again and again.

President Truman was succeeded by Dwight D. Eisenhower in January 1953. Ike made a trip to Korea to observe the situation firsthand in December of 1952, after winning the November election. Like Truman, Eisenhower decided the best course lay at the bargaining table, and he announced that he would "concentrate on the job of ending the Korean War." On March 5, Russia's leader, Joseph Stalin, died and his successor, Georgi

Malenkov, seemed amenable to ending the conflict. The first real advance toward peace occurred on March 28, 1953, when Chinese negotiators agreed in principle to exchange sick and wounded prisoners. The exchange, dubbed "Operation Little Switch," was scheduled for late April.

Neither Eisenhower's ascendancy to the office of president nor "Operation Little Switch" are important events in any Korean War film. Eisenhower is referred to in *Truman* and *MASH*, but he is not a major character in a single Korean War film. The sick and wounded prisoner exchange was a huge advance toward peace at the time, but has likewise been ignored.

When President Truman left office, his approval rating was an incredibly low 32%. At home, the Korean War was unpopular, especially after the Chinese entered the battle. "Homefront" films gradually moved from unabashed patriotism in *I Want You* to explorations of social attitudes in America, as in *Japanese War Bride*, and finally to diatribes about the dangers of Communism like *My Son John*. In the 1990s, the dramas *Chattahoochee* and *Three Wishes* looked back at the 1950s and began to expose the fragile and unraveling social fabric of the time as people tried to come to grips with the war and its various destructive effects.

In the meantime, Communist officials launched an offensive to take Pork Chop Hill to claim a final battlefield victory. The battle for Pork Chop Hill raged throughout April 16 and 17, before the U.S. commanders decided to reinforce the meager remnants of men left on the hill to prevent a propaganda victory by the Reds. The fierce battle proved to the Communists that U.S. forces would not back away from a fight if pressured. Air Force bombings of North Korea were increased and dogfights between Air Force Sabre jets and Russian-made MiG fighter jets along "MiG Alley," along North Korea's western coastline, continued and intensified.

The battle for Pork Chop Hill became recognized as a microcosm of the peace process. The film version of *Pork Chop Hill* includes scenes of the political stalemate at Panmunjom between scenes of carnage on the battlefield. The key mo-

ment occurs when the American negotiator realizes that the Communists need proof that America is just as willing to fight and sacrifice lives for symbolism as they are. Once the Communists see that the Americans are willing to replenish their forces on a strategically worthless hill simply to prevent the Reds from claiming a propaganda victory, they pull back.

After "Operation Little Switch," the negotiators worked hard to hammer a final peace agreement, and following extensive wrangling over the prisoner of war issue, an armistice was announced which would begin in June of 1953, three years after the beginning of the conflict. South Korean President Syngman Rhee once again sabotaged the process, announcing that "I will never accept the armistice terms as they stand. The Republic of Korea will fight on, even if it means a suicide, and I will lead them." Rhee ordered South Korean guards to free some twenty-seven thousand anti-Communist North Korean prisoners; only one thousand of them were recaptured. U.S. officials apologized to the Communists for Rhee's self-initiated action and basically blackmailed the South Korean leader into obedience by agreeing to sign a long-term mutual defense treaty and provide South Korea with $200 million in economic aid. With reluctance, Rhee finally agreed to the peace initiatives.

The armistice was delayed into July, and early that month, the Chinese launched their biggest offensive in two years, hoping to claim a battlefield victory before the curtain came down on the conflict in Korea. This was the eighth and final phase of the Korean War. Fighting continued all along the front, including Pork Chop Hill, which was finally sacrificed by the U.N., fearing that the human cost to retain the hill would be prohibitive. The final version of the armistice document was signed at 10:00 on the morning of July 27, 1953, and the resulting cease-fire began twelve hours later. At 10:00 p.m., the guns in Korea finally stopped firing. As reported by soldiers at the time, "the silence was deafening."

The cease-fire is included in several films, some of which explore the mindset of soldiers who are suddenly prohibited from fighting and killing. **War Hunt** *stands apart, showing that one particular soldier has become incapable of altering the savage lifestyle to which he has become accustomed. Other movies which chronicle the hours leading to the cease-fire are* **Sniper's Ridge**, **The Hook** *and the appropriately titled* **Cease Fire**. *While the armistice was a cause for jubilation, these films are remarkably bereft of celebration. They reflect the attitude of the fighting men, which was quite simple and stoic. "At last we get to go home."*

Under the terms of the peace agreement, both sides withdrew some two thousand meters from their front lines to create a demilitarized zone. The zone stands to this day, with North and South Korea separated by wire fences, searchlights and barren ground. Korea's demilitarized zone has lasted longer than the Berlin Wall and remains an enduring, desolate, tragic symbol of an epic battle between Communist aggression and defenders of freedom. The armistice was signed nearly fifty years ago, but there remains today no concrete, final agreement between the two separate and distinct halves of Korea.

THE FILMS

Air Strike

Credits: 1955. Cy Roth Productions. *Distributed by:* Lippert Pictures. *Written, Produced and Directed by:* Cy Roth. *Music Composer and Conductor:* Andre Brummer. *Director of Photography:* Alan Stensvold, A.S.C. *Editors:* Duncan Mansfield, A.C.E. and George McGuire (uncredited). *Original Song:* "Each Time You Leave Me," *by* Sylvia Ostrow and Andre Brummer. *Assistant Director:* Edward Bernoudy. *Sound Supervisor:* Max Hutchinson. *Script Supervisor:* Fred Applegate. *Public Information Officer:* Lieutenant Commander Leo R. Pierson. *Chief Electrician:* Jimmy James. *Grip Department Head:* E. B. "Buzz" Gibson. *Property Master:* Forrest Ricketts. *Sound by:* Sound Services, Inc. *Technical Advisor:* Captain Frank Turner, commanding U.S.S. *Essex* (CVA 9). Not Rated. Black and White. Flat (1.33:1). 63 minutes. Released in July, 1955. Exteriors filmed on board the U.S.S. *Essex*. Not currently available on commercial home video.

Cast: *Commander Blair,* Richard Denning; *Marg Huggins,* Gloria Jean; *Lieutenant Richard Huggins,* Don Haggerty; *Lieutenant John Smith,* William Hudson; *Anthony Perini,* Alan Wells; *David Loring,* John Kirby; *Parks,* Jack Fischer; *Lieutenant Commander Swanson,* William Halop; *Ensign James Delaney,* James Courtney; *G. H. Alexander,* Stanley Clements; the officers and men of the U.S.S. *Essex (CVA 9)*; the "Fighting Falcons" of VF 142 Cougar Squadron.

Historical Accuracy Level: Low. This is a non-specific storyline set after the Korean War with an inept wartime dogfight flashback.

Patriotic Propaganda Level: High. This movie advocates Naval aviation, specifically in regard to aircraft carriers and fighter jets.

Elements: Aircraft Carriers, Military Training, Multiple Wars, Musical Performance, Navy (Aviators).

Air Strike spotlights the difficulties and responsibilities of Naval jet fighter pilots stationed aboard the aircraft carrier *Essex*. Filmed with full cooperation of the Navy and Department of Defense, the movie is intended as a tribute to the Navy's "top guns," though that term is never mentioned by name. The film involves the Korean War only tangentially, through a brief flashback, yet enough to qualify it for the dubious honor of being one of the worst Korean War films ever made.

Aboard the U.S.S. *Essex* in 1954, a squadron of eight Naval aviators fly practice missions near the Middle East. The flyers are led by easygoing Commander Blair (Richard Denning), who believes in persuasion rather than force when dealing with his new pilots. They try to attach some political meaning to the large scale maneuvers with which they are involved and complain to themselves about Lieutenant Huggins (Don Haggerty), a veteran flyer with no patience for the mistakes of the young, particularly Ensign Delaney (James Courtney). Lieutenant Smith (William Hudson) explains that Huggins is

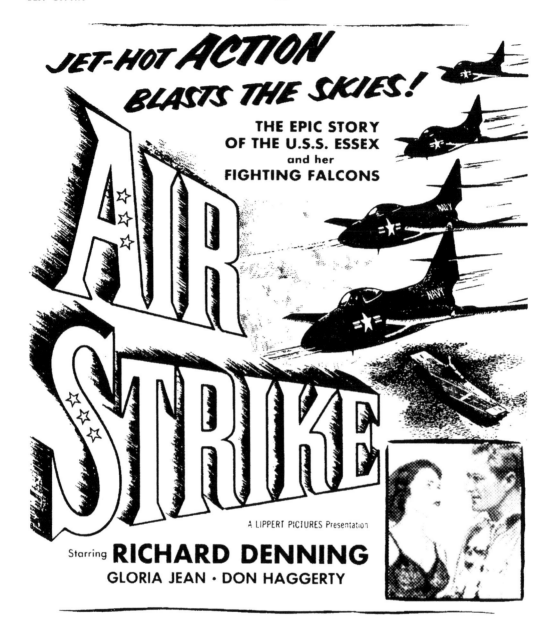

JET-HOT *ACTION* BLASTS THE SKIES!

THE EPIC STORY
OF THE U.S.S. ESSEX
and her
FIGHTING FALCONS

AIR STRIKE

A LIPPERT PICTURES Presentation

Starring **RICHARD DENNING**
GLORIA JEAN · DON HAGGERTY

A low-budget programmer from Lippert Pictures, Air Strike *(1955) describes activities aboard the U.S.S.* Essex *just after the Korean War. The carrier is the focus of the film despite the fact that it is provided with the smallest image in the artwork. Yet the ad is truthful; jets do appear and Gloria Jean can be viewed in her undergarments.*

under pressure to take a shore job from his wife Marg (Gloria Jean), who is seen crooning the song "Each Time You Leave Me" in a flashback.

Blair is reminded of action during Korea (depicted in flashback), when he participated in a dogfight with communist MiG fighters, and Smith explains to the pilots (in another flashback) how Blair won a medal during World War II diving his plane toward and exploding a Japanese cruiser. On a strafing practice mission, Delaney spots a possible enemy submarine periscope and pilot G. H. Alexander (Stanley Clements) is rewarded for being the pilot of the 75,000th aircraft landing aboard the *Essex.*

Huggins grows more irritable, having received a letter from Marg with a personal ultimatum — it's either her or the Navy. Another flashback reveals their most recent argument. Blair and Smith watch the carrier's big guns shoot down a drone aircraft and try to converse about the value of the peacetime Navy over the booming of the guns while patriotic music plays. "What are we doing? We're doing something worthwhile. We're practicing so that other kids can have the same chance we had," contends Blair.

On another mission, the pilots are engulfed in a fog bank. All but two of the flyers return safely to the *Essex* except for Delaney, who is forced to ditch his jet after being waved off (for no explicable reason) and Huggins, whose jet experiences an electrical malfunction and is completely lost in the fog. Blair guides Huggins close to the carrier by radio, but when that fails, Delaney goes up in another jet, after being rescued, finds Huggins in the fog and guides him safely to the carrier's deck before landing himself. Over the carrier's public address system, the captain compliments Blair's squadron, and particularly Delaney, for a job well done.

The movie ends with this epilogue: "The mighty air arm of the United States Navy, with its control of the seas, is a great part of this nation's security. Aggression can be stopped, and peace maintained, with a strong navy. This story is dedicated to the men at sea with wings."

Obviously, *Air Strike* is intended as a stirring tribute to "the men at sea with wings." This production, however, is so bottom of the barrel that the Navy seems barely competent. The vaunted pilots are back-stabbing gossips, completely uninformed about their purpose or mission, who have difficulty just flying in a proper formation. Their leader, Blair, is a slacker who has gained the men's respect merely by leaving them alone while they undermine the morale and effectiveness of the squadron. This is one attempt to depict brave, intelligent heroes where the heroes are certainly not intelligent or interesting enough to merit that attempt.

Things occur in the script which are never properly followed through or which make no logical sense. After their first mission, the eight pilots slowly file into the debriefing room, are introduced by name, and sit for their debriefing; the meeting is then abruptly postponed and ad-

journed. Delaney spots the periscope of a submarine (one which is suspected to be that of an enemy, as no American submarines are reported in the area), is questioned afterward in detail and provides a clear and concise report of his sighting; the suspicious submarine is never mentioned again. Blair takes the time to talk to Huggins about his personal problems, explaining that he both demands and expects "cooperation and loyalty" from his flyers; Blair then strongly hints to the troubled man that he should transfer out of his outfit.

Air Strike is packed full of such nonsense and visual gaffes. More attention is paid to the flyers *drinking coffee* and to the cake which commemorates the 75,000th aircraft landing on the *Essex* than to the various flight scenes, or to the logical incorporation of Huggins' wife Marg into the story. This movie features *five* separate flashbacks! It was written, directed and produced by Cy Roth, who only directed three times in his brief career: *Air Strike, Combat Squad* (another Korean War movie, 1953) and the immortal schlock classic *Fire Maidens From Outer Space* (1956). Without a doubt one of the least talented directors in cinema history, Roth managed with *Air Strike* to make the heroes of his story—the flyers of the United States Navy— seem bullying, blustering and buffoonish.

Blair's flashback of the Korean War is astonishingly inept. Blair is reminded that over Korea he "was jumped by a whole mess of MiGs [the Russian-made fighter jets used by the North Koreans during the war]." For the next two minutes, grainy Korean War footage of Panther jets is mixed with grainier footage of *World War II airplanes* being hunted and shot down. There isn't a MiG in sight during the entire dogfight sequence. At one point, a flaming plane going down catches Blair's attention and he flies in its direction. It is neither seen nor spoken of again.

None of the actors make a favorable impression, including glamorous Gloria Jean, who appears in just two scenes, the first of which is excerpted late in the film. In her musical scene, seemingly staged in a barn, she croons "Each Time You Leave Me" to an unseen audience while Smith, Blair and her husband watch appreciatively from the side, through what seems to be the door of a stable. In her dramatic scene, set in her dressing room, she is wearing only her

From left to right, Navy pilots James Delaney (James Courtney), Anthony Perini (Alan Wells), John Smith (William Hudson) and David Loring (John Kirby) discuss another pilot's comely wife (Gloria Jean, seen in the photo) in Air Strike *(1955).*

underwear (!) and she argues with her husband about his future in the Navy.

The only asset of this travesty is the visual impact of the aircraft carrier *Essex,* and in particular, the takeoffs and landings of its jets. Various angles are employed, some rather spectacularly, to make the jet landings seem as impressive as possible. The real-life action aboard the *Essex* is far more intriguing than anything Cy Roth was able to dramatize, and the all too brief glimpses of life and work aboard the carrier give the film its only sense of realism.

Variety termed *Air Strike* "an unexciting and unimaginatively turned out affair," and "a programmer lacking in just about every element of entertainment," and judged that its "Technical departments are below average." The British Film Institute's *Monthly Film Bulletin* complained that "The very inadequately conceived story and the unconvincing character development prevents this film from achieving any of the excitement one might expect from the type

of subject." In their *Motion Picture Guide,* Jay Robert Nash and Stanley Ralph Ross note that there is "Not a single interesting or thrilling moment in the entire film." They are, unfortunately, absolutely correct.

Air Strike was produced and released by the Lippert studio, which four years previously had struck gold with Samuel Fuller's *The Steel Helmet.* The studio's fortunate luck did not last. Despite full and extensive cooperation from the Department of Defense and the crew of the *Essex,* Cy Roth and Lippert were unable to produce a film even remotely worthy of their subject.

All the Young Men

Credits: 1960. Jaguar Productions. *Distributed by:* Columbia. *Written, Produced and Directed by:* Hall Bartlett. *Associate Producer:* Newton Arnold. *Music: by* George Duning. *Di-*

rector of Photography: Daniel Fapp, A.S.C. *Film Editor:* Al Clark, A.C.E. *Song:* "All The Young Men," by George Duning and Stanley Styne. *Art Director:* Carl Anderson. *Assistant Director:* Lee Lukather. *Set Decorator:* Bill Calvert. *Makeup Supervision:* Ben Lane, S.M.A. *Mr. Ladd's Make-up:* Emile Lavigne. *Hair Styles by:* Helen Hunt. *Sound Supervision:* Charles J. Rice. *Sound:* James Flaster. *Assistant to the Producer:* Ben Mantz. *Technical Advisor:* Lieutenant Colonel C. J. Stadler, U.S.M.C. *Orchestration:* Arthur Morton. Not Rated. Black and White. Flat (1.33:1). 87 minutes. Released in August, 1960. Exteriors filmed at Glacier National Park, Montana. Currently available on VHS home video.

Cast: *Kincaid,* Alan Ladd; *Sergeant Towler,* Sidney Poitier; *Torgil,* Ingemar Johansson; *Cotton,* James Darren; *Wade,* Glenn Corbett; *Crane,* Mort Sahl; *Maya,* Ana St. Clair (Anna Maria Lynch); *Bracken,* Paul Richards; *Casey,* Richard "Dick" Davalos; *Dean,* Lee Kinsolving; *Jackson,* Joe Gallison; *Lazitech,* Paul Baxley; *Lieutenant,* Charles Quinlivan; *Cho,* Michael Davis; *Hunter,* Mario Alcalde; *Korean Woman,* Marie Tsien.

Historical Accuracy Level: Medium. The film's events are completely fictional, but issues of leadership and race were raised at various moments (such as this film's) during the war.

Patriotic Propaganda Level: Low. The motley crew assembled in this Marine Corps unit spend most of their time fighting among themselves rather than battling the enemy.

Elements: Effects on Civilians, Infighting, Integration, Marine Corps, Medicine, Musical Performance, Racism, Winter Fighting.

All the Young Men, released the year following *Pork Chop Hill,* was an attempt to portray the war in contemporary terms, with timely social themes revolving around the unpopular promotion of a black sergeant over a more experienced but lesser ranking white soldier. Hall Bartlett, who served as writer, producer and director on the project, wanted to tell a more symbolic, socially relevant story than had been previously filmed about the war. Ultimately, he was only moderately successful.

On October 11, 1950, an advance Marine Corps unit at Wonsan is assigned to find and hold a strategic farmhouse which guards a mountain pass near Majon-ni and await the arrival of a battalion of American soldiers. Soon after their march through the mountains begins, the platoon is ambushed by Chinese troops and artillery. Only a dozen Marines survive the brutal ambush, and before he dies, the Lieutenant (Charles Quinlivan) instructs Sergeant Towler (Sidney Poitier) to lead the men and continue the mission. The Marines want Kincaid (Alan Ladd), an experienced former sergeant, to lead. They consider him to be their good luck charm, but Kincaid refuses to overrule the Lieutenant's final orders and Towler takes control.

The men march over a ridge while carrying the injured Casey (Richard "Dick" Davalos) on a stretcher, spend some time retrieving Dean (Lee Kinsolving) who slips and falls into a mined ravine, and eventually reach the farmhouse. Movement is seen inside the outer stone wall that rings the farmhouse, so one of the Marines throws a grenade which injures an elderly Korean woman living there with her grown daughter Maya (Ana St. Clair) and Maya's young son Cho (Michael Davis). The Marines move inside, set a watch and tend to the wounded. Most of the men want to leave the farmhouse to the enemy, but Towler asserts his authority and the men back down.

Towler establishes a foxhole as an observation outpost. At the farmhouse, to pass the time, Torgil (Ingemar Johansson) sings a Swedish song about a woman who talks to a tree, Crane (Mort Sahl) improvises a brief comedy routine, Cotton (James Darren) sings "All the Young Men," and they listen to "When the Saints Go Marching In" on Cotton's phonograph. Gunfire brings the men running to the outside wall, where they defend the farm from onrushing Chinese soldiers. The brief battle ends and the men return to their waiting.

Hunter (Mario Alcalde), a Navajo Indian whom Towler calls Chief, moves out on a lone patrol. Crane does another comedy routine while southern racist Bracken (Paul Richards) drinks his fill of wine and attempts to rape Maya. Towler stops Bracken with force while Lazitech (Paul Baxley) is silently killed in the outpost foxhole by the encroaching Chinese. Hunter returns to the foxhole, refuses to provide a password, and is shot by Kincaid. He has been beaten by the Chinese, who were using him to

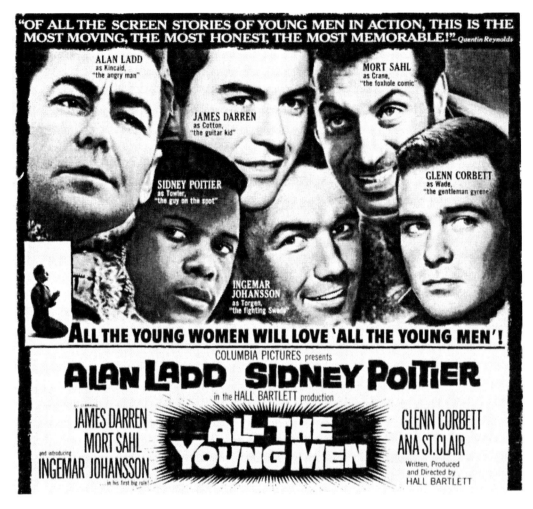

A cross-section of young American manhood is represented in this ad for Columbia's All the Young Men *(1960).* *What Marine squad would be complete without an "angry man," a "guitar kid," a "guy on the spot," a "fox-* *hole comic," a "fighting Swede" and a "gentleman gyrene?" Note also the pitch for a female audience and a crit-* *ical blurb, courtesy of Quentin Reynolds.*

move closer to the outpost, and he dies in Towler's arms.

Another attack begins. The wounded man, Casey, is brought to the wall and given a rifle; he shoots several Chinese soldiers before dying. The Marines hold back the Chinese yet again. To make a point, Towler sneaks up on Kincaid at the outpost (as a Chinese soldier would do). The two men are fighting in the outpost when a tank is heard. Thinking quickly, Towler instructs Cotton to create some Molotov cocktails, which he and Kincaid use to disable and burn the tank and the Chinese inside. The tank runs over Kincaid's leg, however, which must be amputated in order to save his life.

Corpsman Wade (Glenn Corbett) operates on Kincaid, keeping him quiet with wine and Cotton's record of "When the Saints Go Marching In," while Towler keeps Kincaid alive with a blood transfusion. Bracken oversees the transfusion and finally gains some respect for Towler. After the amputation, the Chinese move in with more tanks. The Marines slip out the back gate, taking the Korean family with them. Towler carries Kincaid to the outpost and watches as American jets swoop down and decimate the Chinese with machine guns. Kincaid smiles as Towler adds his own machine gun fire to the din, while "When the Saints Go Marching In" plays in the background.

All the Young Men is a routine, standard war drama which comes replete with familiar and hackneyed situations and clichés. Some individual scenes are effective, such as the tank burning and the amputation sequence, while others are merely listless and tedious. There is little that is original or exciting; the characters are cardboard, stiff and unyielding, and the central situation — a small group trying to survive — is hardly fresh. The one contemporary angle is the racial issue, and that is overplayed and obvious. Hall Bartlett's intent to superimpose hard-edged social drama over traditional war film formula is admirable, but the result is superficial.

Added to those problems, the film is not particularly well made or accurate. It begins with footage of an actual night-time artillery fusillade beneath the credits, which is easily the most dramatic action in the movie. It states that the action takes place on October 11, 1950, near Wonsan, and then depicts the ambush of Marines by Chinese troops. But the Chinese did not enter the war for another two weeks; their earliest known engagement took place October 25 against Republic of Korea (ROK) troops less than forty miles south of the Yalu River, the border between China and North Korea. It would be late November at the earliest before Chinese troops would be in the area where this movie places them in mid–October. A simple change of date would have corrected the mistake and given the film some historical accuracy.

Writer-producer-director Hall Bartlett was most interested in presenting the race relations issue in a confined context. Most of the soldiers in Towler's platoon are surprised that the lieutenant chooses Towler to lead rather than Kincaid because of Kincaid's much broader experience. The lieutenant never discloses why he picks Towler; the answer is certainly one of rank, but there is also a larger reason which is supposed to be evident by the end of the film. Aside from the issue of experience, some of the Marines don't care which man leads them, as long as they stay alive. Two men, however, do not like the lieutenant's choice at all. One of them is Bracken, the southern redneck, who eventually does develop some respect for Towler during the course of the story; the other is Kincaid, who feels that Towler is "a black man with an ax to grind," and who also has some personal dignity to reclaim from the lieutenant's slight.

Sergeant Towler is presented as a Marine put on the spot who admits he doesn't know all the answers, and who is unable to pry them from Kincaid, who is waiting for Towler to fail so that he may claim command. It is shown that Kincaid is worried for the safety of his men, but it is also inferred that Kincaid does indeed feel that he should be leading them. This scenario seems specious, since Kincaid understands rank, was himself busted from sergeant for unspecified reasons (and therefore could blame no one but himself for not being next in line), and didn't seem to mind working under the lieutenant. Professional soldiers are taught to follow orders and that rank is absolute. The men in this movie seem to have forgotten the chain of command.

To some viewers, the movie's central issue of white Marines refusing to respect a black platoon leader might seem banal or hackneyed. While the movie is certainly clumsy in its execution, that central issue was most definitely a viable one during the war. Blacks had served in all of the armed forces during World War II, but mostly in minor capacities, such as stewards and mess hall attendants. It was not until July 26, 1948, that President Truman issued an executive order granting minorities equal treatment and opportunity in the armed services. Two years later, the branches of the armed forces (except for the Air Force, which genuinely strove to integrate rapidly) were still making plans and arguing about details rather than initiating action. The Korean War changed the attitudes of the military leaders, as it proved that keeping minority soldiers segregated from the main fighting forces was wasteful and expensive. Ironically, though the Korean War cost the U.S. and other countries dearly in many ways, it also accelerated the military and social acceptance of integration.

Thus, Hall Bartlett's ambition to depict this socially relevant situation cinematically was a wise one, full of dramatic possibility and commendable purpose. Unfortunately, Bartlett's writing and direction were not as inspired as his ambition. And his use of music, particularly the recording of "When the Saints Go Marching In," which is played three times during the story, including over the climactic battle scene, is puerile.

Private Kincaid (Alan Ladd) leads a Marine platoon in single-file formation through hostile North Korean territory in All the Young Men *(1960). The snowy terrain is actually Glacier National Park in Montana.*

As the film's author, Bartlett is responsible for the stereotypical makeup of the Marine unit, which includes the black sergeant, an experienced but bitter veteran, an Indian scout, a southern redneck, an urban comic, a sensitive Swede and assorted others. Bartlett is also responsible for the lack of any cogent statement about the war itself. The attitudes of the men seem to be straight from standard World War II movies. The closest that the movie comes to profundity occurs when Towler tries to apologize to Maya after Bracken tried to rape her. "Don't judge us the way we are now …Because we are frightened now, because we have seen too much death and we don't understand why, because we have had to bury our friends in places we can't even pronounce."

Casting the role of Towler was an easy choice; Sidney Poitier was the single black actor widely accepted by Hollywood executives and the filmgoing public. Poitier had been representing the black race on screen for the better part of a decade, however, and he was becoming tired of the responsibility. In Carolyn Ewers' book *Sidney Poitier: The Long Journey,* Poitier is quoted as saying "I was unable to work in that movie, even on an elementary level, with any degree of imagination. The producers seemed willing to settle for what would have been the first step in a stage rehearsal and print it."

Alan Ladd is stoic as Kincaid, but the role certainly does not challenge him. The rest of the male cast was culled from charismatic (or sometimes not) young actors from Hollywood and beyond (hence, the title *All the Young Men*). The movie furnished Lee Kinsolving and Joseph "Joe" Gallison with their film debuts, comic Mort Sahl with his second cinematic appearance, Paul Baxley with his third, Richard "Dick" Davalos with his fourth, Glenn Corbett with his fifth and crooner/actor James Darren with his ninth. And in his only Hollywood movie, world champion heavyweight boxer Ingemar Johansson makes a lasting impression as Torgil, the sweet-tempered Swede who sings songs and brandishes a mean machine gun.

Despite the noble intentions of Hall Bartlett, the movie was not well received. The British Film Institute's *Monthly Film Bulletin* commented, "When Hollywood is playing soldiers in a film as painfully self-assertive as this, one wonders what kind of contemporary mentality it means to nourish. Whether this is a war film seasoned with color antagonisms or a race drama in a war setting is not clear: neither theme, in any event, is treated with the slightest concern for its gravity." *Newsweek* summarized *All the Young Men* in this fashion: "The lessons to be gained from this film about the Korean War are that racial tolerance and courage are good, war is hell, and any movie soldier who talks about home is almost sure to be dead inside of fifty frames."

All the Young Men is an undeniably well-intentioned, socially relevant melodrama in the Stanley Kramer mold, but is also one which fails to overcome its own stodginess. Hall Bartlett's production is similar to a pony show, putting its attractive and talented performers through predetermined paces to reach a superficial, predestined conclusion. Despite its contemporary subject, it is neither fresh, innovative nor particularly compelling.

An Annapolis Story

(aka *The Blue and the Gold*; *Navy Air Patrol*)

Credits: 1955. Allied Artists. *Directed by:* Don Siegel. *Produced by:* Walter Mirisch. *Screenplay by:* Dan Ullman and Geoffrey Homes (Daniel Manwaring). *Story: by* Dan Ullman. *Music by:* Marlin Skiles. *Director of Photography:* Sam Leavitt, A.S.C. *Film Editor:* William Austin, A.C.E. *Production Manager:* Allen K. Wood. *Supervising Film Editor:* Lester A. Sansom. *Second Unit Director:* Austen Jewell. *Art Director:* David Milton. *Technicolor Color Consultant:* Mitchell G. Kovaleski. *Recorded by:* Ralph Butler. *Special Effects:* Augie Lohman. *Dialogue Supervisor:* Sam Peckinpah. *Makeup by:* Edward Polo. *Hairdresser:* Mary Smith. *Set Continuity:* John L. Banse. *Set Decorator:* Joseph Kish. *Technical Advisor:* Commander Marcus L.

Lowe, Jr., U.S.N. *Photographic Effects:* Ray Mercer, A.S.C. *Songs:* "Navy Blue and Gold," by Joseph W. Crosley; "The Engagement Waltz," by Marlin Skiles. Not Rated. Technicolor. Flat (1.33:1). 81 minutes. Released in April, 1955. Currently available on VHS home video.

Cast: A. J. "Tony" Scott, John Derek; *Peggy Lord,* Diana Lynn; *J. R. "Jim" Scott,* Kevin McCarthy; *Willie Warren,* Alvy Moore; *Tim Dooley,* Pat Conway; *Watson,* L. Q. Jones; *Macklin,* John Kirby; *Mrs. Scott,* Barbara Brown; *Mrs. Lord,* Betty Lou Gerson; *Connie,* Fran Bennett; *Air Group Commander Austin,* Robert Osterloh; *Boxing Coach,* John Doucette; *McClaren,* Don Kennedy; *Lieutenant Prentiss,* Don Haggerty; *Announcer,* Tom Harmon; *Instructor,* James Anderson; *Superintendent,* John Ayres; *Lieutenant Preston,* Robert Bonoil; *First Classman,* Chris Drake; *Captain Lord,* George Eldredge; *Professor,* Dabbs Greer; *Officer,* Don Keefer; *Storekeeper,* John Lehman; *Pilot,* Sam Peckinpah; *Professor,* Robert Pike; *Tony's Instructor,* William Schallert; *Commander Wilson,* Richard Travis; *narrated by* Richard Carlson.

Historical Accuracy Level: Medium. The story's brothers are fictional, but their journey from the classrooms of Annapolis to dogfighting over Korean waters is certainly plausible.

Patriotic Propaganda Level: High. Filmed with full cooperation of the Navy, this movie is a slick recruiting aid for young men with adventurous souls.

Elements: Aircraft Carriers, Air War, Helicopters, Military Training, Musical Performance, Navy (Aviators), Rescues, Romantic Triangle, Sibling Rivalry.

Conceived as a tribute to the United States Naval Academy at Annapolis, Maryland, *An Annapolis Story* follows an enjoyable—if predictable—path, following a group of friends through the Navy's grueling training program to become proficient pilots. Korea proves to be their destination, as it becomes the world's hottest spot and most in need of Annapolis graduates. Filmed in color (the only Korean War movie of nine made by Allied Artists to be so produced), the movie combines its action with grainy stock footage of actual Naval cadets training and marching, which helps to provide the feel of authenticity.

An Annapolis Story follows the adventures of two brothers as they seek naval glory—and the same girl. Jim Scott (Kevin McCarthy) is the more studious and conservative of the two, while Tony Scott (John Derek) is more charismatic and reckless. Between the brothers is Peggy (Diana Lynn), who at the beginning of the movie is Jim's girl. After months of intensive training, Jim graduates at the top of his class, while Tony is 405th of 550.

The brothers are assigned to more training aboard an aircraft carrier. Tony's plane dives into the ocean upon taking off, but he is rescued by his older brother. Tony is sent back to the States to recuperate from a concussion and is visited by Peggy. Soon he and Peggy are inseparable, and when Jim returns home on leave, he finds that Peggy has switched her affection to his younger brother. Jim is understandably upset and after trying unsuccessfully to defeat Tony in the boxing ring, asks for one of them to be transferred. The request is denied. Jim becomes sullen and ignores both Tony and Peggy.

The Korean War begins. After another graduation, both men and fellow officers Willie Warren (Alvy Moore) and Tim Dooley (Pat Conway) are assigned to Pensacola, Florida, for further flight training, then to Corpus Christi, Texas, to fly jets. Their next stop is Korea. Further training takes place aboard an aircraft carrier, as the fliers learn to land their jets on a runway the size of a rural driveway. Tony tries to make peace with Jim, but Jim still holds a grudge. On a flak suppression mission, the pilots get their first taste of combat and shoot down at least three North Korean "bandits."

On leave in Tokyo, Tony is told by Peggy that she still has feelings for Jim, her first love, and wants to marry him. Tony returns to tell his brother, but is unable to do so before their next mission. Jim's jet is hit and he sustains a head injury. He parachutes into the sea while Tony circles his jet above him, shooting down a "bandit" that tries to disrupt Jim's rescue. Jim is safely rescued by helicopter and transferred to a Japanese hospital. He awakens to find Peggy at his bedside, and they kiss. Tony smiles, genuinely happy for his older brother.

An Annapolis Story's romantic subplot is the film's most unsatisfying aspect. Peggy flits from brother to brother like a baffled butterfly, never quite sure where to land. Her final choice of Jim seems predestined and yet specious at the same time. Ultimately, it doesn't matter. Neither, evidently, did the casting of the brother roles. In his book *A Siegel Film*, director Don Siegel relates that "Derek wanted to play McCarthy's part. I pointed out to Derek that his was the better role, but he obviously didn't believe me. So they changed parts. It actually made not the slightest difference."

To be sure, *An Annapolis Story* suffers from formula plotting and romantic clichés, but it is also directed with economy by Don Siegel, a man who could coax an engrossing story out of the most inane script, and who the next year would produce the enduring paranoia classic, the original *Invasion of the Body Snatchers*. Kevin McCarthy again starred, and Siegel's dialogue director (and personal assistant) on both films (as well as three others) was a young Sam Peckinpah.

The film's lightweight approach to war is evidenced by the brothers' reactions to traveling to Korea, which is presented as simply the natural progression of their military training. Statements about the situation are completely avoided, other than dialogue reflecting the midshipmen's concerns about joining the fighting. Jim thinks the army will take care of the fighting. "How do you think the army will get there?" someone else asks. Once in Korean waters, the Naval aviators merely do their jobs, strafing and bombing targets and occasionally dueling with North Korean pilots. In no other Korean War film is the war viewed so innocuously.

The brothers' military training is stressed throughout the film. The training is shown to be rigorous and demanding, yet is undeniably glamorized. The film's subliminal message seems to be that if these battling brothers can become fine Navy pilots, so can anyone else. As a result, this is a film that surely crosses the border between mainstream entertainment and military propaganda. This is obvious because the film does not criticize the Navy in any way; indeed, it presents life in the Navy as comfortable, exciting and of immense importance. Thankfully, the film is entertaining enough to forgive its dual use as a recruiting tool.

Since the budget allowed for no location

HIGH AS THE SKY!
WIDE AS THE WORLD!

The spectacular times ...
the danger-blazed missions
-- of two guys from Annapolis --
brothers in love with the same
girl...fighting it out all the
way to the China seas!

ALLIED ARTISTS presents

AN
ANNAPOLIS
STORY

starring

JOHN   DIANA
DEREK · LYNN

co-starring KEVIN McCARTHY with ALVY MOORE

A WALTER MIRISCH PRODUCTION

Color by TECHNICOLOR

Directed by DON SIEGEL · Story by DAN ULLMAN · Screenplay by DAN ULLMAN and GEOFFREY HOMES

All of Allied Artists' drama An Annapolis Story'*s (1955) important points are pictured on the poster: the brothers' rivalry, the jets they fly, the love story, the traditions of Annapolis, and even a reference to the war.*

filming (to Siegel's dismay), the director was forced to work on Allied Artists' tiny backlot. Siegel's toughest task was to match existing color stock footage of Annapolis—much of it in 8mm or 16mm formats—with his own movie. He was only somewhat successful, and like every other Korean War film that utilizes existing footage, such shots are easily discernible. Because these shots are in color, however, they do blend into the picture more effectively and they are not the same shots that appear in many of the black-and-white films of the period. Siegel credits his director of photography, Sam Leavitt, for the cohesiveness of the final product.

In his review, *New York Times* critic Howard Thompson wrote, "We defy anybody to cite a cleaner film than this Allied Artists presentation, which has John Derek and Kevin McCarthy engaged in a brotherly tug-of-war over Diana Lynn, one cute dish. Indeed, seldom have so many wholesome, scrubbed-looking young people thronged any picture than they do in this frankly pastel and perfectly legitimate little recruiting poster for our Naval Academy." In their Navy whites, Derek, McCarthy, Moore, Conway, L. Q. Jones and John Kirby certainly do present a clean-cut crew. And it is true that they almost never get dirty, no matter what their duty.

Of course, as a tribute to the Naval Academy, the film presents its underclassmen as eager and receptive, its professors as patient and responsible, and the naval lifestyle as challenging and rewarding. Its propaganda is undeniable, yet it (mostly) avoids jingoism, preferring to stress fundamental themes such as the importance of teamwork, knowing one's job, supporting one's fellows, deferring one's individualism for the greater good, keeping cool under stress, etc. These themes are not hammered but are worked into the story at appropriate points, courtesy of director Siegel. One point not covered is that midshipmen were required to serve not less than three consecutive years after graduation, unless dismissed from the service for academic failure or a major breach of regulations. Marriage, at least at that time, was considered a major breach of regulations, and would lead to dismissal. Therefore, Jim and Peggy would have had to wait for at least two more years before tying the knot.

The Technicolor process gave *An Annapolis Story* a touch of class, and the film performed moderately well at the box office. *Variety* appraised the film positively: "The production is

The Annapolis Naval graduates sit through a briefing in the ready room of an aircraft carrier in An Annapoolis Story *(1955). Tony Scott (John Derek) is in the second row on the left side, while his older brother Jim (Kevin McCarthy) is in the fourth row on the right hand side of the aisle.*

expensive-looking and handsomely mounted, forcefully narrated and well enacted." *Boxoffice* agreed, noting that the screenplay, "while unavoidably resorting to the inevitable clichés, is nonetheless refreshingly wholesome and free of the heel-turned-hero situation. In fact, there isn't a heavy in the film. The yarn offers the usual insight into the always-interesting details of how Uncle Sam's naval officers are trained." *Film Daily* concurred, calling the film a "Box office natural blessed with all the qualities of good entertainment."

An Annapolis Story is a diverting entertainment with a decidedly sunny view of the Navy. It could have been incredibly sappy, but Don Siegel's crisp direction prevents it from turning too syrupy. It would be foolish to take this film too seriously, yet its value as entertainment prevents it from being entirely dismissible.

Back at the Front
(aka *Willie and Joe Back at the Front*; *Willie and Joe in Tokyo*)

Credits: 1952. Universal. *Directed by:* George Sherman. *Produced by:* Leonard Goldstein. *Screenplay by:* Lou Breslow, Don McGuire and Oscar Brodney. *Story by:* Lou Breslow and Don McGuire. *From the characters created by:* Bill Mauldin. *Musical Direction:* Joseph Gershenson. *Original Music:* Henry Mancini (uncredited) and Herman Stein (uncredited). *Director of Photography:* Clifford Stine, A.S.C. *Film Editor:* Paul Weatherwax. *Art Direction:* Alexander Golitzen and Robert Boyle. *Set Decorations:* Russell A. Gausman and Oliver Emert. *Sound:* Leslie I. Carey and Robert Pritchard. *Gowns:* Rosemary Odell. *Hair Stylist:* Joan St. Oegger. *Make-Up:* Bud Westmore. *Assistant Director:* Tom Shaw. Not Rated. Black and White. Flat (1.33:1). Released in October, 1952. Filmed partly in Tokyo, Japan. Not currently available on home video.

Cast: *Willie,* Tom Ewell; *Joe,* Harvey Lembeck; *Nida,* Mari Blanchard; *General Dixon,* Barry Kelley; *Major Ormsby,* Vaughn Taylor; *Sergeant Rose,* Richard Long; *Johnny Redondo,* Russell Johnson; *Captain White,* Palmer Lee (Gregg Palmer); *Ben,* Aram Katcher; *Pete Wilson,* George Ramsey; *Sameko,* Aen-Ling Chow; *Rickshaw Boy,* Benson Fong; *Colonel Harkins,* Tyler McVey; *Corporal,* Paul Smith; *Training Officer,* Guy Williams; *with* (in alphabetical order) Mal Alberts, Howard Banks, Ray Barnes, Lane Bradford, Robert Bray, Ralph Brooks, Earl Brown, Harris Brown, Tom Carr, Dee Carroll, Douglas Carter, Bill Cassaday, Ken Christy, Howard Chuman, Bud Cokes, Pat Combs, Chuck Courtney, Jack Daly, Robert Dane, Van Des Autels, Amy Ding Dong, John Doucette, Norman Evans, Duane Thorsen (Duane Grey), Ted Hecht, Douglas Henderson, Larry Hudson, Frank Iwanaga, Ted Jordan, S. Kawaguchi, Gayle Kellogg, Freeman Lusk, Herbert Lytton, Archer MacDonald, Warren Mace, Clyde McLeod, Rollin Moriyama, John Pickard, Robert Pike, Hugh Prosser, Edward Rickard, Jimmy Shaw, Brick Sullivan, May Takasugi, Claudette Thornton, Roland Varno, George Wallace, Bob Wehling, Gordon Wynn and Mari Young.

Historical Accuracy Level: Low. This follow-up to *Up Front* is even more cartoonish than its predecessor, making no attempt to correspond to reality.

Patriotic Propaganda Level: Medium. Despite their inherent laziness and stupidity, the Army's Willie and Joe do foil an international arms smuggling ring.

Elements: Army, Comedy, Espionage, Japan, Multiple Wars.

Cartoonist Bill Mauldin's famous World War II dogface characters, Willie and Joe, were given their own movie in 1951, titled *Up Front*, starring Tom Ewell and David Wayne in a live-action version of their adventures. Although it could hardly be considered great cinema, *Up Front* proved very popular and spawned a sequel the following year, called *Back at the Front*, with Harvey Lembeck replacing David Wayne as Joe. In the sequel, Willie and Joe find themselves at the periphery of the Korean War, in Japan, and much of the movie was filmed on location at exotic Japanese locales.

After World War II, Willie (Tom Ewell) and Joe (Harvey Lembeck) are still on duty in Italy waiting to return home. Joe suggests enlisting in the inactive reserve, which would result in their immediate discharge. Despite his misgivings, Willie agrees. Years later, the civilians receive recall notices which place them back in the care of the Army. At the induction center, already fed up with the same old army routine, Willie feigns poor hearing and Joe feigns bad eyesight, in order to be discharged. Their ruse almost works, but for a brawl in which the allegedly disabled men overwhelm (offscreen) a bar full of G.I.s. Qualified as fit for duty, they are sent to Camp Drake near Tokyo, Japan.

Unhappy in the infantry, Joe suggests volunteering for the Quartermaster Corps, where the boys find themselves testing army apparel — uniforms, shoes, ponchos and bulletproof vests — under simulated battle conditions. They eventually get a week's leave, and head into Tokyo, despite their conspicuous lack of fresh, clean uniforms. Their dirty appearance causes military policemen to chase them around the city to the Emperor's Palace, where they are rescued by Nida (Mari Blanchard), a sultry and mysterious woman in black who wants to know all about their army service.

Nida suggests the boys freshen themselves at Tokyo Amato's, a local servicemen's club. Willie and Joe sneak in to the "officers only" club, disrupt the bathhouse by fighting their scrub boys, and are forced to escape wearing geisha outfits. They are aided by Johnny Redondo (Russell Johnson), a friend of Nida's, who invites them to his home and entertains them for the evening. The boys are driven to another servicemen's club, where they plan to spend the night, but are arrested for being intoxicated and out of uniform. They are recognized by Major Ormsby (Vaughn Taylor) as being the geishas from Tokyo Amato's and Ormsby sends them to General Dixon to initiate a court-martial. The general overhears that they know Johnny Redondo and releases them; it seems that Redondo is a known arms smuggler whom Dixon has been trying to trap, and the general plans to use the boys as bait.

Willie and Joe are arrested again by Ormsby while sightseeing; the major is then berated by General Dixon for his interference. After meeting with Redondo and arranging to

Marketing for Universal's service comedy *Back at the Front* *(1952) emphasizes "the hilarious NEW adventures" of Willie and Joe in Japan, as "they shake Tokyo apart from Geisha house to Smuggler's dive!" Since this is a comedy, no mention is mde of the Korean War.*

borrow an Army truck so that he can safely deliver a cargo of crab meat, Willie and Joe are arrested yet again by Ormsby, who is promptly tongue-lashed by Dixon. Free once more, with fresh new uniforms provided by the general, the boys unsuspectingly help Johnny Redondo and Nida by delivering their cargo of crab meat to a waiting plane.

Major Ormsby stops the truck of crab meat (which actually carries explosives that are being smuggled to North Korea) per the general's order, but lets it pass when he sees Willie and Joe driving it. Dixon is furious at Ormsby's failure to follow orders and demotes him to a captain. As the loaded plane is about to take off, Dixon arrives and tells the boys that they aided a smuggler. Willie angrily throws a can of "crab meat" at the plane, which explodes and forces the plane to abort its takeoff, and the smugglers

are thwarted and captured. Willie and Joe are commended by General Dixon, who promptly sends them back home so as not to further endanger international relations.

A genial comedy, *Back at the Front* follows Willie and Joe from the end of World War II to Japan during the days of the Korean War, though it must be noted that the war itself is not referred to during the film. At one point, Willie and Joe are stopped by two military policemen, who assume that the boys "have been at the front," and give them directions to the nearest servicemen's club. It is intimated that the smuggled explosives are going to North Korea, though that is never explicitly stated. Nida, in her slinky "black widow" outfit, seems to be spying for the Communists, but again, it is only inferred. But it is because of the Korean War that Willie and Joe have been recalled into the Army,

After being shot while testing bulletproof jackets in the line of duty, Joe (Harvey Lembeck, sitting left) and Willie (Tom Ewell, sitting right) listen dejectedly as the jackets are praised in Back at the Front *(1952).*

and the script is designed to show that even the dumbest and laziest of soldiers — Willie and Joe — can still have an effect on various details of a global conflict.

Back at the Front is less satirical and focused than its predecessor, *Up Front*, and suffers due to the alteration of Joe's basic character. As played by Harvey Lembeck, Joe has evolved into a dogface without a conscience. Every time a situation which offers trouble arises, Joe leads them into it without a second thought for safety, ethics or consequences. Since this is a comedy, the characters have much more latitude, but one wonders why Willie, who can at least sense the approach of danger and trouble, stays with Joe, who continually creates both. The problem actually runs deeper and was described with perfect clarity by the reviewer for *Time*: "Mauldin's pen and ink infantrymen from *Stars and Stripes* were a biting commentary on the long-suffering dogfaces of World War II. By surrounding

Willie and Joe with a threadbare plot and substituting slapstick for the original's realism, *Back at the Front* succeeds in making Willie and Joe more like two-dimensional comic-strip characters than they ever have before."

To be sure, the movie is amusing and at times funny, but it doesn't amount to much. If the "threadbare plot," as *Time* judged it, is examined at all, it makes little sense and undermines the film's entire structure. Flabby writing, however, is not its only problem. One of its chief selling points is the location filming in Tokyo, but even that is unimpressive. Other than some street scenes which fleetingly show various sections of the city, much of the movie takes place indoors until the climactic chase to the airfield. This is the most obvious indication of the movie's low budget and "B" movie status.

Back at the Front was surprisingly popular and well received, considering its low budget and production values. William Weaver of the

Motion Picture Herald was impressed. "The script is constantly a laugh producer to the finish. The direction by George Sherman is a splendid example of proficient timing, shading and changes of pace." The British Film Institute's *Monthly Film Bulletin* commented, "This comic strip brought to the screen (a sequel to *Up Front*) embodies all the things which could happen to two very idiotic G.I.s and in so doing manages to raise quite a few laughs."

The film is certainly silly, but service comedies often are. All in all it is less labored and offensive than many others, and Willie and Joe do, no matter how unsuspectingly, prevent arms from being smuggled to the North Koreans. Fans of this comic subgenre will not be disappointed.

The Bamboo Prison

Credits: 1954. Columbia. *Directed by:* Lewis Seiler. *Produced by* Bryan Foy. *Screen Play by* Edwin Blum and Jack DeWitt. *Story by* Jack DeWitt. *Music Conducted by* Mischa Bakaleinikoff. *Director of Photography:* Burnett Guffey, A.S.C. *Film Editor:* Henry Batista, A.C.E. *Art Director:* Cary Odell. *Set Decorator:* James Crowe. *Assistant Director:* Carter DeHaven, Jr. *Recording Supervisor:* John Livadary. Not Rated. Black and White. Flat (1.33:1). 79 minutes. Released in December, 1954. Not currently available on commercial home video.

Cast: *Sergeant Bill Rand*, Robert Francis; *Tanya Clayton*, Dianne Foster; *Corporal Brady*, Brian Keith; *Arkansas*, Jerome Courtland; *Father Francis Dolan*, E.G. Marshall; *Doc Jackson*, Earle Hyman; *Slade*, Jack Kelly; *Hsai Tung*, Richard Loo; *Li Ching*, Keye Luke; *Clayton*, Murray Matheson; *Pop*, King Donovan; *Jackie*, Dick (Dickie) Jones; *Ramirez*, Pepe Hern; *Pike*, Leo Gordon; *Meatball*, Weaver Levy; *Metaxas*, George Keymas; *Cockney*, Denis Martin.

Historical Accuracy Level: Medium. The Chinese prison camp is presented realistically and without undue exploitation, although the Russians in the story are not credible.

Patriotic Propaganda Level: High. Maintaining one's personal and patriotic integrity is highly emphasized in this psychological exploration of prison camp indoctrination effects.

Elements: Army, Brainwashing, Clergy, Collaboration, Espionage, Peace Negotiations, Politics, Prisoners of War, Red Menace, Repatriation, Secret Missions.

One of the films which examines the plight of Korean War prisoners of war is *The Bamboo Prison*. Released about eight months after MGM's similar but harsher *Prisoner of War*, this is a slightly more serious and believable glimpse of P.O.W. life, though neither film is what one would term absolutely authentic. *The Bamboo Prison* emphasizes the political aspects — Chinese and Russian — governing the prison camp, and depicts the prisoners as pawns in the chess game of international political strategy. Even stronger, however, is its scrutiny of the human nature involved in collaborating in any degree with the enemy, and how such collaboration affects — and defeats — every prisoner.

Exhausted American prisoners are marched into a Chinese prison camp and forced to squeeze into already crowded barracks. One of the new men is Corporal Brady (Brian Keith), who is shocked at the camp's deplorable conditions and the brutality commonly employed by the Chinese guards. Brady challenges the hut leader, Sergeant John Rand (Robert Francis), when he discovers that Rand is friendly to the Chinese, but the other prisoners warn that if Rand is hurt, they will be punished. Rand agrees to collaborate further with the Chinese, even making radio broadcasts against America, and is given "progressive" status, including the freedom to leave the camp and visit a nearby town.

Eventually, Rand is revealed (to the audience) as an American agent and Brady as his contact. They have been assigned to find specific information regarding the whereabouts and condition of thousands of American prisoners for leverage in the Panmunjom peace treaty negotiations. Rand suspects that a British political advisor to Moscow named Clayton (Murray Matheson) who often visits the camp has such records, and so romances Clayton's beautiful Russian ballerina wife Tanya (Dianne Foster) in order to get them.

The Communists have a spy of their own in the camp, however, masquerading as a priest. Father Francis Dolan (E.G. Marshall) moves

YANK PRISONER IN CHINA CHOOSES BAMBOO CURTAIN!

Did Sergeant Fall For Commie Cutie...Or Was He Pushed?

As the heavy-duty trucks rolled away to freedom, Sergeant William Rand, husky American GI, grimly chose to remain behind the bamboo curtain! Sergeant Rand talked freely to reporters and his sensational behind-the-scenes narrative of life in a prison camp had tense drama packed into every minute of his breath-taking story.

Rand carefully went over all details from the day in camp when he first met luscious spy, Tanya Clayton, until the very moment when he turned his back on freedom. In the course of his story, Rand discussed the indomitable spirit of our GI's, the wry humor that was ever-present in the guarded barracks and the infamous brain-washing techniques of the enemy war lords.

His powerful story was carefully noted and has been filmed by producer Bryan Foy for Columbia Pictures. It is called THE BAMBOO PRISON.

TRAITOR? Sgt. Wm. Rand still has us guessing. Is he hero or heel?

PRISON riot breaks out under ruthless rule of infamous Li Chung!

BEAUTIFUL Tanya Clayton has lots of curves and knows all the angles!

Columbia Studios uses a newspaper-like format to advertise its Korean War P.O.W. drama The Bamboo Prison *(1954). With somber pictures of Sergeant Rand (Robert Francis), Li Chung (Keye Luke), Tanya Clayton (Dianne Foster) and rioting prisoners, it successfully captures the spirit of grim desperation that pervades the picture.*

among the men, offering solace and sympathy, collecting information which the Chinese can use against them, and Dolan ultimately realizes that Rand is working against the Communists. Dolan confronts Rand and is killed by him. Clayton discovers that his wife has provided somebody with his top secret information and threatens her (with, appropriately, Russian roulette!) but is killed by Brady, who has escaped the camp with Rand's help to deliver the information to the United Nations authorities at Panmunjom.

The remainder of the prisoners are freed when a truce is declared and the armistice is signed, and all are given a choice of repatriation to America or Communist China. Most, of course, return home, but Rand chooses Communist China. His cover as a collaborator still intact, he rejects a return to America (and faces the shame of his mother, heard on a tape recorder) to continue his important assignment. But before he leaves, he tells Brady and Tanya (who is defecting to America) that he will soon be back.

The Bamboo Prison's villains are not North Korean but rather Chinese and Russian. The enemy here is the insidious spread of communism, and its perpetrators are the Chinese, supported by the Russians. It is a Chinese flag which is in view over the prison camp, while Clayton wields tremendous power at the camp and reports directly back to Moscow. By identifying these targets instead of North Korea, the film is focusing on the larger issue of global communism. This stance is best stated during the scene when black Doc Jackson (Earle Hyman) is interrogated by the Chinese (as well as Rand and Clayton) about his experience with injustice in America. Doc is outspoken and articulate and refutes the notion of Communist superiority, saying "I've decided I'd much rather be black than red," and then suffers a beating for his statement.

The anti–Communist feeling in America was high at the time (1954) and *The Bamboo Prison* provided moviegoers with easy targets for their hate, scorn and ridicule. Even so, red-baiting is downplayed in favor of—for the most part—a well-balanced morality tale of intrigue, courage, honor, loyalty and betrayal. To its credit, it doesn't provide pat solutions to com-

plex problems and its drama rarely seems simplistic. It also avoids the tendency to use physical torture of the prisoners to manipulate audience emotion, which is a tendency that *Prisoner of War* does not resist. The film does not explore the psychological effects of torture or indoctrination to the extent that *The Rack* or *Time Limit* do, but rather examines how collaboration with the enemy affects everyone who is in the prison camp.

The central device of Rand's duplicity does, however, diminish the film's power. Instead of investigating why an American would consciously switch sides to communism, the film "cops out" by revealing Rand to be a double agent. It is a fact that twenty-one American soldiers did, at the end of the war, renounce America and become Communists, choosing to remain in North Korea rather than return home. This film indicates that Rand will follow this path, but then backs away and reveals his true assignment. It would have been a far braver film to depict Rand as a true convert, but no studio at the time would have produced such a story.

The Bamboo Prison can be viewed as an imitation of *Stalag 17*, released the previous year. The Chinese have taken the place of the Nazis, the men band together against a supposed traitor, a secret means of communication is important to the plot and the central character is enigmatic rather than heroic. Both movies are also cognizant of the human suffering taking place in their prison camps. And while *The Bamboo Prison* is surely a more dramatically superficial film than *Stalag 17*, at least it doesn't feature the cloying comedy routines of Robert Strauss and Harvey Lembeck. Instead, there are sly imitations of Cary Grant and Boris Karloff, contributed by Jerome Courtland.

The film's weakest aspect is its dialogue, which ranges from clever to syrupy, especially when it involves Rand's romance with Tanya Clayton. Rand's radio dialogue, when he reviles the American way of life, is also supposed to provide a code to the American authorities who are listening, but this code seems completely specious. Occasionally, the dialogue is poorly underwritten, as when Pop (King Donovan) is killed and Pike (Leo Gordon) yells futilely, "Dirty cruds!"

On the other hand, one of its strongest as-

Corporal Brady (Brian Keith, left) glares at Communist sympathizer—note the armband—Sergeant Bill Rand (Robert Francis) in the topical P.O.W. drama The Bamboo Prison *(1954).*

sets is the use of a double agent priest in the camp. It is a genuine surprise when Father Dolan is revealed to be an enemy agent, and a drinker as well. In their *Motion Picture Guide*, Jay Robert Nash and Stanley Ralph Ross comment that "E. G. Marshall plays a phony priest so well that you want to confess everything to him." The ruse of a priest is especially insidious, of course, for few secrets would be denied to such a figure, especially in a prison camp.

Despite its propaganda quotient and occasionally inane dialogue, however, the movie is compelling, due mostly to its first-rate cast. Brian Keith, E. G. Marshall, King Donovan, Leo Gordon, Earle Hyman, Jack Kelly, Murray Matheson, Keye Luke and Richard Loo all deliver strong supporting performances, with Gordon and Hyman standing out. Fresh from *The Caine Mutiny*, Robert Francis is adequate, if a bit wooden, in the lead. The entire subplot involving ballerina Tanya Clayton's (Dianne Foster) loves and allegiances, however, is ludicrous. *The Bamboo Prison* is not as serious a study

of psyches under pressure as the later gems *The Rack* and *Time Limit*, but its semi-documentary style and active inclusion of political dialogue mark it as thoughtful rather than exploitive. *Variety* termed it a "good actioner," while *Film Daily* appraised it as "a routine film built around a group of soldiers in Communist hands in North Korea, which manages to get across a certain amount of suspense and humor." *The Motion Picture Guide* praises the film: "There is much of merit in this film. It has many interesting plot twists and the theme of Americans turning to Communism under the brainwashing techniques of the North Koreans was, and still is, a fascinating topic."

This prisoner of war drama is not as well known or well remembered as others, but it is worthwhile. It treats the subject of collaboration seriously but without melodrama and does so in a very entertaining fashion. *The Bamboo Prison* is compelling, though it does not shed much light upon its incomprehensible real-life subject.

Battle Circus

Credits: 1953. Metro-Goldwyn-Mayer. *Directed by* Richard Brooks. *Produced by* Pandro S. Berman. *Screen Play by* Richard Brooks. *Based on a Story by* Allen Rivkin and Laura Kerr. *Music by* Lennie Hayton. *Director of Photography:* John Alton, A.S.C. *Film Editor:* George Boemler, A.C.E. *Art Directors:* Cedric Gibbons and James Basevi. *Assistant Director:* Al Jennings. *Recording Supervisor:* Douglas Shearer. *Set Decorations:* Edwin B. Willis and Alfred E. Spencer. *Special Effects:* A. Arnold Gillespie. *Make-Up by* William Tuttle. *Technical Advisers:* Lieutenant Colonel K. E. Van Buskirk and Lieutenant Mary Couch. *Orchestrations by* Robert Franklyn (uncredited). Not Rated. Black and White. Flat (1.33:1). 89 minutes. Released in March, 1953. Filmed in part at Camp Pickett, Virginia. Currently available on VHS home video.

Cast: *Major Jed Webbe,* Humphrey Bogart; *Lieutenant Ruth McGara,* June Allyson; *Sergeant Orvil Statt,* Keenan Wynn; *Lieutenant Colonel Hillary Whalters,* Robert Keith; *Captain John Rustford (Rusty),* William Campbell; *Lieutenant Lawrence,* Perry Sheehan; *Lieutenant Rose Ashland,* Patricia Tiernan; *Lieutenant Jane Franklin,* Adele Longmire; *Adjutant,* Jonathan Cott; *Lieutenant Edith Edwards,* Ann Morrison; *Lieutenant Graciano,* Helen Winston; *Captain Dobbs,* Sarah Selby; *Korean Child,* Danny Chang; *Korean Prisoner,* Philip Ahn; *Sergeant,* Steve Forrest; *Lieutenant,* Jeff Richards; *Captain Norson,* Dick Simmons.

Historical Accuracy Level: Medium. Its view of battlefield surgeons is softly focused rather than sharply etched, but its surrounding atmosphere, particularly regarding a constant lack of supplies and the need to move the camp as the front lines alter, is true to history.

Patriotic Propaganda Level: Medium. While individual characters may be disillusioned or past caring, the film's view of the collective MASH unit is certainly positive.

Elements: Army, Females in the Field, Helicopters, Medicine, Nurses, Rescues, Romance.

Seventeen years before *MASH*, there was *Battle Circus.* Both films share a jaundiced view of the Korean War and the surgeons who struggle every day to save some of its casualties. Both films depict the mental battle those characters face when deluged with a seemingly unending stream of battered humanity. But where *MASH* celebrates the chaos within the war, *Battle Circus* tries very hard to maintain a linear, traditional approach to its subject, even to the extent of imposing an unbelievable love story upon its war drama.

Battle Circus' focus is the 8666th MASH (Mobile Army Surgical Hospital) unit, which is stationed a few miles behind the front lines during the late stages of the Korean War. Three new nurses arrive at the 8666th, including Lieutenant Ruth McGara (June Allyson), who has plenty of care to give wounded soldiers but not enough sense to drop and hide when an enemy MiG fighter strafes the encampment. She is knocked to the ground by Major Jed Webbe (Humphrey Bogart), the company's second surgical officer. Webbe explains the realities of the war to her before receiving news that the camp must move, as the front lines are shifting.

The camp's move is directed by Sergeant Orvill Statt (Keenan Wynn), who choreographs its dismantling as though it were a circus moving from one town to another. Meanwhile, Webbe and pilot Rusty (William Campbell) take a helicopter ride to search for a new camp location and are called upon to collect a casualty while doing so. Dodging enemy bullets, the chopper sets down to find three wounded men. "I thought there was only one," yells Rusty. "That was ten minutes ago," is the reply. The helicopter and its cargo of wounded men return safely to the 8666th.

The camp's eighth move within a month is under way when the convoy comes under sniper fire at night, forcing Webbe to tackle Ruth McGara, again. He makes a pass at her in the back of a truck, but she resists his advances. The following day, the camp is reconstructed in a new location while Webbe is reprimanded by Lieutenant Colonel Whalters (Robert Keith), the company's first surgical (and commanding) officer, for taking foolish and unnecessary risks. Refugees stream past the camp heading south, pausing only for inoculations and hot food. Webbe continues to pursue Ruth, finally winning her affection by operating on a young Korean boy (Danny Chang) with a chest wound whom she had befriended.

Ruth scares him away by referring to

This simple ad for MGM's medical drama Battle Circus (1953) *stresses romance over conflict, but the film's medical aspects are not addressed at all. Also note the reference to* Battleground, *a popular World War II film which MGM had released four years previously.*

commitment, but they finally agree to a relationship the next day during a torrential rainstorm. The other nurses question Webbe's marital status, which prods Ruth to ask him directly. He refuses to answer and finds himself drinking, alone. A windstorm engulfs the camp, but surgery continues. Rusty flies a mission to retrieve whole blood and is on his way back when the storm hits, delaying his return until after dark. Webbe and Statt drive a jeep through the storm to meet him and guide him to the camp with the jeep's headlights. Rusty lands safely, with very little fuel remaining. Rusty provides Webbe with a bottle of scotch, which the surgeon consumes quickly, causing him to be unfit for emergency surgery. Whalters confines Webbe to quarters and tells him to transfer or quit drinking. Webbe apologizes. He and Ruth talk about the past and the possibilities of the future.

More casualties arrive, as well as some North Korean prisoners. One of them (Philip Ahn) has a grenade and threatens to detonate it in the operating room. Ruth takes charge, while the surgeons continue to operate. She approaches the North Korean quietly and takes the grenade as he collapses. Her bravery, and vulnerable crying fit afterward, touch Webbe, bringing them closer together.

The front lines shift again, forcing another move. Shells bombard the camp, wounding Whalters in the leg. Patients are to be evacuated on a hospital train, using a nearby railroad spur, but the train never arrives. Statt organizes a makeshift flatbed car, powered by a truck, to evacuate the most seriously wounded men by rail. Webbe leads the convoy of trucks, carrying the hospital tents, equipment and personnel, and the convoy is detoured twice by enemy activity. At one point, the trucks are emptied of personnel and driven down a steep hill to another road, with men carrying the wounded down the hill on stretchers or on their backs. An Army observer is impressed with the MASH unit's tenacity, saying "They haven't invented a medal yet for those people." The convoy finally arrives at the new camp site and Webbe and Ruth are reunited. The war continues.

Battle Circus is intended as a tribute to the hardworking MASH personnel, and it effectively depicts their struggles against enemy bombardment, hardships of weather, logistical obstacles and simple but deadly fatigue in order to save lives. The film does not glorify these people, but merely presents their situation matter-of-factly, stressing the difficulties inherent in successfully completing their mission. The film lacks the blood and mayhem of *MASH*, but times and standards were different, and Richard Brooks' drama doesn't need flamboyancy. Brooks utilizes one character to embody the difficulties of the situation: Lieutenant Colonel Whalters.

Whalters is the MASH unit's commanding officer and, presumably, best surgeon. While Major Webbe is drinking or pursuing the nurses, it is Whalters who frets over the lack of whole blood, who oversees the camp's operation and who enforces discipline, even concerning Webbe. Whalters works until he's ready to drop and keeps going. Even after being pierced by shrapnel, he tries to rise to facilitate the camp's move. It is this brand of character which best represents the spirit of the MASH unit, and it is very nicely detailed by Robert Keith. A familiar actor who tended toward vacillating characters, Robert Keith here gives a strong performance, projecting skill, authority and compassion. It is a shame that *Battle Circus* is not overly concerned with Whalters' story.

Instead, and to its undeniable detriment, its focus is clearly on the love life of Jed Webbe. Major Webbe appears to be a competent surgeon and isn't afraid of making tough decisions, but when he begins to romantically pursue Ruth McGara, he becomes positively creepy. Webbe starts with standard lines like "What's a girl like you doing in Korea, anyway?" but gradually moves toward harrassment. In the operating room, Ruth asks about the Korean boy. Webbe ignores her concern and asks "When are you getting around to *my* problem?" with definite sexual innuendo. Perhaps this type of "playing hard to get" romance was more effective at the time, but today Webbe's pursuit of his nurse is nothing short of offensive.

Even after he wins her — because traditional Hollywood formula demands that he should — Webbe still acts like a jerk, refusing to provide personal details or admit whether he is married. Over time, he feeds her little tidbits about himself and she devotes herself to him, but the relationship is hardly credible. Unfortunately,

The scene is familiar, but it isn't MASH; *it's Major Jed Webbe (Humphrey Bogart) returning to camp in Richard Brooks' Korean medical drama* Battle Circus (1953).

this relationship is the main focus of the film in between the two moves of the MASH camp which bookend the story. Humphrey Bogart actually makes Jed Webbe too dark for audience empathy, though he does have a couple of nice moments. June Allyson is, as usual, sugary in the role of the greenhorn nurse who doesn't know enough to dodge bullets but seems quite capable of dodging the probing fingers of men. The contradiction doesn't hold water.

The Korean War is simply background to this story. Only the inclusion of the North Korean prisoners, the presence of snipers and a few references to Korean landmarks distinguish this from World War II films. There is a palpable pessimism that pervades the scene, but it doesn't refer to the war per se, but rather the odds of saving lives under such conditions. *Battle Circus* has little to say about the war itself, even though it was filmed and released during the war's final year. The film's brief prologue is self

explanatory: "This is a story about the indomitable human spirit — it takes place in Korea."

Though its central story is unconvincing and trite, the surrounding details are far more effective. The film chronicles the use of helicopters to ferry wounded soldiers and supplies quite authentically, and Rusty's tense search for the camp in the windstorm is a dramatic highlight. Director Richard Brooks endeavors to create a realistic backdrop for his story, and he does succeed in this regard. It is the main characters and their romance which undermines the rest of the story.

Of the other cast members, Keenan Wynn especially acquits himself with dignity. As Sergeant Statt, the former Ringling Brothers foreman who oversees the MASH unit's configuration and deployment, Wynn is efficient and authoritative. The actor is allowed to display his compassionate side when dealing with the young

Korean boy who has taken a special liking to him. And though he doesn't have much dialogue, William Campbell is convincing as Rusty, the brave helicopter pilot. Look fast for Steve Forrest, who portrays a sergeant. And Philip Ahn has an atypical role as the North Korean with the grenade.

When the film stays with the broader picture of the MASH unit, as when Sergeant Statt organizes its dismantling, or shows the controlled chaos in the operating room, the film is effective. Too often, however, it bogs down with the hackneyed romance or presents the other nurses as chickens clucking over Jed the rooster. When the film tries to become personal, it fails completely.

Moira Walsh of *America* explained the film's varying quality in this way: "When the picture is dealing in semi-documentary fashion with logistical problems and the inspiring business of saving lives, it has some very effective moments. In between these, however, it is necessary to put up with a painfully coy and synthetic romance between a cynical, matrimonially once-burned doctor (Humphrey Bogart) and a starry-eyed nurse (June Allyson). The mixture consists of about two parts love to one part war, and in about the same ratio the film is more unpalatable than it is interesting."

Most critics found the proceedings dull or trivial. Arthur Knight of *Saturday Review* thought that "*Battle Circus* fumbles along pretty much at random," *Variety* termed it "routine," while Howard Thompson of the *New York Times* called it "Pure, redundant Hollywood" but liked it a little better than most. *Newsweek* provided the film with its best review, judging the movie to be "A sincere and fairly exciting tribute to the work done by the MASH behind the Korean battle lines."

The film found limited success on its theatrical run, undoubtedly due to its stars. It has not aged well and has been designated a footmark in cinematic history because its subject matter was recycled by Richard Hooker, Ring Lardner, Jr. and Robert Altman two decades later with far greater success.

Battle Flame

Credits: 1959. Allied Artists. *Directed by* R. G. Springsteen. *Produced by* Lester A. Samson. *Screenplay by* Elwood Ullman. *Story by* Lester A. Samson and Elwood Ullman. *Music by* Marlin Skiles. *Director of Photography*: Carl Guthrie, A.S.C. *Film Editor*: William Austin, A.C.E. *Art Director*: David Milton. *Production Manager*: Edward Morey, Jr. *Assistant Director*: Bert Chervin. *Music Editor*: Jerry Irvin. *Sound Editor*: Anthony Carras. *Set Decorator*: Joseph Kish. *Set Continuity*: Virginia Mazzuco. *Recording Engineer*: Ralph Butler. *Wardrobe*: Roger J. Weinberg and Norah Sharpe. *Makeup Artist*: Jack Dusick. *Construction Supervisor*: James West. *Property Master*: Ted Mossman. Not Rated. Black and White. Flat (1.33:1). 78 minutes. Released in July, 1959. Not currently available on commercial home video.

Cast: *Lieutenant Frank Davis*, Scott Brady; *Lieutenant Mary Ferguson*, Elaine Edwards; *Corporal Pacheco*, Robert Blake; *Teach*, Wayne Heffley; *Sergeant McKelvey*, Gordon Jones; *Orlando*, Ken Miller; *Nawlins (New Orleans)*, Arthur Walsh; *Second Lieutenant Wechsler*, Richard Harrison; *Gilchrist*, Gary Kent; *Nurse Fisher*, Peggy Moffitt; *Nurse Claycomb*, Jean Robbins; *Commander Bill Stoddard*, Richard Crane (uncredited).

Historical Accuracy Level: Medium. Its central story is pure hokum, yet it follows its Marines from Inchon to the Chosin Reservoir and Hungnam.

Patriotic Propaganda Level: High. These Marines never lose their fighting spirit, especially when American nurses are captured by the Chinese.

Elements: Bugles, Females in the Field, Marine Corps, Nurses, Rescues, Romance, Winter Fighting.

Battle Flame is a routine war drama which gains some stature by following rather closely several Korean War campaigns. Allied Artists was a minor studio that produced nine different Korean War movies, some of them surprisingly strong and effective, and *Battle Flame* is perhaps the penultimate Allied Artists version of the war. Its approach is more comprehensive and wide-ranging than its other efforts, and it also uses footage from at least three of those previous movies to support its own story.

Battle Flame highlights the U.S. Marine Corps' activities in Korea in 1950. Beginning with the amphibious landing at Inchon, the film uses a great deal of actual combat footage as the Marine Corps pushes east from Inchon and re-takes the South Korean capitol of Seoul. After Seoul is liberated (utilizing footage from *Battle Zone*), the Marines stop to rest and relax. Orlando (Ken Miller) is a former cook who de-scribes mouth-watering meals to the hungry men. Nawlins — actually "New Orleans" with a drawl — (Arthur Walsh) is asked why he joined the Marines. "When I heard the south was fightin' the north, nothin' could keep me out!" he replies. The outfit's leader, Lieutenant Frank Davis (Scott Brady) is reminded of his leg wound and his days at the hospital in Pusan, spent recovering and romancing a nurse, Lieu-tenant Mary Ferguson (Elaine Edwards), seen in flashback.

Corporal Pacheco (Robert Blake), a street-wise youngster with no formal education, be-friends Teach (Wayne Heffley), a college gradu-ate whose wartime specialty is tossing grenades. These men of Able company are sent to an airfield near Seoul, from which an offensive will be mounted. At night, the airfield is raided by North Korean planes, which strafe the men, wounding Orlando, and bomb the planes and equipment. In the hospital tent where Orlando is taken, Davis meets Mary Ferguson again. A group of nurses is helping while their plane is being repaired. Mary tells Davis that she is in-volved with a Navy surgeon and that she was unable to bring herself to tell him earlier. An enemy tank column advances on the airfield, causing an evacuation. The tanks follow the Marines (utilizing footage from *Dragonfly Squadron* and *Battle Zone*), but are attacked and destroyed by Air Force jets.

Time passes. At the end of October, Able company is in frozen North Korea, near the Chosin Reservoir. The Chinese jump into the fight and attack, blowing bugles as they overrun the first line of defense. American artillery dri-ves them back into the hills. Able company is or-dered to march to Chin-yon to eliminate any Reds there, and to watch for survivors of a C-47 plane crash in that area. On the march, a wounded man is found; he is the C-47 pilot, and he tells Davis that the five nurses on board

were taken prisoner by Chinese troops. Davis and his Marines attack Chin-yon (utilizing footage from *Hold Back the Night*) and rescue the nurses. Mary is happy to be rescued, but tells Davis that "nothing has changed" in her per-sonal life. During the action, Teach is killed and Pacheco is devastated by the loss of his friend.

Davis receives instructions to withdraw to Hungnam along with the rest of the U.N. fight-ing forces. Sergeant McKelvey (Gordon Jones) tells the men, "This ain't no retreat, it's a fight-ing withdrawal." The men, with nurses in tow, march toward the sea. They are ambushed by Chinese and suffer heavy casualties before Davis eliminates a machine gun nest with a grenade and Air Force jets swoop in to finish the job. The group continues to march and safely reaches Hungnam, where they are put aboard a troop ship. Actual footage chronicles the true life evac-uation from and subsequent destruction of the Hungnam harbor.

At sea, the men are reunited with the nurses, and Nawlins is kissed by southerner Nurse Claycomb (Jean Robbins) in apprecia-tion on the nurses' behalf for the efforts of the entire company. Davis finds himself talking to Commander Bill Stoddard (Richard Crane), the Navy surgeon to whom Mary Ferguson is en-gaged. Stoddard is a good sport and tells Davis that Mary is crazy about Davis rather than him-self. As Stoddard leaves, Mary appears and they are united in a passionate embrace.

Battle Flame is rather run-of-the-mill dra-matically, though it does contain some clever and effective moments. It follows the familiar pattern of populating Able company with a cross-section of personality types — a southern redneck, an intellectual, a streetwise punk, an Irish sergeant, etc. — and forcing them to band together into an effective fighting unit. This "motley crew" cliche is terribly overused in war films, but it does provide a few telling moments, such as the sequence when Pacheco and Teach attack the village of Chin-yon, Teach is killed and Pacheco mourns his friend.

The inclusion of female nurses in the field suggests exploitation, but this is not the case. The five nurses are never used to titillate the male characters (or the audience) and their pres-ence is plausibly (if rather improbably) ex-plained. In fact, the presence of the nurses gives

FEMALE CAPTIVES OF THE CHINESE REDS!

American nurses trapped in a brutal prison camp ... and a company of U.S. Marines who swore to get them out alive!

BATTLE FLAME

starring

SCOTT BRADY · Elaine Edwards · Robert Blake

AN ALLIED ARTISTS PICTURE

PRODUCED BY LESTER A. SANSOM DIRECTED BY R. G. SPRINGSTEEN SCREENPLAY BY ELWOOD ULLMAN

The producers of Allied Artists' drama Battle Flame *(1959) decided to emphasize the sensational, hoping to lure viewers with the spectacle of "American nurses trapped in a brutal prison camp," and presenting the image of a sexy woman threatened by the Red Menace.*

the Marines' final march an extra dramatic drive and motivational depth to return safely. The romance between Davis and Mary Ferguson is handled especially well; it is realistic in terms of dialogue and emotion and it is nicely staged in brief moments amidst the chaos of war. It also provides some humor, as when Sergeant McKelvey advises his lieutenant to follow the Marine dictum to "fight to the limit and give no quar-ter." McKelvey recommends "a fast, enveloping movement" and is rewarded with a smile from Lieutenant Davis.

The film definitely intends to champion working class soldiers. The enlisted men are given almost as much screen time as Davis, and their various quirks, attitudes and personalities are just as important to the story as his romance. Davis is the highest ranking officer shown regularly, and at the end it is he who wins Mary's heart rather than the Navy commander. Perhaps the ultimate aim of this project was to praise the Marine gyrenes, the men who liberated Seoul and withdrew from the Chosin Reservoir under heavy fire, always bringing their wounded with them. It certainly succeeds in that regard.

It is less successful staging battle action. Most of the major battle scenes are based on those from other Allied Artists films (*Battle Zone*, *Dragonfly Squadron* and *Hold Back the Night*) and liberally use footage from those films. Only the Chinese infantry attack, with its blowing of bugles and night-time running assault, is truly effective. The rest all suffer from choppy editing and, in the case of the tank attack, a strong sense that the sequence is misplaced within the framework of the story. On the other hand, true-life battle footage is also used liberally and it melds into the action more smoothly here than in other Korean War films.

Battle Flame, along with *Hold Back the Night*, also represents the truest glimpse of the winter fighting in Korea. The film emphasizes the country's harsh conditions and shows how soldiers cope with frozen supplies and weapons. Soldiers are seen carrying rations, batteries and medical supplies under their outer clothing to keep them from freezing. The march from the Chosin Reservoir to Hungnam is authentically depicted as being slow, methodical and painful, as the Marines battle the freezing weather as well as Chinese snipers.

Otherwise, the film is strictly routine. Its dialogue is the standard type heard in war films since time immemorial, although Orlando's (Ken Miller's) vivid descriptions of the food that he will eat when he returns to the States provide interesting moments along the way. It is unfortunate that the script wastes its opportunities to say something profound about the war, because it has several chances to do so.

Critics were not impressed with *Battle*

Corporal Pacheco (Robert Blake, foreground) and Sergeant McKelvey (Gordon Jones, above) battle Communist soldiers in the snowy hills of Korea in Battle Flame *(1959).*

Flame. Boxoffice noted that "Other than some rousing battle sequences, however, the picture offers little, either in the story or acting departments, to recommend it." The cast is competent in standard roles, with Robert Blake making the most vivid impression, fifteen years before he became television's Baretta. The film was barely released to theaters, appearing as half of a double feature with the World War II drama *Surrender—Hell!* While its entertainment value is strictly routine, *Battle Flame* deserves some respect for adhering as closely as it does to Korean War history and as a tribute to the Marine Corps, which suffered an inordinately high casualty rate during its vaunted "fighting withdrawal" from the Chosin Reservoir to the Hungnam harbor.

Battle Hymn

Credits: 1957. Universal. *Directed by* Douglas Sirk. *Produced by* Ross Hunter. *Written by* Charles Grayson and Vincent B. Evans. *Music by* Frank Skinner. *Director of Photography*: Russell Metty, A.S.C. *Film Editor*: Russell Schoengarth, A.C.E. *Art Direction*: Alexander Golitzen and Emrich Nicholson. *Set Decorations*: Russell A. Gausman and Oliver Emert. *Sound*: Leslie I. Carey and Corson Jowett. *Special Photography*: Clifford Stine, A.S.C. *Gowns by* Bill Thomas. *Hair Stylist*: Joan St. Oegger. *Make-Up*: Bud Westmore. *Assistant Director*: Marshall Green. *Technical Advisor*: Colonel Dean Hess. *Musical Supervision by* Joseph Gershenson. Not Rated. Technicolor. *Technicolor Color Consultant*: William Fritzsche. CinemaScope (2.35:1). 108 minutes. Released in February 1957. Currently available on VHS videotape.

Cast: *Colonel Dean Hess*, Rock Hudson; *En Soon Yang*, Anna Kashfi; *Sergeant Herman*, Dan Duryea; *Captain Stan Skidmore*, Don De-Fore; *Mary Hess*, Martha Hyer; *Major Moore*, Jock Mahoney; *Mess Sergeant*, Alan Hale; *Lieutenant Maples*, James Edwards; *Deacon Edwards*, Carl Benton Reid; *General Kim*, Richard Loo; *Old Man*, Philip Ahn; *General Timberidge*, Bartlett Robinson; *Lieutenant Hollis*, Simon Scott; *Korean Official*, Teru Shimada; *Major Harrison*, Carleton Young; *Chu*, Jung Kyoo Pyo;

Captain Reardon, Art Millan; *Navy Lieutenant*, William Hudson; *Sentry*, Paul Sorenson; *with* Children of the Orphans' Home in Korea; *introduction by* General Earle F. Partridge, U.S.A.F.

Historical Accuracy Level: High. The film faithfully follows the military career of Colonel Dean Hess, a minister who served as a fighter pilot in Korea.

Patriotic Propaganda Level: High. How can a film that concerns an American fighter pilot who is also a minister and saves hundreds of Korean orphans from death not be considered patriotic?

Elements: Air Force, Air War, Biography, Clergy, Effects on Civilians, Military Training, Multiple Wars, Orphans, Rescues.

Battle Hymn is a largely true, high profile story from the Korean War based upon the actions (and book) of Air Force pilot Dean E. Hess, who also happened to be an ordained minister. Even without his theological background, Hess was a very worthwhile subject for a Korean War film: he was the American officer charged with training the pilots of the Republic of Korea's fledgling Air Force, he almost single-handedly kept the ROK Air Force alive as a military entity, and he somehow managed to fly an astounding 250 missions over a two-year period without a scratch. It is unfortunate, then, that Hess' action-packed career and fascinating background should be trivialized in this overly pious biography which tends to embellish the gulf between Hess' gentle, ministerial side with his vocation of choice—professional fighter pilot.

The film is introduced by General Earle F. Partridge, one of Hess' commanding officers in Korea, as he walks around Hess' F-51 fighter plane. "The remarkable story of Colonel Hess, his poignant and often secret struggle with a problem peculiarly his own, his courage, resourcefulness and sacrifice, have long been a source of inspiration to me and to fighting men who have known him. But the story of Colonel Hess is more than a dramatic demonstration of one man's capacity for good; it is an affirmation of the essential goodness of the human spirit. For this reason, I am happy it is told."

One month after the invasion of Korea, Dean Hess (Rock Hudson) is preaching in Westhampton, Ohio, remembering the World

War II incident (seen in flashback) when, as a bomber pilot, he accidentally bombed an orphanage and killed thirty-seven children. He still feels intensely guilty and applies to be recalled to the Air Force, hoping for an opportunity to assuage his guilt.

In Korea, Hess is assigned to train Republic of Korea pilots on American F-51 planes, ten of which have been donated to establish the ROK Air Force. As Hess begins the arduous task of organizing a base from scraps and training men of a different language how to fly American planes, back in Ohio his wife Mary (Martha Hyer) discovers that she is pregnant, but declines to tell her husband, much to the chagrin of her church elder, Deacon Edwards (Carl Benton Reid). Hess has other children about whom to worry — Korean orphans who crowd around whenever the men dump their dinner remains into the trash cans. Hess encourages the men to pass some of their food to the young Koreans, despite the disapproval of Stan Skidmore (Don DeFore), a pilot who flew with Hess during World War II when he was known as "Killer Hess."

During one training mission, a black pilot, Lieutenant Maples (James Edwards), accidentally strafes a truck carrying civilian refugees and turns to Hess for sympathy. For the first time, Hess, who has not told anyone that he is a minister, is able to give comfort and guidance to a man who needs it. More children appear at the base and begin to seriously interfere with its operation. Hess meets Luan (Philip Ahn), an old Korean who shows Hess a temple where a Korean woman named En Soon Yang (Anna Kashfi) is caring for a group of orphans, and he arranges for the children at his base to join her group. He then persuades his men to occupy their off-hours at the temple, fixing the roof, scrounging for food and supplies and caring for the orphans.

A letter from Deacon Edwards to Hess is read by Stan Skidmore, who announces to the men that Hess is, indeed, a minister. Skidmore resents Hess' secrecy and derides his softness, riling Hess and fomenting trouble among his men. However, the letter also tells Hess about his newborn son, which makes him ecstatic. On a trip to the temple, Hess tells En Soon Yang his good news, and she is happy for him, yet somewhat disappointed because of her own deepening feelings for him.

North Korean and Chinese troops push southward and missions become more frequent. Hess and Skidmore fly a dangerous night mission in rainy weather to isolate and destroy a tank convoy, but during the operation Skidmore's plane is hit. Hess talks his friend down to the ground, but he is badly injured. Hess tells Skidmore not to be afraid and gently eases his conscience and prepares him for the afterlife. Skidmore dies in Hess' arms. Although he has lost a friend, Hess tells Mary in a letter that he has finally "reached beyond myself" and touched someone in a meaningful way.

With the relocation of the ROK Air Force, Hess is given transfer orders, but he ignores them when he realizes that four hundred orphans at the temple are in danger from the advancing Communist forces. En Soon Yang and Hess' men lead the children away from the temple while Hess attempts to commandeer planes to ferry the orphans to safety. After being officially rebuffed several times, Hess joins the marching mob of children, leading them southward. A Chinese plane attacks, strafes the road and shoots En Soon Yang, who dies in Hess' arms after making him promise to save the children. Just as hope seems darkest, five transport planes fly into view, courtesy of a sympathetic general. The children, Hess and his men board the transports and fly to Cheju, an island off the southern coast of Korea, where an orphanage is to be established.

The film's prologue has Hess and his wife, Mary, visiting the orphanage months later, which has been dedicated to the memory of Miss En Soon Yang. The children run outside to meet their savior and surround him with happy smiles and singing.

Battle Hymn is an unusual war film in that so much of its plot and characterization is interlaced with religion and its attendant symbolism. It is not unusual for war films to depict men seeking faith, or a release from guilt, or spiritual redemption, or for a film to utilize religious imagery to support moral stands regarding war, but few films focus on the difficulties of retaining a spiritual core amidst the death and violence of war. Director Douglas Sirk, in his book *Sirk on Sirk*, put the matter this way: "I wanted this film to be about ethics and religion, about mystique, magic and belief." No other

The two conflicting sides of Colonel Dean Hess (Rock Hudson) are amply displayed on the poster for Universal's drama Battle Hymn *(1957). Based on Hess's true experiences, the film attempts to be authentic, exciting and inspirational.*

Korean War film so overtly examines how important religious faith can be to men at war.

Having said that, it must also be noted that no other Korean War film is as filled with the self-righteous platitudes and syrupy situations and dialogue which pervade *Battle Hymn*. While the film's intent is noble, its execution is often maudlin or sentimental rather than dramatic. Perhaps the most blatant example is Stan Skidmore's death scene, when he (who had despised Hess for his ministerial past) reverses character, thus providing Hess with an opportunity to "find himself" as his friend dies, while gazing Heavenward with beseeching eyes and an uplifting heavenly chorus sings "Alleluia" in the background. While some of the religious drama is effective, at other times the film wallows in piety, especially in regard to the unfortunate Korean orphans.

The entire second half of the movie spotlights the very real problem of parentless children caught in the crossfire of the Korean War; in fact, the film's orphans were cast from the Orphans Home of Korea, the very place where they were guided by the real Dean Hess during the airlift later dubbed "Operation Kiddy Car." Such verisimilitude should have helped the film, except that the script falls back on the Hollywood convention of having one cute little orphan boy represent all four hundred of the children. Chu (Jung Kyoo Pyo) is indeed adorable as he tags after Hess, quickly becoming his favorite. Hess and Miss Yang bathe the boy, establishing a possible parental relationship (until Hess tells her that he is already married and expecting a child!), and Hess later personally carries Chu the long miles from the temple to the airfield. While singling out Chu from other orphans simplifies the script, it also renders the others dramatically less important, since Hess isn't seen to care for them as he does for Chu. Critics also noted that the orphans seemed surprisingly healthy, plump and vigorous, considering their struggles.

Douglas Sirk explains in *Sirk on Sirk* that he wanted to analyze the dichotomy of Dean Hess: "He easily combined religion, killing, being a military man and saving children. He was an ambiguous character, in other words highly interesting as a subject for drama. Hess combined a soldier's attitude with a preacher's."

This ambiguousness is central to the story, yet somehow doesn't transfer well onto celluloid. Jim Halliday, who interviewed Sirk for the book, asked "Who was this guy Dean Hess, who was killing people one day and saving kids the next?" Even after Sirk answers the question, Halliday is not satisfied, returning to the subject later, asking "But Dean Hess must have been a very strange guy?"

Sirk attempted to link the two sides of Hess' split personality by utilizing another Hollywood convention — the bottle. Sirk felt that if, when Hess leaves the church in Ohio, and begins to drink, it would signify that "he is a man not able to find his identity, not until he has been killing. At any rate, putting in some structural element like him becoming a drunkard would have strengthened the character." Hess, the film's technical advisor, vetoed the idea because it simply wasn't the truth. He didn't drink. Sirk recalled that "I tried hard to convince him it would make a better movie, and that a guy like him *could* have taken to drink, but he wouldn't hear of it. So he remains this strange guy, which by God he is."

As performed by Rock Hudson, Dean Hess was a guilt-ridden, inarticulate man searching for his place in the world. Hudson loved the idealism and nobility of the role, calling it one of his two favorites, along with the love-struck gardener in another Sirk film, *All That Heaven Allows*. Hudson even resembled the tall, dark-haired Hess to a certain degree, and Hess was said to be thrilled that Hudson was portraying him. Yet director Sirk admits that Hudson may not have been the right choice for the role. "An actor like [Robert] Stack would have been much more fitting, I'm sure. Just think of *Written on the Wind* or *The Tarnished Angels*, a flyer's picture, too. Dean Hess properly cast would have belonged to the gallery of my vacillating characters."

It was especially difficult for Sirk to tamper with Hess' character because Hess was on the set of the film every day as technical advisor. After the war, Hess had served as technical advisor for *Dragonfly Squadron*, which explores the early days of the ROK Air Force, which Hess oversaw. He then wrote his biography (*Battle Hymn*, upon which the film was based), and sold the screen rights for $60,000, which he donated

Colonel Dean Hess (Rock Hudson) attempts to transport hundreds of Korean orphans to safety in Battle Hymn *(1957).*

to the Orphans Home of Korea. As technical advisor, Hess tried to force Sirk to stick to facts when telling his story, but the director was somewhat contemptuous ("But he [Hess] was there on the set the whole time ... trying to make me stick to 'truth.'") and was more interested in amplifying the divergent characteristics of Hess' character than with telling a heroic, true story.

Battle Hymn isn't truthful in some particulars, which tends to weaken the story in favor of Sirk's less effective (and heavy-handed) moralizing. Must a film based on true incidents or characters follow actual events to the letter? No, but when a movie is purported to be a true story, it should have some adherence to what actually happened and respect the spirit of its subject. In this case, not enough respect was paid, and the fault is clearly Sirk's. During the Halliday interview, Sirk actually says, "I don't believe in making biographies." Even so, with Hess as the technical advisor, it is surprising how many important details were changed for the sake of drama.

In the film, Hess rejoins the Air Force several weeks after the invasion of Korea; dramatically, he is searching for meaning in his life by switching from one job at which he feels impotent (the ministry) to another where he feels potent (fighter pilot). In actuality, Hess had been recalled by the Air Force in July of 1948 and assigned to administrative duties in Korea in April of 1950, two months before the invasion. In the film, Hess is assigned to organize the ROK Air Force and train their pilots, which proves to be a difficult, daunting task. In actuality, he almost single-handedly kept the organization alive against the wishes of American military leaders who thought it a waste of manpower and equipment. If anything, the film underdramatizes this aspect of Hess' career.

In the film, Hess is racked with guilt because of his accidental bombing of an orphanage in World War II and is only able to face life again because he saves so many more young lives in Korea. In actuality, Hess claimed that he was not consciously aware of the orphan connection between the two wars and that he was simply doing what he could for innocent people facing a difficult situation. In the film, Hess spends most of his time with the orphans and eventually disregards his own orders that they might be delivered to safety. In actuality, Hess spent most of his time at work, squeezing in time with the children when it was possible. When the Chinese threatened to take Seoul, he worked through channels to secure transport for the children, which was provided by General Partridge, the Air Force officer who introduced the film. Once the orphans were on their way to Cheju, Hess climbed into his fighter plane for another mission.

Finally, the film dramatizes the rescue of four hundred children facing certain deprivation and probable death. In actuality, there were nine hundred and fifty orphans in that situation and fifteen C-47 planes were utilized to transport them to Cheju. Here again, the film actually undermines its drama by not sticking with the truth, although this decision may have been one of simple logistics. One faux pas is intentional, however. When Hess is flying, he wears a naval helmet rather than the standard issue Air Force helmet. Hess had been given a Navy helmet as a gift, and he wore it throughout the war.

While none of these alterations are crucial to the story, they do change the tone of Hess' character, simplifying it to the point of rigid nobility. The script ignores Hess' spectacular mission stories and remarkable administrative feats in favor of the cliches of the unrequited love of En Soon Yang and duty to the children. What might have been a truly fascinating, inspiring chronicle of one man's war within a war is instead a forgettable collection of pious cliches and platitudes about duty and service to God.

Bosley Crowther of the *New York Times* wrote, "This picture doesn't miss a single cliche as it makes a calculated circuit of the old militant sky-pilot plot," and noted that, "It is in the most obvious, mawkish fashion that Douglas Sirk has directed it." In *Saturday Review*, Hollis Alpert complained that, "It may be the script that is at fault for certain moments of obvious sentimentality. Might have been better not to go so all out for that lump in the throat, which is inherent in the material anyway." *Time*'s reviewer began by saying, "*Battle Hymn* pictures the Korean war as a sort of Sunday-school out-

ing at which some of the boys got a little out of control," and finished by noting that, "The sugar count of this picture is so dangerously high that theater managers might be well advised to offer insulin shots in the lobby."

Despite the aforementioned critical barbs and the film's undeniable quantity of sanctimoniousness, audiences flocked to Universal's film, which grossed almost four million dollars, strong enough to place in the top twenty money-making movies of the year. Rock Hudson was named the top box office draw for 1957, based largely upon *Battle Hymn*'s success, and the movie did win a Golden Globe award in a peculiar category, "Best Film Promoting International Understanding." Ultimately the film is just too well-intentioned for its own good and occasionally wallows in the sticky pathos which it should have flown above. Even so, it chronicles one of the most fascinating stories, and people, of the Korean War.

Battle Taxi

Credits: 1955. Ivan Tors Films, Inc. *Released by* United Artists. *Directed by* Herbert L. Strock. *Produced by* Ivan Tors and Art Arthur. *Screenplay by* Malvin Wald. *Based on a Story by* Malvin Wald and Art Arthur. *Music Composed and Conducted by* Harry Sukman. *Director of Photography*: Lothrop B. Worth. *Film Editor*: Jodie Copelan, A.C.E. *Director of Special Effects*: Harry Redmond, Jr. *Assistant to the Producers*: Jack Herzberg. *Assistant Director*: Joseph Wonder. *Art Director*: William Ferrari. *Set Decorator*: Charles S. Thompson. *Sound Effects Editor*: Charles L. Freeman. *Music Editors*: Edward Phillips and Jack A. Goodrich. *Sound*: Frank T. Dyke and Joel Moss. *Propmaster*: Charles Henley. *Wardrobe*: Leonard Mann. *Technical Advisors*: Captain Vincent H. McGovern, Chief of Helicopter Operations, Air Rescue Service, U.S.A.F., Captain Ralph N. Dove, Chief of Information Services, Air Rescue Service, U.S.A.F. Not Rated. Black and White. Flat (1.33:1). 82 minutes. Released in January, 1955. Not currently available on commercial home video.

Cast: *Captain Russ Edwards*, Sterling Hayden; *Lieutenant Pete Stacy*, Arthur Franz;

Though the artwork for United Artists' action drama Battle Taxi *(1955) features rather more action than does the film, it is remarkably representative, with recognizable, specific scenes. The poster even credits the cooperation of various armed services (in tiny type).*

Second Lieutenant Tim Vernon, Marshall Thompson; *Staff Sergeant Slats Klein*, Leo Needham; *Lieutenant Colonel Philip Stoneham*, Jay Barney; *Master Sergeant Joe Murdock*, John Dennis; *Medic Captain Larsen*, Michael Colgan; *Lazy Joker Two*, Andy Andrews; *Blue Boy Three (Gene)*, Dale Hutchinson; *Wounded G.I.*, John Goddard; *Lieutenant Joe Kirk*, Robert Sherman; *Lieutenant Marty Staple*, Joel Marston; *Co-Pilot Harry*, Captain Vincent McGovern; *Lieutenant Smiley Jackson*, Vance Skarsted.

Historical Accuracy Level: Medium. This fictional story incorporates real-life war situations, although distracting a tank with a helicopter is distinctly fanciful.

Patriotic Propaganda Level: High. This tribute to the Air Rescue Service could not be much more patriotic than it already is.

Elements: Air Force, Helicopters, Rescues.

Battle Taxi is a paean to the Air Force's Air Rescue Service, and specifically its helicopter operations. While several Korean War films spotlight the air war waged by the Air Force and the Navy, this is the only one to examine the Air Rescue Service and its importance to the war effort. Possibly concerned that rescuing downed airmen wasn't heroic enough for audiences, the film is filled with aerial action and infers that, all in all, the rescuers would rather be in the thick of the fighting, but that someone has to rescue his fellow fliers.

In Korea, Captain Russ Edwards (Sterling Hayden) commands a portion of the Air Rescue Service, the branch responsible for rescuing wounded U.N. servicemen, and in particular, downed American pilots. Edwards' biggest headache isn't the Communist forces which shoot at the rescue copters, but rather hotshot jet pilot Lieutenant Pete Stacy (Arthur Franz), recently transferred to his command. Stacy continually puts his choppers and crews in harm's way, leading to an inordinate rate of equipment placed out of commission. On his first mission in the film, Stacy uses his H-19 rescue copter to buzz and distract a North Korean tank which is pursuing a group of soldiers. Stacy distracts the tank long enough for a group of F-86 Sabre jets to attack and destroy it.

After Edwards severely reprimands Stacy for his recklessness, Edwards makes his primary concern teaching Stacy the proper and safe methods of rescue work. Edwards forces the former jet pilot to address his former fighter squadron regarding the importance of the rescue unit, and thus forces Stacy to take his job more seriously. Stacy is then transferred to an island rescue base because of a manpower shortage. During a large offensive, Stacy, with co-pilot Tim Vernon (Marshall Thompson) and crewman Slats Klein (Leo Needham), make an easy pick-up and then, low on fuel, divert to make a sea rescue. Almost out of fuel, Stacy lands in enemy territory and finds regular gasoline to fill his fuel tank. The helicopter makes it back to the island but its engine may be damaged from the wrong fuel mixture.

On another mission, Pete has misgivings about landing to pick up a fellow pilot named Smiley Jackson (Vance Skarstedt) because of a possible enemy ambush, but realizes that "that's what we're here for." As Jackson is being retrieved, North Korean gunfire kills him, wounds Stacy, and damages the chopper, which crashes some distance away. Edwards personally captains the rescue mission, bringing a doctor along for Stacy. As medic Captain Larsen (Michael Colgan) treats Stacy's chest wound on the ground, Edwards uses his chopper to divert enemy attention from the real crash scene, and then to rescue Stacy and his crew. At the end of the movie, Stacy, walking with a cane, instructs fighter pilots about the importance and methods of the Air Rescue Service.

Battle Taxi features very little story, yet the film is focused and filled with enough action that it is very effective. Early in the movie — after Stacy's battle with the tank — there is an extended dialogue scene between Edwards and Stacy discussing the differences between jet flying and rescue flying, which is impassioned and forceful. That well-acted scene is important in explaining Stacy's ambivalence toward Air Rescue and establishing the difficulties inherent within the service. Where many Korean War films are talky and often dull, this one has dialogue which is direct and to the point, and which does not impede the pace of the story.

Most of the film is comprised of rescue footage. Though there is some actual combat footage sprinkled thoughout, primarily in the sequence where the big offensive is mounted,

Captain Russ Edwards (Sterling Hayden, right) pointedly tells hot shot air rescue helicopter pilot Lieutenant Pete Stacy (Arthur Franz, left) to stop trying to win the war single-handedly in Battle Taxi *(1955).*

the rescues are not archival. *Battle Taxi* features a great deal of very impressive copter flying done for the movie, over both land and water, involving different types of rescues. The helicopter diversion of the enemy tank in particular is most unusual and fascinating to watch. Another plus is that the cast seem familiar with the equipment and are completely believable in their roles. Credit for the strong aviation values and for the cast's familiarity with the H-19 chopper must be given at least in part to technical advisor Captain Vincent McGovern, who also has a small role as Harry, Edwards' co-pilot in the movie's climactic sequence. As chief of helicopter operations for the USAF Air Rescue Service, McGovern personally made sure that the film was largely accurate and believable, at least in terms of its technical specifications and procedures.

Thus, while *Battle Taxi* may lack the dramatic range of other Korean War films, it is surely among the most truthful. It explores the

various difficulties facing the Air Rescue Service without diluting them, depicts the service's strengths and virtues admiringly and, perhaps most importantly, accurately describes just how tough the job really is for the men who put their own lives on the line to save their fellow fliers. It is a small film in terms of scope, yet it more than fulfills its limited ambition. Its intent as Air Force propaganda cannot be denied, yet that intent is not disagreeable, or unentertaining. The movie really takes no position on the politics of the war itself, preferring to concentrate on the unassailable moral subject of rescues.

As directed by Herbert L. Strock, *Battle Taxi* moves with purpose and, within its dialogue limitations, allows the various characters to develop identifiable personalities. Sterling Hayden gives his standard, professional performance while Arthur Franz makes the biggest impression playing hot shot jet pilot-turned-helicopter jockey Pete Stacy. The various aircraft, in particular the redoubtable H-19 rescue helicopter, are shown to tremendous advantage and regularly upstage the human actors.

Battle Taxi received mixed reviews. *Variety* complained that, "the requisite combat wallop is in short supply," while *Film Daily* judged it a "Fine tribute but only average fare for most audiences"; major magazines did not even review it. On the positive side, *Boxoffice* labeled it, "An authentic and action-packed melodrama" and Charles F. Stevens, writing for *Farm Journal*, noted that, "The fascinating and important work of the rescue helicopters in war-time is shown in careful detail," and declared the film, "exciting."

While *Battle Taxi* is certainly a minor film of the Korean War, it is also one of the more authentic examples of the genre, a no-nonsense action drama which completely fulfills its limited ambitions. Larger-budgeted movies with more far-reaching goals would do well to emulate the example of this simple but effective, well-focused little movie.

Battle Zone

Credits: 1952. Allied Artists. *Directed by* Lesley Selander. *Produced by* Walter Wanger. *Associate Producer:* William A. Calihan, Jr. *Written by* Steve Fisher. *Music by* Marlin Skiles. *Photographed by:* Ernest Miller, A.S.C. *Film Editor:* Jack Ogilvie, A.C.E. *Production Manager:* Allen K. Wood. *Assistant Director:* Henry Hartman. *Research:* Lester A. Sansom. *Technical Supervision:* Captain John M. Terry, U.S.M.C. *Art Director:* David Milton. *Recorded by* Charles Cooper. *Set Continuity by* Gordon Otto. *Special Effects by* Ray Mercer, A.S.C. Not Rated. Black and White. Flat (1.33:1). 81 minutes. Released in October, 1952. Not currently available on commercial home video.

Cast: *Sergeant Danny Young,* John Hodiak; *Jeanne,* Linda Christian; *Sergeant Mitch Turner,* Stephen McNally; *Andy,* Martin Milner; *Smitty,* Dave Willock; *James O'Doole,* Jack Larson; *Lieutenant Orlin,* Richard Emory; *Korean Assistant,* Philip Ahn; *Colonel,* Carleton Young; *Lieutenant Pilot,* John Fontaine; *Officer,* Todd Karnes; *Marine Runner,* Gil Stratton, Jr.

Historical Accuracy Level: Medium.

The film is realistic regarding its Marine Corps combat photographers until they volunteer for a dangerous secret mission.

Patriotic Propaganda Level: Medium. Taking pictures for Uncle Sam has never been so glamorous; the movie, however, retains an objective eye over the conflict.

Elements: Behind Enemy Lines, Combat Photography, Journalism, Marine Corps, Military Training, Romantic Triangle, Secret Missions.

Battle Zone is a standard war film which benefits by following the true course of Korean War events fairly accurately. Its protagonists are combat photographers who have different approaches to the profession, and the film goes to great lengths to explain the intricacies of their job and its importance to the war effort. In that regard, the film retains a jingoistic aspect, but because its protagonists are, by nature, observers, it is able to view the war with an objective distance which other war films do not achieve. Thus, *Battle Zone* seems as much a historical document as a traditional war drama.

Danny Young (John Hodiak) re-enlists in the Marine Corps photographic division at California's Camp Pendleton shortly after the start of the Korean War, where he is reunited with rival photographer Mitch Turner (Stephen McNally), who is now in charge of the photography training program. Their rivalry intensifies when Mitch discovers that Danny has orders providing him freedom from Mitch's command, and Danny discovers that Mitch is now involved with Danny's former girlfriend, Italian Red Cross nurse Jeanne (Linda Christian).

The photographers and their unit accompany the surprise September 15, 1950, Marine landing at Inchon, behind enemy lines, and march and drive with the Marines the twenty-five mile distance to Seoul. Along the way Danny attempts to romance Jeanne, with little success. As the Marines drive the North Koreans northward, they are filmed by the Marine photographic unit. Mitch and Danny engage in a photographic battle of one-upmanship, with each trying to get the most exciting combat footage. Both are upbeat about the course of the war as they head north to the Chosin reservoir area. Quite suddenly, however, they are filming the mass evacuation of United Nations troops

Scenes of war action and the promise of the "first front-line story of the combat cameramen … who blast everything that moves!" provide a fairly truthful account of Allied Artists' drama Battle Zone *(1952). Interestingly, the artwork does not suggest the romantic rivalry between the two photographers, nor the fact that the action takes place in Korea.*

through Hungnam after Chinese Communist troops enter the battle and turn the tide of the fighting.

After the war settles into a standstill the following spring, Mitch initiates a plan for a group of combat photographers to enter enemy territory and film everything in sight, gathering intelligence. Danny joins the special mission, as do fellow photographers Smitty (Dave Willock) and Andy (Martin Milner). South Korean runners act as couriers for the exposed film, but one of those runners is a spy, and recruits a squad of North Korean soldiers who attack the photographers at a farmhouse. Andy and eleven other men are killed, but the survivors capture the enemy soldiers and use their transport truck to drive through the enemy-held city of Wan Ju (while filming, of course) and back toward safety. The men escape from the truck before it is destroyed by a tank at a roadblock, though Danny is grazed in the arm by a North Korean bullet.

At an aid station, Danny sees Jeanne (to get his dressing changed) and finally accepts that she has chosen Mitch over himself, then joins the troops — and friendly rival Mitch — heading back to the front to do their jobs. The war continues.

Battle Zone may seem familiar, because it is patterned after director Raoul Walsh's huge silent-era hit *What Price Glory?*, released in 1926, with Victor McLaglen and Edmund Lowe as Marines fighting in World War I France who both fall in love with Dolores Del Rio. Based on Laurence Stallings' and Maxwell Anderson's play, Walsh's film version brought the brawling Captain Flagg and Sergeant Quirt characters to such popular life that the play's original conclusion (where the two men return to the front and, presumably, death) was altered to a happier ending. In fact, McLaglen and Lowe returned as the Flagg and Quirt characters in three further adventures: *The Cockeyed World* (1929), *Women of All Nations* (1931) and *Hot Pepper* (1933).

At the same time that *Battle Zone* was being made, director John Ford was remaking *What Price Glory?* with James Cagney and Dan Dailey as Flagg and Quirt and Corinne Calvet as Charmaine, the French chanteuse who wins their hearts. The films were released within three months of each other in 1952 and may have

given some viewers a distinct sense of déjà vu. Several critics pointed out the similarities between the stories, often leading their reviews of *Battle Zone* with the phrase "a Captain Flagg - Sergeant Quirt situation," and referring to *Battle Zone* (and Ford's direct remake as well) as pale imitations of a stirring original.

Given the promotional nature of *Battle Zone* and its heavy dependence of aid from the Department of Defense (most of the movie was filmed at Camp Pendleton and quite a bit of actual Korean War combat footage is edited into the action), this low-budget programmer is surprisingly good. It marches at a brisk pace, preventing its rather silly and superficial romantic triangle to impede its progress, keeps its focus on the necessary and difficult jobs of the photographers and steers clear of sentiment and melodrama. And it scores points for painting a realistic, historically accurate view of the Korean War.

Aided by actual film footage of the surprise Inchon invasion, the march to Seoul, the frozen conditions at the Chosin Reservoir (where the Chinese joined the fight) and the evacuation of troops, materiel and refugees from Hungnam, *Battle Zone* comprises a compact history of the first year of the war. It is not a detailed history, but it is accurate and thoughtfully illustrates the war's various stages in an easy to understand fashion.

Since the Marine photographers are firsthand observers of the Korean War (and veterans of World War II), their remarks and attitudes seem more knowledgable and telling. Their critical distance from the action provides a foundation of truth for their thoughts about it. There is very little philosophizing about the war from any of the main characters. From time to time the war's progress is discussed, and everyone is looking to going home for Christmas after, as Danny puts it, "mopping up some straggling North Koreans." It is noteworthy, however, that no one ever questions the war's purpose or rails against the restrictions of the "police action." The characters of *Battle Zone* treat war as a business that will occupy their time and talents until it is over.

The film benefits from the inclusion of interesting details and sequences involving combat photography, such as how (and how not to)

Rival combat photographers Sergeant Mitch Turner (Stephen McNally, left) and Sergeant Danny Young (John Hodiak, right) photograph battle action, capturing images for posterity in Battle Zone *(1952).*

keep cameras steady, what kinds of pictures are surprisingly important, advantages of still over motion photography, and so on. One of the movie's best lines is delivered by Danny (John Hodiak), who makes this complaint during a battle scene which goes into the evening hours: "Ah, we're losing the light! Why can't they fight their battles during the daytime?"

One aspect which clearly stands out is the film's editing. Actual war footage is skillfully blended into and matched with the film's fictional story. In most Korean War films, actual combat footage deviates from its movie host in terms of grain, focus, lighting, point of view, costumes, etc. Such footage is easy to spot because it just doesn't match what the director of photography has shot. In *Battle Zone*, editor Jack Ogilvie mixes war footage into the action unobtrusively; it can usually be spotted, but it doesn't call attention to itself. Care has been taken to ensure that shots generally match, with the result that the film seems more authentic and immediate.

Battle Zone is, of course, a Hollywood fiction, and familiar faces pepper the cast. Martin Milner, who later spent much time on television (*The Trouble With Father, The Life of Riley, Route 66, Adam-12*), plays Andy, the blond photographer who doesn't understand the friendship between rivals Danny and Mitch; Jack Larson (Reporter Jimmy Olson on TV's *Superman*) plays driver James O'Doole; and even Charles Bronson pops up in one brief scene as Smitty's assistant during military maneuvers in California. Korean War movie veterans Richard Emory, Carleton Young, Todd Karnes and Philip Ahn also appear in small roles.

Leading man John Hodiak made other Korean War films as well. Hodiak seems more personable here than in *Mission Over Korea* or *Dragonfly Squadron*, and it is somewhat of a surprise — especially considering the billing — when he doesn't get the girl. McNally, a familiar second lead during the '50s, plays the sterner, more serious character and nicely balances Hodiak's wiseacre. There are moments, however, when

McNally seems to be imitating Humphrey Bogart, even using a similar lisp. Linda Christian is acceptable in a purely decorative role as Jeanne, the nurse who wins both their hearts.

Battle Zone was critically scorned upon its release. Noting its similarity to *What Price Glory?*, Bosley Crowther of the *New York Times* called its story, "hopelessly dull" and judged the finished product "mediocre." *Variety* was a bit brighter, calling it, "an average war film for general bookings, mixing actual combat footage with an acceptable, though standard, story line." Critics agreed that the film's best feature was its adept inclusion of actual location footage from Korea. Despite its timeliness, the film did not perform well at the box office and, along with John Ford's ill-fated remake of *What Price Glory?*, was quickly forgotten.

The movie is patriotic by necessity, but it also presents a largely unemotional view of the Korean War. Its focus is on the friendly rivalry that exists between rival lensmen Mitch and Danny, as they battle for Jeanne's affections and the war's most dramatic photographs. Despite its cheaply staged battle scenes, the film does chronicle the war's progress in a compelling manner without overly simplifying or minimizing its battles. It does have a critical distance absent from other films because its photographers are usually not directly involved in the fighting, and it strives for accuracy in reporting the real situation in Korea.

Bombers B-52
(aka *No Sleep Till Dawn*)

Credits: 1957. Warner Bros. *Directed by* Gordon Douglas. *Produced by* Richard Whorf. *Screen Play by* Irving Wallace. *Story by* Sam Rolfe. *Music by* Leonard Rosenman. *Director of Photography*: William Clothier. *Film Editor*: Thomas Reilly, A.C.E. *Aerial Photography*: Harold E. Wellman, A.S.C. *Art Director*: Leo K. Kuter. *Sound by* Oliver S. Garretson. *Set Decorator*: William L. Kuehl. *Costumes Designed by* Howard Shoup. *Technical Advisor*: Major Benjamin R. Ostlind, USAF. *Technical Coordinator*: Robert Irving. *Makeup Artist*: Gordon Bau, S.M.A. *Assistant Director*: William Kissell. Not

Rated. WarnerColor. CinemaScope (2.35:1). 106 minutes. Released in November, 1957. Currently available on VHS videotape.

Cast: *Lois Brennan*, Natalie Wood; *Sergeant Chuck Brennan*, Karl Malden; *Edith Brennan*, Marsha Hunt; *Colonel Jim Herlihy*, Efrem Zimbalist, Jr.; *Sergeant Darren McKind*, Don Kelly; *General Wayne Acton*, Nelson Leigh; *Stuart*, Robert Nichols; *Barnes*, Ray Montgomery; *Simpson*, Bob Hover; *Sam*, Stuart Whitman; *Airman Rand*, Patrick Curtis.

Historical Accuracy Level: Medium. The evolution of Air Force bombers is sampled but the film is more interested in the fictional dramas which surround its central family.

Patriotic Propaganda Level: High. Service to the Air Force in virtually any capacity is presented as being far more important than similar work in the private sector.

Elements: Air Force, Military Training, Romance.

After the Korean War, the armed forces of the United States altered their guiding philosophies to face the Cold War threat of nuclear warfare. The Air Force, in particular, developed new technology, weaponry and defense systems in response to the Soviet Union's vast nuclear capability. Several post-war movies such as *Strategic Air Command* (1955), *A Gathering of Eagles* (1963) and *Bombers B-52* attempt to depict this adjustment, in terms of military purpose and strategy but also the important human element that supports the technology. Of this trio, *Bombers B-52* is most concerned with the equipment: the gargantuan, 200-ton, intercontinental bomber, the B-52 Stratofortress.

The film begins in Korea in 1950, where a brief dogfight ends in a Russian MiG fighter (doubled by an F-84 Thunderjet) crashing in a fiery explosion. Hot shot Air Force fighter pilot Jim Herlihy (Efrem Zimbalist, Jr.) lands at a small, camouflaged air base and demands that his F-86 Sabre jet be repaired at once, so that he may continue to Tokyo. Crew chief Chuck Brennan (Karl Malden) objects, noting that lighting the repair area would invite air attack, but Captain Herlihy insists. Because of Herlihy's reputation as a "Casanova," Brennan is sure that the pilot's hurry is libidinous in nature. The repair effort is interrupted by enemy fire, but Herlihy's jet is repaired and he departs before a final

The advertising for Warner Bros.' peacetime drama Bombers B-52 *(1957) emphasizes the beauty of Natalie Wood as well as the zooming B-52 jets. Both taglines stress her character's part of the story. Note the box beneath Wood's figure drawing. "You made her a star! You'll love her in this!"*

attack injures one of the ground crew, causing Brennan bitter consternation.

Six years later, Brennan is the line chief for B-47 bombers at Castle Air Force Base in California when Herlihy, now a colonel, is given command of the base. Brennan begins a vacation with his family, wife Edith (Marsha Hunt) and grown daughter Lois (Natalie Wood), traipsing around California and ending on the Gold Rush Quiz television game show, where Brennan wins $4,000 for his knowledge of the baseball poem "Casey at the Bat." Upon returning to Castle, Brennan finds that the base is scheduled to be the home of the new B-52 long distance bombers, and that Herlihy considers it vital that Brennan lead its ground crew maintenance program.

Brennan, however, has other ideas. He is considering an offer to work as line chief for Boeing in Seattle, and the idea of making more money for his family, combined with his dislike of Herlihy, leads him to ask for retirement. Herlihy, under official orders to keep Brennan in the Air Force, persuades him to attend a training seminar regarding the B-52. When he returns, Brennan discovers that Lois is actively dating Herlihy, and Brennan angrily tells his commanding officer to leave his daughter alone. On a test flight piloted by Herlihy and checked by Brennan, the jet's front wheels fail to extend, but Brennan manually activates a relay switch in the wheel bay in the nick of time to avert a belly landing.

Brennan and Lois argue about the respect he receives (and deserves) in the Air Force just before he is ordered to accompany a top secret intercontinental test flight. The B-52 travels to Africa and back, but catches fire over eastern California, causing the crew to parachute over mountainous terrain. Alone, Captain Herlihy lands the B-52 safely at Castle, where the fire is extinguished, saving the aircraft. The crew is collected by Air Rescue, except for Brennan, who cannot be found. As Edith and Lois wait anxiously, Herlihy personally investigates a possible sighting and finds Brennan with an injured leg. Brennan is surprised to see Herlihy, who explains that on that fateful night in Korea, he was under orders to travel to Tokyo *that night* with important information regarding a MiG fighter base. In the hospital, Brennan apologizes to

Herlihy, gives him permission to date his daughter and rejects the idea of retirement from the Air Force, with the blessings of his wife and daughter.

Bombers B-52 is a star-spangled tribute to the Air Force, specifically the ground crew technicians who keep the jets healthy enough to fly. The movie's protagonist has his twenty-year Air Force career called into question by friends and *his own family* and must determine whether he wants to commit more time and effort to the Air Force. The answer is, of course, yes, but only because the Air Force continues to offer him fresh challenges and because his technical expertise is so important to the lives of the men who fly the jets.

On the other hand, the film's propaganda quotient is undermined when the script indicates that the men who report to Brennan are not qualified to take over in his absence, when the B-52's front wheels fail to extend during landing and when the mysterious test panel which prompts the top secret test flight inexplicably bursts into flames. These technical details do not put the Air Force equipment in a good light, but are viewed as unavoidable defects to be discovered and rectified during the test flights. The personnel issue is not handled as well, since most of the men under Brennan's command seem inept, lazy, stupid or simply invisible.

This viewpoint is sustained when Brennan personally spots and captures two suspicious individuals dressed as firemen on the air base. They are "penetration agents," assigned by a general to sneak onto the base and pretend to sabotage the new jet. None of the various security guards identify the ruse; only Brennan detects anything suspicious. In this movie, only line chief Chuck Brennan seems to have the wherewithal necessary to keep the Air Force flying.

In one key scene just before the intercontinental test flight, a general addresses the "big picture" behind the B-52's development. "Now, for centuries it's been the job of a successful general to win wars. But in this nuclear air age, it's the job of a successful general to *prevent* wars. We think that the way to prevent wars, to deter major aggression, is through superior long rage nuclear air power, poised and ready to take off

A ground crew led by Chuck Brennan (Karl Malden, center) begins emergency work on an F-86 Sabre Jet in Korea in Bombers B-52 *(1957). The "Lucky Lady" jet and the metal plating which covers the ground for use as a temporary runway are authentic.*

at a moment's notice." This statement reveals the reasoning behind the Air Force's shift to long range bombers as a nuclear deterrent, and justifies its $9 million investment per aircraft. It explains why the film casts such a worshipful eye on the newest weapon in the Air Force arsenal: the people who designed and built the Stratofortress expected it to save the world. In hindsight, perhaps it did.

The opening scene in Korea is included only to establish the rocky relationship between Brennan, who cares about his men, and Herlihy, who seemingly does not. The brief dogfight is staged with two American jets, one painted to look like a Soviet MiG. On the ground, a tiny studio set is used to depict Korea, enemy MiGs are heard but never seen, and a few nearby explosions are meant to make the characters duck and run for cover. The scene does show that the American repair crews could perform in difficult conditions, but it adds little to the film as a whole and says next to nothing about Korea. Herlihy takes the time to explain away Brennan's bad feelings concerning the episode near the end of the story.

The bulk of the story is dedicated to the dilemma facing Chuck Brennan. Should he stay in the low paying Air Force, working under the command of a man he dislikes, but performing a job he feels is important and for which he is well trained, or should he pursue financial success in the private sector with perhaps less challenging work? Lois personifies the reason for Brennan's soul searching, as she doesn't respect her father, thinking that he is merely one man among many in the service and that he may waste a valuable opportunity to upgrade his status. The film's position is obvious, but it does present both sides of the argument and gives Natalie Wood the occasion to emote and cry about it.

Natalie Wood is the top-billed star of

Bombers B-52, but the real stars are undoubtedly the title aircraft. Wood has a small role, dresses fetchingly and flirts with Efrem Zimbalist, Jr., who went on to star on television's long-running crime drama *The F.B.I.* The most effective human acting belongs to Karl Malden, who is onscreen most frequently and whose character is certainly the most interesting. Malden was the perfect choice for such a professional regular guy role and he carries the movie effortlessly on his broad shoulders.

Bombers B-52 was fairly successful upon its 1957 release. Drawn by artwork of a blossoming Natalie Wood and booming B-52s, audiences made the film a popular success. The film drew mixed reviews, but Howard Thompson of the *New York Times* appreciated the effort: "The simple sound of words in a flight film is for once even more impressive than the propeller droning. Irving Wallace's dialogue is excellent. Furthermore, his unpretentious scenario is credible and persuasive … especially in the hearth scenes, when the beset hero confronts his family with his troubled conscience."

The combination of massive B-52s and compassionate human drama is a winning one, and *Bombers B-52* is able to nicely balance its pro-Air Force slant with a very real story. There is no getting past the film's propaganda, but at least it is presented sensibly, so that viewers can decide on their own whether to swallow it. Beyond that aspect, the film is beautifully photographed and contains an appealing mix of humor and drama. And if the B-52 bombers are not exciting enough, there's always Natalie Wood.

The Bridges at Toko-Ri

Credits: 1955. Perlberg-Seaton Productions. *Distributed by* Paramount. *Directed by* Mark Robson. *Produced by* William Perlberg and George Seaton. *Screenplay by* Valentine Davies. *From the Novel by* James Michener. *Music Score by* Lyn Murray. *Director of Photography*: Loyal Griggs, A.S.C. *Edited by* Alma Macrorie, A.C.E. *Technicolor Color Consultant*: Richard Mueller. *Art Direction*: Hal Pereira and Henry Bumstead. *Second Unit Photography*: Wallace Kelley, A.S.C.

and Thomas Tutwiler, A.S.C. *Set Decoration*: Sam Comer and Grace Gregory. *Special Photographic Effects*: John P. Fulton, A.S.C. *Process Photography*: Farciot Edouart, A.S.C. and Wallace Kelley, A.S.C. *Aerial Photography*: Charles G. Clarke, A.S.C. *Costumes*: Edith Head. *Makeup Supervision*: Wally Westmore. *Sound Recording by* Hugo Grenzbach and Gene Garvin. *Technical Advisor*: Commander Marshall U. Beebe, U.S.N. *Assistant to the Producers*: Arthur Jacobson. *Assistant Director*: Francisco Day. Not Rated. Technicolor. Flat (1.33:1). 102 minutes. Released in January, 1955. Filmed partly on location in Japan and Korea. Currently available on VHS videotape and DVD. Previously available on laserdisc.

Cast: Lieutenant Harry Brubaker, William Holden; *Nancy Brubaker*, Grace Kelly; *Rear Admiral George Tarrant*, Fredric March; *Mike Forney*, Mickey Rooney; *Beer Barrel*, Robert Strauss; *Commander Wayne Lee (Cag)*, Charles McCraw; *Kimiko*, Keiko Awaji; *Nestor Gamidge*, Earl Holliman; *Lieutenant Olds*, Richard Shannon; *Captain Evans*, Willis Bouchey; *Kathy Brubaker*, Nadene Ashdown; *Susie Brubaker*, Cheryl Lynn Calloway; *Assistant C.I.C. Officer*, James Jenkins; *Pilot*, Marshall U. Beebe; *M.P. Major*, Charles Tannen; *Japanese Father*, Teru Shimada; *Chief Petty Officer*, Gene Hardy; *Officer of the Day*, James Hyland; *Bartender*, Robert Kino; *Captain Parker*, Paul Kruger; *Bellhop*, Rollin Moriyama; *C.I.C. Officer*, Gene Reynolds; *Quartermaster*, Jack Roberts; *Flight Surgeon*, Robert A. Sherry; *Air Intelligence Officer*, Dennis Weaver.

Historical Accuracy Level: High. While Toko-Ri is fictional, missions to bomb such bridges were common, and the film represents the single most authentic view of aircraft carrier operations in all of the Korean War film genre.

Patriotic Propaganda Level: High. One line of dialogue says it all: "Where do we get such men?"

Elements: Aircraft Carriers, Air War, Behind Enemy Lines, Bridge Bombing, Combat Photography, Helicopters, Japan, Lonely Wives, Navy (Aviators), Rescues.

Two of the most popular films regarding the Korean conflict star William Holden. Holden had recently (1953) won an Academy Award for *Stalag 17* (which also dealt with war,

THE PAGES AND THE PEOPLE
OF THE GREAT NOVEL COME TO LIFE!

JAMES A. MICHENER'S

THE BRIDGES
AT TOKO-RI

A Perlberg-Seaton production

Live their whole glorious story . . . from the sailors' free-for-all in a rowdy Tokyo night club to split-second action on the carrier deck . . . from the romantic mountain hideaway to the murderous death-trap at Toko-ri!

Color by TECHNICOLOR

"*They kissed as if to use up all the kisses of a lifetime!*"

starring **WILLIAM**   **GRACE**
HOLDEN · KELLY
FREDRIC   **MICKEY**
MARCH · ROONEY

With
ROBERT STRAUSS · CHARLES McGRAW · KEIKO AWAJI
Produced by   Directed by   Screenplay by
WILLIAM PERLBERG and GEORGE SEATON · MARK ROBSON · VALENTINE DAVIES
From the Novel by James A. Michener • A Paramount Picture

References to James Michener's popular book abound on this poster for Paramount's drama The Bridges at Toko-Ri *(1955). The climactic battle is front and center, while line drawings illustrate other episodes of the story.*

set in a World War II prison camp) and followed that triumph with, among others, *The Moon Is Blue, Executive Suite, Sabrina* and *The Country Girl*. Holden continued his phenomenal string of successes by attacking the bridges at Toko-Ri as a naval fighter pilot, and covering the war as a correspondent in *Love Is a Many-Splendored Thing* the very same year.

The Bridges at Toko-Ri was based on a best-selling short novel by James Michener. Michener was instrumental in presenting the Korean War to the American public. He realized that the conflict was unpopular at home and saw that the American fighting men who were sent halfway across the world were getting little support on the home front. Michener's response was to write stories of the men sent to battle. One of his stories, "The Forgotten Heroes of Korea," was made into the film *Men of the Fighting Lady*, in which Michener himself was a leading character (played by Louis Calhern). The biggest success of his early career was the short novel *The Bridges At Toko-Ri*, which describes life aboard the aircraft carrier *Savo*, stationed off the coast of Korea during the war, and focusing on one typical, homesick Navy pilot.

The story begins aboard the *Savo* as a flight of four jets approaches for landing. Helicopter pilot Mike Forney (Mickey Rooney) and airman Nestor Gamidge (Earl Holliman) lift their rescue chopper off the deck and hover nearby in case of trouble. Three jets land safely but one flier reports a flameout and ditches at sea. The pilot is Lieutenant Harry Brubaker (William Holden), and within minutes he spots Forney's signature green top hat and scarf hovering above him and is hoisted to safety. Aboard the *Savo*, after warming up from his dip into the icy sea, Brubaker is invited to visit Admiral Tarrant. The admiral (Fredric March) talks to Brubaker about why certain men like Brubaker are called back into service to fight, and then gives the pilot some news: his wife and children are waiting for him in Okinawa, Japan, where the carrier will dock in three days.

In Okinawa Bay, the air group commander, Wayne "Cag" Lee (Charles McGraw), is angry that the carrier captain is running the engines of strapped down propeller planes to steer the ship, and complains to Admiral Tarrant. When Tarrant reprimands Cag for ignoring channels of command, Cag retreats from his stand and leaves as quickly as possible, incurring Tarrant's low judgment of his fitness. On shore, Brubaker is lovingly greeted by his wife Nancy (Grace Kelly), and two daughters, and settles in for a week's liberty. Later that evening, the Navy flier introduces Nancy to Admiral Tarrant. Their plans are interrupted when a bruised Nestor Gamidge arrives to ask Brubaker to travel with him to Tokyo to bail Mike Forney out of jail. Aware of his debt to Forney, Brubaker agrees, leaving Nancy with Tarrant.

The admiral tells Nancy about her husband's recent sea ditching and reveals the secret that Brubaker will soon be bombing several strategic bridges and facing danger again. Nancy doesn't want to hear or worry about the danger, but Tarrant convinces her that it is best to face trouble than to ignore it. Meanwhile, Brubaker persuades the military police to release Forney and pays $80 for damages. Forney begs Brubaker to talk to Kimoko (Keiko Awaji), the Japanese girl who has thrown him over for a bosun on the *Essex*. Reluctantly, Brubaker follows Forney and Gamidge to a nightclub where Kimiko reiterates that she has "lost her heart" to the *Essex* sailor, and Forney has to be restrained from causing another riot.

Brubaker finally rejoins his wife, who has already gone to bed, and she begs him to tell her about the bridges he will have to face. He calmly describes the importance of the bridges and the hidden defenses surrounding them in the hillsides. Once he has talked to her, Nancy is able to accept the specter of her husband's death. Their week together in Okinawa includes an episode at a nude Japanese bath, where the shy American family is surprised by a Japanese family, and are forced to accommodate themselves to Japanese tradition. Brubaker rejoins the *Savo* refreshed, but also reminded of the toll that his Navy job is taking on his family.

Cag informs his pilots that the Toko-Ri bridges are indeed their next target. Cag elects to fly a photographic reconnaissance mission of the target and chooses Brubaker as his wing man. Armed with only a camera, Cag flies his F-9F Panther jet through a hailstorm of bursting anti-aircraft shells and flak over the four bridges and comes through unscathed while Brubaker orbits overhead. The recon mission disturbs Brubaker, as does the news that the chopper crew of Mike Forney and Nestor Gamidge, whom Brubaker considers a sort of safety net, are being transferred to a rescue boat in Wonsan harbor. As the mission nears, Brubaker becomes increasingly strained.

Three squads of four jets fly toward the target. On the first pass, led by Cag, three of the bridges are damaged. The second pass destroys the fourth bridge, and not a single American jet is scratched. The Navy pilots fly to their secondary target, where an enemy ammunition cache is suspected, and expend their remaining bombs there. Pulling up from the attack dive, Brubaker hears a bang and reports that his jet has been hit. Cag sees the vapor trail from Brubaker's plane and confirms the hit. Brubaker flies toward the sea, but his diminishing fuel forces him to crash-land in enemy territory. Cag covers from above while Brubaker glides to ground and crashes in a valley, then hides in a nearby irrigation ditch. Cag swoops by twice, strafing enemy soldiers who examine the wreckage, and the rest of the squadron follows suit. After the jets leave, four propeller-driven planes (AD-4 Skyraiders) fly into the valley and strafe some more while Forney's rescue helicopter swoops in to get Brubaker.

The helicopter is hit by machine-gun fire, dropping it hard to the ground and killing its motor. Nestor Gamidge jumps to the ground and is shot dead. Forney escapes, grabs Nestor's rifle and joins Brubaker in the irrigation ditch. The AD-4s make a few strafing passes but then leave and Forney tells Brubaker that they are on their own for the night. Enemy soldiers surround the ditch and close in. Forney and Brubaker use their rifles and kill a few of the advancing enemy until they begin to throw grenades. The second one kills Forney and Brubaker runs for his life through the irrigation ditch. He is shot in the leg, and as he attempts to pull his pistol, shot again in the chest and killed.

On board the *Savo*, Admiral Tarrant receives the news that Forney, Gamidge and Brubaker have been killed and is livid. He berates Cag, who defends himself and the mission, despite the loss of three men. "It was a good mission, Admiral!" Cag adds that Brubaker was "his boy" as well as the admiral's. Cag leaves,

and Tarrant admits that his previous judgment of Cag was too harsh. Another squad of jets departs from the carrier deck as Tarrant thinks about Brubaker and wonders aloud, "Where do we get such men?"

The Bridges at Toko-Ri was the first studio-backed big-budget production regarding the Korean War. Based on the bestselling novella by James Michener, it featured recent Academy Award winners William Holden and Grace Kelly as its stars. It was the highest-profile Korean War film of the decade. It has lavish color and aerial photography (instead of relying on combat footage) and benefits greatly from location filming aboard actual aircraft carriers (it was filmed on the *Oriskany*, the *Kearsarge* and the *Princeton*). And it reflects the sentiment of the time, as people both inside the military and out actively questioned America's involvement in a war halfway around the globe.

James Michener was well aware that the Korean War was a divisive subject to Americans, but as he visited the naval aircraft carriers stationed off Korea's coastline, he saw that the men were fighting and dying just as valiantly as they had in World War II, and he became determined to relate their stories to the public. Michener did not promote the Korean War, but rather attempted to raise the consciousness of the public regarding the men who were fighting in it. By indicating that the men who he had witnessed were fighting for the same freedoms and facing the same dangers as those who had fought in previous wars, Michener was promoting support for the men, not the cause. His fiction, along with the war correspondence of Marguerite Higgins, Burton Crane, Keyes Beech and Frank Gibney, among others, reported and interpreted the war for millions of people.

Producers William Perlberg and George Seaton secured the rights to Michener's novel and hired William Holden to star as Brubaker on his condition that the ending, where Brubaker is killed, remain unchanged. They then secured the cooperation of the U.S. Navy and permission to film on board the aircraft carriers on location in the China Sea and Japan. Mickey Rooney spent his spare time on the carrier staging shows for the enlisted men. Holden learned to taxi Panther jets on the carrier deck at sea and romanced Grace Kelly while filming

Lieutenant Brubaker (William Holden) is reunited with his wife Nancy (Grace Kelly) and daughters in Japan during the Korean War in The Bridges at Toko-Ri *(1955).*

concluded in Hollywood. And the second unit crew filmed hours of carrier deck operations, minutes of which appear in the actual film. The movie's verisimilitude can be traced directly to the second unit color photography, which brings alive the action on board the aircraft carrier.

Valentine Davies' script, led by Michener's example, humanizes some of the men who keep the operations running smoothly. Admiral Tarrant maintains a watchful eye over the fleet despite his tragic personal life (revealed to Nancy Brubaker); his only human attribute is to "adopt" the occasional pilot who happens to resemble in some way his deceased son. Mike Forney disregards the captain's order prohibiting his green hat, and cannot control his feelings regarding Kimiko. The ship's landing officer, known as Beer Barrel (Robert Strauss), safely delivers screaming jets onto the pitching carrier deck, but wants nothing to do with the pilots while on liberty. And Harry Brubaker resents being called back into the Navy, pulled away from his family and job, to fight an unpopular war halfway around the world.

Brubaker's situation is the crux of the story. He doesn't understand the reasons why he was chosen to fly in Korea, and he would rather not be there. But that does not stop him from doing the best, professional job of which he is capable. Admiral Tarrant's argument is one of location. "They [Brubaker's friends in Denver] act the way they do because they're [safe and comfortable] there; you don't quit, and go on doing your job, because you're here," he tells Brubaker. He then says "Son, whatever progress this world has made has always been because of the efforts and sacrifices of a few," intimating that, in the case of the Korean War, they are the few. Brubaker suggests that the United States should pull out of the war. Tarrant replies, "Now that's rubbish, son, and you know it. If we did, they'd take Japan, Indochina, the Philippines—where would you have us make our stand? The Mississippi?"

Tarrant acknowledges that the Korean conflict is a "dirty war." He tells Brubaker that "Militarily, this war is a tragedy." But he realizes, and reminds Brubaker (and the audience) that "all through history, men have had to fight the wrong war in the wrong place, but that's the one they're stuck with." As much as Brubaker resents his position, he reluctantly agrees with the admiral's logic. These arguments for U.S. participation in the war were not new, nor were they universally accepted, despite their ostensible irrefutability. These arguments did not provide comfort to the families of the military personnel killed in Korea, as Tarrant realizes when he has to notify Nancy Brubaker of her husband's death. But the movie makes the argument that armed aggression must be countered for the sake of global peace, and that it will cost valuable human lives to do so, and it makes that argument without resorting to false heroism or patriotic fervor.

Indeed, Brubaker's bitterness, revealed in frank conversation with Admiral Tarrant, only serves to authenticate the situation. Brubaker has everything to live for, a fact of which he is reminded by his family's visit to Japan. Yet he willingly serves his country in the battle against aggression, and continues to fly low during his bomb runs and do his job professionally. That professionalism eventually costs Brubaker his life, plus the lives of Mike Forney and Nestor Gamidge, in a stinking North Korean irrigation ditch, but that is one of the unavoidable tragedies of war. Nevertheless, the battle continues, with or without Harry Brubaker.

The brutal deaths of Brubaker, Forney and Gamidge communicate the mortal danger in Korea with emotional force. Heretofore, the battle action was confined to bombing bridges and anonymous stores of ammunition and supplies. Suddenly, two likeable, sympathetic characters are facing encroaching death in a ditch, with a third man, their friend, immediately killed during the ill-fated rescue attempt. Mike Forney dies while trying to protect Brubaker from a grenade, and Brubaker dies as a hunted animal. While their deaths seem incredibly tragic and senseless up close, in the "big picture" of the war, they are merely three more casualties in the ongoing battle against Communist aggression. To its credit, the movie retains its human focus,

as Tarrant rhetorically asks "Where do we find such men?"

Admiral Tarrant is the film's weak link. With seemingly little to do aboard his flagship, he watches for Brubaker, "his boy," at every opportunity. Tarrant is the film's political mouthpiece. It is he who argues that America must be involved in the war for its own protection and he who wonders, "Where do we find such men?" Tarrant tells Nancy Brubaker about his own broken home life — his sons were killed in action and his wife has gone insane — and his confession does seem to console her, though it should truly frighten her that a man with his tragic and unhappy background is in command. Tarrant is meant to be a father figure who has survived war's effects upon his family, but Fredric March portrays him as a man very much still troubled and bitter, and this portrayal cannot help but undermine the structure of the film.

On the other hand, Mike Forney and Nestor Gamidge enliven the story considerably, preventing the drama from darkening the picture. Their exploits in Japan expand the film's perspective and introduce lighter elements while solidifying the bond between themselves and Harry Brubaker. The week that Brubaker spends in Japan with his family not only functions as a device to increase empathy with the flier (and to forecast his death) but as a way to display Japanese customs and sample its culture. This culminates in the bath sequence, where the Brubaker family learns that bathing in the nude with other families is accepted as common in Japan.

The public reception for *The Bridges at Toko-Ri* was tremendous. It became the first blockbuster Korean War film, collecting some $4,300,000 in box office receipts and placing in the top twenty moneymakers for 1955. Its critical reception was no less positive. "The movie version [of Michener's novel] is a remarkable film — remarkable for the caliber of its technical achievements and for the impact and seeming authenticity of its documentary portions; and most remarkable for the uncompromising honesty with which it follows its personal storyline to a grim and altogether un-Hollywoodish conclusion." This assessment was written by Moira Walsh of *America.*

Bosley Crowther of the *New York Times* was

The bridges of The Bridges at Toko-Ri *(1955). This miniature set was used for the climactic air strike in the film, and helped the film win an Oscar for its special effects.*

also impressed. "Its purpose simply is to show the human and professional resolution, organization and sacrifice that prosecution of the war required. And it has fulfilled this purpose in a truly efficient and moving way. One of the best of modern war pictures is *The Bridges at Toko-Ri*." In fact, Crowther made the film his choice as the best film of 1955. *Cue*'s critic judged the film "A taut, thrilling, top-flight documentary drama of men, war, ships and planes. For all the film's explosively exciting naval and aerial action — brilliantly photographed in color — the film is a study of men's minds as well as their military actions."

The Bridges at Toko-Ri was nominated for two Academy Awards. It won the special effects award (over *The Dam Busters* and *The Rains of Ranchipur*), but lost the film editing award to *Picnic* (yet another William Holden picture). It paved the way for future "air war" spectacles such as *The Hunters* and boosted the careers of virtually everyone involved with its production. And though the film has not aged particularly well in some respects, it remains contemporary in its examination of men under the intense pressures of war, and dramatically sound, especially in its brutal, honest conclusion.

Cease Fire

Credits: 1953. Paramount. *Directed by* Owen Crump. *Produced by* Hal Wallis. *Screenplay by* Walter Doniger. *Story by* Owen Crump. *Music Score Composed and Conducted by* Dimitri Tiomkin. *Director of Photography*: Ellis W. Carter, A.S.C. *Edited by* John M. Woodcock. *Camera Operators*: Fritz Brosch, John Leeds, James Miller, Jack McEdward and Robert Rhea. *Editorial Supervision*: Warren Low, A.C.E. *Sound Recording by* Gene Garvin. *Song* "Brothers in Arms" *by* Dimitri Tiomkin and Ned Washington. *Technical Adviser*: Major Raymond Harvey, U.S. Army. *Project Officer in Korea*: Captain Gene M. Brooks, U.S. Army. *Air Force*

Project Officer in Korea: Lieutenant Colonel Fred R. Bates, U.S.A.F. Not Rated. Black and White. Widescreen (1.66:1). Originally relased in 3-D. 75 minutes. Released in November, 1953. Filmed "on the battlefields of Korea." Not currently available on commercial home video.

Cast: *Lieutenant Thompson*, Captain Roy Thompson, Jr.; *Patrol Sergeant Goszkowski*, Corporal Henry Goszkowski; *Kim*, Cheong Yul Bak; *Carrasco*, Private Ricardo Carrasco; *One Ton*, Sergeant Albert Bernard Cook; *Elliott*, Sergeant Richard Karl Elliott; *English*, Corporal Harold D. English; *Eddie "Bad News" Willis*, Private Gilbert L. Gazaile; *Hofelich*, Private Harry L. Hofelich; *Mayes*, Private Johnnie L. Mayes; *Owen*, Corporal Charlie W. Owen; *Pruchniewski*, Private Edmund J. Pruchniewski; *Strait*, Sergeant Howard E. Strait; *Wright*, Private Otis Wright.

Historical Accuracy Level: High. In terms of casting, this film could not be more real, as actual soldiers portray themselves; the story is fictional, but based on actual events.

Patriotic Propaganda Level: Medium. Filmed in documentary style, the film avoids excessive flagwaving in favor of low-key realism.

Elements: Army, Cease-Fire, Musical Performance, Peace Negotiations.

Of all of the films concerning the Korean War, only *Cease Fire* can make the claim of being the most authentic. It was filmed on location in Korea, while the war was still in progress, using actual soldiers as actors! It is a groundbreaking blend of fact and fiction, presenting its real-life situation as a fictional story. Most of the soldiers play themselves, though rank for some of them has changed and one man is given a whole new identity. The story itself is fictional, yet based upon actual, common patrols taking place at the front lines. Perhaps most incredibly, this movie was originally photographed and released in 3-D! Somehow, despite these credentials, the film has been largely forgotten, even though it represents a time capsule of the war in early 1953.

Cease Fire takes place in the waning days of the Korean War, as the peace talks in Panmunjom drag to their conclusion. Two war correspondents, one idealistic and one pessimistic, note the slow progress of the negotiations and wonder about the quiet day up in the hills...

Soldiers of the army's Easy Company are removed from one hill, without waiting for replacements, and therefore think that the war is nearly over. Volunteers for a new mission are needed, however, and fourteen men are selected to make a patrol to a nearby hill called Red Top. They are to probe for enemy activity around Red Top and report on the same. Eleven enlisted men, a medic, and a radio man are led by Lieutenant Thompson (Captain Roy Thompson, Jr.), a no-nonsense leader, into the hills of Korea.

Along the way, the patrol's Korean soldier Kim (Cheong Yul Bak) stops to have a native farmer deliver the news to Kim's pregnant wife that the war will soon be over. The men reach an area of artillery bombardment and Thompson orders them through the live shelling, realizing their chances of being seen will be much greater if the shelling stops. The men pass through safely and find two British soldiers inside a minefield, one of whom has a leg wound. Thompson orders one of his men to stay with the wounded Brit while the other shows them part of the way through the minefield. Kim and radio man Wright (Private Otis Wright) finish the tedious job of leading the men through the remainder of the minefield, step by step.

Crossing a stream, the soldiers are spotted and fired upon; one man is wounded. Two men, Elliott (Sergeant Richard Karl Elliott) and One Ton (Sergeant Albert Bernard Cook) are assigned to flush the snipers into the open. They climb a steep hill, crawl toward the Chinese shooters, and kill them from behind. Wright receives a report that some three hundred Chinese soldiers are in the area, so Thompson leaves four men behind to act as a support group to cover the squad's evacuation and takes the other seven toward Red Top.

Over a ridge of the hill, Thompson sees the Chinese soldiers crossing a valley. Wright radios the information to headquarters just before they are spotted and fired upon. One bullet destroys the radio on Wright's back. Officials at headquarters order artillery bombardment and Air Force and Navy jets into the air to attack the Chinese troops in the valley while Thompson and his men ascend the hill under heavy fire. The battle is fought with rifles and grenades as the Americans slowly move up Red Top. Thompson is hit in the arm and as Kim moves

The poster for Paramount's war drama Cease Fire *(1953) stresses realism, picturing the faces of the men at the front, without resorting to hyperbolic catch-phrases or artwork of superhuman heroics. There is no mention, however, that these men are not actors, but actual soldiers in battle.*

to help him, the Korean soldier is killed. The remaining six Americans reach the top of the hill and kill the remaining Chinese while the valley below the hill is bombed and napalmed by jets.

The hill is reinforced, and as Thompson and his men reach their support squad, they are told that the cease-fire has been arranged to begin that very night at 10:00 p.m., just a little too late for Kim. At Panmunjom, both correspondents are genuinely hopeful for the future.

Cease Fire is the most authentic recreation of the war because of its narrow, defined scope of action, its attention to the detail of war and because its cast has actually served at the front (and would soon again). There are no phony heroics here; the professional soldiers simply go about their business, knowing the odds are that some of them will perish doing so. The only blatantly fictional character is Eddie Willis (Private Gilbert L. Gazaile), called "Bad News" and considered by most of the men (including himself) to be bad luck because several other men near him have died while he has not been scratched. Willis is pushed to the rear of the column as they pass through the minefield and generally shunned until the end of the movie, when he is creased on the arm by a bullet and the jinx is lifted.

The other men are real soldiers, who happen to be making a movie behind the front lines. They talk, bantering back and forth, sing, mostly off-key, and march, trudging along the hills of Korea, just like regular soldiers. For that is what they are. Director Owen Crump procured the participation of the Seventh Division, chose actual soldiers to play his fictional characters and wrote his script at the scene, using the characteristics of the actual soldiers as those of his fictional ones. As Crump was there, writing and planning his story, rumor of an impending cease-fire spread along the line. Crump incorporated that rumor into his story, adopting the cease-fire as an ironic theme to counterpoint the battle action. And though the actual cease-fire did not occur while Crump was filming, the atmosphere of a possible cease-fire is quite realistic.

The movie's simple structure follows a single "quiet day" of a patrol. Several men are injured or killed and three hundred Chinese soldiers are bombed and napalmed, yet in the "big picture" of the war, it is a small skirmish on a relatively quiet day. The film shows in great detail some of the mechanics of war: how many grenades and carbine clips each soldier is to carry, the actual map coordinates of the enemy, the endless tramping up and down soft-soiled Korean hills, the tedious and dangerous method of finding mines. All this furnishes the movie with a verisimilitude that cannot be underestimated.

The film follows the common dictum that even if a cease-fire is close at hand, the war must go on. Keeping the Chinese from gaining last-minute advantages is what spurs the mission and results in assorted wounds to the men and the loss of Kim. This scenario is repeated in several other Korean War films, most notably *Pork Chop Hill*. These films tie the effectiveness of the United Nations negotiators at Panmunjom directly to the effectiveness of the U.N. soldiers holding their ground against Chinese onslaughts just a few miles away.

To make his movie, Owen Crump was provided with a small film crew, members of the Seventh Divison to use as his cast and areas behind the front lines to use for his story. In fact, Crump and his crew were encamped within three miles of Old Baldy and Pork Chop Hill, sites of some of Korea's bloodiest battles. Army equipment and ordnance was provided for battles and Air Force and Navy jets were used to simulate the bombing attack. The men used real bullets and real grenades, as they had no substitutes. As the footage was compiled, Crump sent it to Hollywood for editing. Location filming took three and a half months; the post-production period was as long, and the film was released — in 3-D — in November of 1953, three months after the armistice was signed ending the Korean War.

Producer Hal Wallis had decided not to use Hollywood actors for his cast and was quite pleased with his decision. In an article he wrote for *Reader's Digest*, Wallis tells how he was so impressed with the onscreen charisma of Private Richard Carrasco that he offered the soldier an acting contract. Carrasco, however, turned down the offer and instead rejoined his former company on the front lines, where he was killed shortly before the real cease-fire took effect.

If there is any real defect with *Cease Fire*,

The entire platoon which was filmed for Cease Fire *(1953) is pictured here. These are actual soldiers recruited from the battle lines for the film by director Owen Crump.*

it is the quality of the performances (if you can call them that). These are real soldiers rather than actors, with the result that some line readings are awkward, some of their banter seems forced and they don't have the same timing and tempo as professional actors. Yet the realism they bring to the film is palpable and irreplaceable, and to criticize their acting is to unfairly criticize them.

Critics were laudatory about the experiment that *Cease Fire* represented. Philip T. Hartung of *Commonweal* wrote, "There is no big heroic stuff in *Cease Fire*, no glamour boys wipe out whole regiments, no typical cross-section of American virility in action; but there is heroism and there is plenty of action showing how well-trained men carry out a dangerous mission under fire. *Cease Fire* is an effective war film, and is one of the finest examples of a film in 3D to date." *Look* proclaimed it as "a documentary-type film towering above most Hollywood epics costing twice as much." *Newsweek* termed the

film "remarkable" and noted, "The film has the power of everyday incident. It is also, in most of its footage, a work of art."

Moira Walsh of *America* judged that "*Cease Fire* is about as authentic a reproduction of the combat conditions of today's foot soldier as is likely to be found on any commercial screen" and that "It will furnish an absorbing and salutary vicarious experience for the family." Bosley Crowther of the *New York Times* didn't appreciate the "superfluous and annoying" 3-D effects, but felt that the film itself provided "a harsh, authentic ring. From the routine selection of the detail to undertake the job to the final assault upon a hilltop and the decimation of an enemy force, the operations of the detail are vivid and plausible." Crowther also mentioned that the Production Code had softened the dialogue somewhat, eliminating three "hells" and a "damn" before it was approved.

Perhaps the most expert reaction was given by General William F. Dean, the initial commander of U.S. troops in Korea and who had spent more than three years in a North Korean prison camp. "It was so real it made me sweat," said Dean at a special screening. And in his book *The Lost Films of the Fifties*, Douglas Brode puts the film into historical perspective. "The new realism in the postwar cinema reached an apex with *Cease Fire*, the film which — between Roberto Rossellini's *Open City* (1945) and Haskell Wexler's *Medium Cool* (1969) — must be counted as the most significant experiment at combining fact and fiction."

As Brode notes twice in his comments, *Cease Fire* remains largely forgotten today. Perhaps this is because it boasts no Hollywood names, even though that is one of its greatest assets. Perhaps it is because the film was a participant in the 3-D fad, and few of those 3-D films were taken very seriously. Perhaps it is because people don't know whether to call it drama, documentary, docudrama or some other term. But anyone who encounters it, whether they know the film's incredible history or not, would view a movie that says a great deal of war through the accumulation of details. *Cease Fire* is not overly dramatic or histrionic and it does not attempt to provide a big crescendo of emotion (although Dimitri Tiomkin's song "Brothers in Arms" does become tiresome); it merely tells a simple story and tells it well.

Chattahoochee

Credits: 1990. Hemdale. *Directed by* Mick Jackson. *Produced by* Aaron Schwab and Faye Schwab. *Co-Producer:* Sue Baden-Powell. *Executive Producers:* John Daly and Derek Gibson. *Written by* James Hooks. *Music:* John Keane. *Director of Photography:* Andrew Dunn. *Editor:* Don Fairservice. *Casting Director:* Mindy Marin. *Production Designer:* Joseph T. Garrity. *Production Manager:* Cathy Mickel Gibson. *1st Assistant Director:* J. Stephen Buck. *2nd Assistant Director:* Douglas A. Raine. *2nd 2nd Assistant Director:* Philippe Rene Dupont. *Costume Designer:* Karen Patch. *Production Co-Ordinator:* Kathleen M. Courtney. *Assistant Production Co-Ordinator:* Johlyn Dale. *Production Liaison:* Tani

Cohen. *Mr. Oldman's Dialogue Coach:* Tim Monich. *Script Supervisor:* Sharon "Mae" West. *Location Manager:* Kristi L. Frankenheimer. *Production Accountant:* Derry J. Pearce. *Assistant Production Accountant:* Robert Hartman. *Art Director:* Patrick Tagliaferro. *Construction Co-Ordinator:* Rick Galbraith. *Scenic Artist:* Kenneth G. Deubel III. *Set Decorator:* Celeste Lee. *Leadman:* Patrick T. Cassidy. *On-Set Dresser:* Paul Arthur Hartman. *Swing Gang:* William Rea. *Art Department Co-Ordinator:* Deborah Tagliaferro. *Camera Operator:* Philip Alan Waters. *1st Assistant Camera:* Marco Mazzei. *2nd Assistant Camera:* Lane Russell. *Additional 1st Assistant Camera:* David Luckenbach. *Additional Camera Operator:* Walt Lloyd. *Additional 1st Assistant Camera:* Patrick McArdle. *Additional 2nd Assistant Camera:* Alice P. Taylor. *2nd Unit Director of Photography:* Philip Alan Waters. *2nd Unit 1st Assistant Camera:* P. Scott Sakamoto. *Stills Photographer:* Melinda Sue Gordon. *Sound Mixer:* Ed White. *Boom Operator:* Ken Mantlo. *Gaffer:* Jack Cochran. *Best Boy Electric:* Anthony Beverly. *Electricians:* Brian Robertshaw, Don Kearns and Don Tomich. *Electrician / Grip:* Denny Tedesco. *Key Grips:* Mario L. Davis and Dennis "Dink" Adams. *Best Boy Grip:* Walter "T. J." Johnson. *Grips:* Tim Jones and Bruce "Sarge" Fleskes. *Dolly Grip:* Gary F. Wattman. *Special Effects:* Richard O. Helmer. *Special Effects Assistant:* Jim Schwalm. *Additional Special Effects Assistant:* Cory Faucher. *Property Master:* Deborah Schildt. *Assistant Property Master:* Jane B. Orr. *2nd Assistant Props:* James Scott. *Wardrobe Supervisor:* Shari Griffin. *Wardrobe Assistants:* Kimberley Carleton and David Buckley. *Make-Up Artist:* Gandhi Bob Arrollo. *Hair Stylist:* Michelle Johnson. *Beard Make-Up Artist:* Maureen Stephanson. *Assistants Make-Up / Hair:* Jill Bennett and Theresa K. Stone. *Additional Assistant Hair:* Christopher Cline. *Beards Made by:* Sarah Phillips. *Transportation Co-Ordinator:* Barton James Heimburger. *Transportation Captain:* Richard Sampson. *Camera Truck Driver:* Edward Davis. *Production Van Driver:* George Power. *Honeywagon Driver:* David Walden, Sr. *Star Suites Driver:* David Walden, Jr. *Drivers:* Vicky Ready Lybrand and Joann Bowles Hamilton. *Transportation Assistant:* Cheryl Sampson. *Nurses:* Carolyn A. Evans and Shirley E. Jeter. *Assistant to Mr. Jackson:* Suzie Greene. *Office*

Production Assistants: Emily K. Denton, Janet M. Childers and David M. Thornton. *Casting Assistant*: Dana Zaloom. *Extras Casting*: Charlie Peterson. *Extras Casting Assistant*: Tona Hill. *Unit Publicist*: Steve Newman. *Publicity Consultant*: Andrea Jaffe. *Video Playback*: Sync-Lock. *Stand-In*: Lee Zatkovic. *Caterers*: Tomkats Catering. *Cooks*: Tom Morales, Mark Greiner and Mark Quigg. *Craft Service*: Jamie Amos. *Post Production Executive*: Randy Thornton. *Assistant Editor (UK)*: Emma Hindley. *2nd Assistant Editor (UK)*: Gilmore Smyth. *Assistant Editor (UK)*: Tommy Dorsett. *Apprentice Editor (UK)*: Adrian Smith. *Dubbing Editor*: Colin Ritchie. *Dialogue Editor*: Peter Bond. *Foley Editor*: Richard Hiscott. *Assistant Dubbing Editors*: Sarah Rains, Antonia Van Drimmlen and Les Healey. *Music Scoring Mixer*: Dick Lewsey. *Re-Recorded at* Twickenham Film Studios. *Re-Recording Mixers*: Gerry Humphreys, Dean Humphreys and Jonathan Frankel. *Titles by* Frameline. *Opticals*: Howard A. Anderson Co., Cinema Research Corp. and Studio 51. *Editing Facilities (UK)*: New Central Film Services. *Negative Cutter*: Mary Duerrstein. *Color by* TVC. *Grip / Electric Equipment*: Cinelease. *Travel*: Hoffman Travel. *Insurance Provided by* Bob Jellen and Albert G. Ruben & Co., Inc. *Completion Bond*: Film Finances. *Motion Picture Banking*: Frans J. Afman / Credit Lyonnais Bank, Nederland, N.V. *Payroll Services by* Payments Plus. *Special Thanks to* South Carolina Film Commission; John Lashuma; Residents of Shull Street, Columbia, South Carolina; Maureen Oldman; Leslie Manville and Alfie Oldman. *The entire cast and crew would like to thank* Chris Calhoun and Betty Strickland. Rated R. Color. Dolby Stereo. Flat (1.33:1). 98 minutes. Released in May, 1990. Filmed on location in Columbia and Newberry, South Carolina. Currently available on VHS videotape. Previously available on laserdisc.

Cast: *Emmett Foley*, Gary Oldman; *Walker Benson*, Dennis Hopper; *Mae Foley*, Frances McDormand; *Earlene*, Pamela Reed; *Lonny*, Matt Craven; *Missy*, William De Acutis; *Clarence*, Gary Klar; *Vernon*, Lee Wilkof; *Jonathan*, William Newman; *Dr. Debner*, Richard Portnow; *Harley*, Timothy Scott; *Dr. Harwood*, Ned Beatty; *Morris*, M. Emmet Walsh; *Mr. Johnson*, Whitey Hughes; *Duane*, Wilbur Fitzgerald; *Ella*, Yvonne Denise Mason; *Leonard*, Ralph Pace; *Cop No. 1*, Wesley Mann; *Cop No. 2*, Tim Monich; *Pa Foley*, Laurens Moore; *Ma Foley*, Mary Moore; *Mae's Mother*, Peggy Beasley; *First Woman on Street*, F. Drucilla Brookshire; *Second Woman on Street*, Dorothy L. Grissom Hardin; *Ambulance Driver*, David Fitzsimmons; *Sadistic Attendant*, Gary Bullock; *Goading Attendant*, David Dwyer; *Lucas*, Robert Gravel; *Theo*, Marc Clement; *Dr. Towney*, John Brasington; *Dr. Everly*, Jim E. Quick; *Baker*, C. K. Bibby; *Earl*, Bob Hannah; *Patient Without Shoes*, George Nannerello; *Stream of Consciousness Man*, Ed Grady; *Upside Down Inmate*, Kevin Barber; *Hymn Singing Patient*, James (Fred) Culclasure; *Otell*, Shane Baily; *Inmate in Cesspool*, Kevin Campbell; *Inmate in Movie Theatre*, E. Pat Hall; *Inmate in Tunnel*, Jerry Campbell; *Inmate*, Roger Jackson; *Harwood's Secretary*, Suzi Bass; *Governor's Secretary*, Jill Rankin; *Jimbob*, F. Douglas McDaniel; *Attendants*: Chris Robertson, Bill Collins, Bud Davis and Michael Easler; *Miami Guard*, Randy Randolph; *Miami Nurse*, Kathryn Cobb; *Miami Attendant*, Jim Gloster; *Miami Cop No. 1*, Charles Lawler; *Miami Cop No. 2*, Trader Burns; *Weather Girl*, Kristi L. Frankenheimer; *Quincy Cop No. 1*, Perry Simpson; *Quincy Cop No. 2*, Joe Loy; *Patrolman*, Wallace Merck; *First Guard*, Don Wayne Bass; *Male Nurse*, Mykel Mariette; *First Man at Investigation*, Raul Apartella; *Woman at Investigation*, B. J. Koonce; *Stunt Co-Ordinator*: Bud Davis; *Stunts*: Michael Hanes, Joe Gilbride and Dennis Scott.

Historical Accuracy Level: High. Emmett Foley's personal experiences are chronicled in arresting fashion, though his Korean service is only momentarily glimpsed.

Patriotic Propaganda Level: Low. While Foley's whistle-blowing at the Chattahoochee mental institution is heroic, this is an indictment of 1950s America in many ways.

Elements: Army, Biography, Homefront, Medicine, Post-Traumatic Stress Syndrome, Returning Home, Winter Fighting.

Some Hollywood movies observe war veterans who return home after serving in Korea, but many of those that do (*Hell's Outpost, Going All the Way, A Step Out of Line*, etc.) only use the war as deep background. Aside from the subgenre of "troubled prisoner of war" movies, most of which concern Vietnam veterans, only a handful of others have examined the psychological effects of the war on the human psyche. Of Korean War titles, *Toward the Unknown* and *Strange Intruder* depict examples of stressed veterans; *Chattahoochee* is another.

The film opens in Korea, along the 38th parallel, during the winter of 1952. The scene is bathed in white light and the whistle of wind is heard above the muted noise of rifle shots. Emmett Foley (Gary Oldman) is shooting past the camera, trembling as he does so, and his breathing is ragged. His pupils, shown in close-up, are dilated. Emmett's voice-over narrates the scene: "When you come back a certified hero, it kind of raises people's expectations — [it] makes them think you're a big guy." The scene dissolves to white and advances to Quincy, a small Florida town, three years later.

Emmett Foley walks outside of his home with a handgun. He looks around the suburban street, with its manicured lawns, brightly colored homes and peaceful ambiance and he can't stand it. He begins shooting, disrupting the peace of the neighborhood, and yells for anyone listening to call the police. He returns inside, sweating profusely, reloads, gulps down a glass of water and runs outside to shoot some more, this time wounding a neighbor lady in the leg. The police finally arrive and Emmett moves inside, but he opens the window curtains so that he is completely visible. He shoots at the police, causing them to shoot back, but they miss. After dark, with the entire neighborhood watching the scene, Emmett's wife Mae (Frances McDormand) and sister Earlene (Pamela Reed) arrive and try to talk him out of the house. Instead, he shoots himself in the chest and collapses.

Emmett wakes in a hospital, finding that his suicide attempt failed. After talking to a psychiatrist, and admitting that he was trying to force the police to kill him for $25,000 in life insurance benefits for his family, he is transferred to Chattahoochee, a Florida mental institution.

Conditions at the mental institution are terrible; the patients are generally left on their own, except when they are beaten into submission to stop unruliness. Men unable to clean themselves stay soiled unless helped by other patients. Many of the patients are not mentally impaired at all, but are violent criminals transferred from an overcrowded local penitentiary. One of these men, Walker Benson (Dennis Hopper), quickly becomes Emmett's best friend. Over a long period of time, conditions worsen, people die or simply disappear, and men lose hope. Emmett's sister Earlene visits him often and tries to help, especially after Mae declares that she wants a divorce in order to marry another man.

In 1958, Emmett grows a beard and begins to write letters to the relatives of some of the dead patients. His letter writing lands Emmett in trouble with the head psychiatrist, Dr. Harwood (Ned Beatty), and leads to a period of solitary confinement where Emmett is not allowed to move from a sitting position. One of his letters causes the Supreme Court to order sanity hearings, but Dr. Harwood and his staff merely declare the men unfit for society. Emmett begins to take extensive notes of the beatings, disappearances and deaths at Chattahoochee in his Bible and smuggles the information to Earlene, who writes letters to anyone who might help. Emmett helps Walker Benson to escape, but he stays behind out of a sense of duty to the other patients, and he is then subjected to shock therapy.

Earlene pressures Dr. Harwood to produce her brother, whom she has not seen for nine weeks, and Emmett's life is saved. He is put on heavy sedatives, rendering it difficult for him to communicate, and he finally rebels, refusing to take his medication and fighting the guards, who overpower and carry him, prone and Christlike, from the ward. Emmett wakes to find himself before an investigative committee, one which promises to reform the institution. Emmett Foley is released back into society on September 15, 1959. He says, again in voice-over, "I don't reckon I'm a hero. Sure don't feel like one. I just did what I could."

Chattahoochee is a strong indictment of the mental health care system in America. It is based upon a true story, which, according to the film's epilogue, led to the enactment of one hundred thirty-seven separate reforms. The bulk of the movie is dedicated to dramatizing the dreadful conditions and mistreatment of patients at Chattahoochee, and establishing Emmett Foley as a man whose own personal transgressions are minor compared to the men who kept him and

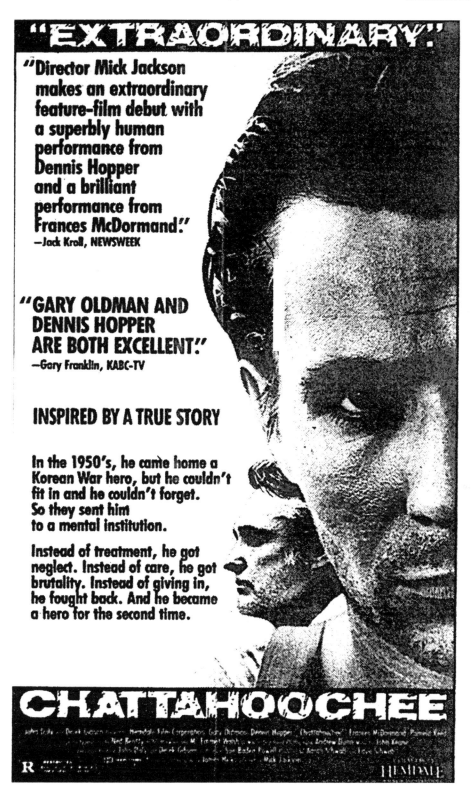

This newspaper ad for Hemdale's social issues drama Chattahoochee *(1990) boasts a rave review, nicely encapsulates the story and presents the noble faces of its protagonists, Gary Oldman and Dennis Hopper.*

many others captive in that living hell. As such, it is a hard-hitting docudrama in the made-for-television mode, although its quotient of profanity, violence and depictions of bodily functions are harsh by television standards.

The movie lucidly examines the nature of heroism. Emmett is obviously frightened in Korea but he does his job; after the war, he cannot reconcile his peaceful, suburban life with his wartime experiences. Although he has won medals for bravery, Emmett is unable to face personal or family responsibility, feels completely isolated, and opts to be killed for the monetary future of his family. In Chattahoochee, Emmett becomes part of an actual community of people, finds his inner courage and stands against the oppression and brutality that poison the facility. Yet, he does not feel that standing against evil makes him particularly heroic. Emmett's voice-over narration at both ends of the film note his difficulty returning home as a hero from the Korean War because of attendant expectations, yet deny any heroism in Chattahoochee for simply "doing what he could."

Director Mick Jackson takes care to subtly contrast Emmett's experiences in the Korean War with conditions at Chattahoochee, and there is no question that he considers Chattahoochee to be much worse. The film's Korean prologue lasts about ten seconds and is bathed in white light and muted sound. The scenes at Chattahoochee last more than ninety minutes, are mostly filmed in dimly lit interiors and occasionally blast the audience with a cacophony of noise. The entire Korean War took three years; Emmett is trapped inside Chattahoochee for four and a half.

The film doesn't explain Emmett's "crazy" episode with the gun, and the one psychiatrist Emmett sees considers his actions desperate enough to confine him to an institution, without providing a diagnosis. Years after this fact-based story took place, psychicatrists diagnosed this type of behavior as "posttraumatic stress syndrome," and it is obvious that this illness is plaguing Emmett Foley. Posttraumatic stress syndrome is symptomatic of people who have experienced a psychologically traumatic event and have not been able to make adjustments. This syndrome is characterized by re-experiencing the event, numbed responsiveness to the environment, guilt feelings, blocked memory, exaggerated startle response and difficulties with concentration and sleeplessness.

At the time of the Korean War, psychiatrists did not have this syndrome narrowed and labeled; they only knew that veterans returning from war sometimes had trouble adjusting back into civilian life. Emmett Foley certainly had this syndrome, and yet it took two years after the war to finally trigger his violent actions. *Chattahoochee* doesn't provide any answers to Emmett's dilemma, nor much of a foundation to explain why he has the syndrome. It simply presents key pieces of his experience and tells his story because it is probably representative of other people's as well, although Emmett left his syndrome-related troubles behind as he began to battle the corruption-riddled Florida mental health system.

The film only touches on the Korean War, depicting ten seconds of a frightening battle in the snow, yet that image represents the dramatic effect that Emmett's wartime experiences had on him during the following years, and juxtaposes Emmett's psyche with that of his peaceful, orderly Florida neighborhood and later, the chaos of Chattahoochee. Perhaps Korea explains why Emmett adapts to and finally triumphs over the evils present at Chattahoochee; he has experienced and survived the chaos and fear of war, so the mental institution's craziness is not all that foreign to him. Emmett's biggest challenge will be to adjust once and for all to "normal" civilian life.

Emmett's return to America is referenced by his voice-over at the beginning, when he says, "When you come back a certified hero, it kind of raises people's expectations — makes them think you're a big guy." This quote describes Emmett's paradox; he does not consider himself a "hero" or a "big guy," and probably does not think anyone else should either. It is Emmett's failure to embody the expectations which others have of him based on his war experiences that ultimately leads to his breakdown. In this way, the film is also an indictment of American society, for having unreasonable expectations of a simple man in the first place.

Director Mick Jackson's debut film reportedly sat unreleased for two years before finally

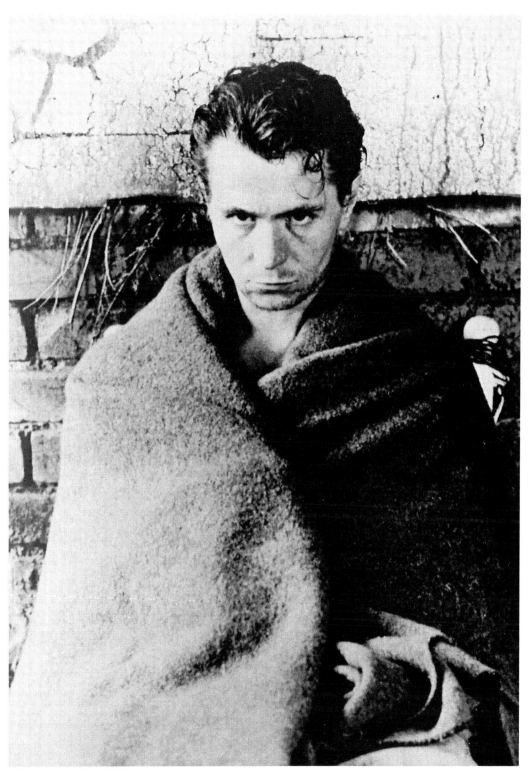

Korean war veteran Emmett Foley (Gary Oldman) *has difficulty adjusting to civilian life in* Chattahoochee *(1990). He finds that life in the Florida mental institution is just as bad as, if not worse than, his experiences under fire in the Korean War.*

appearing in 1990, when it received mainly poor notices. Roger Ebert of the *Chicago Sun-Times* noted that *Chattahoochee* "is a movie that looks and feels authentic. And the performances — especially by Oldman, McDormand and Reed — are strong and well-textured," but then railed against the film's predicatability and inevitable outcome. *Sight and Sound* called it "a remorseless and depressing account of how a decorated war hero, obviously in need of sympathetic psychiatric help, is consigned instead to a Bedlam-like hell-hole presided over by sadistic guards and a complacent doctor."

Chattahoochee is included in this book because its snapshot of the Korean War is so integral to Emmett Foley's character. Despite being terrified, Emmett survived the war only to find that civilian life harbored evils for him that were infinitely worse than the war. War may, indeed, be hell, but there are other hells on earth, as this movie amply displays.

Collision Course: Truman vs. MacArthur

Credits: 1976. David L. Wolper Productions. *Directed by* Anthony Page. *Produced by* Stan Margulies. *Executive Producer*: David L. Wolper. *Associate Producer*: Donald A. Ramsey. *Teleplay by* Ernest Kinoy. *Story by* David Shaw and Ernest Kinoy. *Video*: Dean Terrell. *Video Tape Editor*: Jim McElroy. *Production Designer*: Edward Stephenson. *Lighting Director*: Jim Kilgore. *Technical Director*: Parker Roe. *Associate Director*: Stan Zabka. *Stage Manager*: Peter Barth. *Costumes*: Jack Martell. *Property Master*: Arthur Friedrich. *Make-Up Supervisor*: Ben Lane. *Casting*: Harris and Kleinman. *Audio*: Martin Bolger. *Cameramen*: Lew Adams, Ken Lamkin and Ron Sheldon. *Assistant to the Producer*: Sherry Grant. *Production Assistants*: Marie McKellar, Wendy Winter and Carol Fisher. *Sound Effects*: Neiman-Tillar Associates. *Manager of Production Operations*: Phillips Wylly. *Production Administrator*: Ron Von Schimmelmann. *Post Production Supervisor*: George Taylor. *Video Tape Facilities Provided by* Trans American Video. *Production Supervisor*: Conrad

Holzgang. Not Rated. Color / Black and White. Flat (1.33:1). 100 minutes. Broadcast on January 4, 1976 on ABC television. Videotaped at the Burbank Studios, Burbank, California. Not currently available on commercial home video.

Cast: *General Douglas MacArthur*, Henry Fonda; *President Harry S. Truman*, E. G. Marshall; *Bess Truman*, Lucille Benson; *Averell Harriman*, Lloyd Bochner; *General Omar Bradley*, Ward Costello; *Courtney Whitney*, Andrew Duggan; *General George E. Stratemeyer*, Russell Johnson; *George Marshall*, John Larch; *Charlie Ross*, John Randolph; *Dean Acheson*, Barry Sullivan; *Chiang Kai-Shek*, Richard Loo; *Mrs. Wallace*, Ann Shoemaker; *Jean MacArthur*, Priscilla Pointer; *Times Man*, Paul Lambert; *Associated Press Man*, Howard Hesseman; *Inchon Admiral*, Ben Hammer; *General Collins*, Bart Burns; *Margaret Truman*, Lee Kessler; *General Vandenberg*, John Mahon; *Admiral Sherman*, Michael Fox; *Arthur MacArthur*, Johnston Kelly; *United Press Man*, Ross Durfee; *Air Force General*, Michael Thoma; *Inchon General*, Robert P. Leib; *General*, Ivan Bonar; *Reporters*, Stuart Nisbet, George Kramer and Anthony Herrera.

Historical Accuracy Level: High. This story chronicles the philosophical differences between two legendary American leaders, General Douglas MacArthur and President Harry S. Truman.

Patriotic Propaganda Level: Low. There is no flag waving here; in fact, the film calls into question the personal philosophies and ambitions of America's top leaders during a time of international crisis.

Elements: Army, Biography, Day of the Invasion, Homefront, Journalism, Leaders, Musical Performance, Politics, Red Menace, Returning Home.

One of the most significant battles of the Korean War involved no Communist forces whatsoever. It was the deepening division between President Harry S. Truman and General Douglas MacArthur, the supreme commander of U.N. forces in Korea. Unlike World War II, where total victory was the goal, the delicate balance of power surrounding Korea offered only one politically acceptable answer, which was to fight a "limited war," and to avoid directly involving either China or Russia and thus initiating a third world war. MacArthur felt understandably restricted by the decisions of the Washington policymakers and defied his prohibitions; he challenged the Chinese, which led directly to their entry into the conflict. As a result, he was fired by President Truman, ending a storied and glorious military career with a very public humiliation.

This confrontation and its ramifications are explored in the biographical films *MacArthur* (1977) and *Truman* (1995), but are examined in greatest detail in the 1976 television movie *Collision Course: Truman vs. MacArthur*, in which they are the sole subjects.

Collision Course begins on June 24, 1950, as President Truman (in Missouri) and General MacArthur (in Japan) are informed that South Korea has been invaded. Truman (E. G. Marshall) takes the news calmly, and discusses the invasion's ramifications with his family at dinner; MacArthur (Henry Fonda) immediately asks about Communist troop strength and speed, trying to ascertain the power and intent of the opposition force. The President calls his cabinet together in Washington and resolves to fight a "limited war," unwilling to risk a global confrontation with the Communist superpowers. As the highest ranking officer on the scene, MacArthur is placed in command of the meager U.S. forces in the area. He immediately gives permission to Air Force general George Stratemeyer (Russell Johnson) to attack North Korean planes, airstrips and supplies north of the 38th parallel, as well as south of that predetermined boundary, even though his orders do not explicitly grant him that authority.

On July 19, 1950, with U.N. forces trapped in the southeastern corner of the Korean peninsula dubbed the Pusan Perimeter, Truman and his cabinet discuss whether to accept the offer of troops from Formosa and renegade nationalist leader Chiang Kai-shek. Noting that Chiang wants to regain power in mainland China and is looking for American support to do so, Truman declines the offer and cables MacArthur to inform Chiang of the decision. MacArthur is also in favor of declining Chiang's offer for military reasons, but he feels quite strongly that Chiang, as an anti-Communist, should be supported. MacArthur meets with Chiang (Richard Loo) on July 29 and encourages the exiled nationalist leader to continue to fight against Mao Tse-tung and the Red Chinese. Truman is furi-

ous at what he considers MacArthur's undermining of American policy and sends political advisor Averell Harriman (Lloyd Bochner) to confer with MacArthur. Harriman explains the political situation to the general, but MacArthur is adamant that Chiang be publicly supported. "The Truman doctrine is dedicated to fighting Communism, is it not?" he asks.

Truman's frustration continues when he reads an intended MacArthur speech that strongly supports Chiang, but the President's anger is tempered by MacArthur's daring plan to mount an amphibious assault at Inchon, *behind* the North Korean forces, and cut through their supply lines. At a command meeting in Japan, every operational branch officer objects to Inchon as a landing point, but MacArthur views their objections as insurance for the operation's greatest asset — surprise. In a fiery, heartfelt speech, he implores the officers to support his plan, concluding that "We must act now or we will die." The amphibious landing is successful and turns the tide of the war, gaining General MacArthur the greatest plaudits of his career.

Following the Inchon landing, the U.S. Eighth Army chases the disorganized North Koreans north, back across the 38th parallel and beyond. While Truman and his cabinet members try to decide where and when he should stop, MacArthur continues to push northward. Truman is stunned to hear that an Air Force jet flies some sixty miles into *Russian* airspace and bombs an airfield close to Vladivostok. Truman decides to finally meet MacArthur and resolve their differences. The meeting is to take place on October 15th at Wake Island in the South Pacific, with both men flying to that destination. MacArthur's plane lands first, but then he keeps Truman waiting for some forty minutes on the runway. Truman refuses to leave his plane until MacArthur arrives to greet him. "I'm not going to be downgraded by one of my own generals!" MacArthur finally arrives and the meeting begins. Truman immediately reprimands MacArthur for keeping him waiting, then demands that the general follow his direct orders. No public statements are to be issued by the general unless approved by Truman. After MacArthur assures him that the war will be over by Christmas and that the Chinese have neither the will

Two of the most uncompromising men
the world has ever known...
in a confrontation that could
touch off World War III.

E.G. MARSHALL
is the President

HENRY FONDA
is the General

An ABC Theatre Presentation
"COLLISION COURSE"
Truman vs MacArthur

Special Tonight 9:00 ⑥ ⑦ ⑯ ㉗
Brought to you by Ætna Life & Casualty

The star power of E.G. Marshall and Henry Fonda is presumed to provide the personal fireworks in the premiere of ABC's drama Collision Course:Truman vs. MacArthur *(1976). Interestingly, the description of their "confrontation" is written in the present tense!*

nor the muscle to join the conflict, Truman relaxes. He leaves Wake Island smiling.

Three weeks later, Truman is angry again because the Chinese have entered the war in force. "Either Mac has made a major miscalculation or else he's made this his kind of war," notes Truman's press secretary, Charlie Ross (John Randolph). Truman orders that no bombing take place within five miles of the Yalu River, which divides China from North Korea. MacArthur is livid at the restriction and protests vehemently. Reluctantly, Truman agrees to allow pinpoint bombing of Yalu bridges, providing that Chinese soil remains untouched. Thousands of Chinese troops cross the Yalu and the war begins a new, prolonged phase.

By March, 1951 the two sides have fought to a standstill. Truman is in favor of a cease-fire, but MacArthur wants to drive all of the Communists out of North Korea, using air attacks to slaughter the troops and radioactive waste to pollute their supply lines. The general broadcasts a message demanding immediate Communist surrender and threatening full-scale war. At the same time, a letter from MacArthur to Congressman Joe Martin is read in the House of Representatives, wherein MacArthur states, "We must win. There is no substitute for victory." Truman realizes that he must remove MacArthur now, and his cabinet agrees. A radio broadcast in Tokyo announces the firing, which is communicated to the general by his wife Jean (Priscilla Pointer). His reaction is surprisingly gentle: "Jean, we're going home at last."

MacArthur arrives in New York and is greeted with a mammoth ticker tape parade. He makes a speech at West Point wherein he argues yet again for total victory against the threat of Communism and for support of Chiang Kaishek in Formosa. He quietly concludes his fifty-two years of military service as Truman faces a tremendous public outcry for his controversial decision. Truman is questioned by reporters as to why he sacked MacArthur, and replies that the general repeatedly disobeyed the orders of his superiors and so was fired. "And that's the last damn thing I'm going to say about it!"

Collision Course, its script and dialogue firmly based on actual history, successfully balances the characters and beliefs of two larger-than-life personalities on the pointed, complex question of America's foreign policy in general and that of Korea in particular. Simply put, President Truman was unwilling to risk global war (which very possibly would have included nuclear activity) in a fight to the death with the Communist countries. MacArthur desired a decisive stance against Communism in Korea; he felt that Korea could be unified as a democratic country by pushing the Communists into China and Russia without a catastrophic war, but was willing to fight such a war if it did take place. MacArthur argued for "total victory" so often and so publicly that Truman was eventually forced to sack his prized general simply so that America would present one recognizable face and policy to the rest of the world.

While the film follows (and firmly supports) Truman and the course of history, General MacArthur is provided plenty of opportunity to make his case. From the beginning of the story, MacArthur believes that the Washington politicians have little use for him and will designate someone else to command. He considers it "a miracle" of faith when President Truman names him supreme commander. MacArthur operates within the parameters of his instructions to fight the war, but he does so with the objective of ultimate, total victory. To this end, he allows General Stratemeyer to attack North Korean planes and airfields north of the 38th parallel, he looks the other way when locations in China and Russia are targeted and he plans to drive every Communist past the Yalu River into Asia.

MacArthur could not bring himself to accept the concept of "limited war," wherein enemy aggressors were allowed to retreat, retrench and reinforce their ranks while U.N. or American forces were supposed to wait behind a politically chosen line of demarcation for the enemy's return. He was continually frustrated by political orders he felt undermined his military leadership and by limitations on what he could say publicly regarding the war and its progress. MacArthur's perspective of the war was shared by millions of Americans at the time, and still is today. He always believed that Communism was a threat to be faced and fought wherever and whenever it became aggressive. He would have been astounded to find that Communism was finally defeated by economic realities

President Harry S Truman (E.G. Marshall, left) and General Douglas MacArthur (Henry Fonda, right) find themselves at odds over the Korean War in Collision Course: Truman vs. MacArthur *(1976).*

the general's arrogance and pride, yet shows his quiet, gentle side when at home with his wife and dog Blackie. Fonda articulates the general's positions clearly and furnishes the requisite emotion to make them reasonable. Fonda is not afraid of MacArthur's dark side, revealed when he talks of laying radioactive waste across the Communists' supply lines in North Korea. It is a sure-handed portrayal, factual and effective, from a classic actor.

President Truman is portrayed equally well by E. G. Marshall. Truman is doubly as frustrated as MacArthur, because he is forced to make compromising political decisions rather than clear-cut military verdicts. Marshall portrays Truman as a decent but harried man, trying to maintain the precarious balance of peace in the Far East against a stubborn foe which seems bent on confrontation and bloodshed. Truman is genuinely perplexed when MacArthur exceeds his authority and angry that the general does so even after being told to keep quiet. Truman's anger reaches a boiling point when MacArthur neglects to greet him at Wake Island. He stays aboard the presidential plane, fuming, until MacArthur arrives. It is, of course, a childish reaction, but Truman regards MacArthur's absence as an insult not just to himself but to the authority of his position.

Much time is spent depicting the political side of the equation. Truman was understandably bothered by MacArthur's immense popularity,

and the spread of global unification rather than military force.

The film presents MacArthur's beliefs and judgments logically and dramatically, giving them as much clarity and consideration as possible. The general's brilliant triumph at Inchon is a key point, and is given its due by President Truman, who sends MacArthur a congratulatory cable reading, "Well and nobly done!" But most of all, MacArthur is given humanity by Henry Fonda. The actor chooses to accentuate

and was afraid that he would lose the next presidential election to the general. Truman even exhibits paranoia, questioning whether the Korean invasion was somehow timed to coincide with the presence of MacArthur and ambassador John Foster Dulles in the Far East region. A wise man, Truman listens to the opinions of his cabinet members before making vital decisions, particularly those involving General MacArthur. When it comes time to remove the general, Truman asks for recommendations from his advisors, and the historically important verdict is unanimous. MacArthur must go.

With their differing views on how to handle the Korean invasion and its possibility for a wider-ranging war, it was inevitable that Truman and MacArthur would collide. This talky made-for-television movie dramatizes the conflict between the two men and its worldwide ramifications. The film follows chronological history, bouncing from Truman to MacArthur and back again as they react to the decisions that the other makes. If the film has a flaw, it is a lack of suspense. It does not feature the usual highs and lows of a Hollywood movie; attention must be paid or vital facts may be missed. The film was shot on videotape by stage director Anthony Page, who also helmed two other historical made-for-television movies: *Pueblo* (1973) and *The Missiles of October* (1973).

Of the trio of biographical movies which examine the conflicts between Truman and MacArthur over the course of the Korean War, *Collision Course* remains the most legitimate, balanced view. Ernest Kinoy's fact-based script is superbly enacted by two consummate professionals, supported by a cast of familiar faces. For those who are intrigued by the political power play in America forced by the Korean War, *Collision Course* is indeed a historical treasure trove.

Combat Squad

Credits: 1953. Border Productions. *Distributed by* Columbia. *Directed by* Cy Roth. *Produced by* Jerry Thomas. *Story and Screen Play by* Wyott Ordung. *Music Composed and Conducted by* Paul Dunlap. *Director of Photography*: Charles Van Enger. *Film Editor*: Herry Gerstad, A.C.E. *Production Designer*: Ben Hayne. *Production Supervisor*: Bart Carre. *Assistant Director*: Mack V. Wright. *Script Supervisor*: Dan Alexander. *Wardrobe*: Izzy Berne. *Special Effects*: Donald Steward. *Make-up*: Dan Greenway. *Dialogue Director*: Don Brodie. *Sound Engineer*: Victor Appel. *Set Dressings*: E. H. Reif. *Property Master*: Samuel Gordon. *Optical Effects*: Ray Mercer, A.S.C. Not Rated. Black and White. Flat (1.33:1). 72 minutes. Released in October, 1953. Not currently available on commercial home video.

Cast: *Sergeant Fletcher*, John Ireland; *Martin*, Lon McCallister; *Corporal Gordon*, Hal March; *Brown, the Medic*, George E. Stone; *Jonas*, Norman Leavitt; *Marley*, Myron Healey; *Sergeant Wiley*, Don Haggerty; *Captain Johnson*, Tris Coffin; *Garvin*, David Holt; *Kenson*, Dick Fortune; *Lewis*, Robert Easton; *Yvonne*, Jill Hollingsworth; *Anne*, Linda Danson; *Virginia*, Neva Gilbert; *Patricia*, Eilean Howe; *Colonel*, Paul Keast; *G.I. Hero*, Dirk Evans; *Wounded G.I.*, Bob Peoples.

Historical Accuracy Level: Low. There is nothing specific or significant regarding this film's setting, dialogue or situations.

Patriotic Propaganda Level: Low. This movie does not promote its soldiers, the Korean cause or warfare in general.

Elements: Army, U.S.O.

Some Korean War movies try to encompass the "big picture" of the war, dealing with strategy, political ramifications and key personalities; others, like *Combat Squad*, are merely meant to capture some of the experience that a typical soldier would meet halfway around the world. *Combat Squad* has no pretentions to importance or even timeliness. In fact, the final product is so bland, so run-of-the-mill, that its battles could have been staged anywhere or anytime from World War II to Vietnam. Its lack of detail about the military situation or the enemy is meant to preserve a timelessness, but it really only serves to further dull the lustre of an already boring drama.

Sergeant Fletcher (John Ireland) attempts to lead his squad of soldiers up a hill, but an enemy machine gun emplacement at the mouth of a large cave keeps them at bay. Fletcher requests artillery from Captain Johnson (Tris Coffin) at headquarters, but the shelling is brief and ineffective. Grenade throwers cannot get

The artwork for Columbia's Combat Squad *(1953) suggests masculine bravado "All mud on the outside — all men on the inside!" and hints at romance: "This I like!" Though the soldiers are carrying a flamethrower and a bayonet, there is no mention that they are fighting in Korea.*

close enough, so Johnson sends Fletcher a "Zippo." The flamethrower arrives on the back of Private Martin (Lon McCallister), an inexperienced replacement who does not know how to use it. Fletcher orders his men to encircle the enemy cave, and straps the flamethrower onto his back. A brief firefight ends with Fletcher burning the enemy and exploding their ammo (though the cave itself remains undamaged). The squad is ordered to hold the cave and Fletcher lies down to rest.

Sergeant Wiley (Don Haggerty) passes by with five men to check a nearby road for enemy activity. Sustained gunfire from Wiley's patrol signals a problem, and Johnson sends Fletcher and half of his men to investigate. They find Wiley and his men trapped by enemy soldiers who have barricaded the road. Fletcher and Wiley climb up a hill and around the barricade and Wiley destroys it with TNT, though he is

shot and killed in the process, and another man, Marley (Myron Healey), is wounded. After returning to the cave, Fletcher and his men are withdrawn, to be rested after nearly three months of active duty. They leave, but no replacements arrive to prevent enemy soldiers from retaking the strategically important cave.

Four days of rest are spent marching, constructing tents, listening to regulations and cleaning equipment. Martin is upset because he was not used in either action, but Fletcher still regards him as too inexperienced to trust in battle. Corporal Gordon (Hal March) and Private Jonas (Norman Leavitt) persuade Fletcher to join them in a visit to a U.S.O. club, but even drinking and dancing with lively and attractive women proves unfulfilling to the sergeant. He brightens when told that replacements are available, but there are only three and they are as inexperienced as Martin. Marley rejoins the outfit, as his leg wound was superficial. Captain Johnson arrives and awards Fletcher, Corporal Gordon, Jonas and the medic, Brown (George E. Stone), Silver Stars for their heroism in capturing the cave. Sergeant Wiley gets one as well, posthumously.

Back in the field, Fletcher assigns the men to guard duty in pairs, one replacement with one veteran, hoping to train the youngsters in the art of survival. A night passes with no action and the following day, Johnson orders Fletcher to use the replacements to flush enemy snipers hiding in a nearby woods. Although he has only one month left to go in Korea (after being there more than a year), Fletcher volunteers to lead the patrol himself. Corporal Gordon and Brown, the medic, accompany the patrol into the woods. The U.S. Army soldiers stealthily creep through the woods but an enemy sniper shoots and kills two of the new men, Garvin (David Holt) and Kenson (Dick Fortune), and narrowly misses Fletcher, before being killed by the sergeant. Another sniper kills the third recruit, Lewis (Robert Easton) and Brown. Fletcher uses himself as bait to lure the sniper into firing and only lives because he trips on a log. As he falls, the sniper fires and Martin blasts the man out of a tree. Heading back to camp, Fletcher refers to Martin as "soldier," indicating that Martin has finally been accepted by the topkick.

Combat Squad is a standard coming-of-age war drama which is, unfortunately, peppered with typical platitudes and phrases rather than original dialogue. Fletcher's advice to Marley before battle is, "Don't step on banana peels," and, sure enough, Marley is shot in the leg and falls in a consequent scene. Martin argues heatedly that he is not afraid, but then he sulks like a lonely puppy. The medic Brown timidly volunteers to join each patrol action, "just in case somebody cuts a finger." The men gripe about their duty but do not say anything that hasn't been heard in dozens of other, better war movies.

Occasionally the movie turns inept, as when the men are suddenly informed that they may go into reserve and rest. They leave the cave completely unprotected, even after losing two men in the battle to capture it, and hearing of its special significance to Captain Johnson as an observation post. It is also inconceivable that the cave would be unharmed after Fletcher and his flamethrower detonated the enemy ammunition inside. And later, it is astounding to believe that the captain would force Fletcher to take his four greenest recruits into "a sniper's paradise" and expect any of them to live. Fletcher offers a brief objection but then volunteers to make the suicide mission his own.

Fletcher kills more enemy soldiers *by himself* than the rest of his squad put together. Ironically, while in reserve, Gordon talks about seeing a movie titled *Korea Conquest* where one soldier defeats an entire enemy platoon. At that point, *Combat Squad* is satirizing itself, but does so without acknowledging its own preposterousness. The film is the first (and best!) to be directed by Cy Roth, a thoroughly untalented helmer whose other films (*Air Strike*— the first film in this book — and *Fire Maidens From Outer Space*) were also shot on miniscule budgets with C-list performers. *Combat Squad* was the best film that Roth ever made, but it certainly isn't very good.

The film suffers from the lack of military information. The enemy soldiers are never identified as North Korean, Chinese or even simply Communist. They are merely a nameless, faceless bunch that like to hide behind trees and shoot Americans. The locale is also left open, but it doesn't look anywhere even remotely like Korea. The opening scenes are staged in what seems to be a mining area and the closing woods sequence is a plain forest setting. In almost every way, this movie is bland and unexciting, and that includes the acting. John Ireland is well cast as the crusty sergeant, but Lon McCallister (in his final film role) is too skittish as Martin and George E. Stone's medic Brown is too timid to fully accept. Hal March and Norman Leavitt seem at home in their roles but no one other than Ireland has much to do, and even he doesn't put forth a great deal of effort.

The movie also features an incredible amount of radio traffic between Fletcher and Johnson at headquarters. Fletcher seems to call the captain every five minutes. The film does include a sequence at a U.S.O. club, but this is mainly for comedy relief (Jonas gets a girl, Gordon doesn't) and change of scenery than for any real dramatic purpose. The U.S.O. girls could

Under fire from an enemy machine gun, Sergeant Fletcher (John Ireland, left) radios for help and instructions in Combat Squad *(1953), while an unidentified soldier listens intently.*

have enlivened the film a great deal, but they too are given absolutely nothing to do. Absolutely no music is performed, which is actually surprising, considering the time period and the tendency for U.S.O. numbers in other Korean War films.

Combat Squad was released in October 1953, soon after the cease fire took effect, and therefore probably seemed dated even then. The British Film Institute's *Monthly Film Bulletin* judged that the film "keeps rigidly to a formula, and direction and playing are unenterprising." *Variety* characterized it as "passable filmfare for the kind of bookings it will rate" and noted, "Setup doesn't demand much in the way of performances so the cast strolls through the plot without straining." *Film Daily* was more positive, calling *Combat Squad* an "unpretentious and moderately effective delivery of a simple war story."

Originally produced by Jerry Thomas for a company called Border Productions, the film was purchased outright and distributed by Columbia. That explains the tiny budget and lack of scope that plagued the film's production, but it doesn't make it any better today. *Combat Squad* is one of the duller, less ambitious, and more inept Korean War films ever made.

Cry for Happy

Credits: 1961. William Goetz Productions. *Distributed by* Columbia. *Directed by* George Marshall. *Produced by* William Goetz. *Screen Play by* Irving Brecher. *Based on the Novel by* George Campbell. *Music*: George Duning. *Director of Photography*: Burnett Guffey, A.S.C. *Film Editor*: Chester W. Schaeffer. *Art Director*: Walter Holscher. *Set Decorator*: William Kiernan. *Make-Up Supervision*: Ben Lane, S.M.A. *Hair Styles*: Helen Hunt. *Costume Designer*: Norma Koch. *Production Assistant*: Milton Feldman. *Assistant Director*: George Marshall, Jr. *Recording Supervisor*: Charles J. Rice. *Sound*: Lambert Day. *Orchestration*: Arthur Morton. *Technical Consultants*: Vice Admiral Robert F. Hickey, U.S.N. (Retired) and Aki Mizuno. Not Rated. Eastman Color. CinemaScope (2.35:1). Lenses by Panavision. 110 minutes. Released in March, 1961. Filmed in Yokosuka, Japan. Previously available on VHS home video.

Cast: *Chief Andy Cyphers*, Glenn Ford; *Murray Prince*, Donald O'Connor; *Chiyoko*, Miiko Taka; *George Washington Suzuki*, James Shigeta; *Harue*, Miyoshi Umeki; *Hanakichi*, Michi Kobi; *Admiral Bennett*, Howard St. John; *McIntosh*, Joe Flynn; *William Williams (Lank)*, Chet Douglas; *Koyuki*, Tsuruko Kobayashi; *Mrs. Bennett*, Harriet E. MacGibbon; *Endo*, Robert Kino; *Izumi*, Bob Okazaki; *Chaplain*, Harlan Warde; *Camille Cameron*, Nancy Kovack; *Lieutenant Glick*, Ted Knight; *Lyman*, Bill Quinn; *Keiko*, Chiyo (Ciyo) Nakasone.

Historical Accuracy Level: Low. This comedy has no relation to reality; the Korean War is a mere backdrop for the romantic antics of its Navy photographers.

Patriotic Propaganda Level: Medium. Navy photographers are depicted as conniving hustlers who eventually heed their consciences and help Japanese orphans.

Elements: Combat Photography, Comedy, Japan, Journalism, Navy (Sailors), Orphans, Romance.

Cry for Happy is an unofficial remake of *Teahouse of the August Moon* and also borrows elements (and cast members) from *Sayonara*, with which it shares a producer. These movies were at least partly filmed in Japan and strive to illustrate — to various degrees — what Japanese life is really like, and also promote tolerance and understanding between the former world war combatants. While *Sayonara* is dramatic in nature, comedies like these as well as *Back at the Front*, *The Geisha Boy* and *My Geisha* presented filmmakers opportunities to film in new, relatively unexplored locations and occasionally comment upon our own society by contrasting it with that of Japan.

Cry for Happy is set in Yokosuka, Japan, in 1952. Andy Cyphers (Glenn Ford) is chief of the U.S. Combat Camera Unit, currently housed in a vault of the Kobe bank. Cyphers does not run the unit "by the book," a fact which is soon discovered by the three assistants assigned to him, who are replacing his former assistants who were all killed or wounded while covering the Korean War. The assistants, Murray Prince (Donald O'Connor), George Washington Suzuki (James Shigeta) and William Williams, better known as "Lank" (Chet Douglas), agree to keep quiet if Cyphers' Japanese friend and filmmaker Mr. Endo (Robert Kino) will find them a place to live other than the crowded bank vault.

After photographing a naval operation near the Korean coast (which results in Cyphers and Murray falling into the water and requiring rescue), the American quartet is assigned to cover a press conference about American civic involvement in Japan. Each of the armed services is represented except for the Navy, so Cyphers creates a story about a fictitious orphanage that his Navy buddies are funding. In a display of false modesty, Cyphers refuses to provide details to the press, and soon forgets about the lie when the photographic unit is given ten day's liberty. Endo places the photographers at his cousin's house, unaware that four geisha girls and their "mama-san" Chiyoko (Miiko Taka) have returned early from a trip. The Americans convince the girls to allow them to stay, and are invited to Endo's film premiere.

Endo's film is a Japanese western titled "The Rice Rustlers of Yokohama Gulch." Reporters spot Cyphers carrying a baby and assume it's one of his orphans. Admiral Bennett (Howard St. John) and his wife (Harriet E. MacGibbon) agree to publicize the humanitarian effort and Cyphers is forced to enact his lie. Chiyoko suggests turning her geisha house into an orphanage for a day, using neighborhood children to fool the Navy brass. The ruse works and the Navy photographers are celebrated as humanitarian heroes. A reporter named McIntosh (Joe Flynn) wants to adopt one of the babies, but his efforts are denied by one of the geishas, who is disguised as an administrator.

Murray falls in love with Harue (Miyoshi Umeki), but her poor father has agreed to let her marry a wealthy local businessman. Murray and Cyphers persuade the U.S. Navy to hire her father, a former Navy captain named Izume (Bob Okazaki), as a consultant, thereby providing him with a prestigious position. When the

The advertising for Columbia's service comedy Cry for Happy *(1961) is filled with sexual innuendo, but makes no mention at all of the Korean War. It does, however, reference two previous cinematic adventures in Japan,* The Teahouse of the August Moon *(1956) and* Sayonara *(1957). At least the geisha house ad design is innovative.*

ten day liberty comes to an end, Murray marries Harue and Suzuki marries Hanakichi (Michi Kobi). Lank and his geisha, Koyuki (Tsuruko Kobayashi), are unable to come to romantic terms. Now out of the geisha business, Chiyoko, with the help of Cyphers, turns her house into the Andy Cyphers Orphanage and begins accepting actual orphans.

Cry for Happy is a sturdy example of a cross-cultural comedy. The men from America are placed in Japan and find it difficult, but enjoyable, to adapt to the Japanese world. This type of comedy became popular during the 1950s as the world situation changed. When Russia and Communist China were identified as the most menacing threat to America's national security, European and southeast Asian countries were gradually accepted as friendly. American cinema became truly international, as foreign-language films found acceptance in the U.S., and American filmmakers began to explore the world in their films. One of the results from this exchange was the genre of the cross-cultural comedy.

These films are intended to break down cultural barriers by showing that people all over the world are basically the same, while at the same time providing a new, exciting environment for American filmmakers to explore. Although the intent behind *Cry for Happy* and other cross-cultural comedies is occasionally high-principled, the resulting films are all too often lumbering farces which resort to slapstick chases and innuendo concerning geisha girls instead of insights

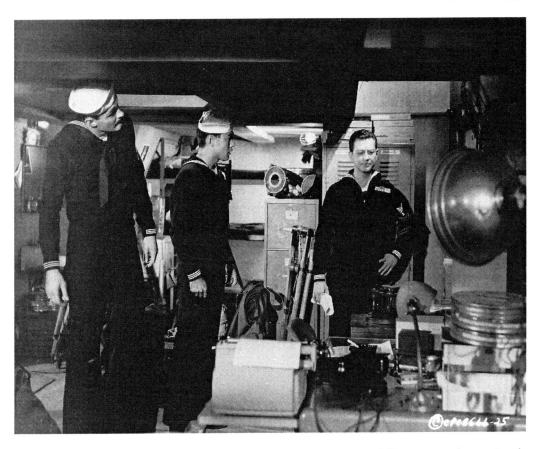

Three photographers of the U.S. Combat Camera Unit— Lank (Chet Douglas, left), George Washington Suzuki (James Shigeta, center) and Murray Prince (Donald O'Connor, right)— report to their new assignment in Yokosuka, Japan, which happens to be located in an unused bank vault, in Cry for Happy *(1961).*

into the Japanese culture. Unfortunately, *Cry for Happy* is a prime offender.

Much of its threadbare plot revolves around the Americans' ignorance of the code of the geisha. Murray Prince (Donald O'Connor) spends a great deal of time and effort trying to persuade Harue (Miyoshi Umeki) to cozy up to him and is insulted when she resists his advances. The other men each experience the same result, all because they assume that geisha girls are specifically trained to pleasure men, particularly American sailors. This misunderstanding, which really isn't humorous at all, lasts far too long before it is resolved. At its best, the idea of horny sailors trying to seduce geisha girls is amusing; at its worst, it represents the overbearing attitude that the American way should naturally take precedence over the local Japanese culture. Indeed, the geisha girls do everything in their power to comply with the Amer-

icans' often unreasonable demands, even to the point of turning their geisha house into an orphanage.

Such racial and sexist condescension occurs throughout the movie, all in the name of good-natured comedy. Perhaps most troubling is Endo's movie-within-a-movie, "The Rice Rustlers of Yokohama Gulch." Endo's homage to the American western is undeniably amusing, but at the same time it reinforces the point that the Japanese cannot do anything as well as the Americans. The fact that Endo intended his film to be dramatic rather than funny is even more damning. Throughout the film, the Japanese people are used and manipulated by the Americans, and yet they do not protest, all because this is supposed to be a comedy.

The Korean War is background to the sailors' antics, even when they become involved in an actual operation, fall into the sea and require a quick rescue. And even though Cyphers has lost three assistants in action, the movie does not dwell on these aspects of war, because, of course, they aren't funny. Well, neither is much else in this pathetic romp around Japan.

Glenn Ford reprises his role from *Teahouse of the August Moon* virtually intact. Donald O'Connor plays his horny sailor role with far too much seriousness; at times Harue (Miyoshi Umeki) actually seems afraid of his interest. The other men have little to do, and the Japanese women are only there to tempt the men, instruct them in the history of the geisha and eventually marry (or in Lank's case, desert) them.

Critics justly lambasted this turkey, with Moira Walsh of *America* noting "In this case, nearly everything goes wrong at once. The jokes don't seem funny, the sailors' mistaken inferences about the nature of geisha girls seem dirty, and the heroes' gold-bricking strategems seem seriously dishonest rather than good, clean, iconoclastic high spirits." *Time* termed the movie "…yawn for sleepy."

Cry for Happy was one of the final American comedies to explore the culture of Japan during that trend; by the time of its release in 1961, the genre had been extensively mined. The only fresh note is Endo's movie, and while that is funny, it also reinforces the racist attitudes prevalent in the film. All in all, *Cry for Happy* is a very unhappy movie.

Dragonfly Squadron

Credits: 1954. Allied Artists. *Directed by* Lesley Selander. *Written and Produced by* John Champion. *Music Composed and Conducted by* Paul Dunlap. *Photographed by*: Harry Neumann, A.S.C. *Film Editor*: Walter Hannemann, A.C.E. *Supervising Editor*: Lester A. Sansom. *Production Manager*: Allen K. Wood. *Music Editor*: Eve Newman. *Assistant Director*: Rex Bailey. *Technical Supervision*: Colonel Dean Hess, U.S.A.F. *Art Director*: David Milton. *Unit Manager*: Edward Morey, Jr. *Special Effects*: Augie Lohman. *Recorded by* Charles Cooper. *Makeup Artist*: Norman Pringle. *Set Decorator*: Robert Priestley. *Set Continuity*: Ted Schilz. Not Rated. Black and White. Flat (1.33:1). Originally filmed in 3-D.

82 minutes. Released in March, 1954. Previously available on VHS home video.

Cast: *Major Matthew Brady*, John Hodiak; *Donna Cottrell*, Barbara Britton; *Doctor Steven Cottrell*, Bruce Bennett; *Dixon*, Jess Barker; *Captain MacIntyre*, Gerald Mohr; *Captain Warnowski*, Chuck Connors; *Captain Vedders*, Harry Lauter; *Anne Taylor*, Pamela Duncan; *Captain Wyler*, Adam Williams; *Captain Taylor*, John Lupton; *Captain Liehtse*, Benson Fong; *Captain Wycoff*, John Hedloe; *Texas Lieutenant*, Fess Parker; *with* Richard Simmons and Gene Wesson.

Historical Accuracy Level: Medium. Although it takes some factual liberties, the film is largely accurate in its portrayal of the South Korean Air Force's poor condition at the beginning of the war.

Patriotic Propaganda Level: Medium. America is there to save the day for the South Koreans, but their own effort to build an Air Force is also extolled.

Elements: Air Force, Air War, Army, Day of the Invasion, Espionage, Females in the Field, Military Training, Politics, Romantic Triangle.

Dragonfly Squadron, perhaps more than any other Korean War film, reflects a missed opportunity. It's script, by producer John Champion, adheres closely to facts in its dramatization of the state of the South Korean Air Force before the invasion and doesn't allow a romantic subplot to unduly intrude upon the proceedings. The film's technical advisor was Air Force colonel Dean Hess, the man who was in charge of preparing the South Korean Air Force as the war began, and many of the cast and crew had previously been involved in various Korean War films. With these assets, this movie should have turned out much better than it finally did.

In May of 1950, Major Matt Brady (John Hodiak) of the Air Force is assigned the task of training South Korean pilots in American planes, just in case noted North Korean troop concentrations north of the 38th parallel indicate trouble for South Korea. Brady and his capable executive officer, Captain MacIntyre (Gerald Mohr), arrive at Kong-ju to find the small air base rather disorganized. Brady calls a meeting on May 28 and informs the men that their South Korean pilots are scheduled to leave the base in twenty-five days — half of the normal training period — as skillful F-51 Mustang pilots.

Brady has an additional problem, of a personal nature. He arrives in Korea to find that Donna (Barbara Britton), a woman who left him six months earlier, is working at the local Red Cross outpost with her husband, Doctor Cottrell (Bruce Bennett), who she thought was dead at the time of her romance with Brady. When Cottrell escaped from a prisoner of war camp in Indo-China, Donna immediately went back to his side, with no regrets. Still, she has feelings for Brady, and vice versa.

The South Korean pilots train constantly, and the Air Force men begin to resent the pace. One of the most popular pilots dies in a crash and the men blame Brady, even after MacIntyre finds evidence of sabotage. Two days before the pilots are to finish training, South Korea is invaded. The South Korean pilots are trucked to the Kimpo airfield near Seoul, while the Americans stay behind for evacuation to Japan. The Red Cross civilians evacuate, except for Doctor Cottrell, who refuses to leave, and faces an almost certain death by remaining. Brady asks for permission to stay and keep the field open for American planes, and is allowed to do so. The remains of an infantry battalion, led by Captain Warnowski (Chuck Connors), arrive to help defend the base. The airfield is attacked in a North Korean air raid at night, and all of the training planes are destroyed. The next day, a North Korean saboteur is found by Warnowski's men, and executed by the South Koreans.

Unable to stop the North Korean tank column sweeping toward them, Brady and Warnowski lead the remaining Americans through the hills toward the sea. At an aid station, Brady is reunited with Donna Cottrell, who learns that her husband has been killed. The aid station is evacuated as the tanks rumble into range and attack. American jets arrive in time to stop the tanks; the United States has officially entered the war. The battered Americans continue toward the safety of the coast and, ultimately, Japan.

Dragonfly Squadron could have been one of the most authentic, realistic and dramatic of all Korean War films; but it isn't. Perhaps the first mistake involving the project is its title. In Korean War parlance, the term "dragonfly " was occasionally applied to the unarmed L-5 monoplanes used by Air Force artillery spotters and reconnaissance cameramen. These planes buzzed around but could inflict no damage, thus the term "dragonfly." The Columbia film studio released a movie about the brave pilots of these airplanes called *Mission Over Korea* (which also starred John Hodiak) the year previous to *Dragonfly Squadron*'s release.

Another problem is the inclusion of a romantic triangle. Romance often seems contrived in war movies, and this one, where Donna Cottrell is torn between idealistic husband Steven and tough, virile Matt Brady, is obvious and ignoble. Reference to Steven's death at the aid station as the survivors prepare to escape the tank onslaught, occurs as a tidy afterthought, allowing the interrupted lovers to reunite. Thankfully, the romance angle is subordinate to the film's real action, which is far more realistic (most of the time).

The film never excels, but it does spotlight the difficulties the Americans had in training South Korean pilots to fly F-51 Mustangs. According to the film's script, the Air Force anticipated the invasion and was busy trying to train South Korean pilots who could then defend their homeland. Actually, American officials knew of North Korean troop movements and displays of military bravado, but the actual invasion caught everyone by surprise. Hess, whose book *Battle Hymn* was filmed in 1957, Colonel Dean Hess was placed in charge (by the flip of a coin) of the real-life training program only after the invasion had already occurred.

The Far East Command donated ten propeller-driven F-51 Mustangs, in which the best South Korean pilots would be trained. The Mustangs were the only planes that the United States was going to make available to the South Koreans that could battle on an even basis the Russian-built Yak-9 fighters which the North Koreans were flying. Even so, ten planes was a pathetic number for an air force. But it was a start.

The film details some of the training procedures, such as learning the cockpit area while blindfolded, through which the veteran pilots were indoctrinated in the minutiae of the American plane, and it manages to convey a sense of

The poster for Allied Artists' action drama Dragonfly Squadron *(1954) emphasizes battles between tanks and airplanes and adulterous romance.*

the teamwork between the cultures necessary for such a project to work. This section of the story should have been the film's most effective strength, but it remains underdeveloped and thin. Although the film does reflect the true story in general, it is shapeless rather than focused, vague rather than precise, and is not particularly interesting. Little is done with the South Korean pilots, who should have been one of the film's main points of interest. The intricacies of learning another culture's language, terms and specific technological data could have been presented in an informative, dramatic and entertaining manner, but that is not the case here.

Dragonfly Squadron does build a sense of dramatic urgency as the North Koreans invade and push toward the Kong-ju airfield. As the Americans wait for transport and the Communist tanks creep closer, the uneasy mood is conveyed very well. One aspect that helps build the

tension is that the characters do not understand whether or not they are at war. Several people ask "Are we in it?" or similar questions which Brady is unable to answer because of the few days it took for President Truman to commit United States military forces to the area. Until the moment at the film's end when American jets come screaming out of the sky and blast the North Korean tanks, the characters' fate is in political limbo.

The air action depicted in *Dragonfly Squadron* is not of a high quality. There are a number of stock footage shots used in the action and some of them do not match at all. At least two sequences show Air Force jets (Shooting Stars) attacking tanks, but are interspersed with shots displaying propeller-driven planes instead of the jets. Even the ground battles are tainted, as when Donna Cottrell and the Red Cross convoy happen across two enemy tanks. The shots of those tanks are taken from an earlier Allied

Major Matthew Brady (John Hodiak) prepares to fly another training mission in Dragonfly Squadron *(1954). The character of Brady is similar to that of Colonel Dean Hess, the chaplain whose career was chronicled in* Battle Hymn. *Hess was placed in charge of training South Korean pilots early in the conflict, and served as technical advisor on this film.*

Artists release, *Battle Zone*, which, coincidentally, also starred John Hodiak. It is unfortunate that the historically accurate sensibilities of the script are undermined by the battle footage chosen for use by Allied Artists.

The film is matter-of-fact in its chronicling of the invasion and the American reaction, and benefits from this approach. One episode which works particularly well involves the identity of the saboteur. Sabotage is plainly identified early in the film, but Brady and MacIntyre are too preoccupied and busy to find the saboteur. After the air raid, which is expected, Captain Warnowski's men discover the saboteur, a woman working in the base hospital, and hand her over to the South Koreans. Within moments, she is executed for her treasonous actions. This episode has a powerful dramatic impact without being falsely embellished.

Dragonfly Squadron was John Hodiak's third and final Korean War movie. After two more films, Hodiak suffered a heart attack and died at the age of forty-one. A handsome, capable actor in regimented roles, Hodiak came to represent capable American soldiers professionally doing their jobs in his trio of Korean War movies. Of the other cast members, Chuck Connors easily makes the best impression as Warnowski, a pessimistic, battle-weary infantryman who seems to know how to survive.

The film's reviews were mixed. The British Film Institute's *Monthly Film Bulletin* commented, "This a fairly straightforward story of the Korean war, efficiently presented; there is little exaggeration or distortion, a little crude anti-Soviet propaganda which is almost incidental, and the usual one or two coincidences. The war scenes are well done and the love interlude is rather played down." *Film Daily* called it "a grim, rather frighteningly real portrayal of the start of hostilities in Korea." Opposite reactions were found in *Variety*, which dubbed the film "a passable program feature," and *Boxoffice*, which denounced it as a "sorry saga of that [Korean] war, not boasting a single redeeming feature."

Dragonfly Squadron is certainly not the movie it could have or should have been. Had a larger studio been entrusted with its development, the results might have been better, although the major studios released Korean War films that were just as ordinary and much worse. It is a passable time filler, and an intriguing glimpse of the military situation in Korea just before and immediately after the invasion.

The Eternal Sea

(aka *The Admiral Hoskins Story*)

Credits: 1955. Republic. *Directed by* John H. Auer. *Produced by* Herbert J. Yates. *Associate Producer:* John H. Auer. *Screen Play by* Allen Rivkin. *Story by* William Wister Haines. *Music:* Elmer Bernstein. *Director of Photography:* John L. Russell, A.S.C. *Film Editor:* Fred Allen, A.C.E. *Art Director:* Frank Hotaling. *Assistant Director:* Gene Anderson, Jr. *Sound:* T. A. Carman and Howard Wilson. *Set Decorators:* John McCarthy, Jr. and George Milo. *Costume Supervision:* Adele Palmer. *Special Effects:* Howard and Theodore Lydecker. *Makeup Supervision:* Bob Mare. *Technical Advisors:* Lieutenant Joseph D. Adkins, U.S.N. and Lieutenant Colonel Edward R. Kandel, U.S.A.F. *Optical Effects:* Consolidated Film Industries. Not Rated. Black and White. Flat (1.33:1). 103 minutes. Released in May, 1955. Not currently available on commercial home video.

Cast: *Admiral John M. Hoskins*, Sterling Hayden; *Sue Hoskins*, Alexis Smith; *Admiral Thomas L. Semple*, Dean Jagger; *Seaman Zugbaum (Zuggy)*, Ben Cooper; *Dorothy Buracker*, Virginia Grey; *Captain Bill Buracker*, Hayden Rorke; *Captain Walter Riley*, Douglas Kennedy; *Captain Walter F. Rodee*, Louis Jean Heydt; *Lieutenant Johnson*, Richard Crane; *Admiral Arthur Dewey Struble*, Morris Ankrum; *Admiral "L. D.*", Frank Ferguson; *Admiral William F. Halsey*, John Maxwell; *with* James Best and Tom Powers.

Historical Accuracy Level: High. With few liberties, this documentary-style biography chronicles much of Admiral John Hoskins' celebrated naval career.

Patriotic Propaganda Level: High. If this biography does not inspire patriotic pride for Hoskins and the Navy, then few films will.

Elements: Aircraft Carriers, Air War, Biography, Disability, Lonely Wives, Multiple Wars, Navy (Aviators), Navy (Sailors).

A very good film with a terrible title, *The Eternal Sea* chronicles the life-affirming story of the Navy's Admiral John M. Hoskins, a man who overcame physical adversity (and a great deal of bad timing) to fulfill his dream of commanding an aircraft carrier. In an era when handicapped people were not given the opportunities of others, Hoskins, by sheer force of will, proved that he could ably command even after the loss of his lower right leg. This is more than an inspirational story, however. Hoskins was also a visionary, a ranking officer in the Navy who believed that modern jets not only could operate from aircraft carriers, but that it was necessary for them to do so. Within five years or so, Hoskins almost single-handedly dragged the U.S. Navy into the modern jet age.

The Eternal Sea begins in a small American town in 1943, where a sinister figure lurks outside of a family home in the middle of the night. Warned of his presence, a woman and her three children cower as the intruder circles their home. The intruder is revealed as Captain John M. Hoskins (Sterling Hayden), home after months at sea. His wife Sue (Alexis Smith) and his two boys embrace him, but his young daughter does not remember him. Hoskins has only seven hours of leave before reporting again, most likely to take command of the U.S.S. *Hornet*. At a briefing, Hoskins is told by his friend and mentor, Admiral Thomas Semple (Dean Jagger), that the *Hornet* has been sunk, and that Hoskins is to instruct naval pilots at Quonset Point, Rhode Island.

Two years later, Hoskins is assigned to command the U.S.S. *Princeton*, taking command from Captain Bill Buracker (Hayden Rorke). When Hoskins arrives on the *Princeton*, however, Admiral William F. "Bull" Halsey (John Maxwell) delays the change in command, as Buracker and his ship are to lead the invasion of the Philippines. Hoskins is invited to stay on board as "prospective Captain," and he gladly does so, knowing that he will take command when the current operation concludes. In the Leyte gulf, the ship is attacked by Japanese kamikaze pilots, the last of whom successfully hits the target, causing a massive fire. Hoskins helps fight the fire on the top deck when an explosion severely wounds his lower right leg. Hoskins is transported to a hospital ship where his right leg is amputated just below the knee.

Captain Hoskins is transported back to the States by plane, and when he reads that an aircraft carrier is being readied to replace the *Princeton*, he diverts the plane to Philadelphia. There, he checks himself into the Naval hospital which overlooks the shipyard and begins rehabilitation with a wooden leg. Sue visits him but is disturbed by his dogged new attitude. Admiral Halsey visits him and suggests retirement; Hoskins insists that he is not ready to retire. Halsey considers it a moot issue because anyone with a debilitating injury is automatically retired. But Hoskins wants to command the new *Princeton* and makes no secret of his desire. He even visits the shipyard to inspect the construction, first on crutches and then without them. Eventually he falls, hurting himself and his wooden leg.

A review board is convened to determine Hoskins' status. Admiral Semple unearths an old Navy regulation which could keep him active, but gives it to Sue to make a final determination. Sue wants her husband to stay at home, or at least on land, but she does send it (anonymously) to him before the review board makes its final decision. The regulation, which states that no one can be forcibly retired without their consent, prevents the board from ending Hoskins' active career, but the *Princeton*'s captain still has not been chosen. At the ship's christening, Admiral Semple announces that Hoskins has been chosen to command the new carrier. Hoskins says, "Today I am the proudest of all Americans," and dedicates the ship to Bill Buracker, his friend and rival for the job.

World War II ends, and Captain Hoskins turns his attention to preparing the Navy to accept fighter jets on its carrier flight decks. He writes a letter to the Navy which results in his reassignment back in the States, to supervise tests to study the possibility of landing jets on

A STORY OF HEROIC GREATNESS...
inspired by the depth of a woman's love!

HERBERT J. YATES
presents

The
ETERNAL SEA

STARRING STERLING HAYDEN ALEXIS SMITH DEAN JAGGER
WITH BEN COOPER · VIRGINIA GREY · RICHARD CRANE
Screen Play by ALLEN RIVKIN · Story by WILLIAM WISTER HAINES
Associate Producer-
Director JOHN H. AUER   A REPUBLIC PRODUCTION

The artwork for Republic's The Eternal Sea *(1955) emphasizes the female and romantic aspect of its story, though the film itself does not. Nowhere is the biographical nature of the story indicated, nor is Admiral Hoskins identified by name.*

aircraft carriers. Sue is glad to have her husband, who is now promoted to the rank of admiral, back home with her family. Hoskins proves that jets can take off from and land on the small area provided by carrier decks and persuades the Navy to proceed. Hoskins even flies the first actual test from a carrier in the Pacific himself. The first use of the carrier-based jets comes as the Korean War begins.

Hoskins is given command of the Seventh Fleet from his flagship, the U.S.S. *Valley Forge*. During the early days of the war, the jets fly bombing and strafing missions against enemy tanks and troop movements; later, they provide air cover as the Inchon invasion takes place. The *Valley Forge* is sent home for a refit, and Hoskins decides that it is time to retire. Instead, he receives orders to report to Pearl Harbor, where he is offered two high-level naval jobs and given a day to decide which one he would prefer. Sue arrives in Hawaii and dances with her husband at a dinner given in his honor. Hoskins insists that he wants to retire and spend time with her.

On his way to the meeting, Hoskins stops at the airport and talks to a planeload of wounded men returning from Korea. At the meeting, he declines both jobs and tries to put his motivation into words. He has treated his own injury as a challenge, one which allowed him to set a precedent for the handicapped. He requests to work fulltime with the Military Air Transport Service (MATS) to help the wounded men returning home from war. Admiral Semple happily agrees, noting, "Either one of these jobs would have made you a big man. But this makes you a great one. The job's yours." Hoskins tells Sue about his change of heart, and she understands completely. The film ends with an image of a cross accompanied by a chorus singing the "Battle Hymn of the Republic."

The Eternal Sea differs from most other Korean War movies in that its characters and action are entirely authentic. This movie joins the biographical film *Collision Course: Truman vs. MacArthur*, as the "truest" of Korean War films, with *Battle Hymn*, *The Great Impostor* and *The McConnell Story* somewhat further behind but still notably faithful to reality. And like *Collision Course*, Admiral Hoskins' story works well because it sticks to the facts and doesn't try to pump any additional drama into what is already a fascinating, inspirational story. Indeed, the most melodramatic scene in the film is the very

first one, with a shadowy figure trying to enter the Hoskinses' darkened home. After that odd introduction to Captain Hoskins, the story is told as straightforwardly as possible, with little sentimentality or pathos.

The success of the drama hinges largely upon the portrayal of Hoskins by Sterling Hayden. A large, quick-talking, quick-thinking actor, Hayden was unafraid of making his characters somewhat unsympathetic. As Hoskins, Hayden reveals glimpses of a sharp temper, overriding ambition and innate stubbornness, but those qualities simply make the officer more human. Hayden has few close-ups in the movie; his most effective shot takes place when he attaches his prosthetic leg for the first time and slowly moves toward the camera. The beads of sweat and restrained grimace of pain on Hayden's face are evidence of the difficulty Hoskins faces in ever walking again, and that shot establishes the mental and physical toughness that defines Hoskins' character. Hoskins also expresses warmth and gratitude to his naval friends, and Hayden reveals more of this sensitive side of his nature than he does in most other movies. Though Hayden had a limited range as an actor, this is one of his better performances, one for which he was particularly well cast.

The other naval officers are nicely portrayed by such familiar actors as Dean Jagger, Hayden Rorke, Douglas Kennedy, Louis Jean Heydt, Morris Ankrum and Frank Ferguson. Jagger is terrific in a very sympathetic role as Hoskins' mentor and friend Admiral Thomas Semple, and Frank Ferguson makes a strong impression as an admiral mysteriously initialed "L. D.," who doesn't share Hoskins' belief that jets are the future of naval aviation. Only two women are included in the story, the wives of Hoskins and Bill Buracker. They are portrayed by Alexis Smith and Virginia Grey, and they deliver the standard Hollywood portrait of wives worried about their men at sea.

It is while at sea that the movie attains its highest level of verisimilitude. Filmed on board the aircraft carriers U.S.S. *Philippine Sea*, U.S.S. *Kearsarge* and the *Valley Forge* (Hoskins' flagship during the Korean conflict), the movie stages its various carrier scenes very convincingly, and depicts authentic aircraft carrier operations without becoming too detail-oriented. The film does

Commander Sala (Arthur Space), Captain Riley (Douglas Kennedy) and Rear Admiral Buracker (Hayden Rorke) try to aid Admiral John Hoskins (Sterling Hayden), whose right leg has just been seriously injured during a kamikaze air attack in the Gulf of Leyte battle during World War II, in The Eternal Sea *(1955).*

not dwell on the technical difficulties of, for instance, transferring the injured Hoskins in a steel stretcher basket from one ship to a hospital ship by rope and pulley. It is simply presented as a necessary facet of combat, and is shown mainly to establish that Hoskins has changed locations. If the film has one aspect which keeps it from excellence, it is this tendency to underplay its more dangerous and suspenseful situations.

The film's most important theme is represented by Hoskins' effort to remain on active status in the Navy. After Hoskins loses his lower right leg, everyone, including his own wife, expects him to retire. But he argues that his mind wasn't in his right foot, and that he is just as capable an officer as before, though perhaps not quite as mobile. The stand that John Hoskins made to fulfill his commitment to duty, along with an arcane naval regulation, forced the Navy

to reevaluate its position on disabilities and paved the way for other wounded people to stay in service to their country. This theme is reinforced at the end of the picture, when Hoskins chooses to spend his time working with the Military Air Transport Service to develop better ways of helping the wounded soldiers returning from overseas. It is all true, and Hoskins' noble effort to help other disabled people adjust to their handicaps would be reason enough for an inspirational film to be made about his life.

But there was more to Admiral Hoskins than a desire to help others and serve his country. He was a visionary who saw that fighter jets could and should be based on the mobile launch platforms of aircraft carriers. He presented his theories to the Navy and fought to have them evaluated. When given the opportunity, he proved that his ideas worked and successfully adopted them into his command of the Seventh

Fleet. When the Korean War began, it was aircraft based on the *Valley Forge* that made the first naval air strikes. The entire strategy of the air war in Korea was possible only because Hoskins had the foresight to support jet operations on carriers. Had all jet operations during the war been based in Japan (the nearest land bases to Korea), the war might well have taken a different, less successful, direction.

Admiral John Hoskins was an important naval officer and an inspirational human being, whose military career has been fashioned into a fine movie. Critical reaction of the time was mixed. *Variety* called it "a good accounting," but noted that it was overlong. *Film Daily*'s critic wrote "The story is told simply and straightforwardly, with very little ornamentation and emerges as a highly exploitable, and thoroughly enjoyable, picture." Lee Rogow of the *Saturday Review* disliked its "straight-line development." He wrote, "There is a certain amount of uplift here, but little excitement." *Newsweek* enjoyed Sterling Hayden's performance, but felt the movie was "too long in the telling."

Little seen today, and encumbered with a title that does little to recommend it, *The Eternal Sea* is nevertheless one of the better military biographies. Its perspective on the Korean War is not sharply focused, but it shines light on the area of aircraft carrier operations that is perhaps taken for granted. It is also an uplifting personal story of a man who did not allow a physical disability to prevent him from fulfilling his dreams.

The Fearmakers

Credits: 1958. Pacemaker Productions. *Distributed by* United Artists. *Directed by* Jacques Tourneur. *Produced by* Martin H. Lancer. *Associate Producer*: Leon Chooluck. *Screenplay by* Elliot West and Chris Appley. *Based on the Novel by* Darwin Teilhet. *Music Composed and Conducted by* Irving Gertz. *Director of Photography*: Sam Leavitt, A.S.C. *Editor*: J. R. Whittredge, A.C.E. *Art Direction*: Serge Krizman, S.M.P.A.D. *Assistant Director*: Eugene Anderson, Jr. *Property Master*: Irving Sindler. *Set Decoration*: James Roach. *Makeup Artist*: Dave Grayson. *Wardrobe*: Frank Roberts.

Sound: John Kean. *Lighting*: James Almond. *Associate Editor*: Paul Laune. *Music Editor*: Harry Eisen, C.M.E. *Sound Effects Editor*: James Nelson, M.P.S.E. *Script Supervisor*: Dolores Rubin. *Optical Effects*: Westheimer Company. Not Rated. Black and White. Flat (1.33:1). 84 minutes. Released in September, 1958. Currently available on VHS home video.

Cast: *Alan Eaton*, Dana Andrews; *Jim McGinnis*, Dick Foran; *Lorraine Dennis*, Marilee Earle; *Vivian Loder*, Veda Ann Borg; *Harold "Hal" Loder*, Kelly Thordsen; *Senator Walder*, Ray Gordon; *Rodney Hillyer*, Joel Marston; *Army Doctor*, Dennis Moore; *Doctor Gregory Jessup*, Oliver Blake; *Senator Walder's Secretary*, Janet Brandt; *TWA Stewardess*, Fran Andrade; *Barney Bond*, Mel Torme; *Man Speaking in Conference Room*, Robert Carson.

Historical Accuracy Level: Low. Communist activity in the United States is described, and overemphasized, in this political espionage thriller.

Patriotic Propaganda Level: High. A stressed veteran from Korea discovers and foils a Communist influence-peddling scheme that the U.S. Senate could not uncover!

Elements: Army, Brainwashing, Politics, Posttraumatic Stress Syndrome, Prisoners of War, Red Menace, Repatriation, Returning Home.

A handful of movies have attempted to delve into the psyches of Korean War veterans who, as former prisoners of war, return to the United States and find it difficult to "fit in." Some, like *The Rack, Time Limit* and *Toward the Unknown* emphasize the guilt that still racks veterans who cracked under the pressure of torture, while others, such as *Chattahoochee, Strange Intruder* and *The Fearmakers* depict the psychological problems of veterans who have not yet recovered from their stays in Communist captivity. *The Fearmakers* describes one veteran's attempt to return to normal within abnormal circumstances, and extends the Communist threat from the battleground of Korea to the exalted halls of power in Washington, D.C.

Behind the opening credits of *The Fearmakers*, a gaunt and bearded Alan Eaton (Dana Andrews) is beaten mercilessly in a Chinese P.O.W. camp during the Korean War. Then, along with other prisoners, he is transported to a repatriation location and released. There is no advance notice of his repatriation; it is a complete and stunning surprise to Eaton. Stateside, Eaton sees an Army doctor (Dennis Moore) who warns him that he is still under stress, and that effects of his two year stint in captivity may remain for months. The Army doctor advises Eaton that if he begins to suffer from severe headaches, he should seek medical help immediately.

On a TWA plane to Washington, D.C., Eaton meets Doctor Gregory Jessup (Oliver Blake), a nuclear physicist who chairs the Committee for the Abolition of Nuclear Warfare, and who strongly hints that Eaton would be welcome to join his cause. Jessup also tells Eaton that his profession of public relations has changed for the worse during his incarceration and is now seen as suspect rather than prestigious. In Washington, Eaton goes directly to his public relations firm, Eaton, Baker Associates, and finds that his partner, Clark Baker, has sold the business without informing him and has since died in an automobile accident. Eaton almost collapses from the shock, and accuses new owner Jim McGinnis (Dick Foran) of fraud; McGinnis produces genuine contracts of the sale and offers Eaton a consulting position for old times' sake.

Eaton visits Senator Walder (Roy Gordon), a former client of his public relations company, who informs him that Eaton, Baker Associates is now a high-powered lobbying firm, and is to be investigated by Walder's Senate committee on lobbying abuses. "It's a pretty fine line between being a paid consultant or a paid foreign agent. We think Jim McGinnis may have crossed that line," says the senator. Eaton agrees to join his former firm and act as a spy for the Senator. Walder also introduces Eaton to Rodney Hillyer (Joel Marston), a *Washington Post* reporter who suspects that Clark Baker's death was not accidental at all, but murder.

Eaton accepts McGinnis' offer to consult, and begins to work closely with Barney Bond (Mel Tormé), McGinnis' right-hand man, to familiarize himself with the firm's current accounts. Eaton also attempts to befriend McGinnis' secretary, Lorraine Dennis (Marilee Earle). With nowhere to stay in the city, Eaton calls upon Hal and Vivian Loder (Kelly Thordsen, Veda Ann Borg), boarding house operators who

were recommended by Doctor Jessup. The Loders welcome Eaton, but his sleep is disturbed by their arguing and by nightmares of his time in the Chinese prison camp. In the morning, Eaton finds Vivian searching his suit; she then attempts to seduce him. As Eaton leaves, he is forced to defend himself from her jealous husband, whom Eaton swiftly subdues with karate chops.

At the office, Barney Bond sidesteps Eaton's interest in the firm's biggest client, referring his questions to McGinnis. Eaton persuades Lorraine Dennis to help him; she steals McGinnis' file key and gives it to Eaton. Barney Bond tries to ask Lorraine for a date but is interrupted by McGinnis, who then presses Eaton to convince Senator Walder to rehire the firm for his public relations work. After everyone else leaves the office for the day, Eaton nearly faints while talking to Lorraine Dennis. Eaton and Lorraine meet at a nearby restaurant and discuss things with the reporter, who informs them that the two alibis for McGinnis' whereabouts during Clark Baker's auto accident were Gregory Jessup and Hal Loder.

Eaton returns to the office to examine McGinnis' master card survey index, hoping to prove that McGinnis is controlling the firm's raw survey data for his own purposes. He is discovered by McGinnis and Hal Loder, who freely admit that they killed Clark Baker and forged the firm's sale documents and threaten to eliminate Eaton unless he joins their effort to place Communist agents inside the government. Eaton resists and is beaten by Loder, and then watched by Barney Bond while McGinnis and Loder leave to capture Lorraine Dennis. Eaton wrests Barney's gun from him, but faints while trying to call Senator Walder. When Barney Bond realizes that Lorraine is to be killed along with Eaton, Bond fights with Loder and is shot.

McGinnis and Loder drive Eaton and Lorraine toward the river, where they are to be disposed, but Senator Walder calls the office and a dying Barney Bond tells him of the plan. Eaton pretends to faint and grabs Loder's gun, shooting Loder and crashing the car in front of the Lincoln Memorial. As the police arrive, Jim McGinnis tries to escape, but Eaton follows and knocks him senseless down the memorial steps. Senator Walder arrives and thanks Eaton for his

The Fearmakers (1958), United Artists' timely drama about "influence peddling," is sold as an espionage thriller in this poster. The figure with a gun just to the left of Dana Andrews is none other than Mel Tormé!

patriotism, and Eaton and Lorraine walk away, arm in arm, toward a happy future together.

The Fearmakers is an antique from the time following the Communist witch-hunts of the early 1950s. Thankfully, it is not as frenetic as it might have been; indeed, director Jacques Tourneur carefully crafts his drama in terms of human consequences rather than political hysteria. While the Communist plot to infiltrate the American government is regarded as real and frightening, Tourneur wisely focuses (most of the time) on the people rather than the plot. Normal, working-class Americans are considered to be completely ignorant of the threat—and the film targets its audience among this group. But ignorance is not judged harshly; even the people who work directly with the Communist agents (such as Lorraine Dennis and Barney Bond) are seemingly unaware of the propaganda they are unwittingly helping to spread.

Even Alan Eaton, though he is suspicious of his former firm's work, is astounded at the depth and breadth of the Communist plot. Eaton is informed of the true situation by Senator Walder, but it is up to him to face the Communists alone. This is nothing new for Eaton, because he survived for two years in a Chinese prison camp during the Korean War. For him, the fight is merely a continuation of the one he left behind in Korea when he was finally repatriated. Still, there is no question that he is shocked to the core to find that Communist agents are at work in the nation's capital, at a firm in which he invested years of his life and professional effort. That is why, despite debilitating headaches that lead to fainting spells and greater risks to his health, Alan Eaton digs until he uncovers the truth. Just as he knocks Loder unconscious during the film's climax at the Lincoln Memorial, Eaton says, "This is for Clark Baker and a lot of guys in Korea!"

The film paints the concept of Communist infiltration from an intriguing perspective, using the public relations field as its canvas. Based on the novel by Darwin Teilhet, *The Fearmakers* proposes that Communists might actively infiltrate and control the fields of public relations and political lobbying, thereby insidiously convincing people to support their positions and candidates without even realizing it. Is such misdirection possible? Of course it is. As recently

as the 1990s, several candidates from the Lyndon LaRouche party won state elections before they were revealed to be members of this extremist group. If anything, the film underplays the possibilities that exist for people to infiltrate the American government. This path finally led, of course, to the nightmare vision of *The Manchurian Candidate*.

Some of the film's rhetoric rings hollow, specifically regarding Gregory Jessup's complaints that science is being used strictly to develop weapons, but occasionally, the film hits an issue squarely on the head. Late in the movie, Eaton and Lorraine Dennis are talking, and he describes the shortcomings of polling a limited number of people. She then asks, "Doesn't that give a few people an awful amount of power?" and she is right. Eaton is aghast that his former public relations firm may be altering the opinions of the everyday people who have been surveyed, but the film (perhaps inadvertently) also asks the larger and more important question of whether such surveys actually mean anything. Eaton is the first to admit that most survey statistics can be manipulated to support any side or cause; it is his (and the film's) contention that the *questions* are the key to the answers.

Another intriguing aspect is the film's handling of Eaton's imprisonment in a Chinese prisoner of war camp during the Korean War. During the opening credits, Eaton is seen being interrogated and beaten. He is gaunt and hungry, bearded and dirty, unable to look anywhere but down at his feet. Eaton's condition is by no means exaggerated; the majority of returning American P.O.W.s had experienced malnourishment and ill treatment during their captivity. After months in a hospital, Eaton is pronounced healthy enough to return home, though he is warned that some symptoms (dizziness, fatigue, headaches) may continue for months. These are symptoms of what is now known as posttraumatic stress syndrome, a condition which afflicted many returning veterans. Circumstances force Eaton to ignore his illness, but ultimately he is temporarily incapacitated by it. Without treatment—and an end to his stressful situation—Eaton would surely suffer a physical or mental breakdown.

McGinnis knows Eaton's personal history, but spares him no embarrassment or suspicion.

Korean War veteran (and former P.O.W.) Alan Eaton (Dana Andrews, seated, right) discovers that his public relations firm business has been sold while he was away at war, in The Fearmakers *(1958). Explaining the situation to Eaton are Jim McGinnis (Dick Foran, left), Barney Bond (Mel Torme, center) and Lorraine Dennis (Marilee Earle).*

On several occasions McGinnis refers to Eaton's brainwashing in detrimental terms, offering his opinion that Eaton is crazy. It may seem odd that such a supporter of Communist beliefs would harangue Eaton about brainwashing, but the film's position is that a Communist agent would use any means of gaining control or superiority over someone else, even if it involves deriding a Communist technique. Ultimately, it is Eaton who accuses McGinnis of brainwashing the American people, saying, "You're peddling poison to put in their minds!"

Unfortunately, the "poison" is never exhibited. The film's biggest weakness is its vagueness as to how public relations polls can be used to elect enemy agents. There is one scene which refers to surveyors being told how to handle specific groups (Jews, labor unions), but the details remain unspecific. While the generalities of the Communist plot seem threatening, there are no specific details to ensure its frightening effectiveness.

The film also treads on thin ice by nominating Senator Walder and his committee to maintain objectiveness during their investigation of political lobbyists. The senator says all the right things, and he has Eaton's unflinching support to comfort the audience, but the spectre of a McCarthy-like congressional committee conducting a witch-hunt in the nation's capital looms large in the background. It is a credit to director Tourneur that such contradictory elements remain in balance throughout the film.

Except for the characters of Hal and Vivian Loder, who seem to be caricatures rather than characters, the film's roles are nicely conceived and played. Dana Andrews is appropriately sincere as Alan Eaton, although his sudden headaches and fainting spells are not very convincing. Marilee Earle is excellent as Lorraine Dennis, and Dick Foran is properly bilious as Jim McGinnis. The strangest sight has to be singer Mel Torme, in a rare dramatic role as milquetoast Barney Bond, constantly perspiring and wiping his face with a handkerchief whenever Lorraine Dennis is in view. Torme overplays Barney's nervous nature and his death scene borders on the absurd.

The Fearmakers was perhaps made a little too late to be taken very seriously. Two years after the allegorical *Invasion of the Body Snatchers*, the political threat featured in *The Fearmakers* seems not only tame, but outdated. The film was barely released at all, and never found an audience. In his book about director Jacques Tourneur, *The Cinema of Nightfall*, Chris Fujiwara judges "*The Fearmakers* isn't a failure — but neither is it a film strongly marked by the director's personality." In their *Motion Picture Guide*, Jay Robert Nash and Stanley Ralph Ross give the director more credit. "Tourneur's fresh direction keeps the film from becoming just anti-red propaganda."

The Fearmakers is a time capsule from an era when filmmakers were still trying to examine and explain the effects of Communist influences on our culture. The film tries to responsibly relate an area of threat while remaining hopeful and patriotic. The result is a very uneven, but oddly satisfying mixture of rhetoric and entertainment.

Field of Honor

Credits: 1986. Oranda Films. *Distributed by* The Cannon Group. *Directed by* Hans Scheepmaker. *Produced by* Menahem Golan and Yoram Globus. *Executive Producer*: Henk Bos. *Screenplay by* Henk Bos. *Story by* Henk Bos and Felix Thyssen. *Music*: Roy Budd. *Director of Photography*: Hein Groot. *Editor*: Victorine Habets. *Art Direction*: Young Woo Do. *Make Up Artist*: Michael J. Mills. *Sound*: Tom Tholen. *Sound Mixers*: Ad Roest and Tom Tholen. *Special Effects*: Jim "Slim" Ballard and Bob Wasson. *Pyro Technics*: Moon Girl Lee, Jung Il Lee and Won Gu Lee. *Animal Trainer*: Karl Mitchell. *As-sistant Animal Trainer*: Mauray Sweeney. *First Assistant Director*: Dae Hee Kim. *Second Assistant Directors*: Hee Chul Lee, Han Woo Jung, Il Soo Oh, Dennis Cristen and Pavel Marik. *Producer's Assistant*: Mrs. Park. *Production Managers*: Jong Ho Joo and Sang Moo Ahn. *First Assistant Camera*: Soon Kwam Lee. *Second Assistant Camera*: Dong Sam Lee. *Loader*: Han Soo Jun. *Clapperboard*: Mi Sun Park. *Camera Reports*: Mi Kyung Song. *Chief of Lighting Department*: Eep Chun Choi. *Electricians*: Man Chang Park, Hoon Song and Jong Hwan Park. *Stills*: Tae Sik Lee. *First Assistant Sound*: Roberto van Eyden. *Second Assistant Sound*: Dae Lim Choi and You Gong Kim. *Wardrobe*: Ja Ohk Shin and Michael J. Mills. *Prop Masters*: Tae Woo Lee, Han Sang Kim, Sung Gi Kim and Kyung Sub Bae. *Script*: Pavel Marik. *Script Assistant*: Jorge Heredia. *Sound Effects*: Tom Tholen, Heinz Bauer and Willi Kluth. *Dialogue Editor*: Tom Tholen. *Effects Editor*: Marc Nolens. *Assistant Editors*: Jorge Heredia, Peter Reef and Barry V. D. Sluis. *Projectionist*: Johan Oosterbroek. *Casting Adviser*: Hans Kemna. *Coordination Extras*: Gill Bowman and My Son Lee. *Graphics*: Emile Molhuysen. *Titles by* Optical Arthouse. *Syncnumbering*: J.M.S. Rushes Service. *Publicity*: Bert Anthoniesse and Margriet Denneman. *Travel Coordinator*: Willem Hakkaart. *Accountancy*: Hans Schellingerhout. *Documentation*: Rut V. D. Pol and Frans Smits, Jr. *Military Adviser*: Peet van Haalem. *Producer's Haircut by* Michael J. Mills. *Music Composed, Orchestrated and Conducted by* Roy Budd. *Recorded at* the Forum Studio, Rome, Italy. *Engineers*: Franco Patrignani and Franco Finetti. *Music Coordinator*: Nino Dei. *Music Editor*: Joe Illing. *Produced by* Roy Budd. *Korean Production Management*: Woo Jin Film. *Managing Director*: Jim Woo Chung. *Film by* Fuji. *Laboratories*: Cineco, the Netherlands and Saebang, the Republic of Korea. *Post-Production Facilities*: Cinetone and Meta Sound, the Netherlands. *Film Mixed at* Meta Sound, the Netherlands. *The Producers wish to thank*: the Army of the Republic of Korea; the Authorities and Citizens of Uncheon; Gerrit Visscher; the Royal Dutch Army; the Royal Dutch Arms and Army Museum in Delft, the Netherlands; the Royal Netherlands Embassy in Seoul, the Republic of Korea; the Korean Immigration Office; Mr. Sae Il Kang; Korean Air. *Special Thanks to*

Charles Lee. Rated R. Fujicolor. Dolby Surround Stereo. Widescreen (1.85:1). Released in June, 1986. Filmed on location in the Republic of (South) Korea. Currently available on VHS home video.

Cast: *Sire (Sergeant Daakonen)*, Everett McGill; *Tiny*, Ron Brandsteder; *the Lieutenant*, Bart Romer; *Taihutu*, Annies de Jong; *Sun Yi*, Hey Young Lee; *Applesan*, Dong Hyun Kim; *Kim (the boy)*, Min Yoo; *Brammetje*, Marc van Eeghem; *Wiel*, Frank Schaafsma; *Leen*, Guus van der Made; *Chinese Medic*, Jae Ho Choi; *Journalist*, Mike Mooney; *Platoon Sergeant*, Jon Bluming; *Truck Driver*, Fritz Homann; *Radioman*, David Hartung; *Pimp*, Yung Guk Chung; *Kim's Mother*, Kyung Ai Yoo; *Desperate Mother*, Ji Young Kim; *Little Girl*, Kyong Lan Kim; *Gabriel*, Shalom Mazar; *Jeepdriver*, Gill Bowman; *Soldier*, Reiner Dremmel; *Chinese Soldiers*, Choon Gil Hong, Bu Yang Park, Yong Guk Jung, Sung Yun Hong, Dal Ho Kil, Gap Sung Na and Sang Ho Choo.

Historical Accuracy Level: Medium. This movie has an authentic grit, but it is nearly impossible to believe that one soldier could have experienced what Sire does.

Patriotic Propaganda Level: Low. This ugly view of war is not patriotic in any way.

Elements: Dogs, Effects on Civilians, Females in the Field, Orphans, United Nations Forces.

The most modern of Korean War films is probably this Dutch movie, which takes great pains to avoid sentimentalizing the war. *Field of Honor* dramatizes the war in all of its ugliness. Its soldiers are not heroes, nor do they attempt heroic acts. They are men trying to survive until it is their turn to be rotated home, trying to enjoy the few good aspects of war in between the bloody battles. *Field of Honor* is not a pleasant film; it is rated R for blood and gore, for sexual scenes, nudity and rape, and for raw language. It is, in all respects, a modern version of the war, complete with a modern sensibility that is almost completely lacking in the films made during and immediately after the war.

Field of Honor is the ostensibly true story of one of the 3,418 men who served in the Dutch Infantry Battalion in Korea in 1951. His name is Sergeant Daakonen (Everett McGill), and he is known simply as Sire. As the movie begins, he emerges from a Korean brothel, naked but for a bow tied around his phallus. He takes a quick dip into a rain barrel (into which he urinated moments before) and washes his hair with scotch. Another Dutch soldier, Tiny (Ron Brandsteder), arrives with news that the Chinese are approaching and that their outfit will be moving immediately. Sire dresses and two soldiers try to sober another named Wiel (Frank Schaafsma), who is a virgin no longer. When the brothel pimp asks for $40, Sire clubs him to death and gives the pimp's money to the women of the brothel.

One week later, the Dutch infantrymen creep toward a small village. Sire leads the way into the village, followed by the other men and Chippy, a dog which has followed Sire since he left the brothel. The village is quiet and empty. A soldier shouts and Sire fires as a reaction, killing a young woman. Sire chastises the soldier, telling him to only yell after identifying a threat, and tells Applesan (Dong Hyun Kim), their Korean translator, to tell the young woman's grieving mother "Accident. Very sorry." Sire sits by himself, cursing the unnecessary, irresponsible death.

The outfit's young, inexperienced, by-the-book lieutenant (Bart Romer) orders Sire to dispose of Chippy, so Sire trades the dog to an American journalist for a typewriter. In a town, Sire sees the young boy Kim (Min Yoo), whom he had earlier advised to make money shining shoes, and Kim offers his sister to Sire for sex. Sire takes Kim, Kim's sister Sun Yi (Hey Young Lee) and their mother (Kyung Ai Yoo) to the soldiers' barracks and allows his colleagues to trade food and money for sex with the women. As the men are to move to the front lines the next day, several agree. The lieutenant questions Sire's motives, but Sire responds, "Gang shagging these two is an act of charity," and he means it. The party is interrupted by explosions and fire as a group of Chinese soldiers march into camp disguised as Koreans and begin a sneak attack.

The Chinese decimate the Dutchmen. The following morning, Sire awakens alive but with a bullet in his thigh and his head covered in blood. After the Chinese move away, he finds Tiny still alive, but with his skin roasted. Sire shoots Tiny, ending his agony. Then Sire digs

A wounded Dutch soldier nicknamed Sire (Everett McGill) rummages through a destroyed building for food and shelter during the Korean War in the Dutch film Field of Honor *(1986).*

the bullet out of his own leg with a knife. Sire finds Applesan with a belly wound, his intestines open to the wind. He covers Applesan's belly with his helmet and crawls under a truck to recuperate. Chinese soldiers awaken him as they destroy the abandoned trucks, and cause the truck under which Sire is hiding to roll onto his foot, trapping him. A soldier tosses a grenade near Sire's cover, but it does not explode. Applesan sings to himself, yells in agony and dies. Sire, still trapped, is awakened by rats, feeding on his former friend. Chippy arrives and is chastised by Sire for not fending off the rats. Then a Chinese medic (Jae Ho Choi) hears Sire humming to himself and finds him. The medic pushes the truck's wheel off of Sire's foot and sets its broken bone. He speaks English and tells Sire that he will go to a prisoner of war camp. Sire refuses and makes a feint for the grenade lying nearby. The medic dives onto it and the grenade explodes. Sire gets up and limps away, followed by Chippy.

Sire hides in an area of two or three de-stroyed shacks. Chippy alerts him to a presence nearby, but no one can be seen. Chinese soldiers drive past and Sire decides to reconnoiter the area. Sire leaves Chippy tied up and climbs a hill to a bunker that overlooks the road. The bunker is abandoned, but from there Sire sees someone beating Chippy. Sire shouts and futilely shoots, but the dog is gone when he returns. Angrily, Sire detonates grenades to kill anyone hiding in the shacks, but no one is present. Finally, he sits down on a log and plays a harmonica, waiting to be attacked like his dog. When the attack comes, it is Sun Yi who tries to kill him. Sire calms the young woman and finds that Kim is also alive but in shock. Their mother is dead. Sun Yi has killed Chippy for food, and Sire helps keep Kim alive by chewing the raw meat and then putting it into Kim's mouth, to be swallowed more easily.

A Chinese soldier finds their hiding place and tries to rape Sun Yi; her screams bring Sire, who breaks the soldier's neck from behind. The sounds of battle move closer, so Sire moves the

Korean kids to the bunker on the hillside. Soon, Chinese soldiers are staggering past, under artillery fire from behind. Some of them try to access the bunker, but Sire shoots them. A grenade is tossed in; Sire tosses it back out, killing more men. Another is tossed in and kills Sun Yi, but Sire kills the remaining Chinese aggressors. Sire waits until the U.N. troops begin marching past, following the Chinese retreat, and then rejoins the war. The Dutch platoon members are astonished to find Sire alive. The lieutenant asks, "Will I see you in a couple of days?" and Sire grimly smiles. He and the boy Kim walk away from the front, back toward the aid station.

Field of Honor is a grim, unrelenting view of war which does contain the cliches and stereotypes present in the majority of other war films, but which also focuses on the dirty details of survival that other movies regularly gloss over. Because of the film's Dutch origins and perspective, its view of war is certainly different and probably more authentic than the traditional Hollywood view. And while the actors' Dutch accents give the dialogue a distinctive sound, director Hans Scheepmaker attempts to make Sire's singular experience of war a universal one that people everywhere can comprehend.

Sire is a traditional loner character, tough and flinty on the surface, but with a core of honor and integrity beneath. He is a man, however, who relishes the basic necessities of life and sees nothing wrong with taking advantage of opportunities to enjoy himself. He partakes of the brothel and even arranges for Kim's mother and sister to prostitute themselves to his comrades, because he believes that sex is good for himself and the men. Yet he makes sure that the women benefit from the action, even to the extent of killing a pimp. While his actions may seem reprehensible to viewers, Sire's statement that "Gang shagging these two is an act of charity" is debatably true under the circumstances. It is a sad fact that human dignity and innocence are the first casualties of war.

Later, when Sire finds Sun Yi and Kim, he takes responsibility for them because it was he who brought them to the soldiers' barracks. It is a mark of Sire's sense of honor that he tries to provide for the Korean youth in the story, even as he takes advantage of their poverty. He even forgives Sun Yi for killing Chippy. The dog represents Sire's tie to civility, and the most emotion he displays is when he sees Chippy being beaten to death. At that moment, he screams and shoots his rifle, uncaring of the danger or consequences of his actions.

Ultimately, this story is about survival. Sire, while a competent and brave soldier, is not heroic. He does manage to kill some Chinese soldiers in the firefight at the barracks and the attack on the bunker, and a few others in between, but his wartime experience cannot be viewed as heroic. Sire is simply fighting to survive. Kim and Sun Yi are simply trying to stay alive while their country erupts in violence all around them. Tiny is just trying to finish his year-long hitch and then return to an easy life in the Netherlands. Nobody in this story is trying to be heroic. War is not about heroism; for most people most of the time, it's about surviving and returning home intact.

For that reason, *Field of Honor* stands virtually alone among Korean War films. Its sentiments were echoed later in such films as *Saving Private Ryan* and *The Thin Red Line*, and occasional earlier films such as *All Quiet on the Western Front* and *Attack* also contain not only the same survival perspective but the horror of war's devastation. And yet, like General George S. Patton, quoted in *Patton* as saying about war, "I do love it so," the film acknowledges that some people seem specially adapted to fight and seem lost when not doing so. Sire is such a character.

Sire is played with hangdog intensity by American actor Everett McGill, who the same year also played Clint Eastwood's uptight commanding officer in *Heartbreak Ridge*. McGill proves with roles in this film and the earlier *Quest for Fire* that he is comfortable without clothes, and his lanky, sinewy physicality is just right for the tough-to-kill veteran soldier. It also helps that he is a relative unknown; Sire would be a very difficult role for a well-known and well-liked actor to portray.

Field of Honor was shown at the Cannes film festival in 1986 and played briefly in American theatres later in the year. *Variety* complained that "most of the fatalities incurred with this peculiar Dutch production will occur in the audience, which gets talked to death. That would be okay if [the] pic had something to say, but the Dutch-accented English dialogue makes the thin 'war is heck' message unintelligible." While the accents are odd, they are certainly intelligible, and the film presents an uncompromising look at the effects of war, not only on the people who travel halfway around the world to fight it, but mostly upon the people whose country and lives are devastated. *Field of Honor* is not a pretty film to watch, nor is it meant to be enjoyed. This movie does an admirable job of depicting war as the personal and unglorified hell that it truly is.

Fixed Bayonets!

Credits: 1951. 20th Century Fox. *Directed by* Samuel Fuller. *Produced by* Jules Buck. *Screenplay by* Samuel Fuller. *Suggested by a Novel by* John Brophy. *Music by* Roy Webb. *Director of Photography*: Lucien Ballard, A.S.C. *Film Editor*: Nick De Maggio, A.C.E. *Art Direction*: Lyle Wheeler and George Patrick. *Set Decorations*: Thomas Little and Fred J. Rode. *Wardrobe Direction*: Charles LeMaire. *Musical Direction*: Lionel Newman. *Orchestration*: Maurice de Packh. *Makeup Artist*: Ben Nye. *Special Photographic Effects*: Ray Kellogg. *Sound*: Eugene Grossman and Harry M. Leonard. *Technical Adviser*: Captain Raymond Harvey, U.S. Army. Not Rated. Black and White. Flat (1.33:1). 92 minutes. Released in November, 1951. Not currently available on commercial home video.

Cast: *Corporal Denno*, Richard Basehart; *Sergeant Rock*, Gene Evans; *Sergeant Lonergan*, Michael O'Shea; *Wheeler*, Richard Hylton; *Lieutenant Gibbs*, Craig Hill; *Whitey*, Skip Homeier; *Vogl*, Henry Kulky; *Walowicz*, Richard Monohan; *Ramirez*, Paul Richards; *Mainotes*, Tony Kent; *Borcellino*, Don Orlando; *Paddy*, Patrick Fitzgibbon; *Medic*, Neyle Morrow; *Griff*, George Wesley; *Bulcheck*, Mel Pogue; *Zablocki*, George Conrad; *Bigmouth*, David Wolfson; *Husky Doggie*, Buddy Thorpe; *Lean Doggie*, Al Negbo; *Fitz*, Wyott Ordung; *Jonesy*, Pat Hogan; *G.I.*, John Doucette; *G.I.*, James Dean; with Bill Hickman and Kayne Shew.

Historical Accuracy Level: Medium. This film's rear-guard engagement is fictional, but the atmosphere teems with authenticity, courtesy of writer-director Samuel Fuller.

Patriotic Propaganda Level: Medium. Some flag-waving is evident, and the soldiers heroically rise to the occasion when the battle is toughest.

Elements: Army, Bugles, Infighting, Winter Fighting.

Samuel Fuller's second Korean War film is far different and much more traditional than his previous one, *The Steel Helmet*. Where Fuller's first opus is, at times, a symbolic struggle, and takes place in the steaming Korean summer, *Fixed Bayonets!* is squarely a physical struggle (although psychological stresses are endured as well) against the frozen climate of wintry North Korea. The enemies are also different: North Koreans in *The Steel Helmet*, Chinese in *Fixed Bayonets!* Most of all, *The Steel Helmet* examines the role of the individual caught in the midst of battle, while *Fixed Bayonets!* depicts the need for the men of a particular platoon to work together as a team in order to survive.

It is winter in North Korea as *Fixed Bayonets!* begins. Military officials discuss the situation, as two companies have already been heavily "chewed up" by Chinese forces. The decision is made to leave one platoon of forty-eight men behind to act as a rear guard while the main body of fifteen thousand troops moves away and reorganizes. This platoon is to give the impression that the entire American force is still present and active, bluffing the Chinese and giving their own troops a chance to regroup on the opposite side of a large river several miles away. The platoon members watch in hushed silence as their fellow soldiers trudge past them toward a much safer position. As soon as the main force departs, the men get busy, chopping down trees to block the mountain pass, digging machine gun posts, planting mines and trying to keep warm in the sub-freezing temperatures.

The platoon is led by Lieutenant Gibbs (Craig Hill), aided by Sergeant Lonergan (Michael O'Shea) and Sergeant Rock (Gene Evans). Fourth in the chain of command is Corporal Denno (Richard Basehart), who is terrified of having to take command and who has yet to kill an enemy soldier. The platoon finishes its preparations and disperses, waiting for the Chinese to make their move. The first attack is heralded by bugles, but fought with mortars and artillery, with the Americans claiming first blood.

Chinese artillery chases most of the men into a hillside cave, where they seem safe from bombardment. Following the skirmish, however, Lieutenant Gibbs is killed outside the cave by an enemy sniper.

Sergeant Lonergan takes charge and orders two soldiers to an outpost to warn of enemy action. The others spend time in the cave talking about their situation, their pasts and each other. Denno is called a coward by Mainotes (Tony Kent) and responds by knocking his fellow G.I. backwards into a stream and slapping

Fixed Bayonets! (1951) was Samuel Fuller's second film about the Korean conflict within a year. 20th Century–Fox's usual publicity hyperbole overshadows the timely message at bottom left: "The biggest story in the world today ... told while it's happening! Written at bayonet point by the U.S. infantry!"

him, proving to Mainotes that he is not afraid to fight. Rock stops the argument and orders the men to warm their feet by putting all their bare feet together and rubbing them. Rock sees that one foot is purple and numb; it turns out to be his own. Privately, Denno asks Rock to demote him to a private because he doesn't want responsibility, noting that when he was previously in charge of men, things went wrong, and that he doesn't want to inadvertently cause the deaths of his colleagues.

Bugles blow again, echoing through the snow-ridged hills. Lonergan orders two men to get one of the bugles. They return — one of them wounded — with an enemy horn, which know-it-all Whitey (Skip Homeier) blows loudly, confusing the Chinese buglers and commanders and ending the raucous concert. One of the outpost men, named Bigmouth (David Wolfson), is reported missing, so Lonergan goes looking for him. Lonergan finds Bigmouth dead, frozen stiff, and is then shot by a Chinese sniper. Stumbling back through the snow, Lonergan collapses in the minefield that the men have established. The medic (Neyle Morrow) bravely walks into the minefield to save the sergeant, but explodes one of the mines and dies. Denno slowly steps into the minefield and succeeds in retrieving his commanding officer. Lonergan, however, is dead when Denno rests him in the snow.

Now in charge, Sergeant Rock orders his men to construct snowmen and adorn them with helmets to simulate live soldiers, and place them in exposed positions. The Chinese use mortar fire to destroy the dummies, revealing their positions for American mortars to destroy them. Rock lectures the men about Chinese approaches and tactics, but a trio of men led by Griff (George Wesley) is silently killed by the Chinese anyway. A mortar and machine gun attack barricades everyone in the cave. Twenty-one men are left, and Rock reminds them that they only need to hold the position for another hour to ensure the safety of the main unit. A Chinese sniper shoots into the cave and the bullet ricochets until it hits Rock in the belly. Denno tries desperately to save him, but Rock dies quietly, in a sitting position.

A few of the men try to persuade the others to leave immediately, but Denno, now in charge, forces them to stay. They remain in the cave for the last hour, quietly thinking about their homes and whether they will ever see them again. At 9:00, Denno orders the men out and away from the cave. As they leave, they hear the approach of an enemy tank. The tank fires, destroying their barricade of the pass. Denno decides to try to ambush the tank when it reaches the pass, creating a new, heavier, more impenetrable barricade. He positions men with bazookas on both sides of the pass and waits while a Chinese soldier scouts the terrain. At the last possible moment, Denno shoots the soldier and the bazookas fire, setting the tank ablaze. More Chinese soldiers follow, and Denno and his men fight their way back to the river, which they cross safely. Denno is the last man to cross the river.

Fixed Bayonets! is a fairly straightforward, typical winter war film which benefits from strong individual performances, authentic dialogue and a grim, unrelenting view of wartime conditions. Writer-director Samuel Fuller, himself a decorated World War II hero, infused his Korean War films with first-hand knowledge of war and the ways in which soldiers cope with their fears of death. Fuller's films are blunt, brutal and usually devoid of extraneous sentiment. Characters are differentiated by their nationalities, their jobs and their personalities. Though many of Fuller's characters are skeleton-thin on paper, he excelled at choosing actors who could "flesh them out" and create engrossing portraits from his bare-bones profiles.

A former reporter, Fuller directed in that style, making his point early (the lead) and then filling in the background and motivation. *Fixed Bayonets!* begins with a jeep racing through the snow and being blown off a road by mortar fire. Two soldiers are then heard talking about the key to leadership. One says, "It takes more than brains to be a general. You've got to have the guts to lead." Then the credits begin, but the movie's premise and point have already been made. Korea will be a bloody battle, and the men who lead will have to rely on more than their intellects. Corporal Denno has not yet been introduced, but his psychological stigma has.

Denno's fear of assuming responsibility for other men's lives is vividly realized in the script. Every decision made by the platoon's leader, no matter how seemingly insignificant, puts someone at risk. Gibbs, Lonergan and especially Rock are viewed as tough, competent soldiers who make decisions based on a mixture of sound military training and common sense. Yet, by the time Denno is forced into a role of leadership, the platoon has lost more than half of its men. It is to quell incipient panic in the men that forces Denno to finally take charge, because he knows that they still have a mission to complete, and that a unit without strong leadership would not last long. And he finds, much to his surprise, that once the burden of responsibility is assumed, that the added pressure brings out the best in his training and intellect. Denno ultimately discovers his courage and pride when he participates as the leader of the platoon.

Writer-director Fuller is not concerned with making "important" statements about war in general, or the Korean War in particular. The politics of the situation do not interest him; indeed, his script jokes about the political term for the war. One soldier says, "They told me this was goin' to be a police action," and another asks, "So why didn't they send cops?" Fuller's intention (especially as a former journalist) is to uncover the "truth" regarding men in war. The interaction and dialogue between the nicknamed soldiers are all based on Fuller's own experiences in the First Infantry Division (the "Big Red One," the eponymous story of which later became his crowning movie) during World War II. The ways in which the soldiers grouse while sitting still and waiting or actively preparing for an enemy attack ring true because they are observances of human nature in those very situations. The scope of Fuller's drama is narrow; he is less concerned with the "big picture" of the battle than with the intimate details of the lives of the men fighting that battle. The movie does not have the sweeping grandeur of a war epic because it is more interested in how the individual participants of war face the danger and survive. Fuller crystallized his point in *The Big Red One* thirty years later, but it is certainly present in *Fixed Bayonets!*: "Surviving is the only glory in war."

Fuller was a filmmaker who, out of necessity, was forced to get the most out of his usually meager budgets. *Fixed Bayonets!* was a low-budget film, shot on 20th Century–Fox back lots and interior sets. So, while other Korean War films display the rugged, open terrain of Korea and emphasize the space of the place, Fuller's film does the opposite. Much of the film is set within the cold, dripping confines of the cave, forcing the men to interact closely with each other and their uncomfortable but protective setting. Even the outside scenes, shot with hazy lighting and visually confined within the contours of steep hillsides, seem tightly confined and almost claustrophobic at times. This feeling is emphasized by the knowledge that anyone who strays too far from the perimeter will soon perish. The result is an unusually taut war story in which the protagonists are not only faced with a physical enemy, but are also constricted in terms of space and a deadly climate as well. Unfortunately, one of the byproducts of filming on a studio set is the lack of one authentic detail: although it is supposedly bitterly cold, no one's breath steams when they speak.

Adding further tension to the situation are the machineries of war itself. The minefield does not claim any enemy lives during the course of the story, but it does kill the medic and delays Lonergan's rescue long enough to force his death. Enemy snipers kill several men, including Gibbs and Rock, and mortar attacks are the most devastating of all. Sergeant Rock uses a clever idea to trick the Chinese into revealing their mortar position in order to destroy them. Rock warns his men about the slow, cautious approach tactics of the Chinese, but they are still eliminated by that threat, even when they know it's coming. Finally, the enemy tank arrives, the deciding factor in the standoff. Only Denno's ingenuity — and bravery — prevents that tank from routing and destroying the remainder of his platoon. The movie celebrates the common sense and fighting know-how of the American soldiers while avoiding the traditional and inspiring "fighting spirit" sentimentality common to this type of war story.

Fuller's characters are certainly not filled with fighting spirit. They are not glory seekers or patriotic flag-wavers; they are merely simple, ordinary men. More than any other factor, that truth — that the men who fight are the same, common men who live in every town on every street — is what Samuel Fuller desired to convey and establish. For Fuller knew that combat is

As the other members of his platoon watch, Sergeant Rock (Gene Evans, foreground right) fixes his bayonet and prepares for battle in Fixed Bayonets! *(1951).*

itself a great common denominator, one that powerfully humbles (and sometimes destroys) each person that experiences its terrifying reality. He had experienced it several times and survived, and he wanted to show audiences that other people — regular, common joes — could do so as well. Fuller's idea of heroism, practiced by the entire cast, is simply to face the danger head-on and try to do one's level-headed best in the face of fear.

Fuller achieved his goal by working his cast to its limits. On the set, he forced the actors to carry full sixty-pound backpacks and climb up and down the hillsides just as real soldiers would do in Korea. Fuller did not want his cast to act as if they were tired; he worked them until they *were* exhausted, and that condition does translate to the screen. The minefield section of the set was particularly icy, and several cast members and extras were slightly injured making their way around and through it.

Although most of the cast consists of vaguely familiar faces (including a quick glimpse of young James Dean at the very end of the movie), Fuller hired two top actors of the early 1950s to portray Rock and Denno. Gene Evans had a long, rather ordinary Hollywood career, except for the three consecutive starring roles he found in Sam Fuller movies. In the two Korean War films, Evans essentially plays the same character, a gruff, bear-like sergeant equally skilled at "sniffing out" the enemy and taking care of his men. With his short, curly hair and beard and compact but powerful build, Evans was not a prototypical leading man, but he had the essence of world-weary cynicism and battle-tested intellect that Fuller wanted for his sergeants, Rock and Zack. For Denno, Fuller chose Richard Basehart, an introspective actor who excelled at portraying troubled men who ultimately learn the value of human companionship.

Astute critics enjoyed Fuller's approach to war drama. Philip T. Hartung of *Commonweal* wrote, "*Fixed Bayonets!* is an exciting war movie and one that directs our attention where it should be more often: on our fighting men in Korea." Manny Farber of *Nation* gushed, "Funny, morbid; the best war film since *Bataan*. I wouldn't mind seeing it seven times." In their voluminous *Motion Picture Guide*, Jay Robert Nash and Stanley Ralph Ross recount the film's most valuable asset: "There is nothing glamorous about this film, as Fuller documents the mental and physical strain the infantryman must undergo, a grimy, bone-weary situation where hope comes down to the ability to wield the cold steel of a bayonet."

But not everyone enjoyed it. Bosley Crowther of the *New York Times* judged that "Mr. Fuller's latest film is lacking in any qualifications that might raise it above the routine. Its action appears staged and synthetic, its characters are all conventional types and its standard of heroism is an ability to stand firm and kill." *Newsweek* noted, "The film, which has a great deal of suspense and excitement, remains a vivid picture of combat and does scant justice to the individual human dilemmas involved in the tragic scene." And even *Variety*, in a mostly positive review, indicated that "The failure of the cast members' breath to steam in the frozen Korean mountains is a tipoff that the scenes were lensed on a warm studio set."

Fixed Bayonets! was released during the first efforts to reach a truce in Korea, and benefited at the box office from its timeliness. It was unfavorably compared to *The Steel Helmet*, Fuller's other Korean War film, which had premiered earlier in 1951. For the first year and a half of the war, it was the two films from Sam Fuller which conveyed to the public the struggle of American soldiers in a faraway land. Together, with their summer and winter climates, their North Korean and Chinese antagonists and, perhaps above all, the pragmatic presence of Gene Evans, these two movies best represent a powerful, personal vision of the Korean War.

Flight Nurse

Credits: 1953. Republic. *Directed by* Allan Dwan. *Produced by* Herbert J. Yates. *Written by* Alan LeMay. *Music:* Victor Young. *Director of Photography:* Reggie Lanning. *Film Editor:* Fred Allen, A.C.E. *Special Photography:* Ellis F. Thackery. *Art Director:* James Sullivan. *Assistant Director:* Herb Mendelson. *Sound:* Earl Craine, Sr. and Howard Wilson. *Costume Supervision:* Adele Palmer. *Set Decorations:* John McCarthy, Jr. and Charles Thompson. *Special Effects:* Howard and Theodore Lydecker. *Makeup Supervision:* Bob Mark. *Hair Stylist:* Peggy Gray. *Technical Advisors:* Colonel Phil B. Cage, U.S.A.F. and Captain Lillian M. Kinkela, U.S.A.F. (AFNC). *Optical Effects:* Consolidated Film Industries. Not Rated. Black and White. Flat (1.33:1). 90 minutes. Released in November, 1953. Not currently available on commercial home video.

Cast: *Lieutenant Polly Davis,* Joan Leslie; *Captain Bill Eaton,* Forrest Tucker; *Captain Mike Barnes,* Arthur Franz; *Lieutenant Ann Phillips,* Jeff Donnell; *Private Marvin Judd,* Ben Cooper; *Sergeant Frank Swan,* James Holden; *Lieutenant Kit Ramsey,* Kristine Miller; *Captain Martha Ackerman,* Maria Palmer; *Lieutenant Tommy Metcalf,* Richard Simmons; *Flight Engineer,* James Brown; *Sergeant Jimmy Case,* Hal Baylor; *Doctor Peterson,* Thomas Browne Henry; *Lieutenant Will Cary,* Richard Crane; *Sergeant,* Richard Wessel; *Chopper Pilot,* Paul Livermore; *G-2 Captain,* Morris Ankrum; *First Sergeant,* Frank Savage; *Second Sergeant,* Harry Lauter; *Captain,* Pat Waltz; *Patient from Copter,* Tony Dante; *Rifleman,* Carl Switzer; *Gus,* James Young; *Longfaced North Korean,* Weaver Levy; *G.I. Charles,* Ted Ryan; *Corporal,* Eddie Ryan; *A.P.,* William Leslie; *British Pilot,* James Lilburn; *British Nurse,* Mary Flynn; *Psycho,* Sumner Williams; *P.O.W.,* David Bair; *P.O.W. Marine,* Gene Collins; *Sergeant,* Gayle Kellogg; *Operations Officer,* Gil Harman; *G.I.,* Michael Hall; *First Patient,* Robert Crosson; *Second Patient,* Isaac Jones; *Third Patient,* Ted Donaldson; *Australian,* Booth Colman; *G.I.,* Leon Tyler; *Patient,* Chuck Courtney; *G.I.,* Steve Wayne; *Patient,* Freeman Morse; *Surgeon,* Robert Shayne; *Patient,* Sam McKim; *Madonna,* Suzanne Alexander; *Mother,* Ruth Clifford; *Best Girl,* Sally Fraser; *Mother,* Helen Spring; *Glamor Girl,* Beverly Cottrell; *Florence,* Kathleen Case; *Medic,* Fred Hartsook; *Geisha Girl,* Esther Lee; *Nurse,* Marilyn Lindsey.

Historical Accuracy Level: Medium.

The film roughly follows the path of the Korean War, but only when it suits the story.

Patriotic Propaganda Level: High. If these nurses had wings, they would be angels.

Elements: Air Force, Females in the Field, Medicine, Nurses, Rescues, Romantic Triangle, United Nations Forces.

Some war movies tailor their stories to follow the path of history, allowing actual events and circumstances to affect the lives and destinies of their characters, while others keep their narratives focused squarely on their plot formulas and stock characters, and wedge historical facts into their stories where it proves convenient. *Flight Nurse* is a prime example of the latter category, where actual Korean War history is merely a background to the romantic longings of a particular woman in the war zone. Though obviously well-intentioned, the film is grandiose and sanctimonious when it should be human and honest.

Lieutenant Polly Davis (Joan Leslie) is an Air Force flight nurse who arrives in Japan for service transporting wounded men from the battlefields in Korea. She is expecting to be met by fiancé and helicopter pilot Mike Barnes, but he is nowhere to be found. However, C-47 pilot Bill Eaton (Forrest Tucker) takes an instant liking to Polly while transporting her to Korea. Polly is surprised by the number of refugees streaming southward beneath the plane as it flies to Seoul, and shocked by the youth and condition of the wounded soldiers with whose care she is entrusted on the return trip. Polly uses narration to describe her feelings when seeing "Your sons." The damaged young men see Polly as they wish — as a dream girl, the girl next door, or an angel — and they appreciate her presence. On her first trip with wounded men, Polly is forced to operate in flight, and saves the life of a young man. This dedication causes Bill Eaton to decide that she is the girl for him.

Eaton visits Polly at her quarters in Tokyo but finds that Mike Barnes (Arthur Franz) has beaten him there, and that Polly is excited to see her fiancé. Eaton leaves quietly, accepting the situation. Her brief interlude is broken when Barnes receives orders to return to the front and continue rescue operations. Polly returns to work caring for "the beat up boys" from several different countries participating in the fighting.

The Communists are approaching Seoul, and Kimpo airfield is mortared by guerillas and strafed by enemy planes. Eaton saves Polly and they watch American pilots shoot the North Korean planes out of the sky. Theirs is the last plane out of Seoul and is forced to fly at hazardously low levels to avoid friendly artillery fire, but they make it safely to Tokyo with another load of wounded men.

Two rescue helicopters are reported missing; one of them is Mike Barnes'. Polly is confident that Barnes is still alive, but his own roommate has given up hope. Barnes is alive, though wounded. He sees Polly at the airfield but turns away so that she will not see him in his suffering, and he is transported to a Japanese hospital. The Air Force pilots and nurses are held inside the Pusan Perimeter until the situation stablizes. Eaton finally confesses his love for Polly and kisses her, but she reminds him that she belongs to Mike Barnes. The Inchon invasion takes place, which Polly refers to as "the counterpunch we've been awaiting for so long," and the pilots and nurses get back the job of saving lives.

Searching for Barnes in an Army hospital, Polly enters a room where an Army investigator (Morris Ankrum) is questioning prisoners of war who have returned from Korea. One of them, Private Marvin Judd (Ben Cooper), tells of prisoners marching fifteen to twenty miles a day without food or water, then being herded into a cave, shot, and sealed inside. Judd feigned his own death, crawled out of the cave and was recaptured. Later, he and other men were forced to dig their own graves, then were shot and pushed into them. Again, Judd pretended to be killed and was again buried alive beneath his own countrymen. Hours later, he dug through the shallow dirt and somehow escaped. Polly is distraught by the idea that Mike Barnes could have been treated in a similar fashion; for the first time, she wonders if he really is dead.

Bill Eaton has a birthday party, but Polly does not attend. After discovering that Barnes' dog tags have been discovered, Polly wanders into the party, dazed with the thought that her fiancé is dead. Eaton protects her from the nightly raid of "Bedcheck Charley," a North Korean pilot with terrible aim who drops a single grenade each evening, and tucks her safely in

Several episodes from the film are evident in this poster for Republic's patriotic drama Flight Nurse *(1953), but romance seems to be the most important.*

bed. Eaton, and Polly's aide, Frank Swan (James Holden), argue that she should be grounded, and the lead nurse, Martha Ackerman (Maria Palmer), agrees. But another nurse arrives with news that Barnes is recuperating at the Itazuke hospital in Japan, and Ackerman sends Polly on the next plane to Japan to meet him.

The flight is Bill Eaton's, and carries one patient who is tied down so he can't hurt himself and another patient who has experienced Communist brainwashing. During the flight, the tied down patient gets loose and opens the emergency door, which blows off and damages the C-47's horizontal stabilizer. The plane is forced to ditch at sea, and Polly is knocked unconscious by the crash. Everybody gets into life rafts and the group is rescued the next morning by an amphibious plane. Polly is sent to Japan to recover. She narrates the story of finding Mike Barnes and their mutual decision not to marry. Barnes is sent home to Rocking Chair, Texas,

while Polly returns to the Air Force for service aboard Bill Eaton's new plane. She informs Eaton that she is available and they resume their duty to "get some guys out of there."

Flight Nurse is a well-intentioned drama that buries surprisingly brutal and honest glimpses of the war beneath a trivial romantic triangle and dialogue so painful it makes one's ears bleed. The film treats the admittedly noble subject of nursing care with so much sanctity that its human element is absent. Its prologue describes the nurses as "Angels of Mercy" and Edith A. Aynes' "The Nurses Prayer" is quoted not once, but twice, backed by a heavenly chorus. Perhaps the worst element is Polly Davis' narration, as she describes her thoughts and feelings amidst the brutality of war. While heartfelt, Polly's sanguine reflections about "the boys" are often so saccharine or told with such purple prose that any sincerity is lost amidst her trite drivel.

Yet, in other ways, the film's perspective of the war is dark and ominous. The stream of wounded is never-ending. During the Pusan Perimeter scene, the fighting men are described as confused and dazed, losing hope with every Communist attack. Bill Eaton says, "The war's quitting us." But then the Inchon landing provides "the counterpunch we've been awaiting so long." While this is not great drama (or dialogue), this sequence does provide an authentic feel for the history which surrounds the characters.

History is definitely the background, however, as the insipid love story dominates the center stage of the film. It seems as though Polly travels to Korea to be reunited with Mike Barnes as much as or more than she desires to help the wounded. Polly's romances never captivate audience interest because her fiancé is bland and her admirer is rugged, and that is the extent of their personalities. And her idyllic plan to retire and relax in Rocking Chair, Texas, with Mike Barnes never seems real. It is not until the fateful ditching of the plane, when Polly gets unceremoniously knocked in the head, that she gains a true sense of herself and her importance to the war effort.

As a tribute to nurses, the film fails because it trivializes their duties and does not allow them to develop into characters. Polly's fellow nurses are merely gossips and man-hunters who happen to spend some of their time saving lives. Polly's romantic follies continually intrude upon her professional duties, and yet she seems almost superhumanly capable. Sadly, nursing is the least realistic aspect of this story.

Far more credence is given to the testimony of Private Marvin Judd, who describes North

Lieutenant Polly Davis (Joan Leslie) takes the pulse of a patient while her aide, Sergeant Frank Swan (James Holden), watches with concern in Flight Nurse *(1953).*

Korean atrocities in vivid detail to an army investigator. In the midst of the romantic adventure of the Korean War, this horrifying vocal depiction of brutality and cruelty, in which Judd faces and identifies the scarred Communist leader who executed dozens of Americans, is startling and dramatic. Critics of the time questioned its inclusion in the film. *Variety*'s critic wrote, "Of questionable taste are several sequences where atrocities of Chinese and North Korean Communists against United Nations troops are unreeled. The American public as well as most other peoples are already well acquainted with the inhuman practices of the Reds and an entertainment motion picture is scarcely a forum to refresh one's memory on gruesome war crimes." One may debate that last point, but the interrogation sequence certainly seems out of place in the context of this romantic folly. Yet it is unquestionably the most effective sequence in the movie.

The film also makes a point to identify the other countries participating in the United Nations effort in Korea. At one juncture, a doctor shows Polly around his very international hospital, where there are two Brits, a Greek, a Filipino, two Turks, three South Koreans, a Canadian, a Thailander, a medic from India, a Dutch flier, two Frenchmen, a New Zealander and a Belgian, besides the Americans in residence. It is a nice reminder that the U.S. troops were not fighting — or suffering — alone.

Flight Nurse does also feature a historical character only mentioned in one other Korean War movie: Bedcheck Charley. A Korean pilot in an antiquated biplane, Bedcheck Charley (or "Five o'clock Charley") as he came to be known, flew over hospital units behind the battle front. He would swoop low over hospital encampments late in the afternoon, wave to the doctors and nurses, then toss a grenade out of his plane to detonate harmlessly once he had flown past. In the movie, he is referred to with just the briefest of history, and quickly departs. The legend of Bedcheck Charley was explored in much greater detail in the television series version of *M*A*S*H*, where the character appeared in multiple episodes.

Despite the presence of Joan Leslie, who daringly appears in a bra in her first scene, the film did poorly. Most critics felt the mixture of romance, nobility and tragedy was uneven and not particularly entertaining. Oscar A. Godbout of the *New York Times* summarized the film in this manner: "Using every cinematic cliche in a script by Alan LeMay that included rhymed streams of consciousness, Allan Dwan, the director, chose to depict truly heroic actions with mediocrity." *Variety* judged that "Allan Dwan's direction in this Herbert J. Yates presentation appears to be so hampered by the rambling script that his guidance never welds the film into a cohesive unit." *Flight Nurse* remains an overwrought drama with a mixture of intriguing ingredients which could have blended into something much more special.

For the Boys

Credits: 1991. All Girl Productions. *Distributed by* 20th Century–Fox. *Directed by* Mark Rydell. *Produced by* Bette Midler, Bonnie Bruckheimer and Margaret South. *Co-Producer*: Ray Hartwick. *Executive Producer*: Mark Rydell. *Screenplay by* Marshall Brickman, Neal Jiminez and Lindy Laub. *Story by* Neal Jiminez and Lindy Laub. *Music by* Dave Grusin. *Musical Sequences Devised by* Joe Layton. *Executive Music Producer*: Joel Sill. *Director of Photography*: Stephen Goldblatt, A.S.C. *Edited by* Jerry Greenberg and Jere Huggins. *Production Designer*: Assheton Gordon. *Casting by* Lynn Stalmaster. *Costume Designer*: Wayne Finkelman. *Associate Producer / Second Unit Director*: Chris Wilkinson. *Associate Producer*: Kate Long. *Unit Production Managers*: Eduard D. Markley and Ray Hartwick. *First Assistant Director*: Alan B. Curtiss. *Second Assistant Directors*: Liz Ryan and John Rusk. *Art Directors*: Diane Wager and Don Woodruff. *Set Decorator*: Marvin March. *Supervising Sound Editor*: Kay Rose. *Supervising Music Engineer*: Robert Schaper. *Supervising Sound Editor*: Curt Sobel. *Sound Mixer*, Jim Webb, C.A.S. *First Assistant Editor*: Kathryn Camp. *Chief Lighting Technician*: James Plannette. *Key Grip*: Charles Saldana. *Property Master*, Louis Fleming. *Construction Coordinator*: Dennis Dewaay. *Special Effects Coordinator*: Allen Hall. *Stunt Coordinator*: Mic Rodgers. *Key Costume Supervisor*: James Tyson. *Transportation Coordinator*:

Dan Anglin. *Location Manager*: Richard Davis. *Executive Production Accountant*: Garrison Singer. *Script Supervisor*: Kerry Lyn McKissick. *Production Coordinator*: Pam Cornfeld. *Assistant to Mark Rydell*: Debbie Leonard. *Character Aging Makeup by* Gaglione and Drexler, Inc. *Designed by* John Gaglione, Jr. *Assistant Art Director*: Gershon Ginsburg. *Set Designers*: Richard Lawrence, Peter R. Romera and Julia Levine. *Leadman*: Jack Eberhart. *Production Illustrator*: David Negron. *Art Department Coordinator*: Kevin Constant. *Set Dressers*: Gary Daspit, Frank Flores, Gregori Renta, Randy Severino and Tommy Samona. *"A" Camera Operator / Steadicam Operator*: Steve St. John. *"B" Camera Operator*: David Golia. *First Assistant Cameras*: Gearey McLeod and Baird Steptoe. *Second Assistant Cameras*: Emil Hampton and Susan Beth Horton. *Assistant Chief Lighting Technicians*: Andrew Nelson and Curtis Foster. *Rigging Gaffer*: Paul Ary. *Rigging Key Grip*: Johnny London, Jr. *Rigging Grip*: David Henderson. *Electricians*: Mike Dechellis and John Gutierrez. *2nd Company Grips*: Hal Nelson and Art Garcia. *Dolly Grips*: Tony Garrido and Craig Garfield. *Technocrane Operator*, Simon Jayes. *Boom Operator*: Doug Vaughn. *Playback Operator*: Harrison "Duke" Marsh. *Utility Sound*: Anna Delanzo. *Sound Reinforcement*: Gary Raymond. *Key Aging Makeup Artists*: Jill Rockow and Michelle Burke. *Lab Crew*: Dawn Severdia, Donna Drexler and Anthony Frederickson. *Makeup Artist for Bette Midler*: Bob Mills. *Makeup Artists*: Frank Griffin, Ron Berkeley, Fred Blau, Dennis Liddiard and George H. Edds. *Body Makeup*: Kaori Turner. *Costume Supervisor*: Sandra B. Jordan. *Assistant to the Costume Designer*: Antonio Martinez. *Men's Key Costumer*: Joe McCloskey. *Women's Key Costumer*: Michelle Kupraska. *Costumer for Bette Midler*: Pam Wise. *Set Costumers*: Diana Wilson, Gilbert S. Hernandez and David Page. *Costumers*: Diane McCloskey, Tony Velasco, Mark Weitzman, Don Richardson, Deanne Ssllner, Stephen Chudej, Amelia Craig Andrews, Bernadette O'Brien, Valerie O'Brien, Elizabeth Sortor and Nava Sadan. *Tailor*: Alfonso Roman. *Hairstylists*: Hazel Catmull, Shirley Crawford and Ellen Powell. *Hairstylists for Bette Midler*: Barbara Lorenz and Carol Meikle. *Second Second Assistant Director*: Robert Huberman. *Assistant Production Coordinator*: Sharyn Shimada. *Production Assistant to Mark Rydell*: Will Plyler. *Assistant to Bette Midler*: Karen Douglass. *Assistant to Bonnie Bruckheimer*: Crystal Carter. *Assistant to Margaret South*: John Mullican. *Assistant to James Caan*: David Keane. *Assistant to Joel Sill*: Marylou Eales. *Assistants to Joe Layton*: Kirby Ward, Maia Winters and Naomi Buck. *Assistant Props*: Scott Leslie, Hope Parrish, Bill Petrotta, Jim Stubblefield, Dean Wilson and Glen Feldman. *General Foreman*: Stephen Fegley. *Prop Shop Foremen*: Isadoro Raponi and Willard Livingston. *Plaster Foreman*: Ray Lopez. *Sign Writer*: Joe Hawthorne. *Paint Foreman*: Robert Clark. *Special Effects Crew*: Gary Karas, Joe Montenegro, Pat Domenico, Michael Schorr, Michael Menzel, Dale Ettema, Michael Roundy, Jay Bartus, Joao Rocha, Michael Tice and Joe Pancake. *Assistant Editors*: Jeff Hodge, Suzy Elmiger and Mark Sadusky. *Apprentice Editors*: Cynthia Kimoto and Jeffrey Cranford. *Music Editor*: Ellen Segal. *Digital Music Systems*: Tim Claman. *Music Advisor to Mark Rydell*: Morgan Ames. *Scoring Mixer*: Don Murray. *Sidelines Musicians Supervisor*: John E. Oliver. *Sound Editors*: Richard L. Oswald, Chester L. Slomka, David Spence, Gordon Davidson, Teri E. Dorman and Milton C. Burrow. *Supervising ADR Editor*: Victoria Sampson. *ADR Editor*: Linda Folk. *Supervising Foley Editor*: Solange Schwalbe-Boisseau. *Foley Editors*: Scot Tinsley and Valerie Davidson. *First Assistant Sound Editor*: Blake Cornett. *Assistant Sound Editors*: Robb Wilson, Jerry Pirozzi, John Dronsky. *Rerecording Mixers*: Donald O. Mitchell, Robert Schaper and Frank Montano. *ADR Mixers*: Thomas J. O'Connell and David Miranda. *Recordists*: Walter Gest and Greg Gest. *Foley by* Taj Soundworks and Ed Bannon. *Foley Artists*: Kevin Bartnof and Hilda Hodges. *Foley Mixer*: James Ashwill. *Foley Recordist*: Marilyn Graf. *Voice Casting*: Barbara Harris. *Special Visual Effects by* Syd Dutton and Bill Taylor of Illusion Arts, Inc. *24 Frame Video Displays by* Video Image. *Video Image Staff*: Gregory L. McMurry, Rhonda Gunner, Richard Hollander and John C. Wash. *Technical Advisor for "Awards" Video Playback*: Steve Howard. *Video Image Coordinator*: Janet Earle. *Technical Supervisors*: Monte Swann and Doug DeGrazzio. *Video Tape*: Phil Silver. *Negative Cutter*: Sunrise Film, Inc. *Color Timer*: Mike Stanwick. *Assistant Locations*: Jody

Hummer, Joe Doyle and Steve Levine. *Transportation Captain*: Stanley Webber. *Transportation Co-Captain*: Clayton Bartholomew. *Production Accountant*: Bob Gordon. *Assistant Accountants*: Gary McCarthy, R. Blaine Currier, Dina Sobalvarro, Lisa Knudson and Marci Graber. *Construction Accountant*: Carmen Avila. *Casting Associate*: Michael Orloff. *Extras Casting*: Central Casting / Jim Green, Cenex Casting / Sam Lynn. *Unit Publicist*: Ellen Pasternack. *Still Photographer*: Francois Duhamel. *Photo Murals*: Frooz Zahedi. *Production Assistants*: Susie Brubaker, Wendy Davison, Marc Hammer, Kristie Hart, Susan Hellman, Suzanne Hilyard, Todd Leslie, Helen Mendoza, Elizabeth Pryor, Sol Rivera, Scott Robertson, Deering Rose, Amy Rydell and Nelsie Spencer. *Aerial Coordinator*: Chuck Hood. *Medical Consultant*: Walter D. Dishell, M.D. *Voice Coach for Mr. Caan*: Seth Riggs. *Craft Service*: Jamie Kehoe and Jack Klein. *Standby Painters*: Robert Stephens and Paul Campanella. *Set Medic*: Elizabeth Tanza. *Location Projection*: J. Dolan Projection Units. *Projectionist*: Lee Tucker. *Stand-Ins*: Nancy Fisher, Stan Rodarte, Steve Sturla and Dan Carey. *Second Unit—Director of Photography*: David Wagreich. *First Assistant Director*: Liz Ryan. *Camera Operator*: Steve Smith. *First Assistant Camera*: John Connell. *Key Grip*: Mike Krevitt. *Stunts*: Chris Tuck, David Burton, Greg Barnett, Doc D. Charbonneau, Eric Chambers, Doc Duhame, Steve Davison, Norman Howell, Annie Ellis, Buddy Joe Hooker, Marcia Holley, Gene LeBell, Matt Johnston, John Meier, Eric Mansker, Carol Neilson, Bennie Moore, Robby Robinson, Manny Perry, Danny Rogers, Mic Rodgers, Tim Trella, Keith Tellez, Tierre Turner, William Washington, Scott Wilder and Dan Wynands. *Music Consultant and Soundtrack Album Producer*: Arif Mardin. *Song and Music Consultant*: Marc Shaiman. *Songs*—"Dreamland" *written by* Dave Grusin and Alan and Marilyn Bergman; "Shake Me Good" *written by* Aina and Bob Marlette, *produced by* Bob Marlette, *performed by* Aina; "The Girl Friend of the Whirling Dervish" *written by* Al Dubin, Johnny Mercer and Harry Warren, *produced and arranged by* Marc Shaiman; "Do You Believe" *written by* James Cammarata, Francis Poeve and Michael Licata, *produced and performed by* Beat Goes Bang; "Wake Up Each Morning With Bai-leys" *written by* Dave Grusin and Marshall Brickman, *produced and arranged by* Dave Grusin; "Billy-A-Dick" *written by* Hoagy Carmichael and Paul Francis Webster, *arranged by* Marc Shaiman, *produced by* Arif Mardin with Marc Shaiman; "Dixie's Dream" *written and arranged by* Marc Shaiman, *produced by* Arif Mardin; "I Remember You" *written by* Johnny Mercer and Victor Schertzinger, *versions arranged by* Dave Grusin, Marty Paich, Marc Shaiman and Peter Matz, *produced by* Arif Mardin with Dave Grusin; "I'll Walk Alone" *written by* Sammy Cahn and Jule Styne; "The More I See You" *written by* Mack Gordon and Harry Warren; "For All We Know" *written by* J. Fred Coots and Sam M. Lewis; "Vicki and Mr. Valves" *written by* Lenny LaCroix, *arranged by* Marty Paich, *produced by* Arif Mardin with Dave Grusin; "Every Road Leads Back to You" *written by* Diane Warren, *performed by* Gary LeMel; "P.S. I Love You" *written by* Johnny Mercer and Gordon Jenkins, *arranged by* Marc Shaiman, *produced by* Arif Mardin with Dave Grusin; "Crossroads" *written by* Robert Johnson, *performed by* Cream; "Underneath the Arches" *written by* Bud Flanagan; "Green Onions" *written by* Steve Cropper, Al Jackson, Jr., Lewie Steinberg and Booker T. Jones, *performed by* Booker T. and the MGs; "A Nightingale Sang in Berkeley Square" *written by* Manning Sherwin and Eric Maschwitz; "I Apologize" *written by* Al Goodhart, Edward G. Nelson and Al Hoffman; "Land of 1000 Dances" *written by* Chris Kenner and Antoine Domino; "The White Cliffs of Dover" *written by* Walter Kent and Nat Burton; "In My Life" *written by* John Lennon and Paul McCartney, *produced by* Arif Mardin and Marc Shaiman; "Symphonie Espagnole" *written by* Eduard Lalo, *performed by* Tamaki Kawakubo; "Stuff Like That There" *written by* Jay Livingston and Ray Evans, *arranged by* Billy May, *produced by* Arif Mardin with Dave Grusin; "Come Rain or Come Shine" *written by* Johnny Mercer and Harold Arlen, *arranged by* Dave Grusin, *produced by* Arif Mardin with Dave Grusin; "Baby, It's Cold Outside" *written by* Frank Loesser, *arranged by* Marc Shaiman, *produced by* Arif Mardin. *Special Thanks to* Robert J. Litt, Michael Herbick, 8th Air Force Historical Society, 311th Army Reserve Corp Support Command, the Family of Pat O'Brien, the Family of Al Jenkins and The Citadel, the Military College of South Carolina. *Cranes and Dollies by* Chapman. *Remote Crane by* Technocrane. *Rerecorded at* Goldwyn Sound Facilities, Warner Hollywood Studios. *Title Design*: Anthony Goldschmidt. *Titles and Opticals*: Pacific Title. Rated R. Color by DeLuxe. Panavision (2.35:1). Dolby Stereo. Cinema Digital Sound. 145 minutes. Released in November, 1991. Currently available on VHS home video and DVD. Previously available on laserdisc.

Cast: *Dixie Leonard*, Bette Midler; *Eddie Sparks*, James Caan; *Art Silver*, George Segal; *Shephard*, Patrick O'Neal; *Danny* (in Vietnam), Christopher Rydell; *Jeff Brooks*, Arye Gross; *Sam Schiff*, Normal Fell; *Loretta*, Lori Brenner; *Luanna Trott*, Rosemary Murphy; *Phil*, Bud Yorkin; *Wally Fields*, Jack Sheldon; *Vicki*, Karen Martin; *Margaret Sparks*, Shannon Wilcox; *General Scott*, Michael Green; *Corrine*, Melissa Manchester; *Stan*, Steven Kampmann; *Milt*, Richard Portnow; *Myra*, Pattie Darcy; *Army Messenger*, Beau Dremann; *Danny* (at 4), Jameson Rodgers; *Stage Manager*, Gary Gershaw; *Dancing Airman*, Jim Raposa; *Audience Airman*, Patrick White; *Band Person*, Christopher Kaufman; *Captain*, James Patrick; *Niles LaGuardia*, Chris Wilkinson; *Nervous Production Assistant*, Andrew Bilgore; *Danny* (at 12), Brandon Call; *Ann Sparks*, Hayley Carr; *Kate Sparks*, Kimberly Ann Evans; *Merry Sparks*, Kelly Noonan; *TV Censor*, John O'Leary; *TV Stage Manager*, Stewart J. Zully; *Showgirls*, Deborah Stern, Heidi Sorensen; *Sponsor #1*, Bruce Gray; *Sponsor #2*, Richardson Morse; *Sponsor #3*, Matthew Faison; *Green Room Page*, Carey Eidel; *Merrill*, Richard Hochberg; *Dressing Room Page*, Andy Milder; *Wounded Marine*, Thom Adcox; *Corpsman on Battlefield*, Andy Lauer; *Marine Sergeant*, Billy Bob Thornton; *Captain Donelson*, John Doolittle; *Marine Driver*, Sal Landi; *Marine Who Stops Trucks*, John Ruskin; *Corpsman at MASH*, Marc Poppel; *Marine at MASH*, Gabe Bologna; *Violinist*, Tamaki Kawakubo; *Vice Admiral*, Mark Roberts; *Navy Commander*, Robert Clotworthy; *Major at the Firebase*, Tony Pierce; *Roberts*, Xander Berkeley; *Janie*, Maia Winters; *Cameraman*, D. David Morin; *TV Director*, Walter C. Miller; *Assistant Director*, David Selberg; *Technical Director*, Alan Haufrect; *Associate Producer*, Annie Prager; *Executive Producer*, Barry Michlin;

Teleprompter Operator, Sherlynn Hicks; *Stan's Assistant*, Maggie Wagner; *Lou Presti*, Leonard Gaines; *Photographer*, David Bowe; *Awards Conductor*, Morgan Ames; *Caretaker*, William Marquez; *Jeep Driver*, Fred Parnes; *Ida Silver*, Esther Jacobs; *Commander at the Citadel*, Garrison Singer; *1950's TV Show Dancers*, Connie Chambers, Janice Cronkhite, Kirk Hansen, Melissa Hurley, Lynnmarie Inge, Theresa King, Steven Majewicz, Paula Nichols, Jody Peterson, Amy Rydell, Susanne Sullivan, Michael Telmont, Paul Michael Thorpe, Kristi Zlock; *Awards Dinner Dancers*, Lada Boder, Ken Molina, Sheri Norwood, Tita Omeze, Raymond Rodriguez, Rick Gavin Tjia, Natsuo Tomita, Jerald Vincent, Beverly Ward, Kirby Ward; *Soldier in Crowd*, Vince Vaughn (uncredited extra); *Michael Leonard*, Arliss Howard (uncredited).

Historical Accuracy Level: Medium. The film spans three wars and does its best to separate and differentiate them, although its war scenes are not specific regarding location or time.

Patriotic Propaganda Level: High. Through it all, no matter what is happening to them personally, these U.S.O. performers keep singing.

Elements: Army, Females in the Field, Marine Corps, Multiple Wars, Musical Performance, U.S.O., Winter Fighting.

For the Boys spotlights an uneasy relationship between a popular entertainer and a brassy singer who becomes his partner on U.S.O. tours and television, but it also examines the American perception of three global conflicts and contrasts them against each other. World War II, Korea and Vietnam are each presented differently in terms of soldier behavior and attitude while the film's fundamental core — U.S.O. tours — remains fundamentally the same over time. The result is an accurate microcosm of America's perception of war as it evolved through three separate global confrontations.

The film is mounted as a flashback from the present day, as production assistant Jeff Brooks (Arye Gross) arrives to escort singer Dixie Leonard (Bette Midler) to an awards dinner, where she and former partner Eddie Sparks are to be presented with the Presidential Medal for their years of public service. Dixie doesn't want to attend, and she reluctantly tells Jeff why.

FOR THE BOYS

This simple image perfectly describes 20th Century–Fox's musical drama For the Boys *(1991) without any fanfare. Bette Midler is front and center as a U.S.O. entertainer, with support from James Caan. Midler's company, All Girl Productions, produced the film, and Midler garnered an Academy Award nomination for her vivid portrayal of singer Dixie Leonard.*

Eddie Sparks (James Caan) is a Bob Hope-like entertainer in the midst of a U.S.O. tour in 1942 England who needs a new singer. On the recommendation of his comedy writer Art Silver (George Segal), he agrees to try Silver's niece Dixie Leonard, a talented but struggling singer.

Dixie is an immediate hit with the soldiers, singing "Stuff Like That There" and "P.S. I Love You," but Eddie doesn't care for her penchant for vulgarity. Nevertheless, Silver and the other members of Eddie's contingent convince him to let her stay. Some time later, while entertaining the troops in North Africa, Eddie arranges for a surprise reunion (onstage and filmed for publicity) for Dixie and her husband Michael (Arliss Howard, uncredited), where she sings "Come Rain or Come Shine" to her happy husband. The very next scene is Michael's funeral.

After World War II, Eddie and Dixie star in a popular television variety show. Dixie tries to raise her young son, Danny, whom Eddie spoils and thinks of as his own boy (he has three daughters, but doesn't seem to care for them). Soon after the Korean War begins, Eddie announces that he is organizing another U.S.O. tour and publicly pressures Dixie into accompanying him again.

Korea is a muddy mess, its roads choked with refugees and their livestock, and the U.S.O. stars, accompanied by gossip columnist Luanna Trott (Rosemary Murphy), seem to be going nowhere. Word arrives that the Chinese "have jumped in with both feet," so the Christmas show is cancelled and the "V.I.P.'s" are evacuated. Their evacuation truck is commandeered to transport soldiers wounded in an ambush to safety, and Dixie helps stop the bleeding of one of the soldiers. Unfortunately, he dies before they reach medical help, and Dixie is traumatized. Shaken by the violence and death surrounding them, Eddie and Dixie find themselves alone together in a truly hostile environment and for the first and only time, they spend the night with each other.

In Japan, they are honored with a dinner, which is spoiled by television sponsor Shephard's (Patrick O'Neal's) insistence that Art Silver be fired because of his alleged Communist leanings. Eddie reluctantly agrees and Dixie physically attacks him for his betrayal of her uncle, shoving Eddie into a large cake. Years later, Eddie approaches his estranged partner with a proposal to tour Vietnam with yet another show. The hook is that Dixie would be able to visit her grown son Danny, whom she has not seen since his enlistment in the Army.

In Vietnam, Eddie and Dixie are heli-coptered to a hilltop bunker where they spend some time with Danny (Christopher Rydell) and Dixie sings a quiet version of "In My Life" to his fellow G.I.s. A Viet Cong rocket attack prematurely ends the concert and the lives of several soldiers, including that of Danny, who dies in his mother's arms.

Having told her story to Jeff Brooks, Dixie changes her mind and quickly dresses for the awards dinner. She and Eddie meet before the show and squabble over the meaning and personal losses of their lives. Dixie stays behind while Eddie accepts the Presidential Medal, but comes onstage to rescue him when he falters during his speech while remembering the death of Danny, the boy whom he loved like a son. Together again, they banter, dance a brief soft shoe routine and sing their signature closing tune, "I Remember You."

For the Boys is primarily a show business biography of two people who bond together for professional success while not really liking each other personally. For dramatic tension, Eddie Sparks is conceived as an irresistible, skirt-chasing superstar whose come-ons do not entice the honorable Dixie Leonard, and whose influence over the years reduces the dignity and happiness of her life. Key to this relationship is the affection which Eddie shows Danny, Dixie's son. Without a son of his own (though he has three darling daughters), Eddie becomes a surrogate father to the boy — to Dixie's chagrin. This portion of the film is formulaic and only occasionally effective, although it does help to develop and humanize its stiff characters.

The film's real impact lies in its U.S.O. shows, its behind-the-scenes glimpses of the staging process and the ways in which the shows (and particularly their reception) reflect the values of the time.

As filmed by director Mark Rydell, the U.S.O. shows themselves are entertaining, fun and often touching. In London during World War II, the troops are enthusiastic, but not wild. They appreciate the sexy frolicking of leggy Vicki (Karen Martin) and love the bawdy repartee between Eddie and Dixie, and her song "Stuff Like That There." They also understand and respect the feeling behind Dixie's ballad "P.S. I Love You," in which, lighted only by soldiers' flashlights, Dixie walks among the men, greeting and momentarily making human contact with them. It is this type of genuine feeling to which the soldiers — and, reluctantly, Eddie — respond.

The scene is repeated in North Africa, as Eddie arranges to have Dixie and her husband Michael reunite on stage. Although the argument can be made that Eddie is only creating publicity, Eddie's actions are more altruistic than that. He sincerely wants Dixie to be happy and does what he can to make her so. Dixie responds appropriately and sings "Come Rain or Come Shine" to her appreciative husband (and soldiers), but this sequence works best as an explanation of Eddie's psyche. (A trivia note: "Come Rain or Come Shine" was not written until after the war concluded in 1945.)

The U.S.O. show in Vietnam is rowdier than that of World War II, with a palpable sense of danger and ugliness. The show has remained basically the same and still features a leggy dancer, this time named Janie (Maia Winters), and in a white go-go outfit. Unlike London, where the uniformed soldiers watched and whistled, these grimy, casually dressed soldiers get up on stage, bump and grind with Janie and are on the verge of stripping and raping her before Eddie puts a stop to their frenzy.

Dixie is introduced and one of the young punks yells "Show us your tits!" This single line of dialogue represents the moral decay which has occurred between World War II and Vietnam and which serves to define a generation. Nonplussed, Dixie tells the boy that doing so would give him a heart attack and decides to appeal to the soldiers' hearts. She sings a soft ballad, "In My Life," directly to the young soldiers and gives the Beatles tune a whole new dimension. To their credit, the men respond just as their forefathers did twenty-five years earlier, with quiet understanding and appreciation for the genuine emotion in the tribute being sung to them. It is the musical highlight of the movie.

The Korean War is afforded just ten of the film's one hundred forty-five minutes, but those ten minutes provide the symbolic and emotional links between World War II and Vietnam. The mud and stink of Korea provide an important counterpoint to the other wars. The soldiers in Vietnam may be dirty but at least their base is orderly; there is nothing remotely orderly about

the campaign in Korea. Korean wagons are overturned and Marine transport trucks are stuck in the mud. Refugees crowd the thin roads and are resolutely ignored by the Americans. Worse yet, some are chased away from a warm fire and insulted by a Marine sergeant (Billy Bob Thornton in a tiny role) for the sake of the visiting show business V.I.P.s. Columnist Luanna Trott is aghast at the refugees' abject poverty, attributing it to a "lack of national character." Art Silver's retort is more to the point: "Lady, they don't have any shoes."

Neither the World War II scenes (which show no battles) nor the Vietnam era sequence (in which Dixie's son Danny is killed before her eyes) depicts the turmoil of war on helpless civilians. The Korean War segment does, with force. It also brings the true nature of war home to Eddie and Dixie, when they are forced to help a group of wounded Marines. Dixie is overwhelmed by the number of brave American boys lost, but more by the immediate sensation of having a wounded man's blood spray in her face and the death of that young man despite her best efforts to save him. This brief segment defines the harsh conditions of war and infers why it is important to stage the U.S.O. shows for the boys.

The film also mentions the Chinese entry into the war, which occurred during late November of 1950. In the movie, it is merely another burden added to an already impossible situation for the Marines, one which foretells a long, continued battlefront. It is the loneliness and desolation of Korea which finally drives Eddie and Dixie into each other's arms and which initiates the key scene in the characters' lives. Eddie and Dixie might have found some happiness together, but Eddie's reaction — fear of being discovered by columnist Luanna Trott — dispels any romantic notion held by Dixie. From that point on, they are partners only in the professional sense of the word.

The Korea sequences are followed by a ten minute segment in Japan during the Korean War, where the spectre of McCarthyism rears its ugly head. Eddie is pressured into firing his longtime pal and comedy writer Art Silver because of Art's outspokenness and obstinate refusal to kowtow to conservative standards. This is when Dixie makes her stand against Eddie,

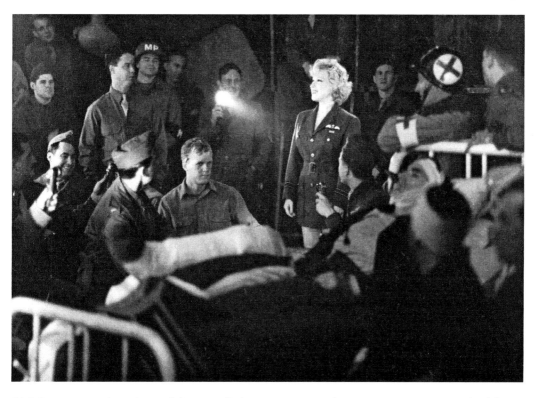

U.S.O. entertainer Dixie Leonard (Bette Midler) improvises a song during a power outage in England during World War II in For the Boys *(1991). Dixie and partner Eddie Sparks (*James Caan*) would return as entertainers to the fronts of the Korean and Vietnam wars as well.*

breaks up the act and gives up her lucrative career, all because she can longer stand the duplicity and faithlessness of show business, as personified by Eddie Sparks.

The primary force behind *For the Boys* was Bette Midler and her production company, All Girl Productions. As Dixie, Bette Midler is given an open stage and she fills it with verve and charisma. *For the Boys* is truly Bette's movie and she shines, capturing a 1991 Oscar nomination for best actress and winning that year's Golden Globe for best performance by an actress in a comedy or musical. Dixie is an often brassy character, but Midler is most effective in the quieter, more thoughtful moments of the movie, when she is able to reveal the warmth and charm beneath Dixie's often ribald personality.

James Caan seems like an odd choice to portray Eddie, but his harder edge as an actor is necessary for the character, and Caan surprises with his musical abilities. It is true that Eddie's superstar status is inferred rather than displayed but this doesn't detract from the film's effective-ness. At the time of its release, the casting of Caan was maligned by many, but his talent is undeniable. If the character grates, that is simply because it was the conception of the filmmakers that it should, and Caan performs to a tee.

Both stars, however, are poorly presented in the last section of the film, the dinner where Eddie and Dixie are to be awarded the Presidential Medal. Made up in garish old age makeup which makes them look as though they have just been embalmed, Caan and Midler putt around the stage like doddering wax figures before relaxing into an old song and dance routine. Hollywood films have always had difficulty presenting young or middle-aged performers as convincingly old, but the makeup and attendant services used in this sequence are embarrassingly bad.

The film received a blow after its initial release when longtime U.S.O. performer Martha Raye sued Midler's company, All Girl Productions, alleging that Raye's career was the actual basis for the movie. Three years later the case finally went to trial and Midler denied that her film had anything to do with Martha Raye. "The stories have no resemblance except for one thing—they both were entertainers during wartime," she testified. The Los Angeles court ruled in Midler's favor and the case was dismissed.

Bette Midler poured her heart and soul into the project and was devastated when the public did not flock to see the film. "I sulked and cried for so long after *For the Boys*, I didn't think anybody wanted to see me again." Part of the film's problem is its length; at 145 minutes it is a long movie, but it actually should have been longer. There is a pivotal romantic scene between Dixie and her husband in North Africa that was omitted from the final cut. The scene, which is included on the film's laserdisc release, explains the feelings Dixie has for her husband and why, after his death, she resists other men and becomes a bitter old woman. This scene's omission caused actor Arliss Howard to ask that his name be withdrawn from the credits and seriously dilutes the power of the middle of the film.

Even without that scene, most critics felt the movie was overlong, even as they differed as to its quality. Amy Dawes of *Variety* called the film "a big, creaky balloon of a movie that lumbers along like a dirigible in a Thanksgiving parade, festooned with patriotic sentiment." *Time*'s Richard Schickel argued that "*For the Boys* is an ambitious film, but it wears its ambitions lightly and lovably." In *Newsweek*, David Ansen praised the movie's ambition: "For a big, glitzy Hollywood entertainment, Rydell's movie opens a surprising number of wounds, and warns us to suspect the very glamour it revels in. It's no small accomplishment."

During its production the film, to everybody's surprise, suddenly reflected real life when President Bush announced the beginning of "Operation Desert Storm," and dozens of servicemen who were acting as extras in the film were assigned to duty in the Persian Gulf. Thus, Midler and company found themselves entertaining troops preparing for war, just as Dixie Leonard and Eddie Sparks would have done some forty years previously.

For the Boys succeeds in many respects, particularly in comparing and contrasting percep-tions of three global wars. The script is not as complex as it could have been, but it does not soft-sell its characters or wartime situations. Its flaws are that of overkill, such as having Dixie present on the very day and at the very time of her son's death, and omission, as not fully displaying the entertainment virtuosity of Eddie Sparks or the depth of her romance with husband Michael. Nevertheless, *For the Boys* is an emotionally involving musical drama with a very noble cause at its core.

Geisha Girl

Credits: 1952. Breakston-Stahl Productions. *Distributed by* Realart. *Produced and directed by* George Breakston and C. Ray Stahl. *Associate Producers*: Irene Breakston and Eugene W. Wooten. *Original Story and Screen Play by* C. Ray Stahl. *Music Composed and Conducted by* Albert Glasser. *Director of Photography*: Ichiro Hoshijima. *Editorial Supervision*: Irving M. Schoenberg, A.C.E. *Production Coordinator*: Edward Lord. *Art Direction*: Seigo Shindo. *Sound Recorder*: John C. Carter. *Dance Specialties*: Matsudo. *Assistant Director*: Robert Clark. *Optical Effects*: Consolidated Film Industries. *Liaison Officer*: Captain Richard Finiels, U.S. Army. Not Rated. Black and White. Flat (1.33:1). 67 minutes. Released in May, 1952. Filmed on location in Japan. Currently available on VHS home video.

Cast: *Rocky Wilson*, William Andrews (Steve Forrest); *Peggy Burns*, Martha Hyer; *Archie McGregor*, Archer MacDonald; *Nakano*, Tetsu "Teddy" Nakamura; *Police Inspector*, Heihachiro "Henry" Okawa; *Zoro*, Dekao Yokoo; *Michiko*, Michiyo Naoki; *Betto*, Ralph Nagara; *Professor*, Tatsuo Saito; *Fumi*, Ikio Suwamura; *Tanaka*, Shinzo Takada; *Stripteaser*, Pearl Hamada; *with* Sergeant Benny Teitel, U.S. Army, Corporal Charles Zanolli, U.S. Army, and Private Richard Wiederholt, U.S. Army.

Historical Accuracy Level: Low. History is overwhelmed by espionage and comedy in this romp which was filmed entirely in Japan.

Patriotic Propaganda Level: High. Two army dunderheads and a pretty secret agent save the world from diabolical Japanese scientists who manufacture atomic pills!

Elements: Army, Comedy, Espionage, Japan, Musical Performance, Red Menace, Romance, "Somewhere in Korea."

Geisha Girl is the second feature filmed in Japan by producer George Breakston, and like its predecessor, *Tokyo File 212*, it is only marginally about the Korean War. During the war years Breakston produced, co-wrote or co-directed three films in southeastern Asia, two of which featured actress Martha Hyer and all of which employed actual (albeit rather low-budget) location filming. Breakston's trio of films are hybrid comedy-action-travelogue-thrillers which promise sights never before seen but ultimately fail to deliver any kind of quality entertainment.

"Somewhere in Korea," two Army servicemen wait to board a plane for Okinawa, Japan. They are Rocky Wilson (Steve Forrest, billed as "William Andrews") and Archie McGregor (Archer MacDonald, a tall, gangly Jerry Lewis-type comedian) who have just finished a year of duty in Korea. On the flight to Japan, Rocky tries to court stewardess Peggy Burns (Martha Hyer), but Peggy is more interested in her real job as an American espionage agent. Her assignment in Japan is to find a scientist who has created atomic pills with tremendous explosive power for a devious businessman named Nakano (Tetsu "Teddy" Nakamura).

Rocky and Archie want to sight-see in Tokyo but many areas are off-limits to men in uniform. So they trade their uniforms for civilian clothes in Nakano's black market store, unaware that the atomic pills just happen to be in Archie's new jacket (except for one pill, which is to be used as an international demonstration of the discovery's power). Nakano's men shadow Rocky and Archie to the Bamboo Club, where Peggy witnesses a pickpocket try to steal something from Archie's jacket. She joins the two Americans as they tour the city of Tokyo at the behest of Nakano, who has befriended them.

Nakano invites them to his geisha house, where Archie takes an instant liking to Michiko (Michiyo Naoki). Nakano instructs his geisha girls to retrieve the pills from Archie, but they are unsuccessful. Peggy contacts the police inspector, who assigns Zoro (Dekao Yokoo), a clever hypnotist, to help recover the pills. Zoro hypnotizes Nakano just as he is about to take the

pills from Archie, but Zoro then hypnotizes himself before he can deliver them to Peggy. Archie somehow retains possession of the deadly pills and nearly eats one at dinner (he's a hypochondriac who carries his own stash of vitamins). Meanwhile, a newspaper reports — in English — that an island in the South Pacific has mysteriously disappeared.

Rocky and Archie are followed and then chased by Nakano's men around Tokyo, through a geisha house, a kabuki theatre and a national shrine, and the two Americans do not have any clear idea why. After some romancing with Michiko and Peggy and much mugging from nearsighted Archie, the two Americans are finally confronted at Nakano's geisha house by the villains, and a wild chase ensues before Zoro "freezes" everyone in place with his hypnotic stare. The deadly atomic pills are retrieved and the American soldiers are sent home in the custody of Peggy Burns.

Geisha Girl was a silly, ridiculous excuse for location filming in Japan, but it was, evidently, the best that Breakston and partner C. Ray Stahl could produce. It attempts to be timely, linking the "Red Menace" Communist threat of atomic power to the Korean War. Further, Nakano's plan of infiltrating and then destroying ten key cities with the atomic pills is diabolical, worthy of a James Bond movie. How then can one explain the secret atomic pill factory (with a scientist whose face is never seen) in the back of a *haberdashery*, and the total idiocy of placing the invaluable pills in the pocket of a jacket available for sale? Who is Nakano anyway, and how does he happen to control the world's most ingenious weapon?

This goofy movie isn't concerned with such trivia; it is much more interested in showing how regular American guys can have a good time in Japan, disrupting a kabuki performance or romancing geisha girls in a national garden and shrine. Writer-directors Breakston and Stahl go to the trouble of introducing Japanese customs and cultural icons, only to ridicule and spoil them for the sake of very labored comedic entertainment. Their approach to the material is that Japanese culture makes a vivid background for the childish antics of their wacky American stars. Only this approach explains why chases are staged through geisha houses, the national

Realart's Geisha Girl *(1952) relies on sexual enticement ("Revealing!") to find its audience, revealing nothing about its story. Leading lady Martha Hyer is nowhere to be seen, and the tagline, "A Night in a Geisha House!" was the film's original title. The movie was actually filmed in Japan, as is noted, but that in itself is not a mark of quality.*

garden and especially the kabuki performance, during which Rocky and Archie dress in kabuki costumes and interrupt the performance on stage before running away.

The only funny side to this debacle is Zoro, the crazy character who takes immense pleasure in hypnotizing everyone around him, especially the policemen who have hired him. It is genuinely amusing when the master hypnotist accidentally hypnotizes himself while shaving. Accompanied by cartoonish but appropriate pop-whiz-bang sound effects, Zoro's escapades are without doubt the most creative and entertaining comic interludes in the film.

The rest of the movie is less entertaining. Newcomer Archer MacDonald acts like a lanky, nearsighted Jerry Lewis while Steve Forrest, billed as William Andrews as he had not yet changed his name at that point, plays his role completely straight. Forrest, who in real life is actor Dana Andrews' younger brother, made several other Korean War films over the next few

years, but this one was his first. Also playing her role straight is Martha Hyer, who at the time was married to the film's co-director, C. Ray Stahl. "Ray is a brilliant boy and marriage to him was a constant travelogue," Hyer remarked in a 1955 interview with Hedda Hopper. "We went all over the world making pictures — he produced them and I acted in them. I might add they were very bad. We made two in Japan, and lived there a year, moved to Australia, spent a year in London and finally wound up on a safari in Africa. We saw the world all right, but our marriage was a flop. I left him in Africa, came home and filed for divorce."

Martha Hyer is not the only person to recognize the inferiority of *Geisha Girl*. *Variety* termed it "a feeble effort, an excuse to work in some native backgrounds," and added, "Acting is weak, direction poor and photography far from firstrate." The British Film Institute's *Monthly Film Bulletin* concurred. "The film's only asset is the interest of the Japanese locale."

Rocky Wilson (Steve Forrest, left, billed as "William Andrews") tries to keep buddy Archie McGregor (Archer MacDonald, center) from flipping his lid over pretty stewardess Peggy Burns (Martha Hyer) in the comedy Geisha Girl *(1952).*

To be sure, *Geisha Girl* is a poor excuse for a movie, one which doesn't take seriously the parameters it has established for itself. It is actually a lowbrow comedy with the format of an espionage thriller. Although it was filmed in Japan, it unfortunately retains the most inane of American comedy traditions. And in terms of Korean War films, it is tangential at best, supporting the unwritten but highly accurate rule that movies that begin with the phrase "Somewhere in Korea" are almost always notoriously bad.

Glory Alley

Credits: 1952. Metro-Goldwyn-Mayer. *Directed by* Raoul Walsh. *Produced by* Nicholas Nayfack. *Story and Screen Play by* Art Cohn. *Musical Director*: Georgie Stoll. *Director of Photography*: William Daniels, A.S.C. *Film Editor*: Gene Ruggiero, A.C.E. *Choreography by* Charles O'Curran. *Orchestrations by* Pete Rugolo. *Art Directors*: Cedric Gibbons and Malcolm Brown. *Recording Supervisor*: Douglas Shearer. *Set Decorations*: Edwin B. Willis and Keogh Gleason. *Special Effects*: A. Arnold Gillespie. *Montage Sequences by* Peter Ballbusch. *Leslie Caron's Costumes by* Helen Rose. Not Rated. Black and White. Flat (1.33:1). 79 minutes. Released in June, 1952. Not currently available on commercial home video.

Cast: *Socks Barbarrosa*, Ralph Meeker; *Angela*, Leslie Caron; *The Judge*, Kurt Kasznar; *Peppi Donnato*, Gilbert Roland; *Shadow Johnson*, Louis (Satchmo) Armstrong; *Gabe Jordan*, John McIntire; *Sal Nichols (The Pig)*, Dan Seymour; *Himself*, Jack Teagarden; *Doctor Robert Ardley*, Larry Gates; *Jabber*, Pat Goldin; *Spider*, John Indrisano; *Domingo*, Mickey Little; *Dan*, Dick Simmons; *Terry Waulker*, Pat Valentino; *Frank, the Policeman*, David McMahon; *Newsboy Addams*, George Garver.

Historical Accuracy Level: Low. This film creates a world of its own, unconcerned with any ties to conventional reality.

Patriotic Propaganda Level: Low. Although Socks Barbarosa wins the Congressional Medal of Honor, he does so for the worst of reasons.

Elements: Army, Bridge Bombing, Congressional Medal of Honor, Musical Performance, Mystery, Returning Home, Romance.

One of the stranger films concerning the Korean War is *Glory Alley*. The war is not even mentioned during the first half, and then is only used to provide the protagonist an opportunity to prove that he is not cowardly. The film's view of heroic servicemen returning home, however, seems authentic and realistic, given the circumstances, and is one of the few good examples of this situation in the Korean War film oeuvre.

In New Orleans, *Daily Picayune* columnist Gabe Jordan (John McIntire) says farewell to his colleagues before he takes another job. He describes Glory Alley, the area of his regular beat on Bourbon Street, as "a block of square guys, with round edges," and a place where unexpected beauty can be found amidst the dregs of society. He describes the biggest story he never put to paper, the complete story of Socks Barbarrosa…

Jordan's flashback begins as prizefighter Socks Barbarrosa (Ralph Meeker) prepares to fight a championship bout. He has thirty-three consecutive wins, twenty-eight of them by knockout. As the fight is about to begin, Socks suddenly exits the ring and runs back to his dressing room. His fight manager, Peppi Donnato (Gilbert Roland), and friend Gabe Jordan try to reason with him, but Socks swears never to fight again. A scuffle ensues and a blind man named the Judge (Kurt Kasznar) is accidentally knocked to the ground. A picture of Socks knocking down the Judge is taken and printed in all the newspapers, and the prizefighter is branded a coward.

Later, Socks meets his opponent in the ring, privately, and flattens him. Socks talks to his longtime girlfriend, Angela (Leslie Caron), who works as a singer and dancer at a nightclub called Chez Bozo. She doesn't understand his actions and warns that her father, the Judge, may no longer approve of their relationship. In the Punch Bowl Bar, the neighborhood hangout, the Judge publicly decries Socks as a coward and admonishes him to stay away from Angela. Peppi, who owns the bar, offers Socks a partnership in it, but Socks is too proud to accept and instead spends a few weeks boozing.

Eventually, Peppi persuades Socks work as a backup bartender and Socks dries out.

After a run-in with a local hoodlum nicknamed the Pig (Dan Seymour), regarding the disposition of prizefighter Newsboy Addams (George Garver), Socks decides to join the Army and prove his bravery in the Korean War. Months later, Socks aids American servicemen under heavy fire, explodes an important bridge under enemy control and is wounded. For his efforts, Socks is presented the Congressional Medal of Honor, and upon his return to New Orleans, toasted with a hero's parade and numerous speaking engagements. Soon, however, the situation returns to its pre-war condition, with the Judge refusing to believe that Socks is anything but a coward.

Socks presses Angela to marry him, but she refuses, noting that taking care of her father is her first priority. Seemingly by chance, an eye specialist, Doctor Robert Ardley (Larry Gates), examines the Judge and an operation is planned. The Judge reneges when he discovers Socks has

This newspaper ad for MGM's "lusty tale of life and love in New Orleans," Glory Alley *(1952), wisely promotes lovely Leslie Caron and swinging Satchmo, Louis Armstrong, over its hackneyed boxing storyline.*

arranged the operation, but Angela and Doctor Ardley convince him that Socks has his best interests at heart. Doctor Ardley tells them how generous Socks has been to his clinic and explains how Socks survived a brutal childhood, which culminated in a serious beating that required forty-nine stitches. Later, Angela reveals to her father that she has been working as a dancer for years to support him (he thought she was studying to become a nurse).

The Judge reconsiders and has the operation, which fails, but he is now able to admit his error regarding Socks' character. Finally accepted by her father, Socks tells Angela that the fear of being ridiculed for the jagged scar on his head is the reason he ran away from his championship fight. Angela chides him for his foolish vanity and for being afraid to remove his ever-present hat. Socks finds his courage, removes his hat, thus winning Angela's respect, and, as the story ends, re-enters the boxing ring and finally claims the championship that should have been his two years previously.

Glory Alley is a ludicrous movie based upon a ridiculous premise, and it is a credit to the acting of Leslie Caron and Gilbert Roland that it is even watchable. The entire story hinges upon the moment when Socks Barbarrosa (whose name is misspelled on his boxing robe) runs from the championship fight. At that moment, it is obvious that he is bothered by something, but the ultimate explanation — that he was afraid the audience would ridicule the forty-nine stitch scar which is hidden by his hair — is utterly beyond belief. Why wasn't he worried during his previous thirty-three fights? The scar is meant to be psychological as much as physical, but it nevertheless remains a specious reason for his retreat.

A short time after he avoids the fight (and then privately pummels his opponent, thereby showing the audience his courage), Socks is accepted by the vast majority of the Glory Alley denizens. Only the Judge remains steadfastly against Socks and his plans to marry his daughter. Nevertheless, Socks hatches a scheme to join the Army and commit an act of courage so unmistakable that even the Judge would have to forgive him. After months of waiting, an opportunity presents itself on the banks above the Yalu River.

Socks and his platoon sergeant witness American soldiers wounded and trapped near a bridge. The sergeant sees no hope for the men, saying, "They're in God's hands now." Socks knows that this is his only chance for glory and runs down the hill, joining the endangered men. He helps one man, then rushes to a point near the bridge where the detonator was left, and with bullets whizzing by, connects the wires to the terminals and explodes the bridge, killing the Communist troops charging across it. For his bravery under fire, Socks is awarded the Congressional Medal of Honor.

The single worst fault of this movie is the attitude regarding the Medal of Honor. Socks sees it as a vindication of his character and journeys to Korea for the express reason of winning it. Upon his return to New Orleans, Socks enjoys the attention that it brings for a time, then cannot understand why the attention dwindles. He is told that "other men are coming back and they've got medals, too," but Socks is embittered and even considers sending it back to the president. Angela sets him straight, saying "The Medal of Honor is just that, an honor. Not a meal ticket," and Socks forlornly decides to keep it.

The whole scenario involving the Medal of Honor is cheap and tawdry, revealing Socks as an opportunistic heel completely unsympathetic to the suffering and sacrifice of others. He clearly has no concept of the medal's significance and his pursuit of it for its attendant glory is quite sickening.

The Korean War sequence is also staged poorly. The only time American soldiers were within striking distance of the Yalu River (the border between North Korea and China) was during the fall and winter of 1950, when the area was frozen solid. The river country climate seen in *Glory Alley* is not wintry at all, and the river viewed in the film is far too small to represent the Yalu, which is quite broad and deep, roughly equivalent to the Ohio River. All in all, the film's war elements were handled inappropriately.

The rest of the movie isn't much better. The "mugs and pugs" of *Glory Alley* are mostly cardboard characters played with antipathy by bored actors. Only Leslie Caron, as the ballerina-turned-hoochie dancer Angela, and Gilbert Roland as Peppi, Socks' genuine friend, manage

The Judge (Kurt Kasznar, center) refuses to alter his low opinion of Socks Barbarrosa (Ralph Meeker, right), even after Socks returns from the Korean War with the Congressional Medal of Honor. Also in Socks' corner are Shadow Johnson (Louis Armstrong, left), and promoter Peppie Donnato (Gilbert Roland, middle right).

to rise above the material. Also in the cast is Louis (Satchmo) Armstrong as Shadow Johnson, the Judge's aide. Caron sings and dances to "When She Dances" and "St. Louis Blues," while Armstrong plays and sings "That's What the Man Said" and the title song. Except for the inclusion of Caron's exquisite legs, the musical numbers are not at all memorable.

Bosley Crowther of the *New York Times* bemoaned the "waste" of Leslie Caron (who had graced *An American in Paris* the previous year) and termed the finished product "this ridiculous fiction," while Jay Robert Nash and Stanley Ralph Ross judged the film "a weak psychological drama" in their *Motion Picture Guide*. *Time* concluded that "*Glory Alley* is a fair-to-middling jazz act slowed down and for long stretches absolutely halted by a heavy burden of story interest." *Glory Alley* performed sluggishly at the box office and did not further the careers of anyone involved.

The film was helmed by legendary one-eyed director Raoul Walsh who, despite a lengthy and acclaimed career, foisted two of the worst Korean War movies of all time on unsuspecting audiences. *Glory Alley* is one, *Marines, Let's Go* is the other. Together they would comprise an unbelievably bad double feature. Walsh made some great adventure and gangster films early in his career, but these two films prove that he was out of his element when he explored the Korean War.

The Glory Brigade

Credits: 1953. 20th Century Fox. *Directed by* Robert D. Webb. *Produced by* William Bloom. *Written by* Franklin Coen. *Musical Direction*: Lionel Newman. *Director of Photography*: Lucien Ballard, A.S.C. *Film Editor*: Mario

Mora. *Art Direction*: Lyle Wheeler and Lewis Creber. *Set Decorations*: Fred J. Rode. *Choreography by* Matt Mattox. *Makeup Artist*: Ben Nye. *Special Photographic Effects*: Ray Kellogg. *Sound*: W. D. Flick and Harry M. Leonard. *Assistant Director*: Eli Dunn. *Technical Adviser*: Captain William J. Knickerbocker, C.E., U.S.A. Not Rated. Black and White. Flat (1.33:1). 82 minutes. Released in August, 1953. Filmed on location at Fort Leonard Wood and Lake of the Ozarks, Missouri. Not currently available on commercial home video.

Cast: *Lieutenant Sam Prior*, Victor Mature; *Lieutenant Niklas*, Alexander Scourby; *Corporal Bowman*, Lee Marvin; *Sergeant Johnson*, Richard Egan; *Corporal Marakis*, Nick Dennis; *Sergeant Chuck Anderson*, Roy Roberts; *Private Stone*, Alvy Moore; *Private Taylor*, Russell Evans; *Sergeant Smitowsky*, Henry Kulky; *Private Ryan*, Gregg Martell; *Captain Adams*, Lamont Johnson; *Captain Davis*, Carleton Young; *Major Sauer*, Frank Gerstle; *Lieutenant Jorgenson*, Stuart Nedd; *Private Nemos*, George Michaelides; *Captain Charos*, John Verros; *Sergeant Lykos*, Alberto Morin; *Sergeant Kress*, Archer McDonald; *Colonel Kallicles*, Peter Mamakos; *Chaplain*, Father Patrinakos; *Greek Soldiers*, John Haretakis, Costas Morfis, David Gabbai, Nico Minardos; *Medic*, George Saris; *Colonel Peterson*, Jonathan Hale.

Historical Accuracy Level: Medium. This movie's mission is fictional, but soldiers of Greek and other nationalities often teamed with Americans for specialized assignments during the Korean War.

Patriotic Propaganda Level: High. The film promotes cooperation between countries to fight the threat of Communism.

Elements: Army, Behind Enemy Lines, Bridge Bombing, Helicopters, Infighting, Racism, Rescues, United Nations Forces.

The Glory Brigade is a Korean War movie with the moral message that people from various backgrounds can and should team together to face and defeat the common enemy of Communism. It is more concerned with depicting strife between American and Greek personnel on the Allied side, however, than with exploring any real Korean war issues. Unfortunately, it is definitely a "B" grade movie with little action, complexity or style to recommend it.

The film opens with American soldiers retreating across a river over a pontoon bridge, which they promptly explode before North Korean forces can use it against them. Soon, a mission calls for a platoon of American combat engineers to ferry a platoon of allied Greek soldiers across that same river for a reconnaissance mission. Lieutenant Sam Prior (Victor Mature) volunteers his squad because he is half Greek himself, and is proud and anxious to introduce his men to some genuine Greek soldiers. The river crossing goes well, but after the Greeks set off, a skirmish with Communist forces leads Prior to believe that the Greeks have surrendered. He sends most of his platoon back to the river to cross and bring back heavy weaponry, but those men are killed on the beach by North Koreans, and Prior is devastated at having sent his men to their deaths.

When only some of the original Greek soldiers return, Prior doesn't believe their battle story because their bayonets are clean. He forcibly takes command of the joint force, striking inland to finish the assigned reconaissance, against the wishes of the Greek leader, Lieutenant Niklas (Alexander Scourby). They destroy a tank and raid an ammo dump, replenishing their dwindling supplies. Prior is surprised, and somewhat ashamed, to find that the Greeks clean their weapons *immediately* after battle, explaining why there were no blood stains on them earlier.

At the ammo dump, a wounded soldier from New Zealand informs Prior and Niklas that the North Koreans are establishing an armored force and plan to attack soon. Lt. Niklas retakes command, with Prior's quiet consent, and begins heading the group back to the river, using a bulldozer and trailer to transport the wounded. Another tank arrives and is destroyed by American demolitions expert Corporal Bowman (Lee Marvin). It becomes clear that they will not reach the beach by daylight, so the Greeks resign themselves to battle, sending the Americans ahead to deliver the vital information regarding the North Korean armored force.

Prior and his men reach the river and see that the North Koreans are building a bridge just underneath the river's surface. The Americans sneak away and at the beach rendezvous, are joined by the previously missing Greek soldiers,

The marketing campaign for 20th Century–Fox's drama The Glory Brigade *(1953) suggests battle action but focuses on the various characters, promising that "you'll never forget 'em." The poster artwork seems to indicate singing, happy-go-lucky soldiers, an inaccurate portrayal at best.*

who surrendered to and then escaped from the North Koreans. Prior uses their radio to communicate the news to headquarters and request rescue, then leads all of the men back to the remaining Greek force. The united forces head for the highest hill and are rescued by helicopter as the relentless Communist forces attack from below, even while being fire-bombed by American jets. The movie ends with American tanks crossing the underwater bridge, pushing into Communist territory, as Prior, Niklas and their men watch from the vantage point of their rescue helicopter.

The Glory Brigade is a routine war film with an agreeable premise: that the various national fighting forces in Korea need to work together,

without rancor, to complete their military objectives. It is an obvious point and one worth repeating, though perhaps not to the extent shown in this film. The American squad is comprised of many nationalities already, further making the point that skin color and ethnic origin should not matter when it comes to working together to win a war. Once the mutual trust between the groups is established, they help and support each other when the going gets rough. The film works a little too hard to make this point, occasionally becoming melodramatic and using some really cornball dialogue, but its intentions are certainly noble.

Attention is focused, particularly early in the story, on the mistrust that exists between the

Following the massacre of half his platoon, Greek officer Lieutenant Nikias (Alexander Scourby) completes a grave for one of his countrymen in The Glory Brigade *(1953).*

Americans and the Greeks. The Americans first meet the Greeks as they are celebrating, dancing in a circle and drinking brandy. Just before they first cross the river, the Greek troops stop to pray and sing. These customs are alien to the Americans, and do not engender trust in their Greek colleagues. When some of the Greeks are captured by the North Koreans, Bowman says, "Those Greeks are no lousy good," and most of the army men agree with him. It is only after the Greeks have proven themselves in battle — and explained to Prior why their bayonets are always clean — that they are accepted as equals by the Americans.

As a war film, *The Glory Brigade* is strictly routine. There is no real sense of time or place;

the men could be in any war at any time, fighting any battle. Unlike some of the major Korean War films of the period, there is little bitterness expressed by the soldiers about fighting an unpopular war in a foreign land. However, the film does express the horror of war to strong effect, particularly when Prior and his men find the remains of their platoon on the beach. Unhappily, the low-budget production does not support the script very well. The river doesn't seem nearly as difficult to cross as it is said to be, and the terrain looks like any number of southern state parks (it was filmed in Missouri).

Victor Mature has the lion's share of the dialogue and gives a steady, understated performance. Lee Marvin wears glasses as the demolitionist, Bowman, and has little to do other than grumble once in a while about the Army and explode something. Alexander Scourby is solid and convincing as the Greek leader, Niklas, and other familiar faces such as Alvy Moore, Nick Dennis, Carleton Young, Lamont Johnson, Archer MacDonald and Henry Kulky fill the supporting roles. Like the United Nations forces it portrays, the cast is an ensemble meant to work smoothly, with each man doing his part. Though the movie certainly practices what it preaches, it could have used a bigger budget, a better script and some exciting action.

Originally titled *Baptism of Fire*, the film did have one fatal mishap. While filming at Lake of the Ozarks in Missouri, boatman Jess Wolf was killed when a demolition charge accidentally exploded beneath his boat. Two other men were injured, but Wolf was the only fatality in the accident.

Like other low-budget Korean War films, *The Glory Brigade* passed through theaters without much fanfare or business. Howard Thompson of the *New York Times* wrote that the movie "falls short in general impact and conviction," but he praised "the picture's frank, sincere plea for true, democratic understanding and harmony, in appraising the friction of a United Nations unit of Americans and Greeks." The British Film Institute's *Monthly Film Bulletin* noted that "*The Glory Brigade* has the distinction of being the first film about the Korean War to consider in any detail the relations between the allied troops. It begins quite promisingly, but the quarrels at every lull in the fighting between Niklas and Prior, and the facile and arbitrary resolution, give the story an all too contrived appearance."

The Glory Brigade is a standard war film with the novel twist of teaming Greek soldiers with Americans. It was the first Hollywood film to seriously explore relations between international partners during the war, and remains one of the few to do so even today. Its noble intentions, however, are somewhat offset by its generally routine script and production. The movie's concept is innovative, but its execution is not. It is certainly watchable and occasionally exciting, but it is never special.

The Great Impostor

Credits: 1960. Universal. *Directed by* Robert Mulligan. *Produced by* Robert Arthur. *Screenplay by* Liam O'Brien. *Based upon the book by* Robert Crichton. *Music by* Henry Mancini. *Director of Photography*: Robert Burks, A.S.C. *Film Editor*: Frederic Knudtson, A.C.E. *Art Directors*: Alexander Golitzen and Henry Bumstead. *Set Decorations*: Julia Heron. *Sound*: Waldon O. Watson and Frank Wilkinson. *Music Supervision by* Joseph Gershenson. *Make-Up*: Bud Westmore. *Hair Stylist*: Larry Germain. *Assistant Director*: Joseph Kenny. *Technical Advisor*: Commodore James Plomer, R.C.N. Not Rated. Black and White. Flat (1.33:1). 112 minutes. Released in November, 1960. Currently available on VHS home video.

Cast: Ferdinand Waldo Demara, Jr. *(aka Martin Goddard, Doctor Robert Lloyd Gilbert, Ben W. Stone, Surgeon Lieutenant Joseph C. Mornay and others)*, Tony Curtis; *Captain Glover*, Edmond O'Brien; *Warden Chandler*, Arthur O'Connell; *Pa Demara*, Gary Merrill; *Catherine Lacey*, Joan Blackman; *Abbot Donner*, Raymond Massey; *Brown*, Robert Middleton; *Ma Demara*, Jeanette Nolan; *Eulalie Chandler*, Sue Ane Langdon; *Cardinal*, Larry Gates; *Clifford Thompson*, Mike Kellin; *Barney*, Frank Gorshin; *WAC Lieutenant*, Cindi Wood; *Hotchkiss*, Richard "Dick" Sargent; *Young Fred Demara, Jr.*, Robert Crawford; *Farmer*, Doodles Weaver; *Executive Officer Howard*, Ward Ramsey; *Doctor Hammond*, David White; *Captain Hun Kim*, Philip Ahn;

Senior Officer, Herbert Rudley; *Defense Lieutenant*, Jerry Paris; *Doctor Joseph C. Mornay*, Harry Carey, Jr.; *Ben W. Stone*, Willard Sage; *Father Devlin*, Karl Malden; *Young Priest*, Patrick Curtis; *Prisoner*, Joe Gray.

Historical Accuracy Level: High. Though criticized by its real-life subject, the film does remain faithful to his exploits during the Korean War.

Patriotic Propaganda Level: Medium. The movie does not promote chameleonism, but Ferdinand Demara's adventures are certainly appealing.

Elements: Biography, Comedy, Courts-Martial, Medicine, Romance, United Nations Forces.

Perhaps the most unusual true story from the Korean War was that of Ferdinand Waldo Demara, Jr., who became widely known as the "Great Impostor" due to his penchant for assuming the identities and responsibilities of other people, usually with great success. During the Korean War, Demara enlisted in Canada's Royal Canadian Navy as a surgeon, trained himself by reading medical books and successfully operated on several people before publicity about his medical prowess exposed his charade.

The Great Impostor begins near the end of its story, as teacher Martin Goddard (Tony Curtis) is identified as Ferdinand Waldo Demara, Jr. and arrested. While being transported to jail, Demara recalls his youth ...

Demara's parents (Gary Merrill and Jeanette Nolan) can barely keep the family afloat financially and seem trapped within their own lives. Determined not to fall into the same trap, Demara joins the Army, but is rejected for officer candidate school because he has not graduated from high school. He deserts the Army and joins the Marines under the identity of a Harvard professor. When told that his background would be investigated, Demara fakes his own death and joins a monastic order, inspired by a talk with his hometown priest, Father Devlin (Karl Malden).

Demara finds that he is not suited to be a monk and he soon leaves, only to find himself in prison after driving a fertilizer truck while drunk. In prison, he interviews warden Ben W. Stone (Willard Sage) and after being released, assumes Stone's identity at a southern prison,

working as a consultant. Impressed by Stone's humanistic philosphies (gleaned from the real warden Stone), Warden Chandler (Arthur O'Connell) gives Stone control of the difficult maximum security area. Demara slowly persuades the prisoners to trust him by giving them limited freedom and treating them with dignity. Just as he is making solid progress, a prisoner transferred from Demara's former prison recognizes him, resulting in Demara's abrupt departure from the prison without a word.

Demara visits his hometown and relates his adventures to Father Devlin. The priest is aghast, but Demara seems more comfortable in other people's identities. "Even I liked myself," he says. Next, Demara joins the Royal Canadian Navy as a surgeon, Doctor Joseph C. Mornay. He is assigned to Halifax, Nova Scotia, where he meets and falls in love with Navy nurse Catherine Lacey (Joan Blackman). He tries to reveal his secret to her but cannot; in some desperation he asks for active sea duty in the Korean War for the opportunity to repent for his past military desertions and to avoid commitment with Catherine.

Mornay's first task upon boarding the destroyer *Cayuga* is to pull an abscessed tooth which is bothering Captain Glover (Edmond O'Brien). Mornay is aided by a novice medical assistant, Hotchkiss (Dick Sargent). This sequence is played for comedy, as Mornay gives Glover three shots of novocaine, which freezes the ship's captain in place and causes him to sleep for a few days after the procedure. The ship sails into an operational area and is approached by a boat with wounded ROK soldiers. Mornay, aided by Hotchkiss and Korean Captain Hun Kim (Philip Ahn), is forced to operate on three badly injured Korean commandos and medically treat another sixteen. He does so without a single fatality.

Mornay progresses to the island of Chinnampo, where he establishes a hospital hut and continues to treat the sick and injured, even going so far as to undertake a lung resection, guided by doctors over the radio. The publicity raised by Mornay's good works becomes Demara's undoing, as the real Doctor Mornay reveals himself in Canada. Demara faces a court-martial by the Royal Canadian Navy, but he persuades the court that letting him disappear

The marketing campaign for Universal's The Great Impostor *(1961) intimates that the title character, chameleon Ferdinand Demara, Jr. (Tony Curtis), changed identities for amorous reasons. The film itself paints a far different picture.*

would be in its best interest. The film flashes forward to the present, as Martin Goddard is being transported to the mainland, but he disappears again before the boat docks. The police begin a manhunt for Demara, and one of the detectives put on the case is none other than Demara. The words "The End" appear on the screen, but Demara shakes his head benignly, smiling at the camera.

The Great Impostor is a lighthearted, amusing glimpse of a fascinating individual, one who evidently felt more comfortable as other people than as himself. The film is not especially deep and does not seem overly concerned with exploring Demara's psychological needs, but such an investigation would be dramatic rather than humorous. Director Robert Mulligan's approach is definitely one of curiosity rather than scrutiny. He chronicles Demara's adventures with a light touch and an absence of moralizing, and he al-

lows the dramatic episodes to develop from the situations and Demara's character without adversely affecting the film's tone. Mulligan is determined to tell Demara's story in a simple, entertaining fashion, and Demara's incredible exploits — and expertise — are most definitely worth watching.

The film's most effective segment is the prison sequence, as Demara puts Warden Stone's humanistic philosphies to a real-life test. Demara enters the maximum security area unprotected among the roughest prisoners and earns their trust. The most dramatic moment occurs when he must physically take away a weapon from one of the prisoners. The prisoner, Clifford Thompson (Mike Kellin), wants Demara to take the knife (actually a spoon) away from him to save face, but Demara needs Thompson's help in order to do so. Then, just as Demara is to be made deputy warden and marry the warden's

Captain Glover (Edmond O'Brien, left) of the Royal Canadian Navy questions ship's doctor Lieutenant Joseph C. Mornay (Tony Curtis, center) regarding the condition of the Korean refugees aboard this ship in The Great Impostor *(1961).*

daughter, he is recognized. The loss that registers on Demara's face and posture is enormous and makes palpable Demara's sorrow at having to give up yet another dream.

The Korean War sequence begins with comedy, as Demara is engaged to pull the captain's tooth. It plays well to audiences, but this is the one episode which is not really in keeping with the movie's tone because Captain Glover (Edmond O'Brien) is sedated with novocaine to the point of mummification. The real comedy is watching Executive Officer Howard (Ward Ramsey) and Hotchkiss (Dick Sargent) squirm as Demara gives the captain his shots.

The Korean War sequence then turns dramatic, as Demara is forced to treat the South Korean commando team. His brief prayer before beginning to operate, "Help me, dear God. I don't want to kill anybody," is heartfelt and to the point. And because he has taken his disguise

seriously and studied medicine full time since becoming Doctor Mornay, he doesn't kill anybody. He does what he believes the real doctor would do, continuing to treat people to the best of his ability.

And that is the key to Demara's character. No matter what role he assumes, he tries to live it, to fulfill it, to the best of his own ability. And he does. While Demara's motives are strange, there is no doubting his professionalism. When his court-martial is arranged, just about everyone with whom he worked seems willing to testify on his behalf because they believe in him. That faith is just another of the incredible circumstances of the story of Ferdinand Waldo Demara, Jr.

Doctor Joseph Mornay was in actuality Doctor Joe Cyr of Grand Falls, Nebraska. It was 1951 when Cyr read about his own surgical prowess in Korean waters. Doctor Cyr notified the authorities and Demara was quickly relieved of duty. Demara had successfully removed one man's appendix and saved another man who had a bullet lodged within one-quarter of an inch of his heart. Demara was discharged from the Royal Canadian Navy on November 21, 1951. He was never charged with practicing medicine without a license because he had gone to the trouble of procuring licenses from several countries under his alibi. Years later, by sheer coincidence, the actual Doctor Cyr began work at a hospital in California where Demara was working under his own real name as a chaplain, having foregone his chameleon ways.

The Korean War sequence also spotlights a little seen aspect of the war, that of the United Nations ships that cruised off-shore during the war, awaiting military orders or injured people to treat. Canada's contribution to the war effort included three destroyers, one army brigade and one air transport squadron. The destroyers cruised around the Korean peninsula, escorting aircraft carriers, conducting patrols, searching for submarines and tending to men evacuated from the battle areas. Denmark had contributed a hospital ship, but other ships were also utilized to a lesser extent for this purpose. This is the only Korean War movie to depict this aspect of the war.

The Great Impostor is an entertaining movie because of its unlikely story, its attitude of bemusement and winning performances from Tony Curtis, Karl Malden and the supporting cast. Curtis is perhaps too individualistic to portray chameleon Demara, but he exudes just the right insouciance and devilry for the part. More than a few critics complained about the casting of Curtis, but Robert Mulligan wasn't trying to make an exposé, and therefore didn't need Laurence Olivier. He was making a movie about a rascal, and that's exactly whom he cast.

The film itself generally received positive reviews, such as A. H. Weiler's judgment in the *New York Times*: "A dedicated team working for Universal-International has turned out an amusing, and occasionally fascinating, comedy-drama about the career of one of the most amazing—and likable—contemporary charlatans, Ferdinand W. Demara, Jr."

The Great Impostor, while not a great movie, is a perfect example of how a small episode taken from a momentous event such as the Korean War can be developed into an intriguing and entertaining feature film. The movie sticks to the facts of Demara's case, yet it is not a documentary. It is a sly and amusing wink at a public personage whose motivations and attitudes will never be truly known or understood. It is a fascinating display of human nature which blends fact and fiction, truth and myth. Most of all, it is a very entertaining motion picture.

Hell's Horizon

Credits: 1955. Wray Davis Productions. *Distributed by* Columbia. *Written and Directed by* Tom Gries. *Produced by* Wray Davis. *Associate Producer:* Ralph Freed. *Music Composed and Conducted by* Heinz Roemheld. *Director of Photography:* Floyd Crosby, A.S.C. *Edited by* Aaron Stell, A.C.E. *Production Manager:* Rex Bailey. *Art Director:* Al Goodman. *Set Decorator:* Darryl Silvera. *Assistant Director:* Bill Calihan. *Technical Advisor:* Robert Brubaker. *Sound:* Ralph Butler. *Makeup Artist:* Lou Fillipi. Not Rated. Black and White. Flat (1.33:1). 78 minutes. Released in December, 1955. Not currently available on commercial home video.

Cast: *Captain John Merrill*, John Ireland; *Sami*, Marla English; *Paul Jenkins*, Bill Williams; *Sergeant Al Trask*, Hugh Beaumont; *Buddy Lewis*, Larry Pennell; *Jockey*, Chet Baker; *Captain Ben Morgan*, William Schallert; *Corporal Pete Kinshaw*, Jerry Paris; *Sergeant Earl Maddox*, Paul Leavitt; *Lieutenant Harry Murphy*, John Murphy; *Lieutenant Ed Houseman*, Wray Davis; *Colonel Baer*, Mark Scott; *Major Naylor*, Kenne Duncan; *Lieutenant Chapman*, Don Burnett; *Dixie*, Stanley Adams.

Historical Accuracy Level: Low. The film's bombing mission is fictional, and its scenes in Japan are not realistic at all.

Patriotic Propaganda Level: Medium. The B-24 bomber crew does eventually achieve its objective, but the film does not champion its characters.

Elements: Air Force, Air War, Bridge Bombing, Infighting, Lonely Wives, Romantic Triangle.

A typical Korean War film advertisement, focusing on everything but the real story of Columbia's drama Hell's Horizon *(1955). The artwork features American fighter planes, though none appear in the film. Marla English (and her cleavage) is the big draw here, though Chet Baker and His Trumpet are also touted. Note also the oblique reference to* The Bridges at Toko-Ri *at bottom left.*

Hell's Horizon is a turgid drama revolving around an American flight crew sent on a dangerous Korean War bombing mission. Its structure is a simple and straightforward telling of the mission, from the introduction of the crew through the official briefing and preparations for flight to the actual ten-hour mission, culminating in a crash landing at the film's climax. The basic idea for the film is sound — an examination of the crew facing a dangerous mission has great dramatic potential — but the wooden script, leaden acting and lack of realistic detail fail to provide the film with enough lift to leave the ground.

While based in Okinawa in 1952, American flight crews wait for the foggy weather to lift so that missions can be flown over Korea. It has been six weeks since one particular crew has seen action, and they spend their time complaining to each other about their relative problems. Al Trask (Hugh Beaumont) worries about his wife's fidelity and drinks to relieve his doubts. The crew's co-pilot, Paul Jenkins (Bill Williams), spends his time writing letters to his eight-year-old son. Jockey's (Chet Baker's) solace is his trumpet, which he plays almost constantly, to the consternation of some of the other men. Two men in the crew have a shared interest: a beautiful half-caste Okinawan girl named Sami (Marla English), who earns money by gathering and cleaning the officers' clothing. Courting her are pilot John Merrill (John Ireland), who explains to Sami that he can provide for her better than anybody else, and Buddy Lewis (Larry Pennell), who simply loves her. Merrill uses his rank to send Buddy on an errand so he can romance Sami; Buddy returns with news that they have been assigned to a mission.

The Air Force has assigned this unnamed, unnumbered crew to a dangerous mission to bomb the main bridge spanning the Yalu River connecting North Korea to Manchuria. It is dangerous because they are not to venture into Manchuria under any circumstances (it would raise a public relations stink) and because they will have no fighter cover for their B-24. The Air Force brass is betting that the foggy weather will hold all the way to the target and keep enemy MiGs on the ground. Since the crew's regular radar operator is hospitalized, they are provided with green replacement Ben Morgan (William

Schallert), a recent arrival who has never flown a mission, or heard a gun fired in anger.

Buddy makes a quick trip to the local village to profess his love to Sami, who agrees to marry him, if he makes it back alive. He barely makes it back to the base in time for the mission. It's a ten-hour mission, and the first four hours are deadly dull, though Morgan is so nervous that he cannot bring himself to eat the sandwich packed for his lunch. As the bomber nears its target, flak begins and Morgan becomes so nervous that he cannot read his radar. The weather clears, however, and bombardier Murphy (John Murphy) is able to destroy the target without Morgan's aid. However, MiG fighters have been launched and attack the B-24 before it can climb back into cloud cover.

Gunners shoot down several MiGs during the dogfight, but flight engineer Ed Houseman (Wray Davis, who also produced the film) is wounded and Jockey is killed by enemy fire. More importantly, one of the plane's fuel tanks has been breached and is leaking fuel, unnoticed by the crew. The voyage back home is uneventful until the first motor quits. It was Trask's job to check on the fuel gauges, but he was so upset by a letter from his wife — in which she tells him that she has found someone else — that he has been unable to function. The crew lightens the plane of everything not nailed down, including their parachutes, to conserve fuel, and guilt-ridden Trask aids the effort by hurling himself out of the plane and into the sea.

The plane's second motor (of four) gives out, but Merrill guides it gingerly back to the base. When the landing gear jams, a crash landing is called for. The plane lands safely, but then catches fire. Each man escapes safely, but Merrill goes back into the plane to bring out Jockey's body. As the men disperse after the hazardous mission, Merrill gives Buddy a pendant he took earlier from Sami and advises the flier to marry the girl. Buddy finds Sami waiting for him and they embrace.

Murky is the most descriptive word for *Hell's Horizon*. Murky describes the film's weather, the melodramatic love triangle and the mission itself. In order to provide some sparks, writer-director Tom Gries cast Marla English, a beautiful but bland woman in a provocative blouse (emphasized in the film's publicity), but the role is essentially empty and English cannot fill it with her personality. The love triangle between Merrill, who desires Sami as he desires all women; Buddy, who loves Sami unconditionally; and Sami, who loves Buddy but wants Merrill's security, is obvious, flat and acted without passion. As with many films concerning the military, the attempt here to humanize the military men by giving them a romantic interest only serves to weaken the central story and pad the film's running time.

On the military side, *Hell's Horizon* is less turgid but no more exciting. As an examination of a single mission and the experiences of the crew before and during that particular mission, the film is fundamentally stable, but not exemplary. The routine script allows no room for more than the stock characterizations familiar to most B-actioners. The film's fatal flaw is that it tries to tell a universal story (what a bombing mission is really like) instead of an individual story. Since Gries does a poor job of creating true individuals instead of types and does not give the crew an authentic identity, the result is that the film is not often believable or interesting, and is often substandard.

The film's political stance involving the Yalu bridge the crew intends to bomb is interesting.

Paul Jenkins (Bill Williams, left) tries to make Ed Houseman (Wray Davis, right) comfortable after Houseman is wounded during a bombing raid in Hell's Horizon *(1955).*

The crew is told that they are going alone because a single plane is needed for precision bombing, and contact with the Manchurian side of the river is not permitted. Even in 1952, well after the Chinese had entered the war, care was taken to avoid provoking the Chinese by the Air Force, which attempted to avoid directly bombing their territory. Dogfights also occurred over Korea; fighter jets were prohibited from crossing into Chinese air space.

One of the film's more interesting flaws is its use of stock military footage. The weather is so bad in the movie that planes on both sides are grounded; however, at the Yalu River target there is no such problem, and later, when the bomber comes in for its crash-landing in the fog, visibility is clear. Inconsistency is one thing, but this is a bit much. And during the dogfight between the bomber and the MiGs, there are many shots of the Russian-made fighters flying past and being shot down. Several of these stock shots are taken from the perspective of pursuing fighters, including a few where the pursuing plane actually flies through the smoke and debris of the damaged MiGs. Though this is the most exciting footage in the movie, it is obviously not from the perspective of a bomber, and because it isn't authentic to the situation, detracts from the effectiveness of the film. Those shots call attention to themselves because they just don't fit.

Though *Hell's Horizon*'s mission takes place over Korea, there isn't much visible difference between this setting and a World War II setting. The film plays like a standard WWII action film with little detail (other than those of the mission briefing) to distinguish its setting. At one point, an officer interrupts a fight in the men's quarters, saying, "The war's in Korea, men," just to remind the audience which war it is watching. As for its moral stance on the war, Bill Williams sums it up when asked why he is involved. "For all the corny reasons. Got an 8-year-old boy that's growing up in this sick world. And if it takes this kind of surgery to cure it, then I want to help." Even the patriotic angle reflects the World War II films of a dozen years earlier.

The human action is familiar and uninvolving. Wisecracking Jerry Paris seems to be the most well-adjusted of the crew. Audiences today are amused to see Hugh Beaumont, who

went on to play father figure Ward Cleaver in *Leave It To Beaver*, crack up and throw himself out of the plane. This was the film debut of jazz trumpeter Chet Baker, who has lines like, "Hey, man, wasn't that gorgeous?" after watching the Yalu River bridge blow up. He is the crew's only casualty. John Ireland plays the heel with so much authority that when he finally lightens his personality the change simply does not ring true. And Larry Pennell as Buddy is just plain wooden. Buddy may have the best intentions for Sami, but his lack of personality is almost total, and it is beyond belief that she would pay any attention to him.

Hell's Horizon was not popular, either critically or commercially. *Variety* judged it a "Poor quality Korean bomber melodrama," and commented, "Little novelty or freshness. Just a rehash of better films of the past," while *Boxoffice* gave "To the film editor and to writer-director Tom Gries an 'A' for effort," but noted, "That they missed their goal by a country mile is attributable to several self-evident productional and literary shortcomings."

Writer-director Tom Gries, whose first film this was, certainly had good intentions for it; unfortunately, good intentions do not always lead to a good movie. *Hell's Horizon* is a well-meaning failure, a routine, mostly boring account of men facing down the demons inside themselves and surviving to fight another day.

A Hill in Korea
(aka *Hell in Korea*)

Credits: 1956. Wessex Film Productions. *Distributed by* British Lion Films. *Directed by* Julian Amyes. *Produced by* Anthony Squire. *Executive Producer:* Ian Dalrymple. *Screen Play by* Ian Dalrymple, Anthony Squire and Ronald Spencer. *From the Novel by* Max Catto. *Music Composed by* Malcolm Arnold. *Director of Photography:* Freddie Francis. *Film Editor:* Peter Hunt. *Music Played by* The Royal Philharmonic Orchestra *and Conducted by* Muir Mathieson. *Art Director:* Cedric Dawe. *Camera Operator:* Arthur Ibbetson. *Assistant Director:* Ronald Spencer. *Production Manager:* William Kirby. *Sound Supervisor:* John Cox. *Sound Recordists:*

Buster Ambler and Bob Jones. *Continuity*: June Randall. *Make-up*: Trevor Crole-Rees. *Wardrobe*: John McCorry. *Chief Electrician*: Maurice Gillette. *Second Assistant*: David Bracknell. *Third Assistant*: Peter Parsons. *Production Secretary*: Isabelle Byers. *Focus Puller*: Derek Browne. *Clapper / Loader*: Ronald Anscombe. *Sound Camera Operator*: Derek Tate. *Boom Operator*: P. Dukelow. *Sound Maintenance*: E. Vincent. *Still Cameraman*: Norman Hargood. *Publicity*: Joy Raymond. *Assembler*: M. Hart. *Second Assistant*: John Poyner. *Assistant Wardrobe*: Brian Owen-Smith. *Assistant Art Director*: William Hutchinson. *Scenic Artist*: Basil Mannin. *Assistant Make-up*: Tom Smith. *Cashier*: Donald Palmer. *Property Chargehand*: Bernard Murrell. *Second Prop*: Arthur Ferrigno. *S / B Carpenter*: Edward Ponsford. *S / B Stagehand*: Frederick Snell. *S / B Painter*: Lyndon Ball. *Grip*: Frank Howard. *Special Effects*: Roy E. Whybrow. Not Rated. Black and White. Flat (1.33:1). 81 minutes. Released in October, 1956. Filmed at Shepperton Studios, England. Currently available on VHS home video.

Cast: *Lieutenant Butler*, George Baker; *Corporal Ryker*, Stanley Baker; *Sergeant Payne*, Harry Andrews; *Private Docker*, Michael Medwin; *Private Wyatt*, Ronald Lewis; *Private Sims*, Stephen Boyd; *Private Lindop*, Victor Maddern; *Private Rabin*, Harry Landis; *Private O'Brien*, Robert Brown; *Private Neill*, Barry Lowe; *Lance-Corporal Hodge*, Robert Shaw; *Private Kim*, Charles Laurence; *Private Matthews*, Eric Corrie; *Private Henson*, David Morrell; *Private Lockyer*, Michael Caine; *Private Moon*, Percy Herbert.

Historical Accuracy Level: Medium. Though fictional, this story is generally authentic in terms of its British perspective and action encountered in Korea.

Patriotic Propaganda Level: High. The movie is dedicated to National Servicemen, who comprise the bulk of the patrol and who acquit themselves honorably in battle.

Elements: Air War, Bugles, Infighting, United Nations Forces.

England was one of twenty-three countries which contributed men, materiel or medical aid to the Korean War effort, and British soldiers are seen in quite a few Korean War movies. But this is the only British-produced film that deals with England's direct participation in the war. As such, *A Hill in Korea* occupies a unique niche among Korean War films; it is also notable for its cast and crew, which features several up-and-coming stars and filmmakers-to-be. It also stands on its own as an intriguing chronicle of the war, depicting tactics and strategy on both sides while retaining a sharp focus on the men who suffer and die during the fighting.

A Hill in Korea, or *Hell in Korea* as it is also known, chronicles a sixteen-man patrol's deceptively simple assignment to investigate whether a small village is inhabited by enemy forces. Ten of the British soldiers — including their inexperienced new leader, Lieutenant Butler (George Baker) — are National Servicemen, conscripted into duty in Britain, then assigned to Korea. The other six are regular soldiers, veterans who seem harder and tougher than their servicemen cohorts. After reconnaissance, the patrol moves quietly into a small village of thatched huts. The only people they find are two Korean men who claim that Chinese forces are somewhere to the north. Butler allows them to go free. At the edge of the village, they watch as Private Matthews (Eric Corrie) kicks in a hut door and is killed as the hut explodes. The Koreans run from the scene, but are killed by Corporal Ryker's (Stanley Baker) rifle fire.

Their assignment complete, the patrol begins to march back, but is intercepted by a Chinese force of two platoons. The Brits spy them first and Butler decides to divide his force. Four men, including Butler, are to remain on their present hillock and engage the enemy while the other eleven are to flank right and escape without being observed and bring back help. The eleven, led by Sergeant Payne (Harry Andrews), march away, leaving Butler with Lance Corporal Hodge (Robert Shaw), Private O'Brien (Robert Brown) and talkative Private Rabin (Harry Landis). They use branches to raise a dust cloud, fooling the Chinese into thinking there is a large force to fight.

Bugles and whistles blow and thirty or more Chinese soldiers attack straight up the hillock; they are decimated by the Brits' machine guns. A second wave is also driven back, while none of the British men are injured. A bit later, the Chinese attack again, around both flanks of the hillock, and again they are driven back. A few Chinese soldiers are still alive after the skirmish and one of them tosses a grenade that Hodge leaps upon, saving the others with his own death. Butler is startled by the arrival of Sergeant Payne; the rest of the British were intercepted by another Chinese force and forced to retreat. Payne looks down the hill at the multitude of dead Chinese and tells Butler, "You lot certainly did your bit."

The Britishers move back to the village, pursued by the Chinese. The radio is not working correctly, as it is not handled properly by Private Wyatt (Ronald Lewis). In the darkness, the Chinese arrive and begin burning the huts; the Brits sneak away and climb a nearby hill, on top of which is a Korean temple. Along the way

as they journey up the hill, Wyatt becomes so exhausted that he simply tosses away the radio. Chinese soldiers on horseback pass nearby and Private Sims (Stephen Boyd) slips noisily and is shot before the cavalry officers are killed. Sims is aided up the hill to the temple, where Wyatt is told to care for him and not to leave him alone.

Butler and Payne decide on a defensive strategy and have the men dig slit trenches to forward outposts. Butler has doubts about his own leadership, but Payne commends him for keeping his head under fire and even has nice words for the men. "City types," he says, "but when you get the frills off of 'em, they're as good as any." In the temple, Sims dies suddenly and

A British infantry patrol finds Hell in Korea *(1956). This drama from Wessex Film Productions was originally titled* A Hill in Korea, *but changed for its American release. The scene in the ad is actually from the film, as a handful of British troops hold back a Chinese platoon.*

Wyatt begins to crack psychologically. Butler tells him to "show some guts" and Ryker threatens to kill him. The men spend the night quietly.

At dawn, beneath the warm sun, a few of the men play soccer on the temple porch before Butler ends their fun. More Chinese cavalrymen appear and are killed by Ryker, who shoots them from one of the outposts. Butler tells Payne to arrange aircraft recognition panels on the ground, in case friendly jets pass overhead. The outfit's Korean scout and translator, Private Kim (Charles Laurence), has been sent to find an escape route, should one be necessary. The rumblings of a tank are heard and the men prepare for battle. Anti-tank experts Private Docker (Michael Medwin) and Private Lindop (Victor Maddern) take their bazooka to one of the outposts with Payne and successfully explode the tank. They return to the temple safely, but Ryker is wounded in the battle and dies shortly thereafter. Later, Kim is seen by Butler and Payne trying to return to the temple but he is killed by Chinese snipers before reaching safety.

Another night passes in the temple, punctuated by sniper fire and the sound of continuous bombing in the distance. Wyatt finally cracks and tries to surrender to the Chinese; the response is a frightening hail of bullets. Butler orders a breakout at dawn and orders the men to eat the last of their rations. The dawn brings jet fighter-bombers, which fly over the hill and bomb the temple, killing Lindop and angering the others. Private Moon (Percy Herbert) is killed by the Chinese, who tramp relentlessly up the hill toward the temple. The jets fly over again, but this time bomb the advancing Chinese soldiers, having seen and identified the recognition panels. A few Chinese survive the bombing and trap O'Brien in one of the outposts. Payne and Butler try to rescue him, but are also held back by machine gun fire. Wyatt runs down the hill toward the Chinese and is killed, but his diversion allows Butler to use a grenade to eliminate the threat. After three days and two nights of combat and imminent danger, Butler and six men return to their home base.

A Hill in Korea sounds and feels authentic in its depiction of conditions in Korea. Admittedly, the hills of England do not look much like Korea, but aside from that slight drawback, the film does a fine job of capturing at least some of the nuances of the Korean War. Its depiction of Chinese tactics — an initial overpowering rush, followed by probing flank movements — and bugling before an attack is accurate and framed very effectively by noted cinematographer Freddie Francis. In addition, this is one of only two films (along with *Hold Back the Night*) to feature Chinese cavalrymen on horseback, an unusual sight that tended to unnerve the U.N. troops which encountered them.

In its second half, the film also utilizes its Korean temple setting quite nicely. This setting is reminiscent of the temple in *The Steel Helmet*, and both films emphasize the image of looming, benign, stone Buddha figures watching silently while small, seemingly insignificant men wage war upon one another. At its climax, the film shows the temple being blasted by jet fighter-bombers, a sad but accurate testament to the destructive effects of war on the Korean way of life. It is also significant that the film does not shy away from the image of so-called "friendly fire"; that is, U.N. jets bombing U.N. soldiers. This unfortunate situation occurred many times during the war, particularly early in the campaign, as South Korean soldiers were mistaken for North Koreans, and in air combat situations, where jets dropped their deadly payloads a bit ahead of their targets. It also occurred with artillery fire, and was viewed by infantrymen as an unhappy by-product of the fighting.

Like all war films, the interaction of the men who are forced to live, suffer and die together provides much of the drama. Here, Private Rabin (Harry Landis) produces much of the dialogue and the film's humor, continuously complaining about being in Korea and fantasizing about returning home to England. Most of the other men get their chance to reveal a bit about themselves, but none to the extent of Rabin. The most poignant character is undoubtedly Hodge (Robert Shaw), who explains that he was a hotel valet who wanted to become a farmer before being conscripted into National Service and finding himself in Korea. Naturally, he is killed soon after revealing so much of himself to his colleagues.

The issue of National Service is central to the film; in fact, the movie is dedicated to

"National Servicemen and Drafted Men of the Free Nations." In 1947, Britain's ruling Labour party instituted mandatory military service for most men between 18 and 26, calling the practice "National Service," for a duration of eighteen months. Some of the young men were assigned to the Royal Navy or the Royal Air Force, but the majority were sent to the British Army and asked to work shoulder-to-shoulder with regular soldiers, sharing the same dangers at half the pay. After the war began, National Servicemen were sent to Korea at an ever increasing rate, and their conscription period was extended from eighteen months to two years. In the final year of the war, British units sent to Korea were largely comprised of National Servicemen.

In the film, ten of the sixteen soldiers are National Servicemen and most of them have never faced fire before. Nevertheless, the Servicemen — including their relatively inexperienced leader, Lieutenant Butler — prove themselves in battle to be just as tough and rugged as the regular soldiers with whom they are fighting. Butler is guided by veteran Sergeant Payne, but Butler's decisions are sound and his judgment keeps the men alive against an outnumbering hostile force.

The servicemen, much more than the regular soldiers, are viewed as a variegated force, as they would be from a forced conscription that crosses social and economic lines. Thus, there is Rabin, the talkative Jew; carefree Londoners Docker and Lindop; Matthews, a quiet lad from Kent; and cowardly Wyatt. The downside of conscription is represented by Wyatt, an insecure introvert who places more importance on his own comfort than the platoon's safety. Butler is forced to work with Wyatt, and tries his best to teach Wyatt how to soldier properly, but the man is a lost cause. Wyatt's dereliction of duty causes several casualties, including, finally, his own.

The film is starkly realized by director Julian Amyes, who moved from feature direction

The anti-tank specialist, Private Docker (Michael Medwin, left) takes aim at an enemy tank with his bazooka while Sergeant Payne (Harry Andrews, right) waits nervously in the British adventure A Hill in Korea *(1956).*

into television production. Noted cinematographer Freddie Francis and film editor Peter Hunt later became directors themselves. This picture was Robert Shaw's second film appearance, one which he considered to be "a nice part," as Lance Corporal Hodge. It was Michael Caine's first role and as Private Lockyer, he has only one line, spoken after Ryker is killed. "Pity. He was the toughest bloke we got." In his autobiography, *What's It All About?*, Caine recalls the making of the movie and its reception. "After a year of waiting for the perfect moment, with true movie genius they premiered the film on the night that we invaded Suez. The picture went straight down the pan, and my movie career along with it." It would take Michael Caine another decade to become an international star, but his first film, while not financially successful, is one of the better Korean War films.

Variety called *A Hill in Korea* a "well-made war episode ... exciting but unpretentious," and noted, "The director has handled the story with simplicity, there being no mock heroics, no jealous motives, no major private issues to be settled, each man fulfilling his distasteful job to the best of his inexperienced capacity." The critic for the British Film Institute's *Monthly Film Bulletin* was less impressed: "Dedicated to National Service men [*sic*] everywhere, this film concentrates on one fictitious but feasible incident and follows the fashionable formula of combining competently staged combat scenes with some investigation of the personalities involved. Unfortunately, an insufficiently perceptive approach fails to fuse the two elements satisfactorily. Character is adequately sketched into a suitably laconic script, although the human relationships remain only partially developed. This is regrettable since most of the playing is quite capable."

As one of the few Korean War films to chronicle United Nations — rather than purely American — activities, *A Hill in Korea* is informative. As an examination of the British experience during the war, it is invaluable. *A Hill in Korea* is not a great film, and it shares some of the pitfalls of Hollywood's war films: a few too many characters, some of which are simply bodies rather than personalities; a limited amount of action because of budget or script constraints; a common, sometimes pedestrian view of men in

war. But it succeeds in overcoming its faults and presents an earnest, enlightening view of untested men facing battle in a foreign land. It is a film which becomes more meaningful on repeat viewings and one which nicely complements familiar American perspectives on the Korean War.

Hold Back the Night

Credits: 1956. Allied Artists. *Directed by* Allan Dwan. *Produced by* Hayes Goetz. *Screenplay by* John C. Higgins and Walter Doniger. *From the Novel by* Pat Frank. *Music by* Hans Salter. *Director of Photography*: Ellsworth Fredericks, A.S.C. *Film Editor*: Robert S. Eisen. *Production Manager*: Allen K. Wood. *Production Assistant*: Austen Jewell. *Assistant Director*: Don Torpin. *Music Editor*: Harry Eisen. *Sound Editor*: Charles Schelling. *Art Director*: Hilyard Brown. *Set Decorator*: Joseph Kish. *Set Continuity by* Richard M. Chaffee. *Recorded by* Ralph Butler. *Wardrobe*: Bert Henrikson. *Makeup*: Emile Lavigne, S.M.A. *Property*: Sam Gordon. *Technical Advisor*: Lieutenant Colonel Harold S. Roise, U.S.M.C. Not Rated. Black and White. Flat (1.33:1). 80 minutes. Released in July, 1956. Not currently available on commercial home video.

Cast: *Captain Sam McKenzie*, John Payne; *Anne Franklin McKenzie*, Mona Freeman; *Lieutenant Lee Couzens*, Peter Graves; *Sergeant Ekland*, Chuck Connors; *Kitty*, Audrey Dalton; *Beany Smith*, Bob Nichols; *Tinker*, John Wilder; *Ackerman*, Bob (Robert) Easton; *Kato*, Stanley Cha; *Papiro*, Nicky Blair; *Major Bob MacKay*, John Craven; *Lieutenant Colonel Toomey*, Nelson Leigh.

Historical Accuracy Level: High. Korean War history is followed faithfully, although the central story is fictional and somewhat fragmented.

Patriotic Propaganda Level: High. These Marines follow their commander, and his bottle of scotch, everywhere.

Elements: Bugles, Helicopters, Lonely Wives, Marine Corps, Multiple Wars, Romance, Winter Fighting.

One of the more inventive, and yet historically accurate, portrayals of the war is to be found in *Hold Back the Night*, a film based upon the novel by Pat Frank. The conceit of the story is a bottle of Scotch that has been carried from battle to battle from the dark days of World War II to the "advance in another direction" in Korea. Flashbacks illustrate the well-traveled bottle's history and introduce elements of romance into the story, and yet the film retains its central thread, chronicling the orderly retreat of U. N. forces from the Chosin Reservoir to safety at the port of Hungnam with a higher level of accuracy and truth than most other Korean War films.

Hold Back the Night begins in November of 1950, as Captain Sam McKenzie (John Payne) leads his platoon of Marines toward the Chosin Reservoir in frozen northern Korea. The men of Easy Company talk of the war's quick finish. Sergeant Ekland (Chuck Connors) asks about a possible promotion. Private Beany Smith (Bob Nichols) gets drunk and tries to force himself on a Korean woman, but is stopped and punished by McKenzie. Lieutenant Lee Couzens (Peter Graves) warns McKenzie about Beany's abuse of alcohol, which reminds McKenzie about his own bottle of Scotch. He checks to make sure it is still unbroken, then tells Couzens that it was a gift just before the battle of Guadalcanal.

A flashback to 1942 introduces Anne (Mona Freeman), a beautiful blonde who wants McKenzie to save the bottle "for a time when things couldn't get worse, or for some great victory." Though Anne wants to marry, McKenzie backs away, not wanting to make her a widow at Guadalcanal.

Couzens is surprised that McKenzie still has the Scotch. Both men are surprised by Lieutenant Colonel Toomey's (Nelson Leigh's) news that the Chinese have joined the war and are advancing toward and around their forces. Toomey orders a "fighting withdrawal" back to the 8th Army and the sea at Hungnam, where they will be evacuated. Easy Company is to forge down a road parallel to the main regiment, warn of Chinese movements from the west, and engage the enemy if necessary.

In Melbourne, Australia, after the stinking jungle of Guadalcanal, there was Kitty. McKenzie suggests that Kitty (Audrey Dalton) and he open his bottle of Scotch, and she agrees. Then she tells him of her husband, who is either missing or dead. She listens to the radio every night at 12:30 a.m., when the Japanese broadcast names of their prisoners, five at a time per broadcast, to learn of his fate. McKenzie realizes that he is intruding, apologizes to her and leaves with his bottle intact.

Soldiers are hunched in the cold, wintry trenches of Korea. Couzens sneaks up on a soldier who has started a small fire and demonstrates how the Chinese would kill him. Suddenly, bugles blare and the Chinese attack in force. After a brief but bloody battle, the Chinese pull back with a solid assessment of the American forces. McKenzie orders sock changes twice daily as the men march south toward Hungnam, fifty miles away. Fifteen miles later, the Chinese attack with mortars and machine guns, inflicting heavy casualties. McKenzie begs command for a helicopter to transport his wounded men to safety, but is denied. Instead, he sends half of his men over the mountains with eight litter cases to an airstrip which he hopes has not yet fallen into enemy hands.

A small, bombed-out town is encountered, and Couzens suggests backing into it with a truck, using it like a tank. The strategy works and a force of Chinese soldiers is massacred. A helicopter is sent to McKenzie's force with food, medical supplies and ammunition, and it leaves with the five worst casualties. Only twenty-nine able-bodied men are left. Couzens suggests leaving the wounded behind, which infuriates McKenzie.

He is again reminded of the Scotch and remembers San Francisco after the end of World War II. He visits Anne, only to find that she is seeing an Air Force officer. McKenzie storms away and gets drunk, but not on Scotch. Anne finds him in his hotel room, where he shows her the unopened bottle, cries despondently and confesses his love for her. They marry.

McKenzie puts the bottle away again and the men continue to march. For three days, the men march through sporadic mortar and sniper fire. Their remaining truck is destroyed and Couzens is wounded. The following morning, the men refuse to march any further. McKenzie breaks out his bottle of Scotch and offers the men drinks, but only when they reach the Hungnam perimiter, seven miles away. The men

A suggestive line drawing of passion overwhelms the indicated combat action in Allied Artists' drama Hold Back the Night *(1956). The film's flashbacks, however, do not fulfill the promise of the illustration. Nowhere is the Korean War indicated, nor is there a mention of the bottle of Scotch that triggers the narrative's episodes.*

rise, their thoughts on liquor rather than their terrible situation, and trudge onward. They are followed by men of the Manchurian Cavalry on horseback, who watch them from the high ridges of the surrounding hills. They eventually attack, killing the bazookaman Ackerman (Bob Easton) and wounding young Tinker (John Wilder), before being eliminated.

Within four miles of safety, an enemy tank is waiting to spring a trap. Leaving the wounded men behind for the moment, the men walk down the road into the trap while McKenzie and a bazooka squad circle opposite the tank. The ruse works and the tank is destroyed, although McKenzie is shot in the abdomen. A helicopter arrives and takes McKenzie and two other wounded men to safety. The rest of the men, now led by Ekland, continue to march. They reach the Marine perimeter and ride into Hungnam in Marine jeeps. The bottle of Scotch, which McKenzie entrusted to Ekland to serve to the men, is returned to McKenzie unopened. He agrees once again to "save it for an important occasion."

Hold Back the Night uses its flashback structure to introduce a female element into the story, but one which does not interfere with its main story. Shown in two scenes, Anne (Mona Freeman) represents military wives and girlfriends who try to provide their men with inspiration and support when the men leave for war and love when they return. She offers to marry McKenzie before he goes off to war, but he is realistic enough to realize that an absent (or dead) husband would be a burden. When he returns to her, unannounced, and finds her with an Air Force flyer, McKenzie is distraught, but Anne loves him enough to ignore her own wounded pride and forces her way through his drunken disappointment to tell him the truth. She makes him understand that she loves only him, and marries him.

The other female role is Kitty (Audrey Dalton), seemingly a one-night stand for McKenzie, but a woman who reveals the other, darker side of being a military wife. She is alone, waiting for word on the life or death of her husband in Singapore. She tries to open her heart to McKenzie but is ultimately unable to do so; he experiences the same feelings and they mutually agree to end their evening without things going

any further. Kitty symbolizes the wives who anxiously wait for news of their husbands during war, who try to go on living but find it difficult to do so without knowing what has become of the men to whom they have devoted their lives.

The bottle of Scotch is the story's way of reminding McKenzie (and the audience) of the woman back home, of the familiar place that awaits him after his tour of duty. Anne gives him the Scotch and simply asks that he save it for a special occasion, a moment when her gift might be properly appreciated. Her request is what triggers his memories of peacetime life, what makes the liquor so special to him. The Scotch becomes McKenzie's good luck charm, and the ultimate supposition is that he'll never drink it.

Those brief sequences are important to the story, but like *Retreat, Hell!*, this film is primarily concerned with telling at least part of the story of the great "fighting withdrawal" of the U.S. Marine Corps from the Chosin Reservoir to the port of Hungnam in the bitterly cold months of November and December 1950. Hundreds of thousands of Chinese troops had moved across the border into North Korea in the previous weeks under cover of darkness and were waiting for U.N. soldiers to reach the Chosin Reservoir area. The Chinese struck, hard, beginning on November 25, 1950, at a thinly-spread, relaxed enemy that thought the war would be over by Christmas.

Hold Back the Night does not document the widespread Chinese attack in detail, but rather concentrates on Easy Company, a real outfit (though this story is fictional) that is assigned to parallel the main regiment on a secondary road. Easy Company experiences many tactics that the Chinese used, beginning with bugle blowing. Chinese leaders commanded their troop movements with bugles and whistles, sounds that often frightened the U.N. troops more than the Chinese bullets. This is one of the relatively few Korean War films to cite the use of bugles, despite their widespread use by actual Chinese troops. Easy Company is attacked and literally overrun by hordes of enemy soldiers who suddenly pull back to their own lines. The Chinese predilection for pinpoint mortar fire and use of snipers and tank traps is also depicted, and the

Sergeant Ekland (Chuck Connors, left) and Captain McKenzie (John Payne, right) face a cold winter in Korea in Hold Back the Night *(1956).*

film even shows the involvement of the Manchurian Cavalry! Through it all, Easy Company must fight its way to Hungnam, through which the U.N. forces are to be evacuated and redeployed.

The details of the long march are thoroughly developed. McKenzie insists that the men change socks twice daily to prevent their feet from freezing. McKenzie relies heavily upon his officers, Lieutenant Couzens and Sergeant Ekland, to prod and police the troops while he oversees the operation. The difficulties of transporting the wounded are discussed at length and the men learn to rely upon themselves and each other as their motorized equipment freezes and fails.

The film also seems to be an accurate, if somewhat mild, representation of the winter conditions in Korea. Most Korean War films are set in the hot summer months of the war (it's cheaper and easier to stage) but much of the

heaviest fighting took place during November and December of 1950 in North Korea in temperatures that dropped to 30 or even 50 degrees below zero at night. *Hold Back the Night* does an adequate job of relating such conditions, although the temperature never seems very cold because the men's breath isn't always visible. In real life the snow was much deeper, the winds were much fiercer and the conditions were much colder.

Hold Back the Night is both historically accurate and dramatically sound. John Payne, Peter Graves and Chuck Connors are each exemplary in their roles and the supporting cast members fill their roles capably as well. Mona Freeman is satisfactory as Anne, and Audrey Dalton as Kitty is very affecting when she describes the circumstances surrounding her husband's fate. The film is tautly directed by Allan Dwan, a long-time veteran helmer who had brought *Sands of Iwo Jima* to the screen seven years earlier, and also made the Korean War film *Flight Nurse* in 1953. Dwan's association with the Marines was to continue in 1967 when, at age 82, he was preparing another Korean War battle film titled *Marine!*, but the sale of the Warner Bros. studio to Seven Arts resulted in that project's abandonment.

The film received moderate reviews. *Variety* called it "a good entry," while *Film Daily* noted, "It is strong on ability." *Boxoffice* was most laudatory: "Realistically staged and impressive are the battle sequences of this thoughtfully produced screen version of the widely read novel by Pat Frank. Add to such noteworthy mountings the fact that the picture is expertly directed by Allan Dwan and boasts splendid performances by virtually every member of the dominantly male cast, and the sum conclusion earmarks the offering as a well-above average war picture." Commercially, the film was one of Allied Artists' larger hits.

Hold Back the Night is inventive, stylish and truthful. It is appropriately sensitive in its romantic sequences and violent on the battlefield. It chronicles the Marine Corps' historic "fighting withdrawal" without undue jingoism, preferring to emphasize the realism of the grim situation. It may not be as deep and resounding a success as *Pork Chop Hill*, but it is a vigorous, dynamic and essentially truthful movie about the war in Korea.

The Hook

Credits: 1963. Perlberg-Seaton Productions. *Distributed by* MGM. *Directed by* George Seaton. *Produced by* William Perlberg. *Screen Play by* Henry Denker. *Based upon the Novel* L'Hamecon *by* Vahe Katcha. *Music Composed and Played by* Larry Adler. *Director of Photography*: Joseph Ruttenberg, A.S.C. *Film Editor*: Robert J. Kern, Jr. *Art Direction*: George W. Davis and Hans Peters. *Set Decoration*: Henry Grace and Keogh Gleason. *Assistant Director*: Donald Roberts. *Make-Up by* William Tuttle. *Recording Supervisor*: Franklin Milton. Not Rated. Black and White. Panavision (2.35:1). 98 minutes. Released in February, 1963. Partially filmed on and around Catalina Island, Cal-

ifornia. Not currently available on commercial home video.

Cast: Sergeant P. J. Briscoe, Kirk Douglas; *Private O. A. Dennison*, Robert Walker (Jr.); *Private V. R. Hackett*, Nick Adams; *Kim, the Prisoner*, Enrique Magalona; *Captain Van Ryn*, Nehemiah Persoff; *Lieutenant D. D. Troy*, Mark Miller; *Steward*, John Bleifer; with Frank Richards, Barnaby Hale, John Alderson and Anders Andelius.

Historical Accuracy Level: Low. This movie raises a moral question rather than telling a realistic or authentic Korean War story.

Patriotic Propaganda Level: Low. The soldiers depicted in this story are not the types used to promote recruitment in the Army, and their ethics are highly questionable.

Elements: Army, Cease-Fire, Infighting, Prisoners of War, Racism.

Made a decade after the end of the Korean War, *The Hook* is an examination of the morals of war as they apply to a North Korean prisoner in the hands of three American soldiers. To its credit, the film tackles issues of conscience which are largely absent from films in the war genre; unfortunately, the film is oppressively didactic, telegraphing its noble intent from the very beginning and rarely allowing the human drama of the situation to overcome its admittedly admirable message.

The Hook begins with four Army soldiers loading drums of fuel onto a freighter ship. Their task is interrupted by a North Korean bomber which, though smoking from the tail, is still operative. The bomber destroys a truck loaded with fuel, killing Lieutenant Troy (Mark Miller), before its fliers parachute out of the burning plane which then crashes into a nearby hill. One of the North Korean fliers survives his fall and is pulled ashore by Private Dennison (Robert Walker). Sergeant P. J. Briscoe (Kirk Douglas) and Private Hackett (Nick Adams) set fire to the remaining American equipment on the beach and board the freighter, reluctantly bringing the North Korean flier (Enrique Magalona), who is now their prisoner, with them.

The freighter's skipper, Captain Van Ryn (Nehemiah Persoff), assigns to Briscoe responsibility for the prisoner. At sea, Briscoe radios for orders and is told to deliver the fuel as quickly as possible. He is told by a South Korean major that

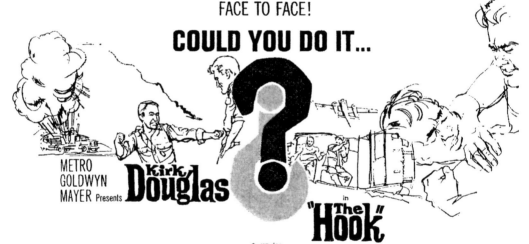

IT IS ONE THING
TO DROP A BOMB AND KILL
AN IMPERSONAL ENEMY
YOU WILL NEVER SEE.
IT IS QUITE
ANOTHER THING
TO KILL A MAN,
A HUMAN BEING,
FACE TO FACE!

COULD YOU DO IT...

METRO GOLDWYN MAYER Presents **Kirk Douglas** in "The" **Hook**

Co-starring

Adams Nick · **Walker** Robert

NEHEMIAH **PERSOFF** ENRIQUE **MAGALONA**

Screen Play by HENRY DENKER   Based on the novel *L Hameçon* by VAHÉ KATCHA   Directed by GEORGE SEATON   Produced by WILLIAM PERLBERG   MGM
in **PANAVISION**

THEATRE

The central ethical question of MGM's drama The Hook (1963) *is posed on this poster. Other posters for the film also used the ?/ hook symbol, but referred to the plot obliquely, leaving its question, story and meaning in doubt.*

the U.N. headquarters has been extensively damaged in an air raid which also destroyed a hospital and a school. Korean civilians have rioted and killed the North Korean prisoners who were held at the headquarters; Briscoe is instructed to kill his prisoner, saving the civilians the trouble.

Briscoe agrees with the order, but Captain Van Ryn is not sure that Briscoe can follow it. He arranges for a lavish dinner for the Americans and their prisoner and reminds them that differences between people do not have to lead to bloodshed. After dinner, Briscoe and Dennison, who is against killing the prisoner, argue about the humanity of the Korean people. Briscoe works himself into a frenzy of anger and shoots the "gook," wounding, but not killing him. Briscoe then orders Dennison, the principled private, to do the deed, ostensibly to toughen the young man who Briscoe considers "soft," but Dennison refuses. Using a Korean/English dictionary, Dennison attempts to establish some communication with the prisoner, but only learns the man's name, Kim.

Killing Kim then becomes Private Hackett's assignment, but Dennison persuades Hackett that killing an unarmed prisoner is inhumane. Hackett has been Briscoe's personal attendant since the sergeant helped him out of trouble once before, but Dennison convinces Hackett that Briscoe's control over him is also unnecessary. Briscoe supplies Hackett with bourbon, hoping to trigger Hackett's rage, but Hackett pursues Briscoe with the gun instead of killing the prisoner. Late at night, Dennison and Hackett agree to put the prisoner on a lifeboat and set him free; their plan is interrupted by Briscoe, who is then forced to rescue both Dennison and the prisoner from the sea.

Briscoe finds himself unable to kill Kim either, and so radios headquarters to surrender himself for failing to follow a direct order. To his surprise, he learns that the armistice has been signed and the war is over. Meanwhile, the prisoner escapes into the cargo hold and attempts to sabotage the ship. The three Americans follow the prisoner, trying to communicate to him that he is free because the war has ended. Kim corners Briscoe with a razor and yells something in Korean. Convinced that Kim is about to attack, Briscoe jumps him and wrestles the razor away from the North Korean, killing him in the fight. Dennison tells Briscoe that Kim was yelling "I can't! I can't!" and, like the three Americans, was not able to kill his enemies face to face. Kim is buried at sea and the ship sails on.

The Hook attempts to explore the depths of inhumanity on a very personal level. There is no doubt that Kim is responsible for the death of Lieutenant Troy, and the message received from the South Korean major is quite clear in its demand that Kim be eliminated. Briscoe accepts the order calmly, perceiving its sense and justice. But when the time comes to actually kill the man — to point a gun at a silent, staring, suffering human being and pull the trigger — even nineteen-year veteran Briscoe finds the task not only distasteful but impossible to countenance. The story's rather obvious messages are that compassion and humanity can and should guide one's behavior, even during time of war, and that every human life, even that of one's enemy, has a nobility and right to exist when not engaged in the activities of war.

These points are made pointedly by Private Dennison, who saves Kim's life on the beach, deflects Briscoe's first shot, and actively tries to set Kim free on a lifeboat, thereby endangering himself. It is Dennison who discovers the photo of Kim's family, rendering the prisoner more human to his captors, and who repeatedly tries, albeit unsuccessfully, to communicate with the foreign flier. Dennison is the conscience of the American group and the film. He cannot stand by, quiet and unconcerned, as Briscoe orders and carries out Kim's execution; his own education and morals (for which Briscoe taunts him) force him to at least speak out against an action he considers morally wrong.

Dennison's stand against Briscoe also results in Hackett's eventual rebellion against the sergeant. As Briscoe's lackey, Hackett occupies a comfortable and protected niche in the Army, but only at the expense of his own personality and freedom. Dennison persuades Hackett to once again become his own man, which almost leads to Briscoe's murder. Yet the three professional soldiers continue to work together, and this is seen in the climactic search for Kim in the cargo hold. And at film's end, on deck after Kim's burial at sea, the three men, now fully-formed individual personalities, gravitate toward each other at the ship's railing. Despite their differences, they still feel an affinity for each other — for their own kind.

The film's messages are delivered with little ambiguity or subtlety, which may be appropriate in time of war, but which diffuses their effectiveness on screen. Despite some noteworthy widescreen cinematography and solid acting from its players, the film is too often preachy and monotonous. When Briscoe only wounds the prisoner, it is obvious that he will not be able to kill the man, and neither will anybody else. Only the film's dramatic conclusion, when

Dennison (Robert Walker, Jr., right) tries to prevent Sergeant P.J. Briscoe (Kirk Douglas, left) from shooting their North Korean prisoner in The Hook *(1963).*

Kim escapes into the cargo hold, contains any suspense, and even that is oddly undermined when Kim is rather easily killed by Briscoe in hand-to-hand combat. That ending is supposed to be ironic, but it only makes one wonder why Briscoe couldn't have shot straight an hour earlier.

The main reason to watch *The Hook* is its acting. Kirk Douglas is, as always, bright and intense in his role, and Robert Walker, Jr. (son of the late Robert Walker and Jennifer Jones) is excellent in his film debut. Nick Adams is properly weasel-like as Hackett and Nehemiah Persoff is cunningly noble as Captain Van Ryn. Perhaps the best performance is given by Enrique Magalona as Kim, the North Korean prisoner. Magalona was a very popular actor in the Philippines, with over seventy movie roles to his credit, when he was signed for *The Hook*. Magalona provides Kim with quiet, stoic humanity, refusing to show fear in the face of death, and

trying to communicate through his eyes. He only made one other English language film, *A Yank in Vietnam*, released in 1964.

Critics were not particularly kind to *The Hook. Newsweek* liked the acting but deemed that "The sentimentality of the script is insurmountable." Arthur Knight in *Saturday Review* was slightly more favorable: "Well acted, reasonably dramatic, and unflinchingly high-principled, *The Hook* speaks for humanity, which is no small thing in the context of today's movies. The only trouble is, it speaks a little too much." Bosley Crowther of the *New York Times* concluded that "An issue of such doubtful occurrence and so little urgency is labored to death."

While most other war films are content to stage battlefield heroics, *The Hook* goes further and examines the very nature of killing. Its very storyline is a moral question with which its characters grapple for the length of the film. It deserves some respect for its novel approach and sturdy craftsmanship. Ultimately, however, *The Hook* settles for familiar attitudes and platitudes regarding humanity, thereby diluting its effectiveness.

The Hunters

Credits: 1958. 20th Century-Fox. *Produced and directed by* Dick Powell. *Screenplay by* Wendell Mayes. *Based on the Novel by* James Salter. *Music*: Paul Sawtell. *Director of Photography*: Charles G. Clarke, A.S.C. *Film Editor*: Stuart Gilmore, A.C.E. *Art Direction*: Lyle R. Wheeler and Maurice Ransford. *Set Decorations*: Walter M. Scott and Bertram C. Granger. *Executive Wardrobe Designer*: Charles LeMaire. *Makeup by* Ben Nye, S.M.A. *Hairstyles by* Helen Turpin, C.M.S. *Aerial Photography by* Tom Tutwiler, A.S.C. *Second Unit Direction by* James C. Havens. *Assistant Director*: Ad Schaumer. *Technical Advisers*: Major Robert E. Wayne, U.S.A.F. and Captain Vernon L. Wright, U.S.A.F. *Sound*: E. Clayton Ward and Harry M. Leonard. *Special Photographic Effects*: L. B. Abbott, A.S.C. 20th Century-Fox wishes to thank the Department of Defense and the United States Air Force for their assistance in the production of this motion picture. *Color Consultant*: Leonard Doss. *CinemaScope Lenses provided by* Bausch and Lomb. Not Rated. Color by De Luxe. CinemaScope (2.35:1). 108 minutes. Released in August, 1958. Currently available on VHS home video.

Cast: *Major Cleve Saville*, Robert Mitchum; *Lieutenant Ed Pell*, Robert Wagner; *Colonel "Dutch" Imil*, Richard Egan; *Kristina Abbott*, May Britt; *Lieutenant Carl Abbott*, Lee Philips; *Lieutenant Corona*, John Gabriel; *Colonel Moncavage*, Stacy Harris; *Korean Farmer*, Victor Sen Yung; *Korean Child*, Candace Lee; *Casey Jones*, Leon Lontoc; *Sergeant*, John Doucette; *Korean Bartender*, Vinnie De Carlo; *Captain Owynby*, Larry Thor; *Gifford*, Ralph Manza; *Japanese Clerk*, Nobu McCarthy; *WAF Lieutenant*, Nina Shipman; *Mrs. Mason*, Alena Murray; *Major Dark*, Jay Jostyn; *Jackson*, Robert Reed; *Greek Sergeant*, Jimmy Baya; *with* John Caler, Bob Olen, Mae Maeshire, Frank Kumagai, Chiyoko Tota Baker, Kam Tong, Rachel Stephens, Mary Song, James Yagi, Whamok Kim, Mabel Lim and Frank Tang.

Historical Accuracy Level: Medium. Its Air Force action and atmosphere seem quite authentic, but the personal stories of its pilots are unconvincing.

Patriotic Propaganda Level: High. These jet jockeys represent the ultimate individual freedom and responsibility available to a pilot during wartime.

Elements: Air Force, Air War, Behind Enemy Lines, Infighting, Japan, Lonely Wives, Romantic Triangle, United Nations Forces.

Five years after the end of the Korean conflict, 20th Century-Fox released its big-budget version of the air war, *The Hunters*. Based on a well-received novel by James Salter, produced and directed by film star Dick Powell and featuring some high-powered talent, the film was the second highest-profile film of its time to chronicle the air war. Only *The Bridges at Toko-Ri* had a more distinguished pedigree. Like its predecessor, *The Hunters* features top-flight, exciting aerial scenes which maintain a high level of audience interest. The dramatics on the ground tend toward the Ross Hunter style of glossy soap opera, however, and prevent the film from becoming a major triumph.

In 1952 Japan, Air Force pilot Major Cleve Saville (Robert Mitchum) reports for assignment in Korea. He is introduced to Lieutenant Carl Abbott (Lee Philips), with whom he will be flying. Abbott is drinking heavily and passes out in a taxi before Saville can deliver him to a dinner date. That date is Kristina (May Britt), a Norwegian blonde who enlists Saville's help to get Abbott to her home. Saville takes an instant liking to Kristina, but brakes his feelings when he discovers that Kristina is Mrs. Carl Abbott.

In Korea, Saville and Abbott report to Colonel "Dutch" Imil (Richard Egan), who knew and flew with Saville during World War II. Imil is glad to see his friend, and makes sure that Saville realizes the situation. "Anybody tell you it's a stinking war?" he asks. Saville replies, "Nobody but everybody." Imil outlines the war's rules — that American jets cannot cross the Yalu River into Chinese airspace, but Chinese MiGs are free to attack whenever and wherever they please — and sends Saville into the air for a check run in an F-86 Sabre jet. Imil assigns his second

The poster artwork for 20th Century–Fox's adventure drama The Hunters *(1958) is dominated by vapor trails and drawn arrows which suggest flight. This CinemaScope production, directed by Dick Powell, was a major undertaking five years after the end of the Korean conflict.*

in command, Colonel Moncavage (Stacy Harris), to "bounce" Saville; that is, to act as a hostile enemy, surprise Saville, and engage him in a chase. Warned of Moncavage's assignment by wingman Lieutenant Corona (John Gabriel), Saville is prepared and able to evade Moncavage and actually switch positions in mid-air. Saville remains glued onto Moncavage's tail until ordered to break away.

Saville meets Kristina while in Japan on leave and they have lunch. Saville learns that Abbott does not pay much attention to his beautiful wife, and despite a reluctance to become involved with another pilot's wife, he kisses Kristina and tells her that he is falling in love with her. Kristina responds, feeling the same way, but asks Saville to protect her husband, whom she still loves. Saville leaves before anything sexual happens, and sees Abbott arrive as he is leaving. Abbott and Kristina talk and make some progress toward repairing their fractured relationship.

After a brief indoctrination period, Saville is awarded a flight command comprised of himself, Corona, Abbott and hot dog pilot Ed Pell (Robert Wagner), who speaks largely in jive terms. On their first flight together, Pell dives in front of Saville and destroys a MiG, leaving Pell's wingman, Corona, vulnerable. Corona's plane is hit and eventually crashes upon returning to the airfield, killing the young pilot. Saville and Abbott both place the blame for Corona's death on Pell, but Imil likes Pell's enthusiasm and flying ability, and forces Saville to promote the hot dog to "element leader." When he sees Pell later, Saville slugs him and warns him to fly properly or face the consequences.

A flying montage takes place, and Pell and Saville are seen accumulating MiG kills. With fifteen kills between them, they are to be decorated as aces (having accumulated five kills or more) in Japan. Saville visits Kristina, taking her sailing and shopping. He kisses her but cannot allow himself to take sexual advantage of her, though she seems willing to accept his advances. They decide that their love is "out of time, out of place" and reluctantly draw away from each other.

Back in Korea, Abbott informs Saville that ace Chinese MiG pilot "Casey Jones" (Leon Lontoc) is back in action and has killed Colonel Moncavage. Abbott, a confessed coward, asks Saville for a chance to duel Casey Jones to prove his manhood, but Saville refuses. Then Abbott offers him his wife as a trade for the favor of facing Casey Jones and Saville slaps him. A mission to provide air cover for parachuting food and supplies to trapped soldiers brings the fliers in contact with the Chinese MiGs. Saville shoots down one MiG while Casey Jones nails Abbott's jet. Abbott parachutes safely to ground and Saville battles Casey Jones, flying low over the terrain and high into the sky before destroying the MiG ace. Saville notes where Abbott lands and belly lands his Sabre Jet nearby. He finds Abbott hanging from a tree, bleeding from an abdominal wound. Saville carries Abbott away as hostile North Korean troops pursue them. The Communists are strafed by Ed Pell, who parachutes out of his jet as it runs out of fuel and joins his friends.

Five days later, the trio of fliers is still missing and Kristina is told by an Air Force official that their chances for survival are slim. Meanwhile, behind enemy lines, Saville, Pell and Abbott hide in caves away from the rain and enemy soldiers. Saville and Pell find and kill two enemy soldiers, which provides them with dry clothes and some hot food. They carry Abbott on a stretcher to the Imjin Baptist mission, where they rest. A Korean family finds and helps them, cooking fresh meals for the exhausted men. Enemy soldiers see the smoke and attack, killing the Korean family as the hiding Americans watch, horrified and angry. Saville and Pell use "potato masher" grenades to stop the soldiers' truck as it leaves and Pell massacres the Communists with a machine gun as Saville is shot in the arm.

Abbott is loaded onto a rickshaw wagon pulled by Ed Pell and the injured Saville, and the trio of men again walk toward friendly lines. After hours of exhausting travel, they are finally greeted by a Greek patrol. In a Japanese hospital weeks later, Abbott tells Kristina that he is to be sent home to America, and that "I remember how it was and I want it to be that way again." She agrees to accompany him and to try again. Imil visits Saville and apologizes to him, saying, "Maybe a man is never what you think he is. Maybe he isn't even what *he* thinks he is." And Kristina says goodbye to Saville, who is actively looking forward to rejoining the fight in Korea.

The Hunters combines Korean War aerial drama — in beautiful De Luxe color and widescreen CinemaScope photography — with more turgid human drama on the ground involving sexual desire and fears of inadequacy. Taking its lead from the novel, Wendell Mayes' screenplay does not downplay the potent sexual symbolism of the Sabre jets and their pilots. Saville and Pell, with their good looks, fast jets and ascending record of enemy kills, are as virile as can be. Carl Abbott, however, is inadequate both sexually and militarily; his wife is unsatisfied and he has yet to shoot down an enemy plane. Abbott becomes so desperate that he offers to trade Saville rights to his wife for the opportunity of proving himself a man in battle. Such heavy-handed dramaturgy serves to make the characters symbolic and certainly diminishes the film's ultimate effectiveness.

Yet the love story also serves to characterize Cleve Saville as a man of principle. Despite his lust for Kristina, Saville allows himself only a few kisses. The civilized rules of conduct with married women do not favor him, but he follows them out of principle and becomes her friend rather than her lover. And solely because of his feelings for her, Saville does protect Carl Abbott, even to the extent of sacrificing his jet and possibly his life to save the man. There is a nobility to the character of Cleve Saville, and it is to the credit of Robert Mitchum that Saville's nobility never becomes sanctimonious.

Mitchum was persuaded to accept the role by Dick Powell and an incomplete treatment of the script. In an oft-repeated quote to Roderick Mann in London's *Sunday Express* in 1978, Mitchum tells how he was "tricked" into the part. "I never take much notice of scripts. Dick Powell once sent me thirty pages of a script, saying how good it was. And it seemed fine to me.

Hot-shot pilot Lieutenant Ed Pell (Robert Wagner, left) amuses fellow jet jockey Lieutenant Corona (John Gabriel, center), but not squadron leader Major Cleve Saville (Robert Mitchum, right) in The Hunters *(1958).*

I got to fly a fighter plane and spend a lot of time in the Officer's Club in Japan. Then he sent me page thirty-one. And I found out my plane crashed and I spent the rest of the film carrying some fellow on my back." Powell had also planned location filming in Japan, but budgetary constraints kept the production on the 20th Century-Fox ranch in California.

On the ground, the film often seems labored. Besides the turgid love triangle, there is Ed Pell's brash character; he arrives on the scene as if from a sock hop. The other pilots are confident and low-key about their abilities. Not Pell. "I'm hot! I'm on fire!" he exclaims to Saville, adding that everything is "George." It is true that Pell's energetic boorishness does enliven the proceedings, but it does so intrusively at times. By the end of the film, of course, Pell has learned how to control his emotions and the value of protecting one's fellow fliers. He follows Saville's lead in protecting Carl Abbott and rather foolishly joins them behind enemy lines. As portrayed by Robert Wagner, Ed Pell comes of age in Korea and finally accepts adult values.

In the air, the film's production is solid. Even the critics who ridiculed its drama lauded its flying scenes as realistic and exciting. The aerial photography, supervised by Tom Tutwiler, is well done in the *Top Gun* fashion, though it is not as frenetic. One can usually tell the F-86 Sabre jets from the Russian-built MiGs, even though the MiGs are actually reconfigured F-84 Sabres, painted in Communist colors. The editing of the aerial scenes is crisp and quick and enough dialogue is provided to keep the action concise. There are three aerial sequences (plus the montage), and they all feature dogfights rather than the more standard Korean War tactic of bombing. Sabre jets are fighters, and the movie (and source novel) utilizes the more masculine and heroic action of air-to-air combat rather than the more passive and less exciting action of bombing for its drama.

Only a few Korean War films actively depicted the sky battles in "MiG Alley," and *The Hunters* does so with better aesthetics and greater excitement than *Sabre Jet* or *The McConnell Story*. Until the advent of *Top Gun* and its imitators, *The Hunters* remained the premier jet air-to-air combat film in terms of its aerial proficiency.

The final half-hour of the film occurs on the ground behind enemy lines, as Saville and Ed Pell attempt to transport the wounded Carl Abbott back to friendly territory. This section of the movie, which Robert Mitchum found so tedious to make, is altogether different from what transpired before, but well-made in its own right. The trio of fliers are in desperate straits, hiding in a cave from the rain and the searching enemy soldiers, and then watching helplessly as a kindly Korean family is murdered for aiding them. This final act of the film delineates the nature of the enemy with cold, hard realism and nicely balances the respect that MiG pilot Casey Jones previously earned.

The Hunters does not spend much time with the philosophies of the war. Early on, Carl Abbott calls it "a lousy war" twice and Dutch Imil terms it "a stinking war," and Saville has one speech which encapsulates the public's apathy about it. "The war has a bigger meaning. The only trouble is it came along too soon after the real big one. It's hard to sell anybody on it." The men obviously don't care for their war, but every Air Force pilot and officer does his job to the utmost of his ability. The film does not flinch from portraying the fliers as arrogant juvenile delinquents (Ed Pell), cowardly, impotent wiseacres (Carl Abbott) or jaded hardcases (Dutch Imil), but in each and every case, the flawed men who fight for freedom do so willingly and without fail.

While not acclaimed, many critics enjoyed *The Hunters*. Moira Walsh of *America* commented, "It is almost axiomatic that a film about aerial warfare will be more impressive when it is in the air than when it settles back to earth. This one, which concerns jet fighter pilots during the Korean War, is no exception. Nevertheless, it is well worth seeing." Howard H. Thompson of the *New York Times* asked, "How are the aerial combat scenes? Dandy — all they should be. On the ground, this 20th Century-Fox release is okay — but no more." In his book *War Movies*, Brock Garland judges the film to be "An entertaining movie whenever the camera focuses on the action, but the lukewarm performances of [May] Britt and [Robert] Wagner and the trite romantic subplot keep it from being a great one."

The film's negative reviews even mentioned

its aerial proficiency. *Newsweek* felt that the movie was "a dud," but praised its action scenes. "The distinction of *The Hunters*, which tries to focus on the speedy figures cut by our jet set during the Korean conflict, lies in some stirring sequences of aerial battle." And *Time*, while deriding the drama as "knackwurst," wrote that director Powell "would have been even smarter to hire some tanker planes and never bring the jets down at all."

Even with its flaws, the movie was popular with the public, though not to the extent that *The Bridges at Toko-Ri* had been. It was Dick Powell's biggest success as a director and set the standard for aerial footage for decades to come. And though the film sidesteps taking a real, substantive stand on the political issues that it raises regarding the war, it is an exciting adventure when it remains in the skies above Korea. According to Stephen Pendo in his book *Aviation in the Cinema*, "the real flying was done by ten crack fighter squadrons at Luke Field, Arizona." As often happens in films about flying machines, the real stars of the movie are not the actors, but those flying machines. That is certainly the case with *The Hunters*.

I Want You

Credits: 1951. Samuel Goldwyn. *Distributed by* RKO Pictures. *Directed by* Mark Robson. *Produced by* Samuel Goldwyn. *Screenplay by* Irwin Shaw. *Based on Stories in* The New Yorker *by* Edward Newhouse. *Music by* Leigh Harline. *Director of Photography*: Harry Stradling, A.S.C. *Film Editor*: Daniel Mandell, A.C.E. *Art Director*: Richard Day. *Costumes*: Mary Wills. *Assistant Director*: Ivan Volkman. *Set Decoration*: Howard Bristol. *Makeup*: Pat McNalley. *Hair Stylist*: Marie Walter. *Sound Recorder*: Fred Lau. Not Rated. Black and White. Flat (1.33:1). 102 minutes. Released in December, 1951. Currently available on VHS videotape.

Cast: *Martin Greer*, Dana Andrews; *Nancy Greer*, Dorothy McGuire; *Jack Greer*, Farley Granger; *Carrie Turner*, Peggy Dow; *Thomas Greer*, Robert Keith; *Sarah Greer*, Mildred Dunnock; *Judge Jonathan Turner*, Ray Collins; *George Kress, Jr.*, Martin Milner; *Harvey Lan-*

drum, Jim Backus; *Mrs. Celia Turner*, Marjorie Crossland; *George Kress, Sr.*, Walter Baldwin; *Ned Iversen*, Walter Sande; *Gladys*, Peggy Maley; *Anne Greer*, Jerrilyn Flannery; *Tony Greer*, Erik Nielsen; *Gloria*, Ann Robin; *Caroline Krupka*, Carol Savage; *Train Porter*, James Adamson; *Art Stacey*, Harry Lauter; *Bartender*, Frank Sully; *Porter*, Robert Johnson; *Taxi Driver*, David McMahon; *Girl*, Melodi Lowell; *Soldier*, Jimmy Ogg; *Secretary*, Jean Andren; *Mr. Jones*, Charles Marsh; *Another Candidate*, Don Hayden; *Woman*, Dee Carroll; *Fat Boy*, Lee Turnbull; *Albert*, Ralph Brooks; *Sergeant*, Roland Morris; *Man*, Al Murphy; *Extra*, Paul Smith.

Historical Accuracy Level: Medium. The story is non-specific regarding the war, but is a balanced, fairly honest glimpse of an American town affected by the war.

Patriotic Propaganda Level: High. Despite its balance, the film most certainly promotes patriotism during the war, urging America's young men to enlist and fight.

Elements: Army, Homefront, Multiple Wars, Red Menace, Romance.

I Want You was producer Samuel Goldwyn's ambitious follow-up to his Oscar-winning success *The Best Years of Our Lives* of five years earlier. Goldwyn assembled an impressive, attractive cast, hired scribe Irwin Shaw to connect various stories by Edward Newhouse which had appeared in the *New Yorker* into a coherent script, and devoted his studio's resources to crafting an intelligent, moving film about the effect of the Korean War on everyday American citizens. He was moderately successful, though not to the extent that he wished, and public indifference has, over the years, veiled *I Want You* in relative obscurity.

The story centers on the Greer family who reside in an unnamed American city of thirty thousand people in the year 1950. The family patriarch is Thomas Greer (Robert Keith), a World War I veteran who has developed a successful construction company with the help of his adult son, engineer Martin (Dana Andrews). Martin, who saw service in World War II, and his wife Nancy (Dorothy McGuire) have two children, a nice home and a bright future. Thomas' youngest son is Jack (Farley Granger), a young lad fresh out of high school who drives around town in a noisy hot rod and who is not

No
three
words
ever
meant
so much
to so
many
people...

"I don't care ... I don't care ...
I can't be left alone
anymore ... I love you!"

"I WANT YOU"

"My outfit's being shipped
out ... overseas ... next week.
It's my last chance to kiss
an American girl!"

from SAMUEL GOLDWYN
comes the most moving story of our day

starring

DANA ANDREWS · DOROTHY McGUIRE
FARLEY GRANGER · PEGGY DOW

with ROBERT KEITH
MILDRED DUNNOCK · RAY COLLINS
Directed by MARK ROBSON
Screenplay by IRWIN SHAW

Distributed by RKO Radio Pictures, Inc.

Love and romance are the focus of "the most moving story of our day," the homefront of America during the (unmentioned) Korean War, in RKO's drama I Want You *(1951). This is a classy advertisement compared to many other war dramas, using the three word title for two separate but equally important meanings.*

looking forward to the upcoming selective service draft. A third Greer son, Riley, was killed in action during World War II.

Jack spends his time wooing Carrie Turner (Peggy Dow) as she returns home from college, but she doesn't want to get serious with men until she's twenty-five. Carrie's father, known as the Judge (Ray Collins), is the chairman of the town's draft committee and doesn't approve of his daughter's relationship with the hot-rodder. Greer and Sons is awaiting a big contract that will ensure the firm's continued growth, and employee George Kress (Walter Baldwin) asks Martin to write a letter to the draft board on behalf of his son, George Jr. (Martin Milner), asking for a deferment. Martin considers the request but refuses, later taking the same stance when his brother Jack is called to duty.

George Kress, Jr. is about to leave for Army basic training, so Martin offers to buy him a beer. George is refused because he is still a minor, and he is teased about it at the bar. Just then, however, a radio news broadcast announces that American troops will be shipped to South Korea to fight the invading North Korean army. Realizing that George Jr. will now be entering a real war, the bartender serves the young man.

Jack also prepares to join the army, though he believes that Carrie's father has railroaded him into service to keep him away from Carrie. In basic training, George Jr. finds Jack and they unsuccessfully attempt to find George Jr. some "romance" before he is shipped overseas. Martin is visited by his former squadron commander Harvey Landrum (Jim Backus), who tells Martin that he has decided to re-enlist and that he would like Martin to join him; that he has, in fact, officially requested Martin for his runway-building outfit. After some soul searching, Martin agrees, over Nancy's objections. And George Jr. is reported missing in action.

As both of her remaining boys prepare for war, Sarah Greer (Mildred Dunnock) finally expresses her anger, knocking all of her husband's displayed World War I memorabilia to the floor and castigating him for instilling a patriotic fervor in their sons even though he has always lied about his own military history, having served as a general's aide in Paris and never hearing a shot. Thomas admits his charade to Martin, who understands and confesses that he has known for years. Martin leaves and Jack returns to town, on leave, to marry Carrie Turner and enjoy a quick honeymoon. The Greer family carries on, although temporarily without two of its men.

I Want You is an earnest attempt at capturing the disruption of the American way of life by the prospect of yet another international conflict. From its very first shots, it makes the persuasive case that the characters (and thus, the audience) must look beyond their town's borders to the big picture, and must take the necessary steps to ensure that the orderly, peaceful life they know and cherish is not threatened. Those first shots are aerial shots of the town, which Dana Andrews describes in a voice-over: "This is how it might look to a bird, or to a bomber pilot straightening out for his run over the target…" Right from the start, the comfortable, middle-class American way of life is viewed as precarious, depending on a strong civil commitment from its citizens that includes active support of military defense.

I Want You strongly supports United Nations military intervention in Korea with the goal of stopping Communist aggression as quickly and thoroughly as possible. Several Korean War films feature characters — usually soldiers already in the fight — who actively question what they are doing halfway around the world from their homes, but the point of this film is that battle is unavoidable. Harvey Landrum replies to Martin Greer's question of whether the fight will do any good this way: "Who knows, I hope so. But if they know we have planes all over the world ready to hit them at a moment's notice, they'll think twice, or three times, or a dozen times before hitting us. Maybe they'll never do it. And I know we won't start anything. It isn't peace exactly — I don't know what you'd call it — but I must say I prefer it to war."

The film occasionally uses frightening verbal images (some said paranoid visions) to enforce its points to susceptible audience members. When Jack is called in front of the draft board, Judge Turner asks him three seemingly innocuous questions: if he did not like his job, would he quit; does he have a picture hanging in his room; and has he recently been awakened in the middle of the night and been frightened?

Jack answers "No, why should I be?" Judge Turner explains his questions: "You shouldn't and you weren't. But there are places in the world where you might have been. Places where, if there'd been a knock on your door at night, your mother might not see you for the next ten years, and never known the reason why. Places where you might be expected to hang someone's portrait in your room, and not necessarily someone you liked. And if you grew tired of your job, you might have to ask your boss if you could quit. Would you like to be living in a place like that?"

In another scene, the Greer's British neighbor, Caroline Krupka (Carol Savage) describes to the Greer's young boy (who is playing with a model B-17 bomber) how she and her family were bombed in London and buried underneath rubble for days. The boy doesn't comprehend her pain, but it is obvious that Caroline Krupka is still grieving for the loss of her family and in some ways still feels guilty about being the only member of her family to survive. While it is undeniable that these kinds of scenes are meant to stir emotions and find support for the film's political and moral stances, it must also be noted that they are, for the most part, skillfully woven into the story above the level of basic propaganda.

Though the basic story is set during the Korean War, it is really about men going to war in general. The film does not make moral or political distinctions between World War I, II or the Korean situation. A war is a war, and men have to go. The crux of the story revolves around their willingness to do so.

This is best exemplified by George Kress's efforts to keep his son, George Jr., out of the

Jack Greer (Farley Granger, center) is drafted to fight in Korea in I Want You *(1951) and his family sends him off with the usual mixture of pride, love and sorrow. Left to right, Dana Andrews, Dorothy McGuire, Peggy Dow, Farley Granger, Mildred Dunnock and Robert Keith.*

army. Unwilling to lose his only son, Kress swallows his pride and asks Martin Greer to term the boy "indispensable" to Greer's construction business. Martin refuses and later has to face Kress' disappointment when George Jr. enters the army and anger when the young man is declared missing in action. Martin also has the opportunity to keep his brother Jack from the same fate, and is actually asked to do so by their mother. Again, he cannot in good conscience write the letter. Finally, Martin himself decides to forego his own "indispensable" label and reenlist to help Harvey Landrum build airstrips. It is this lack of selfishness which the movie promotes, the idea of putting larger ideals ahead of one's own ambitions, at least for a short while.

The film's most obvious weakness is not its quotient of propaganda, which is present but not obtrusive, or its presentation, which is always professional, but rather its tendency to slip into soap-opera melodrama. The young lover characters, Jack and Carrie, seem to be incorporated merely to draw a younger audience to the theater, and their rocky relationship, although tastefully presented, consumes an inordinately large amount of screen time without contributing much drama. Also, near the story's end, as Martin and Jack are going off to war, there is perhaps more emotional leave-taking than necessary.

Even with this tendency and a second half that drags, *I Want You* remains an involving, thought-provoking film. One might think that it would be dominated by its male characters, but that isn't the case at all. The Greer women and Carrie Turner are as important to the story as their men, and each of these women has at least one powerful scene when they contest the ways in which their men are directing their lives. The scene in which Sarah Greer (Mildred Dunnock) determinedly rips her husband's World War I memorabilia down and denounces his false heroism has always been acknowledged as the finest in the film, but there are other very effective scenes as well, and the cast performs at a uniformly high level.

I Want You is one of the few movies about the American homefront during the Korean War. It realistically depicts the war as noise in the background of everyday life, occasionally rising to a level that cannot be ignored. The intention of the filmmakers was to force the characters to face, understand and learn to live with the effects of another war and to implore the audience to do the same. In this regard, although the film was timely and reminded many of *The Best Years of Our Lives*, the filmmakers largely failed. *I Want You* was a box office flop and was negatively reviewed in most major periodicals.

"Lord knows where it has gone, but Mr. Goldwyn's touch is simply not here. His director, Mark Robson, has heretofore exhibited some capabilities and so has his writer, Irwin Shaw. I guess the main trouble is that our vastly troubled times cannot be dealt with by ringing in the same old quickie set of platitudes. The result always seems to look, no matter how close it comes to actual problems and fears, simply like another of those staple mixtures of soapsuds and molasses." So judged Hollis Alpert in *Saturday Review*.

Newsweek decided that "Throughout the film the American scene is demeaned by being made a stereotype, and Samuel Goldwyn's latest effort suffers irremediably by it." *Time* concurred, noting, "But most of the time, *I Want You* uses its characters as puppets in an object lesson, moving too dutifully through their paces to command belief." Robert Hatch of the *New Republic* was not impressed at all. "As a nation, we discovered propaganda late in the day, but now we're shooting it into ourselves like dope fiends. We don't publish facts any more; we sell slogans. Goldwyn accordingly is doing only his patriotic duty, but I wonder if a country defends itself the better for being fed pink marshmallows until it retches."

Not everyone disliked the film. *Variety* termed it "prestige filmmaking," although its review was moderate in tone. Philip T. Hartung in *Commonweal* defended the film's approach to its material: "*I Want You* doesn't come up with pat answers to today's national and international problems, but it does say very effectively that the holiday of drifting is over, and if we prefer our kind of country and government, we've got to fight for it on all fronts wherever they are. At times *I Want You* is raw and grim in putting over its points, and at times it approaches the sentimental; but it is never just a recruiting poster for our white bearded Uncle Sam or for Sam Goldwyn's business. It is a well-made human drama to which attention must be paid."

Audiences did not heed Mr. Hartung's advice, for the movie was not successful. It did receive one Academy Award nomination, for best sound recording. As head of Goldwyn's sound department, Gordon Sawyer was named as the nominee, although the film's actual sound recorder was Fred Lau. Ultimately, the sound recording Oscar was presented to *The Great Caruso*. *I Want You* was Peggy Dow's ninth and final film. She married in 1951 and promptly retired from acting. On the other hand, Mildred Dunnock was making just her third cinematic appearance. For her fourth, *Death of a Salesman*, also released in 1951, she gathered the first of two Academy Award nominations she would receive during the decade. She lost to Kim Hunter for *A Streetcar Named Desire*.

I Want You is a time capsule of the American climate during the Korean War. As one of the few films of its time to attempt to depict how Americans at home viewed the conflict halfway around the globe, it occupies a specific niche in Hollywood history. Whether the film is an idealized, sanitized version of (admittedly white) middle-class life which tries to crudely manipulate its audience or is an honest, emotionally engrossing view of everyday Americans facing difficult choices is entirely dependent on the viewer.

Inchon

Credits: 1982. One Way Productions. *Distributed by* MGM and United Artists. *Directed by* Terencc Young. *Produced by* Mitsuharu Ishii. *Special Advisor:* Sun Myung Moon. *Associate Producer:* Matsusaburo Sakaguchi. *Screenplay by* Robin Moore and Laird Koenig. *Story by* Robin Moore and Paul Savage. *Music by* Jerry Goldsmith. *Director of Photography:* Bruce Surtees. *Supervising Film Editor:* Gene Milford. *Associate Director:* Sung Ku Lee. *Production Supervisor:* Guy Luongo. *Consulting Film Editor:* Bill Cox. *Film Editors:* John W. Holmes, A.C.E., Peter Taylor, Dallas Sunday Puett and Michael J. Sheridan. *Art Directors:* Pierluigi Basile and Shigekazu Ikuno. *Unit Production Manager:* Brad H. Aronson. *1st Assistant Director:* Gianni Cozzo. *Supervising Sound Editor:* Gordon

Daniel. *Sound Editors:* Greg Dillon, James Fritch, Ed Sandlin, Andrew Herbert and Martin Tomson. *Supervising Music Editor:* Len Engel. *Orchestrations by* Arthur Morton. *Location Production Managers:* Roberto Cocco, Young Sil Park and Minoru Kurita. *Location Managers:* Frank Ernst and Se Hyung Lee. *Production Auditor:* Robert F. Kocourek. *Production Coordinator:* Kiyotaka Ugawa. *Associate Production Manager:* Toni Ermini. *Assistants to the Producer:* Robert M. Standard, Kyung Do Park, Kayo Inoue, Takehiro Ono, Kazuhiro Horimoto and Hiroko Otsuka. *Casting Director:* Jack Baur. *Assistant Editors:* Franca Silvi and George Martin. *Production Assistants:* Sean Ferrer and Miko Brando. *Assistants to the Director:* Eva Chun and Katinka Revedin. *Script Supervisors:* Yvonne Axworthy and Francesca Roberti (2nd Unit). *Dialogue Coach:* Juliet Nissen. *Laurence Olivier's Dialogue Coach:* Robert Easton. *Military Advisor:* General Samuel Jaskilka, U.S.M.C. (Retired). *U.S. Eighth Army, Korea Liaison Officers:* Lieutenant Commander Freeman Neish (Retired) and Major Arthur Jungwirth. *ROK Armed Forces Liaison Officer:* Major Sang Don Park. *Sound Engineers:* David Hildyard and Yoji Hiyoshi. *Camera Operators:* Rick Neff, Cesare Allione, Otello Spila, Yonero Murata and Duk Chin Kim. *Still Photographers:* Akira Nakayama and Sergio Strizzi. *Unit Publicist:* Lou Dyer. *Set Decorators:* Kyoji Sasaki, Francesco Chianese and Ho Kil Kim. *Property Master:* Graham Sumner. *Optical Special Effects: Production Manager:* Dennis Hall. *Designer:* Geoff Drake. *Cameramen:* Alex Thompson, Robert Cuff and Bunzo Hyodo. *Special Effects Supervisors:* Fred Cramer and Kenneth Pepiot. *Gaffers:* Charles Holmes, Kazuo Shimomura and Jung Nam Cha. *Key Grip:* Charles Saldana. *Stunt Coordinators:* Ed Stacey and Remo de Angelis. *Arms and Weapons Specialist:* Carl F. Schmidt. *Action Vehicles Supervisor:* Woodrow McLain. *Extra Coordinator, U.S.:* Major Greg Vito Anders. *Extra Coordinator, Korea:* Do Soon Im. *Ms. Bisset's Costumes Designed by* Donfeld. *Military Wardrobe Costumer:* Jules Melillo. *Civilian Wardrobe Costumer:* Gloria Musetta. *Korean Wardrobe Costumer:* Haei Yoon Lee. *Wardrobe Accessories:* Jae Shik Pak. *Wardrobe Assistants:* Susan Moore and Maya Ryan. *Make-Up:* Gianni Morosi and Nilo Jacoponi. *Laurence Olivier's Make-Up:* Peter

Robb King. *Ms. Bisset's Make-Up*: Chuck Craft. *Hairdresser*: Giancarlo De Leonardis. *Ms. Bisset's Hair Styles*: Darby Hoppin. *Filmed with* Panavision equipment. *Post-Production Facilities*: 20th Century–Fox Film Corporation. *Re-Recorded at* 20th Century-Fox and Gomillion Sound, Inc. *Supervising Re-Recording Mixers*: Theodore Soderberg and Don McDougall. *Mixers*: Paul Wells, Douglas Williams, David Dockendorf and John Mack. *Main Title Created by* Kaleidoscope Films, Ltd. and Cinema Research Corporation. *Designed by* Michael Salisbury. *Cinematography by* William Fraker, A.S.C. One Way Productions, Inc. *wishes to express its thanks and gratitude to the following organizations for their help and support*: U.S. Department of Defense; U.S. Eighth Army, Korea; Ministry of National Defense, Korea; ROK Army, Navy and Air Force; Ministry of Culture and Information; Ministry of Government Administration; Ministry of Transportation; Ministry of Communications; Ministry of Finance; Ministry of Education; Ministry of Justice; Ministry of Home Affairs; Shilla Hotel; Hyatt Regency, Seoul; City of Seoul; City of Inchon; City of Waegwan; Motion Picture Promotion Corporation; Armed Forces Film Production, M.N.D.; War History Compilation Committee, M.N.D.; Pohang Steel Company; Korea Folk Village; Little Angels School. Rated PG. Color by DeLuxe and Technicolor. Dolby Stereo. Widescreen (1.85:1). Originally 140 minutes. Released for a limited run in May, 1981 before being re-edited. Released at 105 minutes in September, 1982. Filmed on location in Seoul and Inchon, Korea, as well as Rome, Italy and Dublin, Ireland. Not currently available on commercial home video.

Cast: *General Douglas MacArthur*, Laurence Olivier; *Barbara Hallsworth*, Jacqueline Bisset; *Major Frank Hallsworth*, Ben Gazzara; *Saito-san*, Toshiro Mifune; *Sergeant August Henderson*, Richard Roundtree; *David Feld,* * David Janssen*; *Park (The Bridegroom)*, Nam Goon Won; *Turkish Brigadier*, Gabrielle Ferzetti; *Longfellow,* * Rex Reed*; *Marguerite,* * Sabine Sun*; *Jean MacArthur*, Dorothy James; *Lim*, Karen Kahn; *Mila*, Lydia Lei; *General Almond*, James Callahan; *Pipe Journalist,* * Rion Morgan*; *General Collins*, Anthony Dawson; *Admiral*

Sherman, Peter Burton; *Lieutenant Alexander Haig*, John Pochna; *Turkish Sergeant*, William DuPree; *Ah Cheu*, Grace Chan; *Jimmy*, Nak Hoon Lee; *President Rhee*, Kwang Nam Yang; *North Korean Commissar*, Il Woong Lee; *Barbara's Driver*, Yung Hoo Lee; *Admiral Doyle*, Mickey Knox; *GHQ Officers*, Richard McNamara and Gordon Mitchell; *Admiral Lawson*, Robert Spafford; *Officer aboard Mount McKinley*, Franco Ressel; *Smallest*, Ji Sook Choe; *Small*, Joon Sook Choe; *Middle*, Hye Yun Choo; *Big*, Hyun Joo Kwak; *Biggest*, Jung Sook Hong; *Voice of President Truman*, Ed Flanders; *Stuntman*, Phil Chong.

Historical Accuracy Level: Medium. The Inchon landing did take place, but hopefully the real event was not as pretentious as this movie.

Patriotic Propaganda Level: High. This movie celebrates MacArthur's triumph, but also promotes South Korean patriotism and involvement as well.

Elements: Army, Biography, Day of the Invasion, Effects on Civilians, Females in the Field, Japan, Leaders, Marine Corps, Navy (Sailors), Orphans, Secret Missions, United Nations Forces.

Inchon is a legendary cinematic adventure, not because of any great artistry, but due to its chaotic production, ridiculous casting choices and incredible expense. There is also the matter of its "special advisor," Reverend Sun Myung Moon, whose organization paid for the production. All of these behind-the-scenes struggles would be unimportant if the film was well made, but *Inchon* is a badly written, overacted fiasco which trivializes the single most important American operation during the Korean War and manages to distort (in small ways) history along the way. *Inchon* became legendary as one of the worst films of all time even before its general release. And though it really isn't as horrible as its reputation, it is undeniably a silly, mindless movie concerning a subject that deserves much more respect than it received.

Inchon actually begins on the day of the invasion, June 25, 1950. Barbara Hallsworth (Jacqueline Bisset) is shopping for antiques in a village about ten miles south of the 38th parallel

---

*Edited out of the 105 minute version; not listed in those credits.

when the booming of artillery signals the approach of the North Korean army. Barbara, in her car, joins a stream of civilians that soon becomes a river of people running from the invaders. Russian-made North Korean tanks forge along the dirt roads with soldiers manning—and using—the machine guns on South Korean civilians. Near Inchon, Major Frank Hallsworth (Ben Gazzara) of the Marine Corps advises his mistress Lim (Karen Kahn) and her father, Saito-san (Toshiro Mifune), to leave their home and find safety elsewhere. He tells Lim that he will soon be divorcing Barbara and that he and Lim will then be together.

General MacArthur (Laurence Olivier) is briefed on the developing situation by his ever-present aide, Lieutenant Alexander Haig (John Pochna). Frank Hallsworth and his aide, Sergeant August Henderson (Richard Roundtree), travel to the front by jeep and report to MacArthur that the South Korean or ROK (Republic of Korea) troops are being slaughtered. Hallsworth and Henderson barely escape themselves as the Communist tanks advance. Barbara Hallsworth and her driver are endangered when North Korean planes strafe the refugee column; the driver is killed. Barbara drives slowly southward, alone amidst a throng of frightened civilians carrying their possessions on their backs.

Hallsworth and Henderson reluctantly provide a ride to a cute Korean girl named Mila (Lydia Lei), who is traveling to Seoul to marry. They deliver her to the train station, where her betrothed, Park (Nam Goon Wan), is waiting. Then they each search for Barbara, separately. Henderson finds Barbara near the Han River bridge, instructs her to keep moving south and gives her a revolver for protection. On the bridge, an old man stops her car long enough for five orphan children to climb inside. Reluctantly, Barbara allows them to stay as the car inches forward. A North Korean tank comes within sight of the bridge and begins shooting at it. Before the tank can cross, South Korean soldiers finish rigging the bridge with dynamite. A loudspeaker warns the people on the bridge—including newlyweds Mila and Park and Sergeant Henderson—to jump off. Then the bridge is destroyed. Barbara's car begins to slide backward into the river, but several soldiers grab it and drag it forward to safety. Following the

bridge's destruction, Mila and Park are on opposite sides of the river.

MacArthur is named supreme commander of U.N. forces and considers it a miracle that so many countries are banding together to fight Communist aggression. Park is conscripted into the *North Korean* army and forced to shoot South Koreans who refuse to cooperate. MacArthur flies over the battlefield with Frank Hallsworth and his other officers and receives the inspiration for an operation at Inchon. He sends Hallsworth to Osan for first-hand information. Hallsworth and Henderson watch as eager Marine units are ripped apart by the advancing T-34 tanks. MacArthur regrets the Osan loss of life but indicates that the North Korean forces are widespread and vulnerable. He is confident that the Pusan Perimeter will hold. On the road south to Pusan, Barbara uses the revolver to shoot a man who tries to take her car. She stops where dozens of people have been murdered and sees Mila, who collapses from exhaustion. Mila joins the orphans in Barbara's car and helps to take care of them until they reach St. Mary's Mission, where the orphans are welcomed.

A North Korean column stops to conscript a group of peasants into their army. The Communists are killed by the armed peasants, who are actually soldiers led by Hallsworth and Henderson. They recognize Park, who shoots the North Korean leader who forced Park to kill his own countrymen. Hallsworth makes Park his personal aide. MacArthur presents his plan for "Operation Chromite"—an amphibious landing at Inchon—and every single branch of his command objects. The general dismisses their objections and wins them over by the force of his personality and reputation. The officers agree to his plan, with the caveat that the operation will be cancelled if a strategic lighthouse at the channel leading to Inchon's harbor is destroyed, as its lamp will be necessary to light the treacherous pathway for the Navy ships. MacArthur agrees and assigns Hallsworth to ensure that the lighthouse lamp stays lit.

Hallsworth meets his wife Barbara at a villa; the meeting has been arranged by Henderson. Though the orphans are there with Barbara, he does not see them. They discuss the future and then sleep together. Hallsworth,

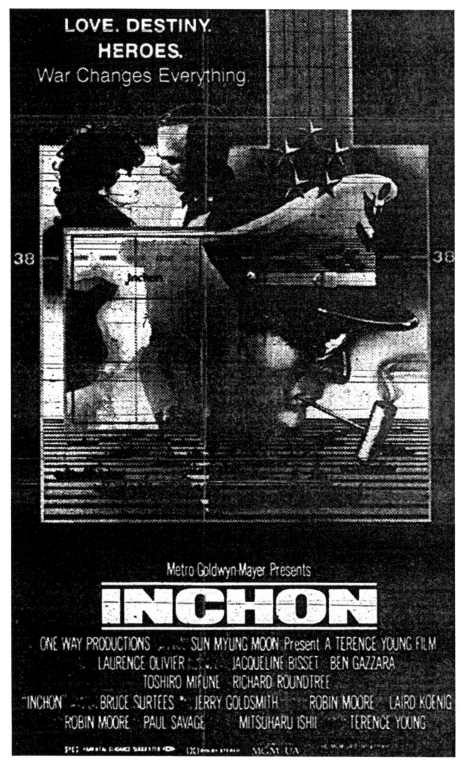

An interesting understated poster for MGM's war drama Inchon *(1982) features explanatory artwork of Korea, battleships and the visage of General Douglas MacArthur, along with stars Jacqueline Bisset and Ben Gazzara. Its tagline, "Love. Destiny. Heroes. War Changes Everything" is prattle, but at least it isn't overly intrusive.*

Henderson and Park lead a Turkish commando brigade to the lighthouse in the middle of the night as two hundred fifty Navy ships approach the channel to Inchon harbor on September 14. Frank's mistress Lim arrives with up-to-date charts of the channel, provided by her father. Then her father arrives with news that the channel has been mined. Saito-san and Hallsworth take a rubber raft into the channel and the elderly Korean connects the mines together. An enemy patrol boat approaches but sees nothing. The mines explode and the lighthouse lamp is turned on. The Navy ships begin their passage, but a North Korean guard shoots the light, once again plunging the channel into darkness. The commandos fight to control the lighthouse while MacArthur nervously awaits on board the lead ship.

Finally, MacArthur decides to cancel the operation. He recites a long resignation letter and just as he finishes, the beacon is relit. The operation steams forward and MacArthur sends reinforcements to guard the light. The Inchon landing goes as planned, with jets protecting the approach of the Marines and Army soldiers landing in transport ships. As tanks roll off transports and into the city, the North Koreans panic and run. Within hours, the city is taken. Hallsworth, still at the lighthouse, sees that Park has been killed. He was shot in the back, yet was still able to relight the lighthouse lamp before dying. Then Saito-san shows him that Lim has been killed, shot while taking part in the commando raid.

Barbara says farewell to the five orphans at an orphanage, then joins her husband at Government House in Seoul as General MacArthur presents South Korean President Syngman Rhee (Kwang Nam Young) a country over which to rule. MacArthur hugs the happy South Korean leader, then recites the Lord's Prayer as the music swells and the movie ends.

Inchon is intended as a tribute to General Douglas MacArthur and his amazing plan to turn the tide of the Korean War. Such a tribute should have made an engrossing, inspiring film, but this version of that remarkable event is prosaic, silly and dull. Director Terence Young was unable to breathe life into the pedestrian script from Robin Moore and Laird Koenig, despite a budget which continually increased with time. The movie trivializes "Operation Chromite," which is staged almost as an afterthought to the soap-opera relationship between the Hallsworths. The movie obscures history beneath the ludicrous plot point involving the lighthouse and its importance to the mission. And despite the eager participation of American and Korean military forces to chronicle this historic event, the participation of the Unification Church's leader — who was later jailed for tax evasion — cast a pall around the movie's release that could not be diffused.

The film's first mistake is to include the fictional Hallsworth couple. Their estranged relationship is badly written, even by soap opera standards. Frank and Barbara have one scene together and it seems completely devoid of any passion or affection. As Barbara, the lovely Jacqueline Bisset travels around Korea in a polka dot halter top and other designer clothes while dozens of civilians are killed or tortured around her. The juxtaposition in imagery, reportedly insisted upon by Reverend Moon, is not to her favor. Barbara is then saddled with five orphan children, which, while noble, is a blatant plea for sympathy and pathos. Their cuddliness is exaggerated to the extent that their very presence is difficult to tolerate.

Frank Hallsworth is a Marine major, yet he visits or confers with Army general MacArthur constantly. He seems to have no immediate superior officer or specific orders regarding his actions. He travels all over Korea with Sergeant Henderson, reporting from the front directly to MacArthur in two scenes, disguised as a peasant and fighting the North Korean army in another, and searching for his wife in between. He is MacArthur's only choice to lead the assault on the crucial lighthouse, and he interrupts that duty to help Saito-san explode the mines in the channel from a rubber raft. If ever a cinematic character threatened to win a war single-handedly, it is Frank Hallsworth.

Hallsworth is played with stoic blandness by Ben Gazzara, who invests the same trifling amount of emotion in scenes with his wife and mistress as he does his battle scenes. When Frank's mistress Lim is killed, his grief is expressed by merely shaking her father's hand! Centering the emotional investment of a motion picture around such a generic, boring character is a deadly mistake.

The movie's main character, however, is the larger-than-life General Douglas MacArthur, and to portray the legendary military leader, producer Mitsuharu Ishii hired legendary actor Laurence Olivier. Lord Olivier was paid $1.25 million dollars for the role and undeniably threw himself into it with abandon. He endured four hours of makeup each day, including a putty nose, false chin, toupee and even lipstick, mascara and rouge, applied because of MacArthur's reputation as a vain man. Told by Alexander Haig that MacArthur's speech patterns were similar to those of W. C. Fields, Olivier affected an accent that hints at high comedy, which is accentuated by his rolling eyes and seemingly nervous energy. And yet because Olivier does seems to take the role seriously the result is one of the strangest performances of a major historical character ever seen on film.

The film was critically drubbed, but many critics had interesting things to say about Lord Olivier. "Saddest of all is Laurence Olivier. Can this really be the greatest living actor, with his ghastly waxworks makeup, speaking in an eargrating travesty of an 'American' accent?" asked Jack Kroll of *Newsweek*. Robert Hatch of the *Nation* was more eloquent in his criticism: "His MacArthur visage looks like a papier-mache death mask, and his weak and reedy conversational voice (intended, I believe, to suggest sardonic Yankee wit) sounds like an emanation from the tomb. He displays a geriatric sprightliness that is just short of a buck and wing." But Vincent Canby of the *New York Times* enjoyed Olivier's hamminess, claiming that Oliver "provides the kind of outrageous performance that cannot be demurely described. His eyeballs roll up under heavy lids as he's conning the general staff with mock humility. When he catches a glimpse of a bust of Julius Caesar in his office, he does the sort of flinch affected by W. C. Fields on colliding with a small, disgusting child."

Whether Olivier ventured into self-parody with his portrayal of General MacArthur will be debated for years. What cannot be denied is the sheer perversity of the choice. In the annals of Hollywood's long history of miscasting actors in roles (John Wayne as Genghis Khan in *The Conqueror*, William Bendix as Babe Ruth in *The Babe Ruth Story*, etc.), Olivier as General Douglas MacArthur is near the top of the list.

The film does a much better job of depicting conditions in South Korea at the time of the invasion and the effects of that brutal onslaught on its populace. The sequences which mark the day of the invasion seem authentic, even with the inclusion of the beautiful Miss Bisset in the middle of the refugee parade. Scenes where the North Koreans murder helpless South Korean civilians are depicted regularly, and though many critics attributed their inclusion to the wishes of anti-Communist "special advisor" Sun Myung Moon, such scenes are consistent with actual history. The North Koreans killed a great many South Koreans in the first flush of battle lust and later conscripted many — as is the case with Park, the bridegroom — to serve menial functions in their army. In this respect, at least, the film sticks to the facts.

It does not, however, portray the demolition of the Han River bridge accurately. The movie dramatizes the arrival of a North Korean tank spurring the South Korean army to demolish the bridge, after it gives a brief warning to the people still on the bridge. This, unfortunately, is a blatant attempt of the producers to rewrite history. In reality, the South Korean ROK's army chief of staff, General Chae Pyong Duk, known as "Fat Chae," ordered the bridge blown as soon as he had crossed it in retreat, at 2:15 a.m. on June 28, even though there were hundreds of civilian refugees and military personnel traversing the span at the time. Though North Korean forces were still reputed to be six to eight hours away, Fat Chae, a *South Korean* general, panicked and destroyed the bridge, along with hundreds of his own people. As the episode appears in the film, it can only be interpreted as an overt attempt to rewrite history and obscure some of the shame associated with the actual event.

Although almost three months passed between the invasion and the Inchon landing, those three months are reduced to just a few minutes in the movie, which posits that MacArthur received the "divine inspiration" for the amphibious assault at Inchon very early in the war, during a reconnaissance flight. How MacArthur would know that such an operation would be necessary so soon in the fighting is never explained.

The briefing for "Operation Chromite" is

handled well and is generally accurate, except for a number of details regarding the lighthouse, the assault plan and General MacArthur's emphasis on the religious righteousness of the cause. In reality, the assault took place at dawn, negating the need to protect a lighthouse even if one was present. There was an island guarding the channel, Wolmi-do, also known as Moon Peak Island, with enemy artillery that had to be silenced before the invasion could proceed, but that was done at dawn on September 15 and no U.S. or U.N. lives were lost. The episode of Hallsworth and Saito-san removing the mines from the channel is pure Hollywood hokum. MacArthur was present on board the *Mount McKinley* that morning, confident in his plan. Though he was known to pray for guidance, MacArthur felt solely responsible for the operation. *Inchon*'s occasional scenes of MacArthur invoking spiritual help are the wish of Reverend Moon, who wanted to interject a spiritual element into the proceedings. Editorially, this seems to be the extent of Moon's direct participation in the project.

The lighthouse sequence, which delays the actual invasion until it concludes, is labored and overdone. It features the commandos dressed and madeup in black for stealth, yet Frank Hallsworth stands next to the white lighthouse in such a way that his shadow, complete with semi-automatic rifle, towers twenty feet above him and could not help but attract attention. The bridegroom, Park, seems to be the only person who knows how to operate the beacon (wouldn't the commandos have been trained for that?), but he is shot in the back after the initial lamp is destroyed. Somehow, he pulls himself up ladder rungs to the top and relights the lamp. Even so, that piece of heroism is performed offscreen! The beacon alights for the second time, the Navy's ships move forward, and only then does MacArthur order Hallsworth's commandos reinforced. This sequence, which is unquestionably weak, is rendered imbecilic by the

In perhaps the worst miscasting of his career, Sir Laurence Olivier portrays General Douglas MacArthur in the Sun Myung Moon production of Inchon *(1982). Here, MacArthur reflects upon the history of warfare, gazing at a bust of Julius Caesar with a look that speaks volumes.*

fact that it did not happen, nor could it have. The ships traversed the Flying Fish Channel in daylight!

The actual invasion seems anticlimactic and dull. The twenty or so ships seen landing a few hundred troops on the Inchon seawall are a far cry from the 230-ship fleet gathered to actually deliver some fifty thousand troops to the site. Though this sequence of the movie was filmed on location, it is also true that Inchon is not a particularly scenic location. The result is that this military operation seems routine and not very dangerous to the men advancing into harm's way. The movie does not capture — at all — the effort and skill necessary to surmount the incredible difficulties and obstacles of MacArthur's greatest achievement, "Operation Chromite."

Despite their best intentions and a reported $46-48 million worth of expenditures, making it the most expensive movie ever made to that time, producer Mitsuharu Ishii and "special advisor" Sun Myung Moon realized that their 140-minute movie was a dud. Over a period of months following a disastrous May 1981 preview run, the film was reshaped and reedited. The biggest change was to completely remove three characters and their storylines. In the original version, David Janssen played cynical reporter David Feld, who questioned American involvement in the region, and former film critic Rex Reed played an art critic named Longfellow who is sent to Korea as a war correspondent. This was Reed's second film appearance following the dreadful *Myra Breckinridge* (1970), also a "worst movie of all time" candidate. The third character to be jettisoned was Marguerite, a friend and source of David Feld's, played by Sabine Sun. The three characters are nowhere to be found in the truncated 105-minute version, and choppy editing suggests that they are missed. Sadly, David Janssen died before the shorter version was finalized, and thus does not even appear in his final film.

That *Inchon* is not very good should be obvious. Jack Kroll of *Newsweek* dubbed it "a turkey the size of Godzilla" and argued, quite convincingly, that "*Inchon* is the worst movie ever made." Roger Ebert of the *Chicago Sun-Times* declared, "This is the most lead-footed, one-dimensional, predictable, dumb, uninvolv-

ing war movie I've ever seen." Other critics followed suit, and *Inchon*'s reputation grew steadily worse. It grossed about $3 million, or roughly one-sixteenth of its budget. But *Inchon* did win some awards. It was nominated for five "Razzie" awards, denoting the worst films and performances of the year, and garnered four wins: worst picture, worst screenplay, worst director (Terence Young tied Ken Annakin for *The Pirate Movie*), and Laurence Olivier nabbed the worst actor prize. Only Ben Gazzara, nominated for worst supporting actor, lost, to Ed McMahon in *Butterfly*.

But *Inchon*'s lasting legacy is due to the participation of Reverend Sun Myung Moon and the Unification Church. Producer Mitsuharu Ishii, a Japanese newspaper tycoon, was also a devoted "Moonie," and persuaded Moon to become a movie mogul. During the production, it was thought that Ishii was the man in charge, as he arrived on the set with suitcases, from which he paid for everything in cash. Eventually it was revealed that Moon's Unification Church was providing the cash. As soon as this information became public, American and Korean military cooperation ended and both governments requested that they not be acknowledged in the credits. Reports surfaced that Moon had laced the film with pro-Unification Church sentiments and that he was going to use the film as a recruiting tool. That is perhaps the main reason why people stayed away from the film in droves, but the truth is that Moon's philosophies do not encumber the film in any significant way.

It is true that Moon is strongly anti-Communist, but so are most Americans, and the plot of the movie can hardly be attributed to Moon since it generally follows the history of the time. Moon's influence is felt in scenes when MacArthur seeks spiritual guidance for the situation in Korea, and even then, the theme is mild rather than strident. Certainly few, if any, of the other characters seek spiritual guidance. Judging from *Variety*'s review of the 140 minute version in May 1981, the original cut may have included a stronger religious slant. "A major battle of the Korean War is given a decidedly religious viewpoint," the review states, later noting "heavy emphasis on divine guidance." But the 105 minute general release from 1982 does not overly emphasize the aspect.

Inchon is definitely Hollywood hokum, through and through, and no amount of tampering from Sun Myung Moon during production or afterward was going to change that. In case anyone cares, producer Ishii appears in the final scene in military uniform, standing behind MacArthur, grinning at the camera. His dream of appearing in a big Hollywood film came true, and only the privilege cost his benefactor some $48 million.

Iron Angel

Credits: 1964. Ken Kennedy Productions. *Written and Directed by* Ken Kennedy. *Producer*: Pete Foley. *Photographed and Edited by* Murray De'Atley. *Camera Operator*: William Troiano. *Special Effects*: Harry Woolman. *Sound*: William Watson. *Script Clerk*: Hannah Scheel. *Chief Grip*: George McDonald. *Unit Manager*: Floyd J. Newton. *Property Master*: Mike Ezzes. *Title Art*: Emmett Lancaster. Not Rated. Black and White. Flat (1.33:1). 84 minutes. Released in April, 1964. Filmed on location around Phoenix, Arizona. Not currently available on commercial home video.

Cast: *Sergeant Walsh*, Jim Davis; *Reb*, Donald "Red" Barry; *Nurse Laura Fleming*, Margo Woode; *Corporal Walker*, R. Wayland Williams; *Private Drake*, Dave Barker; *Lieutenant Collins*, Joe Jenckes; *Captain*, Tris Coffin; *Buttons*, L. Q. Jones; *North Korean soldier*, John S. Hirohata.

Historical Accuracy Level: Low. While set in Korea, the film is unconcerned with any historical relationship to the war.

Patriotic Propaganda Level: Medium. Its characters are heroic, but there is no overt flag-waving or patriotism in its sparse script.

Elements: Ambulance, Army, Females in the Field, Infighting, Nurses, Racism.

In the early and middle 1960s, several low-budget independent films were made about the Korean War. *Iron Angel*, from Ken Kennedy Productions, is an obscure example of this trend. Filmed in rugged American terrain chosen to resemble Korea, these films were produced on shoestring budgets. They have somewhat familiar faces in the cast and feature rented or bor-rowed equipment and uniforms. They were often written and directed by aspiring filmmakers hoping to make their mark with a bang, so to speak. This movie was filmed in Arizona with several recognizable cast members, but it failed to spark audience interest.

In the mountains of North Korea in 1950, men of the "Crazy Fox" company are assigned to find and destroy a North Korean gunpost which overlooks a key road and is blocking the "Circus Tiger" convoy. Lieutenant Collins (Joe Jenckes) is to lead the patrol, for which he particularly includes Sergeant Walsh (Jim Davis), whom he considers cowardly for surviving a patrol in which all the other men were killed. Four other men are also chosen and they march into the hills. One of the men is the talkative Buttons (L. Q. Jones), who uses humor to hide the fear which he feels.

The squad is spotted by the North Korean machine gun nest, which fires upon the Americans. Reb (Donald "Red" Barry), a southern redneck, says sardonically, "I wish somebody would tell them gooks this is a police action. They think it's a war." Collins and Walsh attack the nest; Walsh's gun jams but Collins destroys it with a grenade, and is shot while doing so. Reb checks Walsh's rifle, which fires easily. Collins calls Walsh a coward and then dies, leaving Walsh in charge of the patrol. Walsh decides to continue the mission, hoping to meet the convoy on the road ahead.

The men find a Red Cross ambulance stranded in a creek, with an attractive nurse lying nearby, unconscious. Because she is soaking wet, she is undressed and placed under blankets (offscreen) by Walsh, despite Reb's repeated desire to do the job. Meanwhile, the men retrieve the ambulance and repair its engine. Nurse Laura Fleming (Margo Woode) awakens, dresses, argues with Walsh about his intended use of her ambulance as transport and drives away in a huff. She inadvertently drives toward enemy lines and slowly runs out of fuel. Eventually, the walking soldiers reach Fleming and the ambulance, explain the situation to her and take a break. Reb discovers a picture of Collins in the ambulance, but doesn't tell the nurse of her fiancé's fate.

Their break is interrupted by a North Korean jeep patrol. The men hide in the ambulance

IRON ANGEL

STARRING JIM DAVIS DONALD BARRY

MARGO WOODE R. Wayland WILLIAMS

Special Guest L. Q. JONES

PRODUCED BY PETE FOLEY WRITTEN & DIRECTED BY KEN KENNEDY

"Citizen soldiers—instant heroes!" is the tagline for the independent production Iron Angel *(1964), made in Arizona by Ken Kennedy Productions. The images are taken directly from the film and indicate a lack of action. The film does, however, acknowledge that it is about the Korean War with its reference "Less than a mile from the parallel…"*

and massacre the Communist patrol when they move toward Fleming, but the black soldier, Corporal Walker (R. Wayland Williams), is wounded in the leg during the firefight. While tending to Walker's leg, Fleming finds Collins' dog tag and asks Walsh about his death. Reb blames Walsh and tries to goad the sergeant into a fight. The enemy jeep provides the Americans with fuel and a map, showing that another North Korean gun emplacement is located nearby which also threatens the convoy. Walsh takes Buttons, Reb and Drake with him to eliminate the second machine gun nest, leaving Walker with Fleming in the ambulance. Walker talks to Fleming about Collins' death, blaming it on circumstance and bad luck.

In the hills, the men have trouble pinpointing the machine gunners' location. Walker tries to start the ambulance but faints, so Fleming takes over and slowly drives the ambulance along the road as a target, drawing fire from the nest. Walsh and Drake crawl forward and destroy the gun emplacement, but not before Reb is wounded in the shoulder and Buttons is blinded by a grenade and dies of his injuries. The convoy arrives, so Fleming bids goodbye to Walsh, puts Reb and Walker (who now smoke together as friends) in her ambulance, and drives toward the 101st Field Hospital. Walsh and Drake hop onto a truck and head back into action.

Iron Angel intends to be a gritty glimpse of the Korean conflict, but its character stereotypes and cliches prevent the film from achieving any level of effective drama. Sergeant Walsh is alleged to be a coward, but he is clearly not cowardly. Lieutenant Collins is a one-dimensional hard case. Buttons is the talkative comic relief, pretending to create a fine French dinner from K rations and dying bravely (and blindly) in the climactic skirmish. Reb is the southern redneck, a man of no principles and no tolerance who by the story's conclusion learns to accept a black soldier as his equal. Corporal Walker is the understanding black man and the conscience of the outfit, who is tolerant of Reb's jibes and who watches over the other men. Drake is the Bible reader, a quiet man with little personality.

Into this routine situation with stock characters is thrown nurse Laura Fleming. Her character is refreshing but not very original. An attractive brunette, she outranks every man in the patrol and follows regulations to the letter. She argues with Walsh about the value of women in the combat area and yet proves his point by refusing to allow guns in the ambulance and threatens the safety of the entire squad (and herself) when she drives away rather than bend her principles to the logic of the situation. Later, of course, when given the chance, she acquits herself with heroism and valor, slowly driving the "iron angel" through enemy fire.

The movie's only features of interest are its use of an ambulance and its placement of a woman in the field alongside the men. The ambulance is the "iron angel" of the title; it says so right on the front bumper. It is used by the Americans to travel around Korea and by the North Koreans as target practice. Placing Laura Fleming in the midst of the action perks up the men. Buttons is quite happy at the thought of having her around during the days — and nights — of their patrol, while Reb states idiotically that he thinks she is "a war follower," and likes to be near the fighting men. After their initial encounter with Fleming, however, the men's lechery quickly disappears, replaced with the feeling that she has no business being in Korea.

Fleming argues that she is a surgical nurse with special training needed in a war zone, and that hundreds of lives may depend on her efforts in Korea. Walsh has trouble getting past his macho pride, repeating that "women have no place in the combat area." Fleming leads the men into trouble with her bullheadedness, but she also helps heal those who are injured and ultimately risks her life for their survival. Over time, she becomes an accepted part of the team.

There is little that is fresh or original about *Iron Angel* and quite a bit that is old hat and repetitious. The dialogue is dull and the action is not particularly exciting. Some scenes are shot "day for night," a sure sign of production economy, and the music heard in the film is comprised of material licensed from music libraries. In fact, the film twice uses Trevor Duncan's "Grip of the Law" music, which over time has become well known as the main theme from *Plan Nine From Outer Space*, Edward D. Wood, Jr.'s grave-robbing opus, long considered one of the worst films of all time. The acting is generally bland, although L.Q. Jones and Margo

Nurse Laura Fleming (Margo Woode) attempts to drive her title ambulance to safety from behind enemy lines in Iron Angel *(1964).*

Woode make better impressions than their costars.

The issue of racism is raised, rather half-heartedly, as Reb needles Walker, calling him "night fighter" and refusing to make him coffee. Walsh's response to the situation is brief and terse. "You guys knock it off. That war is over." By movie's end, of course, all is forgiven, but only after Walker proves his heroism and selflessness to the redneck. The film is not concerned with the Korean location or enemy soldiers at all; this war could be happening anytime or anywhere. The film's only concession to Korea is to label the North Korean soldiers "gooks."

Iron Angel passed through theatres in early 1964 with little fanfare and was quickly forgotten. *Boxoffice* gave the film half-hearted praise, noting "The juvenile trade in drive-ins will find this to their liking and identify with the characters, who are among the most misshapen our Army has produced." Even with its familiar faces and familiar music, however, the movie is not very exciting and certainly not very ambitious. It rests in the lower rungs of war films, whether set in Korea or any other conflict.

Japanese War Bride

(aka *East Is East*)

Credits: 1952. Bernhard Productions. *Distributed by* 20th Century-Fox. *Directed by* King Vidor. *Produced by* Joseph Bernhard. *Co-Producer*: Anson Bond. *Screenplay by* Catherine Turney. *Story by* Anson Bond. *Music*: Emil Newman and Arthur Lange. *Photographed by* Lionel Lindon, A.S.C. *Film Editor*: Terry Morse, A.C.E. *Assistant to Producers*: Paul Guilfoyle. *Production Manager*: Percy Ikerd. *Art Director*: Danny Hall. *Comptroller*: Monte Kennedy *Sound*: Vic Appel and Ed Borschell. *Casting Director*: Maxine Marlowe. *Set Decorator*: Murray Waite. *Makeup*: Gene Hibbs. *Wardrobe*: Izzy Berne and Adele Parmenter. *Assistant Director*:

Wilbur McGaugh. Not Rated. Black and White. Flat (1.33:1). 91 minutes. Released in January, 1952. Partially filmed on location around Salinas, California. Not currently available on commercial home video.

Cast: *Tae Shimizu*, Shirley Yamaguchi; *Lieutenant Jim Sterling*, Don Taylor; *Art Sterling*, Cameron Mitchell; *Fran Sterling*, Marie Windsor; *Ed Sterling*, James Bell; *Harriet Sterling*, Louise Lorimer; *Eitaro Shimizu (Grandfather)*, Philip Ahn; *Emily Shafer*, Sybil Merritt; *Shiro Hasagawa*, Lane Nakano; *Mrs. Milly Shafer*, Kathleen Mulqueen; *Ted Sterling*, Orley Lindgren; *Woody Blacker*, George Wallace; *Emma Hasagawa*, May Takasugi; *Mr. Hasagawa*, William Yokota; *Tae's Mother*, Shizue "Susie" Matsumoto; *George Kioto*, Weaver Levy; *Man at Fish Market*, Jerry Fujikawa; *Japanese Servants*, Chieko Sato, Tetsu Komai; *Old Japanese Woman*, Hisa Chiba; *Man at Lettuce Plant*, David March.

Historical Accuracy Level: Medium. This film represents a generation of war brides brought to America; the Korean War is mere background to the story.

Patriotic Propaganda Level: Low. The movie is an indictment of American racial attitudes and takes some swipes at Japan's for good measure.

Elements: Army, Homefront, Japan, Racism, Returning Home, Romance.

After serving in World War II (and, to a lesser extent, Korea), many American soldiers brought "war brides" home — foreign-born girls whom the soldiers had courted and married while on duty overseas. As these women were mixed into America's melting pot, it was inevitable that clashes would occur over differences in customs, language, religion and appearance, and that prejudice would surface. Post–World War II movies like *Teresa* dramatized the plight of beautiful young brides trying to find happiness in America; the plainly titled *Japanese War Bride* continued that cinematic tradition into the era of the Korean War.

In the forty-five second opening sequence, Lieutenant Jim Sterling (Don Taylor) is found on a bloody Korean battlefield, the only soldier left alive after a massacre. Jim awakens in a Japanese hospital where he has been recuperating for a month, and tells Red Cross nurse Tae Shimizu

(Shirley Yamaguchi) how much she has meant to him for the past two weeks. Tae is embarrassed by the depth of Jim's feelings, but she does not forbid him from seeing her. When he is well, Jim visits her home to ask Tae's nearest relative, her grandfather Eitaro (Philip Ahn), for permission to marry her. With some reluctance, Eitaro grants the request.

The newlyweds arrive in Salinas, California, and Jim, now a civilian, introduces Tae to his family. Jim's brothers Art (Cameron Mitchell) and Ted (Orley Lindgren) like Tae immediately, while their parents Ed (James Bell) and Harriet (Louise Lorimer) are not quite as charmed. Art has recently married, and his wife Fran (Marie Windsor) is outwardly friendly but inwardly cold to Tae. Jim and Tae move into the Sterling house with the rest of the family.

Jim busies himself with the family lettuce farm, leaving Tae with much free time. She meets the Japanese neighbor family, the Hasagawas, and befriends Shiro (Lane Nakano) and his sister Emma (May Takasugi), but the refusal of their father to accept American customs or friends prevents the two families from having real friendship. Meanwhile, Fran grows jealous of Jim's infatuation with his wife and gradually adopts a strident tone toward Tae and all things Japanese.

With his family's help, Jim begins to build a house for himself and expectant mother Tae. As time progresses, tensions grow between Tae, who is always defensive, and the Sterling women, who always seem to be watching for Tae to make mistakes. At a party given by Jim's former girlfriend, Tae is harassed by a drunken oaf who assumes that she is a geisha girl. Jim slugs the drunkard, who promptly knocks Jim senseless. Tae is distraught but Jim comforts her as best he can. Tae has a baby boy with Japanese features and names him James Sterling, Jr. The baby brings Harriet closer to Tae, leaving Fran feeling alone in her prejudice and jealousy.

A letter is sent to Ed Sterling suggesting that the baby is really Shiro Hasagawa's, and Jim explodes in anger, leaving for the night and vowing not to live in a house where everyone is against his wife. Tae, believing Jim's break with his family is her fault, leaves with the baby, going to the Hasagawas for help. They send her to Monterey to stay with family until she can

"Why did he have to marry someone like you...!"

"Don't Call My Wife a Geisha Girl!"

The story of a miscegenetic love!

JAPANESE WAR BRIDE

20th CENTURY-FOX RELEASE

starring **Shirley YAMAGUCHI · Don TAYLOR**
CAMERON MITCHELL · MARIE WINDSOR

Discrimination and hatred threaten to tear apart a "miscegenetic love" in 20th Century–Fox's social drama Japanese War Bride *(1952). Beautiful Shirley Yamaguchi (center) is caught between her jealous sister-in-law (Marie Windsor, left) and her temperamental husband (Don Taylor, throwing a punch at right).*

raise enough money to return to Japan. Jim returns and is stunned to find that Tae has left. Fran begs him to let her go and finally admits that she wrote the inflammatory letter. Art finally takes charge of his wife, slapping her into submission and apologizing to his brother.

Jim goes to the Hasagawas and persuades them to tell him where Tae has gone. He finds her in Monterey, where she is seriously consid-

ering suicide. He prevents her from jumping into the Pacific Ocean and promises her that everything will be all right.

Japanese War Bride follows the lead of its title and tells its story plainly and with few frills. As directed by King Vidor, the story moves forward quickly and obviously, eschewing romantic cliches in favor of limited character development and story structure. The Korean prologue is very brief, taking just forty-five seconds to establish that Jim Sterling is a brave and lucky soldier, the only survivor of a bloody slaughter. There are just two scenes set in Japan, the majority of which are devoted to Jim's meeting with Eitaro Shimizu, as Jim attempts to follow Japanese custom, though he barely comprehends its rituals and nuances.

The remainder of the story deals with life in rural California, where some people have neither forgotten nor forgiven Japanese actions during World War II. The location of Salinas was chosen in part because of those festering memories. It was here that several Japanese-Americans returning home from the war were met with violence and hatred, and the situation took some months to settle. The movie's character of Milly Shafer cannot condone Jim's choice of a bride because her son died during the Bataan death march; many members of Salinas' National Guard shared that same fate. Thus, the Salinas area was chosen for both topicality and verisimilitude.

The prejudice against Tae is not depicted as pervasive. It is held by various individuals in various degrees. A comment here or there is about as public as it becomes, and yet its damage is tremendous. Those few comments set Jim's temper on edge, ruin the Sterling's "peaceful Sunday afternoon" and ultimately threaten to tear Jim and Tae's marriage apart. The most insidious prejudice originates in Fran, who is jealous of Tae's place in Jim's life, as Jim seems to have been her first choice among the Sterling men. Fran allows her jealousy to drive a wedge into the trust of Jim's marriage, and she ultimately writes the letter that threatens not just Jim, but the security of the entire family. By providing Fran with a sexual motive for her prejudice, however, the movie also sidesteps its social implications, and gives Art an easy way to rectify the family situation.

It is also uncomfortably real that the Sterling family manages to silently ignore the problem until the letter, ostensibly from the Farmer's Association, arrives at their home. Only when it seems that some neighboring farmers have taken offense at the Japanese appearance of the baby, and that offense seems to imperil the Sterling's social position and ability to make a living, does positive action become necessary. Here the movie indicates that when racism becomes an economic issue, it becomes important. And though that is a point which really should not be so, it is undeniably true, especially in America.

Had the film focused more upon the social prejudice of others, it might have been more forceful in its condemnation of such prejudice. Likewise, if the heroine had been Korean, the story would have a more timely and controversial impact.

Nevertheless, the drama works because all of the characters, including Fran, are solidly rooted in real life and react as real people to real concerns. The drama is low-key, but it is authentic and completely understandable. Another plus is that the movie avoids preachiness, preferring to make its moral points through realistic dialogue rather than through heavy-handed direction, symbolism or melodrama. Its stance against racism is perfectly obvious, and it never becomes sanctimonious.

Though the film begins in Korea, the war is barely mentioned again. At one point in the hospital, Jim tells Tae that "I grew to hate the country [Japan, where he was stationed] — but then I was sent to Korea." The dread on Jim's face and his still painful arm wound reveal his true feelings about fighting in the "Land of the Morning Calm." Although the war is still ongoing when Jim returns to America with Tae (in 1952), no one in California discusses the progress or conditions of the war, or the people returning from it. It's as if it doesn't exist, even though Jim is a walking reminder of the fate of many young men serving halfway around the world. Psychologically, of course, it may be easier for the characters to deal with the war by ignoring it.

The cast — with the exception of Don Taylor, who doesn't seem suited for the dramatic rigors of his role — perform quite ably. As Tae, Shirley Yamaguchi is excellent — lovely enough to believe Jim would fall in love with her so quickly and talented enough to convince audiences that Tae is just as complex as any American-born woman. Tae's grandfather, Eitaro, is portrayed by Philip Ahn. If Ahn seems familiar, it may be because he has appeared in more Korean War films than any other Asian-American actor. Almost always seen as a wise old man,

Cultures clash in Japanese War Bride *(1952). American soldier Jim Sterling (Don Taylor, left) follows Japanese custom and asks farmer Eitaro Shimizu (Philip Ahn, right) for permission to marry his daughter Tae (Shirley Yamaguchi).*

here Ahn is provided with an opportunity to create a fully rounded character, one who balances knowledge and values of both cultures.

Japanese War Bride received mixed reviews upon its release in January 1952. *Newsweek* called it "In good part an intelligent and sensitive story" but lamented that it "turns dramatically sour … into a flare-up of personal bitchery." *Time* found it to be a "skin-deep drama" and A. H. Weiler of the *New York Times* judged that even with commendable performances, "except for its occasional moments of tension, the trials of *Japanese War Bride*, as set down in Catherine Turney's script, have the impact of a twice-told tale." *Variety*'s reviewer liked it more, praising its direction, music, photography, and especially acting.

The reviewers were unanimously agreed that Shirley Yamaguchi was terrific in the lead role. Born Yoshiki Yamaguchi, she made a name for herself as an entertainer in Japanese-occupied China as Li Xianglan (or Ri Koran in Japanese)

before visiting the United States in the early 1950s. She married sculptor Isamu Noguchi in 1952 and only made three more films before retiring to Japan. Twenty years later, she was elected to the House of Councillors, Japan's upper body of parliament, where she has served ever since. Once a promising Hollywood newcomer nicknamed both "the Betty Grable of the Orient" and "the Judy Garland of Japan," Shirley Yamaguchi brings the sensitive character of Tae Shimizu to glowing life in *Japanese War Bride*, the best American forum for her talents.

Jet Attack

(aka *Jet Squad*; *Through Hell to Glory*)

Credits: 1958. American International Pictures. *Directed by* Edward L. Cahn. *Produced by* Alex Gordon. *Co-Producer*: Israel M Berman.

Associate Producer: Mark Hanna. *Executive Producer*: James H. Nicholson. *Screenplay by* Orville H. Hampton. *Story by* Mark Hanna. *Music Composed and Conducted by* Ronald Stein. *Director of Photography*: Frederick E. West, A.S.C. *Film Editor*: Robert S. Eisen. *Production Supervisor*: Bartlett A. Carre. *Art Director*: Don Ament. *Assistant Director*: Robert Agnew. *Assistant Art Director*: Danny Heller. *Set Decorator*: Harry Reif. *Properties*: Karl Brainard and Richard M. Rubin. *Script Supervisor*: Judith Hart. *Assistant Film Editor*: Joyce Sage. *Sound Editor*: Joe Von Stroheim. *Music Editor*: Charles Clement. *Wardrobe*: Marjorie Corso. *Hair Stylist*: Edith Keon. *Make-up*: Ernie Young. *Sound*: Ben Winkler. *Production Assistant*: Jack Diamond. Not Rated. Black and White. Flat (1.33:1). 68 minutes. Released in March, 1958. Currently available on VHS videotape.

Cast: *Captain Tom Arnett*, John Agar; *Tanya*, Audrey Totter; *Lieutenant Bill Claiborne*, Gregory Walcott; *Lieutenant Sandy Wilkinson*, James Dobson; *Major Wan*, Leonard Strong; *Radioman Chick Lane*, Nicky Blair; *Captain Chon*, Victor Sen Yung; *Dean Olmstead*, Joe Hamilton; *Major Garver*, Guy Prescott; *Colonel Catlett*, George Cisar; *Muju*, Stella Lynn; *Colonel Kuban*, Robert Carricart; *Orderly*, Weaver Levy; *Phillips*, Paul Power; *Air Police Sergeant*, Hal Bogart; *WAAC Corporal*, Madeline Foy; *Signalman*, Robert Gilbreath.

Historical Accuracy Level: Low. Any connection between this movie and reality is entirely coincidental.

Patriotic Propaganda Level: Medium. Jive-talking jet jockeys rescue an old scientist and steal a MiG fighter jet for good measure.

Elements: Air Force, Air War, Behind Enemy Lines, Espionage, Females in the Field, Rescues, Secret Missions, "Somewhere in Korea."

Jet Attack, also known by the titles *Jet Squad* and *Through Hell to Glory*, is perhaps the most ludicrous of all Korean War movies. Financed on a shoestring budget by American International Pictures, *Jet Attack* is an unmitigated disaster on every level of filmmaking. Associate producer Mark Hanna is credited with the original story idea and must bear the blame for this ridiculous movie.

"Somewhere in Korea," Air Force pilots Tom Arnett (John Agar) and Sandy Wilkinson (James Dobson) provide air cover for a special mission. Scientist Dean Olmstead (Joe Hamilton) is testing new communications equipment (based on a completely spurious scientific theory) while flying low over North Korean terrain. After successfully testing the equipment, the plane is attacked by Russian MiG fighters and is shot down before Tom and Sandy can destroy the MiGs.

Later, word reaches the Air Force that Olmstead may have survived the crash (despite the fact that the plane exploded), so Tom, rough tough Bill Claiborne (Gregory Walcott) and radioman Chick Lane (Nicky Blair) are parachuted into North Korea to find the scientist, if he is alive. The three men are attacked on the ground by North Koreans, but are rescued by a large guerilla force of South Korean soldiers. Tom makes contact with Tanya (Audrey Totter), a Russian medical aide who successfully protected and smuggled him out of the country once before. Tanya promises to check all the area hospitals for any signs of Olmstead. While waiting for word from Tanya, the guerillas check area prison camps and the Americans argue about whether Tanya can be trusted.

Tanya manipulates her boss, Colonel Kuban (Robert Carricart), into inspecting the area hospitals, but raises the suspicions of Russian security office Major Wan (Leonard Strong) while doing so. Kuban and Tanya find Olmstead, unconscious (but talking), in one of the hospitals and Kuban guesses at the scientist's importance. Tanya returns to the guerillas to arrange a rescue while Major Wan sets a trap at the hospital. Tanya and Tom (who poses as a Russian doctor) arrive at the hospital, secretly drug Olmstead into a coma, pretend that he has died and take the body outside, where Major Wan springs his trap and initiates a firefight which kills most of the South Korean guerillas. Tom, Bill and Tanya escape with Olmstead, while Chick Lane is captured and tortured by the sadistic Major Wan.

At the planned rendezvous point, two truckloads of Russian soldiers intercept the American helicopter sent to pick up Olmstead, wounding Sandy, who is piloting the rescue copter, and killing Bill and Tanya. Tom and Sandy spy a pair of waiting Russian MiGs and

The artwork for American International's programmer Jet Attack *(1958) promises amazing air battles, "jet propelled dames!, jet jockies! (sic) and blazing excitement!" The film itself delivers none of these promises. There are more jets on the poster than appear in the film, and curiously, the exploding jet on the poster is an American fighter rather than an enemy MiG, none of which are pictured.*

steal them. Tom—with Olmstead stuffed into the cockpit with him—flies to safety while Sandy sacrifices himself and his MiG to protect his friend and the scientist. The movie ends with Olmstead questioning whether his rescue was worth all the loss of life, and being assured that it was.

All of *Jet Attack*'s elements are inept. The script purports that Olmstead "has found a way to bounce UHF waves off the heavy-side layer like broadcast wavelengths," which is, of course, B-movie scientific doubletalk. Because Olmstead is the only scientist who can figure out this technical marvel that allows radio contact with planes flying at low altitudes, more than half of the cast perishes trying to get him back. When Olmstead's plane is shot down, a man can be seen ejecting, not just once but *twice*, but the Air Force brass doesn't see it, even when film of the crash is replayed for them. And though the movie features a fair amount of action, both on

the ground and in the air, it can never escape its own sheer folly.

Jet Attack attempts to use the double-agent ruse to build suspense. The Air Force brass introduce Tanya as the woman who previously saved Tom's life, then question Tom as to her trustworthiness. Though Tom has no doubt as to Tanya's sympathies, Bill stubbornly refuses to believe that a Russian woman would help the Americans rather than the North Koreans. Even when she brings word of Olmstead's whereabouts and imminent incarceration, Bill defies logic and declares that Tanya must be leading them into a trap. In a better movie, this kind of red herring might work, but here it just makes Bill seem like an idiot.

Thankfully, the love interest angle is kept to a minumum. Tom and Tanya do share a few tender moments together, but not enough to slow the film. More ridiculous is the relationship between Chick and Muju, which is expressed by having Muju (Stella Lynn) excessively caress Chick's earlobes and, later, by getting him drunk. There is more affection shown between the men for each other (depicted by having them drink, fight and work together) than for any of the women in the picture.

If the movie's scenario is to be believed, the American Air Force in South Korea consists of about twenty jets and a similar number of men, only a few of which are to be entrusted with special mission status. All of the combat scenes consist of familiar stock combat footage, with closeups of actors John Agar, James Dobson and others inserted into the airborne action. The one asset is Ronald Stein's decent music score, which is better than this type of film usually contains.

The film's perspective of the Korean War contains none of the standard situations or storylines. Its take on the war is entirely fresh and new, but it is also incredibly stupid. The movie posits that special, secret missions undertaken by fun-loving fighter pilots are the key to beating the Communists, probably because the Commies are just too square to dig democracy. American International intentionally tried to lure a younger audience to the movie with a combination of heroic young star faces (John Agar, James Dobson and Nicky Blair), pretty young figures (Audrey Totter and Stella Lynn) and colloquial dialogue. Various characters spout hepcat phrases like "Nest to Skyhawk, coming in strong and groovy," "It's a gasser up here. The blue yonder is really wild," and "With wings you swing, without a pair you're nowhere." Bill (Gregory Walcott) refers to both of his buddies as "schmoes." This is not exactly standard military protocol.

Variety and *Boxoffice* both termed *Jet Attack* "a good war feature" when the film was released as part of an American International Pictures twin-bill with the World War II melodrama *Suicide Battalion,* but they were definitely in the minority. Jay Robert Nash and Stanley Ralph Ross were closer to the truth when

The heroes of Jet Attack *(1958): From left to right, Bill Claiborne (Gregory Walcott), Sandy Wilkinson (James Dobson) and Tom Arnett (John Agar) are castigated by Colonel Catlett (George Cisar).*

they assessed the film in their *Motion Picture Guide*. The first line of their review says it all: "One of the worst films ever made about war." Harry Medved and Randy Dreyfuss chose *Jet Attack* as an entry for their book *The Fifty Worst Films of All Time*, forever placing the film in an elite class.

Jet Attack remains a quick, cheap, poorly written and acted exploitation picture with nothing important or entertaining to say about anything. As Tom Arnett, John Agar sums up the Korean conflict this way: "This lousy war." Change the last word to "movie" and *Jet Attack* is perfectly summarized.

Korea Patrol

Credits: 1951. Jack Schwarz Productions. *Distributed by* Eagle-Lion. *Directed by* Max Nosseck. *Produced by* Walter Shenson. *Executive Producer*: Jack Schwarz. *Story and Screenplay by* Kenneth G. Brown and Walter Shenson. *Music by* Alexander Gerens. *Director of Photography*: Elmer Dyer, A.S.C. *Film Editor*: Norman Cerf. *Assistant Director*: Harry Franklin. *Sound Engineer*: Earl Snyder. *Properties*: Monroe Liebgold. *Art Director*: Fred Preble. *Special Effects*: Robert Mattey. *Makeup*: Harry Thomas. *Wardrobe*: Mickey Myers. Not Rated. Black and White. Flat (1.33:1). 59 minutes. Released in January, 1951. Not currently available on commercial home video.

Cast: *Lieutenant Craig*, Richard Emory; *Kim*, Benson Fong; *Sergeant Abrams*, Al Eben; *Ching*, Li Sun; *the Girl*, Teri Duna; *Corporal Dykes*, Danny Davenport; *Murphy*, Wong Artarne; *Lee*, Harold Fong; *Captain Greer*, John Close; *Major Wald*, Richard Barron.

Historical Accuracy Level: Medium. Apart from the U.N. Security Council footage, this film is not at all an accurate portrayal of the first days of the war.

Patriotic Propaganda Level: Medium. The soldiers do complete their bridge bombing mission, but this film would never be a recruiting tool for the army.

Elements: Army, Bridge Bombing, Day of the Invasion, Females in the Field, Sibling Rivalry, United Nations Security Council.

It was a mere seven months after the invasion of South Korea that the first American films about the conflict were released to theaters. Samuel Fuller's *The Steel Helmet*, and Max Nosseck's *Korea Patrol* were released almost simultaneously in January of 1951, with Lew Landers' *A Yank in Korea* arriving in theatres a few weeks later. *The Steel Helmet* was acknowledged as a powerful and stylish exploration of war, and today is considered one of the classic Korean War films. *Korea Patrol*, with a brief fifty-nine minute running time and absence of exciting action or drama, was quickly paired with another Eagle-Lion release, *Prehistoric Women*, for double feature duty.

Korea Patrol commences with actual footage of an emergency meeting of the United Nations Security Council after the Communist invasion of South Korea. A resolution is quickly adopted for a North Korean withdrawal to north of Korea's 38th parallel. A narrator then intones that fewer then five hundred American soldiers were in Korea at the time of the invasion, as part of the U.S. military advisory group, and that this is the story of one patrol, the first U.N. force to see action.

On the day of the invasion, Lieutenant Craig (Richard Emory) and a patrol of five other men, whom he describes as "a couple of Tuesday night soldiers and some Korean scouts in pup tents," are relaxing, playing craps and discussing where a possible North Korean attack might take place. Craig receives a radio call informing the patrol of the invasion and ordering the men to execute plan "Mabel," which is to hold or destroy a particular bridge which the North Koreans will need to cross. Two other patrols are to rendezvous with Craig's to accomplish the mission. Craig, his two enlisted men and three Korean scouts march through the Korean forests, hide from an enemy plane, and continue to march toward their objective.

At headquarters, word arrives that the two other patrols have met the enemy and been obliterated. A Korean runner named Ching (Li Sun) is sent to find Craig's patrol and deliver supplementary orders. Ching locates Craig's patrol and is reunited with his brother Kim (Benson Fong), its chief scout. Kim is surprised to see his brother, "especially in that [South Korean] uniform." Ching tells Lieutenant Craig that they will have to detour to a nearby construction site for dynamite to be used on the bridge. The men bed down for the night, within earshot of enemy voices.

Kim raids the construction site alone, retrieves a case of dynamite and silently kills the two guards who follow him. The dynamite is fused and distributed among the seven men. Craig asks Kim about his brother Ching, who Kim fears would collaborate with the North Koreans if given the chance. Craig talks to his subordinates, Corporal Dykes (Danny Davenport) and Sergeant Abrams (Al Eben), about their personal lives and the reasons why they joined the Army. The patrol again marches toward the bridge and encounters the enemy. One Korean scout, Lee (Harold Fong), is killed and Dykes is injured in the skirmish. Mortally wounded, Dykes sets his dynamite, crawls toward the enemy soldiers and blows them all to pieces.

Having seen the horror of war firsthand, Ching tries to persuade Kim to betray the Americans, but Kim resists. The men come upon a farmhouse where a Korean girl (Teri Duna) is being held prisoner. They kill the North Korean guards and rescue the girl, retreating into the forest. The other Korean scout, Murphy (Wong Artarne), is shot in the belly and dies; Sergeant Abrams is knifed in the back shortly thereafter. Lieutenant Craig and Kim decide to forge ahead with the mission and give the girl a rifle to guard Ching, who has already run away once before being stopped.

The girl tells Ching what a coward he is being, and what the North Koreans are doing to South Korea and its people. Ching is ashamed of himself and inspired to act. With her blessing, Ching takes the rifle and follows his brother into danger. Near the bridge, Kim is wounded in the leg and Craig is shot in the arm. Still, they fight on. Ching arrives, shoots some North Koreans, takes the dynamite and destroys the bridge just as the first North Korean tanks are crossing it. Having successfully completed the job, Ching, Kim and Lieutenant Craig walk (and limp) back toward their own forces, remembering their dead comrades. The girl is nowhere to be seen.

Korea Patrol is an odd, low budget programmer. Rushed into production after the South Korean invasion, it combines a bit of action and a lot of sneaking around with actual footage of a U.N. security session. The result is uneven and rarely satisfying. Executive producer Jack Schwarz deserves some credit for having the idea to include the United Nations material to preface his story; only *A Yank in Korea* also incorporates such authentic history directly into its plot. Having said that, it is also important to note that the U.N. material has little value other than its curiosity factor and seemingly misplaced verisimilitude.

There is no standard character development to speak of in *Korea Patrol*. Its characters are skeletal outlines, barely fleshed out by its cast. The only standout is Benson Fong as Kim, the Korean scout who refuses to consider collaboration with the North Koreans. When Kim says to his weak-willed brother Ching, "Right now we are going to blow up that bridge. It is the most important thing in our lives!" it is delivered with some fortitude. The action is, unfortunately, rather slow to begin and involves a great deal of skulking around in bushes. The climactic bridge bombing is actually combat footage rather unskillfully blended into the action.

What is interesting about the film is the slow and steady elimination of most of its characters, just as in war. Of the seven men on this fateful patrol (including Ching, the runner who joins them), four are killed outright and two of the three survivors are injured. Virtually no other Korean War film boasts such a realistic and devastating body count. The only other intriguing situation in the film is the relationship between the Korean brothers, Kim and Ching. Kim realizes that the Americans are there to defend South Korea, while Ching initially believes that the foreigners are the real enemy, not understanding the aggressive motives of the Communist-led North Koreans. As he sees the murderous plunder of Korea by the North Koreans, some of whom may be blood relatives, Ching gradually realizes the gravity of the situation. Eventually, he decides to fight for his homeland and earns the respect of his brother in the process.

Two other factors about *Korea Patrol* are noteworthy. While other facets of the war were more glamorous, such as the jet-fueled air war, much of the action in the Korean War concerned

A behind-the-lines drama!

the STORY OF SEVEN... SEVEN HARD-HITTING SOLDIERS, AND A NATIVE GIRL — SLUGGING IT OUT, BLASTING THEIR WAY TO GLORY!

KOREA PATROL

Richard EMORY · Benson FONG

AL EBEN · LI SUN · TERI DUNA · DANNY DAVENPORT

AN EAGLE LION CLASSICS RELEASE

Rousing patriotism is the call for audiences to attend Eagle Lion's action drama Korea Patrol *(1951). "Seven hard-hitting soldiers, and a native girl—slugging it out, blasting their way to glory!" Minimal artwork depicts only two identifiable soldiers (Benson Fong, left and Richard Emory, center), and, of course, the "native girl" (Teri Duna).*

Six men on routine patrol listen to the news of the Korean invasion on their radio in Korea Patrol *(1951). From left to right, Wong Artarne, Al Eben, Li Sun, Danny Davenport, Benson Fong and Richard Emory.*

the bombing of bridges. As one of the first movies about the conflict, this movie establishes bridge bombing as an important effort designed to hinder the enemy and gain time for United Nations forces to be collected and placed in the field. As Korean War films multiplied, bridge bombing continued to be an important focus, in films as disparate as *The Bridges at Toko-Ri*, *Glory Alley* and *Return From the Sea*. It also happens that *Korea Patrol* is one of just a few Korean War films to deal with the actual day of invasion as events were occurring. Since there were few Americans in Korea at the time of the invasion (June 25, 1950), most movies begin days, weeks or months after the war has already begun, or else use the invasion news to move their characters to Korea shortly thereafter. Only *Korea Patrol* has a handful of Americans trained and in place on the day of the invasion. The movie has such a low budget and narrowly focused script that it does very little with those men, but they are on hand.

The film abounds with stock footage taken from battlefields which is used to pad the running time and fill in the gaps in the story. This footage does not match the rest of the film, making it seem even more hackneyed than it is. And a major plot line remains dangling at the film's conclusion: What happened to the girl? She is last seen upbraiding Ching for refusing to defend his own country. When Ching leaves the girl behind in the forest, her story evidently ends.

The film's notices were uniformly poor. *Boxoffice* warned that "Productionwise, the feature is a patent cheater, even in the most modest budget category. The location-exposed footage is skimpy, under-cast, awkwardly directed and amateurishly delineated." *Film Daily* remarked, "Handling lacks credence, polish, performances." And the British Film Institute's *Monthly Film Bulletin* commented, "The makers seem to have sacrificed every other consideration to the desire to produce a topical picture, and the result is an improbable story, crude characterisation, and poor technical quality."

Korea Patrol has remained virtually unseen since its initial release more than fifty years ago. As a historical artifact it retains some value, but dramatically it is dull and uneventful. The messages that it contains about the tragic nature of war are delivered awkwardly and without subtlety. It could have been a movie that reflected interest in the war, but that role was quickly filled by *The Steel Helmet*.

Love Is a Many-Splendored Thing

Credits: 1955. 20th Century–Fox. *Directed by* Henry King. *Produced by* Buddy Adler. *Screenplay by* John Patrick. *Based on* "A Many-Splendored Thing," *by* Han Suyin (Dr. Elizabeth Comber). *Music*: Alfred Newman. *Director of Photography*: Leon Shamroy, A.S.C. *Film Editor*: William Reynolds, A.C.E. *Art Direction*: Lyle R. Wheeler and George W. Davis. *Set Decorations*: Walter M. Scott and Jack Stubbs. *Special Photographic Effects*: Ray Kellogg. *Wardrobe Direction*: Charles LeMaire. *Song*: "Love Is A Many-Splendored Thing," *by* Sammy Fain and Paul Francis Webster. *Orchestration*: Edward B. Powell. *Assistant Director*: Hal Herman. *Makeup by* Ben Nye. *Hair Styling by* Helen Turpin. *Sound*: Alfred Bruzlin and Harry M. Leonard. Not Rated. Color by DeLuxe. *Color Consultant*: Leonard Doss. CinemaScope (2.55:1). *CinemaScope Lenses by* Bausch and Lomb. 102 minutes. Released in August, 1955. Filmed on location in Hong Kong. Currently available on VHS and DVD. Previously available on laserdisc.

Cast: *Mark Elliott*, William Holden; *Doctor Han Suyin*, Jennifer Jones; *Mr. Palmer-Jones*, Torin Thatcher; *Adeline Palmer-Jones*, Isobel Elsom; *Doctor John Keith*, Murray Matheson; *Ann Richards*, Virginia Gregg; *Robert Hung*, Richard Loo; *Nora Hung*, Soo Yong; *Third Uncle*, Philip Ahn; *Suzanne*, Jorja Curtright; *Suchen*, Donna Martell; *Oh-No*, Candace Lee; *Dr. Sen*, Kam Tong; *Fifth Brother*, James Hong; *Father Low*, Herbert Heyes; *Mei Loo*, Angela Loo; *Rosie Wu*, Marie Tsien; *Nurses*, Barbara

Jean Wong, Hazel Shon, Jean Wong; *Intern*, Kei Chung; *Officer*, Henry S. Quan; *British Sailor*, Ashley Cowan; *Wine Steward*, Marc Krah; *General Song*, Joseph Kim; *Hotel Manager*, Salvador Basquez; *Dining Room Captain*, Edward Colmans; *Fortune Teller*, Leonard Strong; *Wives*, Aen Ling Chow, Stella Lynn, Irene Liu; *Aunt*, Beulah Kwoh; *Second Brother*, Howard Soo Hoo; *Third Brother*, Walter Soo Hoo; *Elder Brother*, Keye Luke; *Old Loo*, Lee Tung Foo; *Gate Keeper*, John W. T. Chang; *Soldier*, Weaver Levy; *English Secretary*, Eleanor Moore.

Historical Accuracy Level: Medium. These characters are based on real people, but seem to have detached themselves from the history which surrounds them.

Patriotic Propaganda Level: Low. The film shines as a travelogue of Hong Kong, but its real purpose is to indict racism and criticize the war which deprives its heroine of personal happiness.

Elements: Air War, Journalism, Racism, Red Menace, Romance.

This enormously popular love story doesn't have any connection to the Korean War for some eighty minutes, until the correspondent portrayed by William Holden is sent to cover the story when the North Koreans cross the 38th parallel in June of 1950. The war then intrudes on the tender love story, as it did for so many real people, in startlingly tragic fashion. Based upon an autobiographical memoir by Dr. Han Suyin (a pseudonym for Dr. Elizabeth Comber), with fictionalized names in deference to the family of the real-life London *Times* correspondent with whom she had become involved, the movie remains faithful to its source while emphasizing some elements more than others and altering specific details for no apparent reason.

In 1949 Hong Kong, Dr. Han Suyin (Jennifer Jones), a Eurasian woman—half-English and half-Chinese—is a respected physician at the Victoria Hospital. A young Chinese girl (Candace Lee), dubbed "Oh-No" by Suyin, has been hit by a car and is her latest patient. Fellow physician Dr. John Keith (Murray Matheson) senses that Suyin is overburdened by work and takes her to a party, where she is forced to defend herself to Mr. and Mrs. Palmer-Jones (Torin Thatcher and Isobel Elsom), the snobby English couple who run the hospital. Retreating

The love story is the prime focus of 20th Century–Fox's drama Love Is a Many-Splendored Thing *(1955), which became an international sensation. Somehow, however, the stars' positions hardly seem romantic.*

from their inquisition, the attractive Suyin is pursued by an American correspondent, Mark Elliott (William Holden). He pesters her with a dinner invitation, but she demurs. She asks John Keith about Mark Elliott and discovers that he is married.

Elliott persists in asking Suyin to dinner and she finally accepts. They find that they have much in common, but Suyin insists that she is not interested in becoming involved with the brawny American, especially as he is married. Suyin meets an old friend named Suzanne (Jorja Curtright), a woman who is also Eurasian but who hides her Asian background and who advises Suyin to do the same. Dr. Keith advises Suyin not to become involved with Elliott, and Suyin says that such warnings may pique her interest.

Elliott and Suyin meet for an afternoon of swimming. They swim across a bay to the house of Suyin's friends, Robert and Nora Hung (Richard Loo and Soo Yong). After an enjoyable afternoon, Elliott and Suyin are taken by boat back to the beach, where Suyin warns Elliott not to complicate their friendship, but Elliott tells her he loves her. She again warns him not to wake "a sleeping tiger" and he suggests meeting the next day. She tells him of a tree on the hill above the hospital and they arrange to meet. Despite her misgivings about love, she is thrilled to see him and they begin their affair in earnest.

Suyin is contacted by her Chinese family and arranges to travel back to her homeland for the first time in a decade. Suyin and Elliott argue about the difficulties surrounding their love and he angrily leaves her. She travels to Chungking and is welcomed back by Third Uncle (Philip Ahn) and her Chinese family. Her youngest sister, Suchen (Donna Martell), has shamed the family by moving into a foreign-born neighbor's house, where she thinks she will be protected if and when the Communist Chinese forces take power. Suyin convinces her to move back home by offering to arrange a passport for her to leave China. Mark Elliott arrives, having followed Suyin to China, and asks her to marry him. She agrees and asks Third Uncle for his blessing. Despite Third Uncle's objections concerning Elliott's foreignness, the blessing is given.

Elliott and Suyin return to Hong Kong, and Elliott continues to Singapore to obtain a divorce from the wife he has not seen in six years. He returns with bad news; his wife has refused to grant the divorce. Suyin understands, and continues to love him openly. Oh-No improves and Suyin begins to consider taking care of the girl, whose parents have never been found. Elliott is sent to Macao for a story and arranges for Suyin to meet him there. Before she leaves, Suyin is warned by Mrs. Palmer-Jones that her affair is too indiscreet for the conventions of the English blue bloods. Suyin ignores the warning and meets Elliott in Macao. Their time together is cut short when Elliott receives word that South Korea has been invaded and that he will be sent there immediately.

The lovers return to Hong Kong and say goodbye beneath the tree upon the hill above the hospital. Elliott leaves without knowing that Suyin has lost her residency at the hospital because of their relationship. Suyin takes Oh-No when she leaves the hospital and moves in with the Hungs, across the bay. She looks for medical positions but her scandalous reputation precedes her and no hospital will hire her. Elliott writes from Korea; the second scene of his writing is cut short when a North Korean plane drops a bomb directly on the shelter protecting him. Suyin hears that Elliott has been killed and doesn't want to believe it. But then she reads the words in his latest letter and realizes the truth. She runs to the tree on the hill above the hospital and remembers him and all that he meant to her as the music swells and a chorus sings the title song.

Love Is a Many-Splendored Thing was a popular, best-selling book which eloquently describes the social difficulties surrounding cross-cultural relationships. Its unusual title is adapted from a line in Francis Thompson's religious poem *The Kingdom of God*, which is recited by Mark Elliott to Han Suyin during a romantic scene in the film. While the book's social criticism is deemphasized in the film version, the project remains a timely, contemporary lesson that human feelings of love and tenderness need have no social restrictions. The movie's message about love is clear: the English people who gossip behind Suyin's back are mean-spirited snobs, while Suyin's Chinese family are viewed as well-meaning but naive regarding anything with larger ramifications than family issues. And despite

Suyin's initial reluctancy to experience love once again, that love is seen as the force that reinvigorates her, that provides her with the will to truly live.

The film emphasizes Elliott's marital status as much or more than the lovers' differences in skin tone. Although the details of Mark Elliott's in-name-only marriage seem to be public knowledge, it is his married status which the "proper" English hospital administrators (and Dr. Keith as well, to a lesser degree) use to discredit Suyin's reputation. Elliott has not even seen his wife in six years, and never wants to again (and vice versa), but the fact of his marriage is used to represent the racial issue by writer John Patrick and director Henry King.

Dr. Han Suyin (Jennifer Jones) and boyfriend Mark Elliott (William Holden) meet under the tree at the top of the hill overlooking Hong Kong in the romantic drama Love Is a Many-Splendored Thing *(1955).*

Instead of harping on the racial difference between Elliott and Suyin — which itself is deemphasized by casting Jennifer Jones as Han Suyin — the filmmakers use the sticking point of Elliott's previous marriage to make the same moral points.

The Korean War is a late addition to the movie and telegraphs the tragic finale to the love story. In reality, Han Suyin's lover was killed with two other correspondents when their jeep ran over a mine, but the film gives Mark Elliott a nobler death at the hands of the Communist enemy. In Korea to report "the cold facts of war," Elliott is witness to the larger picture of the same racism and aggression that threatens Suyin. His experiences are not detailed, though they might have reinforced the movie's message about tolerance. Elliott's death (besides being true) is a necessary conclusion to the romantic life of Suyin. The only way that the love story could retain its beauty and power is to end it, heroically, before it could become ordinary.

The love story itself borders on schmaltz and occasionally crosses the line into sticky sentimentality, but for the most part manages to convey the complex feelings of two people who find in each other a common understanding. This adult relationship is finely detailed by writer John Patrick; it is his literate, sensitive script which prevents the story's drama from degrading into soap opera posturing. The two lead characters are embodied by previous Oscar winners Jennifer Jones and William Holden.

Jennifer Jones is wonderful as Han Suyin. Even though she doesn't look Oriental at all, Jones injects a strong measure of Chinese sensibility, posture and grace into the role and is utterly convincing. Presented in fourteen stunning Chinese-themed gowns as well as a sleek bathing suit, Jones is glamorous and sexy, and offers occasional glimpses of the woman beneath her often reserved character. Han Suyin is a rarity in American cinema, an independent, strong-willed woman who does not need the love of a man to complete her life. She is happy before she meets Mark Elliott and she will survive without him. For her efforts, Jones was nominated for her fifth Academy Award in twelve years. She lost to Anna Magnani for *The Rose Tattoo*. William Holden is solid as Mark Elliott, though it is apparent he has a less detailed character with

which to work. Attractive and engaging, he is a good match for Jones in the movie, despite reports that he and Jones did not get along at all behind the scenes. Nonetheless, their onscreen chemistry is powerful and brought droves of people into theatres.

The film, preceded by the incessant playing of the title song (sung by a chorus and written by Sammy Fain and Paul Francis Webster), was a huge success, grossing more than $4 million in its initial release. It was nominated for eight Oscars, including best picture, actress, color cinematography, color art direction-set decoration, color costume design, song, scoring of a dramatic or comedy picture and sound recording. It won three Oscars, for song, score and costume design.

While the public flocked to theatres to see the film and radios played the theme song for months, some critics were bowled over by the romance. Fred Hift of *Variety* gushed, "It's an unusual picture in many ways, shot against authentic Hong Kong backgrounds and offbeat in its treatment, yet as simple and moving a love story as has come along in many a moon." The *Hollywood Reporter* termed it a "beautiful and sensitive motion picture"; *Newsweek* judged that "the love story is completely persuasive" and summarized it as "fine talk in the Far East."

Other critics were more reserved in their praise for the project. *Time* called it a "morass of sentimental fudge." Bosley Crowther of the *New York Times* dubbed it a "dew-dappled romance" and complained about the preponderance of talk. However, the public loved it and it remains a glossy example of "woo-pitching, Hollywood style," as film historian Lawrence J. Quirk likes to say. It is true that the film has little to say about the Korean conflict, but it does spotlight an all-too-common result of the war for many people, particularly women, around the world: the end of their love stories.

MacArthur
(aka *MacArthur, The Rebel General*)

Credits: 1977. Universal. *Directed by* Joseph Sargent. *Produced by* Frank McCarthy. *Executive Producers*: Richard D. Zanuck and

David Brown. *Written by* Hal Barwood and Matthew Robbins. *Music by* Jerry Goldsmith. *Director of Photography*: Mario Tosi, A.S.C. *Film Editor*: George Jay Nicholson, A.C.E. *Special Visual Effects by* Albert Whitlock. *Production Designer*: John J. Lloyd. *Chief Technical Advisor*: D. Clayton James, Ph.D. *Set Decorations*: Hal Gausman. *Sound*: Don Sharpless and Robert L. Hoyt. *Sound Effects Editor*: Jim Troutman. *Music Editor*: Morrie McNaughton. *Unit Production Managers*: Ernest B. Wehmeyer and James R. Nicholson. *First Assistant Director*: Scott Maitland. *Second Assistant Director*: Donald E. Zepfel. *Assistant to the Producer*: John E. Nyhuus. *Stunt Coordinator*: Joe Canutt. *Make-up*: Jim McCoy and Frank McCoy. *Hair Stylist*: Michael Corsentino. *Matte Photography*: William Taylor and Dennis Glouner. *Titles and Optical Effects*: Universal Title. *Second Unit Cameraman*: Richard E. Brooks. *Orchestrated by* Arthur Morton. *Scoring Mixer*: Dan Wallin. Rated PG. Technicolor. Panavision (2.35:1). 128 minutes. Released in June, 1977. Currently available on VHS and DVD. Previously available on laserdisc.

Cast: *General Douglas MacArthur*, Gregory Peck; *President Harry S. Truman*, Ed Flanders; *President Franklin D. Roosevelt*, Dan O'Herlihy; *General Sutherland*, Ivan Bonar; *General Marshall*, Ward Costello; *Colonel Huff*, Nicolas Coster; *Mrs. MacArthur*, Marj Dusay; *The Secretary*, Art Fleming; *Admiral King*, Russell D. Johnson; *General Wainwright*, Sandy Kenyon; *Representative Martin*, Robert Mandan; *Colonel Diller*, Allan Miller; *Colonel Whitney*, Dick O'Neill; *Admiral Nimitz*, Addison Powell; *General Sampson*, Tom Rosqui; *General Eichelberger*, G. D. Spradlin; *Admiral Halsey*, Kenneth Tobey; *General Walker*, Garry Walberg; *General Marquat*, Lane Allan; *Television Reporter*, Barry Coe; *General Krueger*, Everett Cooper; *General Harding*, Charles Cyphers; *Prettyman*, Manuel De Pina; *Castro*, Jesse Dizon; *General Shepherd*, Warde Donovan; *Aide*, Jerry Holland; *Admiral Doyle*, Philip Kenneally; *Admiral Leahy*, John McKee; *General Kenney*, Walter O. Miles; *General Blamey*, Gerald S. Peters; *General Collins*, Eutene Peterson; *Ah Cheu*, Beulah Quo; *General Derevyanko*, Alex Rodine; *Prime Minister Shidehara*, Yuki Shimoda; *General Bradley*, Fred Stuthman; *Admiral Sherman*, Harvey Vernon;

Lieutenant Bulkeley, William Wellman, Jr.; *Emperor Hirohito*, John Fujioka (uncredited); *Prisoner of War*, Robert V. Barron (uncredited); *Douglas*, Shane Sinutko (uncredited).

Historical Accuracy Level: High. Douglas MacArthur's military career is faithfully recreated, if somewhat truncated, from the Philippine Islands through Korea.

Patriotic Propaganda Level: High. The film celebrates the general's brilliant military successes more than it examines his ultimately flawed character.

Elements: Army, Biography, Japan, Leaders, Multiple Wars, Navy (Sailors), Politics, Red Menace, Returning Home.

Perhaps the most dynamic public figure during the Korean conflict was General Douglas MacArthur. Within the span of one year he was thrust into command, prevented the North Koreans from forcing U.N. troops off of the Korean peninsula, orchestrated a brilliant tactical maneuver at Inchon, drove the North Korean forces back to China, failed to recognize the Chinese threat, fought the combined Communist forces to a standstill and forced President Truman to fire him because he questioned orders he could not fully support. MacArthur was, indeed, a man of almost mythic proportions and capabilities, and this biography attempts to explore his personal and public history.

The film begins at West Point, as General Douglas MacArthur (Gregory Peck) gives his famous "Duty, Honor, Country" speech, then flashes back to the Philippine Islands during World War II, three months after the Japanese attack at Pearl Harbor. MacArthur visits a hospital established in a tunnel and tries to cheer his wounded men. Soon, he is ordered out of the Philippines by President Roosevelt (Dan O'Herlihy), but rather than travel by submarine, the general and his family transit the sea between the Philippines and Australia by gunboat, proving that the Japanese blockade can be circumvented successfully. In Melbourne, MacArthur makes his famous "I shall return" speech and begins to work with Australian officials on offensive strategy.

While the Australian military is determined to defend their island, MacArthur is equally determined to attack the Japanese. The Allied forces strike in New Guinea and begin to leapfrog past Japanese strongholds and raid the enemy's supply lines. The general begins to fight some political battles as well, ultimately meeting with and convincing Roosevelt and his staff that the Philippines must be liberated. Months later, MacArthur fulfills his promise and returns to the Philippines. He visits a prisoner of war camp and is welcomed by American prisoners, some of whom he left behind in the islands to fight on their own two years previously.

Roosevelt dies and Harry S Truman (Ed Flanders) becomes president. MacArthur despises the use of the atomic bomb (which thwarted his plans for a grand invasion of Japan), but welcomes the end of the war. He devotes himself to rebuilding Japan and its economy, and accepts the pledge of the new Japanese prime minister to completely dismantle its armed forces. For the next few years, MacArthur oversees the reconstruction and westernization of Japan, and becomes a hero to the Japanese people in the process. The general allows his name to be considered for the 1948 presidential primary, but he is soundly beaten and admits to himself that politics are not his forte. This period of his life and career comes to an abrupt end when South Korea is invaded.

MacArthur considers the opportunity to fight as "one last gift to an old warrior." He visits South Korea and witnesses for himself the destruction wrought by the North Korean invaders. The general visits Formosa and encourages Chiang Kai-shek to build forces in resistance to mainland China, hoping to be able to utilize Formosa's soldiery to help save Korea. Truman orders MacArthur to keep Chiang Kai-shek out of the fight, which infuriates the general. "It's my destiny to defeat Communism, and only God or those Washington politicians will keep me from doing it!" he rants. Nevertheless, he works with General Walton Walker (Garry Walberg) to hold the Pusan Perimeter while forces can be organized, and plans a counteroffensive invasion at Inchon.

A White House conference considers MacArthur's plan. One officer summarizes the plan's downside: "If every possible handicap were listed [for an invasion], Inchon has them all." The president believes in MacArthur, however, and the operation is authorized. On board one of the many invading ships, MacArthur ex-

presses his doubts, realizing that seventy thousand men are at risk, but those doubts fade when the first objective, the island of Wolmi-do, falls in just fifty-eight minutes. Within days, the North Koreans are retreating and MacArthur's forces are pursuing them into North Korea.

President Truman decides to meet MacArthur and does so at Wake Island. Truman is angry to be kept waiting, but MacArthur is apologetic and assures the president that he has no further political aspirations, warning him instead about the ambitions of Dwight D. Eisenhower. The general also assures his leader that the Chinese will remain out of the war, and that the war should be over by Christmas. On Thanksgiving, a tentful of soldiers is killed by Chinese soldiers, signaling China's entry into the war. MacArthur is furious that the Communist Chinese have joined the fight, but is even more angry when the politicians limit his military options, telling him that Chinese territory and air space are off-limits and suggesting that he bomb only "the southern half" of the bridges connecting China to North Korea. "For the first time in military history, a commander has been denied the use of his military power to safeguard the lives of his soldiers and the safety of his army."

After the battle lines stalemate at around the 38th parallel, again, Washington officials begin to seek a cease fire, but MacArthur demands a complete Communist surrender, to be made personally to himself. Truman has no choice but to dismiss his most popular general and sends him a telegram telling him so. Mrs. MacArthur (Marj Dusay) breaks the news to him during dinner; the general's response is a long sigh. "We're going home at last."

MacArthur receives the largest ticker-tape parade in U.S. history, then addresses Congress (his famous "Old soldiers never die" speech) and demands a complete military victory. Despite his popularity, it is not MacArthur but Eisenhower who receives the Republican nomination for president in 1952. MacArthur is supportive of Eisenhower, calling him "the best clerk who ever served under me." The general returns to West Point, and the present, to finish his speech — and his incredible military career.

MacArthur is a standard military biography in the *Patton* mold. Made and released seven

He fought wars and won them. He defied Presidents – and might have been one.

The most controversial American hero of our time ...and one hell of a man.

Four years in preparation and production.

GREGORY PECK as

General

Douglas MacARTHUR

A RICHARD D ZANUCK/DAVID BROWN PRODUCTION

ED FLANDERS · DAN O'HERLIHY · Written by HAL BARWOOD & MATTHEW ROBBINS · Music by JERRY GOLDSMITH · Directed by JOSEPH SARGENT

Produced by FRANK McCARTHY · A UNIVERSAL PICTURE · TECHNICOLOR®

PG PARENTAL GUIDANCE SUGGESTED

THEATRE

Patriotism rings throughout this ad for Universal's biography MacArthur *(1977), "the most controversial American hero of our time…" Also prominent on the poster are Presidents Truman (Ed Flanders, left) and Roosevelt (Dan O'Herlihy, right).*

years after *Patton*, *MacArthur* is clearly meant to emulate its popular Oscar-winning predecessor. Like General George S. Patton, General Douglas MacArthur became a larger-than-life figure during the second world war, and yet somehow remained enigmatic despite his worldwide fame. Patton's celebrity ended with the war, but MacArthur's accomplishments continued through peacetime and into the Korean War. The argument can be made that MacArthur's greatest deeds came after World War II, and that his ultimate demise resulted from his own inability to adapt to the concept of "limited war," a concept which he found illogical. It is, in fact, MacArthur's personal flaws which make him, like Patton, such a fascinating character.

Hoping to catch *Patton*'s lightning in a bottle, Universal followed the same basic structure for its biography. The difference between the two films, and their portraits of legendary military leaders, is that *Patton* fully develops its characters while *MacArthur* never really allows its characters to live and breathe. *Patton* features two fascinating characters — Generals Patton (George C. Scott) and Omar Bradley (Karl Malden) — who demonstrate not only why they were regarded as brilliant military men but also how such men are able to live with such awesome responsibility and continue to function professionally amidst the chaos of war. On the other hand, *MacArthur* chronicles just one man (while many other characters are present, they are merely standard military and political types) and never allows its subject to overcome his own public image. As portrayed in the film, MacArthur is a brilliant man with uncommon foresight, but he almost completely lacks dynamism. He holds himself physically in check, preferring to judge people and events over his familiar corncob pipe rather than to actively participate. Notoriously vain, MacArthur would rarely venture anywhere without a clean, pressed uniform and sunglasses; while the film remains faithful to these characteristics, because MacArthur rarely even becomes dirty he seems aloof and detached from the action surrounding him. This effect is no doubt intended, but it also prevents MacArthur from becoming an inspiring presence (such as Patton) and prevents the film from fulfilling its dramatic promise.

The film also pales in comparison to *Patton* in its battle scenes. *MacArthur*'s battle scenes are adequate but rarely exciting. They seem small in scale and not particularly intense. The Inchon invasion represents the key defining moment of General MacArthur's Korean War leadership, but the sequence is disappointingly unimpressive. A few shots of Naval ships bombing the coast are viewed, and most of the sequence takes place on the command ship, as MacArthur voices his doubts about the operation. This was the most inspiring, risky episode in MacArthur's military career, but instead the film treats it as an unlikely victory during which the usually composed MacArthur actually expresses self-doubt.

The film's Korean War sequences are given just as much weight as the World War II sequences. When MacArthur first hears about the invasion of South Korea (in a scene not based on fact — MacArthur was awakened with the news), he considers it to be another chance to finish his military career with honor. The general soon finds that winning the war will be more difficult than he expected, and takes it upon himself to recruit help from Chiang Kai-shek. When his efforts are rebuffed by the president, MacArthur discovers that his concept of total victory is not shared by Washington's politicians, and he cannot understand why. That single difference of philosophy leads to his eventual dismissal and public humiliation.

MacArthur regarded the Red Menace of Communism as the ultimate American enemy, and pledged himself against its spread. The movie spotlights the general's feelings regarding Communism but doesn't emphasize them as strongly as it should. For instance, it briefly mentions his plans to poison the Communist supply lines with radioactive waste, but the film backs away from depicting the general as a radical who would seriously consider such a plan, preferring to veil such extreme sentiments. Ultimately, it seems that MacArthur was fired because he was stubborn and could not coexist with President Truman on the public stage. The truth is more complex, of course, and is really based on MacArthur's refusal to compromise in any way regarding the fight against the Communist cause. The film's biggest weakness is its failure to fully explore this basic philosophical difference between MacArthur and President Truman.

As an examination of MacArthur's persona, the film is rewarding because it shows at least glimpses of the majority of MacArthur's most historic and noteworthy public moments, as well as momentary views of the private man. Judged simply as a career overview, the film is worthwhile, especially to people unfamiliar with MacArthur, his accomplishments in two world wars and his leadership in reconstructing Japan. But it rarely digs past the surface of MacArthur's image to reveal the multi-faceted man beneath.

To portray MacArthur, director Joseph Sargent chose commanding actor Gregory Peck, who had also starred in the Korean War classic *Pork Chop Hill*. Peck studied MacArthur's

2093-33

President Harry S Truman (Ed Flanders, left) meeets General Douglas MacArthur (Gregory Peck) for the first time in MacArthur *(1977). Their disparate views on the direction of the Korean War led to an untimely and unfortunate political confrontation, which MacArthur lost decisively.*

mannerisms and speech patterns incessantly. The actor came to feel that MacArthur was indeed "a very, very great man," and desperately wanted to convey the general's complexities and contradictions. As filming progressed, Peck sent memos to producers noting his growing dissatisfaction with the film's lack of dramatic bite. "There is going to be a softness at the core of the picture. It is going to lack edge and force in building up to the dramatic conflict that brought MacArthur down," read one such memo. Another, after completion of the film, summarized Peck's disappointment:

> I thought we had a chance at some degree of greatness, a powerful emotional historical drama, a cause celebre in film. In the name of 'balance' we are giving them instead of kind of military tear jerker. It is a terrible disappointment to me because I will never again have

such a part. I don't think I failed to deliver, but the picture as directed deliberately diminishes the character in colour, dimension and impact.

Critics generally agreed with Peck's assessment of the final product. Kathleen Carroll of the *New York Daily News* wrote, "it misfires almost completely. Unlike the snappy, smartly executed *Patton*, *MacArthur* is so stiff-necked and generally undistinguished that it leaves one wishing that Hollywood had allowed this old soldier to fade away quietly." Judith Crist of *Saturday Review* noted, "A lack of feeling — more specifically a lack of viewpoint — appears to be the hallmark of *MacArthur*." *Newsweek*'s Jack Kroll was more impressed, stating that the film "doesn't have the flair and panache of *Patton* but in many ways it cuts deeper and churns up more food for thought."

If *MacArthur*'s notices were disappointing,

its box office take of just over $8 million was even more so, but it had the bad luck to be released during the same summer as a phenomenon called *Star Wars*. Gregory Peck gives a studious interpretation of the man and the film is constructed so that MacArthur dominates every scene of the movie, but the result is less dynamic than reverential. *MacArthur* is generally compelling because of its controversial subject and his undeniable achievements, but it could have been one of the greatest war studies ever made.

The Manchurian Candidate

Credits: 1962. M. C. Productions. *Distributed by* United Artists. *Directed by* John Frankenheimer. *Produced by* George Axelrod and John Frankenheimer. *Executive Producer:* Howard W. Koch. *Screenplay by* George Axelrod. *Based upon a Novel by* Richard Condon. *Music Composed and Conducted by* David Amram. *Director of Photography:* Lionel Lindon, A.S.C. *Film Editor:* Ferris Webster. *Production Designer:* Richard Sylbert. *Assistant Director:* Joseph Behm. *Assistant Film Editor:* Carl Mahakian. *Costumes by* Moss Mabry. *Janet Leigh's Hair Styles by* Gene Shacove. *Assistant Art Director:* Philip M. Jefferies. *Set Decorator:* George R. Nelson. *Dialogue Coach:* Thom Conroy. *Operative Cameraman:* John Mehl. *Costumer:* Wesley V. Jefferies. *Property Master:* Arden Cripe. *Hair Stylist:* Mary Westmoreland. *Makeup Artists:* Bernard Ponedel, Jack Freeman and Ron Berkeley. *Special Effects:* Paul Pollard. *Sound Mixer:* Joe Edmondson. *Script Supervisor:* Amalia Wade. *Sound Effects Editor:* Del Harris. *Music Editor:* Richard Carruth. *Re-Recording:* Buddy Myers. *Music Recording:* Vinton Vernon. *Photographic Effects:* Howard Anderson Co. *Jewels by* Ruser - Beverly Hills. *Maps provided through the courtesy of* American Map Company, Inc. Rated PG-13. Black and White. Widescreen (1.77:1). 126 minutes. Released in October, 1962. Re-released in February, 1988. Currently available on VHS home video and DVD. Previously available on laserdisc.

Cast: *Bennett Marco,* Frank Sinatra; *Ray-*
mond Shaw, Laurence Harvey; *Rosie (Eugenie Rose),* Janet Leigh; *Mrs. Iselin (Mother),* Angela Lansbury; *Chunjin,* Henry Silva; *Senator John Iselin,* James Gregory; *Jocie Jordon,* Leslie Parrish; *Senator Thomas Jordon,* John McGiver; *Yen Lo,* Khigh Dhiegh; *Corporal Al Melvin,* James Edwards; *Colonel (Milt),* Douglas Henderson; *Zilkov,* Albert Paulsen; *Secretary of Defense,* Barry Kelley; *Holborn Gaines,* Lloyd Corrigan; *Berezovo,* Madame Spivy; *Medical Officer,* Whit Bissell; *Mrs. Melvin,* Mimi Dillard; *Officer,* Anton Van Stralen; *Grossfeld,* John Lawrence; *Bobby Lembeck,* Tom Lowell; *Ed Mavole,* Richard LePore; *Berezovo,* Nick Bolin; *Silvers,* Nicky Blair; *Little,* William Thourlby; *Freeman,* Irving Steinberg; *Haiken,* John Francis; *Manager,* Lou Krugg; *Benjamin K. Arthur,* Robert Riordan; *Gomel,* Reggie Nalder; *Miss Gertrude,* Miyoshi Jingu; *Korean Girl,* Anna Shin; *Chairladies,* Helen Kleeb, Maye Henderson; *Reporters,* Mickey Finn, Richard Norris, John Indrisano; *F.B.I. Men,* Mike Masters, Tom Harris; *Soprano,* Marquita Moll; *Convention Chairman,* Robert Burton; *Secretary,* Karen Norris; *Gomel,* Bess Flowers; *Nurse,* Jean Vaughn; *Policeman,* Ray Spiker; *Jilly,* Merritt Bohn; *Photographer,* Frank Basso; *General,* Harry Holcombe; *Page Boy,* Ray Dailey; *Party Guests,* Julie Payne, Lana Crawford, Evelyn Byrd; *Women in Lobby,* Estelle Etterre, Mary Benoit, Rita Kenaston, Maggie Hathaway, Joan Douglas, Frances E. Nealy; *Men in Lobby,* Ralph Gambina, Sam "Kid" Hogan, James Yagi, Lee Tung Foo, Raynum K. Tsukamoto; *narrated by* Paul Frees.

Historical Accuracy Level: Low. The film is highly implausible in terms of the war and Communist ability to completely brainwash a soldier, but its very improbability is what makes the film so dramatically compelling.

Patriotic Propaganda Level: Low. The story can certainly be read as a dire warning that our country is not prepared for psychological attacks.

Elements: Army, Brainwashing, Congressional Medal of Honor, Espionage, Infighting, Mystery, Politics, Posttraumatic Stress Syndrome, Prisoners of War, Red Menace, Returning Home, Romance, Secret Missions.

The story told in *The Manchurian Candidate* begins in Korea but its ramifications involve three international superpowers — China, Russia and the United States — when a minor incident that takes place during the Korean War blossoms into events that would change world history. Made in 1962, *The Manchurian Candidate* was highly lauded, only to be shelved for twenty-five years following the assassination of President John F. Kennedy (who, ironically, was a big fan of the movie). Re-released in 1988 to universal acclaim, John Frankenheimer's prophetic political thriller was found to be just as contemporary and meaningful as it had been during its initial release, and possibly more so. There are some very good Korean War movies to be found in this book; *The Manchurian Candidate* is the greatest, dwarfing all others in terms of concept, style and execution. It is a cinematic masterpiece.

The Manchurian Candidate commences during Korea in 1952, as a night patrol of eleven Americans led by Captain Bennett Marco (Frank Sinatra) and Sergeant Raymond Shaw (Laurence Harvey) are led into an ambush by Korean scout Chunjin (Henry Silva). The Americans are knocked unconscious and airlifted by helicopter into the dark night. Weeks later, Raymond Shaw returns to America to receive the Congressional Medal of Honor. His dignified arrival is disrupted by his manipulative mother (Angela Lansbury) and clownish stepfather, Senator John Iselin (James Gregory), who take the opportunity to trumpet Raymond's relationship. Raymond informs his parents that he will not be living with them, but will instead take a newspaper job in New York with a publisher of whom his mother disapproves. "That *Communist*?" she roars.

Two years after the war's conclusion, Bennett Marco, now a major stationed back in the States, begins to suffer a recurring nightmare. He and the other members of the patrol are attending a garden party, where an elderly woman is touting the merits of hydrangeas. Inexplicably, Chinese and Russian officers are also present, although not all of the time, and Raymond Shaw politely strangles fellow soldier Ed Movole (Richard LePore) with a knotted scarf ...

Marco meets with Army brass about his nightmare, but is diagnosed with delayed stress and is assigned to lighter duties in the public relations office. At a press conference with the Secretary of Defense, Marco is unable to prevent an uproar when Senator Iselin proclaims that he has a list of 207 Communists in the armed forces. Moments later, away from the press, Iselin changes his number to 104, then to 275.

Meanwhile, another member of the patrol, Al Melvin (James Edwards), also experiences trouble sleeping. His nightmare is more detailed than Marco's, and depicts Raymond Shaw's killing of Bobby Lembeck (Tom Lowell) with a pistol. Following his wife's advice, Melvin writes a letter to Raymond asking him for help. Before Raymond can respond, however, he is "triggered" by a command issued over the telephone. Melvin's letter is forgotten as Raymond, in a zombie-like state, reports to a hospital where his indoctrination is checked by Chinese psychologist Yen Lo (Khigh Dhiegh) and Russian colleague Zilkov (Albert Paulsen). The two men discuss Raymond's future as a secret weapon and send him on a test run, during which Raymond kills his boss, publisher Holborn Gaines (Lloyd Corrigan), and assumes Gaines' position.

Bennett Marco, unable to sleep securely, is relieved of duty. On a train to New York, he meets a beautiful woman named Rosie (Janet Leigh) and they establish a rapport. Marco goes to Raymond's apartment and finds Chunjin, whom Raymond has just recently hired as a valet. Marco instantly recognizes Chunjin and attacks him. The two men battle using karate chops and judo flips, destroying much of the apartment. Marco is arrested and calls Rosie, the only person he knows in New York. She pays his bail and takes him home with her, telling him she has cancelled her marriage engagement so that they may be together. Marco visits Raymond, learns of Melvin's letter, and travels to Washington to assemble the pieces of the growing mystery.

Marco identifies photographs of Yen Lo and Zilkov — confirming identifications made by Melvin hours earlier — and is then placed in charge of an Army-C.I.A.-F.B.I. investigation of Raymond Shaw. Meanwhile, Senator Iselin begs his wife to choose a specific, easily remembered number of Communists for his mudslinging. She watches him pour Heinz ketchup on a meal and chooses 57.

Marco and Raymond get drunk together, causing Raymond to reminisce about the only time in his life when he was "lovable." It was the

United Artists' advertising campaign for The Manchurian Candidate *(1962) reveals little about its story and urges moviegoers to arrive on time. Its impact stems from its unique line drawings of familiar crime action.*

summer before he joined the army, and he fell in love with Jocie Jordon (Leslie Parrish), the daughter of Senator Thomas Jordon (John McGiver), an arch-enemy of Raymond's mother. A flashback, narrated by Raymond, revisits this happy time, which ends when his mother forces Raymond to write a particularly nasty letter to the Jordons. Back in the present, when meeting Marco in a bar, Raymond is accidentally "triggered" into travelling to Central Park and jumping into its lake. Marco remembers the triggering device, the queen of diamonds card, and guesses that it is meant to represent Raymond's mother.

Raymond's mother arranges a costume party to welcome Jocie Jordon back to America after her years in Paris. Raymond is to be given his final instructions at the party, but that plan goes awry when Raymond sees Jocie, whose costume is the queen of diamonds. They run away and marry, making Raymond the happiest he has ever been. Marco tells Jocie that Raymond is mentally sick and gives her two days with him before Raymond is to be interrogated. When Raymond happens to hear that Iselin is threatening to impeach Senator Jordon, Raymond moves to stop his mother's political machinations. Instead, she is revealed to be his American controller and orders him to kill Senator Jordon. Raymond goes back to the Jordons in his indoctrinated, zombie-like state and calmly shoots Senator Jordon, who is holding a carton of milk. Jocie hears the killing and interrupts it; Raymond kills her as well. As he leaves the Jordon house, tears stream down his unemotional face.

Marco reads of the Jordon assassination and realizes that it was done by Raymond, although he blames himself for delaying Raymond's interrogation. Raymond contacts Marco and they meet. With a deck of queen of diamonds cards, Marco learns the whole story of their brainwashing and then "smashes the links," hopefully curing Raymond of remote control. Raymond still does not know what his ultimate mission is, so Marco allows him to go free, hoping that Raymond will tell him when it is finally revealed.

The political convention takes place at Madison Square Garden, and Senator Iselin has been nominated for vice president. Raymond's mother instructs her son to wait until a specific moment during the presidential nominee's acceptance speech and then shoot him through the head. Iselin will then lift the body, make an emotional speech and be swept into the White House. Raymond's mother apologizes to her impassive son for involving him as the assassin; the Communist leaders decided to use Raymond in order to control her, but she vows to grind all who oppose her into the dirt. She kisses her son for the final time — a long, lingering kiss on the lips.

Raymond Shaw enters the convention dressed as a priest and climbs to an unused spotlight room, where he sits and waits. With no contact from Raymond, Marco finally goes to the convention, hoping for a miracle to prevent Raymond's mysterious mission. During the national anthem, Marco sees the light from the spotlight room and rushes up the stairs. Raymond prepares his rifle and at the specific point in the nominee's speech, shoots twice. His first bullet kills Senator John Iselin, the second kills his mother. Marco arrives in the spotlight room moments after the shots. Raymond tells him, "You couldn't have stopped them. Nobody could have." He then puts the rifle in his mouth and pulls the trigger.

Afterward, Marco reads descriptions of Congressional Medal of Honor winners to Rosie. He then recites his own version of what Raymond Shaw's should say: "Made to commit acts too unspeakable to be cited here, by an enemy who had captured his mind and his soul — he freed himself at last, and in the end, heroically and unhesitatingly, gave his life to save his country."

The Manchurian Candidate is a masterwork of suspense and terror. It perfectly captures the paranoid mood of the Cold War, when McCarthyism (represented by John Iselin) was branding all who disagreed with its tenets as Communists. At the same time, it highlights an elliptical, far more fiendish Communist advance, one aimed at securing the highest place of power in American politics as a secret stronghold. The film depicts the long-standing socialist practice of rousing the rabble with boisterous rhetoric to camouflage its true intentions, and the success of that tactic is what makes the film so frightening. While the sinister story ventures away from reality at times, and the capability for brainwashing is tremendously overstated, the film's possibilities are so mind-boggling and engaging that audiences are captivated.

The film's most famous sequence is, of course, the brainwashing itself. Excerpted in the nightmares of Al Melvin and Bennett Marco, the brainwashing sequence, with its circling dolly movements and transmogrification from genteel garden club to psychological examination and back again, is the work of director John Frankenheimer and director of photography Lionel Lindon. With little instruction in the script for this crucial sequence, Frankenheimer simply improvised, tracking his camera around an expanded set, with the intent of reediting the footage later. Once viewed, however, the brilliant sequence was left virtually intact.

No other film has utilized the notion of "brainwashing" as well as this one. The Chinese, aided by the Russians, use a sophisticated new technique which relieves the subject of all guilt or remorse. Thus, Raymond Shaw becomes a weapon, able to kill fellow soldiers Ed Mavole and Bobby Lembeck calmly and dispassionately, and unable to remember the murders afterward. Raymond's brainwashing, perhaps aided by the "check-up" and fine tuning two years later, holds tenaciously; under tight Communist control, he commits three more murders (including that of his newlywed wife!) before his ultimate mission takes place.

The other men in the patrol, however (all of whom are named after cast and crew members of the *Phil Silvers Show*!), experience some breakdown of the brainwashing effects over time. Both Al Melvin and Bennett Marco experience recurrent nightmares which reveal confusing details about their ordeal, and it is very possible other surviving members of the patrol are suffering the same fate. Since the focus of the brainwashing experiment is on Raymond, it is likely that the indoctrination of the other men is less severe, and thus diffuses more rapidly. Also, only Raymond is subjected to a check-up, while the other men are left alone. This becomes the only weakness of the Communists' plan, as Marco gradually deduces what really happened on that patrol in Korea and that his friend Raymond is in terrible trouble.

The film's most classic and effective scene, reminiscent of the best work of Alfred Hitchcock, is Raymond's murder of the Jordons. Raymond politely confronts Senator Jordon in his kitchen, as the senator is about to enjoy a late night snack. Raymond calmly raises his silenced pistol and shoots Jordon through a carton of milk the senator is holding. The milk flows out of the carton as the body drops to the floor. Moments later, Jocie sees Raymond shoot her father in the head (to ensure death) and screams. Without hesitating, Raymond shoots Jocie in the chest as she rushes toward him. Raymond then leaves, calmly and quietly, his face impassive except for tears streaming from his sad eyes.

The scene is shocking and brutal, but also incredibly tragic, as Raymond and Jocie were just married and happy a few scenes previously. It is in this scene that the audience — and Raymond — experience the emotional impact of the evil that the Communists have inflicted upon him.

The most shocking revelation is, of course, the identity of Raymond's "American controller." The first clue is when Marco remembers the queen of diamonds card as "the second key to the mechanism," and that it was chosen because it was reminiscent of Raymond's mother. Still, when his mother reveals herself to be the top Communist agent in America, audiences are stunned. The very idea is diabolical! Raymond's mother, whose first name is never mentioned and whose role as candidate's wife seems to be firmly cast, has already been shown as duplicitous, dominating and ruthless. She tells Raymond (who cannot interact with her in his trance) that she will stop at nothing to take power and that the Communists will be "… ground into the dirt for what they did to you and what they did in so grotesquely underestimating me," thereby revealing her true, egomaniacal character. Then, by kissing her son farewell as she does, with incestuous overtones and a real longing for absolution, Raymond's mother seals his fate. Such a complex, monstrous characterization is sheer brilliance, and it is played ferociously by Angela Lansbury, who was just three years older than "son" Laurence Harvey when the film was made, and who received an Oscar nomination for her work.

Harvey and Frank Sinatra contribute sterling performances as well. Sinatra plays Bennett Marco and functions as the film's explaining tool; the audience learns of things mainly through his eyes. Marco is a strong character, able to overcome the debilitating mental confusion of his mind to once again become a professional soldier, investigating the mystery involving his friend with sense and compassion. Sinatra also broke one of his fingers chopping down on a table in the fight scene with Henry Silva.

Marco also becomes entangled with Rosie (Janet Leigh), in what remains the film's strangest and most enigmatic relationship. The dialogue between the two when they meet and talk on the train is often absurd, with non-se-

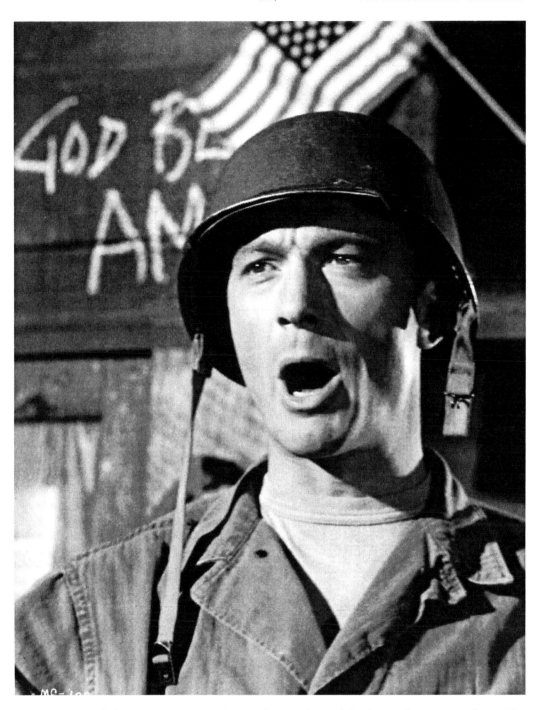

Sergeant Raymond Shaw (Laurence Harvey) is an abrasive platoon leder during the Korean conflict in The Manchurian Candidate *(1962). After the war, every one of his fellow soldiers inexplicably refers to him as "the kindest, gentlest man I've ever met."*

quiturs and little real communication. It's almost as if the characters are talking to themselves rather than to each other, and yet they do connect. It is Rosie's calming, reassuring influence that saves Marco from mental collapse, and he gives her someone for whom to care. Critic Roger Ebert of the *Chicago Sun-Times* put forth this theory to explain their behavior:

My notion is that Sinatra's character is a Manchurian killer, too — one allowed to remember details of Harvey's brainwashing because that would make him seem more credible. And Leigh? She is Sinatra's controller.

While Ebert's theory of Marco remembering details for credibility's sake seems weak and unjustified, his notion of Rosie as Marco's controller is thought-provoking. As Ebert writes, "This possible scenario simply adds another level to a movie already rich in intrigue," and he is correct. Regardless of the "reality" of the situation, the bizarre byplay between Marco and Rosie does make the film more hallucinatory and compelling.

But it is Laurence Harvey as Raymond Shaw who makes everything work. The Lithuanian-born actor specialized in charmless opportunists, and ensured that Raymond was, indeed, without charm or personal magnetism. That worked in the script's favor, supporting the irony of his patrol mates' unemotional claim that "Raymond Shaw is the kindest, bravest, warmest, most wonderful human being I've ever met in my life." Yet Harvey also releases Raymond's unfulfilled longing for Jocie Jordon during his drunk scene with Marco, where he bemoans not being "lovable." And when he returns from his reunion with Jocie, Raymond is a new man, happy and energetic, even cracking a joke. Harvey is totally convincing as a man who has suddenly found the love he thought was lost to him forever. But Harvey's greatest achievement lies in his reserve during the last act of the film, as Raymond learns of his fate and calmly decides for himself how he will die. His most effective moment comes as he leaves the Jordon house after killing the Senator and Jocie. He walks away, unhurried and unemotional in his trance, yet tears streak down his face, revealing the inner torment that indoctrination cannot prevent.

The Korean War is background for this story, but it is essential background, for it is the only time and place that perfectly aligns the participants and opportunities of the story. The international conflict allowed China and Russia to work together (never admittedly, of course) and to experiment on captured United Nations soldiers. Many prisoners of the time told of harsh, barbarous methods of converting U.N. soldiers to Communist ideology, though none approached the scope of the plan in *The Manchurian Candidate*. One can even infer that the war was undertaken for just such an opportunity, though the film does not say so.

Korea is unimportant in the movie's scheme of things; it is dwarfed by the actions and intricate plans of Communist China and Russia. The Communist threat to democracy is the villain, one which insidiously twists the concept of rewarded heroism — specifically utilizing our highest military honor, the Congressional Medal of Honor — for its own evil usage. The ways in which both the Congressional Medal of Honor and the accepted role of wife and mother are turned inside out and used against America indicates just how deceitful the Cold War has become, according to the story's perspective. And yet, the film offers hope, based on the inner workings of free people's minds, that no matter how diabolical the subterfuge employed by our enemies, free people can still prevail.

Aside from its elements of suspense and high drama, the movie is also wildly satirical. Pauline Kael, judged "It may be the most sophisticated political satire ever made in Hollywood." Other critics of the time — from both sides of the political spectrum — found the film subversive, and demanded its withdrawal. In the *Saturday Review*, Arthur Knight stayed on the fence, writing that "Without question, it is the best-told story of the year. Without question, it is also the most irresponsible." Ironically, the head of United Artists, Arthur Krim (who was also the national finance chairman of the Democratic Party), had to be persuaded to make the film in the first place because he felt it was un-American. Moira Walsh in *America* summed up the controversy this way: "I cannot, however, join in the chorus denouncing the film as irresponsible. Curiously enough, this charge seems to emanate from positions fairly far out on both ends of the political spectrum. In neither case does the charge seem to have been honestly thought through or persuasively stated." She concluded with this sage bit of advice: "I also think a citizenry that is not protected from the yearly flood of specious campaign oratory is in no great need of being protected from *The Manchurian Candidate*."

The Manchurian Candidate was both damned and praised on its initial release. *Time's* critic concluded that "It tries so hard to be different that it fails to be itself." The *London Sunday Times* termed the film "an insolent, heartless thriller," and Bosley Crowther of the *New York Times* decried the film's lack of focus. "Whatever chance of balanced satire and ironic point there might have been in the subtle equating of these two firebrands [Raymond Shaw and Johnny Iselin] is lost in the script of George Axelrod."

On the other hand, the *New Yorker*'s Brendan Gill loved its melodrama: "Many loud hurrahs for *The Manchurian Candidate*, a thriller guaranteed to raise all but the limpest hair." And *Variety*'s Vincent Canby wrote, "Every once in a rare while a film comes along that 'works' in all departments, with story, production and performance so well blended that the end effect is one of nearly complete satisfaction. Such is *The Manchurian Candidate*, George Axelrod and John Frankenheimer's jazzy, hip screen translation of Richard Condon's bestselling novel." Canby went on to note that "One of the brilliant achievements of the film is the way Axelrod and Frankenheimer have been able to blend the diverse moods, including the tender and explosively funny as well as the satiric and brutally shocking."

Many critics seemed to enjoy the film as a potboiler, but refused to take it seriously. Or else they took the opposite approach, taking the picture far too seriously and refusing to enjoy it.

The movie was nominated for two Academy Awards in 1962: the film editing of Ferris Webster and the supporting actress performance of Angela Lansbury. *Lawrence of Arabia* won the film editing prize while Patty Duke took home the Oscar for portraying young Helen Keller in *The Miracle Worker*. Lansbury did win the Golden Globe best supporting actress award,

The famous brainwashing "tea party" sequence in The Manchurian Candidate *(1962), in which Bennett Marco (Frank Sinatra, left), Raymond Shaw (Laurence Harvey, center, yawning) and Bobby Lembeck (Tom Lowell, right) receive instructions from their Chinese interrogators.*

and was named best supporting actress by the National Board of Review for her performances in two John Frankenheimer films, *All Fall Down* and *The Manchurian Candidate.*

John Frankenheimer should have been Oscar nominated for the director award, but was not. Frankenheimer generously spread credit for the film around: "*The Manchurian Candidate* is a classic example of the old adage — you are no better than your material. Richard Condon wrote a great book. Everything that critics praise in the film is in the book — the dream sequence, the scene in the train, the character of Raymond's mother and so much more. In fact, there are three or four scenes from Condon's book that we were unable to put in the film - something I have always regretted. George Axelrod wrote a marvelous screenplay, which I followed faithfully. The actors were wonderful. The cameraman, Lionel Lindon, was the finest I ever worked with. In short, *The Manchurian Candidate* was one of those experiences where everything went right."

Following the assassination of John F. Kennedy in 1963, the film was quietly shelved. The most widely reported reason for this is that United Artists executives felt that the film struck entirely too close to reality and they were ashamed of being associated with it, but this has been refuted by all parties involved. The film was not widely promoted by United Artists to begin with, and by their accounting, had never made a profit. Over the years, attempts to reissue the title by the studio were refused by Frank Sinatra, who had placed a lot of faith in the film and was angry that the studio had not supported the film and were still claiming that it had never been profitable. Finally, in early 1988, the film was re-released, to glowing reviews, and made quite a bit of money. In 1994, the film was named to the National Film Registry, the first Korean War film to be so honored.

The Manchurian Candidate is an amazing movie, filled with enough suspense and classic moments to fill three films. It was vividly directed by John Frankenheimer, a stylish virtuoso then at the top of his powers, and it has stood the test of time, outlasting many of its contemporaries in the public memory. It is an atypical Korean War film, but one which, through a remarkable and dazzling story cour-tesy of Richard Condon, perhaps best represents the ultimate Communist threat to democracy, one which, thankfully, has never come to pass.

Man-Trap

(aka *Man in Hiding*)

Credits: 1961. Tiger Productions. *Distributed by* Paramount. *Directed by* Edmond O'Brien. *Produced by* Edmond O'Brien and Stanley Frazen. *Associate Producer:* Sam E. Waxman. *Screenplay by* Ed Waters. *Based on a Novel* Taint of the Tiger *by* John D. MacDonald. *Music:* Leith Stevens. *Director of Photography:* Loyal Griggs, A.S.C. *Edited by* Jack H. Lippiatt. *Art Direction:* Hal Pereira and Al Roelofs. *Process Photography:* Farciot Edouart, A.S.C. *Costumes:* Edith Head. *Set Decoration:* Sam Comer and James Payne. *Assistant Director:* Tom Shaw. *Makeup Supervision:* Wally Westmore, S.M.A. *Hair Style Supervision:* Nellie Manley, C.H.A. *Sound Recording:* Philip Mitchell and John Wilkinson. Not Rated. Black and White. Panavision (2.35:1). 93 minutes. Released in September, 1961. Not currently available on commercial home video.

Cast: Mathew Jamison, Jeffrey Hunter; *Vince Biskay / Arturo del Garza,* David Janssen; *Nina Jamison,* Stella Stevens; *Liz Addams,* Elaine Devry; *Ruth,* Virginia Gregg; *Vera Snavely,* Dorothy Green; *E. J. Malden,* Hugh Sanders; *Paul Snavely,* Frank Albertson; *Cortez,* Arthur Batanides; *Puerco,* Perry Lopez; *Fat Man,* Bernard Fein; *Lieutenant Heissen,* Tol Avery; *Ralphie Turner,* Bob Crane; *Yolande Thaw,* Lisa Seagram; *Arlene Anders,* Ann McCrea; *Bobby-Joe,* Mike Vandever; *Zargosa,* Raoul De Leon; *Paul Finnerty,* Frank Tom Bank; *Chauffeur,* J. Lewis Smith; *Motorcycle Officer,* George G. Dockstader; *Room Clerk,* George Mather; *Photographer,* Byron C. Fromme; *Truck Driver,* George Sawaya; *Officer,* Clyde McLeod; *Murray,* Michael St. Angel; *Man,* Cosmo Sardo; *Woman,* Ann Carroll; *Man,* Joe Brooks; *Woman,* Gaylen McClure; *Marine,* Jim Cody; *Oriental Men,* Yuki Shimoda, Lynell Katsutaro and Tanigoshi; *Marine,* Chuck Morrell; *Bellhop,* William L. Mullikin; *Mexican Policemen,* Henry T. Delgado and Joseph A. Raciti; *Mexican Woman,* Laurette

Luwez; *Mexican Border Guard*, Donald A. Diamond.

Level of Historical Accuracy: Low. This is a non-specific storyline featuring a vague raid into Korea by Marine Corps personnel.

Patriotic Propaganda Level: Low. This film spotlights a group of very unhappy people.

Elements: Behind Enemy Lines, Marine Corps, Rescues.

Man-Trap is one of several movies which utilize the Korean War to establish a relationship between two men that is later tested by some event (commonly, a woman). Many war films depict ways in which men bond together under fire and how those men come to depend upon each other even after they return from combat. Other movies show how men who dislike each other — but who share the common background of having experienced action together — retain the protective characteristic of "watching the other fella's back" from habit and conscience. To varying degrees, *Bombers B-52*, *The Manchurian Candidate*, *Not with My Wife, You Don't!* and even *Strange Intruder* explore such relationships, but *Man-Trap* is without doubt the most lurid of this group. Its Korean War prologue is included only to establish bonds between two men, one of whom owes his life to the other.

U.S. Marines make a small raid into Korea in 1952. One of the men, Vince Biskay (David Janssen) is trapped on a ridge by Chinese snipers. Vince is shot in the leg and the right hand, losing his thumb and index finger. Another soldier, Matt Jamison (Jeffrey Hunter), comes to Vince's rescue, jumping the Chinese soldiers and bayonetting them. Matt carries Vince to the beach, but one of the Chinese snipers survives and shoots Matt in the head before being killed by another Marine. Vince and Matt are carried to the Marines' inflatable raft, where Vince pledges to split any future money he makes with his unconscious friend.

Eight years later, Matt Jamison is a successful associate in a construction firm, but his marriage is a shambles. Matt spends time kissing his secretary, Liz Addams (Elaine Devry), and looking for an escape from his alcoholic, oversexed wife Nina (Stella Stevens). Deep in debt, Matt tries to leave the construction firm, but boss E. J. Malden (Hugh Sanders), who is also Nina's father, reveals that Matt owes too much money to leave. Malden actually suggests "squeezing the subcontractors for kickbacks," but Matt is too honest to force other people to pay for his mistakes. Suddenly, Vince Biskay re-enters his life, with a plan to make a cool one million dollars. Unbeknownst to them, however, Vince is being followed and watched.

Biskay has been masquerading in Central America as Arturo del Garza, and has arranged to intercept a suitcase full of cash stolen from a Latin American dictator to buy armaments for the dictator's enemies. By stealing the suitcase at the San Francisco airport and returning it to the dictator, Vince will earn $1 million. Vince wants his old buddy to drive the getaway car; the money will be evenly divided between them and an arms sale will be prevented. Matt refuses and tries to patch up his ailing marriage with Nina. She responds by clubbing him in the head with a fireplace poker and threatening to leave him. Matt comes close to killing her, but then decides that Vince's plan offers the best solution to his problems and drives to San Francisco.

Matt and Vince rehearse the interception plan several times and discuss every eventuality. On the day of the robbery, the San Francisco airport is besieged by fans of a young rock and roll singer whose cheering disrupts the delivery of the cash. Three Latin American hoods who have been following Vince since his arrival in California open fire in the crowd killing the man with the suitcase and badly injuring Vince. Matt comes to Vince's rescue again, getting him and the suitcase into the getaway limousine and escaping the scene. They are followed by the hoods, who shoot at the car, disrupting a local parade. Eventually, the hoods are stopped and they flee on foot while Matt and Vince drive away with the money.

To Matt's surprise, the suitcase contains $3,650,000, and Vince admits to stealing it with no intent to return it for the $1 million reward. Matt uses some of the money to procure a doctor for Vince and then takes him home. Nina agrees to stay while Vince recuperates, and soon her husband finds her in bed with him. A newspaper report that Vince is staying with Matt forces him to hide Vince at Nina's father's cabin in the mountains. While the men are gone, Nina has a drunken fit, yelling at her housekeeper

Sex and violence are draws in Paramount's lurid drama Man-Trap *(1961), directed by actor Edmond O'Brien. Though Jeffrey Hunter and David Janssen are top-billed, the movie's marketing focuses on up and coming star Stella Stevens.*

Ruth (Virginia Gregg), and falls to her death over the upstairs railing. Matt returns home, finds Nina's body, and buries it at one of his construction sites. Matt drives to the mountain cabin and tells Vince to take the money to Mexico in Nina's car. Vince agrees and leaves with all the money. Matt then calls Liz Addams, confesses to the robbery and asks for her help. She agrees to meet him.

The three Latin American hoods find Matt at home and beat him bloody, reinjuring his head wound from Korea (for which he received a metal plate) to such an extent that Matt cannot remember the immediate past. Liz arrives and finds him unable to recall the robbery or Nina's death. She takes him to the police, where Ruth has already revealed how Nina died. Meanwhile, Vince crosses into Mexico safely.

He stops at a cantina, ill from his long trip, and drinks two beers. When he realizes he doesn't have the dinero to pay for them, he jumps into Nina's roadster and speeds away, but Mexican police open fire. In the resulting crash the car overturns, spilling the large denomination American money onto the ground all around Vince, who is killed. Matt vaguely recalls burying the money at the construction site; when Nina is uncovered instead, his memory comes back with devastating effects. Police lieutenant Heissen (Tol Avery) comforts Liz Addams, assuring her that Matt will be treated well. "The right thing will be done."

Man-Trap is a time capsule from the early 1960s in several respects. First is the accent upon melodrama over traditional drama. Director Edmond O'Brien (a noted, Oscar-winning actor in his own right) chose to exaggerate important elements of the story and sensationalize aspects rather than make them convincingly real. Thus, the character of Nina is spectacularly flamboyant and completely over the top. A beautiful, alcoholic nymphomaniac, Nina is easily the most memorable character in the piece, but her bitchery is so pronounced that it soon becomes tiresome. This type of character — sexually intense and provocative in a loud, overbearing manner — became popular in the late fifties and continued to appear throughout the decade of the 1960s, before evolving into a quieter, more sinister type of vixen.

Another dated aspect centers on the neighbors. Several times during the story, middle-aged neighbors of the Jamisons have rambunctious, alcoholic parties, at which Nina is a featured performer. The film hints, non-explicitly, that these neighbors engage in wife swapping and other sexual shenanigans. Their favorite game is "Braille," wherein men try to identify their wives by touch alone. This hyperactive frenzy of repressed suburban sexuality, highlighted by Nina shooting people with her "martini pistol," dates the film more than any other single aspect. Yet its inclusion is deliberate, because *Man-Trap* is an indictment of greed and corruption on both personal and professional levels.

The neighborhood parties are indicative of the film's view that modern life in America is hollow at its center. The rampant carnality at which the film hints points to a complete loss of societal integrity, and only Matt Jamison actively battles that loss. Matt is an honest man trying to provide value to his construction clients, but even his own father-in-law actively encourages him to cheat them. "Now I know where Nina got her sense of values," Matt comments. He is trapped in a loveless marriage, and his open affair with secretary Liz Addams is tearing her conscience apart. At one point Liz cries, "I've lost my sense of values! What's happened to me?" Moreover, Matt's quest for career success parallels the destructive effects of the robbery. Every person who comes in contact with the stolen Latin American suitcase full of money loses his or her life or freedom, just as Matt literally loses part of his mind. In this movie, it seems that the only place of honor, at least for Matt, is on the battlefield.

Indeed, personal honor is rare in the *Man-Trap* universe. Both Vince and Nina chide Matt for his ethics; in fact, Nina becomes so infuriated at husband "Sir Mathew" that she clubs him in the head with a fireplace poker. Of all the characters, Vince Biskay represents the worst of human nature. Seemingly a good guy in Korea, eight years later he is cheating the Latin American dictator for whom he works (disguised as Arturo del Garza), persuading his best friend to help him in a robbery and then nonchalantly bedding Matt's wife. That Vince meets a violent end is predestined; it is surprising that he does not take more people with him when he goes.

Director Edmond O'Brien invests the film with moral warning, but in doing so unfortunately emphasizes the tawdry aspects of humanity. His directorial style is never less than obvious, but he utilizes techniques such as split-screen effectively, and the film is never dull. Under O'Brien's direction, Jeffrey Hunter and David Janssen deliver decent performances, but while she is onscreen, Stella Stevens is the whole show. As Nina, Stevens cuts loose, spitting verbal jabs and insults like an angry cobra and using her steamy sexuality to ensnare virtually every other male in the cast. Matt's other love, Liz Addams, is played by Elaine Devry, whose voice rarely rises above a whisper in contrast to Stevens' verbal fireworks.

Apart from its melodramatic tone, the film's other major problem is Liz Addams. Her

Vince Biskay (David Janssen, left) and Mathew Jamison (Jeffrey Hunter, right) examine the cash netted from their robbery of a Latin American courier in Man-Trap *(1961). Biskay's shirt is bloody from a gunshot wound, and his right thumb and index finger are not visible, because they were shot off in a shore raid during the Korean War during the film's opening sequence.*

initial appearance is the film's worst scene, as she is used to explain Matt's situation to the audience in between kisses with him. In that scene, she asks questions about the metal plate in his head (pawing him as if to feel the plate beneath his skin), about Vince (whom he hasn't seen in eight years) and about Nina (whom the audience has not as yet seen). In later scenes, Liz overcomes her role as a plot device, but it is difficult to believe that Matt would be interested in her when he has Nina at home waiting for him. His affair with Liz also makes Matt a less honorable character, even after Nina's infidelities are revealed. Ultimately, the movie would be better off without her.

The robbery segment is intriguing but also exposes the film's meager budget and necessary minimalism. It is rather poorly staged, and the car chase scene is silly rather than exciting. The Korean War prologue is another disappointment, obviously filmed at a local beach. And it

is obvious that this prologue is merely included to introduce Vince and Matt and establish their friendship. The film has nothing at all to say about the Korean War, which is disappointing considering its indictments of society at large. In this case, the war is, like Liz Addams, simply a plot device.

Man-Trap was one of two David Janssen films in 1961 which dealt with the Korean War in some regard (*Twenty Plus Two* is the other), but even Stella Stevens' supercharged performance failed to attract people to theatres, and the melodrama was seemingly too tawdry to attract critical attention. In their study *The Motion Picture Guide*, Jay Robert Nash and Stanley Ralph Ross summarize the film thusly: "Good performances are wasted in a script filled with absurd situations." Perhaps the most absurd, if trivial, aspect of the film is now its most noteworthy. The leader of the drunken neighborhood revelers, Ralphie, is portrayed by Bob

Crane, the *Hogan's Heroes* actor who was later murdered and then publicly revealed to be a sex addict. It is unfortunate that this "life imitates art" aspect has become the film's lasting legacy.

Marine Battleground

Credits: 1966. Paul Mart Productions. *Distributed by* Manson Distributing Corporation. *Directed by* Manli Lee and Milton Mann. *Produced by* Paul Mart and Sun Won. *Executive Producer:* Michael F. Goldman. *Associate Producer:* Sy De Bardas. *Screenplay Adaptation by* Milton Mann. *Screenplay by* Han-chul Yu, Burton Moore and Tom Morrison. *Based on a Story by* Kook-jin Jang. *Music by* Jaime Mendoza-Nava. *Directors of Photography:* William Hines and Jingmin Su. *Film Editor:* Milton Mann. *Art Directors:* Wally Moon, Sungchil Hong and Tod Jonson. Not Rated. Black and White. CinemaScope (2.35:1). 88 minutes. Released in 1966. Partly filmed on location in South Korea. Not currently available on commercial home video.

Cast: *Nick Rawlins*, Jock Mahoney; *Nurse Young Hi Park*, Pat Li (Pat Yi); *Young Hi Park (as a child)*, Young-sun Jun (Youngson Chon); *Squad Leader*, Dong-hui Jang (Tong-hui Chang); *Private Ku*, Dae-yup Lee (Tae-yop Yi); *Private Bong Ku*, Bong-su Ku (Pong-su Ku); *First Patient*, David Lowe; *Second Patient*, Lloyd Kino; *with* George Zaima. *Note:* actor names are taken verbatim from the film's pressbook; actor names in (parentheses) are taken from other sources.

Historical Accuracy Level: Medium. This story personalizes the Inchon landing from a South Korean perspective, though it does falsely include Chinese troops.

Patriotic Propaganda Level: High. American Marines adopt a South Korean orphan and inspire her to become a nurse.

Elements: Effects on Civilians, Females in the Field, Journalism, Marine Corps, Medicine, Multiple Wars, Nurses, Orphans.

Marine Battleground is an independently produced co-production between the United States and South Korea which dramatizes the invasion at Inchon from the perspective of a young Korean girl who is orphaned in the bat-

tle. The girl, Young Hi, is adopted by a Marine platoon which takes her into battle as they secure the city. She remains at headquarters while the Marines wage a fierce battle, from which only two Marines return. Young Hi survives the war and dedicates her life to nursing, inspired by the protectiveness of the Marines who saved her. The beginning and ending of the film are set in Vietnam, as the beautiful nurse (played by Pat Li) describes her childhood during the Korean War to visiting journalist Nick Rawlins (Jock Mahoney).

The movie sounds like an authentic version of the Inchon landing (no copy of the film could be found for review), but its own publicity material undermines its realism. The pressbook describes that after the orphan girl is left at headquarters, "The [Marine] platoon has been informed that a trap is being set for the incoming Chinese invaders." It should read "by" instead of "for," but the real faux pas is that the Chinese didn't enter the war for another two months. The pressbook states "The movie-going public will see the Red Chinese soldier as he really appears in battle. He is under the influence of narcotics when attacking, with total disregard for his own safety as he becomes a part of a suicide attack." While Chinese soldiers did take part in sacrificial attacks, there is no evidence that they were drug-addled when doing so, and, to belabor the point, such Chinese troops were certainly not present at Inchon.

The film seems to focus on nurse Young Hi Park's devotion to the Marines, both in Korea and Vietnam, inspired by their kindness and protectiveness of her as a young orphan. She attempts to explain this devotion to journalist Rawlins by relating her personal experiences in the long Korean War flashback that is the main story. As such, it seems to be a personal and involving story rather than "The All Out Story of the Hell-Blasting Marines!" that its publicity promises.

Marines, Let's Go

Credits: 1961. 20th Century–Fox. *Produced and Directed by* Raoul Walsh. *Screenplay by* John Twist. *Based on a Story by* Raoul Walsh.

Music: Irving Gertz. *Director of Photography*: Lucien Ballard, A.S.C. *Film Editor*: Robert Simpson, A.C.E. *Art Direction*: Jack Martin Smith and Alfred Ybarra. *Assistant Director*: Milton Carter. *Makeup by* Ben Nye. *Hairstyles by* Helen Turpin. *Sound*: Bernard Freericks and Warren B. Delaplain. *Technical Adviser*: Colonel Jacob G. Goldberg, U.S.M.C. *Orchestration*: Edward B. Powell. *Song* "Marines, Let's Go" *by* Mike Phillips and George Watson, *Sung by* Rex Allen. *Main Title by* Pacific Title. Not Rated. Color by DeLuxe. CinemaScope (2.35:1). 103 minutes. Released in August, 1961. Partially filmed on location in Japan. Not currently available on commercial home video.

Cast: *Skip Roth*, Tom Tryon; *David Chatfield*, David Hedison; *McCaffrey*, Tom Reese; *Grace Blake*, Linda Hutchins; *Russ Waller*, William Tyler; *Ina Baxter*, Barbara Stuart; *Newt Levells*, David Brandon; *Chase*, Steve Baylor; *Hawkins*, Peter Miller; *Ellen Hawkins*, Adoree Evans; *Pete Kono*, Hideo Ikamura; *Hank Dyer*, Vince Williams; *Song Do*, Fumiyo Fujimoto; *Yoshida*, Henry Okawa.

Historical Accuracy Level: Low. These Marines have very little analogy to their real-life counterparts, and their actions are often absurd.

Patriotic Propaganda Level: Medium. Despite their flaws, these Marines can fight.

Elements: Comedy, Effects on Civilians, Japan, Marine Corps, Musical Performance, Romance, Secret Missions.

Marines, Let's Go follows a group of hell-raising Marines from the front lines in Korea to a quiet hotel in Japan for a week of rest and recreation and back again. It is intended as a well-meaning tribute to the fighting spirit of the Marine Corps, but the film is so loud, grotesque and insipid that it can only be an embarrassment to the long and honorable Marine Corps tradition.

In Korea, war correspondent Hank Dyer (Vince Williams) describes some of the fighting men of the 1st Marine Division. Dyer profiles Skip Roth (Tom Tryon), a conniving Marine known as "the Brain"; David Chatfield (David Hedison), a Back Bay aristocrat; and McCaffrey (Tom Reese), a large, scar-faced, veteran leatherneck demoted to a private's rank, whom the others naturally follow. The Marines enter the fray, spot a Chinese mortar emplacement,

grenade it and capture the surviving soldiers. After the skirmish McCaffrey and Chatfield argue, while Dyer informs the men of an impending furlough and McCaffrey of his impending promotion to sergeant. Chatfield visits his beautiful Korean girlfriend Song Do (Fumiyo Fujimoto) and her father. They talk of the war, and of McCaffrey, whom Chatfield admires and who he wishes would approve of him as a Marine.

The Marines are sent to Yokuska, Japan on leave, providing McCaffrey a chance to relax before receiving a decoration. They stop at the Hotel Okamoto and con their way into restricted rooms (because Roth has lost their money) telling the hapless hotel manager that they are on a secret mission that involves the Japanese government. A phony radio transmission to the hotel from "headquarters" — actually Marine Pete Komo (Hideo Inamura), standing outside the hotel — persuades the hotel manager to cooperate, but it is intercepted by officials at military intelligence, who suspect that some sort of espionage operation is taking place. Roth decides that McCaffrey should not be promoted to sergeant (again) for his own good, and attempts to spur the big Marine into a fight by writing him a "secret admirer" letter. But McCaffrey refuses to lose his temper and the Marines go to a nightclub for an evening of entertainment. Meanwhile, Russ Waller (William Tyler) reacquaints himself with old flame Ina Baxter (Barbara Stuart) and "Gunny" Hawkins (Peter Miller) attempts to have a proper honeymoon with his wife.

At the Gaiety club, Marine Newt Levells (David Brandon) sees former love Grace Blake (Linda Hutchins) in the audience and follows her home. McCaffrey receives another "secret admirer" letter from Roth, but again laughs it away. He goes backstage to meet three dancer sisters and becomes embroiled in a fight with a Navy sailor who has reached the girls first. Military police arrive and find McCaffrey hiding under the dancers' makeup table. At Grace's house, Newt learns that after their brief romance Grace was sent to a Japanese prison camp and became a prostitute in order to maintain her lifestyle. She still entertains professionally, so Newt leaves, his romantic illusions destroyed.

The next day, McCaffrey receives a medal

for heroism. The presiding officer says, "I've never known a better fighting man nor a more troublesome citizen." McCaffrey is warned to stay out of trouble; he quickly makes a date with the three dancer sisters. Dave Chatfield receives a letter from Song Do, which sparks visions of terror in his mind as she describes the Chinese moving closer to her home. McCaffrey visits the three sisters and meets their brother Fuji, a national wrestling champion. While talking to them, McCaffrey discovers that Roth is the author of the secret admirer letters; McCaffrey invites Roth to join the party, and then tells Fuji that Roth is their enemy. Roth arrives and is chased away by the wrestler; McCaffrey leaves, ostensibly to procure a marriage license and to arrange immigration to America for the entire family.

A despondent Newt is robbed at a bar, so the Marines go to his defense, and bring back the bar's juke box, booze and women for a party at the hotel. Military intelligence intercepts a radio signal and arrives at the hotel to find a hoedown in progress. The Marines are corralled for court-martials when an alert calls for all Marines to report for duty immediately. They find Russ Waller ready to go AWOL with Ina Baxter and persuade him to rejoin the outfit. They are sent back to Korea.

An amphibious landing takes place, with the Marines

The Marines in the 20th Century–Fox comedy Marines, Let's Go *(1961) laugh, live and love their way through Hokosuka, Japan on furlough before returning to fight in Korea. The poster plays up the movie's comedic aspects rather than its military ones.*

(3

moving into the Chinese front lines. Chatfield explores a wrecked house and realizes that it was Song Do's home. He is shot in the shoulder while trying to aid a dying British soldier, but escapes and finds a group of Korean civilians, among them Song Do and her father. Chinese soldiers are summoned but killed by McCaffrey, who arrives in the nick of time. A captured Chinese soldier informs them that the valley ahead of advancing American troops is mined with explosives. McCaffrey locates the control post, grenades it and disarms the explosive charges before being shot in the back by a dying Chinese soldier. With his last breath, McCaffrey shakes Chatfield's hand and says, "You're OK." Roth takes over the outfit and the war continues.

Marines, Let's Go is without doubt one of the worst Korean War movies ever made. It marks a low point for director Raoul Walsh, who also helmed the far below average Korean War drama *Glory Alley*. While Walsh is renowned for suspenseful, hard-hitting dramas such as *The Public Enemy* and *White Heat*, there is nothing noteworthy about *Marines, Let's Go*. It is supposed to be a rollicking comedy about a group of lecherous, boozing, hell-raising Marines who may act like louts on leave but who are courageous and dependable in battle. But there is nothing funny about such characters, at least not as presented here. There is absolutely no chemistry between the actors, all of whom seem to be trying to upstage the others. The characters are without charm and wit, and their wild and woolly adventures in Japan are cringe-inducing rather than amusing.

Much of the film is given to contrasting American culture with Japanese culture. In *every instance*, the American soldiers are viewed as thoughtless interlopers who do not and perhaps cannot comprehend the intricacies of Japanese customs. The resultant collision between American and Japanese customs is supposed to be funny, with the big, dumb Americans brawling and stumbling their way through Japan, and the kindly Japanese people ready and willing to forgive any transgression, but such antics are grating and embarrassing rather than humorous. And instead of exposing its characters (and the audience) to samples of some actual Japanese culture, as is done in *Sayonara*, the film spot-lights a nightclub with scantily clad dancing girls.

Beneath the comedy, the film also features some serious themes, but these are as witless as or perhaps more so than, the alleged comedy. David Chatfield loves a Korean woman, Song Do, and constantly worries about her. Eventually, he arrives to find her home destroyed, while she and her father are missing. There is no suspense and little drama in this plot; it is all too obvious and moralistic. There is a serious subplot regarding Newt Levells discovering that his former girlfriend is a high-priced prostitute; this sequence is painful to watch because it should brim with melodrama and overtones of tragedy, when in effect, all it really does is reinforce the theme that women are nothing but trouble to a good Marine. This low opinion of women is also demonstrated by the Marines' constant pursuit of them as sex objects, and Russ Waller's near-abandonment of the corps for a tryst with Ina Baxter. As Waller and the Marines drive away from Ina Baxter, one of them yells, "Goodbye, tramp." Ultimately, these Marines seem to reject women in favor of brawling and hell-raising in general.

The Korean sequences feature combat action and seem far more exciting than those set in Japan, but even here, Walsh is ineffective. The first sequence, when the men demolish a mortar emplacement and capture the survivors, takes place so rapidly and uneventfully that it seems simple. The final sequence makes little sense, with the Marines divided into two groups to bypass a hill, tramping through interminable underbrush and then finding Song Do's wrecked home and a group of hiding Korean civilians. And then to have the valley lined with explosives, with a control post close enough for McCaffrey to attack it single-handedly, is simply not believable. McCaffrey's death is telegraphed early, and his final, dying approval of Chatfield is ludicrous.

Another problem surrounds the character of Dyer, the war correspondent. The film begins with his descriptions as he is writing a book about the 1st Marine Division. Then he is never seen or mentioned again. Why use the device of a narrator at the beginning and then completely forget about him? At the very least, his voice should be heard at the ending, commending

Private Skip Roth (Tom Tryon, driving the jeep) escapes with a geisha girl as his fellow Marines (from left to right, Hideo Ikamura, David Hedison, William Tyler and Tom Reese) follow expectantly in this publicity still from Marines, Let's Go *(1961).*

McCaffrey's final heroic acts. But no, there's simply no mention of the character, his book, or his fate.

Of the actors, only Tom Reese deserves any praise. David Hedison has virtually nothing to do and Tom Tryon is competent but unexciting as Skip Roth. As McCaffrey, however, Reese actually creates a larger-than-life caricature of a Marine. With his scar-lined face, broad shoulders and volatile temperament, McCaffrey is occasionally amusing as he buffoons his way through Japan. Tom Reese's performance is the only reason to watch this turkey, and it alone cannot redeem the film.

Marines, Let's Go was reviled at the time of its release. Moira Walsh of *America* wrote, "In any case, the picture seems by turn embarrassingly childish, excessively sentimental and unnecessarily offensive." Howard H. Thompson of the *New York Times* commented, "As an extremely roundabout, hollow and often exasperating trib-

ute to American fighting men in Korea — bearing down hard on their braying, drunken antics in town — this 20th Century-Fox film is no credit to anyone." Over the years, its reputation has worsened. In his book *War Movies*, Brock Garland judged, "A blemish on the great Raoul Walsh's movie war record, this tepid tale of Marines on leave in Japan will either embarrass you or put you to sleep." And Edward F. Dolan, Jr. in *Hollywood Goes to War*, minces no words. "At the very opposite end of the spectrum is what may well be the worst film made about the Korean War — *Marines, Let's Go.*"

In his book, Garland asserts that Walsh was considered to direct *PT 109*, the biographical film about John F. Kennedy's wartime experience, but that after seeing *Marines, Let's Go*, Kennedy insisted on another director. Whether or not this story is true, there is no denying that *Marines, Let's Go* is a mindless, numbing movie with very little to recommend it to anyone.

MASH

Credits: 1970. Aspen Productions. *Distributed by* 20th Century–Fox. *Directed by* Robert Altman. *Produced by* Ingo Preminger. *Associate Producer*: Leon Ericksen. *Screenplay by* Ring Lardner, Jr. *From the Novel by* Richard Hooker. *Music by* Johnny Mandel. *Director of Photography*: Harold E. Stine, A.S.C. *Film Editor*: Danford B. Greene. *Song* "Suicide is Painless" *by* Johnny Mandel and Mike Altman. *Art Direction*: Jack Martin Smith and Arthur Lonergan. *Set Decoration*: Walter M. Scott and Stuart A. Reiss. *Orchestration*: Herbert Spencer. *Sound*: Bernard Freericks and John Stack. *Special Photographic Effects*: L. B. Abbott, A.S.C. and Art Cruickshank. *Titles by* Pacific Title. *Unit Production Manager*: Norman A. Cook. *Assistant Director*: Ray Taylor, Jr. *Medical Advisor*: Doctor David Sachs. *Assistant to the Producer*: Y. Ross Levy. *Makeup Supervision*: Dan Striepeke. *Makeup Artist*: Lester Berns. *Hairstyling by* Edith Lindon. *Football Sequence Choreographer*: Andy Sidaris (uncredited). Originally Rated R. Re-released as PG. Color by De Luxe. Panavision (2.35:1). 116 minutes (either version). Released in January, 1970 (R version). Re-released in 1973 as a PG version. Currently available on VHS (R or PG versions) and DVD (R version). Previously available on laserdisc (PG version).

Cast: Captain Benjamin Franklin "Hawkeye" Pierce, Donald Sutherland; *Captain John Francis Xavier "Trapper John" McIntyre*, Elliott Gould; *Captain Augustus Bedford "Duke" Forrest*, Tom Skerritt; *Major Margaret "Hot Lips" Houlihan*, Sally Kellerman; *Major Frank Burns*, Robert Duvall; *Lieutenant Colonel Henry Blake*, Roger Bowen; *Father John Patrick "Dago Red" Mulcahy*, Rene Auberjonois; *Staff Sergeant Vollmer*, David Arkin; *Lieutenant Maria Schneider "Dish,"* Jo Ann Pflug; *Corporal Walter "Radar" O'Reilly*, Gary Burghoff; *Captain Oliver Harmon "Spearchucker" Jones*, Fred Williamson; *Captain Ezekiel Bradbury "Me Lay" Marston IV*, Michael Murphy; *Lieutenant Leslie*, Indus Arthur; *Private Seidman*, Ken Prymus; *Sergeant Gorman*, Bobby Troup; *Ho-Jon*, Kim Atwood; *Corporal Judson*, Tim Brown; *Captain Walter Kosciusko "Painless Pole" Waldowski*, John Schuck; *Lieutenant Storch*, Dawne Damon; *Captain "Ugly John" Black*, Carl Gottlieb; *Captain*

Bridget "Knocko" McCarthy, Tamara Horrocks; *General Charlie Hammond*, G. Wood; *Private Lorenzo Boone*, Bud Cort; *Captain Murrhardt*, Danny Goldman; *Captain Bandini*, Corey Fischer. *Hawkeye's Son (age 5)*, Stephen Altman; *Nurse Corps Captain*, Cathleen Cordell; *Colonel Merrill*, J. B. Douglas; *Corporal*, Tom Falk; *Motor Pool Sergeant*, Jerry Jones; *Second Lieutenant*, Harvey Levine; *Pretty WAC*, Monica Peterson; *Nurse / Pin-up Model*, Samantha Scott; *Correspondent*, Diane Turley; *Korean Doctors*, Dale Ishimoto and Weaver Levy; *Korean Prostitute*, Hiroko Watanabe; *Japanese Nurse*, Sumi Haru; *Japanese Golf Pro*, John Mamo; *Japanese Caddies*, Susan Ikeda and Masami Saito; *Japanese Servant*, Yoko Young; *Football Players*, Tommy Brown, Buck Buchanan, Jack Concannon, Ben Davidson, John Myers, Noland Smith, Fran Tarkenton, Howard Williams and Tom Woodeschick; *Offstage Dialogue*, David Arkin, Ted Knight, Marvin Miller and H. Lloyd Nelson; *General Hammond's Aide,* Rick Neilan.

Historical Accuracy Level: Medium. While the characters' rebellious hijinks may seem too outrageous to believe, such behavior was common behind the front lines of the Korean and Vietnam wars.

Patriotic Propaganda Level: Low. The medical personnel are certainly heroic, but the film's attitude is decidedly anti-war and the military establishment is consistently ridiculed.

Elements: Army, Clergy, Comedy, Females in the Field, Helicopters, Infighting, Medicine, Musical Performance, Nurses, Racism.

The single most famous movie about the Korean War must be *MASH*. The original novel by Richard Hooker (a pseudonym for Doctor Richard Hornberger and William Heinz) spawned several literary sequels as well as this celluloid version, which was hugely popular and nominated for five Academy Awards including best picture, which in turn begat a hugely popular television series lasting eleven seasons, which in turn begat two more television series (*Trapper John, M.D.*, lasting six seasons and *AfterMASH*, lasting two). The project was director Robert Altman's first major success and launched his career, as well as that of several of the actors in the cast. And though it is ostensibly about Korea, there is no doubt that the movie's pointed satire and unsubtle under-mining of authority are intended as direct commentary on our participation in the Vietnam War, which was a major social cause at the time of its filming. *MASH* is, indeed, a film with many facets.

Two new surgeons arrive in Korea: southerner "Duke" Forrest (Tom Skerritt) and New England native "Hawkeye" Pierce (Donald Sutherland). Duke mistakes Hawkeye for his driver, but Hawkeye doesn't mind and enjoys driving a stolen jeep. They drive to the 4077th MASH (Mobile Army Surgical Hospital) unit, only three miles from the front lines, and have lunch before reporting to Lieutenant Col-onel Henry Blake (Roger Bowen). Both men make passes at a pretty nurse, dubbed Lieutenant "Dish" (Jo Ann Pflug) by Duke, but it is Hawkeye who succeeds in adding her to his surgical team. Duke and Hawk-eye are billeted with religious zealot Major Frank Burns (Robert Duvall) and within days are demanding that Frank be removed from *their* tent and stealing his Korean ser-vant, Ho-Jon (Kim Atwood), for their own care.

The other demand they make is for a "chest cutter." A mysterious figure arrives in camp in answer to their request, whom Hawkeye finally recognizes as former col-lege quarterback "Trapper John" McIntyre (Elliott Gould). Soon afterward a new chief nurse, Major Margaret Houlihan (Sally Kellerman), arrives by helicopter. Trapper John joins Duke and Hawkeye in their tent, dubbed "the Swamp," while Houli-han proves to be an ally to Frank Burns. Doctors and nurses work hard in the oper-ating rooms, so they tend to play hard when they are off duty. When Henry leaves on an overnight trip, the party lasts long into the night. Frank and Houlihan dis-cover a passion for each other; their love-making is broadcast all over the camp as a practical joke. Hawkeye goads Frank into attacking him the next day by mocking his encounter with "Hot Lips"; Frank becomes so upset that he is sent back to the States in a straitjacket.

The company dentist, "Painless Pole"

The original movie artwork for 20th Century–Fox's comedy MASH (1970) combines cheesecake with a definite anti-authoritarian attitude. Its tagline, "M*A*S*H gives a D*A*M*N," is inscrutable and it is rated R.

Walter Waldowski (John Schuck), who is renowned as "the best equipped dentist in the army," suffers an episode of impotence and decides to kill himself. He turns to his friends for advice, and Trapper John suggests using "the Black Capsule." Painless is feted with a dinner which is staged as a "Last Supper" tableau, and then laid inside a coffin and given a tranquilizer while his assistant, Private Seidman (Ken Prymus), sings the ballad "Suicide Is Painless." Hawkeye persuades Lieutenant Dish, whom he has been yearning to bed, to spend the night with Painless in the coffin. She does so, and transfers to another camp the next morning with a smile. Painless returns back to normal and does not even recall the idea of suicide.

Duke bets Hawkeye that Hot Lips Houlihan is not a natural blonde, and others join the betting. Most of the camp appears for her undraping, which occurs while she takes a shower. Hot Lips screams at Henry Blake about her humiliation but he only adds to it. Hawkeye takes Ho-Jon to Seoul, hoping to prevent the young man's mandatory service in the Korean military. Hawkeye's plan does not work, and Ho-Jon is kept in Seoul.

Trapper John is ordered to Japan to perform surgery on a congressman's son, and he takes Hawkeye with him. Carrying golf equipment and calling themselves "the pros from Dover," the two surgeons create havoc in the strict military hospital run by Colonel Wallace C. Merrill (J. B. Douglas). They successfully operate on the congressman's son and discover that their anesthesiologist is Hawkeye's friend "Me Lay" Marston (Michael Murphy), who moonlights as a medical consultant at the "New Era Hospital and Whorehouse." The three men break the military hospital's rules by bringing in a "native" civilian child for treatment, and when Merrill objects, they overpower him with anesthesia and photograph him with a Japanese prostitute to prevent him from raising any more trouble for anyone.

Back at the 4077th, Hawkeye and Trapper John operate in their golfing duds and discover that Duke has been making time with Hot Lips. Henry Blake is contacted by General Charlie Hammond (G. Wood), who has a letter of complaint from Hot Lips; Henry advises the general to ignore it. General Hammond visits the camp and arranges a football game between his outfit (the 325th) and the 4077th. Hawkeye persuades Henry to transfer a neurosurgeon to the camp, one Captain Oliver Harmon "Spearchucker" Jones (Fred Williamson), formerly of the San Francisco 49ers pro football team. With Jones as a running back and Trapper John as quarterback, the team actually has a chance to win.

The 325th takes an early lead in the game, as Jones is not playing in the first half in order to increase the odds, and General Hammond's team leads 16-0 at halftime. The bet is doubled, with 3-1 odds. The 325th's lead evaporates quickly once Jones enters and dominates. The game is littered with injuries on both sides as play continues. With seconds to go and the 4077th down 16-12, Jones calls a special play. The center is made an eligible receiver, keeps the ball and runs downfield while the other team chases the quarterback. The 4077th wins the game 18-16 and a purse of over $5000.

After months of duty, Hawkeye receives news that he and Duke can return home; he interrupts Duke's surgery to tell him. "Right now?" Duke asks. "You mind if we get out of this guy's brain first?" replies Duke's assistant. The camp's chaplain, Father "Dago Red" Mulcahy (René Auberjonois), blesses their jeep; there is no other ceremony for the departing surgeons. Hawkeye and Duke drive away in the same stolen jeep in which they arrived.

MASH is a revolutionary film in many ways. Above all it is about revolution; revolt against accepted authority in particular. Filmed at the height of protest against American involvement in the Vietnam War, the film used its Korean War setting to depict the madness of war as it was currently occurring in Vietnam. Realizing that an anti-war film set in Vietnam would not be made at the time, director Robert Altman simply altered his criticisms of the Vietnam situation into criticisms of the Korean situation. He explains the point during his audio commentary on the the film's DVD: "We were dealing with the Vietnam War. The script was about the Korean War, but all of the political attitudes and the irreverance and the criticisms and everything we did was at Nixon and the Vietnam War. We used the Korean War as a surrogate for the Vietnam War."

The director felt that it was wrong for

Re-rated PG for its 1973 re-release, MASH's *new advertising campaign focused on its popular breakout stars, but retains its distinctive emblem.*

Americans to be in Korea at all. "Our security was never endangered, we were never in danger of being attacked, it was all terror that people like Joe McCarthy and the general right wing set up," he states on the film's DVD audio commentary. Those sentiments have some credence when applied to American involvement in Vietnam, but they fly in the face of historical judgments about Korea. Despite his reference to Senator Joe McCarthy, Altman's statements provide further proof that *MASH* is intended as a commentary about Vietnam rather than Korea.

From the very first scene, military authority is mercilessly derided. Because the motor pool sergeant (Jerry Jones) exhibits sneering condescension, Hawkeye simply takes the jeep without waiting for proper authority. As Hawkeye drives away, the sergeant and two military policemen give stumbling chase, but the sergeant is so insulting to the policemen that they finally beat him rather than chase the jeep. Henry Blake commands the 4077th, but it is clear that he is barely competent and that anybody can get away with just about anything under his watch. Frank Burns is a man of integrity — he doesn't drink or smoke and he prays sincerely for the souls of everyone he knows — yet he is goaded into maniacal rage simply to be rid of his haughty manner and religious fervor.

Religion is another target of the film's pointed satire. Frank tries to improve the mind and spirituality of Ho-Jon by teaching him to read from the Bible. Duke gives the young man a girlie magazine, and in the context of the movie, the girlie magazine does Ho-Jon more good. Frank's fervor is mimicked by Hawkeye and Duke, who lead the camp in a rousing rendition of "Onward Christian Soldiers." Frank confesses his feelings for Hot Lips with the phrase "God meant us to be together," and she opens her blouse to him, replying, "His Will be done!" Father Mulcahy, the camp's Catholic chaplain, normally a figure who ought to command respect, calls himself "Dago Red" and seems to be the most naive person in the war. Mulcahy is unable to help the dentist, "Painless Pole" Waldowski, with his impotence problem and cannot bring himself to give absolution for Painless' phony suicide, yet he does bless the jeep at the end of the movie (based, Altman says, on an actual army prayer). Altman stages Painless' final meal as DaVinci's painting *The Last Supper* and employs sex with Lieutenant Dish as the cause for Painless' resurrection. In the chaos of war, organized religion is placed on the same low level as military authority.

The ridicule of authority extends to Colonel Merrill's military hospital in Japan, where the surgeons' rebellion reaches its zenith. Determined to play a few rounds of golf while in Japan, Trapper John and Hawkeye travel in their golf clothes and utterly destroy the orderly hospital routine to schedule themselves time on the links. Later, they bring a Korean baby to the military hospital for treatment, and when Merrill objects, the surgeons overpower and anesthetize him, and take photographs of him with a Korean prostitute as blackmail insurance. The surgeons are never actually seen playing golf in Japan, though it is to be assumed that they do.

The film condemns military conformism and celebrates its characters' wild, unique individuality. Characters who support the military establishment — Frank Burns, Hot Lips Houlihan, Staff Sergeant Vollmer, and to an extent, Henry Blake — are consistently denigrated, ridiculed and humiliated. Frank is taken away in a straitjacket because he cannot adapt to the "new reality" of young, wiseacre healers with irreverent attitudes. Hot Lips is publicly humiliated until she loses her haughtiness, gradually accepts her nickname, secretly sleeps with Duke and generally becomes as raucous as everyone else. By the time of the football game, she is the team's head cheerleader and has seemingly lost all of her intelligence. Throughout his career, director Altman has faced occasional charges that his films are sexist and misogynistic. It can certainly be argued that a lowly view of women is present, if not omnipresent, in this film, although Altman insists that "I'm showing you the way that I observe how women were treated."

Yet, despite these characters' lunatic actions and anti-authoritarian attitudes, they are also very conventionally noble and endearing. None enjoy the war, but everyone does his duty to the best of his ability under the circumstances. That simple fact is the key to the appeal of the movie. Hawkeye, Trapper John and Duke can complain about Korea to their heart's content, but once they are in the operating room, they are professionals and they save lives. It is understood that their rebellion against authority is simply to cope with the pressures of on-the-fly surgery. Henry is a buffoon, but he's also an efficient administrator and does what he can to take care of his personnel. Dago Red is naive and irritating but he is certainly well-intentioned and he also

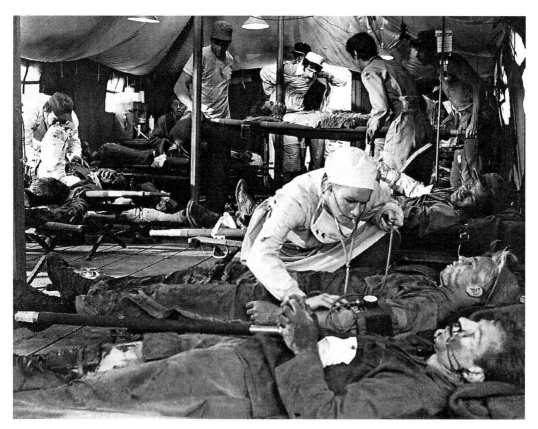

The 4077th MASH doctors experience a typical hectic day in the operating room. Nurse Houlihan (Sally Kellerman) checks a patient's blood pressure in the foreground while Trapper John (Elliott Goulld) dresses for yet another operation in the background. Robert Altman's MASH (1970) showed the results of the fighting as it really was — bloody.

assists in the operating room when necessary. While the film seems to endorse disobedience (for the psychological good of its characters), it also refuses to allow its characters to protest without good reason. Except for some boorish behavior, the surgeons and nurses remain faithful to their medical duty and faithful to the army.

The film is also effective because it eschews overt sentimentality. Under another director (some seventeen refused the assignment before Altman was hired), the characters might have been far more traditional and techniques to encourage audience empathy might have been employed. That isn't the case here. Early in the story, Hawkeye begins to take care of a stray dog, which he names Pup Pup. The dog is only seen a few times and in the final scene, is simply left with Trapper John without any emotional dramaturgy. Likewise, Hawkeye and

Duke are given no formal good-byes when they leave. Trapper encourages them to "get out before they [the army] change their mind." No one attends the departure of Hawkeye and Duke, or that of Lieutenant Dish earlier. People come and go and the bloody work continues. The film, like the war, has no actual ending; it merely stops when its participants leave.

The Korean War is always present, supplying the MASH unit with casualties, but it remains in the background of the story. The only gun in the film belongs to the referee at the football game. The characters never discuss, nor are they provided with, news of the war, except for one instance when General Hammond tells Henry Blake that the battle for "Old Baldy" (a hill and major battleground in Korea) has concluded. "Who won?" asks Henry, though he truly doesn't care. Only three miles from the front, the camp is — except for the influx of casualties—almost completely removed from the reality of the war. In this limbo, it is easy, if not imperative, for the people of the 4077th to unleash their wild and crazy impulses.

MASH is also revolutionary in cinematic terms. Altman's use of overlapping dialogue recalls Howard Hawks' technique but goes much further, creating situations where several characters speak at once and it is up to the audience to decipher which dialogue, if any, is important to hear. Much of the dialogue is reportedly improvisation by the actors, trying to ground their characters in the everyday, routine small talk so common to people who both live and work together. Altman's utilization of sound extends off the screen as well. The public address system announcer (four voices are heard, including Ted Knight's, but David Arkin's is the most recurrent) becomes an important character, introducing Japanese versions of popular American songs, stuttering through illegible announcements of medical jargon and describing the featured movie of the week (three movies are mentioned, one being *The Glory Brigade*, which, incidentally, was released two years after the action in *MASH* takes place).

Visually, Altman describes a Korea full of movement. People seem to be always rushing or driving in and out of frame, maintaining the perception that life at the 4077th is constantly busy. The cinematography in the operating rooms also shows action, though its characters are often standing still. Bodies spurt blood, hands move in a flurry of activity and the dialogue is quick and sharp, all contributing to a tense atmosphere which actually resists movement because rapid, spatial motion in the operating room would be disastrous. Kinetic action returns to the forefront during the football game. Altman uses the football game to emphasize the irony of violence: on the football field, healers dedicated to saving human life are literally beating the sense out of each other. Altman also moves his camera freely in tracking shots, crane shots, helicopter shots and especially zooms, adding to the movie's illusion of constant motion.

It is to writer Ring Lardner, Jr.'s credit that the movie never preaches about its subject. The characters do not indulge in coffee-counter philosophy about the war; they are too busy trying

to protect their psyches from its effects. The film wisely exhibits the war's most devastating effects in the hospital's operating rooms, where young men bleed profusely, lose limbs and occasionally die. As noted by Brock Garland in his book *War Movies*, the filmmakers "underline the charnel-house atmosphere of Richard Hooker's novel and make vividly graphic the futility of attempting to save young lives and repair battle casualties while their superiors are dedicated to killing people." This poignancy is ever present, as the MASH personnel try to enjoy their hours offduty while casualties mere yards away suffer and often perish.

Lardner's script became a springboard from which Altman and his cast could leap, and they did just that. Episodic rather than narrative, the script provided a framework which allowed the actors to improvise. Both Lardner and Robert Altman grabbed credit for the witty and clever banter of the characters, and each contributed to the final product, as did the actors themselves. Lardner was upset that his script was not filmed as written, but the director had a larger vision in mind. Ultimately, the lion's share of credit for the dialogue must fall to Altman, who encouraged his cast to experiment and included a number of the improvisational takes in the final cut. It is the script's deadpan, often cruel humor which keeps it fresh, hip and contemporary thirty years after its initial release. "I wonder how a degenerated person like that [Hawkeye] could have reached a position of responsibility in the Army Medical Corps," asks Hot Lips rhetorically. "He was drafted," intones Father Mulcahy.

One aspect which is fondly remembered but which really does not add much to the film's power is the climactic football game. Choreographed by Andy Sidaris, a filmmaker who later became famous for making cheesy action films in Hawaii with buxom *Playboy* playmates as sexy secret agents, the football game turns the film into a cartoon, stressing the physical cruelty of the match. Altman tries to equate the violence of the football game to the violence of combat, using the sequence as what he calls a "battlefield metaphor." There is a montage in the second half of injured players being carried off the field which ends with a player colliding with and knocking over a row of viewers in wheelchairs.

The "pros from Dover" (Elliott Gould and Donald Sutherland) are driven to a round of golf after a special assignment to operate in Seoul in MASH *(1970).*

But the football game lasts much longer than necessary and, apart from a few cheap laughs, contributes little to the movie's theme. Incidentally, besides "Spearchucker" Jones (Fred Williamson, making his feature debut), several pro football players appear in the game, including Fran Tarkenton, Jack Concannon, Noland Smith and Buck Buchanan.

Another flaw is the music score. Composer Johnny Mandel composed a haunting, poignant ballad, for which the director's son, Mike Altman, provided lyrics that are alternately profound and superficial. The power of the song, "Suicide is Painless," is undeniable, and the song is featured over the opening and closing credits as well as during the "Last Supper" sequence, for which it was specifically written. Besides that song, however, Mandel's score consists of loud, fast, brassy marching songs which reach an almost unendurable, accelerated crescendo during the football game. The brassy music is meant to underscore the game's raucous humor, but it mainly induces headaches in the audience.

The film's most unsatisfying aspect revolves around Ho-Jon, the Korean houseboy who is inducted into the Korean army despite Hawkeye's admirable, if unethical, efforts to prevent his conscription. Ho-Jon is last seen in Seoul, remaining with a Korean doctor and presumed to be drafted into the army. Later, however, a casualty arrives in the MASH operating room with gunshot wounds to the chest; a nurse comments that he is "a prisoner of war." That casualty is Ho-Jon, though his face is obscured. No mention of his identity is made, though Trapper John and Hawkeye do try to save his life. After the football game, there is a scene in which the winnings are being divided in a tent; a jeep drives slowly past with a corpse shrouded in a white sheet plainly visible. Hot Lips and Hawkeye both turn to glance at the white-sheeted corpse being driven away, then return without comment to the matter at hand. That corpse is Ho-Jon's. Most of Ho-Jon's story was deleted from the final cut of the film, leaving the glimpses that remain ambiguous and frustrating because the operating room and tent scenes are obviously supposed to indicate something important. Incidentally, the loose thread of Ho-Jon's fate was eventually adapted as the principal plotline of the television pilot for the *M*A*S*H* series.

MASH was released in 1970, soon after many filmmakers' utilization of sex, nudity, profanity and violence forced the Motion Picture Association of America to adopt its first movie rating code. *MASH* was certainly risqué for its time, containing a little bit of nudity, some profanity and a hearty helping of blood in the operating room sequences, and was threatened with an X rating. The film was finally granted an R rating but three years later, with some of the language redubbed, it was re-released as a PG-rated feature. These then-daring elements insured a young audience for the film, and it was a massive success, earning more than $36 million in its initial release. Today, these elements seem tame, and it would certainly rate a PG-13 rating at most. But in 1970, this was a controversial, adult movie. Critic Richard Schickel described the effect of the film this way: "*MASH* challenges us as few comedies — few movies of any kind — challenge us. It asks us to see with some of the alertness, some of the courage its makers did. Some will turn aside from it, but a film like this is what the new freedom of the screen is all about. It redeems a great many of the abuses of that freedom that we have endured in the past few years."

The movie made stars of its leads, Donald Sutherland and Elliott Gould, and of Sally Kellerman, who received an Academy Award nomination for her portrayal of Hot Lips Houlihan. Acclaim and fame did not extend to the third lead, Tom Skerritt, who is just as good as Sutherland and Gould in the film. One reason may be the film's preview, which spotlights "two indispensible military surgeons" instead of three, ignoring Duke. Skerritt did eventually become a television star in *Picket Fences* and has amassed a very respectable career, but he never received the attention lavished upon Sutherland and Gould. The other intriguing detail involving casting is the large number of actors making their debuts in the film. No less than thirteen performers are listed after the term "Introducing ..." during the opening credits, including Fred Williamson, Jo Ann Pflug, Gary Burghoff, John Schuck and Bud Cort, all of whom fashioned, as did Skerritt, respectable acting careers.

Not quite three years after the initial release of the film, its television adaptation was broadcast on CBS. Despite low ratings during its first season, *M*A*S*H* the television show became a phenomenon which lasted eleven years and two hundred fifty-one episodes. Its finale, *Goodbye, Farewell and Amen*, remains the most watched television entertainment broadcast in history. The television version tones down the film's raucous, crude humor, replacing it with more sentimental, character-driven humor, but it also considerably deepens those characters, creating far more audience identification and empathy with them. Robert Altman dismisses the series, saying, "The television version of *M*A*S*H* is the most insidious kind of propaganda. I think it's terrible. It says — no matter what platitudes they use — that the guys with the slanted eyes are the bad guys. They don't show the blood, the horror. They don't make you pay for the laugh. It's only done for commercial reasons. That isn't the reason I did the movie; it isn't the reason the artists involved did it. There was a point to be made, and we made it." Despite Altman's reservations, however, the television version of *M*A*S*H* has easily supplanted the film in the world's consciousness as the single most famous, artistic, influential and beloved representation of Americans in the Korean War.

Critics lavished either praise or damnation on the film. Pauline Kael of the *New Yorker* called it "a marvellously unstable comedy, a tough, funny and sophisticated burlesque of military attitudes that is at the same time a tale of chivalry. It's a sick joke, but's also generous and romantic — erratic, episodic, full of the pleasures of the unexpected." Kael's summation that "*MASH* is the best American war comedy since sound came in, and the sanest American movie of recent years," was widely quoted and helped persuade critics and audiences alike to give the challenging film a chance.

The film won the prestigious Golden Palm award at the Cannes Film Festival and was named the best film of the year by the National Society of Film Critics. It was nominated for five Academy Awards, including best picture, and won for best adapted screenplay; and was nominated for six Golden Globe awards, winning three: best motion picture (musical or comedy), best director and best screenplay. In 1996, this landmark film was named to the National Film Registry, the second Korean War film to be so honored (the first was *The Manchurian Candidate* in 1994).

MASH (the famous asterisks are absent in the movie's actual title, although they appear everywhere in its advertising) is a raucous remake of *Battle Circus*, made with far less melodrama and far more realism. More of a political statement than a document about war, the film nevertheless shines a bright light on how people who are exposed to the brutality of war fight its psychologically numbing effects. It is a landmark movie full of dichotomies — it is funny yet blasphemous, childish yet adult, cartoonish yet somber and insane yet sensible — which challenges the audience to formulate its own opinion about the craziness of war. *MASH* is not a perfect movie, nor could it have been made before it actually was in 1969-1970. Together with its television offspring (despite Robert Altman's objections), *MASH* is a counter-cultural phenomenon that, for better or worse, has become the most famous Hollywood representation of the Korean War.

Mask of the Dragon

Credits: 1951. Spartan Productions. *Distributed by* Lippert Pictures. *Directed by* Samuel Newfield. *Produced by* Sigmund Neufeld. *Screenplay by* Orville Hampton. *Music by* Dudley Chambers. *Director of Photography*: Jack Greenhalgh. *Film Editor*: Carl Pierson. *Production Manager*: Bert Sternbach. *Assistant Director*: Stanley Neufeld. *Set Decorator*: Harry Reif. *Set Construction*: Tom Kemp. *Sound*: Glen Glenn. *Makeup Artist*: Paul Stanhope. *Wardrobe*: Al Berke. *Handknits and Fashions*: Diane. *Special Effects*: Ray Mercer, A.S.C. Not Rated. Black and White. Flat (1.33:1). 53 minutes. Released in March, 1951. Not currently available on commercial home video.

Cast: *Phil Ramsey*, Richard Travis; *Ginny O'Donnell*, Sheila Ryan; *Murphy*, Sid Melton; *Major Clinton*, Michael Whalen; *Lieutenant Ralph McLaughlin*, Lyle Talbot; *Terry Newell*, Dee Tatum; *Lieutenant Daniel Oliver*, Richard Emory; *Professor Kim Ho*, Jack Reitzen; *Mister Moto*, Mr. Moto (Charles Iwamoto); *Kingpin*, Karl Davis; *Television Show Host*, John Grant; *Singers*, Curt Barrett and the Trailsmen; *Chin Koo*, Eddie Lee; *Grantland*, Ray Singer; *Sarah*, Carla Martin; *with* Barbara Atkins and Dick Paxton.

Historical Accuracy Level: Low. The war is mere background for an unbelievable story about smuggling.

Patriotic Propaganda Level: Low. Comedic murder mysteries generally have little or no patriotic content.

Elements: Army, Comedy, Espionage, Musical Performance, Mystery.

An obscure entry in the Korean War film directory is *Mask of the Dragon*, a low-budget B-movie from Lippert which deals with smuggling. The movie also attempts, rather unevenly, to blend comedy into its dramatic structure, featuring a motley gang of criminals who might be considered lovable bumblers if they refrained from killing people. The film plays its smuggling story fairly straight, yet parodies the conventions of the genre and specific subjects like television, martial arts and hucksterism. It even allows the lead actor, Richard Travis, to directly address the audience at the end of the film.

Mask of the Dragon begins in what seems to be a small suburb of Seoul, where U.S. Army soldier Lieutenant Dan Oliver (Richard Emory) steps into a curio shop. He is asked to transport a museum piece — a football-sized jade dragon — to another curio shop in Los Angeles for several hundred dollars. Oliver questions shop owner Chin Koo (Eddie Lee) as to the legality of such transport, but is reassured by the Korean's answers. In need of the money, Oliver agrees. Upon his return to Los Angeles, Oliver immediately visits the office of the Oakleaf Detective Agency, which he co-owns. Oliver telephones his partner Phil Ramsey (Richard Travis) from the office, but is knocked unconscious and then stabbed to death during the call by two thugs, a large brute named Kingpin (Karl Davis) and a small wiseacre named Murphy (Sid Melton).

Ramsey and his girlfriend Ginny O'Donnell (Sheila Ryan) rush to the Oakleaf office and find Oliver dead, his luggage rifled through, and the only remaining clue being a brochure for the Jade Lotus curio shop. Lieutenant Ralph McLaughlin (Lyle Talbot) of the police department and Major Clinton (Michael Whalen) of the army are assigned to investigate the Oliver murder case, which becomes more complex with the arrival of Terry Newell (Dee Tatum), Oliver's fiancé, who is looking for a souvenir he might have brought back from Korea. Ramsey determines to solve the murder of his partner on his own.

Ramsey visits the Jade Lotus and becomes suspicious when the owner, Professor Kim Ho (Jack Reitzen), sells some small "immortal" figurines to other people but refuses to sell one to him. Ramsey leaves and is abducted by Kingpin, Murphy and an oriental martial arts expert, Mr. Moto (Mr. Moto; actually Charles Iwamoto). The thugs beat the blindfolded private eye, demanding Oliver's package. Ramsey doesn't know anything and is beaten unconscious. He is freed by an unseen woman, and returns to his office and finds that it has been ransacked. Ramsey visits the local television station where Terry Newell and Curt Barrett and the Trailsmen sing. Terry tells Ramsey that she told Dan Oliver what the package was and that Oliver was attempting to catch the criminals in the act of receiving it when he was killed. Before she can say more, Terry is summoned to sing on camera, and as she begins she is killed — knifed in the back from behind a curtain.

Ginny retrieves a package from the post office, in which Oliver mailed her the jade dragon. Ramsey takes the figure to the Jade Lotus, hoping to provoke Kim Ho into revealing its secret. Meanwhile, Ginny discovers from McLaughlin that Kim Ho is a dangerous criminal, and she sends the police to the curio shop to rescue Ramsey. Kim Ho offers Ramsey $700 for the object, but Ramsey asks for $2000. Kim Ho delays and Ramsey realizes he is in danger. He sneaks into the basement and is caught by the thugs and Major Clinton, who is working with the smugglers. Mr. Moto is told to kill Ramsey and attempts to do so while the other men return to the shop. Ramsey breaks free and fights Mr. Moto while the police arrive and arrest the others. The police and Ginny run downstairs to find that Ramsey has somehow conquered the martial arts expert.

Newspaper reports reveal that uranium was concealed within the jade dragon and that the smuggling ring has been broken. McLaughlin tells Ramsey and Ginny that the contraband uranium was contained in the small "immortal" figurines "for the retail trade." The movie ends as Ramsey reenters his detective office, looks directly into the camera and says, "the movie ends when the hero captures the bad guys."

Mask of the Dragon is a perfect example of a B-movie. It is cast with lesser known but familiar actors (Richard Travis, Lyle Talbot, Richard Emory and Sid Melton), paced with a quick tempo, lensed on simple, often sparse sets, and weaves its completely ridiculous story around a timely subject. The simple smuggling story that takes place in Korea and Los Angeles during the war is the type of story which is well told in B-movie formulas, but the film's final minute is almost too ludicrous to describe.

Uranium? Transported from *Korea*? Uranium *"for the retail trade"*? If the contraband were opium, the movie would make sense. But *uranium*? The choice of uranium ignores all logic, since Korea has no natural uranium deposits and had no nuclear capability when the movie was made in 1951. The characters handle the jade dragon (and its uranium) quite carelessly, completely ignorant of its radioactive secret, and yet nothing happens to any of them. Had uranium (especially in its powdered form) actually been in the jade dragon, everyone who handled it would require hospitalization and treatment for radiation poisoning. The reference to the "retail trade" is utterly preposterous if indeed the contraband is uranium. The people who buy the "immortals" statuary act like drug addicts, not like people who need uranium. It seems likely that uranium was chosen because it taps into the fear of such volatile, fissionable material falling into Communist hands, and that its selection as contraband was made after filming was completed for reasons of timeliness rather than story sense.

As an espionage story, it is also weak. It was not unusual for American soldiers to bring "souvenirs" back from wartime service, and the notion of a soldier making a delivery for a Korean

Villainous henchman Murphy (Sid Melton, left, in disguise as a Chinaman) and Phil Ramsey (Richard Travis, right) tussle over the Jade Dragon in Mask of the Dragon *(1951). The Jade Dragon is the key to the film's murder mystery.*

business is certainly believable. But who would willingly hand a treasure of uranium to a relatively unknown American soldier? And when Oliver reaches Los Angeles, he is eliminated far too easily to believe, especially after it is revealed that he was aware of what he was carrying.

The film is more successful as a comedy, although its comedic elements do not blend well with its sinister, melodramatic story. The thugs who kill Oliver and menace Ramsey are played jovially by Karl "Killer" Davis, Sid Melton and Charles "Mr. Moto" Iwamoto. The dimunitive Sid Melton in particular brings a gusto to his role as Murphy, the wisecracking thug with a knife who also dons a Fu Manchu mustache with goatee and Chinese robes and tries to lure

customers into the Jade Lotus. In one scene, Murphy tries to learn judo from the much larger Mr. Moto, and the comedy in that scene seems as if it is from a completely different movie.

Mask of the Dragon does not take itself seriously, and lampoons a few targets, most particularly television. The Los Angeles set of KLBC, the local television station, is the cheapest, seediest looking studio imaginable. The television programming is almost burlesque, with host Johnny Grant completely comfortable hawking cheap alarm clocks between musical acts. When Terry Newell is killed on camera, the television cameras swing to a simple card announcing "technical difficulties." The film also parodies the preponderance of crass advertising, with the abovementioned alarm clock sequence and Murphy's oriental act outside the Jade Lotus. He brings people into the shop with a mix of hucksterism and comedy, all delivered in a bad Chinese accent. "Ah yes. See Chiang Kai-shek and his cousin Cancelled Check. Ah yes."

It is also one of those Korean War films which utilize the war setting while saying absolutely nothing about the war. Dan Oliver is completing his final day as a soldier in Korea when he agrees to transport the jade dragon to America. Afterward, the war is no longer mentioned, even though the uranium contraband should seemingly be connected to the war effort.

Released through Lippert Pictures as half of modest double features, *Mask of the Dragon* quickly disappeared from public view. *The Hollywood Reporter* enjoyed it, calling it "an action-ful programmer" and noting that "the story holds interest, the acting is good and Samuel Newfield's direction fills it with pace and plenty of punch." *Variety*, on the other hand, was less impressed. "Attempting a combination of comedy and mystery, this entry fails to score in either department." The film remains unknown today, a comical but obscure footnote in cinema history.

The McConnell Story

(aka *Tiger in the Sky*)

Credits: 1955. Warner Bros. *Directed by* Gordon Douglas. *Produced by* Henry Blanke. *Screen Play by* Ted Sherdeman and Sam Rolfe. *Story by* Ted Sherdeman. *Music by* Max Steiner. *Director of Photography*: John Seitz, A.S.C. *Film Editor*: Owen Marks, A.C.E. *Art Director*: John Beckman. *Sound by* Charles B. Lang. *Set Decorator*: William L. Kuehl. *Wardrobe by* Howard Shoup. *Second Unit Director*: Russ Saunders. *Dialogue Supervisor*: Leon Charles. *Makeup Artist*: Gordon Bau, S.M.A. *Technical Advisors*: Colonel William L. Orris, U.S.A.F. and Captain Manuel "Pete" J. Fernandez, U.S.A.F. *Orchestrations by* Murray Cutter. *Assistant Directors*: Chuck Hansen and William Kissel. Not Rated. Warner Color. CinemaScope (2.35:1). 107 minutes. Released in September, 1955. Currently available on VHS home video. Previously available on laserdisc.

Cast: Joseph C. "Mac" McConnell, Jr., Alan Ladd; *Pearl "Butch" Brown*, June Allyson; *Ty Whitman*, James Whitmore; *Sergeant Sykes*, Frank Faylen; *Bob*, Robert Ellis; *Newton Bass*, Willis Bouchey; *Mom Brown*, Sarah Selby; *First M.P.*, Gregory Walcott; *Mechanic*, Frank Ferguson; *Red*, Perry Lopez; *Second M.P.*, John Pickard; *Pilot Instructor*, Dabbs Greer; *Medical Corps Instructor*, Edward Platt; *Blonde Woman*, Vera Marshe; introduced by General O. F. Weyland, U.S.A.F.

Historical Accuracy Level: High. Korean War ace Joseph McConnell is the subject, and the film chronicles his story, and the evolution of the Air Force, faithfully.

Patriotic Propaganda Level: High. This movie could double as a recruiting poster for young Air Force fliers.

Elements: Air Force, Air War, Army, Biography, Lonely Wives, Military Training, Multiple Wars, Red Menace, Returning Home, Romance.

Apart from President Truman and General MacArthur, very few actual military men during the Korean conflict have had their stories told in Hollywood movies. One of those few is the Korean War's first triple jet ace, Captain Joseph C. McConnell, Jr. Over the skies of Korea, a pilot was termed an ace only after downing five Russian-made MiG jets. There were thirty-nine such aces over the three-year span of the war. A double ace was a man who downed ten MiGs; only eight men qualified for double ace status. The triple ace level was fifteen MiG kills; only McConnell (with sixteen) and Captain James Jabara (with fifteen) attained this plateau. It is also worth noting that one of *The McConnell Story*'s technical advisors, Captain Manuel "Pete" J. Fernandez, was third in MiG kills during the war, with fourteen to his credit, just missing the triple ace level.

The McConnell Story begins with Joseph "Mac" McConnell (Alan Ladd) in the Army in 1942, training with the Medical Corps in Massachusetts, but spending his money on flying lessons in hopes of transferring to the Army Air Corps. McConnell ends one flying lesson by parachuting out of the plane, evading and then hiding from military police at the home of Pearl Brown (June Allyson), a woman with whom he quickly falls in love. Within a few weeks, Pearl, who Mac (and everyone else thereafter) calls "Butch," has sweet-talked his mean sergeant into approving their marriage. Mac and Butch marry and move to a cramped apartment in Texas, where he has been assigned as a medical student.

Before very long, Mac flunks out of medical school, but takes the opportunity to enroll in a flight training program in Washington. Butch is pregnant, and moves back to her family's Massachusetts home to wait for him. Mac does well at flight school, aided by a new friend, Ty Whitman (James Whitmore). Mac misses the birth of his first daughter, but is assigned to navigator training and he and Butch move back to Texas. A year later, Mac is sent to Europe as a navigator, spending the rest of World War II on bombers. After the war, Mac agrees to take a desk job in order to stabilize his family, and they move to Nebraska, where they welcome another baby girl to the family.

Ty Whitman arrives, sees that Mac is unhappy in his job, and offers him the chance to fly jets in the newly created Air Force. Mac jumps at the opportunity and quickly becomes a fully trained fighter pilot. The McConnells transfer to California, where a baby boy is added to the mix, and then to Anchorage, Alaska, where his family lives in a small trailer while he flies above them. It is there that Butch reads of the invasion of South Korea. Another transfer puts them back in California, in Apple Valley, where Mac signs the papers to buy a parcel of land. This is where he will build the McConnell home — after he returns from Korea.

In Korea, Mac is reunited with Ty Whitman, now his commanding officer. Whitman briefs the new pilots with this perspective: "You see, Korea is a testing ground for the Reds. If their arms succeed against us here, then there will be no place in the world that is safe." Mac's first action as an F-86 Sabre jet pilot is to protect a helicopter rescue of downed fliers. MiGs attack and a dogfight ensues in which Mac and his Sabre, christened "Beauteous Butch," shoots down two enemy jets. Soon he is the third highest ranking ace in Korea with ten kills. At home, Butch listens to a radio broadcast which describes how Mac was shot down, but safely rescued from the sea. When Mac scores his fifteenth kill he becomes the first triple jet ace in history. His sixteenth is his last because Ty

Whitman orders McConnell home. The publicity-minded policy makers have decided that he is more valuable as a live symbol of excellence than as a dead hero.

Mac returns home to Butch, and to meet the president. At Apple Valley, the McConnells are presented with a beautiful ranch home by their proud and happy neighbors, led by Newton Bass (Willis Bouchey). After the war, Ty Whitman returns to California and asks Mac to test the new generation of Sabre jets. Butch objects, asking why her husband has to be the one to risk his life, but Mac accepts the challenge with her ultimate consent. Mac flies the jet through the sound barrier and fully explores its capabilities with little trouble, until the fateful day when the controls freeze at low altitude and the jet crashes, killing him. Butch is disconsolate, but Ty Whitman takes her to the airfield and shows her another model of the jet her husband was testing. She sees that the young pilot isn't afraid to fly it and that Mac's input about the machine will make it safer for all who follow in his footsteps.

The McConnell Story was filmed and released in 1955, two years after the end of the Korean War. Captain McConnell died in that test flight just before the story of his military career was to go before the cameras, and his death was then written into the film.

One rather surprising aspect of the production is that it does not emphasize McConnell's speedy ascent as an ace. The air war in Korea lasted three years and MiGs were introduced about six months into the campaign, in November of 1950, but Joseph McConnell didn't even arrive in Korea until late 1952. Within nine months, McConnell scored more MiG kills than anyone else during the war, and he was shipped home before the war ended. He was also battling more experienced MiG pilots than had been flying earlier in the war, according to several Korean War historical evaluations. The film spends so much time on the earlier parts of McConnell's life that his Korean exploits seem almost anti-climactic and are not depicted as thoroughly as they deserve to be.

McConnell's career and family life are explored in some detail, although everything prior to military years is completely ignored in the script. His background and childhood are never

TOLD TO THE THUNDERING THROB
OF A THOUSAND ROARING JETS!

The hair-raising, trail-blazing glories of the steel-nerved 'Sky-Tiger' who became America's first Triple Jet Ace...and the real-life, real wonderful love story of 'Butch'— the beautiful bundle of courage who became his wife.

WARNER BROS. PRESENT **ALAN LADD · JUNE ALLYSON**
"THE McCONNELL STORY"
WARNERCOLOR CINEMASCOPE STEREOPHONIC SOUND
Also Starring **JAMES WHITMORE** Screen Play by TED SHERDEMAN and SAM ROLFE
MUSIC BY MAX STEINER Produced by **HENRY BLANKE** Directed by GORDON DOUGLAS

The marketing for Warner Bros. biography The McConnell Story *(1955) emphasizes the "Sky-Tiger's" human side over his daredevil heroics, and takes care to credit "the beautiful bundle of courage," his wife "Butch."*

even mentioned, while his chief characteristics seem to be an obsessive urge to fly and a casual rejection of military authority when it doesn't suit his own plans. It is intimated that this rebellious streak, this individuality, is what makes McConnell a natural flier and fighter pilot. Yet the Army never takes advantage of McConnell's talents and the Air Force is also slow to value him. Indeed, the Army in particular is shown to be less than intelligent in its evaluation of personnel.

The film ably displays the differences in air battle between World War II and Korea. The B-17 bomber for which McConnell navigates lumbers across the sky, drops its heavy load and tries to fly home while being pursued and wounded by smaller, quicker fighter planes. In fact, in that brief scene, a prototype German jet is viewed which sparks McConnell's imagination. In Korea, Mac pilots powerful, speedy fighter jets which flash across the sky, dodge enemy fire and destroy enemy aircraft only in close combat. The film does a nice job of following the Air Force — and thus moving the audience — into the jet age. It follows this theme past the Korean War and into the realm of test piloting, where the aircraft are still experimental in design and the danger to pilots was much higher.

In terms of the overall view of the Korean War, the film's perspective is narrow. It is only interested in McConnell's record and his friendship with mentor Ty Whitman. The other fliers

Joseph "Mac" McConnell, Jr. (Alan Ladd) prepares to fly his Sabre Jet over Korean skies in The McConnell Story *(1955). The irony is that Ladd was actually terrified of flying.*

are not individually named, and Whitman is a composite character based on several of McConnell's commanding officers. The air war is viewed as a series of skirmishes with the Chinese-piloted Russian-made planes over North Korea. Whitman urges his pilots to destroy the enemy, for he understands that only after suffering great losses will the Communists end their aggression.

Director Gordon Douglas does introduce as much warmth and humor as the story will take, from the first fateful meeting between Mac and Butch while he evades the military policemen who are after him, through his punishment tours in Washington when he learns that he is a father. The love story between Mac and Butch is given a great deal of emphasis in the film and it works, despite some syrupy passages, largely because its two stars, Alan Ladd and June Allyson, also happened to fall in love while on the set. Both performers were married at the time, and both stayed with their spouses, but the feelings between them are palpable on the celluloid. Happily, one true-life aspect is not visible: Alan Ladd's fear of flying. Ladd was terrified of air travel and refused to fly whenever possible. Yet his portrayal does not betray this consuming fear.

The film benefits from crisp CinemaScope photography and actual use of military hardware rather than stock footage (although the World War II bomber belly landing scene is stock). Its editing is judicious, particularly when Ty Whitman breaks the news of Mac's death to Butch, and her tearful reaction is unheard beneath the roar of the "missing man" formation which flies overhead at that moment. The story itself is properly heroic and usually compelling, although it does eventually drift into piousness about duty, honor and sacrifice. Its dialogue is also worth mentioning; it is realistic and authentic except for the occasional florid phrasing by Ty Whitman: "Go, Tiger! You own the sky!"

In their book *The Films of Alan Ladd*, Marilyn Henry and Ron De Sourdis judge the film honestly. "If all this sounds a little saccharin — it is. Most of the Hollywood biography cliches are present — the hero's dedication above and beyond the call of duty, his mission and his dream, his loving, self-sacrificing wife who understands her husband's greater responsibilities. But newspaper briefs on the real McConnells give every impression that they were indeed (at least in public moments) as they were presented here." *Variety* recommended *The McConnell Story* as "A tasteful, thrilling motion picture," while *Time* groused about its platitudes and familiar situations. "It declares a ringing hail and farewell to the hero, with all the domestic and military taradiddle that Hollywood finds necessary on such occasions." Its evaluation ended with this summation: "*The McConnell Story* is an instance in which simple human dignity has been clobbered by commercial cuteness."

The McConnell Story is by no means a great movie, nor an incisive biography of a war hero. But it does tell an interesting story and has some success dramatizing key moments in an important life. Its real value is that its emotions ring true. McConnell's story is always compelling and occasionally exciting. It largely avoids becoming military propaganda, although the ultra-noble ending does venture into that territory. Ultimately, it is a decent movie about a decent man who found great success when finally allowed to fulfill his dreams.

Men in War

Credits: 1957. Security Pictures. *Distributed by* United Artists. *Directed by* Anthony Mann. *Produced by* Sidney Harmon. *Screenplay by* Philip Yordan. *Based on a novel* ("Day Without End" [Combat]) *by* Van Van Praag. *Music by* Elmer Bernstein. *Director of Photography:* Ernest Haller, A.S.C. *Film Editor:* Richard C. Meyer. *Assistant Director:* Leon Chooluck. *Supervisor:* Irving Lerner. *Production Design:* Lewis Jacobs. *Technical Advisor:* John Dickson. *Special Effects:*

Jack Erickson and Lee Zavitz. *Costumer:* Norman Martien. *Property Master:* Elmer Stock. *Sound Effects Editor:* Henry Adams. *Music Editor:* Robert N. Tracy. *Editorial Associate:* Toni Roelofsma. *Script Supervisor:* Michael Preece. *Sound:* Jack Salomon. *Make-up Artist:* Layne Britton. *Special Photographic Effects:* Jack Rabin and Louis DeWitt. Not Rated. Black and White. Flat (1.33:1). 104 minutes. Released in February, 1957. Currently available on VHS videotape and DVD.

Cast: *Lieutenant Benson*, Robert Ryan; *Sergeant Montana*, Aldo Ray; *The Colonel*, Robert Keith; *Sergeant Riordan*, Phillip Pine; *Sergeant Lewis*, Nehemiah Persoff; *Corporal Zwickley*, Vic Morrow; *Sergeant Killian*, James Edwards; *Sergeant Davis*, L. Q. Jones; *Private Meredith*, Scott Marlowe; *Private Maslow*, Adam Kennedy; *Private Haines*, Race Gentry; *Private Ackerman*, Walter Kelley; *Private Penelli*, Anthony Ray; *Private Christensen*, Robert Normand; *Private Lynch*, Michael Miller; *Korean Sniper*, Victor Sen Yung.

Historical Accuracy Level: Medium. The battle action which takes place, excepting the state and fate of the Colonel, is scrupulously authoritative.

Patriotic Propaganda Level: Low. The intent of this project is to depict the grim, nasty business that is war, not to promote it.

Elements: Army, Disability.

"Tell me the story of the foot soldier and I will tell you the story of all wars."

This statement, shown before the beginning of *Men in War*, provides the film with a noble intent which it only partially fulfills. While the main storyline concerns the regular infantry soldiers — the grunts — and conveys well the confusion and frustration of men alone in the field isolated from their command, the secondary plot concerning the madness of the Colonel has little to do with foot soldiers, and actually distracts attention from the primary story until it is explained during the film's explosive climax.

Men in War takes place in Korea on September 6, 1950, roughly two months after the invasion. As dawn arrives, thirteen soldiers in the platoon led by gaunt and grizzled Lieutenant Benson (Robert Ryan) are spread throughout a gully, sleeping or on guard duty. One soldier finds that his relief has been killed during the night, and being justly frightened, sets off a round of futile firing by the platoon. Benson stops the shooting, organizes his men and points them toward Hill 465 some twenty miles away, where they are to rendezvous with the remainder of the 34th Division.

After marching single file for a time, they spy a jeep speeding crazily across the Korean landscape, and heading straight for them. Benson stops the jeep, which is driven by Sergeant Montana (Aldo Ray) and carrying the Colonel (Robert Keith). When he learns that the Colonel is unable to speak and is strapped into the jeep for his own safety, Benson commandeers the jeep and orders Montana to join his outfit, at least until they reach Hill 465. Montana is unwilling to subordinate himself to Benson, but reluctantly does so. When a sniper destroys the platoon's radio, Montana tracks down and kills the sniper, proving to Benson his superior survival skills.

The men march on. Trailing as rear security, Sergeant Killian (James Edwards) sits down for a few minutes and is killed, quietly and brutally. Montana is assigned to the rear position and he too sits. Montana expects the attack and kills his assailants, but not before the platoon's location is broadcast to Korean artillery. In pairs, the men are sent forward through artillery fire. Later, in a forested area, Sergeant Lewis (Nehemiah Persoff) discovers that their path is mined; he panics and is killed by one of the mines as he attempts to run away. Montana captures a North Korean soldier, whom Benson then forces to lead his men through the minefield.

At last Hill 465 is attained, but the 34th Division is nowhere in sight. The North Korean prisoner is sent up the hill as a decoy and is shot from above. Soldiers appear, who yell "G.I.!" and "American!" down to the platoon and encourage them up the hill. Montana spots the ruse and kills the North Koreans wearing American uniforms, thus saving the platoon once again. Benson is disgusted that Montana had no proof of the ambush and could have killed Americans. "God help us if it takes your kind to win this war." Montana asks for and receives permission to take the jeep and the Colonel away.

Reconnaissance proves that the North Koreans hold the hill and are waiting for the Americans to attack. After much anguish, Benson decides to attack with his twelve men in two groups, taking the most forward position himself. Montana prepares to drive off with the Colonel, telling him, "I miss hearing you call me son," thus revealing the feeling between the two men. The attack begins and Benson uses grenades to blow up a machine gun nest before he is wounded. Two of Benson's men attempt to rescue him and are quickly killed. One by one, the men are pinned down and killed as they try to move up the hill. The Colonel finally snaps out of his funk, frees himself from the jeep, takes Montana's rifle and joins the attack, knocking out a machine gun nest before being gunned down. Montana arrives at the Colonel's side in time to hear him murmur "Son" and die.

Most of the American soldiers die in the battle, but Montana and Benson fight on. They lie low for a while, share a cigarette, muse about the friends they've lost and vow to attack again. Montana dons the company's flamethrower and burns out the remaining machine gun nest and, with one other soldier left alive, they capture the hill. As the 34th Division begins to arrive, Benson, wounded and bone-weary, reads aloud the names of the soldiers to whom he will posthumously award Silver Stars.

Grim and gritty, *Men in War* fulfills its intention of providing a realistic and truthful view of warfare. Completely devoid of patriotism, the film primarily focuses on the foot soldiers' most basic duty — simple survival. By depicting the difficulty of just staying alive in this situation, *Men in War* examines not only the futility of war but its very essence. Two of the men in Benson's platoon — Killian and Lewis — are killed as a result of their own mistakes. Two more soldiers are killed when they leave their relatively safe position in order to carry the wounded Benson back to safety. Two more are killed by gravity, when hand grenades dropped by the North Koreans roll down Hill 465 to the Americans and explode.

Stupidity, heroism, chance. No matter what the reason and no matter how noble the intent, the result is the same. Six men are dead. That's the essence of war.

One of the men, young Corporal Zwickley

SECURITY PICTURES INC. presents

ROBERT RYAN ALDO RAY

MEN in WAR

THE PART OF THE MILITARY MACHINE THAT BLEEDS!

"One more step and I'll fill your guts with lead!"

...NOW IT EXPLODED OUT INTO THE OPEN—THE TRIGGER-HOT HATE BETWEEN THE LIEUTENANT WHO'D LEAD HIS MEN ANYWHERE—AND THE SERGEANT WHO'D FOLLOW HIM INTO HELL...JUST TO GET EVEN!

H   É   A   T   R   E

co-starring ROBERT KEITH · with PHIL PINE · VIC MORROW · NEHEMIAH PERSOFF · JAMES EDWARDS · Screenplay by PHILIP YORDAN

Based on the novel "COMBAT" by VAN VAN PRAAG · Music Composed and Conducted by ELMER BERNSTEIN · Directed by ANTHONY MANN · Produced by SIDNEY HARMON · Released thru UNITED ARTISTS

4 Cols. x 125 Lines—500 Lines (36 Inches)   Mat 401

Personal conflict between Sergeant Montana (Aldo Ray, left) and Lieutenant Benson (Robert Ryan, right) is the focus of this ad for United Artists' drama Men in War *(1957), which slightly exaggerates their stormy relationship.*

(Vic Morrow), feels too sick to march or fight when he is introduced early in the film. Zwickley is watched over and protected by Killian, until Killian's death. Zwickley tries to save his friend, and takes his death hard. Slowly, he learns to take on more responsibility, even asking for an important assignment (utilizing a bazooka) in the climactic battle. When Zwickley dies, along with most of the other men who have become familiar, the film's message is again

The faces of war: Lieutenant Benson (Robert Ryan, left) and Sergeant Montana (Aldo Ray, right) discuss their upcoming assault on Hill 465 in Anthony Mann's Men in War *(1957).*

hammered home. War is a deadly pursuit, and most of the men who fight are doomed, no matter their intelligence, race or personality. Ultimately, the side with the remaining soldiers left alive, however few they may be, is the victor.

The North Korean soldiers in *Men in War* are guerilla fighters and snipers, silent and deadly. Even the soldier who is captured attempts to lead the Americans into an ambush. Contrasted with the grousing Americans, the North Koreans are quiet and patient, waiting for opportunities to pick off the enemy one by one. Such tactics, which would be used later in Vietnam, disheartened American soldiers because they were so difficult to defend against or to prevent. The film vividly depicts the unrelenting sense of danger which American soldiers had to face under such conditions.

The primary plotline is handled well with Benson, alternately tough and paternal,

doggedly leading his men toward perceived safety. The secondary plot which presents Montana as the Colonel's guardian is much less successful. Until the climactic battle, when Montana speaks to the Colonel as a repentant son might speak to his father, the relationship between the two men, and the inability of the Colonel to speak or show emotion, is ineffective and distracting. In the context of this realistic arena of war, this subplot is decidedly unrealistic.

Ultimately, however, it is Montana who gives the film its power. Robert Ryan is gritty and determined as Benson, but his role is a straightforward, by-the-book leadership role. Montana (Aldo Ray) is an atypical soldier with uncanny instincts and a keen understanding of the enemy. Though Benson is disgusted by Montana's brutality, it is the burly sergeant's quick thinking and decisive actions which continually save the lives of Benson's men, which

Benson eventually learns to appreciate. When the two men finally join forces for the final attack, it is an unbeatable combination of brains, toughness and determination.

Ryan and Ray balance each other beautifully, as each character (and actor) sizes up the other, and the tension between them gives the film a sharp edge. In smaller roles, James Edwards and Vic Morrow do well, though Robert Keith as the Colonel has a thankless role, and seems foolish in it.

Though *Men in War* is a fine chronicle of the basic elements of warfare, it isn't a particularly exciting film. It avoids standard cliches of war films but also lacks the familiar build-up and release of inflated dramatic sequences common to those movies. The low-key approach to the subject is quite appropriate, but it doesn't draw viewers into the action the way that big battles do. And while the film seems authentic and genuine, it's also quite depressing. Almost everybody dies, and there's no glory in the victory of the survivors, other than their very survival. *Men in War* provides a penetrating view of the unrelenting *work* of war.

Critics generally found the film insightful and worthwhile. *Newsweek* praised Anthony Mann's unusual approach: "Because the makers of this ordinary-size black-and-white movie have done it the hard and unusual way — exploited silence rather than noise, detail instead of big effects, acting instead of acrobatics, and striven mightily to be true — *Men in War* is much more persuasive than most of its whopping and colorful war-story predecessors." Hollis Alpert of *Saturday Review* concurred: "There is remarkable camera work, magnificent realistic studies of men faced with an all but hopeless situation, and some stunning, quite harrowing suspense as one gets the idea that the platoon is surrounded by a quiet, remorseless enemy." The British Film Institute's *Monthly Film Bulletin* judged that "*Men in War* is, perhaps, one of the most realistic of American war films."

Others did not dispute the film's technical expertise, but wondered whether yet another "war is hell" picture was really necessary. Audiences seemed to agree, were slow to respond to the drama, and the film was largely forgotten. Today, mainly due to the respect given director Anthony Mann for his insightful films of the

1950's (most notably his tough westerns), it is considered one of the better Korean War films and a telling examination of the futility of war.

Men of the Fighting Lady

(aka *Jet Carrier*; *Panther Squadron*)

Credits: 1954. Metro-Goldwyn-Mayer. *Directed by* Andrew Marton. *Produced by* Henry Berman. *Screenplay by* Art Cohn. "It is based on events published in the *Saturday Evening Post* under the titles 'The Forgotten Heroes of Korea' by James Michener and 'The Case of the Blind Pilot' by Commander Harry A. Burns, U.S.N." *Music by* Miklos Rosza [uncredited]. *Introducing* "Blind Flight," *Composed and Conducted by* Miklos Rosza. *Director of Photography*: George Folsey, A.S.C. *Film Editor*: Gene Ruggiero, A.C.E. *Art Directors*: Cedric Gibbons and Paul Groesse. *Set Decorations*: Edwin B. Willis and Keogh Gleason. *Assistant Director*: Joel Freeman. *Recording Supervisor*: Douglas Spencer. *Special Effects*: A. Arnold Gillespie and Warren Newcombe. *Make-Up by* William Tuttle. *Technical Advisor*: Commander Paul N. Gray, U.S.N. Not Rated. Technicolor. *Technicolor Color Consultant*: Alvord Eiseman. Flat (1.33:1). 79 minutes. Released in May, 1954. Currently available on VHS videotape. Previously available on laserdisc.

Cast: *Lieutenant (j.g.) Howard Thayer*, Van Johnson; *Commander Kent Dowling*, Walter Pidgeon; *James A. Michener*, Louis Calhern; *Ensign Kenneth Schechter*, Dewey Martin; *Lieutenant Commander Ted Dodson*, Keenan Wynn; *Lieutenant Commander Paul (Cat) Grayson*, Frank Lovejoy; *Ensign Neil Conovan*, Robert Horton; *Lieutenant (j.g.) Andrew Szymanski*, Bert Freed; *Commander Michael Coughlin*, Lewis Martin; *Cyril Roberts*, George Cooper; *Lieutenant Wayne Kimbrell*, Dick Simmons; *Pilot White*, Chris Warfield; *Pilot Johnson*, Steve Rowland; *Pilot Brown*, Ed Tracy; *Ensign Dispatcher*, Paul Smith; *Officer*, John Rosser; *Replacement*, Ronald Lisa; *Szymanski's Son*, Teddy Infuhr; *Mrs. Szymanski*, Sarah Selby; *Dodson's Sons*, Jerry Mathers, Ronald Stafford, Joseph "Bucko"

Stafford; *Mary Reynolds*, Ann Baker; *Home Movie Commentator*, Jonathan Hale; *Mrs. Dodson*, Dorothy Patrick.

Historical Accuracy Level: High. The stories which comprise the film are based on true incidents recorded by James Michener, who himself is a character in this story.

Patriotic Propaganda Level: High. A naval recruiting video, which also strongly supports U.S. involvement in the Korean War.

Elements: Aircraft Carriers, Air War, Bridge Bombing, Disability, Helicopters, Journalism, Military Training, Navy (Aviators), Rescues.

One of the many "air war" films set during the Korean conflict, *Men of the Fighting Lady* is unique in its setting: most of the action takes place aboard or begins from the aircraft carrier *Yorktown*, though the Navy's "Fighting Lady" is never specifically identified by name, number or nickname during the film (except in the title). In fact, shortly after the Korean war drew to a close, the *Princeton* served as the primary filming location for "Jet Carrier," as the movie was first proposed to be titled.

The narrative structure of the film is also unusual. Writer James Michener (Louis Calhern) is brought to the "Fighting Lady" so that he may be told two particular stories by the carrier's flight surgeon, Commander Dowling (Walter Pidgeon), with the hope that Michener would then write and publish the stories back in the States. For simplicity's sake, the movie's narrative infers that Michener did write the stories which were eventually made into this very movie, but in fact (and stated before the film's opening credits) Michener wrote only one of them, while U.S. Naval Commander Harry A. Burns wrote the other; both stories were published in the *Saturday Evening Post* during 1952.

Both of the stories Michener is told relate to how the jet fighter pilots aboard the "Fighting Lady" react to the imminent danger of their missions as well as the interminable loneliness and homesickness which plague them between flights. The first story examines the notion of heroism, as evidenced by Lieutenant Commander Paul "Cat" Grayson (Frank Lovejoy), a flight leader who continually takes his squadron of eight Panther jets lower and lower to shoot and bomb targets in Korea. Before one flight, the

pilots bet on the lowest altitude they will use; Lieutenant Commander Ted Dodson (Keenan Wynn) wins the pool when they attack on their third pass at two hundred feet. Grayson's plane is hit by flak, however, and he bails out on the way back to the carrier. He is rescued from the frigid sea by the helicopter that hovers close by the flight deck waiting for each jet to return safely.

Dodson, an awarded veteran of World War II, speaks up against what he views as Grayson's foolhardy risk-taking, but most of the men seem to side with Grayson, who believes that the only way to damage the Korean rail system — their current target — is at close range. On the next mission, Lieutenant j.g. (junior grade) Howard Thayer (Van Johnson) is hit at an altitude of one hundred feet and is forced to circle the carrier while the other pilots land their jets ahead of him, in case of a mishap. Thayer lands his plane safely and Dodson counts fifty-nine holes in it. After this, Grayson is told to attack from no lower than eleven hundred feet, or face grounding.

Grayson and the squadron comply, but Dodson is hit by flak anyway and spectacularly crashes into the deck of the carrier trying to land after the others and burns to death. Showing his human side for once, Grayson asks flight surgeon Dowling why he's still alive after taking so many chances while Dodson, who played it safe, has died. "God wraps his arms around crazy characters like you, "Dowling answers. "I don't know why." They toast Dodson's memory.

The second story involves the squadron's next mission. They bomb the Wonsan railroad yard (for the twenty-seventh consecutive time), then search out targets of opportunity. While attacking a bridge, Ensign Kenneth Schechter's (Dewey Martin's) jet is hit and he is at least temporarily blinded. Thayer sees the jet head skyward and follows it, urgently trying to make contact. Thayer discovers that it is his roommate, Schechter, who has been wounded and talks to him over the radio, calming him and turning him back toward the sea. Thayer continues the conversation to keep Schechter from blacking out or giving up, and eventually guides him back to the carrier.

Since Schechter can neither bail out because the ejection mechanism has been fouled,

M·G·M presents the heroic story of what happened to the
"MEN OF THE FIGHTING LADY"

THRILLS IN COLOR!
SMASHING THROUGH THE THRILL
BARRIER... MGM's THUNDERING DRAMA
THAT HAS ALL THE FURY, SWEEP
AND POWER OF THE NAVY'S
GREATEST WEAPON...
THE JET PILOT!

DOROTHY PATRICK
as the girl back home.

STARRING
VAN JOHNSON·WALTER PIDGEON·LOUIS CALHERN
DEWEY MARTIN·KEENAN WYNN·FRANK LOVEJOY

Screen Play by ART COHN Based on James A. Michener's "FORGOTTEN HEROES OF KOREA" and Comdr. Harry A. Burns' "CASE OF THE BLIND PILOT"
Photographed in ANSCO COLOR · Print by TECHNICOLOR · Directed by ANDREW MARTON · Produced by HENRY BERMAN
AN M·G·M PICTURE

This cluttered ad for MGM's drama Men of the Fighting Lady *(1954) emphasizes uplifting, inspirational heroism (as seen in the faces of the six male stars) and zooming jets which seem as though they are about to crash into the* Fighting Lady *aircraft carrier.*

nor ditch into the sea because of his weakened condition (he would not be able to climb out of the jet before it sank), Thayer decides to talk his friend down onto the carrier — it is his only chance. After one aborted pass — which frightens everyone on deck and in the audience — Thayer successfully guides his roommate down onto the carrier deck, then is able to land safely himself once Schechter's jet is cleared away.

The jubilation on board the "Fighting Lady" lasts into the Christmas party which the pilots attend. Home movies of some of the pilots' families back home are displayed. Thayer's father is interviewed, as is Schechter's pretty girlfriend, which draws catcalls from the appreciative male audience. Then the crowd quiets as Ted Dodson's wife and three sons are seen wishing their father a happy birthday and merry Christmas, with presents for both occasions.

Men of the Fighting Lady ends with James Michener learning that Schechter is headed back to the states, still partially blind, to study economics, and thanking Dowling for the stories to tell. Michener told his story in the Saturday Evening Post in an article called "The Forgotten Heroes of Korea," a paean to the naval aviators keeping the world free from aggression. In the article, Michener writes, "At home we seem even yet unable to realize that in Korea a tragic few have been nominated to fight the battle of the entire free world," and asks his audience to give those men "remembrance and support."

Though the film is most definitely a patriotic tribute to the men and machines of the United States Navy, it also most certainly questions the mission, the reasoning behind sending Americans to toil, and often die, in eastern Asia. When Commander Dowling meets Michener, he compliments the writer on his South Pacific tales of World War II, then remarks, "Why couldn't you stop while you were ahead? Even Shakespeare couldn't make this dirty little war romantic."

Dowling goes further when the pilots are seen for the first time, narrating over the action: "They know there are no answers as to why they are here. They've been told it's a police action, which makes them cops. And others have told them that they're containing a blaze, which makes them firemen. All they know is they're buying time. Now and then, paying with a life." Later, trying to calm Ted Dodson, Dowling is pragmatic: "I didn't ask for this war, any more than you did. But I'm here. Let's hope it stops a bigger one."

That last remark, "Let's hope it stops a bigger one," is at the heart of the movie. That one line gives every man aboard the carrier a reason to carry out his orders to the best of his ability. Even though flight surgeon Dowling (the highest authority shown aboard the carrier in the film) can and does question why he is fighting this "dirty little war," deep down he knows there is a basic reason which cannot be ignored. The pilots understand this as well and take their turns bravely, hoping to survive and make it back safely to the States, where they feel that a largely disinterested populace doesn't support them.

Michener addresses this directly in his *Post* article. "I hold their [naval pilots in Korea] heroism to be greater than what I witnessed in 1941–45, for then the soldier on Guadalcanal could feel that his entire nation was behind him, dedicated to the job to which he was dedicated. Civilian and soldier alike bore the burden. But today the fighter in Korea cannot feel this sense

of identification with his own nation. When the men of Marshall Beebe's squadrons go forth to hold the enemy, they are, I am ashamed to say, alone."

Combating that domestic reaction to the Korean conflict was one of the reasons this movie was made. Movies like *Men of the Fighting Lady*, *The Bridges at Toko-Ri* and *The McConnell Story* attempt to present a realistic military and political look at the Korean conflict while entertaining audiences and perhaps provoking some thought along the way. As stated plainly in the opening credits, *Men of the Fighting Lady* is "dedicated to the remarkable men who run the machines of war." The movie tries, with varying degrees of success, to depict the dangers of being a fighter pilot in Korea.

Of course, the naval pilots are seen as heroic. Taking off from and landing a jet fighter on an aircraft carrier is one of the most demanding piloting jobs in the world under normal conditions; doing it continuously while attempting difficult and hazardous missions during a thoroughly unpopular war in foreign waters half a world away from home only makes it that much harder. But they are also human, griping about this and that, missing their families, wanting the personal freedom they are defending for others.

The movie's biggest asset is the location filming on an actual aircraft carrier (in this case, the *Princeton*). Many of the film's seventy-nine minutes are devoted to the ship and the jets which she carries. Planes emerge with their wings folded up like bats' from below decks, are pulled by hand into position and lined up behind the catapults, and are then sent off one by one to zoom loudly over the calm sea. There are even point-of-view shots from the carrier deck as a jet takes off above the camera and from inside the cockpit of one of the jets as it is launched. This documentary approach may lack the human touch, but it is fascinating nonetheless. Within a few minutes, an entire squadron of jet fighters is aloft and heading for combat, because of the choreographed efforts of the carrier's support staff, and it's a wonder to behold.

Landings are even more interesting and suspenseful. Again, point-of-view shots are employed to give the audience a taste of what it is actually like to land a speeding jet fighter on a

Writer James Michener (Louis Calhern, right) meets the carrier's medical officer, Kent Dowling (Walter Pidgeon, left), and Lieutenant Wayne Kimbrell (Dick Simmons, center) in Men of the Fighting Lady *(1954).*

moving area the size of a rural driveway. Most of the takeoffs and landings were filmed on site; but for Dodson's fatal crash, film editor Gene Ruggiero used black-and-white 16mm footage of an actual carrier crash, had it hand-colored frame by frame to match the Ansco color of this film, and inserted it in place. The result fooled Department of Defense officials, who reportedly asked Ruggiero where he found the color footage. While the crash itself is horrifying, the frame by frame painting is tipped off by the color of the sky in the background, which subtly changes as the jet crashes. Incidentally, this specific footage has been used many times since, in war films chronicling carrier use from World War II such as *Midway* (where only the actual crash, not the approach, is seen) to modern thrillers like *The Hunt for Red October*.

Judicious use of the military hardware keeps the film's boredom factor low. In many low-budget films such as *Jet Attack*, stock shots of jets taking off and landing are completely boring because they are not intercut with the human action and are repeated interminably. *Men of the Fighting Lady* intercuts documentary jet flying footage with standard Hollywood process shots of the movie stars pretending to fly. In addition, the film presents an actual helicopter rescue of a downed pilot from the sea, thereby displaying another aspect of the naval program.

One area where the film falls short is its use of actual Korean combat footage when depicting strafing and bombing runs of the Panther squadron. Some of the shots work well and are consistent with the altitudes of the attacking jets, but as the film moves on, that consistency rapidly deteriorates, and the combat photography becomes repetitive. Apart from this quibble, however, the film's photography is very good and the military footage supplied by the Department of Defense is well utilized.

When James Michener and Commander Harry Burns wrote their *Post* articles, they wrote about the real people involved in the actual incidents. For the movie, Commander Paul Gray became Paul "Cat" Grayson, even though Gray served as the film's technical advisor. However, Lieutenant Andrew Szymanski (Bert Freed) remained the same in both versions. Howard Thayer and Ken Schechter are taken directly from Commander Burns' story; the other characters in the movie, including Dowling and Dodson, seem to have been created by screenwriter Art Cohn, who has done a decent job of melding such disparate stories into an entertaining narrative.

Van Johnson, as Thayer, imbues his character with just the right amount of personal integrity. Interestingly, his character is very similar to that of Lieutenant Maryk, the naval officer he played in *The Caine Mutiny* the same year. Frank Lovejoy is properly pugnacious as working-class squadron leader Grayson and Keenan Wynn does well as the squadron's conscience, Dodson. As flight surgeon Dowling, Walter Pidgeon seems vaguely uncomfortable and does most of the moralizing of the piece; he is the weakest of the main players, perhaps because his role is largely undefined. Dewey Martin has little to do during the first half of the film, then hams it up in the last half as blinded Kenneth Schechter. Louis Calhern has what amounts to a cameo appearance as Michener, though he seems well cast. Look fast for Jerry Mathers, pre–*Leave It to Beaver*, as one of Ted Dodson's sons in the home movie shown to the pilots.

Overall, the critical response to *Men of the Fighting Lady* was positive. Moira Walsh of *America* wrote that the film "in general draws a modestly convincing picture of combat routine and the men who carry it out. These latter emerge as diverse personalities with no clear idea of what they are fighting for, a certain amount of understandable bitterness and cynicism concerning the disinterest on the homefront and a devotion to duty and to one another which gives

the lie to their disenchanted utterances." Both *Time* and *Newsweek* commended the film's documentary-style approach, while noting the script's inadequacies.

It was one of the biggest hits of the year for MGM, continuing the trend of money-making military films, which recently had included *From Here To Eternity*, *The Caine Mutiny*, and *Stalag 17*, and which would lead to *Battle Cry*, *Mister Roberts*, *The Bridges at Toko-Ri* and *Strategic Air Command*, all of which became huge hits. *Men of the Fighting Lady* should be counted as one of the most successful Korean War films, both artistically and financially.

Mission Over Korea
(aka *Eyes in the Sky*)

Credits: 1953. Columbia. *Directed by* Fred F. Sears. *Produced by* Robert Cohn. *Screen Play by* Jesse L. Lasky, Jr., Eugene Ling and Martin M. Goldsmith. *Story by* Richard Tregaskis. *Musical Director:* Mischa Bakaleinikoff. *Director of Photography:* Sam Leavitt. *Film Editor:* Henry Batista, A.C.E. *Art Director:* George Brooks. *Set Decorator:* Frank Tuttle. *Assistant Director:* James Nicholson. *Sound Engineer:* George Cooper. *Technical Adviser:* Captain Paul F. Hopkins. Not Rated. Black and White. Flat (1.33:1). 85 minutes. Released in August, 1953. Not currently available on commercial home video.

Cast: *Captain George Slocum,* John Hodiak; *Lieutenant Pete Barker,* John Derek; *Kate,* Audrey Totter; *Nancy Slocum,* Maureen O'Sullivan; *Sergeant Maxie Steiner,* Harvey Lembeck; *Corporal Swenson,* Richard Erdman; *Clancy,* William Chun; *Major Hacker,* Rex Reason; *Singing Soldier,* Richard Bowers; *Lieutenant Jerry Barker,* Todd Karnes; *Major Kung,* Al Choi; *Pilot,* Dabbs Greer.

Historical Accuracy Level: Medium. Based on true incidents and situations, the film also meanders along its own path some of the time.

Patriotic Propaganda Level: High. During a highly dangerous war, this film promotes pilots who fly unarmed photographic reconnaissance aircraft!

Elements: Air Force, Air War, Combat

Photography, Military Training, Orphans, Romance, Sibling Rivalry.

One of the more authentic Korean War films is this minor programmer, which bolsters its routine story with stock footage which is blended into its storyline better than most other films of the period. *Mission Over Korea* tells the story of the observation pilots who fly unarmed monoplanes (L-5s) over battlefields and hostile territory, looking for enemy targets. Pilots of these aircraft communicate with artillery on the ground, helping to pinpoint target areas.

As the movie opens, Captain George Slocum (John Hodiak) and Lt. Jerry Barker (Todd Karnes) are instructing Republic of (South) Korea soldiers on the intricacies of using observation planes in battle. Training is the keyword, as it is 1950 and the war has not yet begun. The ROK major (Al Choi) remarks to Slocum that twelve weeks earlier his soldiers were field workers and he was an insurance salesman. Jerry Barker's brother Pete is assigned to join the outfit, but it is Slocum who is assigned to fly to Japan to meet him and escort him to Korea.

As he approaches Japan in his L-5, Slocum is greeted by another, which flies loops around him and even accompanies him upside down for a time. Its pilot is Lt. Pete Barker (John Derek), who assumes that his brother Jerry is in the other plane. On the ground, Slocum lectures Pete that there are only three L-5s in their outfit and Pete has just endangered two of them. After visiting the provost marshal's office for unauthorized stunt flying, Slocum reunites with his wife and kids, whom he hasn't seen in months. Pete tries to pick up a nurse named Kate (Audrey Totter), who tells him to cool his jets.

The North Koreans invade South Korea, so Slocum and Pete are sent back to Korea. Low on fuel, they land at their base near Seoul, which is now burning and littered with dead bodies. They find Jerry, still alive but badly injured, and try to carry him to safety, but North Korean attackers kill him. A hand-to-hand battle ensues, but Slocum and Pete kill their attackers. They are immediately assigned to fly two civilians to safety, and Slocum takes along Clancy (William Chun), a Korean teenager whom he has befriended.

Pete, thinking of his dead brother and a letter which Jerry wrote to him, flies too high and invites an attack from a North Korean plane, which then switches to Slocum's tail. Slocum eventually eludes the attacker, leading it into a hill. Upon landing, Slocum lectures Pete again and angrily informs him that their two passengers were a U.S. senator and the President of Korea.

While Slocum gets their new orders Pete fits a rocket launcher below the wing of his L-5. They take off again and soon spot enemy tanks. Pete attacks them with his rocket launcher and is shot down by a tank's machine gunner. Slocum leaves Pete where he is (he can't land anywhere nearby) and reports Pete's predicament. He is assigned to drop plasma to a cornered unit, and takes one of his mechanics with him. Swenson (Richard Erdman) expresses his displeasure at the situation, exclaiming, "I hate this police action. I'm no cop!" but drops the needed plasma on target. Even with bullet holes in its gas tanks, the plane makes it back, and repairs are begun. Pete arrives, escorted by some ROK troops, and he and Slocum snarl at each other.

Down to just one plane, Slocum and Pete share flying duty, filmed in montage. At an encampment one night, North Korean troops suddenly attack, wounding Slocum. As the battle rages, Pete flies Slocum to a hospital where Kate takes charge of him. Pete is criticized by commanding officer Major Hacker (Rex Reason), for taking the plane and then learns that Slocum has died of his wounds. Kate visits Pete and persuades him to carry on Slocum's burden of work. Clancy, the Korean boy whom Slocum befriended, hears of Slocum's death, removes his prized combat boots and walks away, never to be seen again.

Pete installs a wide-band radio in his plane so that he can talk to jets as he does with ground artillery and lead them to targets. Major Hacker gives Pete a photographic assignment and Pete takes along his other mechanic, Maxie (Harvey Lembeck), to take the photos. Spying a tank ambush behind their lines, Pete contacts a nearby jet squadron and guides them to the tanks. An explosion injures Pete, and Maxie is forced to fly and land the plane from the back seat. The plane cracks up spectacularly and burns as the two men are pulled out and carried away to safety. Then a narrator intones, "This was not the end, but the beginning…"

Although the description of Mission Over Korea's *"seeing eye dogs of the Artillery" is essentially accurate, the pictures beneath the title to this 1953 Columbia film hint at more action and romance than there actually is in the movie.*

Mission Over Korea suffers from the normal B-movie maladies of a formulaic script, contrived situations, actors of less than exceptional talent and a general lack of imagination. But the film, at least to some degree, overcomes these shortcomings with its straightforward and constantly moving narrative, well staged and photographed scenes of aviation, earnest performances and, most of all, its outlook regarding the war.

The Korean War is seen as an inevitability, one which nobody wants but which must be faced. The "why" of the war is never deeply discussed or examined. Rather, every character attempts to do his or her duty as best he or she can, under lousy circumstances. This film has a very authentic feel to it as far as the military situation goes: air bases and command centers constantly move, sometimes under fire; civilians are the victims and they are also always on the move, looking for safe places to rest; the work is never, ever done; life is valued but the bigger picture is always kept in focus; people and equipment are overworked, but they are pushed and supported to hold up under the strain.

One of only a few films to address Korea both before and after the invasion, *Mission Over Korea* parallels *Dragonfly Squadron* (which also starred John Hodiak) in its view of the disorganized state of the South Korean Air Force. In fact, *Dragonfly Squadron*, which was filmed and released the year after *Mission Over Korea*, reflects some of the same situations and attitudes as the earlier film. Seen together, they would make an interesting, if repetitive, double feature.

Mission Over Korea's script defies normal Hollywood heroism by showing Pete foul up repeatedly, even after he should have learned his lessons; by killing its main character, Slocum Slocum, (offscreen!) three-quarters of the way into the story; by disregarding several opportunities to

Corporal Swenson (Richard Erdman, left) and Captain George Slocum (John Hodiak, right) examine artillery damage to the wing of Slocum's observation monoplane in Mission Over Korea *(1953). The airplane is an unarmed L-5 monoplane, which was used by the Air Force for reconnaissance and photography.*

introduce romance and sex into the mix; and by ending the story with what can certainly be considered a defeat. As such, it is one of the most realistic — and unusual — Korean War movies ever filmed.

Another plus is the flying scenes, which are nicely done. Other than the standard bluescreen shots of the actors in mock cockpits, the flying sequences which involve the L-5 monoplanes and a few jets as well are expertly photographed and interesting to watch. A few of the landings are quite bumpy, which only adds realism and excitement. At least some of the battle footage is actually from Korea, though its percentage is difficult to ascertain. In any case, the film looks authentic, especially from the air.

While the film's characters and performances are nothing special, one casting note is worth mentioning. Clancy, the Korean orphan, is portrayed by William Chun, the same actor who played Short Round in *The Steel Helmet* two years previously. The role of Clancy is similar to that of Short Round, although more clichéd and less memorable. After Slocum's death, the boy wanders away from the Americans, because Slocum has proven that they also die, just like Koreans.

The film received poor notices, partly due to its release soon after the war finally dragged to a conclusion when people did not wish to be reminded of it. Critic Howard Thompson of the *New York Times* complained that the film "is a sad aftermath to the recent hostilities and would have been even more embarrassing to watch before the armistice." In his book *The Columbia Story*, Clive Hirschhorn labelled the movie "Little more than a compendium of wartime platitudes."

This film was obviously intended as a propaganda tool for the Air Force and its cooperative efforts with the Republic of Korea. This is borne out by the opening sequence and some other moments along the way. But unlike other propaganda pieces in which the flag is waved and the heroes are cheered, *Mission Over Korea* expands its own mission beyond that of propaganda and attempts to relate some of the Korean situation the way it really was. Despite its B-movie origins and limitations, to a large degree, it succeeds.

Mr. Walkie Talkie

Credits: 1952. Rockingham Productions, Inc. *Released by* Lippert Pictures. *Directed by* Fred Guiol. *Produced by* Hal Roach, Jr. *Associate Producer*: Guy V. Thayer, Jr. *Original Story and Screenplay by* Ned Seabrook and G. Carleton Brown. *Music by* Leon Klatzkin. *Director of Photography*: Walter Strenge, A.S.C. *Edited by* Bert Jordan, A.C.E. *Production Manager*: Dick L'Estrange. *Supervising Editor*: Roy Luby, A.C.E. *Art Director*: McClure Capps. *Photographic Effects*: Jack R. Glass. *Sound Engineer*: Howard Fogetti. *Assistant Director*: Dick Moder. *Special Effects*: Ira Anderson. *Song* "I Love the Men," *Music by* Leon Klatzkin, *Lyrics by* Tom Adair. Not Rated. Black and White. Flat (1.33:1). 65 minutes. Released in December, 1952. Not currently available on commercial home video.

Cast: *Sergeant Doubleday*, William Tracy; *Sergeant Ames*, Joe Sawyer; *Captain Burke*, Robert Shayne; *Tiny*, Alan Hale, Jr.; *Colonel Lockwood*, Russell Hicks; *Corporal Jackson*, Frank Jenks; *Entertainer*, Margia Dean; *Lieutenant Kim*, Wong Artarne; *with* William "Bill" Boyett, James B. Leong, John Breed, Peter Ortiz, Walter Ng, Ralph Brooke and Clarence the duck.

Historical Accuracy Level: Low. There is no record of a duck ever being inducted into the U.S. Army.

Patriotic Propaganda Level: Medium. Movies like this make the Army seem like fun.

Elements: Army, Behind Enemy Lines, Comedy, Congressional Medal of Honor, Females in the Field, Infighting, Musical Performance, U.S.O.

There are very few out-and-out comedies about the Korean War. Unlike World War II, which inspired a whole genre of service comedies, there didn't seem to be much to laugh about in Korea. One comedy which harks back to the halcyon days of Abbott and Costello or Bill Mauldin's comic strips featuring dogfaces Willie and Joe (who have their own Korean War movie, *Back at the Front*) is *Mr. Walkie Talkie*. This innocuous little movie is actually the eighth, and final, teaming of William Tracy and Joe Sawyer as Army sergeants Doubleday and Ames. This series, produced by Hal Roach and nicknamed the "Laff Time" series, began in 1941 and followed the Doubleday and Ames charac-

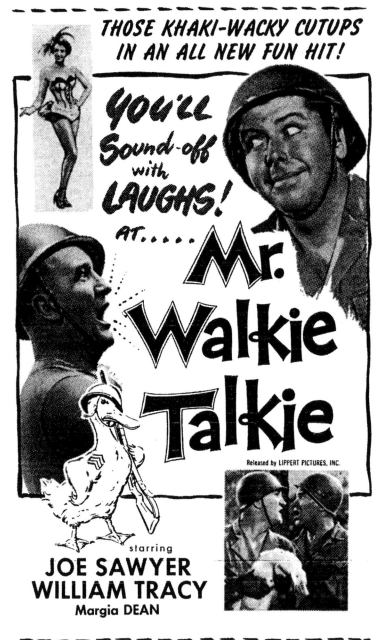

THOSE KHAKI-WACKY CUTUPS
IN AN ALL NEW FUN HIT!

You'll
Sound-off
with
LAUGHS!
AT.....

Mr.
Walkie
Talkie

Released by LIPPERT PICTURES, INC.

starring
JOE SAWYER
WILLIAM TRACY
Margia DEAN

Service humor is the key attraction for Lippert's comedy Mr. Walkie Talkie (1952). This advertisement features U.S.O. entertainer Margia Dean as well as stars Joe Sawyer (left) and William Tracy (right). Although Sawyer is indicated as "Mr. Walkie Talkie," the title actually refers to Tracy as Sergeant Doubleday. Clarence the duck appears twice in the ad; at the bottom, held by Sergeant Amers (Joe Sawyer), and as a stern caricature, complete with rifle, helmet and sergeant's stripes of his own.

Mr. Walkie Talkie begins at the Army's Camp Carver, as Sergeant Ames (Joe Sawyer) is trying to prepare his squad for upcoming war games and trying not to listen to Sergeant Doubleday (William Tracy) recite the history of the rifle. Doubleday is blessed with a photographic memory and often expatiates upon various subjects interminably, much to Ames' consternation. During the war maneuvers, Ames confiscates Doubleday's quail caller and attempts to direct his men using bird sounds. His efforts are disrupted by real quails, which have the soldiers running around in circles. Reprimanded again, Ames begs Captain Burke (Robert Shayne) to transfer him away from Doubleday, so Burke takes Ames with him to Korea.

In Korea, Ames is happy, whistling while Chinese snipers are shooting at him, all because he is away from the non-stop talking of Doubleday. Ames and new buddy Corporal Jackson (Frank Jenks) eliminate a sniper with grenades; to Jackson's great amusement, Ames surrenders to a duck. Ames decides to keep the duck for a future dinner, and so keeps it, feeding it half of his K ration in order to fatten it, and naming it Clarence. Ames and Jackson are in a foxhole (with Clarence in his own, nearby) when badly needed

ters through World War II, the peacetime period and into the Korean War.

reinforcements parachute into the battlefield. Jackson exits the foxhole and Doubleday lands beside his old buddy.

The men march, but Doubleday stops them before they enter a particular rice paddy. Ames uses Doubleday's refusal to move against him, demanding that he be court-martialed, but Colonel Lockwood (Russell Hicks) agrees with Doubleday's assessment that enemy soldiers are nearby, indicated by an absence of cricket noise. Later, the time comes for Ames to eat Clarence, but he cannot bring himself to kill his feathered friend. He asks Doubleday to do it, but he can't kill the duck either. Thus, Clarence becomes part of the army.

A very limited (one girl singer) U.S.O. show is presented in the Korean forest. While Doubleday plays the piano, an entertainer in a skimpy costume (Margia Dean) sings "I Love the Men." Ames is on guard duty, but he fails to notice the Chinese soldier who sneaks behind, then sits beside him to enjoy the show. When the Chinese soldier pulls the pin on a grenade, Doubleday sees him and orders him to stop in Chinese. Doubleday rushes over, grabs the grenade and saves the day by throwing it away. For his negligence, Ames loses his sergeant's stripes, which are instead placed upon Clarence.

Before its radio is destroyed, a squad led by Tiny (Alan Hale, Jr.) and Lieutenant Kim (Wong Artarne) reports that it is trapped near Hill 290. Colonel Lockwood needs a volunteer to contact the squad and lead them out using a complicated artillery schedule. Ames volunteers in order to win back his stripes, and Doubleday memorizes the artillery schedule. Ames is ordered to protect Doubleday, no matter what. The two men sneak through the forest, at first followed by, and then led by, Clarence, who signals them forward and back using his tail. At one point, Clarence is "ducknapped" by the Chinese, who build a fire. Singlehandedly, Ames rushes in and clobbers the entire Chinese squad, saving his feathered friend.

Led by Clarence, Ames and Doubleday locate the squad and, using Doubleday's memorized knowledge, return to safety. Colonel Lockwood is impressed by Ames' effort and begins to type a recommendation for the Congressional Medal of Honor for the newly restriped sergeant. But Ames has had enough of Double-

day's double talk and chases him through the command tent, bringing an end to Lockwood's recommendation and the film.

Mr. Walkie Talkie is an old-fashioned comedy featuring contrasting characters and several different set-pieces from which its laughs are derived. The key elements are the loud, overbearing, short-tempered Sergeant Ames and the quiet, earnest, encyclopedic Sergeant Doubleday. Ames becomes so irritated with Doubleday that he cannot control his emotions, and therein lies the comedy. Audiences wait for Doubleday to embark upon one of his intellectual lectures and then watch happily as Ames' temper explodes and the fireworks begin. At some point during the proceedings, Ames realizes that the two men actually complement each other and tells Doubleday that very thing, but before long, he is at his friend's throat again.

Together, William Tracy and Joe Sawyer made eight films as sergeants Doubleday and Ames, and they probably would have made more but for Tracy's service late during World War II. The films are *Tanks a Million* (1941), *Hay Foot* (1942), *About Face* (1942), *Fall In* (1943), *Yanks Ahoy* (1943), *Here Comes Trouble* (1948), *As You Were* (1951) and *Mr. Walkie Talkie*. Doubleday and Ames served in the Army in all but *Here Comes Trouble*, a color comedy in which Doubleday was a reporter and Ames a detective. These fifty- to seventy-minute comedies were designed as second features on double bills and are all but forgotten today, although they do preserve the legacy of great cinematic comedy teams.

The third most important character in the film is Clarence the duck. Audiences were tickled by the idea of big, lumbering Joe Sawyer going soft over a duck, scooping a foxhole for it and protectively covering it with his helmet, and especially when he realizes with a rare flash of conscience that he cannot cook his feathered friend. Clarence proves himself particularly valuable later on when he leads his keepers through enemy territory, signaling them with his tail. And he provides the movie's biggest laugh when Doubleday discovers that he is not a "he" at all.

More comedy is provided when a Chinese soldier creeps behind Ames during the Margia Dean song, then joins him in his appreciation

A squad surrounded behind enemy lines circles Clarence the duck, whom they trust to lead them back to safety in Mr. Walkie Talkie *(1952). Closest to Clarence from left to right are Sergeant Doubleday (William Tracy), Sergeant Ames (Joe Sawyer) and Tiny (Alan Hale, Jr.)*

of her presentation. Ames and the soldier take turns slapping each other good-naturedly on the shoulders, and the longer that Ames takes to recognize the enemy, the more amusing it is. The first comedy sequence, which has Ames' squad reacting to quail calls, both real and impersonated, is also very well staged, although the shots of quail do not match the live action.

The film obviously had a shoestring budget (the forest is strictly backlot and the U.S.O. only furnishes one girl singer, without piano player!), but it utilizes its people and locations adroitly. Alan Hale, Jr., Robert Shayne, Russell Hicks, Frank Jenks and Wong Artarne fill their roles quite capably, and Sawyer and Tracy are the whole show — other than Clarence, of course. *Mr. Walkie Talkie* is an enjoyably silly, critic-proof movie, one which creates a nostalgia for the cinematic period when wartime escapades could be enjoyed without having to worry for the safety of the characters.

My Son John

Credits: 1952. Rainbow Productions. *Distributed by* Paramount. *Produced and Directed by* Leo McCarey. *Screenplay by* Myles Connolly and Leo McCarey. *Story by* Leo McCarey. *Music Score by* Robert Emmett Dolan. *Director of Photography*: Harry Stradling, A.S.C. *Edited by* Marvin Coil, A.C.E. *Art Direction*: Hal Pereira and William Flannery. *Orchestrations by* Robert Russell Bennett. *Costumes*: Edith Head. *Special Photographic Effects*: Gordon Jennings, A.S.C. *Process Photography*: Farciot Edouart, A.S.C. *Set Decoration*: Sam Comer and Emile Kuri.

Makeup Supervision: Wally Westmore. *Sound Recording*: Gene Merritt and Gene Garvin. Not Rated. Black and White. Flat (1.33:1). 122 minutes. Released in April, 1952. Not currently available on commercial home video.

Cast: *Lucille Jefferson*, Helen Hayes; *FBI Agent Stedman*, Van Heflin; *Dan Jefferson*, Dean Jagger; *John Jefferson*, Robert Walker; *Doctor Carver*, Minor Watson; *Father O'Dowd*, Frank McHugh; *Chuck Jefferson*, Richard Jaeckel; *Ben Jefferson*, James Young; *Bedford*, Todd Karns; *Ruth Carlin*, Irene Winston; *College Professors*, David Bond, Erskine Sanford and Eghiche Harout; *Jail Matron*, Gail Bonney; *FBI Agents*, Russ Conway and David Newell; *Taxi Driver*, Jimmie Dundee; *Government Employee*, Douglas Evans; *Nurses*, Nancy Hale and Margaret Wells; *Boy*, Lee Aaker; *Parcel Post Man*, William McLean; *Cleaner*, Fred Sweeney; *Secretaries*, Frances Morris and Vera Stokes; *Man*, Mishka Egan.

Historical Accuracy Level: Medium. This film's dire warnings regarding Communist infiltration of the American government are undeniably timely, but it would be foolish to take this overblown melodrama very seriously.

Patriotic Propaganda Level: High. Actually, off the charts, as the story's loving mother surrenders her Commie son to the F.B.I. for his own good.

Elements: Army, Collaboration, Homefront, Mystery, Politics, Red Menace, Sibling Rivalry.

Several Korean War films try to capture the feeling of paranoia which swept the country as the threat of subversive Communist elements became widely publicized, but few are as hysterical as Leo McCarey's *My Son John*. The threat of the Red Menace was undoubtedly real and frightening to many people, but cinematic "warnings" such as *My Son John* only served to heighten the hysteria rather than examine the situation rationally. Certainly *My Son John* is well-intentioned, but by insisting that Communist spies could be and, in fact, were the nice boys next door (specifically intellectual, non-athletic types who rejected religion), the film merely contributed to the paranoia that cost thousands of innocent people their reputations, their livelihoods, and in some cases, their very

lives. It remains today an eerie, frozen moment in time, a morality play that hardly seems as though it could have been taken seriously.

On a quiet street, the Jefferson family prepares for church. The parents, Dan (Dean Jagger) and Lucille (Helen Hayes), fuss while the grown boys, Chuck (Richard Jaeckel) and Ben (James Young), toss a football. It is a special Sunday, because Chuck and Ben are in their Army uniforms, and today is their final day at home before travelling to fight in the Korean War. Lucille is sad to see her sons go, but even more melancholy because her eldest son, John, is unable to be present. Chuck and Ben are driven to the train by Father O'Dowd (Frank McHugh). A week later, Doctor Carver (Minor Watson) stops by with some pills for Lucille, to help her through "that time of life," and John (Robert Walker) comes home, entering through the back door. Lucille is overjoyed to see her son, but a stiff formality stands between Dan and John.

The three go to mass, and then John insists that they leave him at a nearby Teacher's College, where he can visit a former professor. John is to receive an honorary degree and deliver a commencement address at his alma mater, and wants his professor's input. On the way home, Dan hits another car, but little damage results. John returns home late and talks to his parents. Dan requests John's help on his upcoming American Legion speech, "Where Are We Headed?" and then sings an ultra-patriotic song. John mimics his father as he climbs the stairs, causing Dan some consternation. Lucille brings him a sandwich and they talk more intimately, but she also feels that he is condescending to her and "making fun of a mother's love." John apologizes and they sing together, lightly parodying Dan's song.

The following morning, the driver of the car which Dan struck (Van Heflin) arrives at the house with an $18 bill for his bent fender. At first hostile, Lucille is soon talking freely about her boys. The driver eventually abandons his quest and rips the bill into shreds. In the evening, father and son discuss John's responses to Dan's speech, all of which are rejected by Dan. The exchange becomes heated and Dan accuses John of sounding like a Communist. Dan becomes so upset that he skips dinner and goes to the Legion hall early to repair his speech. John receives a long distance call and his manner changes. Lucille tells him about the other driver and admits that she told him a lot about John. This troubles John, who decides to fly to Washington (where he works) that night. He reassures his mother that he is not a Communist by swearing on the Bible that he is not. Dan comes home and is encouraged that his son has renounced Communism, but then it occurs to him that Communists do not believe in the Bible. An argument escalates, resulting in Dan

The sensational topic of enemy collaboraion is indicated in the artwork for Paramount's My Son John *(1952). The ad is framed like a "WANTED" poster, and the four boxes promise excitement that this low-key drama does not really deliver.*

bopping John in the head with the family Bible and then pushing his son over a table. Since his pants are ripped, John changes clothing and leaves; Dan is thrown out of the house by Lucille and he returns to the Legion hall to drink. Dan comes home much later, drunk, and talks with Lucille about the state of the American character.

The next day, John calls and asks for his ripped pants, but Lucille has given them to a church clothing drive. John is insistent, so Lucille walks to the church and finds them; she discovers a key in one of the pockets. The driver (Van Heflin) who talked to Lucille arrives again, but this time introduces himself as F.B.I. agent Stedman. He indicates that John is suspected of being linked to a "Red spy ring," the story of which is featured on the front page of the local newspaper. Lucille tells him nothing and flies to Washington. She meets John and is convinced that he is lying to her. She almost gives John the key, but his insincerity prevents her from trusting him. She meets Stedman again at the Tidal Basin, and he provides details about the case which persuade her that John may be involved. She takes the key to a known spy's apartment and tries it; the key opens the door. Faced with the knowledge that her son is a spy, Lucille goes home and cries.

Sick at heart, Lucille asks for Doctor Carver. When Dan goes to get the doctor, John sneaks into the house and tries to force her to give up the key. Lucille wants to believe his lies, but cannot. Stedman arrives and watches quietly while John undermines his mother's sanity and refuses to confess on his own account, despite her begging. Dan and Doctor Carver arrive and John leaves through the back door. He sneaks back in later, and hears his father state that he wants to kill him. Lucille is more forgiving; together they pray for John's soul.

John's conscience finally forces him to admit his treason to himself. He calls Stedman and offers to make a deal. John records his upcoming commencement speech on audio tape and then calls Stedman to set up a meeting. A car follows John's cab and chases it down Pennsylvania Avenue; a hail of machine gun bullets forces it to crash on the steps of the Lincoln Memorial. Stedman arrives and John tells him of the recording before he dies. Stedman listens to it and agrees to play it for the graduating class at John's alma mater. In the recording, John tells of his recruitment by Soviet agents and conversion to Communism. John's voice urges the young men and women to "Hold fast to honor — it's sacred," and admits that he is a traitor and a Communist spy. After the ceremony, Dan and Lucille head for the nearest church to pray for John's soul.

My Son John is, in a word, overripe. While the first half of the story is an often interesting view of small town life and contains some clever dialogue, it loses focus and gains a hysterical tone as it continues. Ultimately it becomes a parable against any mode of liberal thought or action, utterly condemning anyone who isn't a true-blue patriot. John is not like his brothers. They are former football heroes and only seen in uniforms (either athletic or military), ready to fight in Korea. John is a dandy, always impeccably dressed and ironically erudite in manner. He is almost effeminate and quite probably meant to be homosexual, and is unable to protect himself even against a gentle push from his father. Asked if he has a girl, John replies sheepishly, "Oh, Mother!" It is also intimated, though not specifically noted, that John has avoided serving in Korea. Though older than his brothers, there is nothing to prevent him from fighting alongside them, except, of course, a basic unwillingness to serve his country.

Perhaps the most disturbing element of John's condemnation — other than the probability of his intended homosexuality — is the fact that he is an intellectual. While the film hints that homosexuals are Communists, it states far more stridently that intellectuals are, or at least are more likely to become, Communist agents. John's father labels himself dumb or uninformed several times, while John's own intellect is exaggerated. No one in town is smarter than John, but no one else has become a Communist spy. John's climactic speech indicates that the Soviets are constantly recruiting the most intelligent graduates, always searching for new blood. John compares the personal attention he received while being recruited to a drug and insists that he was lured to treason by the promise of free thought. Stating its case in these terms, the movie is clearly condemning such thought, arguing that intellectual Americans are not resilient or tough enough to resist its dangers of ideas. It also intimates that most people are too simple to fall for such Commie nonsense, but that individuals with imagination are susceptible.

The film's warnings about the Communist threat are all-inclusive. By pitting parents against their son, the film actively attempts to persuade its audience that the very possibility of Communist thought rips families apart. At one point, Dan notes that it is a Communist specialty to break up happy homes. And according to the film's sensibilities, the only proper thing to do if one suspects a family member of having fallen under the spell of the Red Menace is to call in the F.B.I.

When the locale switches to Washington, D.C., the movie's propaganda level switches into high gear. Stedman tails Lucille to the Tidal Basin and meets her there, taking the time to point to the Jefferson Memorial, the Washington Monument and the direction of the Lincoln Memorial to inspire her patriotism. The film's only scene of action (a car chase) ends on the steps of the Lincoln Memorial (just as *The Fearmakers* would six years later), with the F.B.I. arriving too late to save John, who simply had to be the sacrificial lamb for the cause of freedom.

Religion acts as a warning sign for spotting Communists in the film. When Lucille suggests John go to mass, he instantly becomes uneasy. John cleverly insults Father O'Dowd and resists active participation in either the church or the American Legion. Lucille tells Stedman that her two boys are "fighting on God's side," and frequently prays for her other son, John. The Bible is a divining rod; Dan concludes that a Communist would not hesitate to use it for his own purposes, and Dan uses it as a literal club to "knock some sense" into his son. Even by having Father O'Dowd transport Chuck and Ben to the train on their first step to Korea, the film is inferring that religion is behind their cause, and that Communists cannot possibly win.

On another level, the film is a fuzzy indictment of the American family unit. Even though the Jeffersons (note the all-American name) have produced two fine football-hero sons who are perfectly willing to fight the good fight, they have also produced John. The father, Dan, is portrayed as an ultra-patriotic, flag-waving, song-singing teacher of young children who

believes that "good old American bromides" will provide the answer to every problem, while the mother, Lucille, is an overprotective, hyperactive imp who frets over each and every occurrence in John's life. Even accepting that John is Lucille's favorite, a Mama's boy of the highest caliber, it is amazing that the other two boys turned out as well as they have from this obviously dysfunctional family.

While the film does not actively deal with the Korean War, its view of America as a homefront during that time of conflict is its primary value. There are two important "homefront" movies, *I Want You* and *My Son John*, and each presents a different perspective as to the state of America during the Korean War. *My Son John* submits that America was just as dangerous a place as Korea because of an abundance of sneaky and cunning Communist infiltrators. One of its many failings is that it seems unneccesary and even foolish to send troops overseas when enemies are in our own back yards. The movie's level of rhetoric and propaganda is so high that audience paranoia is encouraged and expected. On the whole, small town life goes on as it has before, but the exposure of John Jefferson as a spy should alert everyone, everywhere of the imminent danger, and encourage every person to actively watch their neighbors and report any unseemly behavior. And while this approach is founded in common sense, it is taken to such an extreme that civil liberties and personal rights are threatened. This is just a movie, but one simply has to read histories of the Communist witch-hunts of the time to discover how certain segments of the American population were discriminated against and punished for no reason except fear.

The anti-Communist fever which culminated in Senator Joseph McCarthy's personal reign of terror was fueled by speeches, articles and "artistic expressions" such as this movie. Writer-producer-director Leo McCarey, a talented filmmaker who must take full responsibility for this project, had been a willing witness before H.U.A.C. (the House Un-American Activities Committee) and was fervent in his hatred of Communism. He meant *My Son John* to serve as a warning against a threat that he felt many people were either ignoring or cared nothing about, but his "warning" became so

The principals of My Son John *(1952): John Jefferson (Robert Walker, left), Mr. Stedman (Van Heflin, top left), Lucille Jefferson (Helen Hayes, center), Dan Jefferson (Dean Jagger, top right) and Father O'Dowd (Frank McHugh, right).*

inflammatory and virulent that the result is embarrassing. This is especially sad because there are several positives in the film.

McCarey's view of small-town life seems authentic, and the cinematography which depicts the details of the town and its citizens is excellent. Comedy has always been Leo McCarey's hallmark, and there are quite a number of nice comedic touches throughout the story. Some, such as Dan's drunken skirmishes with the lamp and the stairs, are slapstick, while others, such as John's parodying of his father's jingoism, are more pointed or sublime. Whichever the case, these touches of comedy help keep the film light and watchable until the melodrama inevitably takes control. And as dysfunctional as the Jefferson household may be, it is clear that Dan and Lucille truly love each other and belong together.

Unfortunately, the negatives outweigh these positives. The acting of Helen Hayes (who returned to the screen after a seventeen year absence for this role) and Dean Jagger in particular is completely over the top. Watching Helen Hayes lead cheers for the soul of her diffident son ("Take the ball, John! Time's running out! We can't stop that clock! I'm cheering for you, now! My son John! My son John!") makes one's skin crawl. Just as creepy is Dan's unflinching patriotism, which seems dangerous rather than uplifting. At the other end of the acting scale is Van Heflin as the most sensitive, caring F.B.I. agent in the history of cinema.

Robert Walker, who had recently triumphed in Alfred Hitchcock's *Strangers on a Train*, portrays the central character, John. Walker's eloquent manner serve the character well, but one never believes that John *isn't* a Communist spy. Walker died near the end of filming *My Son John*, causing the need for alterations to the final half-hour to properly complete the story. Thus, both Lucille and Stedman have one-sided telephone calls with John in which John doesn't speak; the shots of John speaking from a telephone booth (and later dying) are cribbed from close-ups and outtakes from *Strangers on a Train*. Luckily, Walker had already finished his recording of the final speech before his death, but the scene of an empty podium bathed in a heavenly bright light while John warns the college graduates to beware gifts from strangers is perhaps the most bizarre image from a bizarre movie.

The film was lambasted critically, though it did moderately well in theatres. Otis L. Guernsey, Jr., of the *New York Herald-Tribune* was eloquent in his dismissal of the film: "In effect, McCarey's picture of how America ought to be is so frightening, so speciously argued, so full of warnings against intelligent solution of the problem that it boomerangs upon its own cause and becomes, by mistake, a most vivid demonstration that two wrongs don't make a right." Bosley Crowther of the *New York Times* noted that "it seethes with the sort of emotionalism and illogic that is characteristic of so much thinking these days." Perhaps the most succinct review appears in *The Paramount Story*, in which John Douglas Eames judges it "A ludicrously overdrawn piece of claptrap."

The most amazing fact regarding the release of *My Son John* is that it earned Leo McCarey an Academy Award nomination in the writing (motion picture story) category. While the film lost this award to *The Greatest Show on Earth*, it is astounding that any such honor was even considered for such blatant propaganda. The nomination must be attributed to the anti-Communist feeling sweeping the country at the time, and the belief that such a film was aiding the cause of freedom. Today, the idea that *My Son John* could be taken seriously at all is incredible. Looking back, the film is an invaluable time capsule, however embarrassing it may be.

No Man's Land

Credits: 1964. Cinema-Video International. *Directed, Produced and Written by* Russ Harvey. *Music by* Jaime Mendoza-Nava. *Director of Photography*: James C. Houston. *Film Ed-*

itor: Charles L. Kimball. *Art Direction*: Don Russell. *Makeup*: Nan Ruckman. *Military Advisor and Coordinator*: Tom E. Lytle. Not Rated. Black and White. Flat (1.33:1). 72 minutes. Released in 1964. Filmed near San Antonio, Texas. Not currently available on commercial home video.

Cast: *Corporal Jerry Little*, Russ Harvey; *Anna Wong*, Kim Lee; *Old Sarge*, Lee Morgan; *with* Val Martinez, Tom Lytle, Henry Garcia, Eddie Retacy, Tom Drossis, Lyman Harrison, Don Russell and Percy Barbat.

Historical Accuracy Level: Low. This fictional story seems to have little to do with the actual fighting in Korea.

Patriotic Propaganda Level: Medium. An American soldier matures in Korea, falls in love with a Korean woman and marries her.

Elements: Army, Dogs, Females in the Field, Romance.

Another independent film in the manner of *Iron Angel* and *Sniper's Ridge*, Russ Harvey's production of *No Man's Land* is a low-budget take on the Korean War, filmed in the American southwest, and barely distributed to theaters. The most obscure version of a popular cinematic title—including Charlie Sheen's 1987 action flick and an Oscar-winning 2001 Best Foreign Film from Bosnia—no copy of this version could be found for review.

During the Korean War, Corporal Jerry Little (Russ Harvey, who also penned, produced and directed the film) triggers a major battle by nervously tossing a grenade at noises while on patrol in "no man's land." After the battle between U.S. and North Korean forces, he meets a Korean woman, Anna Wong (Kim Lee), who is walking her dog. They become friends and romance inevitably blossoms. Little is assigned to another patrol, during which an enemy sniper wounds Old Sarge (Lee Morgan). Most of the patrol delivers Old Sarge back for medical treatment, but Little remains in no man's land, finds the sniper and kills him. Little returns with a new understanding of war and a fresh appreciation of life, and arranges to marry Anna Wong.

The film's focus on a soldier who seeks redemption after inadvertently causing the deaths of some of his colleagues is reminiscent of the plot of *A Yank in Korea*. Many entries in the Korean War film oeuvre feature soldiers who mature after making mistakes in battle and viewing firsthand the consequences of their actions. There is little that sounds interesting or original about this project, which was filmed near San Antonio, Texas by star Russ Harvey, who also produced other low-budget action films in this manner, such as *Dungeons of Harrow* (1962). Several cast members also filled roles behind the camera, a common effort on small, independently-produced movies.

Not with My Wife, You Don't!

Credits: 1966. Fernwood-Reynard Productions. *Distributed by* Warner Bros. *Produced and Directed by* Norman Panama. *Associate Producer*: Joel Freeman. *Screenplay by* Norman Panama, Larry Gelbart and Peter Barnes. *Story by* Norman Panama and Melvin Frank. *Music Composed and Conducted by* Johnny (John) Williams. *Director of Photography*: Charles Lang, A.S.C. *Film Editor*: Aaron Stell, A.C.E. *Production Design*: Edward Carrere. *Assistant Director*: Jack Aldworth. *European Photography*: Paul Beeson, B.S.C. *Sound by* Stanley Jones. *Makeup Supervisor*: Gordon Bau, S.M.A. *Supervising Hair Stylist*: Jean Burt Reilly, C.H.S. *Set Decorator*: George James Hopkins. *Choreographer*: Shelah Hackett. *Aviation Liaison*: Hamish Mahaddie. *Miss Lisi's Wardrobe Designed by* Edith Head. *Visual Consultation and Title by* Saul Bass and Associates. *Original Songs* "Not With My Wife, You Don't!," "A Big Beautiful Ball" and "My Inamorata" *by* Johnny (John) Williams and Johnny Mercer. *Second Assistant Director*: Michael Daves. *Scoring Mixer*: Dan Wallin. *Orchestrations by* Jimmy Bryant. Not Rated. Technicolor. Flat (1.33:1). 118 minutes. Released in November, 1966. Currently available on VHS home video.

Cast: *Colonel Tom Ferris*, Tony Curtis; *Julie Ferris*, Virna Lisi; *Colonel "Tank" Martin*, George C. Scott; *General Maynard C. Parker*, Carroll O'Connor; *General Walters*, Richard Eastham; *Sergeant Gilroy*, Eddie Ryder; *Sergeant Dogerty*, George Tyne; *Doris Parker*, Ann Doran; *Nurse Sally Ann*, Donna Danton; *Lillian Walters*, Natalie Core; *Air Police Colonel*, Buck Young; *BBC Commentator*, Maurice Dillmore; *Time Reporter (Chandler McVeigh)*, Robert Cleaves; *Italian Maid*, Karla Most; *Miss Ephron*, Betty Bresler; *Bartender*, Alfred Shelley; *Himself*, Bob Hope.

Level of Historical Accuracy: Low. While the Korean War dogfights seem real enough, on the ground the fighter pilots carry on as if they were in the swinging sixties.

Patriotic Propaganda Level: Low. This comedy lampoons Air Force pilots and brass, and is not in the least concerned with promoting patriotism.

Elements: Air Force, Air War, Comedy, Infighting, Lonely Wives, Nurses, Romance, Romantic Triangle.

Four years before *MASH*, this comedy explored what a hoot the Korean War really was. At least, that was the concept. Actually, *Not with My Wife, You Don't!* is a cute romantic comedy about two boorish, womanizing fighter pilots who battle over a sleek Italian nurse in Korea. As comedies go, it's a lightweight (though overlong) adventure. As 1960s-era Tony Curtis comedies go, it's above average, particularly owing to the unheralded comedic talents of George C. Scott. There's not much to this movie, but it is enjoyable to watch, especially for fans of Curtis, Scott or gorgeous Virna Lisi.

The movie is introduced by an animated creature: the green-eyed monster of jealousy. Bernie (that's its name) talks a bit about jealousy and then disappears after setting the story in London, where Colonel Tom Ferris (Tony Curtis) is organizing the British welcoming party for General Maynard C. Parker (Carroll O'Connor). Ferris is extraordinarily efficient due to his little black book, which is filled with private personal information about the people whom he encounters. Ferris is assigned as General Parker's attache. Ferris is married to beautiful Julie (Virna Lisi), a hot-blooded Italian blonde who collects things in pairs. The Ferrises argue about his devotion to duty (as opposed to his lesser devotion to Julie) and her desire to bear children. Ferris' friendly rival Colonel "Tank" Martin (George C. Scott) arrives unexpectedly, causing Ferris to believe that Tank will make a play for Julie. In the midst of a conference, Ferris thinks back to his flying days with Tank in Korea …

Air Force pilots Tom Ferris (Tony Curtis, left) and "Tank" Martin (George C. Scott, right), battle for the affections of Julie (Virna Lisi) in the Warner Bros. comedy Not with My Wife, You Don't! *(1966). The poster's right panel hints at the film's smarmy, innuendo-laden tone.*

In flashback, an aerial dogfight takes place over Korea, and Ferris' Sabre jet is being chased by a Chinese MiG fighter jet. Tank comes to his rescue and destroys the MiG. Later, at the officers' club, each of them tries to attract a young nurse, but their rivalry leads to a brawl and Ferris is sent to the hospital with a concussion. He awakens to find that Julie is his nurse, and falls in love immediately. Ferris manages to prevent Tank from meeting Julie for a while, but eventually Tank also meets and falls for her. Tank arranges for Ferris to rehabilitate himself in Japan for six months and almost coerces Julie into his bed. Ferris returns to Korea and is surprised to find that Julie loves both of them, and cannot make a choice between them.

Ferris and Tank fly together and again encounter MiG fighters. This time, Tank is shot down and ditches his jet in the Yellow Sea. Ferris is sincerely concerned for his friend, but when news arrives that Tank has been rescued, Ferris burns the message and convinces Julie that Tank has died. They marry. In a hospital bed, Tank reads about the wedding and sends a telegram of congratulations. Julie is overjoyed to learn that Tank is still alive, but she is now Mrs. Tom Ferris.

Back in the present, fourteen years later, Ferris is certain that Tank wants revenge. Ferris is sent on a trip to Copenhagen and Tank springs into action, arranging for Ferris to be sent to Labrador in northeastern Canada for arctic survival tests for two weeks, and aggressively begins to court Julie. While Ferris learns how to cut snow blocks, Tank and Julie are frolicking on a French beach. Julie enjoys the attention (which she has not been receiving from her husband), but refrains from sleeping with Tank after viewing an Italian movie, "Arrivederci Mondo," in which the adulterous characters are transformed into herself, Ferris and Tank — and all of them die.

Ferris discovers that Tank arranged his transfer to Labrador and goes into a rage. He escapes the arctic cold on foot (!), steals a private jet and flies nonstop to Rome. Tank thinks about Julie while flying in close formation and almost crashes, causing him to rethink his amorous goals, and he finds himself frightened when Julie begins talking about babies. Tank tells her that Ferris burned the telegram during the war, but she realizes Ferris did it so that she would marry him. Julie concludes that she doesn't want Tank, but is trapped in his room when General Parker arrives in the adjoining suite. Ferris finds Julie in Tank's hotel suite and brawls with Tank, all the time trying to remain quiet so as not to disturb General Parker. Finally, both officers confess the situation to the general, and the scene freezes. In a sequence similar to the opening, Ferris organizes an awards ceremony to be presided over by General Parker. This time, Tank receives general's stars and Julie watches from the side with two baby boys in her arms, wrapped in blue blankets.

Not with My Wife, You Don't! is a loopy comedy from Norman Panama, who injects his movie with visual gags to keep things interesting. Some of them work, such as the eerie sonic waves which accompany certain long distance telephone calls, and Ferris' low-level jet flight across the Atlantic, which is projected at a faster speed than normal. Others do not, such as Bernie the green-eyed monster of jealousy, the creature that introduces the movie and then abruptly disappears. Writer, producer and director Panama also planned to insert visual messages like "WOW!" and "ZONK!" into his movie at specific times, à la the television show *Batman*, but this plan was, thankfully, rejected. What remains is a movie with some visual style, but which is probably more conventional than originally intended.

The comedy is mostly lighthearted and fun, even while dealing with such subjects as extramarital affairs and death. Because the audience knows what various characters do not, however, these situations are amusing and occasionally even funny. The one aspect which works throughout is the chemistry between the leads. Tony Curtis is (and was) an old hand at this type of comedy, but George C. Scott's comedic appearances are less common. Scott, however, can mug just as broadly as Curtis and seems to really enjoy his role, which makes the movie quite enjoyable. As Julie, Virna Lisi really plays "straight man" to the hijinks of the others, but she is amusing as well, and certainly gorgeous enough to inspire the rivalry between her suitors. Their chemistry together fuels the film, giving it enough gas to push past its silly story conventions.

Lieutenant Tank Martin (George C. Scott) is one of two Air Force fighter pilots who battle over a beautiful French nurse in the comedy Not with My Wife, You Don't! *(1966).*

There are three comedy highlights. One is the extended jet flight across the Atlantic, which involves some great photography and special effects, along with the inspired whining of Sergeant Gilroy (Eddie Ryder). The second is Ferris' arctic adventure, where he is paired with Sergeant Dogerty (George Tyne) and a pack of sled dogs. While the entire sequence is rather silly, it has some funny moments. The third, and best, sequence, is the fight between Ferris and Tank in the hotel suite in Rome. The fight is funny because they are trying to fight silently, so as not to bother General Parker next door, who keeps banging on the wall for quiet. This sequence is full of great physical gags and is, if anything, too brief.

An inventive sequence involves parodying the earnestness of foreign films. Julie goes to see "Arrivederci Mondo" and sees herself and her suitors in the characters that appear onscreen. She is presented with the most extreme result,

in which the husband kills the illicit lovers and then shoots himself, and is shocked into reconsidering her feelings for Tank. The Italian film, shot in black and white, parodies liberal European ethics of love and sex, and has fun with the English subtitles. It's a cute sequence which is made more for effect than for humor.

The Korean War flashback is long and important to the film because it establishes the friendship and rivalry between Ferris and Tank and explains how they met and battled for Julie's affections. Both men are appropriately cocky as Air Force fighter jocks, and the two dogfight sequences shown, though brief, are nicely filmed. Julie is not a convincing nurse, but she looks great. There is one reference to Bedcheck Charlie, who buzzes a bar where Tank and Julie are having a drink. And one serious moment takes place as Ferris is waiting for word concerning Tank, who has crashed into the sea. Ferris is genuinely worried about his friend and joyful when word of Tank's rescue is sent. It should also be noted, however, that a map shows that Tank was shot down east of the Korean peninsula, near Japan. MiG Alley was on the west side of North Korea, and MiGs never flew in the area where Tank supposedly crashed.

The main storyline is interesting, explaining how two friendly rivals battle over the affections of a beautiful woman, but seems a bit thin to carry a two-hour comedy. The movie gently pokes fun at a wide variety of conventions, but never really establishes a central point of view. The performances are fun and the scenery, particularly involving Virna Lisi, is striking. Despite its unwieldy title, *Not with My Wife, You Don't!* was moderately successful and surprisingly earned a Golden Globe nomination as best musical / comedy. Critics generally panned the effort, but *Time*'s reviewer enjoyed the comedy as a guilty pleasure: "And some congratulations are due Director Norman Panama, who keeps this airy nothing whooshing along so briskly that audiences may fail to notice how much of the ho ho is really just ho hum."

Not with My Wife, You Don't! is one of Tony Curtis' better efforts of the 1960s and reveals George C. Scott's fine comedic as well as dramatic talents. Despite its laborious title, it is a witty and sometimes funny comedy which does not say anything profound about love, sex, the military establishment or the Korean War, but it is a pleasant way to spend two hours.

The Nun and the Sergeant

Credits: 1962. Springfield Productions and / or Eastern Film Productions. *Distributed by* United Artists. *Directed by* Franklin Adreon. *Produced by* Eugene Frenke for Springfield Productions, Inc. *Associate Producer*: Harold N. Even. *Screenplay by* Don Cerveris. *Music Composed and Conducted by* Jerry Fielding. *Director of Photography*: Paul Ivano, A.S.C. *Film Editors*: John Hoffman and Carl Mahakian. *Art Director*: Robert Kinoshita. *Production Manager*: Bartlett A. Carre. *Assistant Director*: Robert Agnew. *Costumes by* Marjorie Corso. *Make-up*

Artist: Carlie Taylor, S.M.A. *Property Master*: Ted Mossman. *Special Effects*: Norm Breedlove. *Sound*: Woody Clark. *Production Assistant*: Jack Cash. Not Rated. Black and White. Flat (1.33:1). 73 minutes. Released in January, 1962. Not currently available on commercial home video.

Cast: *Sergeant McGrath*, Robert Webber; *Nun*, Anna Sten; *Dockman*, Leo Gordon; *Pak*, Dale Ishimoto; *Hall*, Hari Rhodes; *Bok Soon*, Linda Wong; *Orville Nupert*, Robert Easton; *Soon Cha*, Linda Ho; *Nevins*, Tod Windsor; *Turnbridge*, Roger Torrey; *Rivas*, Valentin De Vargas; *Johnson*, Gregori F. Kris; *Quill*, Kenny Miller; *Myung Hee*, Caroline Kido; *Mossback*, Norman Du Pont; *Pollard*, King Moody; *Kil Cha*, Yashi; *Ok-Cha*, Anna Shin; *with* Steve Drexel.

Historical Accuracy Level: Low. Using prisoners in suicide missions only happens in the movies.

Patriotic Propaganda Level: Medium. These Marines may be criminals, rapists and killers, but when lives are on the line, they are Marines!

Elements: Behind Enemy Lines, Clergy, Effects on Civilians, Females in the Field, Helicopters, Infighting, Marine Corps, Prisoners of War.

The Nun and the Sergeant is of interest for three reasons. The first is its familiar cast, which includes Robert Webber, Leo Gordon, Hari Rhodes, Robert Easton, Valentin De Vargas and Anna Sten. These recognizable performers help lessen the absurdity of the action. The second reason is that its suicide mission plot predates the similar *Dirty Dozen* by five years, and the similarities between the two adventures is striking. The third reason is that this movie is, by far, the most exploitive Korean War movie in the genre. While other films such as *Operation Dames* and *Iron Angel* position women on the Korean battleground, their hints of sexuality are tempered by sly self-consciousness. This is not the case in *The Nun and the Sergeant*, which constantly puts a group of young Korean girls in physical — and sexual — peril, and tastelessly revels in that prospect.

The Nun and the Sergeant begins in a Marine camp in 1951 Korea. Sergeant McGrath (Robert Webber) is given a new, dangerous assignment. Because he is upset with his own

Good (the nun, Anna Sten) and evil (the soldier, Robert Webber) battle for the souls of the innocent but sexy young school girls in the "incendiary" United Artists drama The Nun and the Sergeant *(1962). The ad emphasizes brute sexuality with both words and images, but does not mention the Korean War locale whatsoever.*

inability to keep his men alive, McGrath decides to take a desperate measure. He visits the Marine prison stockade and, with the warden's help, selects twelve prisoners to accompany him on the new mission. McGrath's Korean aide, Pak (Dale Ishimoto), argues against conscripting the prisoners, but McGrath wants to put men "who don't deserve to live" in danger rather than good American soldiers. McGrath, Pak and the twelve men board a helicopter and begin their mission before the officers at headquarters can stop them.

The helicopter lands in a clearing and the departing Marines are immediately attacked by North Korean soldiers. Two of the men, trying to run for freedom, are shot and killed. The other ten, plus McGrath and Pak, fight back and destroy the enemy patrol. During the attack, an enemy plane bombs a school bus driving through the forest, forcing it off the road. A nun (Anna Sten) and eight teenage, uniformed Korean schoolgirls abandon the bus, running for cover. One of the girls is hit by shrapnel and dies. The Marines catch seven of the girls, but one escapes, though she is never seen or heard from again. The nun wants to take the girls to safety by herself, but McGrath refuses to listen and orders the girls to accompany the men on their mission.

Most of the men don't want to have anything to do with the mission; they would rather rot in the brig than face death in the forest. The meanest prisoner, Dockman (Leo Gordon), slowly recruits the other men into his plan to eliminate McGrath at the earliest opportunity and then take to the hills. Dockman is largely successful, but fails to persuade the group's black medic Doc Hall (Hari Rhodes), or southerner Orville Nupert (Robert Easton), who carries a snake named Pawnee with him, to join the revolt. At night, the nun and her girls camp near, but apart, from the men. The nun is shown to have an injury to her leg, and asks Doc Hall for some bandages for it.

In the morning, the nun takes the girls to a riverbank, where they bathe and swim in their slips. The nun gleefully watches as her charges cavort in the water. Their fun is cut short by McGrath, who berates the nun for letting them make so much noise in enemy territory. The group marches through the forest. Doc Hall sings a goofy song about animals and Nupert unknowingly drops his snake, which Dockman kills. The group reaches a rope bridge above a treacherous gorge. The biggest Marine, Turnbridge (Roger Torrey), is sent across to test the bridge and makes it safely. The rest cross in pairs, one man and one girl, bonding as they face danger together. McGrath and the nun are the last to cross, and do so just before an enemy plane attacks them; no one is hurt.

Dockman prepares to kill McGrath when a Marine named Johnson (Gregori F. Kris) falls into a snake pit, but the Marines rescue Johnson and prevent Dockman from killing McGrath. One girl is missing: it is Soon-Cha (Linda Ho), the girl who was most saddened by the death of the girl — her sister — at the bus. McGrath and the nun begin to search for her and the remainder of the group stops for rest at the ruins of a house. The men tie Pak to a tree so they can roam freely. The schoolgirls find a cache of liquor, causing the men to refuse to "bug out" with Dockman, preferring to stay with the wine and the young women. Everyone gets drunk except for Bok Soon (Linda Wong), the eldest of the girls. Dockman tries to make her more friendly by pouring wine into her, but she repels his advances. He is about to rape her when the other men interrupt. They restrain Dockman and give Bok Soon his belt so that she may beat him.

Meanwhile, Soon Cha has been found at the riverbank. She has fallen into the water, and the nun jumps in to rescue her, but is too weak to do so. McGrath rescues the girl as the nun swims to shore. The trio finds the others just as Bok Soon begins to whip Dockman with his own belt. The nun grabs a rifle and shoots past Dockman, stopping the violence. She then collapses, revealing her poisoned leg. She is placed on a stretcher and the group marches toward the tunnel the Marines have been assigned to destroy. McGrath reassures the nun that nothing further will happen to the girls, at least not from his men. "They may be brig rats, but underneath it all, they're still Marines."

The motley group camps on a hill above the tunnel entrance. McGrath teaches the men his plan and has them recite it back to him. The girls want to take the nun, now very sick, to a hospital, but McGrath refuses to move her until nightfall, when the Marine attack will commence. Bok Soon argues with McGrath unsuccessfully, then runs down the hill toward the tunnel. Dockman follows, trying to stop her, and both are shot and killed by North Korean guards. With the advantage of surprise gone, McGrath orders his men down the hill. The remaining girls pick up the stretcher bearing the nun and head in the opposite direction toward a nearby town. The Marines charge down the hill, yelling and shooting. The tunnel explodes. The movie ends.

The Nun and the Sergeant contains some very interesting ingredients, most of which were put to far better use in *The Dirty Dozen*, but the result is an upalatable mess. The idea of pushing twelve men into combat against their wishes is one full of dramatic potential, but one which is not very realistic. In *The Dirty Dozen*, the prisoners are given a choice of joining the mission, with the possibility of a commuted sentence (or, of course, death) or fulfilling their sentenced punishment. Here, the prisoners are simply chosen by McGrath and the stockade warden and

The Nun and the Sergeant *(1962) predates* The Dirty Dozen *by five years, yet shares the same basic formula. Sergeant McGrath (Robert Webber, facing, center) and the warden of the brig choose the twelve prisoners best suited for a Marine mission which McGrath considers suicide.*

forced to go. A few of the prisoners' histories are summarized by the warden, but their past indiscretions remain largely secret. The result is that the men are not individually recognizable as characters. McGrath's conscription of the men is obviously unfair, but his action is at least given a modicum of motivation, and the unfairness does lead to some sympathy for the men.

If Don Cerveris' screenplay had simply followed this ill-advised mission, and had provided the prisoner-soldiers with authentic characteristics and dialogue, the film might have been more effective. However, this was never meant to be a serious wartime drama. The inclusion of the nun and the Korean schoolgirls irrefutably labels this film as exploitation material. The initial clue to what lies ahead occurs during the opening credits, which are accompanied by drawings of the upcoming action. Included are drawings of two young, topless girls. The film then contains a sequence of the young girls bathing in the

river, watched over by the leering nun. Aside from the sight of a nun gleefully ogling the girls, which suggests exploitation at its worst, this sequence also seems to be edited, perhaps from a longer, more explicit European release. Although the girls bathe in the river, they are not naked, nor are they accompanied by any men. However, stills exist which show North Korean soldiers in the water with the girls, but soldiers are not viewed in the American version of the film. This suggests that part of the sequence was censored for American audiences, and that the excised material is risqué in nature.

The young girls are incorporated into the plot in order to entice the men (and titillate the audience) with sexual innuendo. The girls do provoke the men into advances, particularly Dockman, to whom advance means rape. But in the spirit of these Korean War sex movies, the men remain — incredibly — gentlemen, stopping Dockman before he rapes Bok Soon and offering her a chance for retribution. Though the girls are constantly in moral peril, it is an overstated peril. These Marines, no matter how outwardly unkempt, cowardly or brazen, would never abuse the good will of these young girls.

The military mission in *The Dirty Dozen* is crucial to its story; here, it is a mere afterthought. McGrath does not tell his men what they are doing in the Korean forest until they camp near their target, a tunnel. Then he leads them in a recitation of the plan, a scene which was repeated (and improved upon) in *The Dirty Dozen*. It makes little sense to send a patrol to destroy the tunnel when, as noted by Paul M. Edwards in his *Guide to Films on the Korean War*, bombing from the air would accomplish the same thing, and more quickly. But the mission must go on, and so it does. Amazingly and unfortunately, the mission itself is not shown. The men rush down the hill and shots are heard. This is followed by an insert shot of a tunnel exploding. That's it; the movie is over. Who lives? Who dies? Who cares? Until the final scene, the film is exploitive and dumb; at this point it becomes totally inept.

The Nun and the Sergeant, an independent project from Eastern Film Productions and/or Springfield Productions (one company is listed on publicity material and another on the film itself), was barely distributed by United Artists in early 1962. Despite its familiar cast members and sexual innuendo, the film was ignored by audiences and relegated to obscurity. It is, thankfully, one of a kind in terms of Korean War films, and unless a longer, more explicit version surfaces, should remain in obscurity for a long time to come.

One Minute to Zero

Credits: 1952. RKO Radio. *Directed by* Tay Garnett. *Produced by* Edmund Grainger. *Executive Producer*: Howard Hughes. *Written by* Milton Krims and William Wister Haines. *Music by* Victor Young. *Director of Photography*: William E. Snyder, A.S.C. *Film Editor*: Robert Belcher. *Production Supervisor*: Cliff P. Broughton. *Art Directors*: Albert S. D'Agostino and Jack Okey. *Set Decorations*: Darrell Silvera

and John Sturtevant. *Technical Advisers*: Lieutenant Colonel S. Paul Latiolais, USAF and Captain Edward R. Harrison, USA. *Production Coordinator*: Clarence A. Shoop. *Special Photographic Effects by* Linwood Dunn, A.S.C. *Musical Director*: C. (Mischa) Bakaleinikoff. *Editorial Supervision by* Sherman Todd, A.C.E. *Sound by* Frank McWhorter and Clem Portman. *Wardrobe by* Michael Woulfe. *Makeup Artist*: Mel Burns. *Hair Stylist*: Larry Germain. *Song* "When I Fall in Love" *by* Victor Young. *Song* "Tell Me Golden Moon (China Night)" *by* Norman Bennett and Nobuyuki Takeoda. Not Rated. Black and White. Flat (1.33:1). 105 minutes. Released in August, 1952. Currently available on VHS home video.

Cast: *Colonel Steve Janowski*, Robert Mitchum; *Linda Day*, Ann Blyth; *Colonel John Parker*, William Talman; *Sergeant Baker*, Charles McGraw; *Mary Parker*, Margaret Sheridan; *Captain Ralston*, Richard Egan; *Doctor Gustav Engstrand*, Edward (Eduard) Franz; *Major Davis*, Robert Osterloh; *Major Carter*, Robert Gist; *General Thomas*, Roy Roberts; *Private Means*, Wally Cassell; *Lieutenant Stevens*, Eddie Firestone; *Lieutenant Cronin*, Peter Thompson; *Lieutenant Martin*, Steve Flagg; *Private Noble*, Ted Ryan; *Private Weiss*, Larry Stewart; *Private Chico Mendoza*, Lalo Rios; *Private Jones*, Hal Baylor; *Private Clark*, Tom Carr; *Sergeant Cook*, Tom Irish; *Private Lane (Chef)*, Alvin Greenman; *M. F. Villon*, Maurice Marsac; *Nurses*, Dorothy Granger and Karen Hale; *Mrs. Stuart*, Kay Christopher; *Pilot Norton*, Wallace Russell; *Officer*, Stuart Whitman; *Interpreter*, Owen Song; *French U.N. Woman*, Monya Andre; *Soldiers*, John Mallory (Mitchum), Buddy Swan, William Forest, Tyler McVey, Robert Bray, Ray Montgomery and Al Murphy.

Historical Accuracy Level: Medium. In general terms, the movie follows the first few months of the war, but specific incidents and all characters are completely fictional.

Patriotic Propaganda Level: Medium. These soldiers are in the fight to stay, even if it does result in the massacre of a few hundred civilians.

Elements: Air Force, Air War, Army, Behind Enemy Lines, Day of the Invasion, Effects on Civilians, Females in the Field, Japan, Lonely Wives, Musical Performance, Romance, United Nations Forces.

One of the first Hollywood studio films to portray the conflict in Korea is the RKO production *One Minute to Zero*. Though maverick filmmaker Samuel Fuller had made his pair of Korean War films, the big studios were slow to follow, and it was two years into the war before traditional combat films about the "police action" began to appear. This one, for which RKO and new owner Howard Hughes spent a costly $2,181,000 to produce, covers a lot of territory concerning the war but is only sporadically effective. Today, the film is notorious due to its inclusion of a refugee massacre scene (which the Department of Defense objected to and wanted removed) in which an Army officer reluctantly orders his artillery to bomb a column of refugees which has been infiltrated by North Korean soldiers.

One Minute to Zero opens before the start of hostilities in Korea. While children play, U.S. Army officers Colonel Steve Janowski (Robert Mitchum) and Sergeant Baker (Charles McGraw) advise South Korean troops as to the proper way to disable a tank with a bazooka. A United Nations health commissioner named Linda Day (Ann Blyth) wants permission to go into North Korea to inoculate and vaccinate children there, but she is warned not to do so by Janowski. The next day, the North Koreans invade, waking Janowski and Air Force pilot Colonel John Parker (William Talman) from their sleep in Seoul. The war has begun.

Janowski forcibly removes Linda from harm's way and sends her to safety in Japan. Parker is given command of the Air Force. Time passes, with the U.N. forces in Korea undergoing a pattern of holding, then retreating. Janowski finds a disorganized company and helps Captain Ralston (Richard Egan) coordinate it and make it function correctly. Under Janowski's guidance, the army regulars disable a Russian tank and delay the Communist advance while American jets destroy the tank column and Australian Air Force planes slaughter approaching North Korean soldiers. However, camouflaged enemy soldiers infiltrate the area and attack, wounding Janowski with a grenade. Colonel Parker, who has landed in an L-5 observation plane to evaluate the situation for himself, flies Janowski to a hospital in Japan.

As he recovers, Janowski takes advantage of his non-combat status to romance Linda Day, whose husband was killed during the final year of World War II. She cooks him dinner and they sing a song, "Tell Me Golden Moon," to each other — he in Japanese, she in English. After a few dates, Janowski asks Linda to marry him, but she refuses. The laconic colonel returns to the war, leaving Linda behind with the wives of the pilots at Itazuke Air Force base, who wait for their men to return home to them. She follows him to Korea soon afterward, as the U.N. resumes its inoculation and vaccination program. However, the U.N. crew soon cannot find any refugees to inoculate.

Refugees are being held in one column, as wide as the road and several miles long, by Colonel Janowski. His men inspect the refugees and let them trickle through a few at a time, searching for (and finding) hidden weapons and Communist infiltrators. Estimating that fully half of the refugees are actually enemy soldiers in disguise, Janowski reluctantly decides to take action. From a circling plane, a translator on loudspeaker exhorts the refugees to go back a short distance, to where food and medicine will be provided. If they keep moving forward, they will be shot. Infiltrators with guns keep the mass moving forward, and Janowski instructs artillery to shoot three warning shots over their heads. The refugees press forward and more warning shots are made, landing closer. A final plea is made, with more warning shots. After a long, thoughtful pause, Janowski orders the artillery to fire into the column of people. Dozens of people, both soldier and civilian, are killed before the refugees and enemy soldiers turn and run for their lives. Linda Day arrives on the scene just as the slaughter begins, and she is horrified to find that Janowski has ordered it.

Afterward, the lead U.N. phyisician, Gustav Engstrand (Eduard Franz), asks Linda to sign a statement that the massacre was necessary, but she cannot. The doctor likens the massacre to amputation of a gangrenous body part. Linda continues to believe that the massacre was inhumane until John Parker shows her a group of dead American soldiers, shot and killed with their hands bound behind their backs. He explains that U.N. soldiers are facing this kind of brutality from the Communists constantly. "You just don't believe it until you see it," she says

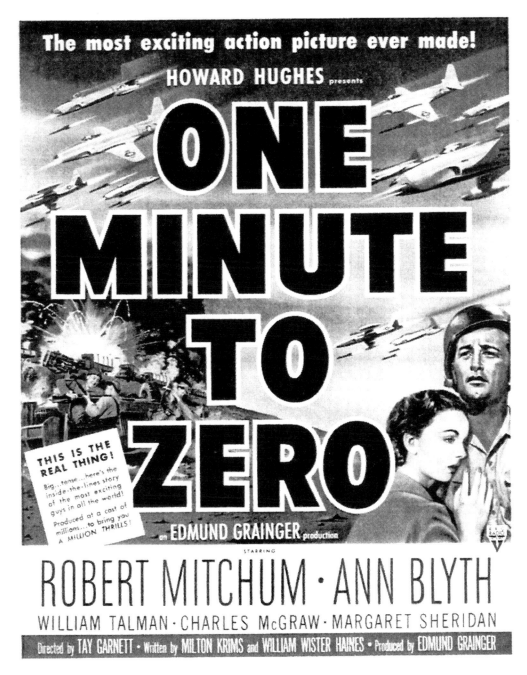

The most exciting action picture ever made!

HOWARD HUGHES presents

ONE MINUTE TO ZERO

THIS IS THE REAL THING!

Big...tense...here's the inside-the-lines story of the most exciting guys in all the world! Produced at a cost of millions...to bring you A MILLION THRILLS!

an EDMUND GRAINGER production

STARRING

ROBERT MITCHUM · ANN BLYTH

WILLIAM TALMAN · CHARLES McGRAW · MARGARET SHERIDAN

Directed by TAY GARNETT · Written by MILTON KRIMS and WILLIAM WISTER HAINES · Produced by EDMUND GRAINGER

RKO's action drama One Minute to Zero *(1952) promises "a million thrills!" because it is "the most exciting action picture ever made!" Obviously, producer Howard Hughes was not afraid to exaggerate. There is more action in the poster, however, than there is in the movie.*

ashamedly and then prays to keep Janowski safe so that he may return to her.

The North Koreans have begun moving their vital supplies at night, safe from air strikes. Colonel Parker attempts an air strike anyway, with flares, but stops it after his first pilot flies into a hill. Janowski devises a plan to block the supply route until daylight, when the convoy can be safely bombed. He leads a platoon of men eleven miles behind enemy lines, blocks the road with fallen trees and overturns the first trucks that arrive at the barricade. Dawn arrives and the battle begins as the Communists attempt to get under cover. Janowski and his men battle all day, holding the convoy together until jets blow it to pieces. They are asked to hold through the night, but are running out of ammunition and personnel. Parker risks a nighttime supply drop, which is successful, but his plane is shot down. He parachutes, but it catches on fire and he dies in a fiery fall to earth.

Morning dawns and General Thomas (Roy Roberts) arrives with reinforcements. Only a few men, including Janowski and Baker are left, but they have stopped the Communist advance. Thomas tells them that the Inchon landing, staged at the same time as Janowski's barricade, was also successful, and that the tide of the war has finally turned. He appoints Janowski to the rank of general. On the way to headquarters in a jeep, Janowski stops when he spots Linda Day. They embrace and she agrees to marry him. Then he continues to his next combat assignment as she asks God to protect the fighting men, guide them to victory and return them safely.

One Minute to Zero is a wildly uneven movie which combines some strong action scenes with a predictable and pat romance. Its perspective on the wives of American fliers waiting in Japan for their husbands to return from their days at war is succinct and accurate, yet the bombing of the refugee column is treated as just another operation. Men on the Korean battlefield are eliminated by the enemy in alarming numbers and with some suspense as to who is next, yet the death of John Parker is telegraphed long before his final mission begins.

The romantic story is rushed and ineffective. Once again, two people who dislike each other upon first meeting find that they are made for each other. In this scenario, Janowski asks Linda to marry him after just a few dinner dates while he is recuperating in Japan. She rightly turns him down, but later changes her mind, even after witnessing the massacre of the refugees. The primary problem seems to be the character of Linda Day. As a health commissioner of the United Nations, Linda possesses a naive, holier-than-thou attitude. Later this softens, but at the beginning of the story, she is quite

irritating. Linda is played by Ann Blyth, a last-minute replacement for Claudette Colbert, who originally signed to portray the role but who was forced to quit after developing pneumonia on location in Colorado. Blyth does the best she can with the turgid role, but apart from the surprisingly melodious song at dinner which she shares with Robert Mitchum, she does not add anything substantial to the film.

Mitchum is his usual sleepy-eyed self as Janowski, heroically placing himself in harm's way for the good of the cause while deflecting any commendation for his actions. Charles McGraw scores as tough Sergeant Baker, ready to follow Janowski wherever he goes, and Richard Egan and William Talman do well in their roles. The various relationships among the men, dictated by rank of course, seem much more believable and realistic than the phony romance between Janowski and Linda Day.

The film briefly addresses the issue of wives of American fliers waiting anxiously for their husbands to return. With just two scenes set at the return gate of Itazuke Air Force Base in Japan, the film conveys the fear and hope of the waiting women far more concisely than the later, overwrought *Sabre Jet*. And when Linda Day is added to the queue of lonely women at the gate, watching as Janowski returns to the war, her personal situation makes their collective emotional dilemma more involving.

Two separate, memorable aspects within the framework of the film point to its own contradictory nature. The first is the inclusion of brief, graphic footage of actual casualties from Korea. At a few key points during the film, real-life footage of charred corpses and dead soldiers with their hands wired behind their backs is glimpsed in order to shock audiences into siding against the perpetrators of such atrocities. The majority of Korean War films employ actual combat footage, but only *One Minute to Zero* inserts such graphic scenes of death within its story. The effect is jarring and sickening. Instead of creating empathy for the U.N. soldiers, it creates antagonism toward the filmmakers. Its unrealistic story does not support the use of such a tactic to reinforce its drama.

The second aspect is, of course, the massacre scene. The majority of the sequence is dedicated to warning the refugees to stop advancing

United Nations worker Linda Day (Ann Blyth) professes her love aand concern for Colonel Steve Janowski (Robert Mitchum) in One Minute to Zero *(1952).*

and to depict the preponderance of Communist infiltrators within their ranks, and the massacre itself is quick and relatively bloodless. As opposed to the U.N. soldiers burned and executed by the enemy, the refugee massacre is seen as a necessary part of war. Although the refugee column contained old people, families and children, the bodies littering the road afterward seem to be adults, many recognizable as enemy agents. The film not only understates the slaughter, but indicates that it was effective in eliminating an enemy threat.

Most remarkable is the insistence that the action was the right thing to do. It is beyond any scope of belief that the lead U.N. doctor (Eduard Franz) would support such an action, let alone ask the only other civilian witness to the slaughter (Linda Day) to also support it in writing. Linda refuses, but incredibly changes her mind when John Parker shows her the executed American soldiers. She says, "You just don't believe it until you see it," referring to the enemy atrocities, and changes her mind about Janowski's tactic of attrition, thereby excusing him of any wrongdoing. According to the film's political and moral stance, Janowski (albeit reluctantly) made the necessary and "right" decision when he bombed the infiltrated refugee column with artillery.

It should also be noted that the conclusion of this scene is ineptly staged. The wide line of refugees was miles long when seen from the air, but after thirty seconds or so of artillery barrage at the head of the column, there are no more refugees to be seen (other than the dead ones in the road). Purportedly, the barrage has driven them back, or off the road into the fields on either side, but in less than a minute the thousands of refugees and their belongings have simply vanished!

The U.S. Department of Defense, along with the Army and the Air Force, had cooperated in the production of *One Minute to Zero*, providing men and equipment for its large-scale scenes and allowing the production to be filmed at Camp Carson, Colorado. Upon seeing the finished product, the DOD requested the refugee massacre sequence be excised or reedited. RKO refused and the DOD removed their official cooperation. The film was released as planned by RKO, without governmental approval, but relatively few people noticed. Even with its brief inclusions of atrocities and the massacre scene, box office business was slow. *Time* magazine noted the controversy in its review: "One sequence, in which Mitchum orders the shelling of a civilian refugee column that harbors Communist guerillas, was found objectionable by the Department of Defense. The producers of the picture refused to eliminate the scene, and it remains the only unusual feature in a formula film."

Nearly fifty years later, the massacre scene became somewhat more notorious when allegations surfaced that American soldiers slaughtered Korean civilians beneath a railroad bridge at No Gun Ri early in the war. A 1999 *Associated Press* story about the incident won the Pulitzer Prize for investigative journalism and led to a full investigation of the event by the U.S. government. The finding was that panicky American soldiers had, on their own initiative, killed some two hundred fifty South Korean civilians, on the belief that at least some of them were enemy agents. President Clinton expressed regret for the incident but did not issue a full apology to the relatives of the victims.

After the No Gun Ri story was released, the massacre scene in *One Minute to Zero* began to serve as "proof" that the event was based on fact. Although the American government is investigating rumors of other such incidents that may have occurred in the early weeks of the war, there is absolutely no evidence that any U.S. or U.N. commander ever ordered his troops to fire upon civilians. The problem of infiltrators moving within refugee columns was a real one; many instances are recorded of attacks on U.N. and U.S. troops from both the front and the rear simultaneously after refugees had passed through battle lines. But General William Dean refused to fire upon civilians. "We won't kill civilians to kill the enemy," he said.

The movie takes a more pragmatic approach to the problem, where Janowski elimi-nates *anyone* who might be a threat, no matter how personally disturbing the action may be to him. Because such massacres did not generally happen in Korea, the film takes a dramatic stance which is directly opposed to the reality of the war. The massacre is a shocking moment in the story, but it is also *an untrue moment*. It simply would not have happened, especially so publicly. Linda Day's eventual acceptance of the massacre completely invalidates her character and acts as a rubber stamp of approval for the action, rendering the film utterly specious.

In his book *Hollywood Goes to War*, Edward F. Dolan, Jr. comments that "The film comes across as a flat, cliche-ridden (all sorts of statements about the futility and cruelty of war) melodrama. It is not even saved by its action sequences." Other critics concurred. Arthur Knight of *Saturday Review* complained that it "is a cheap and routine affair produced to cash in on current headlines but contributing nothing to an understanding of them." The British Film Institute's *Monthly Film Bulletin* argued that "This is poor stuff, long, tedious, violent and unrewarding—for military enthusiasts only."

One Minute to Zero is an often engrossing, often superfluous study of men and women directly affected by the Korean War. Because of its depiction of a civilian refugee massacre, it has attained more notoriety recently than it had during its original release, when it was largely ignored. Marketed with claims of being "The most exciting action picture ever made!" and "Produced at a cost of millions … to bring you A MILLION THRILLS!" the film was overhyped by the Howard Hughes regime and the public failed to respond. It remains a formulaic effort to capitalize upon the war, one which contains perhaps too many elements of propaganda and righteous jingoism for its own good.

Operation Dames

(aka *Girls in Action*)

Credits: 1959. Camera Eye Pictures. *Distributed by* American International Pictures. *Directed and Edited by* Louis Clyde Stoumen. *Produced by* Stanley Kallis. *Screenplay by* Ed Lakso. *Original Story by* Stanley Kallis. *Music Composed* *by* Richard Markowitz. *Director of Photography*: Edward R. Martin. *Production Manager*: Bri Murphy. *Script Supervisor*: Dody Weston. *Unit Manager*: Sumner Williams. *Assistant Director*: Arthur Swerdloff. *Sound and Music Editor*: John Mack. *Sound Mixer*: Jim Fullerton. *Assistant Cameraman*: Victor Fisher. *Set Construction*: Robert E. Maxwell. *Key Grip*: Ray Guth. *Boom Man*: Lou Guinn. *Special Effects*: Howard W. Maxwell. *Make-up*: Trudy Kallis. *Culinary Director*: Lucetta Kallis. *Production Secretary*: Jill Murphy. *Art Assistant*: Greta Davis. *Special Crew*: Kip Lawrence, Dick Thies and Bart Patton. *Art Director*: Marvyn Harbert. *Technical Director*: John Soh. *Original Songs* "Girls, Girls, Girls" *and* "Regular Man" *by* Ed Lakso. Not Rated. Black and White. Flat (1.33:1). 74 minutes. Released in March, 1959. Currently available on VHS home video.

Cast: *Lorry Evering*, Eve Meyer; *Sergeant Jeff Valido*, Chuck Henderson; *Tony*, Don Devlin; *Hal Wilson*, Ed Craig; *Roberta*, Cindy Girard; *Billy*, Chuck Van Haren; *Marsha*, Barbara Skyler; *Dinny*, Andrew Mitchell Munro; *Benny Sullivan*, Byron Morrow; *Stella Sullivan*, Alyce Allyn; *George*, Ed Lakso; *Colonel Johns*, Joe Maierhauser; *Stanley*, Rick Beck-Meyer; *Ed*, Kip Lawrence; *Captain Janise*, Alfred Smith; *South Korean Interpreter*, John Soh; *Sniper*, Keisuke Yoneda; *Special Service Lieutenant*, Bill Palmer; *Korean Boy*, Ray Kamuda; *Sentry*, Bart Patton; *Master Sergeant*, Dick Thies; *First G.I.*, Marshall Steiner; *Second G.I.*, Paul Trinka; *North Korean Scout*, Ted Kawata; *Korean Woman*, Greta Davis; *North Korean Officer*, Mas Nagasawa.

Historical Accuracy Level: Low. The film is non-specific regarding its Korean time and locale and its situations are more absurd than realistic.

Patriotic Propaganda Level: Medium. The film celebrates its U.S.O. performers and Army soldiers, but also offers the opinion that war truly is a dangerous business.

Elements: Army, Behind Enemy Lines, Effects on Civilians, Females in the Field, Musical Performance, Romance, U.S.O.

Operation Dames is a low-budget melodrama centering on the plight of a group of U.S.O. entertainers caught behind enemy lines early in the Korean conflict. This is a tidy example of what author Paul M. Edwards calls the

"sex subgenre" of Korean War cinema, wherein nubile (often well-endowed) women find themselves in peril and must depend upon brave (often lecherous) soldiers for safety and comfort. This small group of films manages to combine the hint of sex with the brutality of violence, thus furnishing their masculine protagonists (and the audience) with both facets of entertainment.

The film begins as a small group of U.S.O. entertainers (three men, four women, two accompanying soldiers) leave an American encampment and head toward Pyong-yi in a transport truck, practicing their catchy song "Girls, Girls, Girls." However, North Korean troops have taken the town ahead and have forced American troops to pull out of their positions. The U.S.O. truck is caught in the middle; it is stopped by two North Korean scouts who kill the liaison officer and wound the driver but who are killed by the entertainers. The troupe, led by Benny Sullivan (Byron Morrow), grab the supplies and belongings from the truck, and despite the protestations of cowardly Hal Wilson (Ed Craig), put the wounded man on a stretcher and head south, back toward safety.

They walk for hours, stop by a stream to refresh themselves, then move again, while North Korean troops pick up their trail. They stop at night and build a small fire, which attracts soldiers—Americans. Five Army men and one British soldier, led by gruff Sergeant Jeff Valido (Chuck Henderson), are astonished to find American civilians, among them pretty women, wandering around the South Korean countryside. The soldiers, of course, instantly begin warming up to the U.S.O. women. After retrieving buxom blonde Lorry Evering (Eve Meyer), who was bathing in a nearby stream—and leaving behind the driver who has died—the group continues the long, dangerous walk south.

A box canyon provides a refuge, and the group rests, exhausted. Gunfire in the morning announces the arrival of North Korean troops, who kill Benny's wife Stella (Alyce Allyn) and two of the soldiers. Distraught, Benny grabs a pack of grenades, ostensibly surrenders to the enemy, and blows them (and himself) to smithereens. Valido orders immediate movement. Resting again later, Lorry talks to Valido

There is little subtlety (or class) in this advertising campaign for American International Pictures' drama Operation Dames *(1959), which displays a great deal of star Eve Meyer and hints at the wild hilarity that, of course, was the Korean War. The film was double-billed with* Tank Commandos, *a World War II drama, everywhere it played.*

(who is on watch) and they discuss their pasts and their desire to be the best at what they do, leading to slapping and kissing. On her way back to the others, Lorry is jumped and cut on the face by a North Korean, whom soldier Tony (Don Devlin) chases down and suffocates.

The group stops again at a farmhouse, where a young Korean boy (Ray Kamuda) is the only survivor of the slaughter of his family.

Valido befriends the boy, but eventually leaves him to his fate. After everyone discards their metal objects and jewelry — anything that might clink or shine — Valido leads them through the North Korean front lines at night, crawling and killing as he goes, to the American battle line, where, wounded, he finally delivers the surviving civilians and his own men to safety.

Operation Dames is by design not a particularly serious war movie. Its inclusion of buxom blonde entertainers imperiled by faceless Reds and wooed by lovesick Army grunts precludes any real artistic ambition. Its drama is occasionally overwrought and its humor often silly. Whatever its weaknesses, however, the production company, Camera Eye Pictures, which had won the 1956 best documentary Oscar for *The True Story of the Civil War*, took the time and effort to infuse its fictional Korean War movie with some grit. Despite its low budget and admittedly lowbrow premise, this film presents a hard, realistic view of war not always seen in the genre.

Most impressive is its view that civilians bear the brunt of warfare. This is a perfectly obvious statement, but many war films choose not to deal with civilians at all and only peripherally refer to war's effects on civilians. Some Korean War films seem more designed to display the latest military hardware (fighter jets, helicopters, aircraft carriers, submarines, etc.) than to depict the effects of the horrors of war upon the Korean people and their homeland. *Operation Dames* boasts little ambition, but this is one aspect which it presents honestly and intelligently.

Though the ranks of the Army are hit hard in terms of casualties, the focus of the film is on the civilian loss of life. In the U.S.O. company, Benny and Stella Sullivan are killed (immediately after they warmly reminisce about their working honeymoon) and the other women are in constant danger of injury, rape or death. At the farmhouse, Valido explains the cold reality of the conflict to Roberta (Cindy Girard), when she asks about the murdered family of the Korean boy. "It's called the spoils of war. Some take money, some take food. That one in there [the North Korean soldier they killed while taking the farmhouse] tried to take a farmer's wife. Looks like he did."

It is also unusual to show the soldiers leaving the Korean boy behind. Even cynical Hal Wilson is surprised. "He's just a kid!" But Valido is adamant, and probably right, that the boy would stand a better chance on his own, among his own people, than with the ragtag group of U.S.O. performers and exhausted Army soldiers. Valido gives the boy their last can of rations and wishes him luck, but is not willing to endanger the rest of the group with a young boy with whom they cannot easily communicate and for whom they cannot responsibly care. In most films, the heroic American soldiers would take the boy with them, rescuing him from a life of poverty and ensuring him a new start in America. That is not the case here; the boy remains on his own.

The movie also features a moral, stated by Lorry to Valido: No matter what, life is worth living. When Lorry asks Valido what he'll do after the Army, he replies (on two separate occasions) "Die." After being cut on the face, Lorry realizes that she will no longer be the beautiful leader of the U.S.O. troupe, and she accepts that, realizing that her life must continue anyway. As Valido is being carried away on a stretcher at the denouement, Lorry again reminds him that "second best is good." Though it is perhaps awkwardly stated, her message is that life itself is worth living, even if one isn't the king or queen of one's surroundings.

The women of the story are viewed as worth fighting and dying for, yet constantly hinder the progress and endanger the safety of the entire group. There is surprisingly little sexual interaction; only Lorry and Valido seem to do more than kiss, and that is offscreen. Buxom Eve Meyer, who plays Lorry Evering, had been *Playboy*'s Playmate of the month for June 1955. There are a few glimpses of Eve with a bare back, but no frontal nudity is shown. Eve married director Russ Meyer, displayed her charms in his 1961 opus *Eve and the Handyman*, and served as associate producer on his later nudie films. But other than those few teasing hints of Lorry without clothing, none of the other women are exploited at all, except, possibly, for Roberta during her song "Regular Man," to which she dances in an old-fashioned provocative manner. Despite its title, *Operation Dames* does not deliver the dames that it promises.

The film does feature two songs written by cast member (and scriptwriter) Ed Lakso, "Girls, Girls, Girls," and "Regular Man." The first song is a catchy little ditty, sung over the opening credits, while Cindy Girard sings the second song in a meadow to the soldiers, accompanied by the U.S.O. musicians. The actors do a nice job of conveying the attitudes of entertainers caught in a situation where their skills are not particularly useful.

Lorry Evering (Eve Meyer) is the comely leader of the U.S.O. troupe caught behind enemy lines in Operation Dames *(1959). Meyer had been the June 1955 Playboy Playmate of the month, the first to be specifically photographed for the magazine, and was married to Russ Meyer, so-called "King of the Nudies."*

Other than its focus on civilian suffering, *Operation Dames* is a disappointment. Its male characters are the familiar, stock roles found in hundreds of other war movies, its performances are unimaginative and stereotypical, its dialogue is standard issue and dull, its romances are trite and unconvincing, its comedy is not very amusing and its drama is not particularly exciting. Only in its surprisingly authentic view of war does the film rise above the ordinary.

The film was not a success, passing through drive-ins on a double feature with the World War II drama *Tank Commandos*. *Operation Dames* does not fulfill its exploitive title or expectations, nor is it exciting as an action picture. It is obviously a low-budget film with limited ambitions; however, even as ordinary as it is, the film does project a gritty perspective of the war which other, more serious films would do well to emulate.

Pork Chop Hill

Credits: 1959. Melville Productions. *Distributed by* United Artists. *Directed by* Lewis Milestone. *Produced by* Sy Bartlett. *Screenplay by* James R. Webb. *Based upon the Book by* Brigadier General S. L. A. Marshall, U.S.A.R. *Music Composed and Conducted by* Leonard Rosenman. *Director of Photography*: Sam Leavitt, A.S.C. *Supervising Editor*: George Boemler, A.C.E. *Production Designer*: Nicolai Remisoff. *Technical Advisor*: Captain Joseph G. Clemons, Jr., Infantry, U.S.A. *Sound Effects Editor*: Del Harris. *Music Editor*: Byron Chudnow. *Sound Recording*: Earl Crain, Sr., and Roger Heman. *Production Manager*: Tom Andre. *Location Manager*: Carl Benoit. *Assistant Director*: Ray Gosnell. *Costumer*: Eddie Armand. *Makeup Supervision*: Frank Prehoda, S.M.A. *Makeup Artists*: Dan Greenway and Stan Smith. *Special Effects*:

David Koehler. *Set Decoration*: Edward G. Boyle. *Director, Second Unit*: Nate Watt. *Assistant Director, Second Unit*: John Bloss. *Director of Photography, Second Unit*: Edwin DuPar. *Script Supervisor*: John Franco. *Casting*: Lynn Stalmaster. Not Rated. Black and White. Widescreen (1.85:1). 97 minutes. Released in May, 1959. Currently available on VHS home video and DVD. Previously available on laserdisc.

Cast: *Lieutenant Joe Clemons*, Gregory Peck; *Forstman*, Harry Guardino; *Lieutenant Walt Russell*, Rip Torn; *Fedderson*, George Peppard; *Peace Conference General*, Carl Benton Reid; *Corporal Jurgens*, James Edwards; *Kern*, Bob Steele; *Franklin*, Woody Strode; *Lieutenant Tsugi O'Hashi*, George Shibata; *Sergeant Coleman*, Norman Fell; *Public Information Officer*, Lew Gallo; *Velie*, Robert Blake; *Corporal Payne*, Cliff Ketchum; *Bowen*, Biff Elliot; *Harrold*, Charles Aidman; *Lieutenant Colonel Davis*, Barry Atwater; *Chinese Broadcaster*, Viraj Amonsin; *S-2 Officer*, Michael Garth; *Lieutenant Cook*, Leonard Graves; *Marshall*, Martin Landau; *General Trudeau*, Ken Lynch; *Sergeant Kreucheberg*, Paul Comi; *Sergeant Kuzmick*, Syl Lamont; *McKinley*, Abel Fernandez; *Corporal Kissell*, Kevin Hagen; *Chalmers*, Chuck Hayward; *Lieutenant Waldorf*, John Alderman; *Saxon*, Gavin MacLeod; *Olds*, John McKee; *Lieutenant Cummings*, Bert Remsen; *Soldier Runner*, Robert Williams; *Radio Operator*, Buzz Martin; *Iron Man*, William "Bill" Wellman, Jr.; *McFarland*, Harry Dean Stanton (uncredited); *Lieutenant Attridge*, Barry Maguire (uncredited).

Historical Accuracy Level: High. Based on a true story and employing real people as its characters, this drama is perhaps the most authentic Korean War movie ever made.

Patriotic Propaganda Level: High. The film does not overemphasize these soldiers' heroism, valor and nobility, but it cannot hide those attributes, and does not try.

Elements: Army, Biography, Bugles, Peace Negotiations.

Among the bloodiest battles fought during the Korean War was the one for control of Pork Chop Hill. This particular battle, which took place on a desolate piece of land that some said was shaped like an elongated pork chop, had vast ramifications regarding the final phase of the war well beyond the territorial dispute of the moment. While the battle was largely insignificant from a tactical standpoint, it became supremely important at the peace talks taking place just seventy miles away at Panmunjom, where it came to represent a test of wills between China and the United States. Because the political battle over Pork Chop Hill became more important to the peace process than the actual battle was to the war, and because the value of human life seemed to sink to its lowest level during that battle (at least in the eyes of the politicians of both sides), the fight for Pork Chop Hill has become emblematic as a paradoxical symbol of the war.

It is the third year of the Korean War, and peace talks are dragging at Panmunjom. During the credit sequence, both Chinese and American negotiators take turns getting angry and leaving the negotiating table. Seventy miles away, at a reserve position near Pork Chop Hill, a Chinese broadcaster (Viraj Amonsin) reminds the American troops in the area that the Korean conflict is now in its one thousand and twentieth day, and that it has produced more American casualties than the American War of Independence. Lieutenant Joe Clemons (Gregory Peck) is badgered by a soldier named Forstman (Harry Guardino) about rotation home, so Clemons recommends he sue the army. Clemons is in charge of King Company, and he greets two new squad leaders, Sergeant Coleman (Norman Fell) and Corporal Payne (Cliff Ketchum), with the news that King Company has been elected to recapture Pork Chop Hill.

Though Clemons is relatively inexperienced, he and Lieutenant O'Hashi (George Shibata) study the layout of the hill and devise a simple plan of attack, which is approved by Colonel Davis (Barry Atwater). Clemons will lead one platoon, O'Hashi another, while a third will be kept in reserve, and the dangerous right flank will be Love Company's concern. Nearly one hundred men are transported close to the hill by truck in the dark; they begin to work their way quietly up the hill under no enemy fire. Clemons radios for a lift of friendly artillery fire to allow his men to pass through; it is granted. In the sudden quiet, the Chinese broadcaster exhorts the Americans to avoid the fight, then plays taps over his loudspeaker, and says sardonically, "Welcome to the meat grinder."

The poster for United Artists' drama Pork Chop Hill *(1959) is rather artistic, with a nicely understated view of star Gregory Peck leading an advancing night patrol. The ad copy at left is intrusive, however, exhibiting mundane and familiar marketing tactics.*

Chinese troops watch from above as the American soldiers climb closer. A soldier named Franklin (Woody Strode) falls and pretends to be hurt, but Clemons realizes that he is trying to avoid the battle and pulls the man to his feet, ordering him to stay close. The men reach the first hill defense, rolls of concertino wire which were reported to be flattened but which are obviously intact. As they begin to cut the wire, the Chinese open fire from above with rifles and machine guns, and toss grenades down the hill. A few of the men lie on top of the wire, allowing others to pass over them. Suddenly, bright lights illuminate the battlefield from behind, making easy targets of the men moving uphill. Clemons angrily radios for the lights to be doused, and moments later, they are. Clemons cuts a passage in the wire and more men pass through. Clemons sees one man, Velie (Robert Blake), wandering up the hill without a rifle and decides to use him as a runner. Velie is sent to contact O'Hashi and picks up a dead soldier's rifle along the way. O'Hashi and his men rush the first trench, driving the Chinese back, and destroy a bunker with enemy soldiers inside.

Chinese swarm the right-hand ridge which Love Company is supposed to defend, and Clemons orders one small squad with a machine gun to hold it until reinforcements arrive. On the way back to Clemons, Velie is stopped by a machine gun post. He uses two grenades to destroy the post, but he is wounded in the arm in the process. Clemons and his men rush the top trench and secure it. Clemons assigns Corporal Jurgens (James Edwards) to watch Franklin, who is still trying to avoid combat. When Franklin takes offense at being watched by Jurgens (both of whom are black), the corporal replies, "I got a special interest in every thing you do." Velie reports back to Clemons, who sends him down the hill to an aid station for his arm wound.

With the battle quiet for the time being, O'Hashi estimates casualties at forty percent. Members of Love Company finally show themselves; there are only twelve men left, and two more die from a shell blast as Clemons and their leader Marshall (Martin Landau) watch, helplessly. In one of the trenches, Chinese soldiers stage a hit and run assault, shooting a few men before disappearing over the crest of the hill. In a bunker, some American soldiers who were under siege by the Chinese are rescued, and the men celebrate. Their celebration is cut short by a well-placed artillery shell which kills several of the men just rescued. One man claims the shell was from an American battery, but Clemons defuses the volatile situation by noting that the shell came from Old Baldy, a hill controlled by Chinese forces. Satisfied that the trenches are secure, Clemons calls in the third platoon as reinforcement, allowing them to spell the exhausted first and second platoons.

Fighting continues and communication breaks down. Clemons is unable to contact upper echelons because the Chinese are jamming radio frequencies, so runners are used as contacts. O'Hashi leads a bayonet charge that expels Chinese from part of the hill. Men are ordered to stay in bunkers for their own protection while not engaged in combat. Velie appears with his arm in a sling, ready again to act as a runner. Forstman and his friend Fedderson (George Peppard) are crossing the hill when Fedderson is hit and killed by a shell blast. Clemons finds Forstman grieving and consoles him, saying, "It's no use trying to figure it out. You just have to keep going."

Clemons has just thirty-five of his original one hundred thirty-five men remaining and ready for battle. Unexpectedly, his brother-in-law, Lieutenant Walt Russell (Rip Torn), arrives with George Company, and Clemons assigns them to the right flank with the remainder of Love Company. Russell is surprised that King Company is so decimated; he was told that George Company would be "mopping up" after King. Then a runner arrives from Colonel Davis ordering Russell's company to withdraw. Clemons is furious and sends the runner back to Davis explaining that King is just barely hanging onto the hill and desperately needs supplies and reinforcements. A smiling public information officer (Lew Gallo) and photographer appear, asking to chronicle the story of King Company's glorious victory. Clemons can't believe that everyone thinks he has taken and is successfully holding Pork Chop Hill. He begs the publicist to tell the Army brass to send him aid, and sends the officer back down the hill to safety.

At headquarters, officers pass the question "Do we still want to hold Pork Chop?" up the ladder of command for a final decision. General Trudeau (Ken Lynch) receives Clemons' plea, but allows the order to remove George Company to stand. He rationalizes the battle as too costly and determines not to waste any more lives fighting for the hill.

Walt Russell takes King Company's wounded with him, leaving behind all of George Company's grenades and ammunition. Just twenty-five able-bodied men are left. Clemons pulls back his perimeter to the hill's crest and the closest trenches. Clemons stumbles across Franklin in a deserted bunker, and the frightened soldier threatens to kill him rather than face a court-martial for cowardice. Clemons calmly persuades him to overcome his cowardice and join the fight. The Chinese broadcaster gives the men on the hill just forty-five minutes to surrender, then spends that time trying to persuade them to do so. The men spend the time talking of home, discussing the details of their lives. The radio interference is stopped and Clemons asks for his force to be withdrawn. General Trudeau orders him to stay put. The date is April 17, 1953.

At Panmunjom, the chief negotiator (Carl Benton Reid) comes to the conclusion that the Chinese will attack Pork Chop Hill as a show of strength. "Its value is that it has no value," he concludes, and asks himself, "Are we as willing to risk lives for nothing as they are?"

Bugles blow and flares illuminate the hill; hundreds of Chinese soldiers attack. The Americans shoot as many enemy as they can, then pull back to a single bunker reinforced with sandbags. A Chinese flamethrower attempts to burn them out, but the men are able to plug openings with sandbags. Then different sounds are heard from outside, as the Chinese soldiers are driven back by arriving Americans. The jubilant soldiers tear away the sandbags, run outside and join the fight, led by Lieutenant O'Hashi, who suffers an arm wound. Clemons is exhausted. Walking down the hill later, Clemons looks at some of the survivors: Velie, Franklin, Jurgens, Forstman. He thinks aloud, "Millions live in freedom today because of what they did."

Pork Chop Hill is based solidly on fact and, though it does take small liberties with actual events, is a faithful recreation of one of the bloodiest battles in U.S. Army history. It is based on Brigadier General S. L. A. Marshall's painstakingly researched account of the battle and the political climate which surrounded it, and is muscularly directed by Lewis Milestone, the man responsible for two other classic war films, *All Quiet on the Western Front* and *A Walk in the Sun*, along with several other well made adventures. *Pork Chop Hill* would complete Milestone's unofficial war trilogy (although he directed several other war films) and be the final major film of the director's long career.

In all three of his renowned war films,

Milestone takes great pains to dramatize the futility of war and its destructive effects on its participants and victims. Yet Milestone also balances his anti-war message with the understanding that there is a nobility in risking one's life for a cause, even when one cannot really comprehend that cause. Thus, the main characters in his war films realize the irony and waste of their battles, yet still strive to be the best soldiers they can be, because that is their mission, their duty. They don't have any choice, especially if they hope to survive. This depth of characterization and ironic realization, done totally without opportunistic jingoism, sets Milestone's movies apart from other war films. Though Milestone's combat sequences can be exciting and thrilling, it is not his intention to make war entertaining. His moral mindset is solidly against the concept of war, even when war is deemed necessary, for the simple and understandable reason that good men die in the fighting, often for no practical reason.

Other Korean War films take the same stance — that the soldiers fighting the war did not really understand or appreciate why they were risking their lives in Korea — but that feeling is best expressed throughout *Pork Chop Hill*, on three separate levels. The infantrymen are aware of the political situation, but most accept the risk with joking cynicism. One notable exception is Franklin, the man terrified of dying for no reason in a foreign land. "I don't want to die for Korea," he exclaims. "What do I care about this stinking hill?" Lieutenant Clemons and the officers are aware that they may be sending their men (and themselves) to their deaths in a pointless fight, but they, too, are powerless to prevent it. Because the officers make the decisions of who goes where and when, it is they who must face the guilt when those men are killed in action. Finally, the chief peace negotiator has an inverse perspective. He also knows that Pork Chop Hill is insignificant in the big battle picture, and that men will die if the hill is to be taken and defended. But he also comes to believe that the sacrifice of some men in one battle may save a far greater number from the same fate later. At his level, the men who must fight and die become statistics, and the war is won by the side with more favorable statistics.

The movie skillfully blends these levels into

Lieutenant Joe Clemons (Gregory Peck) motions his men forward, up the deadly slope of Pork Chop Hill *(1959). For the film, Clemons, then at the rank of captain, served as technical advisor.*

one coherent and pointed view of the atmosphere surrounding the battle for Pork Chop Hill. The audience is provided with the rationale for the decisions made by the Army brass, even though some of the characters are left in the dark. Milestone presents moments of heroism and cowardice throughout, depicting the danger, boredom and fear which every soldier on that hill has to face. It is certainly the most authentic and believable chronicle of the Korean War ever put on film, and if it is not overwhelmingly involving on an emotional level, that may be forgiven because it is so informative and makes such a strong moral point.

James R. Webb's detailed screenplay makes note of simple, yet important, things such as the Chinese method of blowing bugles and whistles before they attack, the sincere persuasiveness of the Chinese broadcaster, the lack of reliable information provided to Clemons before his assault on the hill, the incredibly dumb and mistaken lighting of the hill during the initial assault, the inability of officers to communicate with each other and with headquarters, the hit and run pattern of Chinese soldiers to test American defenses and the importance of sandbags to protect human life. These types of details illuminate the ongoing battle and increase viewer awareness of just how difficult the soldiers' job to stay alive and kill the enemy really is. Unlike other war films with superhero characters who single-handedly destroy entire enemy squadrons, the men of *Pork Chop Hill* are tired and overworked, hungry and grouchy. They are human, and they long to survive.

It is the political perspective which gives *Pork Chop Hill* its greatest effectiveness. The beginning of the film features peace negotiators on both sides becoming angry with the process and leaving. Later, when the American negotiator calls Pork Chop Hill "an insignificant little hill with no importance to you and no importance to us," and the Chinese negotiator arrogantly removes the translator from his ear and stops listening, it is an act more infuriating than any of the preceding battle. It is from this act that the American negotiator determines that the battle for Pork Chop is, in effect, a battle of international wills. The Chinese seem willing to expend men and material to capture and hold this "insignificant little hill," and they will continue to fight until the Americans prove themselves as willing to pour resources into such a cause. Only then, when the Chinese know themselves to be against a tougher, more resilient foe, will they weaken their stance and back away from the battle. That determination saves the lives of Clemons and his remaining twenty-five men, and finally helped bring the three-year conflict in Korea to a close.

The real battle for Pork Chop Hill actually lasted two days and a night, whereas the movie focuses specifically on the battle's second day. And while a few of the men's names were changed — and the character of the cowardly Franklin was invented for dramatic purposes — the film remains remarkably true to actual events. The actual Clemons served as the film's technical advisor, ensuring that his cinematic story remained faithful to his real experiences, and producer/star Gregory Peck was satisfied enough with the story not to try to make it more traditionally heroic. Among both military personnel and movie critics, the film's verisimilitude was noted as its strongest and most valuable characteristic.

The movie's presentation of the Chinese is worth noting. The soldiers themselves are seen as merely individual parts in a vast human tide. While attacking, the Chinese are both fearless and foolish, bravely overrunning American outposts and positions but never trying to protect themselves while doing so, and thus are slaughtered by the dozen. This manner of attacking also represented the Chinese political method of fighting the war, although American and United Nations negotiators took a long time before recognizing it as such. The Chinese negotiator at the peace talks is inscrutable and arrogant, and is meant to signify the intractability of the Communists. The key figure, however, is the Chinese broadcaster. He spends his days teasing and talking to the Americans, attempt-

ing to persuade them to forego the fight for Pork Chop Hill. As played by Viraj Amonsin, the Chinese broadcaster is the conscience of the Chinese people. He believes his side is right, of course, but he personally wants no harm to befall the Americans, whom he recognizes as just as brave as his fellow Communists. His convincingly sincere attempt to prevent the battle adds yet another level of irony to the proceedings.

The film not only avoids a jingoistic tone, but deliberately includes scenes which sharply sketch the U.S. Army's ineffectiveness. Most importantly, the Army officers in charge of running the battle were unsure if their superiors wanted the battle to be fought. As it escalates, the question "Do we still want to hold Pork Chop?" is passed up the ladder of command until someone makes a final decision. Communications between platoon squads is difficult, and between the battle front and the rear headquarters it is nonexistent. Clemons requests supplies and reinforcements multiple times, and somehow the officers at headquarters misunderstand or ignore his requests again and again. The frustrating irony reaches a peak when Clemons' brother-in-law arrives with a fresh company, only to be pulled back hours later, and by the arrival of a public information officer wanting to write a story about the Army's most recent military triumph. Such scenes add greatly to the "madness of war" theme prevalent in Milestone's war films and reinforces, the concept that war is a largely futile exercise.

The battle scenes, filmed in the San Fernando Valley during a forty day schedule of filming, are taut and suspenseful. A majority of the action takes place at night, and those scenes mix shadows and fog with flares and bright searchlights, providing them with a permeating sense of darkness and foreboding. The Chinese preferred to attack under cover of darkness, so the film necessarily and effectively depicts the nuances of night fighting. And despite being filmed in southern California, the film's painstakingly chosen and constructed locations provide it with the feel of Korea, proving again that the illusion of film can be enormously convincing.

Leading the cast is producer/star Gregory Peck as Lieutenant Joe Clemons, and he delivers

The surviving members of King Company wait in a sandbagged bunker on top of Pork Chop Hill, surrounded by the enemy, anxiously hoping for reinforcements to arrive in Pork Chop Hill *(1959).*

a commanding performance. Clemons has doubts about the mission and his own ability to lead, both of which are expressed by Peck in the role, but he is also a smart, hardworking character, and Peck excels at portraying these aspects. Most impressive is how Clemons keeps his wits about him even while his reinforcements are being recalled, and in these scenes, Peck is outstanding. This was the initial offering from Melville Productions, a company founded by Peck and producer Sy Bartlett, and both men did their utmost to present a worthy version of General S. L. A. Marshall's acclaimed book.

Several other familiar faces appear in the supporting cast, though it must be noted that their characters are never fully developed. Harry Guardino and George Peppard play buddies nearing rotation home, while Gavin MacLeod portrays a soldier who loses a foot during the battle. Robert Blake has an interesting role as Velie, whom Clemons assigns as a runner; Blake

also appeared in *Battle Flame* the same year. Woody Strode and James Edwards portray the black members of King Company as two men who have completely opposite views of duty, and Harry Dean Stanton has a small role as a complaining soldier. Martin Landau and Norman Fell play besieged squad leaders. Apart from Peck's, two other impressive performances come from George Shibita as Lieutenant O'Hashi and Rip Torn as Clemons' brother-in-law, Lieutenant Russell. Shibita had been the first Japanese American to graduate from West Point, where he had been a classmate of the real Joe Clemons, and his portrayal is on the same high level as Peck's.

The film's critical reception was tremendous. *Newsweek* led the cheers, proclaiming, "Every hellish moment of *Pork Chop Hill* generates the adrenalin taste of war. Gregory Peck, its star, Lewis Milestone, the director, and Sy Bartlett, the producer — all men of integrity —

have each had experience in making exceptional war movies, but this time they have surpassed themselves." The magazine later noted, "as a totally honest war movie — and a dramatic one — *Pork Chop Hill* is one of the best Hollywood has ever made." Hollis Alpert of *Saturday Review* noted, "The action in *Pork Chop Hill* may occasionally seem confusing, but for this very reason it is more real and more convincing." Stanley Kauffmann of the *New Republic* pronounced it "a lucid and thorough dramatization of one specific action." And in his book *War Movies*, Brock Garland describes the movie as "Perhaps the best film made about the Korean War."

Pork Chop Hill was considered one of the best films of the year and became quite profitable for its studio, but was totally ignored for the Academy Awards. Nevertheless, it stands today as a classic study of war in general and perhaps *the* historical study of the Korean War in particular. No other Korean War film contains as concise a view of the battle front or as pungent a view of the peace negotiations. The film excels in recreating the palpable futility felt by soldiers who fully realize that they may die as pawns in a political war rather than as men in a military action. The film both condemns and praises the American military hierarchy for its actions, and its balanced view is due to the strenuous research work undertaken by the original author, Brigadier General S. L. A. Marshall, who understood that historical truth could only be served by telling the full story, warts and all. *Pork Chop Hill* has retained its sterling reputation for more than forty years and today remains one of the best films produced about the Korean War.

Prisoner of War

Credits: 1954. Metro-Goldwyn-Mayer. *Directed by* Andrew Marton. *Produced by* Henry Berman. *Written by* Allen Rivkin. *Musical Direction by* Jeff Alexander. *Director of Photography*: Robert Planck, A.S.C. *Film Editor*: James Newcom, A.C.E. *Art Directors*: Cedric Gibbons and Malcolm Brown. *Special Effects*: A. Arnold Gillespie and Warren Newcombe. *Assistant Director*: Joel Freeman. *Recording Supervisor*: Douglas Shearer. *Set Decorations*: Edwin B. Willis and Jack D. Moore. *Make-Up by* William Tuttle. Not Rated. Black and White. Flat (1.33:1). 80 minutes. Released in April, 1954. Not currently available on commercial home video.

Cast: Captain Web Sloane, Ronald Reagan; *Corporal Joseph Robert Stanton*, Steve Forrest; *Jesse Treadman*, Dewey Martin; *Colonel Nikita I. Biroshilov*, Oscar Homolka; *Francis Aloysius Belney*, Robert Horton; *Captain Jack Hodges*, Paul Stewart; *Major O. D. Halle*, Henry (Harry) Morgan; *Lieutenant Georgi M. Robovnik*, Stephen Bekassy; *Colonel Kim Doo Yi*, Leonard Strong; *Merton Tollivar*, Darryl Hickman; *Red Guards*, Weaver Levy and Ralph Ahn; *Captain Lang Hyun Choi*, Rollin Moriyama; *Benjamin Julesberg*, Ike Jones; *MVD Officer*, Clarence Lung; *Axel Horstrom*, Jerry Paris; *Lieutenant Peter Reilly*, John Lupton; *Captain*, Stuart Whitman; *Alan H. Rolfe*, Bob Ellis; *General*, Lewis Martin; *David Carey*, Otis Greene; *Sachez Rivero*, Lalo Rios; *Emanuel Hazard*, Lester C. Hoyle; *Donald C. Jackwood*, Roy Boyle; *Jacob Allen Lorfield*, Leon Tyler; *Red Doctor*, Edo Mita; *Captain Fred Osborne*, Peter Hansen.

Historical Accuracy Level: Medium. The film is undeniably overstated in some respects, but its central depiction of the hardships faced by Americans in Communist prison camps contains a great deal of truth, as attested to by real-life survivors.

Patriotic Propaganda Level: High. The Communists can kill our soldiers, but it takes a lot to make them break.

Elements: Army, Brainwashing, Collaboration, Dogs, Medicine, Prisoners of War, Secret Missions.

This was the first Korean War film to document the hardships facing American prisoners of war and to depict the brutality and brainwashing techniques that P.O.W.s faced in Communist prison camps. Rushed into production while the peace talks were concluding in 1953, *Prisoner of War* was released in April of 1954, almost a year after the Korean armistice was signed, but eight months before the next P.O.W. film, Columbia's *The Bamboo Prison*, played on theater screens. Today, *Prisoner of War* is notorious for the presence of Ronald Reagan, later the President of the United States, in a role which calls for him to pretend to support the cause of Communism.

Reagan plays Web Sloane, an army captain who volunteers to gather information for the Army regarding treatment of American prisoners in North Korean POW camps. Sloane, re-ranked as a corporal, parachutes into North Korea and manages to join a parade of American prisoners marching north. Seven hundred eighteen men are forced to march for twenty-one days and are barely fed during the trek; only two hundred eleven reach their destination. Sloane befriends Joe Stanton (Steve Forrest) during the march, and they witness many deaths along the way.

The unnamed prison camp is run by two Chinese officers, Kim (Leonard Strong) and Lang (Rollin Moriyama), but the real power belongs to Russian advisor Biroshilov (Oscar Homolka). The burly Russian subjects the American prisoners to lectures and classes about the "true nature of Communism" and beats those men who actively resist the indoctrination. The first prisoner to cooperate is Jesse Treadman (Dewey Martin), who is named "monitor" of Hut 16 and rewarded with food, liquor and cigarettes for his choice. The other Americans no longer trust Treadman and avoid him whenever possible, but he still attempts to coax the men into cooperating and reaping the rewards.

Sloane tells Stanton that "every man has his breaking point," but Stanton continues to resist and is beaten for his trouble. Stanton manages to adopt and conceal a little lost dog, whom he names Eloise. Prisoner Merton Tollivar (Darryl Hickman) develops appendicitis, and Sloane pretends to cooperate with the Reds in order to get brandy and the opportunity to steal medical supplies. An emergency operation is performed in candlelight by another prisoner, Jack Hodges (Paul Stewart), aided by the men of Hut 16, and Tollivar lives.

The Communists persuade Sloane to broadcast a speech in which he praises their virtues, but a special code word alerts listening American officials that he is lying, and that the Reds are forcing pilots to falsely confess to conducting germ warfare. One pilot, Lieutenant Peter Reilly (John Lupton), is tortured until he agrees to confess. Later, his forced confession is filmed and broadcast to the prisoners, along with another by Web Sloane. Stanton leads a riot as the men destroy the film and the projec-

tion equipment, and a dozen of the men are punished. They are forced to lie in shallow graves beneath the burning sun until they agree to sign a document that states they have neither seen nor been subjected to any wartime atrocities. The prisoners grow weak from hunger and exposure, and Merton Tollivar dies. But the men stand firm until faced with a firing squad; then, all but five agree to their captors' terms. The five remaining resistors are tortured until only Stanton remains opposed to their will. Biroshilov finally breaks Stanton's will by killing Eloise.

Time passes. As the peace talks progress, conditions in the camp improve. The men are "fattened" for health inspections, and games and movies are made available to them. During one film, Stanton sneaks outside, follows the Russian, Biroshilov, and kills him in revenge. Although Colonel Kim wants to punish the prisoners to find the murderer, he receives orders to select twenty prisoners for repatriation. Kim gives Sloane the task of choosing the men to return home, and Sloane chooses some sick or wounded men, and also includes Joe Stanton. Sloane is astonished to hear his own name on the list, and finally discovers that Jesse Treadman is a fellow mole and will be heading to Moscow, continuing the lie that he is a collaborator. The movie ends with Sloane, Stanton and the other lucky prisoners boarding a truck for the long voyage home, while the other prisoners sing their goodbyes.

Prisoner of War is a brutal film in which many of the American prisoners are routinely beaten or punished, and all are subjected to the Pavlovian "conditioned reflex" techniques of the Russian camp advisor. The men are starved, provided with little or no medical care, and forced to undergo lengthy indoctrination classes designed to undermine the American way of life. The Communist leaders are kind and smiling until someone resists their methodology; any such resistors are usually subjected to physical torture. While some critics — and presumably audience members — of the time (including the Department of Defense, which termed these atrocities "a distortion") expressed disbelief that so much physical abuse existed, screenwriter Allen Rivkin claimed to have full documentation of the authenticity of his incidents. Indeed, despite the overtly shocking and cruel nature of

SHOCKING!
YOU'VE
NEVER SEEN
ANYTHING
LIKE IT!

BRAIN-WASHING IN ACTION!
•
BRAVERY UNDER TORTURE!
•
THE TERRIBLE
MARCH NORTH!
•
LIFE IN THE
P.O.W. CAMPS!
•
WHY 21 GI's
DIDN'T COME
HOME!
•
THE NAKED
TRUTH!

M-G-M
presents

PRISONER
OF WAR

STARRING
RONALD REAGAN · STEVE FORREST
DEWEY MARTIN · OSCAR HOMOLKA
Written by ALLEN RIVKIN · Directed by ANDREW MARTON · Produced by HENRY BERMAN.
AN M·G·M PICTURE

This poster for MGM's drama Prisoner of War *(1954) has what amounts to a table of contents for the film, with each topical news item given its own brief exclamatory description. The ad also underscores the film's shock value, declaring "You've never seen anything like it!"*

Sloane's first foray into Korea, when he joins the long march to the prison camp—which is eerily reminiscent of the World War II Bataan "death march"—sets the tone, as an increasing number of men fall by the side of the road to die. The number of dead is eventually established at just over five hundred, though the film shows only a couple of dozen casualties. One troublemaker is even shot in the back during an air raid, reinforcing the point that the Communists were not interested in the value of individual human life, but rather in the spread of their beliefs. Those men who happened to survive were to be indoctrinated into Communist thinking, and those who found value in Communism would spread its seeds later in life. Or so the Reds hoped.

The film mentions brainwashing, and stages much rhetoric supporting the idea of indoctrination, but it really only skims the surface of those terrible psychological tactics. These Communists were far more apt to beat obedience into someone or torture resistance out of someone rather than to actually change that person's way of thinking. In this regard, the film is a throwback to the days and villains of World War II. It does not seriously attempt to depict the state-of-the-art psychological mind attacks which were being attempted in North Korean prison camps.

As a result of its simplistic good vs. evil conflict, the film never fully realizes its potential. The Russian advisor and Chinese leaders are intriguing characters who quickly become one-dimensional because of their reliance on violence. The Americans never lose their identities be-

some of the brutality depicted, the film's tone does ring true, and many returning P.O.W.s gave accounts of prison life that make this film seem tame.

The American prisoners, including Web Sloane (Ronald Reagan, center, with a beard and mustache), huddle around a tiny fire trying to keep warm, in Prisoner of War *(1954).*

cause they are beaten physically, but not mentally. Yes, the Communists use force, or the threat of force, to make the prisoners confess to crimes they have not committed, but the men know that they are lies, and that those lies were told under extreme duress. Some of the men would rather die than lie, and do. But the film argues that surviving is what is most important. Treason is not to be abided, of course, but none of the prisoners is guilty of treason, and therefore they should try to survive, no matter what the Communists make them say.

This simplistic approach to the material skirts around its important issues rather than directly facing them. Because of this, and the undeniable cruelty staged on the screen, *Prisoner of War* was severely criticized. Moira Walsh of *America* decried its "endless succession of physical brutalities visited on wholesome but poorly characterized American types by bestial but slightly comic and more than slightly feebleminded Red automatons." Her review ended with this judgment: "Altogether the film is a

harrowing ordeal and is utterly unrewarding except, I fear, for the sadist fringe of moviegoers to whom it will appeal for entirely wrong reasons."

There is a thin line between representing violence and cruelty on screen for the purposes of drama and reveling, or wallowing, in such carnage. It was the majority opinion of the time that *Prisoner of War* crossed that line. In *Commonweal*, Philip T. Hartung tried to define the line. "If director Andrew Marton had allowed his good cast to carry on in a simple and realistic manner, this film could have been quite instructive. But piling cruelty on torture, the material becomes only a succession of grim details." Arthur Knight of the *Saturday Review* judged that "*Prisoner of War* is a brutal, sadistic, and thoroughly cheap attempt to exploit public interest in a tragic, highly sensitive situation."

While based on factual incidents and testimony from returning American P.O.W.s, the film is exploitive and occasionally ridiculous. Ronald Reagan was the wrong choice for the lead, because he looks as if he could be talked into anything. Interestingly, Reagan narrated a documentary at about the same time called *The Ultimate Weapon: Men's Minds*, in which he argues that American soldiers gave in to Communist brainwashing because of a lack of moral fiber. Steve Forrest is impressive as Stanton, but as soon as he finds the dog, his weakness is revealed. Dewey Martin is adequate as Treadman, but the character is ignored rather than mistrusted or hated by his fellow prisoners.

Prisoner of War is well-intentioned and well-staged. It has more visceral power than the similarly themed *The Bamboo Prison*, but it does not share that Korean War movie's shrewdness. Its lack of intelligence and subtlety, the casting of Ronald Reagan and its insistence on vividly portraying the cruelty of the Communists rather than their cunning are weaknesses that the movie cannot totally overcome.

The Rack

Credits: 1956. Metro-Goldwyn-Mayer. *Directed by* Arnold Laven. *Produced by* Arthur M. Loew, Jr. *Screenplay by* Stewart Stern. *Based on the teleplay by* Rod Serling. *Music by* Adolph Deutsch. *Director of Photography*: Paul C. Vogel, A.S.C. *Film Editors*: Harold F. Kress, A.C.E. and Marshall Neilan, Jr. *Art Directors*: Cedric Gibbons and Merrill Pye. *Set Decorations*: Edwin B. Willis and Fred MacLean. *Recording Supervisor*: Dr. Wesley C. Miller. *Assistant Director*: Robert Saunders. *Makeup by* William Tuttle. *Technical Advisor*: Colonel Charles M. Trammel, Jr., U.S.A.R. Not Rated. Black and White. Flat (1.33:1). 100 minutes. Released in November, 1956. Not currently available on commercial home video.

Cast: *Captain Edward W. Hall, Jr.*, Paul Newman; *Major Sam Moulton*, Wendell Corey; *Colonel Edward W. Hall, Sr.*, Walter Pidgeon; *Lieutenant Colonel Frank Wasnick*, Edmond O'Brien; *Aggie Hall*, Anne Francis; *Captain John R.. Miller*, Lee Marvin; *Caroline*, Cloris Leachman; *Colonel Ira Hansen*, Robert Burton; *Law Officer*, Robert Simon; *Court President*, Trevor Bardette; *Sergeant Otto Pahnke*, Adam Williams; *Millard Chilson Cassidy*, James Best; *Colonel Dudley Smith*, Fay Roope; *Major Byron Phillips*, Barry Atwater; *with* Robert Blake, Dean Jones and Rod Taylor.

Historical Accuracy Level: Medium. This story is a fictional representation of soldiers who confessed to war crimes under Communist brainwashing and torture.

Patriotic Propaganda Level: Medium. The film promotes understanding of the forces facing soldiers in Korea and asks for broader and firmer support of our fighting men.

Elements: Army, Brainwashing, Collaboration, Courts-Martial, Prisoners of War, Returning Home, Sibling Rivalry.

During the final year of the Korean War, stories of American soldiers who had or were collaborating with the Communists became public. A small number of soldiers and airmen confessed to germ warfare activities and other war crimes, and attempted to convince their fellow prisoners to accept Communist doctrine. While some servicemen did convert to Communism, the majority were forced into their actions through brainwashing and/or torture. *The Rack* presents a story of a Korean War prisoner who, after months of duress, finally submits to the Communist indoctrination to which he has been subjected and collaborates with the North Koreans. His story is contrasted with that of another soldier who did not capitulate and a rhetorical question is asked: What would you do?

Army Captain Edward W. Hall, Jr. (Paul Newman) returns home from duty in the Korean War with an injured leg and a great deal of guilt. He has a secret, one which will forever alter his relationship with his proud military father (Walter Pidgeon) and his late brother's widow Aggie (Anne Francis). When Hall is well enough to leave the hospital, he is charged with collaborating with the enemy while being held as a North Korean prisoner of war. Major Sam Moulton (Wendell Corey) finds the case distasteful but undertakes the task of prosecuting Hall in the ensuing court-martial, while sympathetic Lt. Colonel Frank Wasnick (Edmond O'Brien) handles Hall's defense. Hall's father learns of the charges through a military friend, loses his temper and harshly condemns his son for his admitted treason, even suggesting that death would have been more honorable. Aggie tries her best to reconcile the two men.

During the court-martial the prosecution uses the testimony of Captain John R. Miller (Lee Marvin) to show that even when physically tortured, most American soldiers did not reach the point where they would give "aid and comfort" to the enemy. Hall was never tortured, at least not physically. He was held for six months in solitary confinement in a small, wet cellar until, when informed that his younger brother had died in combat, he collapsed emotionally and agreed to sign whatever his captors wanted him to "for a blanket that smelled of fish and urine and three hours of sleep. And at the time, I thought it was a pretty good bargain," states Hall.

Hall's defense is that he was an intensely lonely man — his caring mother died when he was 12 and his martinet father has never embraced him or shown him love — and that the North Koreans used this knowledge against him until he couldn't help himself. Under oath, and honest introspection, however, Hall admits (to the court and to himself) that he never did reach his breaking point, close though he may have come. After this testimony, Hall and his penitent father do their best to start their relationship all over again.

The military court finds Hall guilty of treason. Hall takes the stand one final time and relates that he talked to Captain Miller that morning, and that Miller told him that everybody faces a moment of ultimate choice in their lives. If the right choice is made, it becomes a "moment of magnificence." If not, a moment of regret. Hall wishes that he had not "sold himself short" and prays that other people who face life-altering situations will choose more wisely than himself. He then stands, ready for sentencing.

The Rack is a serious exploration of human nature, specifically of what determines Captain Hall's "breaking point." While movies like *Prisoner Of War* and *The Bamboo Prison* ask the same questions, they do so in far more simplistic ways, and thus provide far more simplistic responses. *The Rack* presents a soldier who *did* surrender and admits to committing treason; it is for viewers to decide how far he was coerced by Communist pressure and to determine in their own minds his degree of guilt. Hall is provided with sympathy and nobility, especially at the end, when he tells how Miller came to understand —

and forgive — his actions. The film rhetorically asks how much psychological pressure a soldier must be able to handle and concludes that soldiers must be better prepared for such duress than Hall was.

This film and *Time Limit*, which was released the following year, are the two films which attempt to make sense of American soldiers collaborating with the Communists. At the end of the Korean War, twenty-one Americans had chosen to remain behind in North Korea, preferring Communism over democracy. Three years later, the American public was still trying to understand the motivations of these men and how someone could be driven to accept beliefs so foreign. Besides those twenty-one, other soldiers had publicly denounced America and had even confessed to fictional war crimes. As with the case of Ed Hall, some of those confessions had been made to secure food, water, comfort or just a brief respite from continual indoctrination. Other prisoners were beaten and tortured until they confessed. Still others were simply afraid, and confessed to avoid any physical or psychological abuse.

The term "brainwashing" came into vogue then, as psychiatrists and military experts explained how the Communists would use psychological tactics to gain prisoners' trust and continually ridicule America. Extra food and privileges were often provided to soldiers who cooperated with the Communists. Men who made public confessions of war crimes, no matter how far fetched such claims might be, were treated well by the Communists and encouraged to persuade others to also make confessions. Communists used these false accusations of germ warfare and other crimes as international propaganda, designed to discredit American involvement in Korea.

The movie focuses on Hall as a person suffering from guilt rather than the larger issue of collaboration and its ramifications. Hall is viewed as a victim of his upbringing, a man who eventually betrays his country because he is not psychologically strong enough to contest the enemy's continual pressure. Hall finally surrenders when he learns that his brother has died; at that precise moment, he decides that the fight is no longer worthwhile. The Communists are described as extremely cunning, and use the news

ALL THE
DRAMA...THE
SUSPENSE...
THE POWER...
OF "THE CAINE
MUTINY"!

M-G-M presents

"THE RACK"

STARRING

PAUL NEWMAN · WENDELL COREY
WALTER PIDGEON · EDMOND O'BRIEN
ANNE FRANCIS · LEE MARVIN

Screen Play by STEWART STERN · Based on the Teleplay by ROD SERLING · Directed by ARNOLD LAVEN · Produced by ARTHUR M. LOEW, JR. · AN M-G-M PICTURE

T   H   E   A   T   R   E

MGM's marketing department obviously had no idea how to promote their drama The Rack *(1956), so they borrowed the prestige of Columbia's* Caine Mutiny. *The artwork provides a sense of the main character's guilt and isolation, but reveals nothing of the plot or the Korean War.*

of his brother's death to assail Hall at the time when he is the most psychologically vulnerable. Although Lieutenant Colonel Wasnick defends Hall in the court-martial and convincingly describes Hall's plight, only Aggie seems to truly understand how her brother-in-law was coerced into treason. While the lawyers battle over the legal points surrounding Hall's actions, Aggie responds to his feelings of guilt and loneliness.

The Rack had its origins in a live television drama by Rod Serling, who had tackled the controversial subject soon after his hit teleplay "Patterns" had aired. The original teleplay was produced for the *United States Steel Hour* on April 12, 1955, with Marshall Thompson as Captain Hall. Wendell Corey co-starred as the prosecuting attorney; he was the only major television cast member to repeat his performance in the film. MGM then bought the property and had a film ready for theatres just one year later.

Captain Edward Hall, Jr. (Paul Newman, right) is sworn in during his court-martial for collaborating with the enemy in The Rack *(1956). Swearing him in is prosecuting attorney Sam Moulton (Wendell Corey, left), while defense counsel Frank Wasnick (Edmond O'Brien, center) watches the proceedings intently.*

This was Paul Newman's third movie performance, after his inauspicious debut in *The Silver Chalice* (1954) and his excellent portrayal of boxer Rocky Graziano in *Somebody Up There* *Likes Me* (1956). Newman takes full advantage of the role, showing his range as the character moves from a scared and confused veteran with a hellish secret to a professional soldier on the witness stand describing the harrowing death march to the North Korean prison camp. His sensitivity is highlighted in the film's most moving scene in a car with Walter Pidgeon (recalling the famous scene between brothers Marlon Brando and Rod Steiger in *On The Waterfront*) as father and son try to find common ground.

In supporting roles, Wendell Corey and Edmond O'Brien clash nicely as the lawyers on both sides of Hall's case, while Lee Marvin is solid as the fellow prisoner who moves from condemning Hall for his weakness to understanding and finally forgiving Hall for his sins. Anne Francis is properly steely and understanding as Aggie, while Walter Pidgeon is excellent as Hall, Sr., particularly late in the story, as he tries to reconcile with his son. Watch for James Best, Robert Blake, Dean Jones and Rod Taylor in small roles.

The Rack received generally favorable notices, such as Arthur Knight's review in the *Saturday Review*: "Paul Newman is superb in the complex role of the accused, Wendell Corey and Edmond O'Brien create warm and human figures as the prosecuting and defending officers in the court martial that dominates the film, and Walter Pidgeon gives one of his finest performances as Newman's father, a hard-shelled colonel whose lack of understanding precipitated his son's breakdown under the Red terror. Like *Marty* and *Patterns*, *The Rack* indicates what vital new subject matter the TV screen is opening up for the movies."

Lawrence J. Quirk of the *Motion Picture Herald* praised the film as "a powerful, moving and adult drama," and stated that "*The Rack* is a provocative and creative piece of work." Paul Newman was singled out by nearly every critic for his sensitive portrayal of the unfortunate prisoner of war. Thanks to his strong roles in this film and *Somebody Up There Likes Me*, Newman was well on his way to becoming a major star.

The Rack is a sensitive, intricate drama which, more than any other Korean War film, explores how some soldiers were at increased risk of accepting indoctrination and collaborating with the enemy. The film does not condone Hall's actions, but does demand sympathy regarding public treatment and punishment of such individuals. Hall is a traitor, but he is certainly not a willing collaborator, and the movie posits that the human situation behind the action is just as important, if not more important than, his act of signing a piece of paper.

The Reluctant Heroes
(aka *The Egghead on Hill 656*)

Credits: 1971. Aaron Spelling Productions. *Originally Broadcast on* ABC-TV. *Directed by* Robert Day. *Produced by* Robert Mirisch. *Associate Producer*: Shelley Hull. *Executive Producer*: Aaron Spelling. *Teleplay by* Herman Hoffman and Ernie Frankel. *Story by* Herman Hoffman. *Music by* Frank de Vol. *Director of Photography*: Arch Dalzell. *Film Editor*: Art Seid, A.C.E. *Art Director*: Paul Sylos. *Assistant Director*: Lou Place. *Music Supervisor*: Rocky Moriana. *Sound Effects*: Gene Eliot. *Property Master*: Jerry McFarland. *Costumes*: Robert Harris, Sr. *Make-Up*: Ted Coodley. *Set Decorator*: Ken Swartz. *Construction Coordinator*: Jesse Stone. *Sound Engineer*: Tommy Thompson. *Unit Production Manager*: William Porter. *Script Supervisor*: Helen Parker. *Recorded by* Glen Glenn Sound. *Production Manager*: Norman Henry. *Casting Supervisor*: Bert Remsen. Not Rated. Color. Flat (1.33:1). Originally broadcast on November 23, 1971. Not currently available on commercial home video.

Cast: *Lieutenant Parnell Murphy*, Ken Berry; *Corporal Bill Lukens*, Jim Hutton; *Private Sam Rivera*, Trini Lopez; *Private Carver Le Moyne*, Don Marshall; *Captain Luke Danvers*, Ralph Meeker; *Sergeant Marion Bryce*, Cameron Mitchell; *Corporal Leroy Sprague*, Warren Oates; *Private Jimmy Golden*, Richard Young; *Corporal Bates*, Michael St. George; *(North) Korean Officer*, Soon-Taik Oh (Soon-Tek Oh).

Historical Accuracy Level: Low. The situation and characters in this adventure are preposterous.

Patriotic Propaganda Level: Medium. This movie promotes the ingenuity and knowledge of the central character, elevating him to sex symbol by story's end.

Elements: Army, Behind Enemy Lines, Bridge Bombing, Comedy, Infighting, Musical Performance, Racism.

Among the oddest of Korean War movies is *The Reluctant Heroes*, an ABC television movie which originally aired in 1971. In the wake of the tremendous success of *MASH*, it should not be surprising that television would attempt its own version of mixing comedy and tragedy within a wartime setting. While executive producer Aaron Spelling and writer Herman Hoffman did choose to follow *MASH*'s example and use Korea again rather than the more timely setting of Vietnam, they also chose a lighter, more traditional storyline, and filled the cast with familiar faces. The result is a strange blend of homespun wisdom, surreal dialogue and B-movie heroics.

The Reluctant Heroes are several individuals from the "36th Recon Company" in Korea. Captain Luke Danvers (Ralph Meeker) orders tough, capable Sergeant Marion Bryce (Cameron Mitchell) to collect volunteers for a five-man fire team, plus a medic. Bryce collects his "volunteers" and escorts them toward Hill 656, where they are to act as an observation post for early warning of any enemy advance. Danvers is ordered to send an army historian, Lieutenant Parnell Murphy (Ken Berry), to accompany the fire team and write a report on its activity. Murphy is found helping local Korean children collect farm animals so that he can teach them the proper way to sing "Old MacDonald Had a Farm," and is sent on his way.

Murphy, a bright, affable, friendly man who dislikes military protocol and who calls everyone by their first name regardless of rank, joins the patrol as it reaches Hill 656, just after southern redneck Corporal Leroy Sprague (Warren Oates) takes offense at the black medic, Private Carver Le Moyne (Don Marshall), which leads to a fight between the two men. At dusk they are attacked by North Korean soldiers, who shoot and kill the patrol's youngest member, Private Jimmy Golden (Richard Young), but who are unable to take the hill after a fierce firefight. Murphy radios Danvers and learns that a major enemy force is advancing toward them, and that their current opposition is most likely a scouting patrol. The men become despondent when they hear American artillery destroy the bridge that they were to use as an escape route. In the middle of the night, the men bury Golden. Sprague starts another argument with

Le Moyne, so Bryce takes the southerner aside and slaps him into obedience.

The next morning, a North Korean sniper obtains a position overlooking Hill 656 and under his direction, a mortar attack ensues. The most cynical of the men is Corporal Bill Lukens (Jim Hutton); yet it is he who spots and shoots the sniper, saving the life of Private Sam Rivera (Trini Lopez). Sprague suggests that they surrender, but Murphy holds up a white flag as an example and it is shot to ribbons. During a firefight, the radio is knocked down the hill. Bryce tries to retrieve it and is shot in the head. Before anyone else can grab it, it is destroyed by enemy fire. Bryce is retrieved and bandaged; his wound is a potentially serious graze. Bryce turns control of the squad over to Murphy. After another mortar attack, Murphy faces down Sprague, who doesn't want to follow the inexperienced egghead, and puts an ancient battle plan into effect.

The North Koreans storm and overrun the hill. Nobody is there. The North Korean commander (Soon-Tek Oh) assumes the Americans have fled, and so sets off in pursuit. After they have left, the Americans emerge from what seemed to be shallow foxholes, in which they had covered and camouflaged themselves. They run down the hill heading north, the direction from which the North Koreans attacked. Finding no one on the south side of the hill, the North Korean commander revisits its crest and discovers evidence of the ruse. The North Koreans pursue the fleeing Americans. Sprague is shot and after some discussion, it is the black medic, Le Moyne, who rescues the redneck and carries him to safety.

Murphy and Rivera discover a North Korean radio, Murphy disguises his voice and, in Korean, orders an artillery strike on Hill 656. The North Koreans are caught unaware by their own artillery and are cut to pieces. Murphy learns from the radio that the enemy is building another bridge, to be used to launch an offensive against the American regiment. He orders his motley crew to destroy the bridge.

From a high vantage point, the ragtag American group watches a North Korean construction team put the finishing touches to a wooden bridge. The men snake down the hill, overpower and kill two guards and start a flatbed

The Reluctant Heroes

Starring Ken Berry

It was a funny way to win a war, but it certainly worked for these way-out warriors.

A World Premiere Movie of the Week

ⓐⓑⓒ 8:30 ⓻ ⑧

Comedy is stressed in this ad for the premiere of the ABC-TV movie The Reluctant Heroes (1971), *with the phrases "a funny way to win a war," and "way-out warriors." The movie itself, however is largely dramatic rather than comedic.*

truck. They drive toward the bridge, exploding fuel drums along the way, causing the enemy soldiers to abandon the bridge to fight. The truck stops just short of the bridge and each man fights his way across, spreading fuel onto the planking as he goes. Rivera throws a grenade to start a fire, but it is a dud. As the North Koreans begin to cross the bridge after them, Murphy fashions a molotov javelin, wrapping his undershirt around a stripped tree branch. He sets it on fire and Le Moyne throws it onto a patch of spilled fuel, igniting the bridge, which then explodes. Murphy, shirtless, and his men walk back to regiment headquarters, where they are received with astonishment by fellow G.I.s and Korean children.

The Reluctant Heroes is an old-fashioned war movie in which a bunch of misfits band together with one purpose and achieve the incredible. This type of plot has been recycled for generations and probably will continue to be forever. When written with strong situations, characters and motivations, it can be very effective. Unfortunately, this movie's situations are as often silly as they are dramatic and its characters are the barest stereotypes. The movie also suffers from a complete absence of subtlety.

The movie is watchable because familiar actors fit their stereotypical roles so well. Ken Berry, best known from the television shows *F Troop* and *Mayberry R.F.D.*, is well cast as effervescent historian Parnell Murphy, an unlikely action hero. Warren Oates plays redneck Leroy Sprague with his usual tenacity, although his friendliness after being shot and then rescued by Carver Le Moyne is not believable. At one point, after Sprague again thanks Le Moyne, Bill Lukens (Jim Hutton) says, "Leroy, if you get any sweeter, I'll get diabetes." Throughout the film, Lukens has wisecracks and asides for every situation, and Hutton delivers them with an effective deadpan delivery. Some are funny, some are probing or scathing, and some are just strange. There is an entire discussion about atheism as the men are burying Jimmy Golden and Lukens criticizes the men for trying to sanctify the occasion.

Cameron Mitchell is perfectly cast as the veteran sergeant Marion Bryce, and his performance is probably the best of the bunch. Don Marshall is solid as Carver Le Moyne, but the role of the put-upon medic is so standard and unremarkable that it is surprising the character is not killed. Trini Lopez plays Sam Rivera as worried and frightened — his is the most sensible reaction to their predicament — and Ralph Meeker is Captain Danvers, the conscientious officer. None of these actors are taxed in their roles.

Filmed on the backlot of Paramount Studios, the film never seems authentic, nor is it suspenseful. Its central gimmick, that Murphy can save the men with military tactics from past battles, is interesting but not effective enough to carry the film. That is because Murphy only works the trick once. Afterward, he destroys the enemy by ordering an artillery barrage in Korean, and the final battle at the bridge is not planned well at all. If Murphy had employed his knowledge of history more than once, the movie's perspective would be far more compelling.

It also suffers from an episodic nature. Every ten minutes or so, scenes build toward a specific moment of realization, and then the camera holds on someone and then fades out. Time for a commercial. Even without commercial breaks, such a structure becomes tedious and monotonous.

The film says nothing new about the Korean War. It could just as easily have been set in either of the two World Wars or Vietnam. Its characterization of the enemy is mostly faceless and unimpressive under any circumstances. The one aspect that rings true is the need for bridge bombing. In the mountainous region of Korea, bridges were important to both sides, at least during the summer months. The film's emphasis on the strategic value of bridges is true and correct.

The Reluctant Heroes remains enjoyable only because of its recognizable cast. It does follow in the footsteps of *MASH* in terms of some irreverence, particularly aimed at the military establishment, but it is rarely funny or even amusing. Though it was heavily advertised as a comedy, the film is definitely a drama, and not a very good one. It is punctuated by Sprague's acts of racism and bigotry, and surprisingly only Sergeant Bryce ever steps in to prevent bloodshed. None of the other soldiers ever says anything to stop Sprague, and just after Jimmy

Sergeant Marion Bryce (Cameron Mitchell, left), Corporal Leroy Sprague (Warren Oates, bottom), Lieutenant Parnell Murphy (Ken Berry, center) and Private Sam Rivera (Trini Lopez, right) attempt to deceive the enemy which surrounds them in the made-for-television movie The Reluctant Heroes *(1971).*

Golden tells Le Moyne that Sprague didn't mean anything by his racist remarks, the young private is killed. It's just another strange aspect to an odd and ultimately disappointing movie.

Retreat, Hell!

Credits: 1952. United States Pictures Productions. *Distributed by* Warner Bros. *Directed by* Joseph H. Lewis. *Produced by* Milton Sperling. *Screen Play by* Milton Sperling and Ted Sherdeman. *Story by* Milton Sperling. *Music by* William Lava. *Director of Photography:* Warren Lynch, A.S.C. *Film Editor:* Folmar Blangsted, A.C.E. *Art Director:* Edward Carrere. *Sound by* Francis J. Scheid. *Set Decorator:* William Wallace. *Technical Adviser:* Captain Benjamin S. Read, U.S.M.C. *Makeup Artist:* Gordon Bau. *Orchestrations:* Charles Maxwell. Not Rated. Black and White. Flat (1.33:1). 95 minutes. Partially filmed on location at Camp Pendleton, California. Released in February, 1952. Currently available on VHS home video.

Cast: *Colonel Steve Corbett,* Frank Lovejoy; *Captain Paul Hansen,* Richard Carlsen; *Private James W. McDermid,* Rusty (Russ) Tamblyn; *Ruth Hansen,* Anita Louise; *Sergeant Novak,* Ned Young; *Captain "Tank" O'Grady,* Lamont Johnson; *Shorty Devine,* Robert Ellis; *Andy Smith,* Paul Smith; *Major Knox,* Peter Ortiz; *Eve O'Grady,* Dorothy Patrick; *Captain Kyser,* Mort Thompson; *Lieutenant Ortiz,* Joseph Keane.

Historical Accuracy Level: High. While its characters are fictional, the story remains remarkably faithful to the general course of the Korean War.

Patriotic Propaganda Level: High. These Marines do not retreat, they merely attack in another direction!

Elements: Air War, Bugles, Marine Corps, Military Training, United Nations Forces, Winter Fighting.

The first cinematic attempt to chronicle some of the actual events of the Korean War was *Retreat, Hell!* Although its main characters are fictionalized, it faithfully follows the First Marine Division, which was involved in several key campaigns during the initial year of the war.

Filmed in and around Camp Pendleton, California, which is reputed to strongly resemble the hills of Korea, the film was made quickly and released just over a year after its events actually took place. The movie functions as propaganda, telling a rousing, inspiring story of Marine fortitude during the harshest of conditions, but does so with respect and humor that sweetens the mix considerably.

As the Korean War begins, the Marine Corps is called upon to furnish a division of men, and they must be provided in a hurry. Colonel Corbett (Frank Lovejoy) is rerouted from a train in Yugoslavia to oversee training, while in Denver, World War II veteran Captain Paul Hansen (Richard Carlson) is reactivated from the reserves. They meet at Camp Pendleton, California, where Corbett names Hansen the commander of Baker Company. Hansen objects, noting a lack of recent experience, but Corbett reminds the captain "You're a Marine, Hansen, and don't you forget it!" and places Sergeant Novak (Ned Young) at his disposal. Corbett's three companies are sent into the hills for training, where they learn how to advance with close air support and practice with flamethrowers, and grenades. One of the Marine recruits, Andy Smith (Paul Smith), defines a Marine as "a gas-operated, rain-cooled, spam-fed semi-automatic weapon who's never been known to have a stoppage," while another, boastful Jimmy McDermid (Russ "Rusty" Tamblyn) silently hopes that he'll be able to live up to his family's Marine tradition.

The men are shipped to Korea. En route, Corbett demands that Hansen learn each of his men's names, service record and capabilities. Corbett worries that because Hansen is married with a family, he will "play it safe," but fellow company commander Captain "Tank" O'Grady (Lamont Johnson) assures the colonel that Hansen will do his duty. The men arrive in time to participate in the Inchon landing. The Navy and Air Force bombard the port city of Inchon, "softening it up" for the Marines, who make an amphibious landing and climb the rocky seawall into Inchon. McDermid is frightened by a dead man who falls on top of him, and cannot bring himself to shoot. Under fire, Hansen delays moving his troops forward and is chastised by Corbett, who reminds him that casualties are

...Then a bunch of husky guys with star-spangled spunk took over!

WARNER BROS.

THE FIGHTIN'EST WORDS IN THE WHOLE FIGHTIN' HISTORY OF THE U. S. MARINES!

"Retreat, hell! We're just attacking in another direction!"
GEN. O. P. SMITH

FRANK LOVEJOY · RICHARD CARLSON · RUSTY TAMBLYN · ANITA LOUISE A UNITED STATES PICTURES PRODUCTION SCREEN PLAY BY MILTON SPERLING AND TED SHERDEMAN DIRECTED BY JOSEPH H LEWIS DISTRIBUTED BY WARNER BROS

Patriotism is the key to this rather sparse poster for Warner Bros.' drama Retreat, Hell! *(1952). General O.P. Smith's famous quote is included, along with character sketches of "husky guys with star-spangled spunk."*

unavoidable. Actual combat footage is shown from the capture of Inchon, mixed with scenes of the characters fighting and marching inland.

The drive continues into Seoul, the capital city of South Korea, where United Nations troops recapture the city, street by street. Hansen tells Jimmy McDermid that his brother is nearby, but the youngster isn't ready to see him because he has yet to prove himself. As Baker Company moves up a street, an enemy sniper halts their advance. McDermid risks his life by running forward under cover of Sergeant Novak, and eliminates the sniper with a grenade. The men continue up the street. Colonel Corbett joins them at a rest stop and talks to Hansen about family life. "I wish I had kids," the colonel says. "You have," replies Hansen, indicating the Marines. "They're all around you." Now proven in battle, McDermid goes in search of his brother, and finds him in a lineup of corpses behind the headquarters building.

Later, a Marine convoy heads into the hills of North Korea, into snow country. South Korean soldiers are among the fighting men, and southerner Andy Smith comments, "This is one war that makes sense. North against South. This time we're fighting on the right side." The men hear the rumor that the fighting will be over by Christmas. Marching up a road with the men near Yudam-ni, Corbett sees tank tracks in the snow. Before a warning can be issued, the men are attacked by men and a tank, which destroys jeeps and trucks. Corbett sends a bazooka team forward but they are killed. Corbett, Hansen and McDermid follow, grab the bazooka and destroy the tank with it while the other men rout the opposition. Corbett makes McDermid his personal driver, removing the youngster from Hansen's command. Captured enemy soldiers are revealed to be Chinese, and the colonel does not know what that means.

Fearing the worst, Hansen commands his

men to dig deep foxholes. McDermid is told that he is to be sent home, as he is the sole-surviving son in his family, but he does not want to go. He asks to spend his last night with Baker Company and is given permission to do so. That night, the Chinese make their first big push, blowing bugles and whistles to frighten and disrupt the U.N. soldiers, and attack en masse. Tank O'Grady is wounded when the Chinese overrun Able Company and Corbett himself shoots three enemy soldiers who swarm into the command tent. After suffering heavy losses, the Chinese retreat, signaled by more bugle blowing. The U.N. soldiers await replacement ammunition and supplies, praying that it arrives before the Chinese attack again. Dawn brings an airdrop of supplies just as the Chinese mount another attack, but Air Force jets bomb and strafe the enemy soldiers, forcing them back and giving the Marines time to rearm themselves.

Colonel Corbett is ordered to withdraw his troops, causing a nearby soldier to say, "You mean retreat?" Corbett replies hotly, "Retreat, Hell! We're just attacking in another direction! That's what the general said, and it's what I say." As Chinese riflemen watch, the Marines begin the long trek to the sea along a snowy, winding narrow road. Hansen is assigned to lead a patrol to chase snipers away; his men patrol the hills above the road. Sergeant Novak commands the Marines to keep moving and stamping their feet to avoid frostbite. A Chinese mortar battery knocks Novak unconscious and kills other men, but is destroyed. A group of British Royal Marines volunteers to patrol the hills and joins Hansen's men. Supplies are dropped to the men on the road, but the progress is slow. Wounded men, including Jimmy McDermid, are found in the hills and brought to the convoy, which finally reaches an airstrip from where the wounded can be evacuated. Corbett is shot and wounded, but orders the medics to patch his wounded arm. Hansen arrives unhurt after being missing and asks where battalion command is.

From his stretcher, Corbett sits up and plants Novak's rifle bayonet-first into the frozen ground. "Right here. Get out the word that the First Battalion forms here. Tell them that we're going to fight our way to the sea on the same road that we came up. If the enemy blocks our road, we'll smash through them. If they blast our bridges, we'll build new ones. If they try to stop us, we'll run right over them. We'll push them back with rifles, bayonets, grenades, our bare fists if we have to, but we're getting to the sea. And we're coming out fighting!"

U.S. planes bomb the hills surrounding the main road and a fighting montage is shown in which the Marines pull closer to their objective. They reach a sign marking four miles to Hamhung and are met by military policemen. Wounded men are transported forward on jeeps while the rest of the Marines, including Jimmy McDermid, Andy Smith and Sergeant Novak, file past on their way to well-deserved food and rest.

Retreat, Hell! uses fictional characters, but its framework faithfully follows the true story of the First Marine Battalion's battles in Inchon and Seoul and their historic withdrawal from the Chosin Reservoir area. The comment "Retreat, Hell! We're just attacking in another direction!" from whence the film derives its title, is a direct quote from General O. P. Smith. Here, Colonel Corbett speaks the words, attributing them to "the general." Thus, while the film does not *exactly* stick to the facts and does not identify the actual soldiers who inspired its story, it certainly adheres to the spirit of the Marines who fought and survived. One of Corbett's rousing speeches is quoted verbatim in the plot synopsis because it is so integral to the film's tone. Corbett's speeches do function as propaganda but they are also accurate depictions of an officer's determination to inspire his troops and keep them alive. History has proven that such determination was effective: some twenty thousand Marines marched into Hungnam and were safely evacuated.

That *Retreat, Hell!* is a tribute to the Marines and their indefatigable spirit is undeniable. The movie depicts the making of Marines through rigorous training methods and tough discipline. Although Marine standards are high, the film shows that men who are willing to follow orders without question and who are physically able to do the difficult work will not only survive, but prosper. Other armed forces also have "tribute" films, but few are as effective as *Retreat, Hell!* is for the Marines because most "tribute" films lack a true test for the men who

A trio of American soldiers, Captain Paul Hansen (Richard Carlson, left), Colonel Steve Corbett (Frank Love-
joy, center) and young Private Jimmy McDermid (Russ Tamblyn, billed as "Rusty" in the film, right), watch
the effects of a bazooka blast on the enemy in Retreat, Hell! *(1952).*

have trained. These Marines are impressive because they move from training directly into battle at Inchon, Seoul and the Chosin Reservoir.
When the film concludes, at the harbor of
Hungnam, the audience knows that these tired,
exhausted Marines will soon be rested and fighting once again against Communist aggression.

The film does not contain rhetoric about
the war; the filmmakers obviously felt that
American involvement was necessary and above
question. Some of the Marines gripe about conditions, and they all look forward to being
"home by Christmas," but none of them talk
about the war in political terms. The single link
to domestic life is the character of Hansen, the
captain called into active service against his
wishes from the reserve. Hansen would rather
not be in Korea, and Corbett worries that
Hansen will "play it safe," and act conservatively
rather than decisively, but Hansen takes his duties seriously and soon learns how to properly

run his company. The movie's philosophical
point is made with Hansen: that even a man
worried about his wife, family and business back
home will act honorably in a crisis for the greater
good.

Perhaps the film's greatest weakness is the
lack of depth of its characters. Hansen is sometimes more a symbol of conscience than a person, and his worrying ways do become gratingly
predictable. Corbett is a soldier's soldier, tough
as nails and impossible to kill. He is given a dynamic, forceful personality by veteran character
actor Frank Lovejoy, who delivered strong performances throughout the 1950s but just didn't
catch enough of the public's fancy to become a
major star. The youngster, Jimmy McDermid,
is a rather trite character, but Russ Tamblyn
brings the necessary energy and vitality to the
part. And as the veteran Sergeant Novak, Ned
Young is competent and trustworthy. The other
characters are not particularly important to the

plot; they represent a cross-section of Americans who found themselves fighting a war half a world away. What is important is the overall story of the Marines and how they faced the test of Korea.

The majority of Korean War films do not concern themselves with rendering accurate, truthful accounts of the action in Korea. Most are fictional by design, and a few of those that claim to be factual, such as *Inchon*, are less realistic than the fictional films. *Retreat, Hell!* is an honorable attempt to chronicle the action faced by the Marine First Battalion. By and large, it is a successful attempt.

Variety called the film "a topnotch war drama," while *Christian Century* noted its "vivid picture of suffering and courage of men in frustrating, unpleasant situations," and "convincing backgrounds and performances." In his book *The Great War Films*, author Lawrence J. Quirk describes *Retreat, Hell!* as "this excellent Korean War film" and especially likes "a superb sequence which depicts a night raid by the Chinese on the ramshackle Marine headquarters."

Joseph Roquemore, in his book *History Goes to the Movies*, also commends the film. "[Director Joseph H.] Lewis' blend of newsreel footage and scripted action delivers a first-rate account of the 1st Marines' Korean tour, from Inchon through the Chosin retreat. Dramatically weak in spots … but scrupulously accurate renditions of the Inchon landings, street fighting in Seoul, and withdrawal to Hungnam make *Retreat, Hell!* a must for Korean War aficionados."

Other Korean War films cover the Inchon landing and the withdrawal from the Chosin Reservoir to Hungnam, but only *Hold Back the Night* does so with the consistent accuracy of *Retreat, Hell!* Despite its stock characters and occasional jingoism, the film is highly engrossing and literate. The detail which is demonstrated in the battle scenes goes far to make the conflict real and authentic, and the film does not shirk from showing the devastating effects of war upon innocent civilians as well as the men who fight. This movie does not decry war, nor does it promote war. It simply shows war the way in which it was fought in Korea.

Return from the Sea
(aka *Home from the Sea*)

Credits: 1954. Allied Artists. *Directed by* Lesley Selander. *Produced by* Scott R. Dunlap. *Screen Play by* George Waggner. *From* Jacland Marmur's *Saturday Evening Post story* "No Home of His Own." *Music Composed and Conducted by* Paul Dunlap. *Director of Photography*: Harry Neumann, A.S.C. *Film Editor*: John C. Fuller, A.C.E. *Production Manager*: Allen K. Wood. *Technical Advisor*: Captain H. H. Connelly. *Assistant Director*: Austen Jewell. *Art Director*: David Milton. *Set Decorations by* Joseph Kish. *Recorded by* Ralph Butler. *Makeup Artist*: Edward Polo. *Hairdresser*: Mary Smith. *Wardrobe*: Bert Henrikson. *Set Continuity by* John L. Banse. *Special Effects by* Ray Mercer, A.S.C. Not Rated. Black and White. Flat (1.33:1). 79 minutes. Released in July, 1954. Not currently available on commercial home video.

Cast: *Frieda*, Jan Sterling; *Chief Petty Officer Charles MacLish*, Neville Brand; *Jimmy*, John Doucette; *Lieutenant Manley*, Paul Langton; *Spike*, John Pickard; *Tompkins*, Don Haggerty; *Smitty*, Alvy Moore; *Cecil Porter*, Robert Arthur; *Pinky*, Lloyd Corrigan; *Doctor*, Lee Roberts; *Harris*, Bill Gentry; *Clarke*, Robert Wood; *Captain*, Walter Reed; *Welch*, Robert Patten; *Barr*, James Best; *Doyle*, John Tarangelo; *with* Bert Arnold, Nick Stewart, Harry Landers and Don McShane.

Historical Accuracy Level: Low. This story is intended to represent good-hearted Navy men everywhere, but seems too far-fetched and unconvincing to accept.

Patriotic Propaganda Level: High. The movie's moral is that even Navy pugs such as MacLish deserve love, respect and happiness.

Elements: Air War, Bridge Bombing, Lonely Wives, Military Training, Navy (Sailors), Returning Home, Romance, Secret Missions, "Somewhere in Korea."

Return from the Sea is a typical example of the routine, pedestrian, low-budget dramas cranked out by small studios (in this case, Allied Artists) soon after the Korean War came to a conclusion. It is a generic war film, one which could have taken place during any international conflict, spotlighting a generic everyman as its main character and relating a bland, predictable

The advertising for Allied Artists' Return from the Sea *(1954) correctly spotlights the romance between wait-ress Frieda (Jan Sterling) and C.P.O. Charles MacLish (Neville Brand), even while dubiously exclaiming "It's the Navy's grandest story!" and not mentioning either World War II or the Korean War at all. Instead, it refers to "that* High and Mighty *blonde" and "that* Riot in Cell Block 11 *guy."*

formulaic plot with a bit of heroism and few surprises.

The film begins "Somewhere off the coast of Korea" (almost always a sign of poor quality entertainment to follow), on board the U.S. Navy destroyer *Morgan*. Chief Bosun's Mate Charles MacLish (Neville Brand) gives his camouflaged landing party final instructions regarding its mission to blow up a railroad bridge. Two boatloads of sailors row in and expertly demolish the bridge, encountering no interference, and saving a Korean family which was camped nearby. Back on the ship, news spreads that the *Morgan* is being sent to San Diego for a month's overhaul, thus providing the men with shore leave at home. They cheer.

In San Diego, MacLish drinks away some of his pay at a bar called "Pinky's" before a friendly waitress named Frieda (Jan Sterling) takes him home. She is attracted by his stated desire to settle down, because she has the same dream, which was shattered when her first husband was killed in the Pearl Harbor attack a decade earlier. She and former brother-in-law Jimmy (John Doucette) befriend MacLish and before long they are house-hunting. By the time the *Morgan* is ready to set sail, MacLish has put a down payment on Frieda's dream home (a yellow house surrounded by avocado trees) and combined their bank accounts.

On patrol in the seas near Korea, the *Morgan* hits an underwater mine and is attacked by North Korean planes. The ship is damaged, the Captain (Walter Reed) killed and MacLish is wounded in the legs in the battle, during which the ship shoots down three enemy aircraft. After some hospital rehabilitation, MacLish, now walking with a cane, is sent home to San Diego. He finds Frieda and they marry. MacLish is summoned back to the *Morgan* where he receives his retirement papers and a gift from the crew before being put ashore for good.

The focus of *Return From the Sea* is firmly on MacLish, one of the CPO's (chief petty officers) who, according to the film's prologue, are "the men who keep this [the Navy's] fighting spirit alive" and "who are responsible for the continuity of our naval tradition." MacLish is meant to be a regular guy, with regular dreams, as well as a hero. He has earned the respect of the ship's crew through hard work and he considers their safety his primary responsibility. But on shore, he's just another "big, homely guy," as Jimmy refers to him. Basing a movie on such an anonymous character is a bit risky, because unless the filmmakers and lead actor can inject some charisma or real drama into the part, the audience simply wouldn't care what happens to him. That, unfortunately, is what happens here.

Neville Brand had served in the U.S. Army for ten years and emerged the fourth most decorated soldier of World War II. He made his film debut in 1948 and most often portrayed Indians, gangsters or Army grunts. This was one of his few starring roles, simply because there weren't many leading parts calling for "big, homely guys." Brand fills his role physically and seems at home on the *Morgan*, but looks lost on land. His romantic clinches with Jan Sterling lack all chemistry and his dramatic skills are not at all impressive. Jan Sterling is slightly better, but her character's desire to spend the rest of her life with MacLish is never convincing.

To make matters worse, the rest of the movie is equally desultory, occasionally even inept. The stealthy mission which opens the movie calls for two boatloads of sailors to demolish a railroad bridge. Only one group of sailors visits the bridge; the others merely watch from the shoreline. No enemy forces guard the bridge, so the commandos' stealth is unnecessary, and furthermore, it is within binocular sight of the destroyer and its big guns. Why couldn't the ship just fire upon the target? Evidently, because the screenwriter said so. And when the bridge finally is destroyed, behind schedule, it is obviously a toy bridge exploded by a firecracker, photographed from a long distance.

As chief Bosun's mate, MacLish is responsible for training the new midshipmen of the crew. His first lesson consists of indicating the bow of the ship, and the stern of the ship to the new men. Wouldn't they have received this information at some time during their shore training?

The Navy's operations during the Korean War are not a popular movie subject. Except for the "air war" films based on aircraft carriers, the Navy is virtually invisible in Korean War films. This film is an effort to publicize the Navy's role

5402-52

C.P.O. Charles MacLish (Neville Brand, left) and Lieutenant Manley (Paul Langton, right) can only watch helplessly as more planes approach their already damaged destroyer off the coast of Korea in Return from the Sea *(1954). The planes they see, however, are their belated air cover.*

in the war, but it is not very exciting. The Navy's missions were largely of support, supplying long range artillery shelling, and personnel for shore raids. Because the North Korean Navy was virtually nonexistent throughout the war, the ships and submarines of the Navy patrolled Korean waters almost entirely unchallenged. It should be obvious, then, that Navy activity did not inspire many cinematic Korean War stories.

That is not to say that the subject is not worthwhile. Filmmakers should be able to fashion an engrossing story from a sailor's love of the sea and his reluctance to leave the life he loves for a woman's care or due to injury. But this particular film, especially once it puts its sailor on dry land, goes soft, losing the dramatic edge that it has at sea. The film's obvious intent is to present a typical Navy story featuring a "regular joe" because the Navy is filled with regular joes and this story is representative of their lives. If so, the Navy is full of brave, ugly men who get drunk and confused whenever they set foot on

solid ground. The Korean War setting is utilized only to insert some action into the proceedings; otherwise, the film could be a tenth-rate *Mister Roberts*. Well-meaning and occasionally authentic though the film is (much of it was filmed on the U.S.S. *Maddox*), it is also poorly made.

Largely ignored upon its 1955 release, the film was precisely targeted by *New York Times* critic Oscar Godbout. "It is so dull and without merit, that those who are seriously interested in seeing how a feature length, theatrical film should not be done, should go see it." He finished with this thought: "The most one can feel is pity and embarrassment at the production's sterile mediocrity." In its *Monthly Film Bulletin*, the British Film Institute concurred, calling the film "slight and unconvincing in substance, conventional in tone and characterisation, and with sentiment of a rather maudlin kind."

Return from the Sea has admirable intentions and some good location shooting on board the destroyer, but its drama is never as compelling as it is dull. These characters are nice people who deserve a nice future, but their movie is too … nice. A harder edge, at least on land, might have provided more drama and made the movie more entertaining. As it is, the film is simply and utterly ordinary.

Sabre Jet

Credits: 1953. Carl Krueger Productions. *Distributed by* United Artists. *Directed by* Louis King. *Produced by* Carl Krueger. *Associate Producer:* Harry Spitz. *Screenplay by* Dale Eunson and Katherine Albert. *Story by* Carl Krueger. *Music Composed and Conducted by* Herschel Burke Gilbert, S.C.A. *Director of Photography:* Charles Van Enger. *Aerial Photography:* Tom Tutwiler, A.S.C. *Film Editor:* Arthur H. Nadel, A.C.E. *Assistant Directors:* Emmett Emerson and Gilbert Mandelik (uncredited). *Art Director:* Jerome Pycha, Jr. *Set Decorations:* George Milo. *Wardrobe:* Oscar Rodriguez and Jackie Spitzer (uncredited). *Sound:* Jack Goodrich and Joel Moss (uncredited). *Assistant to the Producer:* Donald E. Baruch. *Make-up:* Dave Newell and Lou LaCava (uncredited). *Script Supervisor:* Bobbie Sierks. *Special Effects:* Dan Hays. *Negligees for Miss Gray and Miss Bishop Created by* Juel Park. *Music Director:* Irving Gertz (uncredited). *Technical Advisors for the U.S.A.F.:* Colonel Alfred G. Lambert, Jr.; Colonel Clay Tice, Jr.; Major William H. Wescott; and Major Frederick C. Blesse. Not Rated. Cinecolor. *Color Technician:* Roy Tripp (uncredited). *Color Consultant:* Cliff Shank. Flat (1.33:1). 96 minutes. Released in November 1953. Exterior scenes filmed at Nellis Air Force Base, Nevada. Not currently available on commercial home video.

Cast: *Colonel Gil Manton*, Robert Stack; *Jane Carter*, Coleen Gray; *General Robert E. Hale*, Richard Arlen; *Marge Hale*, Julie Bishop; *Lieutenant Colonel Eckert*, Leon Ames; *Helen Daniel*, Amanda Blake; *Lieutenant Crane*, Reed Sherman; *Lee Crane*, Lucille Knoch; *Sergeant Klinger*, Michael Moore; *Susan Crenshaw*, Kathleen Crowley; *Captain Bert Flanagan*, Jerry Paris; *Sergeant Cosgrove*, Johnny Sands; *Lieutenant Bill Crenshaw*, Tom Irish; *Betty Flanagan*,

Jan Shepard; *Major James Daniel*, Ray Montgomery; *Fuji*, Frank Kumagai; *with* Dickie Bellis, Walter Flannery.

Historical Accuracy Level: Medium. The situations in this drama ring true, but the lead characters and their romantic problems do not.

Patriotic Propaganda Level: High. These swooping jets and heroic pilots are poster boys for the Air Force, although, to be fair, the loneliness of their wives is also exposed.

Elements: Air Force, Air War, Journalism, Lonely Wives, Romance.

Of all the films which depict the air war in Korea, *Sabre Jet* is the only one which specifically examines the effect of war on the wives of the fighter jet pilots. The film's focus is divided between jet action in Korea's "MiG Alley" and domestic drama on the ground, with each affecting the other. In terms of intent, it is one of the more ambitious of Korean War films; in terms of execution, it is perhaps the most disappointing.

At the Itazuke Air Force Base in Japan, General Robert E. Hale (Richard Arlen) welcomes a female reporter, Jane Carter (Coleen Gray), who wants to write a story about "women who kiss their husbands goodbye in the morning and wait for them to come home at night. Only, their men haven't had a hard day at the office, they've had a hard day at war." Jane also has another reason for her visit: she wants to return to her estranged husband, Colonel Gil Manton (Robert Stack). He is not happy to see her, or to have their relationship become the gossip of the base.

Hale is surprised that Jane is Manton's wife, but Manton and his wife Marge (Julie Bishop) welcome Jane and throw a party for her so that she can meet the other wives on the base. Jane meets a few other couples and is surprised how well the women seem to be adjusted to the constant danger facing their husbands. She is informed that the Air Force was opposed to letting the pilots' wives stay at Itazuke, but a petition was signed by every woman with a husband and the Air Force wisely backed down. Pilot Bert Flanagan (Jerry Paris) stops by to announce that his wife Betty (Jan Shepard) has just had a baby. After the party, Manton chastises Jane for coming to Japan, and for putting

One of the few movies titled after a specific fighting machine, United Artists' drama Sabre Jet *(1953) features nice, understated artwork, which promises no action it cannot deliver. Curiously, the pilot pictured does not resemble Robert Stack, star of the picture. Ironically, however, the tagline reads "The high and mighty...," the title of an upcoming Stack film.*

her career ahead of her duty as a wife. Angry and tired of fighting, Jane promises to finish her story and then their marriage.

Manton proposes a massive assault against a MiG base near the Yalu River before the rainy season begins, and the mission is approved for two days hence. In the interim, regular missions

are conducted. Manton and Flanagan attack land and river targets, strafing railroads, barges and destroying an ammunition dump. Jane interviews Betty Flanagan and learns that Bert has only five missions left to fly before being rotated back to the States. General Hale orders Manton to spend some time with Jane and she whets his appetite for domestic life (and romance) before a cable from her newspaper spoils his amorous mood.

General Hale flies a reconnaisance mission alone, discovers that their assumed target is incorrect, radios the location of the actual target and is shot down by attacking MiG fighters. Jane witnesses another woman, Helen Daniel (Amanda Blake), lose control of her emotions under the stress, but Marge Hale believes her husband is still alive and refuses to give up hope. Marge's faith forces Jane to question her own actions; she stops work on her story and tries to reconcile with her husband. Manton takes command of the air squadron, and orders Jane to leave. The night before the big attack, neither he nor many of the wives can sleep.

Heavily-laden B-29 bombers take off first, followed by their F-86 Sabre jet and F-80 Shooting Star escorts. The Shooting Stars and B-29s wreak havoc on the North Korean airfield while the Sabres protect the bombers from enemy MiGs. Two B-29s are downed, as are Bert Flanagan's and Bill Crenshaw's (Tom Irish) Sabre jets. Manton downs the MiG which killed Flanagan and Crenshaw. At Itazuke field, the pilots' wives anxiously await the return of their husbands. Thirteen Sabre jets return, although sixteen had departed. Susan Crenshaw (Kathleen Crowley) is devastated. Jane and Gil Manton meet at the gate and embrace, brought together at last by shared danger, sorrow and need for each other.

Sabre Jet begins with this prologue: "This picture is dedicated to the Air Force wives who shared their men with a world made desperate by the most brutal aggressor in history." This rhetoric indicates the simple level of the script. Its premise is dramatically solid and definitely promising, but the interaction between characters is stereotypical and awkward, particularly between Colonel Manton and his wife.

Colonel Manton's character is without doubt the most poorly conceived. An able flier, he is unable to abide his wife's success, and has completely soured on the marriage. His personal unhappiness has bled into his flying and leadership roles in the Air Force as well. Most commanders would ground this sourpuss without hesitation, but here, he is the most crucial man in the air squadron. Manton is played woodenly

by Robert Stack, who acts as if his favorite pet had recently died. In later films with director Douglas Sirk, notably *Written on the Wind* and *The Tarnished Angels*, Stack perfected his brooding, world-weary pessimism, but here he merely seems petulant.

The other characters offer little improvement. General Hale seems like a personable, reasonable commander until he insists on flying a dangerous reconnaissance mission alone (a no-no in the Air Force, which insists on teamwork). Bert Flanagan is happy to have fathered a baby, but nearing the end of his tour in Korea, he is also the obvious sacrificial lamb. The other fliers are bland and insignificant to the story.

The women are the focus, but they, too, are shortchanged by the script. The plight of lonely wives waiting for their husbands to return from dangerous missions is one with plenty of inherent drama and tension; unfortunately, it is also one which easily degenerates into cliché and melodrama. The wives of *Sabre Jet* fulfill those clichés, keeping up brave fronts while their husbands are nearby, chatting gaily to ignore the constant tension, and waiting nervously for their men to return. In their *Motion Piction Guide*, Jay Robert Nash and Stanley Ralph Ross make note that "the pilots and wives' stories are simplistic and melodramatic," and they are correct. The writers have chosen the path of least resistance for their characters; the result is that those characters are neither fresh nor authentic.

Even when its drama is fully formed, the script manages to undermine its effect. Jane is writing a human interest story concerning the pilots' waiting wives and goes about doing so very professionally. Such a story is certainly a valid one (producer Carl Krueger was reportedly inspired by such a feature article), yet Jane eventually abandons her task in the face of her husband's opposition and her growing identification with the role of Air Force wife. At one point, she refuses to become "a little slave to bring your slippers and light your pipe," yet that is precisely what occurs when she relinquishes her career in deference to his. The story would have been better served if Jane had finished and submitted the story, and then resigned from the newspaper to stay with her husband.

Another example is the reaction of General

Concerned and anxious wives of Air Force fighter pilots in Japan wait outside the airfield gate for their husbands to return from missions over Korea in Sabre Jet *(1953). The gate is printed with these words: "Through these portals pass the best jet pilots in the world."*

Hale's wife after his jet is shot down. She is certain he is still alive, leading viewers to believe that she is right and he will return to the story intact. Despite the odds that Hale was killed, Colonel Eckert (Leon Ames) reinforces Marge's faith when he reveals that the Air Force brass think Hale may have been able to bail out and presumably could still be alive. Common sense dictates that the general, attacked and shot down by MiG fighters while alone and unarmed, would not survive. Yet the script stubbornly refuses to permanently eliminate its warmest character.

Another problem is the repeated use of stock battle footage that does not match the movie's fictional story. Most obvious are scenes which allege destruction of specific targets, and then show stock footage of completely different targets being destroyed. The prime example of this is the climactic attack on a North Korean airfield. Some of the targets in the stock footage

used during this sequence have seemingly little to do with airfields. The aircraft which are seen to be attacked and destroyed are propeller-driven planes from World War II. It is a difficult and tedious process to mix the two types of film together believably, but this is a poor sample of such editing.

The editing is also suspect in the sequence when the squadron of F-80 Shooting Stars led by Colonel Manton returns to Itazuke. Almost all of the planes land without fuel pods at the ends of their wings (they are jettisoned when emptied), but as they taxi back to their ready positions, the fuel pods magically reappear. At least the jets are real, even if the principal actors merely climb into and out of them. All scenes pertaining to Itazuke Air Force Base and the North Korean airfield were filmed at Nellis Air Force Base in Nevada, with the full cooperation of the Air Force, which also provided producer Carl Krueger with the color combat footage.

Sabre Jet was introduced at a world premiere in Dayton, Ohio, during a national aircraft show, on September 3, 1953. Along with principal cast members, nine Korean War jet aces were in attendance, including Joseph D. McConnell, Jr., whose own exploits above Korea were dramatized in *The McConnell Story* just two years later.

Despite the huge publicity created by United Artists, the movie was found wanting. Bosley Crowther of the *New York Times* concluded that "The [film's] notion is very tender but the drama is eminently dull." *Newsweek*'s reviewer agreed. "The Cinecolor film has no special illumination to shed on the realities of pain, loss and compassion." *Time*'s critic complained about the coloring process: "The Cinecolor is something to see — all the blondes look like redheads, and the redheads are purple."

The only other note of interest is the title itself. *Sabre Jet* is one of the very rare movies to be named after an actual aircraft (another, *Bombers B-52*, is also a Korean War movie). The F-86 Sabre, built by North American, premiered in 1949 and, along with the F-80 Shooting Star, quickly became identified with the Korean conflict. Nearly ten thousand Sabres were produced, and the jet ultimately served in the air forces of thirty-one countries. As noted, it is one of just a few types of aircraft immortalized in the title of a feature film, yet it would have been better served with a better movie.

Sayonara

Credits: 1957. William Goetz Productions. *Distributed by* Warner Bros. *Directed by* Joshua Logan. *Produced by* William Goetz. *Screen Play by* Paul Osborn. *Based on the Novel by* James A. Michener. *Music by* Franz Waxman. *Director of Photography:* Ellsworth Fredricks, A.S.C. *Film Editors:* Arthur P. Schmidt, A.C.E. and Philip W. Anderson. *Art Director:* Ted Haworth. *Sound by* M. A. Merrick. *Set Decorator:* Robert Priestly. *Costumes Designed by* Norma Koch. *Orchestrations:* Leonid Raab. *Assistant Director:* Ad Schaumer. *Production Associate:* Walter Thompson. *Second Unit Photography:* H. F. Koenekamp, A.S.C. *Dialogue Coach:* Joseph

Curtis. *Makeup Supervisor:* Gordon Bau, S.M.A. *Dialogue Coach for Marlon Brando:* Carlo Fiori. *Matsubayashi Girls Revue Numbers Supervised by* LeRoy Prinz. *Technical Advisor for Japanese Theatre Scenes:* Masaya Fuyima. *Song* "Sayonara (Goodbye)" *by* Irving Berlin. Not Rated. Technicolor. Technirama (2.35:1). 147 minutes. Released in December, 1957. Filmed on location in Kobe, Kyoto, Tokyo and Osaka, Japan. Currently available on VHS home video and DVD. Previously available on laserdisc.

Cast: *Major Lloyd Gruver*, Marlon Brando; *Eileen Webster*, Patricia Owens; *Airman Joe Kelly*, Red Buttons; *Hana-ogi*, Miiko Taka; *Nakamura*, Ricardo Montalban; *Mrs. Webster*, Martha Scott; *Katsumi*, Miyoshi Umeki; *Captain Mike Bailey*, James Garner; *General Webster*, Kent Smith; *Colonel Craford*, Douglas Watson; *Fumiko-san*, Reiko Kuba; *Teruko-san*, Soo Yong; *Consul*, Harlan Warde (uncredited); *with* the Shochiku Kagekidan Girls Revue.

Level of Historical Accuracy: Medium. Though the Korean War is merely a backdrop, the main story involving American men loving and marrying Japanese women is timely and important, genuinely reflecting the era.

Patriotic Propaganda Level: Low. The film portrays the armed services as hopelessly behind the times and unwilling to place the happiness of their personnel ahead of their outdated rules and regulations.

Elements: Air Force, Japan, Marine Corps, Musical Performance, Racism, Romance.

James A. Michener wrote two best-selling books which were made into films that concerned the Korean War: *The Bridges at Toko-Ri* and *Sayonara*. Though *Sayonara* was originally a novel of World War II, filmmakers Joshua Logan and William Goetz updated its era to the Korean War for greater timeliness. America's use of Japan for military bases and as a staging area for the Korean War also lent credibility to Michener's storyline; after World War II, some ten thousand American servicemen defied existing regulations to marry Japanese women. Michener's book, and this extremely popular movie, encouraged the armed services to reconsider and rewrite regulations which prohibited such marriages, and they were eventually changed to reflect greater tolerance and understanding.

In 1951 Korea, Air Force fighter pilot Major

Lloyd Gruver (Marlon Brando) lands his Sabre jet after destroying his eighth and ninth MiG fighters. Rather than feeling jubilant, however, Gruver is distracted by having seen the face of an enemy pilot before killing him. Gruver's introspection ends when he hears that he is being sent to Japan at the special request of General Webster. Before he leaves, Gruver is asked to convince one of his men, Airman Joe Kelly (Red Buttons), to reconsider his request to marry a Japanese woman. Gruver does so, indicating that such an interracial relationship would subject a couple to harsh treatment. At one point Gruver loses his temper and refers to Kelly's fiancée as a "slant-eyed runt," but he quickly and sincerely apologizes. As both men arrive at Itake Air Base in Japan, Kelly asks Gruver to be his best man, and seeing that Kelly will not alter his decision, Gruver reluctantly accepts.

Gruver is met at the air base by General Webster (Kent Smith), his wife (Martha Scott) and their daughter Eileen (Patricia Owens), to whom Gruver is engaged. Eileen quickly falls in love with Japan, and introduces Gruver (and the audience) to various aspects of its history and culture. She also questions why Gruver has not yet pressured her to marry him, and begins to wonder if they will marry. Joe Kelly does marry Katsumi (Miyoshi Umeki), with Gruver serving as best man, in an uncomfortable ceremony during which the chaplain expresses his displeasure. Upon questioning from Gruver, he admits that some ten thousand servicemen have ignored the rule against interracial marriage. Later, however, Gruver is criticed by General Webster and (especially) his wife, neither of whom is in favor of mixed marriages. Mrs. Webster asks Gruver point blank if he is going to marry her daughter, and he cannot answer her. Eileen avoids making a date with him, not wanting to be forced into his arms by her parents.

At a bar, Gruver bumps into Marine Corps captain Mike Bailey (James Garner), whom Gruver had witnessed trying unsuccessfully to bring a Japanese woman into an Americans-only club. Gruver and Bailey become friends and soon trade life histories. Bailey takes Gruver to see where the Matsubayashi girls — famous theatrical performers — live, train and rehearse. Bailey makes a date with his girl, Fumiko-san (Reiko Kuba), while Gruver is immediately

smitten with the show's leading lady, Hana-ogi (Miiko Taka). With spare time on his hands because his job (wangled by General Webster) in Japan is insubstantial, Gruver begins waiting around the Matsubayashi Bridge for Hana-ogi to appear. One day, watching from a distance, he sees that she notices he is not there, and then he knows that she is interested in him. They are finally introduced at Kelly's house, by Katsumi. Hana-ogi has hated Americans since her father and brother were killed in World War II, but she soon melts in Gruver's arms and grows to love him.

Katsumi, Kelly and Hana-ogi teach Gruver about Japanese culture, and soon he is spending all of his time at Kelly's house in a kimono. Meanwhile, Colonel Craford (Douglas Watson) is trying to end American fraternization with Japanese women and complains to General Webster about both Kelly and Gruver. Eileen goes to Kelly's and talks to her fiancé, warning him about Craford's interest. And in a roundabout manner, without precisely saying so, Eileen and Gruver end their romantic involvement. Gruver and Hana-ogi begin their affair in earnest, while Eileen begins spending time with master kabuki performer Nakamura (Ricardo Montalban!).

Colonel Craford announces transfers of men back to the States; all of the men have Japanese wives who must be left behind in Japan. Kelly and Gruver protest, but Craford is insistent, even after he learns that Katsumi is pregnant. Moreover, he orders Kelly's house off-limits to all personnel, including Kelly. Gruver appeals to General Webster, but the general reluctantly agrees with Craford's action, despite Eileen's protests. Gruver tells the Websters he will soon be in the same position as Kelly, because he is planning to marry Hana-ogi. Eileen is angry at her parents' obstinacy and interference and goes to Nakamura for consolation. Kelly refuses to tell his wife about his transfer, hoping to find some resolution. The two couples return home to find Kelly's house being sealed by military policemen, and Gruver is taken into custody. He is told by Webster that he is being transferred back to America and is confined to quarters.

Two military policemen ask Gruver to help find Kelly, who has disappeared. Disregarding

"I am not allowed to love. But I will love you if that is your desire."

MARLON BRANDO AND AN EXQUISITE NEW JAPANESE STAR. THE'
LIVE JAMES A. MICHENER'S STORY OF DEFIANT DESIRE. IT IS CALLED

SAYONARA

FILMED IN JAPAN IN TECHNIRAMA® AND TECHNICOLOR® PRESENTED BY WARNER BROS.

CO-STARRING
PATRICIA OWENS · RED BUTTONS · RICARDO MONTALBAN   MIIKO TAKA
MARTHA SCOTT · MIYOSHI UMEKI · JAMES GARNER

PRODUCED BY   DIRECTED BY   BASED ON THE NOVEL BY   SCREEN PLAY BY
WILLIAM GOETZ · JOSHUA LOGAN · JAMES A. MICHENER · PAUL OSBORN
SONG SAYONARA WORDS AND MUSIC BY IRVING BERLIN · MUSIC BY FRANZ WAXMAN

The forbidden love between Japanese geisha Hana-ogi (Miiko Taka) and U.S. Air Force pilot Lloyd Gruver (Marlon Brando) takes center stage in Warner Bros.' drama Sayonara *(1957).*

his ordered confinement, Gruver takes Bailey with him to Kelly's house, which is surrounded by a crowd of Japanese. Inside, they find Kelly and Katsumi dead, lying together on a bed, hav-

ing committed suicide. A riot begins as Gruver and Bailey leave the house, but they escape unharmed. Gruver searches for Hana-ogi, but she has been sent to Tokyo, to perform in the troupe there. Back in confinement, Gruver is told by Webster that a new law will pass in a month or so which will allow servicemen to bring their foreign-born wives to America with them. However, the news arrives too late for Kelly and Katsumi.

Gruver flies to Tokyo and corners Hana-ogi at the theatre, demanding to know whether she loves him or not. She admits her feelings, but protests that her life is planned and that she has obligations to fulfill. Gruver says, "We've been wasting two good lives trying to do the right thing," and begs her to do the right thing by him. He waits outside for her answer, surrounded by Japanese fans and American reporters. Hana-ogi joins Gruver and tells the crowd that he has asked her to marry him. She publicly agrees to his proposal and the couple drive away to their new life together.

Sayonara is a heartfelt plea for tolerance. The central theme, adapted from the opera *Madame Butterfly*— that mixed-race marriages should be accepted without reservation — is represented by two couples: Gruver/Hana-ogi and Kelly/Katsumi. Kelly's marriage ends in disaster because of the prejudicial stance of the armed forces, which is considerably weakened at story's end by the likelihood of a new law allowing foreign-born wives of Americans to enter the United States. Gruver's upcoming marriage looks to be happier, though not without obstacles, because the couple has seen firsthand the damage that can be caused by racial prejudice. In addition, two other couples, Bailey/Fumiko-san and Nakamura/Webster, indicate that social barriers are being overcome even when the couples may not have marriage in mind as an end result.

The fight against racial discrimination became a personal cause for writer James Michener, who had extensively toured the islands of the South Pacific, and written about their peoples, whom he greatly admired. The year after *Sayonara*'s publication, Michener himself married a Japanese woman (his third marriage), Mari Yoriko Sabusawa, with whom he remained until her death in 1994. This was also a cause close to star Marlon Brando's heart; he had always been drawn to exotic women, a few of whom he would eventually marry, and he had just finished playing a Japanese man in *Teahouse*

of the August Moon and found himself eager to return to Japan and its culture. It was Brando who insisted on Hana-ogi's acceptance of Gruver's love at the finale; Michener's book ends with the two lovers parting. And though Brando's insistence makes the moral point that two people who love each other should remain together despite social opposition, his decision also provides the film with a conventional happy ending, ensuring larger, satisfied crowds at the box office.

Director Joshua Logan and writer Paul Osborn (along with rumored help from Brando) also balance the script by showing Japanese opposition to mixed marriages as well. In fact, Japanese opposition is viewed as stronger; Hana-ogi risks dismissal from the Matsubayashi troupe and is transferred rather than dismissed only because of her immense popularity. The fate which befalls Kelly and Katsumi is predestined by their viewing of the famous Bunraku Mitsuwa puppet show "The Love Suicides of Amijima." As expressed by Katsumi, "It is customary for lovers to die together when they can no longer face life." Ultimately, Kelly truly accepts the Japanese way, sharing death with his beloved rather than facing life alone without her.

Some critics carped that the movie's stance was outdated, as the armed forces were already loosening their regulations, but the film stands against more than prejudicial regulations. *Sayonara* is a basic appeal to people to look past other people's appearances and to respect cultures other than their own. Films set and actually lensed in Japan began appearing in 1951 (the Korean War film *Geisha Girl* was the first to be entirely filmed in Japan), but most efforts tended to ridicule (either slyly or overtly) Japanese customs. *Sayonara* is really the first film to seriously explore post-war Japan, and it does so without forcing its Japanese characters into caricatures.

Along with such projects as *The Defiant Ones, Twelve Angry Men, Love Is a Many-Splendored Thing, Bad Day at Black Rock* and *The Diary of Anne Frank*, this movie proved that Hollywood filmmakers could tackle the serious subjects of prejudice and bigotry and present them in ways that were dramatically compelling. These films are proof that filmmakers could include powerful, socially significant themes in their work and that audiences would embrace

From left to right, Major Lloyd Gruver (Marlon Brando), Hana-ogi (Miiko Taki), Katsumi (Miyoshi Umeki) and Airman Joe Kelly (Red Buttons) watch a Japanese puppet show with grave implications in Sayonara *(1957).*

those films which affected them intellectually as well as emotionally. All of these films are both popular and critically acclaimed, garnering Academy Award nominations (and wins), and while not all of them are great movies, their arguments for tolerance and understanding make all of them important.

Sayonara has other assets. Technically, it is exceedingly well made, with gorgeous widescreen cinematography and exquisitely detailed art direction/set decoration which captures the serene beauty of the film's lovely Japanese locations. Director Joshua Logan includes as many glimpses of Japan's artistic culture as possible, which is the main reason the film lasts two-and-a-half hours. Scenes of puppet theatre, kabuki theatre and revue dance are performed for the main characters, and thus, the movie's audience. The film even details Japanese table manners, further demonstrating the contrasts between Japanese and American lifestyles.

Some viewers may feel that the film is sexist. It is true that Katsumi seems to have little will of her own, and even plans at one point to have her eyelids surgically altered to resemble those of American women, but the other female characters are each strong and self-sufficient. Hana-ogi, though restricted by her role as a Matsubayashi dancer, breaks her organization's rules and makes the decision to love and marry Gruver despite the professional risk. Eileen Webster basically presents Gruver with an ultimatum, and when he does not respond positively, finds someone else for comfort. Mrs. Webster, though obviously the most bigoted person in the story, is also strong-willed and seemingly makes some of the decisions attributed to her husband the general. Therefore, it would be wrong to label the film as sexist, though the position of women in Japan is obviously different than it is in the U.S.

The Korean War is background to the love

stories, but it is important. Gruver is an ace, having destroyed nine enemy jets, and is described as the Air Force "pin-up boy." His most recent "kill" involved seeing the other pilot's face, an image which disturbs the fighter pilot. Gruver thinks long and hard about the fact that his other kills had faces, too. This introspection marks the beginning of Gruver's sensitivity. If the pilot had not been affected by seeing one of his foreign-born victims close-up, he would not be receptive to the possibility of interracial contact. Gruver's thoughts are brought into focus by Kelly, who is adamant in his battle to marry Katsumi, and it is Gruver's acceptance of Katsumi as Kelly's bride — and his gentle marriage kiss of Katsumi — which leads to his affair with Hana-ogi. The film's very stance against prejudice makes it an anti-war film, arguing that peace between races can and must be pursued.

Sayonara was a huge hit, making more than $10 million for Warner Bros., and while that amount seems tiny now, in 1958 the film's gross only trailed that of *Peyton Place* and *The Bridge on the River Kwai*. It was nominated for ten Academy Awards, including best picture, and won in four categories. Red Buttons and Miyoshi Umeki each won supporting performer awards, while the film won the art direction-set decoration and sound categories. Red Buttons also won a Golden Globe award as best supporting actor, while James Garner was listed as one of three most promising newcomer — male(s) at the Golden Globe awards for his role.

Marlon Brando is sensitive and believable as Lloyd Gruver, though his Southern accent (adopted to increase the character's perceived level of prejudice) wears thin over time. It's an interesting characterization because Gruver is occasionally loutish, especially early in the story. Gruver matures throughout, becoming more introspective and sensitive. Leading lady Miiko Taka had no previous acting experience, which sometimes shows, but she also has the star quality needed for the character. Red Buttons and Miyoshi Umeki are excellent, and James Garner is very appealing in his first good role. Patricia Owens is also very good as Eileen Webster, even though her role is the most conventional. An oddity in the cast is Ricardo Montalban, who is inexplicably cast as the kabuki master, Nakamura. Though his performance cannot be

faulted, his casting in the role is misguided and does lessen the significance of Eileen's attraction to the character.

Perhaps surprisingly, many critics panned the film. *Time*'s reviewer felt that "*Sayonara* is a modern version of *Madame Butterfly* which has gained in social significance, but lost its wings — Puccini's music," and complained about Marlon Brando's accent, which "sounds as if it was strained through Stanislavsky's mustache." The British Film Institute's *Monthly Film Bulletin* found that "Not only has the ending of James Michener's novel been reversed, but the whole theme has been emasculated," and opined that "Conflict is reduced to the most facile terms." *Newsweek*'s critic was bored. "The pair [Gruver and Hana-ogi] spend most of two and one-half hours frozen in a dreadful standstill, debating whether to marry." And absolutely no one enjoyed Irving Berlin's screechy title song.

On the other side of the coin, *Variety* dubbed it "a picture of beauty and sensitivity," and Bosley Crowther of the *New York Times* called it "this beautiful, sentimental tale" and highly praised Marlon Brando's performance. Jay Robert Nash and Stanley Ralph Ross summarized *Sayonara* this way: "This updating of the *Madame Butterfly* theme remains a powerful story, well told with a statement on racial prejudice that remains timeless." Over time, the film's critical reputation has increased slightly, though its popularity has certainly diminished. Today, it stands as a well-intentioned and well-crafted entreaty to bring to an end intolerance and prejudice. The film is overlong, but its message remains timeless and its drama compelling.

Sergeant Ryker

(aka *The Case Against Paul Ryker*; *The Case Against Sergeant Ryker*; *Torn Between Two Values*)

Credits: 1968. Roncom Films. *Distributed by* Universal. *Directed by* Buzz Kulik. *Produced by* Frank Telford. *Associate Producers*: Joel Rogosin and Jo Swerling, Jr. *Screenplay by* Seeleg Lester and William D. Gordon. *Story by* Seeleg Lester. *Music by* Johnny (John) Williams. *Director of Photography*: Walter Strenge, A.S.C.

Film Editor: Robert B. Warwick, A.C.E. *Art Director*: John J. Lloyd. *Set Decorations*: John McCarthy and Robert C. Bradfield. *Sound*: Waldon O. Watson and William Lynch. *Assistant Director*: John Clarke Bowman. *Titles by* Universal Title and Optical. *Makeup*: Bud Westmore. *Hair Stylist*: Larry Germain. *Cosmetics by* Cinematique. *Music Supervision by* Stanley Wilson. Not Rated. Pathe Color. Flat (1.33:1). 86 minutes. Originally filmed in 1963 as "The Case Against Paul Ryker" for *Kraft Suspense Theatre*. Released in February, 1968. Currently available on VHS videotape.

Cast: *Sergeant Paul William Ryker*, Lee Marvin; *Captain David Young*, Bradford Dillman; *Major Frank Whitaker*, Peter Graves; *Ann Ryker*, Vera Miles; *General Amos Bailey*, Lloyd Nolan; *Captain Leonard Appleton*, Murray Hamilton; *Sergeant Max Winkler*, Norman Fell; *Colonel Arthur Merriam*, Walter Brooke; *President of the Court-Martial*, Francis DeSales; *Corporal Jenks*, Don Marshall; *Major Kitchener*, Charles Aidman.

Historical Accuracy Level: Low. This story of a traitorous American soldier in Korea is complete and utter fiction.

Patriotic Propaganda Level: Medium. The only group which this movie promotes are the Judge Advocate General lawyers, who solve crimes and dabble in romance.

Elements: Army, Collaboration, Courts-Martial, Espionage, Mystery, Romance, Secret Missions.

Sergeant Ryker is one of the few Korean War films to explore the areas of collaboration and treason, and is the second film featuring Lee Marvin to do so, following *The Rack*. Originally conceived as a two-part episode of NBC's hour-long anthology series the *Kraft Suspense Theatre*, "The Case Against Paul Ryker" had aired on October 10th and 17th of 1963 as *Kraft*'s premiere episode and garnered good reviews and ratings. Five years later, after Marvin's rise to stardom, Universal Studios decided to edit the two-part episode into a releasable feature film to further exploit Marvin's appeal.

Sergeant Ryker begins during the Korean War in 1951. Sergeant Paul William Ryker (Lee Marvin) has been tried and convicted of treason — for collaborating with the North Koreans — and sentenced to death. His wife Ann

(Vera Miles) arrives in Tokyo, where Ryker's military trial is to take place, and persuades prosecuting attorney Captain David Young (Bradford Dillman) to investigate the case on his own, despite orders to the contrary from his boss, Major Frank Whitaker (Peter Graves).

In Seoul, Captain Young and Ann persuade Sergeant Max Winkler (Norman Fell) to help locate the personal belongings of Colonel Chambers, the officer who Ryker claims sent him on a secret mission in North Korea but was killed before Ryker's return. Later, during a confrontation with General Bailey (Lloyd Nolan) and Whitaker, Young puts forth his case to have Ryker's imminent execution at least delayed. Bailey listens to Young's evidence, including the discovery that Chambers' body was not in its grave, and grants Ryker not only a stay of execution, but a new trial, and this time appoints Young as Ryker's *defense* lawyer. Whitaker vows to prosecute the case himself.

Late at night Young visits Ann Ryker to inform her of the retrial; their conversation turns personal and Ann confesses that she loves him more than her husband. As they kiss, General Bailey enters the scene and orders Young to be court-martialed as well, after the new Ryker trial is concluded.

The trial begins. Witnesses support the army's position that Ryker defected to the North Koreans and was returning as a North Korean spy. Flashbacks reveal some of Ryker's initial interrogation upon his return by Captain Appleton (Murray Hamilton) and Young's discovery of Chambers' empty coffin. Two surprise witnesses testify that Ryker knew a current North Korean general when they attended college together back in the States and that Ryker helped that current general interrogate American prisoners of war as a North Korean official.

Young puts Ryker on the stand. Under Whitaker's accusatory cross-examination, Ryker loses his temper, damning himself in the eyes of his judges. When all hope for Ryker seems lost, Winkler innocuously tells Young that he also had a secret assignment from Colonel Chambers, who was concerned about an information leak in his department. With a new lead, Young goes to work. The next day, with General Bailey present, Young recalls Winkler, who tells of his secret assignment to check on a Korean

COMMIE MAJOR...
OR U.S. SERGEANT?
There's a bullet at one end...and a
hangman's noose at the other!

UNIVERSAL
PRESENTS

LEE MARVIN
EXPLODES INTO ACTION AS
"SERGEANT RYKER"

CO-STARRING
BRADFORD DILLMAN · VERA MILES · PETER GRAVES · LLOYD NOLAN

SCREENPLAY BY   STORY BY   DIRECTED BY   PRODUCED BY
SEELEG LESTER and WILLIAM D. GORDON · SEELEG LESTER · BUZZ KULIK · FRANK TELFORD

Based upon the TV Production
"THE CASE AGAINST SERGEANT RYKER"   A UNIVERSAL PICTURE IN COLOR

Though this Universal drama features almost no action at all, the marketing for Sergeant Ryker *(1968) promises plenty. The poster has a distinct resemblance to that of Lee Marvin's previous film* The Dirty Dozen, *in which Marvin truly "explodes into action."*

woman whom Appleton has been seeing. Appleton testifies that he has been keeping company and drinking with this woman; Young then notes that the lady in question has just asked for political asylum at the Soviet embassy, proving that Appleton was the leak that Chambers was so worried about. The defense rests and Ryker is acquitted of treason. After the trial, Ann tells Young that Ryker will never be fully believed despite the acquittal and that she must stay with him. Bailey congratulates Young on plugging the information leak and saving the life of a war hero.

Sergeant Ryker, which has also been released on videotape as *Torn Between Two Values*, is similar in subject to Marvin's earlier film *The Rack*, which starred Paul Newman as the accused soldier and which also had its origins in a television play. Both of these dramas examine dark issues of war — treason and collaboration — although *Ryker* is more of a legal drama of military justice than *The Rack*'s psychological exploration of a soldier under duress. The issue of American soldiers collaborating with the North Koreans and Chinese during the Korean War was a new and disturbing concept to Americans. While *The Rack* dramatizes one soldier's plight, *Sergeant Ryker* focuses on the legal and military implications of a soldier's alleged collaboration.

Very little is revealed about Ryker's alleged treason; he seems to have changed sides simply in order to renew an old friendship with an influential North Korean officer. Upon his return, Ryker does not reveal any secret discoveries or admit that he has learned anything of any importance. Furthermore, the idea that Colonel Chambers would not have left some physical authorization of Ryker's subterfuge is ludicrous and unbelievable. Ryker's "secret mission" is dubious at best; thankfully, it does not obscure the film's target, which is the sensibility of justice in the armed services.

The film offers a fascinating glimpse of military justice. It is very even-handed, depicting the shortcomings of the military court-martial system as well as the noble search for truth. The character of General Bailey, in particular, is representative of such justice: tough, no-nonsense, but ultimately fair and willing to consider all the facts. And like the court-martials in *The Caine Mutiny* and *The Rack*, *Sergeant Ryker*'s also

focuses on the defense of someone who is accused of a crime so heinous that just finding him an attorney at all is a challenge. The film's gimmick of having Young switch sides from prosecutor to defender is intriguing, if highly improbable.

As a vehicle for acting, it is superior throughout, with honors going to Bradford Dillman as Young, the lawyer who sticks to his principles even though he feels that his client deserves whatever fate he receives. Peter Graves and Lloyd Nolan are stalwart as the military brass, while Norman Fell and Murray Hamilton make the most of their supporting roles. Vera Miles is also strong and believable, though her role has some clichés and poor dialogue to overcome. Lee Marvin does well in a surprisingly small role as the sullen title character; although the feature was released to capitalize on Marvin's popularity, ironically, some of his original scenes were cut from the finished film!

The project's television origins are apparent, as most of the drama is confined to the courtroom and Ryker's cell. The editing of the film from the original two-part episode is haphazard and sloppy. Instead of the straightforward chronological approach originally taken, the film starts in the middle of the story and then uses flashbacks to fill in the gaps. The first half is full of gaffes because the location has been changed to Tokyo instead of Seoul. Some dialogue is lost, including General Bailey's decision not to prosecute Young at the end of Ryker's second trial! The worst editing occurs when Young and Ann are traveling to Seoul and are followed, and then fired upon, by a mysterious motorcyclist. In the TV version, the motorcyclist's presence is questioned and has some importance; in the film, however, he is frightened away by added stock footage of jets attacking a road convoy, and is never to be mentioned again.

Howard Thompson of the *New York Times* commented on the film's television origins and gave it a favorable review, noting that "Mr. Marvin and Mr. Dillman are fierce and fine, with firm support from Murray Hamilton, Peter Graves, Norman Fell and that old pro, Lloyd Nolan, who couldn't give a bad performance if he tried."

"The Case Against Paul Ryker," the original NBC *Kraft Suspense Theatre* program, is

Lee Marvin in Communist uniform and dramatic pose for the flashback sequences in Sergeant Ryker *(1968). For whom is he really spying?*

available for viewing at certain locations across the country, such as Chicago's Museum of Broadcast Communications. It is well worth seeing, and is superior to the film version.

Three years after "The Case Against Paul Ryker" aired on NBC, a television show debuted on ABC entitled *Court Martial*, starring Bradford Dillman as Captain David Young and Peter Graves as Major Frank Whitaker. The setting of the show was changed from the Korean War to World War II but the format was essentially the same: the Judge Advocate General's lawyers travel across Europe collecting evidence, then go to trial. *Court Martial* lasted for twenty-six episodes during the 1966 season, though some of them never aired in America.

Still, *Sergeant Ryker* is an interesting, well-acted courtroom drama and study of military procedure. It was distributed by Universal in March 1968, but did little business, despite poster art which depicts Marvin in brutal action,

very reminiscent of the artwork for *The Dirty Dozen*. However, this just isn't the case: *Sergeant Ryker* is not an action film. Of the handful of Korean War films which examine collaboration with the enemy, *Sergeant Ryker* is the shallowest and flimsiest example.

Sky Commando

Credits: 1953. Columbia. *Directed by* Fred F. Sears. *Produced by* Sam Katzman. *Screen Play by* Samuel Newman. *Story by* Samuel Newman and William Sackheim & Arthur Orloff. *Musical Director:* Ross DiMaggio. *Director of Photography:* Lester H. White, A.S.C. *Film Editor:* Edwin Bryant, A.C.E. *Art Director:* Paul Palmentola. *Set Decorator:* Frank Kramer. *Special Effects:* Jack Erickson. *Assistant Director:* Willard Sheldon. *Sound Engineer:* Frank

Goodwin. *Unit Manager*: Herbert Leonard. Not Rated. Black and White. Flat (1.33:1). 69 minutes. Released in August, 1953. Not currently available on commercial home video.

Cast: *Colonel Ed Wyatt*, Dan Duryea; *Jo McWethy*, Frances Gifford; *Lieutenant Hobson "Hobbie" Lee*, Touch Conners [Mike Connors]; *Major Scott*, Michael Fox; *Lieutenant John Willard*, William R. Klein; *Danny Nelson*, Freeman Morse; *Captain Frank Willard*, Dick Paxton; *General Carson*, Selmer Jackson; *Jorgy*, Dick Lerner; *General Combs*, Morris Ankrum; *Major Daly*, Paul McGuire.

Historical Accuracy Level: Low. This story is strictly fictitious from the perspectives of both of the wars which it depicts.

Patriotic Propaganda Level: Medium. These flyboys may not get along with each other, but they know how to fight the enemy.

Elements: Air Force, Air War, Combat Photography, Infighting, Multiple Wars, Romance.

One of the many multiple war scenarios (in which someone serves in both World War II and the Korean War) takes place in this routine Columbia programmer. Its spare sixty-nine minute running time is padded with quite a lot of stock Air Force flying footage from both wars, leaving little time for the airborne actors to emote. But given the pedestrian nature of the script and the direction, that is probably for the best.

Sky Commando begins in the air above Korea, as two American jets — an F-86 Sabre piloted by Lieutenant John Willard (William R. Klein) and an F-80 Shooting Star flown by his brother Captain Frank Willard (Dick Paxton) — fly toward their home base after completing a mission. They are diverted by Colonel Ed Wyatt (Dan Duryea) to attack Red forces on a hill which are trapping some three hundred Marines. As the jets approach, four enemy MiG jets appear and follow the Willard brothers. The American jets are able to bomb the ridge with napalm and rockets, clearing the way for the Marines to pass, before the MiGs attack.

In the ensuing dogfight, Frank Willard nails a MiG but is then shot down (although it is a Sabre jet seen descending toward the ground). John's jet is also hit, but he belly lands his Sabre at the base. He storms into Colonel

Wyatt's office, calls his superior officer a murderer and threatens to thrash him. A general interrupts and berates Frank, sending him to his quarters. He is visited there by Major Scott (Michael Fox) who tries to put Frank's feelings into perspective. Scott tells Frank that he is wrong to blame Wyatt, and tells him a story about Wyatt during World War II ...

In March of 1943, American fliers are based in England and flying missions over Europe. A photographic reconnaissance mission over Bremen, Germany, is postponed due to poor weather conditions. Captain Wyatt is distrusted by his own crew because he recently lost a copilot. He is assigned a new copilot, Lieutenant Hobson "Hobbie" Lee (Mike "Touch" Connors), who warns Wyatt that he does not intend to share the same fate as the previous copilot. Wyatt is also saddled with a female reporter named Jo McWethy (Frances Gifford), who is researching an in-depth article regarding the workings of the reconnaissance outfit.

Wyatt's B-25 Mitchell "The Nemesis" is on its way to France when a wind shift clears Bremen. Over the crew's objections, Wyatt turns the plane toward Germany and flies over Bremen at two thousand feet. The plane is hit by anti-aircraft fire and three men die, and two more, including Hobbie, are wounded. Wyatt orders the load lightened, and everything loose is ejected from the plane — including the three bodies. The two wounded men, Hobbie and Danny Nelson (Freeman Morse), eject and parachute safely to earth while Wyatt successfully lands the wounded plane.

While recuperating in the hospital, Hobbie is told by Jo that one of the airmen thought to be dead on board the bomber actually drowned in the English Channel. Overwhelmed by guilt, Hobbie rejects his own captaincy and asks to be assigned to Wyatt's command, which has moved to North Africa. Hobbie is determined to catch Wyatt unnecessarily risking his crew and to punish him for it. Since Jo has also followed Wyatt to North Africa, Hobbie and Jo begin a romantic relationship. In Casablanca, Hobbie rescues Danny Nelson, who has gone AWOL because Wyatt has demoted him to a private's rank. This act costs Hobbie a night's sleep, which almost results in a crash at takeoff the following day.

608-Line Ad Mat No. 402—4 Cols. x 152 Lines • *This ad also available as 342-Line* Ad Mat No. 302—3 Cols. x 114 Lines.

Action in the air and on the ground is mixed with romance—"Baby, this operation I like"—in Columbia's Sky Commando *(1953). The F-86 Sabre Jets pictured are in the film only briefly, since most of the story takes place aboard B-24 and B-25 bombers during World War II.*

Wyatt and Hobbie finally come to blows, but their fight is interrupted by a general. Both are kept on active status for an important mission to bomb Romanian oil fields. Flying B-24 Liberators, the American pilots bomb the oil fields, but a photographer on Wyatt's plane sees that some of the oil tanks were phony and that the actual tanks were not destroyed. Wyatt's bomber is shot down in Yugoslavia, and Wyatt personally pulls Hobbie and the remainder of his crew from the wreckage, despite a broken arm. The survivors are led to the coast by a partisan named Jorgi (Dick Lerner), who is killed within sight of the sea. Back in a hospital in England, Hobbie learns that the follow-up raid on the oil fields, made possible because of their film of the first raid, was a big success. Hobbie and Jo plan to marry and Hobbie stops blaming Wyatt for the carnage of war.

Back in the present, Major Scott tells John Willard that he has been removed from active status and that Wyatt will be flying John's missions.

Scott leaves John alone, where he cries for the loss of his brother. For the next mission, John assumes his normal role, relieving Wyatt of the chore. As John is about to take off, Major Scott delivers a note to him, making the pilot joyful. Scott tells Wyatt that Frank Willard is alive and in the hands of the Marines. John departs on another mission.

Sky Commando, at its core, is about one single issue: the responsibility of an officer for the welfare of his men. The film pretends to explore that issue during two world wars, but in both instances, the cases against Wyatt are barely credible. During the lengthy World War II flashback, which occupies the bulk of the movie's running time, Wyatt's crew distrusts him because his copilot was killed while Wyatt was in the fuselage instead of the cockpit. Wyatt is cleared of any wrongdoing by an investigation, but suspicion remains. Though a few people make comments, only Hobbie Lee actively attempts to prove Wyatt guilty of negligence. And in Korea, Wyatt's decision to send the Willards

Lieutenant Hobson "Hobbie" Lee (Mike "Touch" Connors, left) is wounded in action and Colonel Ed Wyatt (Dan Duryea, right) watches him with concern in the military aviation drama Sky Commando *(1953).*

to help the Marines is completely clear cut. The film suffers because its drama is artificial, with an obvious moral, and has little basis in reality.

The film also suffers from cheapness. Its opening scene features a jet dogfight where exploding airplanes (in commonly seen stock footage) are suddenly subsitituted for the jets. Frank Willard is flying an F-80 Shooting Star, yet when his jet descends toward the ground, it is a Sabre jet. Perhaps most indicative of the rushed, low quality of the film is that the third-billed star, Mike Connors (then known as "Touch"), has his last name spelled incorrectly in the opening credits.

Some of the air footage, particularly in the lengthy World War II flashback, is impressive. Aficionados of B-25 Mitchells and B-24 Liberators should enjoy seeing these bombers in action, with much footage presented of actual bomb runs. While the dramatics that surround the flying scenes are less than adequate, the flying scenes maintain interest in the story. This factor is also true of the Sabre jets and Shooting Stars in the brief Korean War scenes.

The film is much more interesting as a World War II story, as it depicts action over Europe and Africa, than as a Korean War story. In fact, although the film obviously starts and finishes in Korea, neither that country, nor its war, is ever mentioned by name. Only one battle is shown, which consists of the two American jets bombing a ridge and then engaging two MiGs in a dogfight. No real feeling for the Korean situation is present, whereas the film communicates the World War II situations with much more clarity, detail and skill.

Critics — and audiences — paid little attention to *Sky Commando*. *Variety* called it a "Fair warplane actioner for the program market," and lauded its "generous use of actual combat clips." But it also noted that "the stereotyped characterizations in the script are too formidable a hurdle for any director to overcome." Today the film rests in oblivion, notable only as one of the early features of Mike "Touch" Connors before he found fame as a private eye on television's *Mannix*. As a war film, it is a disappointing presentation of the air war in the skies over Korea, although its World War II scenes are somewhat more effective. The flying machines provide the only real reason to watch the film.

Sniper's Ridge

Credits: 1961. Associated Producers, Inc. *Distributed by* Twentieth Century-Fox. *Produced and Directed by* John Bushelman. *Written by* Tom Maruzzi. *Music by* Richard LaSalle. *Director of Photography*: Kenneth Peach, A.S.C. *Film Editor*: Carl Pierson. *Art Direction*: John Mansbridge. *Production Supervisor*: Harold E. Knox. *Assistant Director*: Ira Stewart. *Script Supervision*: Mel Marshall. *Sound*: Carl Zint. *Makeup*: Ernie Park. *Costumes*: Robert Olivas. *Property Master*: Monroe Liebgold. *Set Decorations*: Harry Reif. *Supervising Sound Editor*: Jack Cornall. *Sound Facilities by* Continental Sound Corporation. *CinemaScope Lenses by* Bausch and Lomb. Not Rated. Black and White. CinemaScope (2.35:1). 61 minutes. Released in August, 1961. Not currently available on commercial home video.

Cast: *Private Scharack*, Jack Ging; *Corporal Pumphrey*, Stanley Clements; *Captain Tombolo*, John Goddard; *Sergeant Sweatish*, Douglas Henderson; *Lieutenant Peer*, Gabe Castle (Gabe de Lutri); *Wardy*, Allan Marvin; *Bear*, Anton Van Stralen; *David*, Mason Curry; *Bo-Bo*, Mark Douglas; *Soldier*, Scott Randall; *Mongolian*, George Yoshinaga; *Gwathney*, Albert C. Freeman, Jr.; *Tonto*, Henry Delgado; *Young Soldier*, Joe Cawthon; *Soldiers*, Richard Jeffries and Thomas A. Sweet.

Historical Accuracy Level: Low. While specific incidents are no doubt truthful, the film as a whole is too angry and melodramatic to represent reality.

Patriotic Propaganda Level: Low. This movie is intent on depicting how cruel and merciless the army and its officers can be.

Elements: Army, Cease-Fire, Infighting.

This odd little movie, filmed in the widescreen CinemaScope process, yet only an hour in length, is full of contradictions. Ostensibly about the conflict among nations in Korea, the film is far more interested in the conflict between men and ideals in the United States Army. As the prologue states, "This is the story of men in battle, fighting the bitter elements, the enemy and most of all — themselves."

Sniper's Ridge is the location of an Army platoon in Korea on July 25, 1953, two days before the official cease-fire is to begin. The army has the high ground, but its soldiers are caught napping by Chinese soldiers, who briefly overrun the ridge, killing several men. The Chinese are routed by Private Scharack (Jack Ging), who almost single-handedly turns them away with his rifle and grenades while World War II hero Sergeant Sweatish (Douglas Henderson) cowers nearby. At the command post, Lieutenant Peer (Gabe Castle) is ordered to make a night ambush patrol in retaliation — with Scharack — even though the cease-fire is so close and Scharack is overdue for rotation back to the States.

When Scharack discovers that his rotation is delayed again, even though three other men are being sent home, he argues heatedly with Captain Tombolo (John Goddard), but to no avail. Disgusted, Scharack commandeers a jeep, drives to a battalion aid station and attempts to be medically discharged for severe headaches. The head surgeon is, in turn, disgusted by Scharack's behavior and orders him to walk back to Sniper's Ridge. There, Tombolo assigns him to dig latrine ditches until darkness falls and the ambush patrol gets under way. A new man, Corporal Pumphrey (Stanley Clements), joins the outfit. He is a buddy of Sergeant Sweatish, whom he knows as a war hero, and has also been witness to Captain Tombolo's cowardice in the face of a fire, from which Pumphrey rescued Tombolo's two children. Tombolo still blames Pumphrey because his wife later divorced him.

The ambush patrol moves down the ridge uneventfully and things stay quiet most of the night. As the men begin to move back up the ridge, however, Lieutenant Peer smells garlic, a sign of the enemy, and the Chinese attack. Soldiers on both sides are killed. Upset by the platoon's failure to win a convincing battle victory, Tombolo orders yet another patrol the next night as soon as darkness falls. Peer objects, noting the cease-fire is to begin at 10:00 p.m., but Tombolo is determined and slaps his lieutenant for back-talking.

In late afternoon, Scharack is digging another latrine ditch when an artillery shell lands nearby but does not explode. When he hears about it, Tombolo orders the men to mark its place, but they refuse, as it has fallen into a suspected minefield. Angry, Tombolo defiantly finds the shell, marks its location and walks back — until he steps on a "Bouncing Betty"

mine. When he steps off, it will explode. Scharack reluctantly takes charge at Sweatish's insistence, and the two men collect flak jackets and wrap them tightly around the frightened captain. Tombolo is told to jump off the mine, but he is afraid to move, frozen in place. Scharack charges the captain and knocks him down as the mine explodes. Captain Tombolo is unhurt but Scharack has wounds to both legs and his left ear. He doesn't mind; he's smiling, for now he has to be sent home. At 10:00 p.m. the cease fire goes into effect; the following morning the men destroy their defensive positions and celebrate the end of the Korean War.

Sniper's Ridge is a rather heated melodrama. So heated, in fact, that the film's major characters, most particularly Captain Tombolo, sweat profusely and constantly. They also snarl and yell at each other most of the time, perhaps because of the heat. Or perhaps the intense heat is meant to symbolize the intensity of men constantly on edge, facing the prospect of death every single day, and the men who sweat the most — Sweatish (note the name) and Tombolo — are the ones most afraid of dying.

There are Chinese enemy soldiers who appear in two scenes to eliminate some of the American extras, but the battle here is clearly staged within the ranks of the American Army. Scharack is angry at everyone because he is not being rotated home, yet he is such a survivor that he is usually able to control his temper enough to lead by example, and the men naturally turn to him for guidance. Tombolo is still angry at himself for failing to save his own children from a fire, and pushes his men to their limits because of his severe guilt. Tombolo will not grant Scharack's rotation because he knows that without Scharack, the Chinese would have already overrun the American positions on the ridge.

Peer seems to know how to lead a platoon, yet continues to lose men at an alarming rate, which gnaws at his conscience. Sweatish knows why his previous valor has turned to caution and occasionally cowardice, but has not found a way to reverse the trend. Pumphrey arrives and tries to help his old friend Sweatish, argues with Tombolo about the captain's divorce and tries to decipher the complex character that is Scharack. The other characters are all unimportant extras

The poster for 20th Century–Fox's tense drama Sniper's Ridge (1961) *is surprisingly representative of the film: bleak, desolate landscape, tedious dangerous patrolling; the promise of confrontation. The only clue to its Korean location is the infamous hill of the title.*

in this war zone and to add more pressure, time is ticking away. Within two days, all military action will end, and the relationships between these incendiary characters must be resolved before the cease-fire.

While some of this melodrama actually works, most of the time *Sniper's Ridge* is simply overripe. Dialogue is barked rather than spoken, Tombolo paces his bunker like a caged animal, the characters are often reduced to caricature and Scharack acts like a wildman. The movie's point may be that the effect of war provokes people into craziness, but there is more repressed rage here than in a major traffic jam. It's overdone.

The movie avoids the usual, formulaic reasons for infighting: privileges of rank, prejudice, rivalry over a woman, etc. In their place are rather simplistic psychological reasons involving guilt, shame and fear, all of which are exaggerated by the inexorable sweating. Even when characters' actions seem sensible, producer/director John Bushelman's attention to their glistening faces seems oppressive.

The presentation of the cease-fire is accurate, except that there was more regular, monotonous shelling in real life, so much so that the silence which followed the 10:00 p.m. deadline actually made many of the soldiers more nervous than the sound of constant bombardment, to which they had become accustomed. The movie also rings true in that it was the next morning, following the quiet night, when realization that the war was finally over was actually felt and celebrated.

Because the cease-fire is so close, the soldiers do not want to heedlessly risk their lives. The first ambush patrol is not questioned, except by Scharack, who should not have been included. But when Tombolo demands another patrol, into enemy territory on the night of the cease-fire, Peer refuses to carry out the order and it is likely that none of the men would have gone. Open rebellion is only avoided because of Tombolo's brush with death on the "Bouncing Betty" mine. The film works hard to accumulate this festering feeling of anxiety and fear, yet it is this very crescendo of emotion which makes the film so overblown and difficult to believe.

As a movie scene, Tombolo's climactic adventure and inability to handle it works very well. It is taut and exciting, plausible and effective. As a denouement, one which teaches Tombolo some humility and humanity, it is thematically less successful because it is Tombolo's own stubbornness and stupidity which place him in danger, and his own fear which, once again, demands action from a braver soul than himself for salvation. Thus, Tombolo's inept attempt at apology the next morning is curtly rejected, and he must live with the fact that the men cannot tolerate him.

The cast surely works hard to convey the feel of battle-weary men who just want to finish their term of service and go home. Jack Ging, John Goddard and Gabe Castle each play their roles with sharp edginess, while Stanley Clements brings a welcome breeze of normalcy with him when he arrives on the scene. Douglas Henderson has perhaps the trickiest role as Sweatish, and earns some empathy with his portrayal. John Bushelman's production values are low: the country looks like California desert (because it is) and during the ambush firefight, a commercial jet can be seen in the background sky in at least two separate shots.

This film is an excellent example of judicious film editing. All extraneous elements are omitted; every shot in the film is designed to depict the volatility of the situation in Korea or keep the story moving to the next confrontation. Its short running time is deceptive, because the film feels like a ninety minute feature — it just omits the character detail that is so familiar to the war genre. The result is an unusual film in which the action begins immediately, and the characters are precisely who they seem to be.

Sniper's Ridge is an interesting little movie, long on the histrionics but short on common sense. Eugene Archer concluded in the *New York Times* that "Perhaps John Bushelman, who produced and directed the Twentieth Century–Fox release, thought to aim this anti-heroic drama at an anti-militaristic contemporary audience. But the whole thing would have flabbergasted Errol Flynn." Positive notices were found in *The Films of 20th Century–Fox*, where Tony Thomas and Aubrey Solomon judge it to be "A modest war picture, but a tautly made one and a good insight into battle fatigue," and the *Encyclopedia of American War Films*, in which Larry Langman and Ed Borg comment, "The action sequences

Sniper's Ridge (1961) features an angry, intense character named Private Scharack (Jack Ging, right), who desperately wants to be sent home. Here, he confronts Wardy (Allan Marvin, left) because his transfer was denied yet again.

are realistic and suspenseful in spite of the skimpy budget."

While it cannot be ranked as one of the best Korean War films, *Sniper's Ridge* is certainly more dramatic and interesting than most. Its high intensity level is refreshing and its simple

yet convincing structure is appreciated. On repeated viewings, the film becomes less strident and more effective. And of the small, independent films which were produced about the war during the 1960s, *Sniper's Ridge* is undoubtedly the best.

Starlift

Credits: 1951. Warner Bros. *Directed by* Roy Del Ruth. *Produced by* Robert Arthur. *Screen Play by* John Klorer and Karl Kamb. *From a Story by* John Klorer. *Musical Direction*: Ray Heindorf. *Director of Photography*: Ted McCord, A.S.C. *Film Editor*: William Ziegler, A.C.E. *Art Director*: Charles H. Clarke. *Sound*: Francis J. Scheid and David Forrest. *Set Decorator*: G. W. Berntsen. *Wardrobe by* Leah Rhodes. *Makeup Artist*: Gordon Bau. *Technical Advisers*: Major James G. Smith, U.S.A.F. and Major George E. Andrews, U.S.A.F. *Musical Numbers Staged and Directed by* LeRoy Prinz. *Songs*: "'S Wonderful" *and* "Liza" *by* George and Ira Gershwin; "You Do Something to Me" *and* "What is This Thing Called Love" *by* Cole Porter; "You're Gonna Lose Your Gal" *by* Joe Young and Jimmy Monaco; "You Oughta Be in Pictures" *by* Edward Heyman and Dana Suesse; "It's Magic" *by* Sammy Cahn and Jule Styne; "Good Green Acres of Home" *by* Irving Kahal and Sammy Fain; "I May Be Wrong, But I Think You're Wonderful" *by* Harry Ruskin and Henry Sullivan; "Look Out, Stranger, I'm a Texas Ranger" *by* Ruby Ralesin and Phil Harris; "Noche Carib" *by* Percy Faith. *Hair Stylist*: Gertrude Wheeler. *Assistant Director*: Mel Dellar. Not Rated. Black and White. Flat (1.33:1). 103 minutes. Released in December, 1951. Filmed primarily at Travis Air Force Base, California. Not currently available on commercial home video.

Cast: *Themselves*, Doris Day, Gordon MacRae, Virginia Mayo, Gene Nelson and Ruth Roman; *Sergeant Mike Nolan*, Dick Wesson; *Nell Wayne*, Janice Rule; *Corporal Rick Williams*, Ron Hagerthy; *Colonel Callan*, Richard Webb; *Chaplain*, Hayden Rorke; *Steve Rogers*, Howard St. John; *Themselves*, Tommy Noonan and Peter Marshall, James Cagney, Gary Cooper, Virginia Gibson, Phil Harris, Frank Lovejoy, Lucille Norman, Louella Parsons, Randolph Scott, Jane Wyman and Patrice Wymore; *Mrs. Callan*, Ann Doran; *Turner*, Tommy Farrell; *George Norris*, John Maxwell; *Bob Wayne*, Don Beddoe; *Sue Wayne*, Mary Adams; *Doctor Williams*, Bigelowe Sayre; *Mrs. Williams*, Eleanor Audley; *Theatre Manager*, Pat Henry; *Chief Usher*, Gordon Polk; *Piano Player*, Robert Hammack; *Captain Nelson*, Ray Montgomery; *Co-Pilot*, Bill Neff; *Ground Officer*, Stan Holbrook; *Flight Nurse*, Jill Richards; *Litter Case*, Joe Turkel; *Virginia Boy*, Rush Williams; *Pete*, Brian McKay; *Will*, Jack Larson; *Nebraska Boy*, Lyle Clark; *Nurses*, Dorothy Kennedy, Jean Dean and Dolores Castle; *Boy With Cane*, William Hunt; *Army Nurse*, Elizabeth Flournoy; *Driver*, Walter Brennan, Jr.; *Lieutenants*, Robert Karnes and John Hedloe; *Boy With Camera*, Steve Gregory; *Morgan*, Richard Monohan; *Soldiers in Bed*, Joe Recht and Herb Latimer; *Doctor*, Dick Ryan; *Crew Chief*, Bill Hudson; *Mis Parsons' Assistant*, Sarah Spencer; *Non-Com*, James Brown; *Waitress*, Ezelle Poule.

Historical Accuracy Level: Medium. "Operation Starlift" was real, but folded before this fictionalized version of its origination played in theaters.

Patriotic Propaganda Level: High. Hollywood stars rally around the boys travelling to and returning from Korea.

Elements: Air Force, Army, Comedy, Homefront, Musical Performance, Returning Home, Romance.

Starlift is the one Korean War film which carries on the tradition of World War II-era all-star jubilees such as *Hollywood Canteen* and *Stage Door Canteen*. It was designed to boost patriotism by featuring a host of Hollywood stars who are seen donating their time and talents to entertaining the troops going to and returning from Korea. Based on an actual project entitled "Operation Starlift," the story dramatizes the origins and evolution of the idea — while adding a romantic backstory — and expands it into a feature film length. The result was intended to be a musical extravaganza with dramatic moments and comedic interludes, but the film is far less effective than it should have been, and not particularly patriotic.

Two Air Force officers are touring the theater district in San Francisco when they spot actress Ruth Roman (portraying herself). Sergeant Mike Nolan (Dick Wesson) introduces himself and asks if she can arrange a meeting between his buddy, Corporal Rick Williams (Ron Hagerthy), and her friend, actress Nell Wayne (Janice Rule), who are both from Youngstown, Ohio. Roman agrees and takes the fliers to her apartment, where they meet Doris Day, Gordon MacRae and James Cagney (all portraying

This marketing for Warner Bros.' musical Starlift *(1951) touts eighteen stars and its music, promoting its patriotic angles at every opportunity. It was made to promote "Operation Starlift," a U.S.O.-type campaign to entertain servicemen travelling to and returning from Korea.*

themselves) while waiting for Nell Wayne. Nell arrives but doesn't remember Williams, even though his father was her dentist. The actresses agree to accompany the fliers back to Travis Air Force Base, because they believe the boys are on their way to the Korean front.

Ruth Roman, Doris Day and Nell tour the Air Force base while the fliers prepare for their trip overseas, and are persuaded to perform some songs for soldiers waiting to leave for Korea. Nell gives Williams a locket and kisses him goodbye. Nell admits to the other girls that "If I took his [Williams'] mind off going to war, even for a minute, I'm glad I came." Colonel Callan (Richard Webb) guides the women to arriving planes, where wounded men are returning from Korea, and then to the hospital, where they are once again persuaded to perform. On the spot, the actresses agree to return in a week and bring some of their friends to properly entertain the waiting and wounded troops, and Colonel Callan agrees to provide their transportation.

One week later, a host of stars arrive at Travis Air Force Base, including Louella Parsons, who has written that Nell and Rick Williams have found love together. Nell finds Williams and Nolan in a plane and believes that they lied to her, when in fact they deliver troops back and forth between San Francisco and Honolulu. Williams, ashamed and embarrassed, asks for a transfer to Korea, but Nolan (who knows no shame) attempts to make time with Virginia Mayo. Nell and Williams are forced to pretend to be in love for the publicity, even to the point of lying about it to their parents.

The studio head (Howard St. John) decides to back the effort to entertain the troops and arranges for a full-fledged show at Travis. Gary Cooper, Frank Lovejoy, Phil Harris, Randolph Scott, Jane Wyman and others take part and greet the men when they are not onstage. Williams' transfer is approved and he prepares to depart, trying to avoid Nell while doing so. She finally finds him and makes a chocolate malt for him, just like she used to when they lived back in Youngstown, and they apologize to each other. Williams' flight is delayed by Nolan so that the couple can have time together, and the next day Williams leaves for Korea with Nell's love and blessing.

Starlift's plot is both formulaic and wafer thin. The romance that blooms between Nell Wayne and Rick Williams is often facile and never convincing. Their story is the link between stars' visits to Travis Air Force Base, but it unnecessarily lengthens an already interminable movie. Indicative of the story's absurdity is the fact that Williams would much rather go to war in Korea than pretend to be Nell Wayne's paramour, even for a short time. And after Nell finds Williams in a transport plane (rather than overseas), their relationship turns not just rocky, but hateful. Their bickering is far too strident in what is supposed to be a pleasant entertainment.

Some of the guest stars have obvious fun during the proceedings, and are thus fun to watch. Phil Harris ceremoniously loses $300 at cards, then narrates the song (which he cowrote) "Look Out, Stranger, I'm a Texas Ranger" without missing a beat. Doris Day sings all or parts of four songs, and Jane Wyman contributes a nice rendition of "I May Be Wrong, But I Think You're Wonderful" in a hospital ward. Others, such as James Cagney and Randolph Scott, have absolutely nothing to do, or, like Virginia Mayo, are asked to perform subpar material.

Comedy is contributed by Dick Wesson as Sergeant Mike Nolan, the aggressive Air Force officer who never takes no for an answer, and has an eagle eye for the ladies. Besides the "Texas Ranger" number which features Gary Cooper and Frank Lovejoy as dueling opponents, a drunken chef routine is performed by the nightclub team of Noonan and Marshall. Marshall is Peter Marshall, who later hosted *The Hollywood Squares* for a fifteen year run.

Even with these musical and comedy performances, however, *Starlift* remains as flat and lumpy as a collapsed soufflé. Its main story is preposterous and unconvincing, full of clichés and hopelessly cloying. While the intention behind "Operation Starlift" was certainly noble, the reality was far less satisfactory. When the idea was first discussed, Hollywood studios contributed $5000 toward the goal of creating an ongoing program of entertainment for the departing and returning soldiers. But when that initial investment had been spent, no new funds were allocated. Thus, "Operation Starlift" died in stillbirth even before the movie was released.

Colonel Callan (Richard Webb) and actresses Ruth Roman (playing herself, center) and Nell Wayne (Janice Rule, right) stand ready to greet wounded soldiers returning from Korea to San Francisco in Starlift *(1951).*

Warner Bros. spent roughly $1,000,000 to film and publicize the *Starlift* film, but did not contribute any further money to the real-life project. The studio used the film to advertise its own stars, even inserting non-performers such as James Cagney and Randolph Scott into the story to increase its box-office potential while refusing to showcase performers from other studios. Perhaps Warners' worst breach of ethics was that some of the film's "guest stars" never bothered to perform at Travis, but the film gives the false impression that they did. This all-star jubilee hit theatre screens just a month after the real "Operation Starlift" closed for lack of funds.

Critics castigated the movie, and Warner Bros. for trying to profit from what was meant to be a charitable event. *Time* detailed the real-life fiasco of "Operation Starlift" in its review and called the film an "ill-starred project." Bosley Crowther of the *New York Times* was far more specific in his complaints. "The

acts are unspeakably slapdash and the romance is painful beyond words." He concluded, "The washout of 'Operation Starlift' is understandable, if it depended upon such 'entertainment' as is exhibited in this film." *Christian Century* was more succinct: "Embarrassing self-praise."

Starlift was intended to infuse audiences with a sense that Hollywood was once again doing its share of charity during a time of conflict. But not enough attention is paid to the actual soldiers for whom the entertainers are performing. It is their reactions which would make the act of performing a valuable function. Only one scene in the base hospital comes close to capturing that feeling. The songs, dances and comedy routines chosen are not patriotic at all, and seem completely random. Worst of all, the film is boring. Rather than creating a thoughtful, endearing show for the fighting men, director Roy Del Ruth fashioned a dull vaudeville dud.

The Steel Helmet

Credits: 1951. Deputy Corporation Productions. *Distributed by* Lippert Pictures. *Written, Produced and Directed by* Samuel Fuller. *Associate Producer*: William Berke. *Music Composed and Conducted by* Paul Dunlap. *Director of Photography*: Ernest Miller, A.S.C. *Film Editor*: Philip Cahn. *Art Director*: Theobold Holsopple. *Set Decorations*: Clarence Steenson. *Assistant Director*: John Francis Murphy. *Special Effects*: Ben Southland. *Sound Engineer*: William Lynch. *Optical Effects*: Ray Mercer, A.S.C. *Makeup*: George Bruce. *Wardrobe*: Alfred Berke. *Dialogue Coach*: Stanley Price. Not Rated. Black and White. Flat (1.33:1). 84 minutes. Released in January, 1951. Currently available on VHS home video.

Cast: *Sergeant Zack*, Gene Evans; *Private "Conchie" Bronte*, Robert Hutton; *Lieutenant Driscoll*, Steve Brodie; *Corporal Thompson*, James Edwards; *Sergeant Tanaka*, Richard Loo; *Joe*, Sid Melton; *Private Baldy*, Richard Monahan; *Short Round*, William Chun; *The Red Major*, Harold Fong; *First G.I.*, Neyle Morrow; *Second Lieutenant*, Lynn Stalmaster; *with* Stuart Klitsner, Leonard Stone, Donica D'Hondt and Russ Hodges.

Historical Accuracy Level: Medium. This classic film is more impressionistic than realistic by design, though many of its individual elements are authentic.

Patriotic Propaganda Level: Low. Fuller's work is rarely meant to induce patriotic fervor; he is dedicated to exploring essential truths of war.

Elements: Army, Medicine, Musical Performance, Orphans, Racism.

The Steel Helmet was the first major Korean War film to play in theatres, and though it was released concurrently with *Korea Patrol* and *A Yank in Korea*, it is the only one of the trio that is remembered today. Samuel Fuller's tribute to infantrymen earns its reputation by eschewing traditional heroism in favor of stressing plain, simple survival. Some Korean War films emphasize patriotism to the point of propaganda; others philosophize about war, establishing a moral stand. A few films, usually considered to be the best of the bunch, examine war as it is without trying to make grandiose statements or create modern myths. These few films are the ones which come closest to the truth of war. For the Korean War, none come closer to essential truth than *The Steel Helmet*.

A steel helmet with a prominent bullet hole remains stationary behind the opening credits. When they finish, the helmet slowly lifts to reveal Sergeant Zack (Gene Evans), who is wounded in the left leg and has his hands tied behind him. Zack crawls through an area rife with dead American soldiers but stops when he hears someone coming. It is a young, barefoot Korean boy with a rifle (William Chun). The boy stops at Zack, bends over and listens to hear if he is alive. The boy cuts Zack's hands free and tells him (in excellent English) that he is South Korean. Zack is glad to be free, but ignores the boy while he quickly eats and drinks. The boy wants to accompany Zack, but the gruff sergeant refuses. Zack limps away but finally turns, realizing the boy might be helpful to him. Dubbing him Short Round, Zack instructs him to put on a dead soldier's shoes and helmet and allows the boy to tag along. They near a statue where two Korean women are worshipping. As they pass, the worshippers open fire. Zack shoots both and discovers that they are Communist guerillas dressed as women. They move forward.

Fog shrouds the Korean countryside, so Zack and Short Round move carefully. They find a black medic, Corporal Thompson (James Edwards), who is searching for survivors from his platoon in the thick fog. Zack explains that his platoon was also decimated by Reds. They decide to stick together and move forward, where they hear others, revealed to be an American squad led by Lieutenant Driscoll (Steve Brodie). Driscoll asks the men to join his squad, but Zack refuses, not wanting to be led by an inexperienced officer. Soon after leaving the squad, Zack, Thompson and Short Round hear gunfire. They return to the squad, which is trapped by two enemy snipers. Zack and the squad's Sergeant Tanaka (Richard Loo) crawl forward, deliberately drawing fire to locate the snipers and then open fire, killing them. Zack agrees to lead the squad and its two pack mules to a nearby Buddhist temple, where they are to establish an observation post, in exchange for a box of cigars.

A group of refugees pass, and Zack orders

The poster for Lippert's war drama The Steel Helmet *(1951) stresses that "it dares tell the TRUTH behind today's headlines!" and promises the "Action story of our fighting G.I.s!" Sergeant Zack's steel helmet, replete with bullet hole, is the artwork's focal point, but the Buddha statue and the Red Major are also included.*

them to be thoroughly searched. They are found to be what they seem, and Zack is satisfied, though Driscoll considers the search to be a waste of time. The men take a break when Tanaka finds a patch of melons, and they reveal some of their personalities. Private Bronte (Robert Hutton) carries a portable organ, given to him by a priest who was later killed. Bronte was a "conscientious objector" during World War II, so Zack abbreviates the phrase and calls him "Conchie." One soldier is silent, refusing to speak; Zack calls him Joe (Sid Melton). Another man is bald (Richard Monahan); he naturally becomes Private Baldy. A dead soldier is found, and Driscoll orders one of his men to retrieve the man's dog tags. That soldier dies when the booby-trapped body explodes. Zack takes the cigars from the dead man's pack, claiming them as his own, and gives them to Short Round to carry.

The soldiers reach the large Buddhist temple safely and install an observation post near its top. The men are awed by the beauty of the temple and the size of the Buddha statue inside; Driscoll asks the men to respect the temple and not damage it in any way. While the soldiers rest and sleep, Joe is placed on watch upstairs. He is stabbed to death by a Red Major (Harold Fong) who has been hiding in the temple. Private Baldy finds Joe and the men search the temple but do not find the intruder. From the observation deck, the Red Major drops a grenade into their midst, but the pin remains in place and the grenade does not explode. Zack finds the Red Major by firing into a statue which he is hiding behind. Thompson treats the Communist's minor chest wound and rejects the Major's argument that because he is black, he should not be fighting for America. The Red Major tries the same argument on Sergeant Tanaka, a Japanese-American, with similar results. They both tell the Red Major to keep quiet.

Private Baldy finally fixes the radio and Zack prepares to take the Red Major to headquarters for interrogation. Short Round goes outside to don his shoes and helmet while Driscoll asks Zack if they can switch helmets for luck. Zack refuses. While they talk, Short Round is shot and killed by a sniper. When the Red Major mocks a prayer written by the boy,

Zack loses his temper and shoots him. Thompson tries to keep the Red Major alive, but his wounds are too massive, and he dies in front of the giant Buddha statue.

Suddenly, Communist forces advance toward the temple. Driscoll radios artillery coordinates and American tanks blast the enemy soldiers. The temple comes under fire as Red soldiers spot the observation post. Zack stands on the lap of the Buddha statue, firing through the stained glass window. Tanaka uses a bazooka to destroy an enemy tank. Bronte takes over the machine gun and slaughters dozens of enemy soldiers before being shot in the head. Medic Thompson takes his place and kills many more.

The beautiful temple is heavily damaged by artillery and rifle fire, but the infantrymen hold their ground. Zack fires until he runs out of ammunition, then is stunned by a close explosion. His mind reverts back to World War II and he talks of "Krauts" before being knocked unconscious by falling debris. Driscoll operates the machine gun, but is shot in the belly and killed. But the Communist rush ends, leaving only Thompson, Tanaka, Baldy and Zack as survivors. American soldiers arrive and lead the four survivors away from the temple. Before he leaves, Zack switches helmets with the dead lieutenant. Last in line, he limps away from the temple and back to the war.

The Steel Helmet was the first serious cinematic exploration of the Korean War, and because writer-producer-director Samuel Fuller focused his talents on demonstrating an authentic feel for the war rather than a judgment of its politics, his drama has retained its relevancy even today. Fuller was unconcerned with trying to explain why Americans were in Korea or rallying his audience around a patriotic cause; we were there, and that was enough. He wanted to provide people with a glimpse of contemporary warfare as he saw it — rough and dirty, exhausting and dehumanizing, messy and uncivilized. Yet, even in the glum, dangerous environment of Korea, men could retain their dignity, protect each other and even laugh now and then.

Although Fuller's vision of Korea (he fought in World War II but never visited Korea) is hampered by meager production values (*The Steel Helmet* was filmed in ten days on a budget

Sergeant Zack (Gene Evans, center) slowly crawls toward a knife, with which he hopes to cut himself free, in The Steel Helmet *(1951). As with Zack, the dead soliders which surround him also have their hands tied behind them. And note the bullet hole in Zack's helmet.*

of $104,000 in Los Angeles' Griffith Park), the forests of his Korea buzz with the imminent threat of danger. Snipers hide in the trees, Red guerrillas dress as peasant women and dead bodies are booby-trapped; nothing in Korea can be trusted. Lieutenant Driscoll tries to lead "by the book," but it becomes evident that Zack's philosophy, which is to stay out of harm's way whenever possible, is the wisest. Zack attempts to teach the men how to survive: he exhorts them to carry all the ammunition they can, chastises them for carrying unnecessary and noisy gear, and provides them with verbal survival clues, but he does so while complaining about their burden on him. Yet it is Zack's experience (and Sergeant Tanaka's bravery) that saves the squad when snipers attack in the forest.

Zack is the main character, but the others deserve closer examination as well. Fuller re-

sisted the common trend to differentiate his soldiers by stereotype; most of them seem interchangable in both appearance and attitude. Those who stand out as individuals do not fit conventional types: Driscoll is inexperienced and does not really seem to care; Thompson, like Zack, is a retread from World War II; Bronte is a conscientious objector who fights as hard as anyone; Baldy is the comic relief, but he's also a competent radio operator; Joe, who does not speak except to the mules, is an enigma; Tanaka is just as cynical as Zack; and Short Round is smart and hopeful, believing in the power of prayers to Buddha.

Short Round's prayers to Buddha inspire Zack to write one for the boy, but the film seems to argue that religion has no power in war. Short Round is killed soon after Zack writes a prayer for him and the beautiful temple is completely desecrated by the climactic battle. The image of Zack standing in the Buddha's lap, firing over its shoulder, is perhaps the most memorable of the entire film. Earlier, Zack finds the Red Major by shooting through various Buddha statues (they fail to protect the Communist), and when the Red Major is dying, Thompson hangs his blood supply from the giant Buddha's hand. Nevertheless, the Red Major dies in front of the beatific, impassive Buddha. In fact, Zack's first skirmish with the Reds comes at a small temple in the fields where Red guerillas disguise themselves as women. The argument is not made explicitly, but events seem to suggest that religion is powerless (and sometimes misused) in war.

An issue which is probed explicitly is racism. Sergeant Zack is casually racist, unintentionally insulting and unaware that he is offensive. He initially refers to Short Round as a "gook" (the term "gook" was perhaps bastardized from *han'guk saram*, an identifying term for Koreans, which incorrectly continued to be used by servicemen to identify any Asian person during the Korean and Vietnam wars), but Short Round objects. "I am no gook! I am Korean!" he exclaims. Seeing that Short Round is offended, Zack refrains from using the word "gook" around him. When he meets the black medic, Corporal Thompson, Zack asks about his military career, saying "You guys" to refer to blacks in the military in general. Thompson listens politely, then tells Zack that he is a soldier who has served in both wars just like the sergeant, and Zack gets the message. Corporal Thompson's color is never mentioned by Zack again.

It is an issue to the Red Major, however. While waiting to be delivered for interrogation, the Red Major tries to start some infighting by questioning why Thompson would fight for a country that mistreats him. He uses the same tactic on Tanaka, whose family spent time in an American concentration camp during World War II. Neither man answers very clearly the Red Major's question, but the results are the same. They both tell him to keep quiet. Each man has faced racism in America and is hopeful that it will gradually recede. They also realize that the Communist cause is racism on a much greater scale. The movie even uses the concept of racism for typically funny, yet truthful, dialogue. Asked how to tell Koreans apart, Zack answers, "He's a South Korean when he's runnin' with ya, he's a North Korean when he's runnin' after ya."

In Fuller's squad, apart from rank and experience, everyone is equal. Short Round is accepted just as much as Sergeant Tanaka, Corporal Thompson or silent Joe. Fuller's army is an equal opportunity employer. Short Round's English is impeccable, which makes him immediately empathetic, but the Red Major's English is equally as impressive. It is interesting that the Red Major is never given the opportunity to speak to Short Round; theirs would be a very interesting conversation.

Short Round is perhaps the movie's key character. He is a Korean orphan, walking barefoot through battlefields, looking for someone to take care of him. He finds and unties Zack, and implores the sergeant to allow him to accompany Zack by telling him, "When you save someone's life, his heart is in your hands." Zack reluctantly agrees, saying, "You can come along, but you're on your own." Short Round represents both innocence and hopefulness and in Fuller's world it is inevitable that he be killed. It is the Red Major's contemptuous reaction to Short Round's prayer (that Zack would like the boy) which provides the movie's climactic moment. The Red Major mocks the prayer, and Zack shoots him. Zack tries to hide his feelings for the boy, but it is obvious that he has grown to cherish Short Round. The boy's death encapsulates Fuller's view of war: that young men kill and are killed, that the good die young, that only the people who use their cunning to survive have the odds in their favor. Incidentally, the character name of Short Round was "borrowed" as an homage to Fuller by director Steven Spielberg when he made *Indiana Jones and the Temple of Doom*.

Zack is the embodiment of Fuller's stance that people must be tough and armor themselves against emotion to survive war. It is Fuller's position that Zack has survived two wars because he constantly surveys situations as they apply to him, and takes as few risks as possible. The battle at the temple, however, takes its toll on the sergeant. At one point, he loses his mind, at least in part, thinking that he is back in Germany fighting "Krauts." He is knocked unconscious, and after waking seems like a zombie, though he is conscious (and empathetic) enough to switch helmets with the dead lieutenant in the final moments. It is Fuller's point that the chaos of war will, eventually, make anyone crazy, but Zack's insanity is an odd and perhaps unnecessary moment in a strong script.

Zack's one moment of unrepressed emo-

Short Round (William Chun, left) and Sergeant Zack (Gene Evans, right) look back on a field of dead American soldiers before searching for other survivors in The Steel Helmet *(1951). Short Round's helmet and boots were taken from the body of a soldier named Pee Wee Johnson.*

tion, shooting the Red Major who mocks Short Round's prayer, was a controversial decision by Fuller because it led many people to label him anti-American. Officials at the Pentagon were upset that an American soldier would be shown shooting an unarmed prisoner and called for alterations in the storyline. Fuller replied by locating several army officers who admitted that such prisoners were occasionally killed in that manner. Fuller's position was that he wasn't imagining the situation but was reporting it. Reportedly other governmental officials did not appreciate the arguments made by the Red Major in the cause of Communism, and accused Fuller of providing Communists with propaganda fodder in his film. In the early 1950s era of Communist witch-hunts and blacklisting, it was brave, if perhaps a bit foolhardy, for Fuller to include such inflammatory topics in his film, but the film is undoubtedly the better for their inclusion.

Fuller's films have always had the reputation of bluntness and a lack of subtlety. *The Steel Helmet* was his first major success, and is unquestionably blunt and occasionally unsubtle. But it explores thorny issues that other films do not dare to suggest, and does so with an honest and authentic approach, searching for truth. The film's quick pacing does not allow its characters to philosophize ad nauseam or to act in an overly theatrical manner. A veteran of World War II campaigns, Fuller ensured that his dogfaces acted like dogfaces, and that his movie reflected real concerns of real people.

The director also imbues his movie with humor. Besides the cynical dialogue that always seems to identify infantrymen, Fuller includes several other comedic moments to lighten the Korean gloom. Silent Joe walks around the temple, trying to find a place where the benevolent eyes of the Buddha do not follow him; Tanaka rubs earth onto Baldy's head, promising that it will lead to hair growth as it did with his own dear mother; Driscoll has a scare when a grenade on his belt loses a pin; Baldy snores with the sound of an incoming shell; the portable organ carries the name of "Fat Paul" (short for "Father Paul"; three letters are missing); Bronte plays "Auld Lang Syne" on the organ and Short Round sings along, claiming that it is the Korean national anthem!

Such moments are entertaining, but they never fully (and are not meant to) hide or camouflage the ever present danger. Viewers are not supposed to forget that Zack was found with his hands tied behind him amidst a field full of dead American soldiers, that Short Round's parents are both dead, that Corporal Thompson's outfit was massacred just like Zack's, or that Driscoll and his men are wandering around the forest in circles. "No one knows where we are but the enemy," one of the soldiers says. Fuller's perspective of the war is bleak and unromanticized. Only four characters survive.

Fuller coaxes strong performances from his largely unknown cast. His original star, Robert Hutton, injured his hand early in the production and his role was reduced, but Hutton is fine as the conscientious objector. Steve Brodie is also good as Driscoll, a role which Fuller felt should have received little audience empathy. Sid Melton and Richard Monahan are amusing as silent Joe and Baldy. Richard Loo and James Edwards are excellent as the Nisei sergeant and the black medic; both actors deliver, arguably, their finest performances in this movie. William Chun is remarkable as Short Round and Gene Evans is perfect as the quintessential Fuller protagonist, Sergeant Zack. The movie simply would not be nearly as good with different actors in these two roles.

The weakest section of the film is undoubtedly the final attack. Fuller had just twenty-five extras and used them intelligently, but the enemy force is considerably smaller than it is described in the movie. In addition, for the first time stock military footage of artillery shooting and the resulting explosions is used, and it poorly matches Fuller's own footage. In this regard, the film is no better than dozens of other Korean War films which used real battlefield footage to avoid spending money on recreations. An indication of how little Fuller had to work with is the enemy tank seen behind some bushes — it is made of cardboard.

Despite its paltry budget, *The Steel Helmet* was a rousing financial success. Its investment was returned tenfold and made Sam Fuller a bankable director, leading to his hiring by 20th Century–Fox. Audiences didn't care that the film was scripted in a week, filmed over the span of just ten days or cost a pittance; they responded to its power. Some arbiters did as well. *Boxoffice* decreed, "Producer-Director Samuel Fuller etched a commanding, albeit sometimes grim, picture of the Korean War as it pertained to the lives - and deaths - of one group of G.I. heroes." *Variety* called it "a grim, hardhitting tale that is excellently told." Arthur Knight of *Saturday Review* remarked, "Samuel Fuller has fashioned a tight, tense, exciting little picture."

Others, such as the reviewers for *Time* and *Newsweek*, found it to be a routine war story. Their judgment, however, has been forgotten; *The Steel Helmet* has, since the time of its release, been considered the single most important film to be made about American participation in Korea. The film does not contain the political ramifications of *Pork Chop Hill* or the impressive production assets of *The Bridges at Toko-Ri* or *The Hunters*. It does not feature a star such as William Holden or Gregory Peck. And Fuller's vision, compelling as it is, is not the brilliant nightmare vision of *The Manchurian Candidate*. Even so, because of its extraordinary timeliness, its finely etched performances, and, most of all, its gritty, unromanticized perspective of war, *The Steel Helmet* remains the single best and most representative Korean War picture ever made.

Strange Intruder

Credits: 1956. Allied Artists. *Directed by* Irving Rapper. *Produced by* Lindsley Parsons. *Associate Producer*: John H. Burrows. *Screenplay by* David Evans and Warren Douglas. *From the Novel* ("The Intruder") *by* Helen Fowler. *Music Composed and Conducted by* Paul Dunlap. *Director of Photography*: Ernest Haller, A.S.C. *Film Editor*: Maurice Wright, A.C.E. *Song*: "Bad For Each Other," *by* Carroll Coates. *Assistant Director*: Kenneth Walters. *Art Director*: Leslie Thomas. *Set Decorator*: Morris Hoffman. *Casting by* Fred H. Messenger. *Make-up by* Willard Colee. *Hairdresser*: Cherie Banks. *Set Continuity*: Bobbie Sierks. *Recorded by* Tom Lambert. *Chief Set Electrician*: Lloyd L. Garnell. Not Rated. Black and White. Flat (1.33:1). 82 minutes. Released in September, 1956. Not currently available on commercial home video.

Cast: *Paul Quentin*, Edmund Purdom; *Alice*, Ida Lupino; *Mary Carmichael*, Ann Harding; *Howard*, Jacques Bergerac; *Meg Carmichael*, Gloria Talbott; *James Carmichael*, Carl Benton Reid; *Parry*, Douglas Kennedy; *Adrian*, Donald Murphy; *Violet*, Ruby Goodwin; *Libby*, Mimi Gibson; *Johnny*, Eric Anderson; *Joady*, Marjorie Bennett.

Historical Accuracy Level: Medium. The prison camp scenes are authentic and gripping, but the rest of the story is a flight of fancy.

Patriotic Propaganda Level: Low. This film explores a stressed soldier's psyche, and is not meant to promote anything relating to war.

Elements: Army, Disability, Posttraumatic Stress Syndrome, Prisoners of War, Returning Home, Secret Missions, United Nations Forces.

Following the Vietnam War, a number of films were made featuring unbalanced veterans returning home to wreak havoc upon the uncaring society which did not want or understand them. This unfortunate stereotype became prevalent in the early 1970s, before the more serious Vietnam War films appeared and examined the veterans' problems with a more objective eye. Set during the Korean War, *Strange Intruder* is an interesting precursor to those stereotypical movies, in that it contains some of the same elements, and yet presents them in a suspenseful rather than exploitive format.

Strange Intruder begins in a North Korean prison camp. American and British soldiers are marched into the camp, carrying leafy branches to use for their bedding. One of the prisoners is Adrian Carmichael (Donald Murphy), a doctor who does everything in his power to keep his fellow prisoners alive, arguing that "The only weapon we have left against these animals is life." His best friend is Paul Quentin (Edmund Purdom), who has a wounded leg, the poor condition of which he is hiding from the guards. After another prisoner dies in Adrian's arms, he attacks a guard and is tied to a tree and lashed as an example to the others. Paul sneaks him water at night, but Adrian is very weak. An air raid commences and the camp itself is bombed. The prisoners take the opportunity to revolt and run free. Adrian collapses, barely alive. He gives Paul a key and a watch containing pictures of his children, and he makes Paul promise to visit his home and kill his children if his wife is still seeing another man, which she had admitted doing in a recent letter. He dies in Paul's arms after Paul makes his promise.

Months later, Paul is released from a psychicatric hospital on a weekend pass. He takes a bus to Adrian's home town, listening to Adrian's voice in his head narrating the journey, prodding him to go forward with his mission. Paul walks into the house, looks around as Adrian's voice describes past events and sits at the piano. His playing lures Adrian's sister Meg (Gloria Talbott) and his parents (Ann Harding and Carl Benton Reid) to the living room, where they sit astonished as Paul relates the histories of objects and people in the room and produces the key which winds the grandfather clock. The Carmichaels welcome Paul into their home, insisting that he remain with them. Paul feels at home and agrees, but he is disturbed to find that Paul's children are staying with Adrian's wife Alice, who has her own home.

Paul plays the piano for the family, including Alice (Ida Lupino), and describes life in the prison camp, telling the Carmichaels how Adrian helped so many people stay alive. Mr. Carmichael is overcome with emotion, hearing how his son lived and died in captivity. Alice takes Paul to her home, but the children are in town at school. Paul is unfamiliar with this home, though Adrian lived there briefly. Alice confirms that she was seeing another man, Howard Gray (Jacques Bergerac), but says that the relationship has been over for some time. While Paul seems satisfied that Adrian's children are safe, Adrian's voice asks Paul to "send them to him," causing Paul to sleepwalk around the Carmichael house.

Promoted as a domestic drama with murderous overtones, Allied Artists' Strange Intruder (1956) is only vaguely represented by its lurid advertising. The movie's central plot of endangered children is only hinted by the tagline "the most terrifying thing that can happen to any woman!" and all Korean War references are ignored.

The next day, Paul and Meg swim together and seem to genuinely like each other, and Mr. Carmichael, who has suffered a stroke and is confined to a wheelchair, tells Paul that his presence has encouraged him to fight the stroke's effects and that he would like for Paul to join the family in Adrian's place, to share their business and home. Paul is overwhelmed by the generous offer, but delays answering it. Meanwhile, Alice speaks to her lawyer, Parry (Douglas Kennedy), about Howard, who is blackmailing her for $10,000. Paul meets Adrian's children and loves them instantly; but he keeps hearing Adrian's voice begging him to keep them from Howard. He has an opportunity to drown them in Alice's well-house, but cannot. At night, Paul sleepwalks again.

Sunday morning, Paul plans to walk the children to church. Adrian's voice is insistent and Paul cannot stop himself from listening to it. He takes the children to the well-house again and leaves them there, returning to Alice's for a knife. Paul finds that Howard is there, demanding more money from Alice. Paul threatens him with the knife, saying, "You can't have them!" The two men fight; Howard knocks Paul down a flight of stairs into the basement and runs away. Paul awakens in bed and immediately asks about the children. They are fine, and visit him briefly. A local doctor judges that Paul is "shell-shocked," and recommends rest. That evening, Paul returns to the psychicatric hospital by bus after promising Alice, the children and the Carmichaels that he will return.

Strange Intruder is a strange-sounding movie, but its dark subject matter is handled very nicely and it is a thoroughly compelling feature. Based upon Helen Fowler's novel *The Intruder*, the film, through careful writing and realistic presentation, makes Paul Quentin's moral dilemma credible and pressing. Screenwriters David Evans and Warren Douglas took pains to provide a wealth of personal detail regarding the characters, which renders them more empathetic and, thus, makes Paul's fatal mission that much harder to accomplish because he likes the Carmichael family and has, essentially, adopted it as his own. And yet, Adrian's call from beyond the grave is fully understandable, especially as Howard Gray's true character is revealed.

The story attempts a very difficult trick: to convince audiences that Adrian's wish to have his own children killed is in any way justifiable, and it succeeds because Adrian in every other respect is such a good person, but when he is betrayed by his wife, he quite understandably cannot abide having another man raise his family. Because Adrian has kept Paul Quentin and the other prisoners alive, Paul feels that he owes his best friend this dying wish, even if it is horrifying to contemplate. Paul also realizes that he will have no life after the deed and tells Meg that he has no future. The moral battle within Paul, as he tries to honor his friend's wish even though it defies society's moral codes (including his own) and would ruin his own life, provides the film with a philosophical framework absent from most other movies.

Of course, Paul cannot kill Adrian's children. Even when he has evidence that Adrian was right about Alice's lover, and spurred by Adrian's voice in his confused mind, he cannot bring himself to kill. And that is precisely the movie's point. Life is worth living, no matter how bad things seem. In the prison camp the North Korean guards killed without conscience. Adrian called them "animals," and he was right. Paul finds in himself the strength to do the right thing, just as Adrian would have done had he returned home alive. Paul discovers that Adrian's life was very rewarding, as he was surrounded by a loving family, and he has the opportunity to partake in the same happiness himself. The film ends with an optimistic view that Paul will return to the Carmichaels, particularly to Meg, and live a fruitful life.

The opening prison camp scene is a brutal opposite of the idyllic life in Adrian's home town. The North Korean guards take pleasure in torturing their prisoners, even past death. They have no respect for their charges and rule with force. This view of Korean War prisoner of war camps is perhaps more one-dimensional than in the full-length movies *The Bamboo Prison* and *Prisoner of War*, but its power and directness is undeniable. Perhaps for a shorthand depiction of the conditions at the camp, the film follows the lead of *Prisoner of War* and visually depicts the guards' harsh treatment of even ill prisoners. And judging from stories of prisoner of war camp survivors from that time, the movie's accuracy is not far off the mark.

Paul Quentin (Edmund Purdom) wonders how he will survive incarceration in a brutal Communist prison camp during the Korean War in Strange Intruder *(1956).*

The Korean War is not mentioned again after the opening scene, except in reference to Adrian. Paul keeps public knowledge of his stay in the psychiatric hospital to himself, as though he is ashamed of not yet adjusting to civilian life. When the doctor terms his condition "shell-shocked" after his fight with Howard, it is the first tangible proof that Paul is still suffering from posttraumatic stress syndrome, though the term had yet to be conceived. The weight of Adrian's final wish is certainly heavy upon Paul's mind, but his observation of cruelty, barbarism and death has also affected him more deeply than he can imagine. The promise of time spent with the supportive Carmichael family, and particularly Meg, is his best hope for complete recovery.

Strange Intruder is very well acted. Edmund Purdom strikes the right balance of emotions as Paul is torn in different directions. Gloria Talbott is fetching and sweet as Meg, and their relationship, which only hints at further affection,

is very nicely enacted. Ida Lupino, Ann Harding, Carl Benton Reid and Donald Murphy (as Adrian) all fulfill their roles admirably. Director Irving Rapper has carefully crafted this most unusual of Korean War films superbly, delivering a smart, suspenseful, thought-provoking film from an idea that perhaps initially seems too shocking (or silly) to believe.

Critics generally praised the film. In their *Motion Picture Guide*, Jay Robert Nash and Stanley Ralph Ross called the film "Far-fetched but handled well." Paul M. Edwards, in his *Guide to Films on the Korean War*, concurred, saying, "it is surprisingly well done." *Boxoffice* commented that "Good taste and good talent combine to successfully elevate this psychiatry-laden drama from the maudlin and depressing experience it might have been, had it been entrusted to less competent hands."

Strange Intruder contains one of the most potentially disturbing elements (the killing of innocent children) in all of Korean War cinema, but does not exploit its subject. Rather, it seeks to explore the brittle psyche of a man caught between his promise to a beloved friend and his knowledge of right and wrong, which has beeen twisted by war. Its subject matter is unusual, but *Strange Intruder* is a forceful drama that provokes thought until its final frame.

A Stranger in My Arms

Credits: 1959. Universal. *Directed by* Helmut Kautner. *Produced by* Ross Hunter. *Screenplay by* Peter Berneis. *Based on the Novel* "And Ride a Tiger" *by* Robert Wilder. *Music Supervision by* Joseph Gershenson. *Director of Photography:* William Daniels, A.S.C. *Film Editor:* Frank Gross, A.C.E. *Art Direction:* Alexander Golitzen and Richard H. Riedel. *Set Decorations:* Russell A. Gausman and Julia Heron. *Sound:* Leslie I. Carey and Robert Pritchard. *Gowns:* Bill Thomas. *Make-Up:* Bud Westmore. *Hair Stylist:* Larry Germain. *Assistant Director:* Phil Bowles. *Special Photography:* Clifford Stine, A.S.C. Not Rated. Black and White. CinemaScope (2.35:1). 88 minutes. Released in February, 1959. Not currently available on commercial home video.

Cast: *Christina Beasley*, June Allyson; *Major Pike Yarnell*, Jeff Chandler; *Pat Beasley*, Sandra Dee; *Vance Beasley*, Charles Coburn; *Virgily Beasley*, Mary Astor; *Donald Beasley*, Peter Graves; *Harley Beasley*, Conrad Nagel; *Marcus Beasley*, Hayden Rorke; *Bessie Logan*, Reita Green; *Colonel Bert Wayne*, Bartlett Robinson; *Congressman*, Howard Wendell.

Historical Accuracy Level: Low. This tale of two downed fliers in the Yellow Sea is neither historically accurate nor is their plight dramatically compelling.

Patriotic Propaganda Level: Medium. Discussion of the Congressional Medal of Honor adds the only propaganda interest to this story.

Elements: Air Force, Congressional Medal of Honor, Infighting, Mystery, Romance.

The Congressional Medal of Honor, which is the highest citation for valor that can be awarded to U.S. military personnel, is an important detail in several Korean War movies, but

in none is it of greater importance than in the glossy soap opera *A Stranger in My Arms*. Although other films make use of the Medal of Honor in their stories, only this one builds its plot around the efforts of a dead soldier's family to secure the honor for their lost son. And while some of the aspects of this movie are surely melodramatic, that should not be said about the discourse involving the Medal of Honor.

A Stranger in My Arms begins some time after the end of the Korean War, as test pilot Pike Yarnell (Jeff Chandler) is grounded for bad judgment in landing his jet on the same runway as another taking off. Yarnell is also urged by his superior officer to attend the dedication of a veteran's hospital in New England, but the pilot refuses. The hospital is to be dedicated to the memory of a navigator killed in the Korean War. Yarnell is visited by Christina Beasley (June Allyson), widow of the navigator, who tries in vain to convince the pilot to attend. They argue, but Yarnell remains steadfast in his refusal. At home, Yarnell cannot sleep. He looks at a set of dog tags and a photo of Christina and recalls (in flashback) floating in a life raft with Donald Beasley (Peter Graves), a man who openly admits to cheating on his wife, wastes several rounds of ammunition shooting at circling shark fins and then tries to drown himself.

In New England, Donald's father Harley (Conrad Nagel) suggests that it might be time for Christina to move away from the Beasley estate and move on with her life, but she doesn't feel ready to do so. Christina explains to Donald's mother Virgily (Mary Astor) that Yarnell expressed no interest in attending and was rude about doing so. Virgily mentions that Yarnell's participation will be necessary to procure a Medal of Honor for Donald, and insists that the first step is to remind the public of her son's heroism. Christina also talks to Donald's younger sister, Pat (Sandra Dee), who is tired of all the fuss made about her dead brother. Virgily controls every facet of the dedication ceremony, until the moment when Christina, speaking about Donald, spots Yarnell in the audience and loses her train of thought.

Yarnell listens to Christina and then Virgily talk about Donald Beasley and recalls Donald's apathy on the life raft during a storm. Donald refuses to help bail, even after Yarnell threatens to throw him overboard. "I'm a coward!" he shouts. "I know it, I know it, I know it!" After the memorial, Yarnell is corralled by Pat and the two spend time in the local malt shop getting to know each other. Virgily knows Yarnell is in town and is desperate to see him. Christina is sent to find him and does so at the malt shop. She persuades Yarnell to visit the family. Virgily tries to impress upon Yarnell that Donald was a popular, heroic young man, but Yarnell doesn't buy the fiction, particularly when she tries to give him one of Donald's medals that Pat, interrupting, claims is hers.

Despite his misgivings, Yarnell stays at the Beasley estate and finds himself drawn to Christina. After a horseback ride, Yarnell expresses his feelings for her and they kiss. The pilot is introduced to Congressman Vance Beasley (Charles Coburn) at a formal dinner where an empty place is left for Donald; his portrait hangs above the table. Yarnell has another flashback about Donald, then listens in horror as Vance asks if he is in favor of Donald receiving the Medal of Honor. Aghast, Yarnell explains the importance of the medal and notes that only four fliers were awarded with it during the entire Korean War. Vance applies pressure and asks him

outright what it would take for Yarnell to change his testimony and recommend a medal for Donald. Yarnell is outraged and leaves. Harley

The artwork for this "emotional shocker" stresses the romantic coupling of Major Pike Yarnell (Jeff Chandler) and Christina Beasley (June Allyson), a situation brought about by the death of her husband during the Korean War, to which Yarnell was a witness. Universal's A Stranger in My Arms *(1959) is definitely a soap opera, and is certainly promoted like one.*

Beasley notes that some men have no price for their integrity, and is called a weakling and a coward by his father Vance. Christina calls the dinner "a rotten business" and runs after Yarnell.

Yarnell accuses Christina of trying to persuade him to lie about Donald, but won't answer her questions about Donald's death. He tells Christina that Virgily hates her, and that Donald hated his mother, but she doesn't believe it. Nevertheless, she returns to confront Virgily and learn the truth. Virgily admits that she was against Donald marrying Christina, and the young widow realizes that it's time for her to leave the Beasley estate. She packs and drives to the town's hotel, where she sees a repentant Yarnell. They drive around, talk about Donald and finally admit their love for each other. They return to the hotel to find the Beasleys waiting for them. In a quiet, dark room connected to the hotel lobby, Yarnell finally tells Donald's parents and widow what happened. "I killed him."

A flashback shows that after eight or nine days, the two men stranded on a drifting life raft are near madness and death. Donald won't stop talking about death and Yarnell is sick of it. He hands Donald his pistol and says, "Make it soon, will you? Don't let me keep you," and turns his back. Donald shoots over Yarnell's head, then shoots himself. Yarnell is mortified that Donald committed suicide, but it is too late. Two days later, the pilot remembers, the raft landed on a coral island and he buried Donald's remains. He admits to lying about Donald's death to spare the family members' feelings.

Yarnell continues to blame himself for Donald's demise, but Christina understands and forgives him. Virgily is aghast that Yarnell lied about Donald's death and threatens to expose him publicly as a liar. Harley finally takes a stand and threatens to leave his wife if she persists in prosecuting the man that kept their selfish son alive for an extra week. Virgily is adamant until Yarnell reveals Donald's dog tags and his will, written on the life raft, which details how much he resented his mother's control of his life. For once, as she reads her son's damnation, Virgily's grief is real. Harley comforts his wife and Christina joins Yarnell for the next step of their lives together.

A Stranger in My Arms is a glossy soap opera in the Universal–Ross Hunter (who produced) style of *Magnificent Obsession, All That Heaven Allows, Imitation of Life* and, later, *Airport*. It is directed by Helmut Kautner, a prominent German filmmaker who only made two English-language movies — *The Restless Years* (1958) and *A Stranger in My Arms* one year later — both of which, incidentally, featured young Sandra Dee. Both of Kautner's English-language projects are melodramatic, dysfunctional family-themed soap operas in the tradition of *Peyton Place*, which had been a monster hit in 1957. After these two movies, Kautner returned to Europe and directed films there until his death in 1980.

That *A Stranger in My Arms* is an imitation of *Peyton Place* is undeniable, and the film also bears a striking resemblance at times to *The Great Man*, a 1956 feature written by, directed by and starring Jose Ferrer. All three films are set in affluent New England and feature a casual disregard for the more dignified aspects of upper class existence in favor of duplicity and betrayal by largely amoral men and women. *Peyton Place* became a giant hit wallowing in its own trashy vicissitudes, while *The Great Man* is a moral parable about a despicable person with a benevolent public facade. *A Stranger in My Arms* attempts to remain on the higher moral ground of Ferrer's film and does manage to stay compelling on its own terms. Its chief fault remains the unyielding stuffiness of its primary relationship between Pike Yarnell and Christina Beasley.

The love that develops between the stoic test pilot and the curious widow never seems particularly real, no matter how impassioned the acting of Jeff Chandler and June Allyson. Their kinship is destined from their first meeting at the air force base and symbolized quite clearly soon after. He flies jets; she races horses; they are both alone and lonely. Their romance quickly blossoms and is encumbered only by the presence of the Beasley family. Such inevitability also surrounds Pike Yarnell's relationship with the deceased Donald Beasley. It is patently obvious that he is hiding the truth about Donald from the family and that sooner or later he will be forced to explain himself. Even with these structural problems, however, the film does maintain viewer interest because the majority of the characters and their dialogue are interesting.

Young Sandra Dee steals the show as Pat Beasley, the teenager who has a more realistic

Air Force fliers Pike Yarnell (Jeff Chandler, left) and Donald Beasley (Peter Graves, right) threaten each other while fighting to stay alive after crashing in the Yellow Sea during the Korean War in A Stranger in My Arms *(1959).*

view of life than anyone else in the household. Her attempts to win Pike Yarnell's heart are sweet and amusing, and she is very fetching and flirtatious in a swimsuit and a kimono. The same year, Dee would find lasting fame the same year in *Imitation of Life* and *A Summer Place*, and as *Gidget*.

Of all the characters in *A Stranger in My Arms*, perhaps the most memorable is Virgily Beasley, Donald's smothering mother. As played by Mary Astor, Virgily directs every scene in the life of the Beasley household and manipulates much of the town of Latham to fulfill her selfish dreams. That is why Donald despised her — she never allowed him to live his own life, but tried to force him to fit into hers. In an unending effort to reap social benefit from her deceased son, Virgily attempts to coax Pike Yarnell to join her plan to posthumously reward Donald Beasley with the nation's highest military honor, the Congressional Medal of Honor.

While Pike Yarnell is polite out of uniform, he does not seem honorable until he discusses the Medal of Honor. Then, his passionate rhetoric about the meaning of the award and the scarcity of pilots having won it in Korea (just four) reveal just how dishonest and dishonorable Virgily's plan truly is. And when Vance asks Yarnell outright what he wants in exchange for the pilot's approval of the scheme, Yarnell is nauseated. He finally understands the political pressure which pushed him to the town of Latham and is sickened by the baseness of the Beasleys' self-serving plans. The Congressional Medal of Honor has been exploited and cheapened in a few Korean War films; here, at least, it is given the respect that it deserves.

Ultimately, Pike Yarnell's flashbacks to the Korean War provide the impetus for the drama and explain his reticence to discuss the past or approve the Medal of Honor for Donald Beasley. Yarnell indicates that he was ordered to Japan to transport Donald to Korea, and that it was Donald's navigational error that landed them in the Yellow Sea. Still, Yarnell kept the despondent coward alive for six days, until the fateful moment when Yarnell foolishly handed Donald a gun. Yarnell then buries the truth with Donald on an island, not to save himself from blame, but to spare Donald's family the truth about his cowardice. At last the truth is heard, though even then it is not accepted by Donald's mother without substantiating evidence. When she is handed that evidence—Donald's will, written in his own hand, describing how he resents her interference in his life—it destroys her. The flashbacks provide the meaning behind Yarnell's reluctance to meet the Beasleys, and illustrate the cowardly character of Donald Beasley. Without the flashbacks, the film would lack balance and not make much sense.

Critics of the time felt, however, that the finished product did not make much sense. Bosley Crowther of the *New York Times* labeled the film "an obvious and labored thing," and eventually judged it "a thin dramatic dud." Moira Walsh of *America* wrote, "*A Stranger in My Arms* is undoubtedly an American soap opera and a peculiarly unconvincing one at that." And Jay Robert Nash and Stanley Ralph Ross call it "a bleary-eyed melodrama" in their *Motion Picture Guide.*

Despite such unfavorable notices, the film did moderate business for Universal and continued the Ross Hunter/Douglas Sirk style of melodrama prevalent at the studio at that time. The film also effectively argues that the truth of any situation ought to be known, and that holding such knowledge back, or ignoring it, is not only morally wrong but unhealthy for everyone. Largely forgotten today, the film boasts a powerful performance by Mary Astor and the charismatic presence of Sandra Dee, elements which overshadow the indulgent romantic interludes between the top-billed stars. In terms of Korean War films, it fits into the majority of routine, talky dramas, with only its discussion of the Medal of Honor offering any extra substance to the viewer.

Submarine Command

Credits: 1951. Paramount. *Directed by* John Farrow. *Produced by* Joseph Sistrom. *Story and Screenplay by* Jonathan Latimer. *Music Score by* David Buttolph. *Director of Photography*: Lionel Lindon, A.S.C. *Edited by* Eda Warren, A.C.E. *Art Direction*: Hal Pereira and Henry Bumstead. *Special Photographic Effects*: Gordon Jennings, A.S.C. and Harry Barndollar. *Process Photography*: Farciot Edouart, A.S.C. *Set Decoration*: Sam Comer and Ross Dowd. *Makeup Supervision*: Wally Westmore. *Technical Advisor*: Rear Admiral Thomas M. Dykers, U.S.N. (Retired). *Costumes*: Edith Head. *Sound Recording*: Harry Lindgren and Gene Garvin. Not Rated. Black and White. Flat (1.33:1). 87 minutes. Released in November, 1951. Not currently available on commercial home video.

Cast: Commander Kenneth White, William Holden; *Carol*, Nancy Olson; *Petty Officer Boyer*, William Bendix; *Lieutenant Commander Pete Morris*, Don Taylor; *Lieutenant Arnie Carlson*, Arthur Franz; *Ensign Wheelwright*, Darryl Hickman; *Alice Rice*, Peggy Webber; *Rear Admiral Rice*, Moroni Olsen; *Commander Joshua Rice*, Jack Gregson; *Lieutenant Barton*, Jack Kelly; *Quartermaster Perkins*, Don Dunning; *Sergeant Gentry*, Jerry Paris; *Admiral Tobias*, Charles Meredith; *Gavin*, Philip Van Zandt; *Sue Carlson*, Noel Neill; *Chief O'Flynn*, Walter Reed; *Chief Herb Bixby*, George Wallace; *Frogman*, John Close; *Major Kim*, Harold Fong; *Ralph*, Gordon Polk; *Man*, Jerry James.

Historical Accuracy Level: Medium. Elements of this story are certainly authentic, but the human drama is too simplistic to accept as historical truth.

Patriotic Propaganda Level: Medium. The characters are not stereotypical heroes, but service under the sea is viewed as exciting and rewarding.

Aspects: Behind Enemy Lines, Lonely Wives, Multiple Wars, Navy (Sailors), Rescues, Romantic Triangle, Secret Missions, Submarines.

Submarine Command was the first of four projects concerning the Korean War which starred William Holden. The others—*The Bridges at Toko-Ri, Love Is a Many-Splendored Thing* and *Toward the Unknown*—would come three years or more into the future, but this tale of submarine action was timely, as it was released around the midpoint of the war. Holden was just coming into his own as a major star, having recently appeared in *Born Yesterday* and *Sunset Boulevard*, and his stature provided *Submarine Command* with more visibility than other films of a similar type.

Submarine Command attempts to relate the physical and emotional difficulties of commanding a submarine and its crew. In 1950, Commander Kenneth White (William Holden) is examining the *Tiger Shark*, a submarine mothballed since the end of World War II, while still trying to accept the validity of his own actions of five years earlier. The story flashes back to August 13, 1945, as the *Tiger Shark* patrols the seas near Japan. The submarine, commanded by Joshua Rice (Jack Gregson), surfaces to rescue a downed American flier, Lieutenant Commander Pete Morris (Don Taylor), a brash officer with the attitude that submariners have things easy.

Early the next day, the submarine spots a Japanese convoy and Commander Rice allows his new executive officer, White, to attack it. White is successful, sinking two ships. The sub surfaces a bit later to rescue survivors and is attacked by a Japanese plane. Unseen by the sub's crewmen, Commander Rice and another sailor are hit by the strafing. They are evidently injured or dead but unable to enter the submarine, so White, as second in command, orders the sub to dive. Petty Officer Boyer (William Bendix) argues vehemently against White's order, but it is carried out. A Japanese destroyer, alerted by the plane, drops depth charges around the *Tiger Shark*, causing pilot Morris to adjust his thinking about the easy life of submariners. The depth charging stops, but the sub is forced to surface due to a deadly chlorine gas smell. The Japanese destroyer does not attack; the radio reports that the war is over.

Four months later the *Tiger Shark* docks in San Diego. White has commanded it since Rice was killed, but he feels inadequate in the role, especially since Boyer continues to resent what he views as White's dereliction of duty. White's fiancée Carol (Nancy Olson) is at the dock to meet the ship along with Pete Morris, but the commander delays seeing her in order to talk to

Mrs. Rice (Peggy Webber) about the death of her husband. She and her father-in-law, Admiral Rice (Moroni Olsen), ease White's mind about his decision, noting that he saved the ship first, as any good captain would have. He rejoins Carol and accepts her offer of marriage.

Four years later, White is reminded of his fateful decision by a newspaper reporter, and White allows his self-hatred, along with frustration from his administrative duties, to make him completely antisocial. Soon, even Carol cannot stand his bursts of anger and boorishness. She and Admiral Rice conspire to find White a job outside the Navy, and he reluctantly resigns. He tours the *Tiger Shark* one final time, bringing the movie to its starting point, and hears in his memory the voices of the day he took command. Carol is waiting for him at the dock, but White is unable to leave the Navy without redeeming himself in some way. She leaves him. White asks Admiral Rice to ignore his resignation and is told that North Korea has that very day invaded South Korea. White will be placed in command of the *Tiger Shark* and sent to sea within two weeks.

Some time later in North Korean waters east of Hungnam, the *Tiger Shark* is assigned to ferry two groups of commandos to the Korean shore in order to disrupt communications during an important paratroop drop designed to free some two hundred prisoners of war. One group of three men, headed by Pete Morris and a Korean officer, Major Kim (Harold Fong), is to destroy a radar shack, while two frogmen are to eliminate a telephone exchange one hundred miles away. The *Tiger Shark* deposits Morris and his men, but develops a propeller problem and falls behind schedule. Needing to make up time, White steers the submarine directly into the harbor to shorten the journey for the frogmen. This decision earns the respect of Petty Officer Boyer, who, like White, was also reassigned to the *Tiger Shark*.

The sub scrapes a mine cable, but enters the harbor safely. Both commando units do their jobs and signal the sub. White surfaces to contact the main command, and Korean shore batteries begin to bombard the enemy submarine. The *Tiger Shark*'s machine guns fire back, but the sub is hit and begins to sink. White and his men abandon ship and swim for shore as the

Paramount presents

SUBMARINE COMMAND

starring
WILLIAM
HOLDEN
NANCY
OLSON
WILLIAM
BENDIX
DON
TAYLOR

The lovers of "Sunset Boulevard" and "Force of Arms," in love again!

Split-second timing by commando raiders wreck enemy communications!

Helicopter transfer in mid-ocean—at Task Force rendezvous for "strike"!

Breathless moments as "The Tiger Shark" invades mine-strewn enemy waters . . . Scenes never before filmed.

THE U.S. SUBMARINE "*Tiger Shark*" IN BATTLE OFF KOREA'S COAST!

★ ★ ★

The Most Daring Naval Rescue Raid Of Our Time!

A JOHN
FARROW
PRODUCTION

Produced by JOSEPH SISTROM · Directed by JOHN FARROW
Story and Screenplay by Jonathan Latimer

Suspenseful submarine warfare is touted, along with romance and "The Most Daring Naval Rescue Raid of Our Time!" in Paramount's multiple war drama Submarine Command *(1951). Interestingly, it is the Korean War rather than World War II that is mentioned in the ad.*

gallant submarine sinks behind them. Fighter jets and planes carrying paratroopers roar overhead, their mission unimpeded by resistance because of the successful commando raids. On the beach in the morning, White and Boyer are reunited with Pete Morris and his men, and Morris tells White the news that Carol is pregnant.

Later, Carol christens a new *Tiger Shark* while Boyer holds the White's baby.

Submarine Command is a fairly standard war story in which one person attempts to make sense of his place in the chaos of war. White's crisis of conscience over the loss of his captain — he calls himself a one-day warrior who lost a

captain and quartermaster during his only battle action — is meant to show the most difficult
aspect of commanding a submarine. This scenario is repeated later in the film when a fire
breaks out as the *Tiger Shark* is being refitted.
Boyer wants to enter the fire area immediately,
but White orders him to don an asbestos suit before doing so. The crewman inside is badly
burned but survives, and once again, White is
commended by Rice for using caution, but
White's instincts were the same as Boyer's, and
he feels that his own precautionary attitude is inadequate. Only in the climactic harbor sequence, when "this time, the odds are in our
favor" does White gamble with the lives of his
men. He finally redeems himself in the eyes of
Boyer, and most importantly, himself.

Admiral Rice twice absolves White of
blame for his conduct, reminding the sub skipper that his topmost priority must be his submarine and crew as a whole, even when White
was forced to sacrifice Rice's own son to protect
the sub. White knows that Admiral Rice is right,
but he has a difficult time living with his decisions.

Although this study of conscience does not
venture into new cinematic territory (several
critics found it "monotonous" or "contrived"), it
is handled with some skill by director John Farrow, and well acted by William Holden. In three
of his four Korean War films, Holden portrayed
military men with deep misgivings about their
own capabilities, men who had to constantly remind themselves of the task at hand and forget
the past in order to successfully accomplish their
missions. The early 1950s were a time when neu-
roses and psychological conditions began to be
included in movies as motivational factors and
protagonists gradually became more troubled.
Holden embodied this trend as well as anyone,
and perhaps more often.

The weakest segments of the film are those
set on land and which concern the deterioration
of White's marriage with Carol. White's sudden relapse into self-hatred and bad manners
isn't always convincing because it is so rapid and
unsupported, and rarely in movies of this type
do wives leave their husbands, no matter how
lonely they are. Thus, it is somewhat of a surprise when Carol actually leaves White. The
script allows Carol to be as strong-willed and in-

dependent as her husband, although their reconciliation is never in question. As Carol, Nancy
Olson gives a strong performance alongside her
frequent costar. This was the fourth collaboration between Holden and Olson within two
years, following *Sunset Boulevard, Union Station*
and *Force of Arms*. Critics began to predict a long
partnership between the two, à la Spencer Tracy
and Katharine Hepburn, but *Submarine Command* was their swan song. They never made another film together.

Another weak link is Don Taylor. His character is rather ill-conceived as a romantic rival
for Carol, and there seems to be no good reason
for White to accept him as a buddy. Dramatically, Taylor is not on the same level as Holden,
and this also works against the romantic triangle's effectiveness. Holden has been quoted as reporting that he and Taylor spent much of the
film drunk, or getting that way. If true, it isn't
revealed in Holden's performance, but there is
some evidence that it affected Taylor's.

However weak the film's landlocked scenes
may be judged, there is no question that the sequences aboard the *Tiger Shark* are superior. Director Farrow was provided with assistance from
the Navy and the Department of Defense to ensure that his sea-going scenes would be as authentic as possible. Filming at Navy bases at
Mare Island and San Diego gives the film the
necessary verisimilitude, and the submarine interiors are all the more effective because they are
real.

The scenes depicting action at the conclusion of World War II are very well done and exciting, particularly the attack on the Japanese
convoy. Details provided here, such as the timing and switching for each individual tube used
by the torpedoman, distinctive sounds of depth
charges and the refusal of Japanese survivors to
accept help from the Americans aboard the sub,
ground the film in reality. And though the plot
device of having to dive the sub while officers remained on deck may seem hackneyed or contrived, it is certainly based on real events which
occurred more often than might be imagined.

The Korean War scenes are less successful.
Because the North Korean Navy was tiny in
comparison to that of the United Nations forces,
submarines patrolling around the Korean peninsula didn't face much opposition. Subs were

Tempers flare aboard the U.S.S. Tiger Shark *as Commander Keith White (William Holden, left) orders Chief Petty Officer Boyer (William Bendix, right) to keep the* Tiger Shark *submerged in* Submarine Command *(1951).*

mainly used to accompany naval surface vessels, conduct reconaissance missions and ferry commando units. While the film's mission is in line with actual usage, most likely two submarines would have been used in real life, and entering the mined harbor entrance would have been frowned upon. The other liability is the model work involved, which is obvious and unconvincing. It is difficult to accept that the loss of a submarine would be considered heroic, no matter how important the mission. Despite these misgivings, the film's final sequence is compelling and at least routinely satisfying.

One major critic was not too disappointed by the movie. Bosley Crowther of the *New York Times* noted that "...the story and the film are perpetually on the verge of an intriguing surprise. For the screen play by Jonathan Latimer is a compact and levelheaded job, the direction of John Farrow is naturalistic and the performers are uniformly good." Crowther didn't like the climactic heroics, however: "But, unfortu-

nately, the story goes sky high at the end in a purely theatrical blowout with the old ship in the Korean War. And also the psychological tension is completely and dismally relaxed in a blood-and-thunder adventure that has the officer recapturing his morale. It is disappointing to see a picture come so close and miss."

Time's critic wrote: "In its dramatic action scenes, *Submarine Command* is directed skillfully enough by John Farrow, but the landlocked portions of the picture occasionally reach nonsensical heights, despite the quietly commanding presence of Actor Holden." *Newsweek* termed the film too divisive: "All hands in the cast perform in the most creditable fashion, and it is regrettable that writer Jonathan Latimer and director John Farrow could not have made the picture more single-minded, fixing its attention hotly either on the drama of submarine warfare or the complexities of the moral conscience."

Ultimately, *Submarine Command* should be viewed as an efficient example of a "multiple war" movie. The film realistically depicts how submarines were utilized in two different wars for two different purposes, noting the versatility and high performance of both men and machine, and it makes a strong case for keeping a fleet of submarines in reserve "just in case." To balance its quotient of propaganda, the film offers a very human study of conscience of men under extreme pressure. Despite some soap opera elements and an admittedly weak conclusion, it is largely successful.

Take the High Ground!

Credits: 1953. Metro-Goldwyn-Mayer. *Directed by* Richard Brooks. *Produced by* Dore Schary. *Associate Producer:* Herman Hoffman. *Story and Screen Play by* Millard Kaufman. *Music Composed and Conducted by* Dimitri Tiomkin. *Director of Photography:* John Alton, A.S.C. *Film Editor:* John Dunning, A.C.E. *Art Directors:* Cedric Gibbons and Edward Carfagno. *Assistant Director:* Jerry Thorpe. *Recording Supervisor:* Douglas Shearer. *Set Decorations:* Edwin B. Willis and Alfred E. Spencer. *Make-Up by* William Tuttle. *Technical Adviser:* Major Walter K. Sims, U.S.A. *Song:* "Take the High Ground!" *by* Dimitri Tiomkin and Ned Washington. Not Rated. Ansco Color. *Color Consultant:* Alvord Eiseman. Flat (1.33:1). 101 minutes. Released in November, 1953. Filmed at Fort Bliss, Texas. Not currently available on commercial home video.

Cast: Sergeant Thorne Ryan, Richard Widmark; *Sergeant Laverne Holt,* Karl Malden; *Julie Mollison,* Elaine Stewart; *Merton Tolliver,* Carleton Carpenter; *Paul Jamison,* Russ Tamblyn; *Elvin Carey,* Jerome Courtland; *Lobo Nagalski,* Steve Forrest; *Donald Quentin Dover IV,* Robert Arthur; *Soldier,* Chris Warfield; *Daniel Hazard,* William Hairston; *Franklin D. No Bear,* Maurice Jara; *Sergeant Vince Opperman,* Bert Freed; *Shorty,* Dabbs Greer; *Moose,* Gordon Jones; *Chaplain,* Regis Toomey; *Woman,* Iris Adrian.

Historical Accuracy Level: High. This drama about army training in Texas is highly authentic and convincing, though its trainees are little more than stereotypes.

Patriotic Propaganda Level: High. The mean drill sergeant will yell and scream at his charges, but deep down, he loves them as if they were his own children.

Elements: Army, Infighting, Military Training, Romantic Triangle.

Because the vast majority of Korean War films feature military hardware, personnel and combat action, and are filmed with the cooperation of one or more armed services, it is natural that at least some of them present scenes of military training. Films like *Torpedo Alley, An Annapolis Story, Retreat, Hell!* and *Submarine Command* contain previously filmed footage of recruits undergoing rigorous training, footage which is supplied by whichever armed service the film is highlighting. Such footage furnishes a dose of realism for the finished product, but it is also evident that the film's actors are absent from such scenes, sometimes distractingly so. *Take the High Ground!* differs in that none of its training scenes are culled from other sources, and it is thus far more effective in making the training seem important to its characters.

Take the High Ground! begins in Korea, in May of 1951, as Sergeant Thorne Ryan (Richard Widmark) and Sergeant Laverne Holt (Karl Malden) lead a squad of infantrymen up a hill under enemy fire. Behind Ryan, a soldier sits on a large rock and takes a long drink from his canteen. His respite is interrupted by a bullet to the temple, which instantly kills him. Ryan, looking back, sees the soldier's unnecessary death and shakes his head sadly. Forging ahead, he clears the enemy machine gunners with a well-thrown grenade, and motions his squad to the top of the hill, to take the high ground.

Two years later, Ryan and Holt are sergeants at Fort Bliss, Texas, charged with indoctrinating new recruits into the ways of the U.S. Army. They greet a lineup of former civilians from various backgrounds, all of whom are to be molded into fighting men. The recruits are given haircuts, issued clothing and equipment and lectured by Ryan on the importance of their rifles. Later, while playing pool with Holt, Ryan is teased by another sergeant, Opperman (Bert Freed), about Ryan's fifteen requests for transfer back to Korea, all of which have been denied, and about his harsh training methods, a subject on which Holt agrees with

This promotional ad for MGM's drama Take the High Ground! *(1953), a movie about basic infantry training, more closely resembles that of a musical comedy. Note the reference to the studio's earlier success,* Battleground, *and the complete lack of references to the Korean War.*

Paul Jamison (Russ Tamblyn), has unforseen difficulties telling his left from his right.

On a rare night in town, the recruits surround lovely Julie Mollison (Elaine Stewart), who buys drinks for them. They are sent back to barracks by Ryan and Holt, spoiling their evening away from the camp. Holt wants to get to know Julie, but it is clear that she is more attracted to Ryan, with whom she argues vociferously. When she begins to collapse, they accompany the drunken young woman home and put her to bed.

The recruits are whipped into shape running obstacle courses and climbing a tall wooden trestle. They are subjected to tear gas, with and without gas masks. Ryan begins to explain why he is so hard on them, and they follow him back into the tear gas room with more stamina. More marching follows, after which the men receive personal mail. Though he is newly married, Elvin Carey (Jerome Courtland) does not know what to write to his bride; sensitive Daniel Hazard (William Hairston) suggests poetry and recites a sample. At a busy restaurant,

Opperman. The young men learn how to march in formation, although the most agile of them,

Ryan joins Holt and Julie Mollison, but intemperate remarks from Sergeant Opperman drive her into the street, crying. Holt follows and comforts her while Ryan fights Opperman in the street, finally learning that Julie left her husband while he was in Korea, shortly before he was killed. Since then, she has been seeing army men almost constantly, out of a sense of guilt.

As Holt spends more time with Julie, his relationship with Ryan deteriorates. Ryan humiliates Merton Tolliver (Carleton Carpenter) for chewing gum during bayonet practice, angering Lobo Nagalski (Steve Forrest) so much that he visits the Army chaplain (Regis Toomey) about his desire to kill the drill sergeant. While cleaning the barracks, the men fool around and have a pillow fight, leaving the place a feathery disaster. Ryan warns them that an inspection is coming, and they thoroughly clean their barracks. Their rifles, however, do not pass inspection, infuriating Ryan, who exhorts them to "Treat your rifle lovingly, as if it were a small child!"

Live ammunition exercises follow, conditioning the men to the sounds and feelings of actual combat. When one soldier stops to drink from his canteen, Ryan takes it away and empties it on the ground, remembering how the same action cost another man his life in Korea. When Holt protests, Ryan insults him, and Holt responds by slugging Ryan and leaving him alone in the field with the men. Later, at the recreation center, no one wants anything to do with Ryan and he leaves. Ryan's worst moment occurs when he scolds Tolliver for poor marksmanship. The recruit then points his rifle at Ryan's belly, threatening to kill him. Ryan slowly places himself between Tolliver and the rifle target, daring him to shoot at the target which can be seen between Ryan's legs. Taking the challenge, Tolliver fires his rifle eight times, hitting or coming close to the target most of the time. Tolliver exits, a marksman at last, and Ryan wipes his sweating face in relief.

Ryan visits Julie's apartment and makes a pass at her, but he does not want to hear about her dead husband so she throws him out. Back at Fort Bliss, Don Dover (Robert Arthur) is afraid to handle grenades, and goes AWOL after Ryan reprimands him. Ryan finds Dover and brings him back, gently admitting that his own father was a deserter, and that Dover would be ruining his life by running away. Ryan learns that Julie is leaving town, and at the train station asks her to marry him. She refuses, acknowledging that he is already married to the army. She leaves, and Ryan and Holt reconcile their friendship without either one saying a word.

On graduation day the now-seasoned recruits form ranks and march around the field in precision to the strains of the title song. Ryan and Holt greet a new batch of civilians and point to the marching men as real soldiers. Ryan directs the marching men around the civilians and onto a departure platform where a train is waiting to take them away. As the soldiers proudly board the train, Ryan and Holt begin the indoctrination of a new group of recruits.

Take the High Ground! is almost entirely focused on the aspects of training inexperienced young men for the rigors of combat. Producer Dore Schary was determined to make his movie as realistic as possible, and, as noted, totally avoided the use of stock footage. The actors portraying the recruits are undergoing actual training procedures on the screen. As a result, Richard Brooks' film is fresher and more immediate than other movies featuring military training, and is without unnecessary pauses (without dialogue) caused by the inclusion of training montages utilizing stock footage.

While the film cuts back and forth between the recruits' training and the romance involving Julie Mollison, it does manage to depict a wide array of training methods, from fitness exercises such as the obstacle course to bayonet practice, showing how and where to inflict lethal damage. Perhaps most impressive is its live ammunition exercise, where the recruits crawl beneath barbed wire and real bullets. In this sequence, the filmmakers pay special attention to the safety devices used to ensure that soldiers are not inadvertently killed. A machine gun is placed within a frame to keep it from dipping, and dynamite (rather than grenades) is exploded within sandbagged pits to prevent debris from injuring the crawling infantrymen.

The film is very successful in presenting to the public a variety of the methods used to train America's fighting men, and does so in an entertaining, compelling manner. This success was

Sergeant Thorne Ryan (Richard Widmark, center) interrupts a messy cleaning of the barracks in Take the High Ground! *(1953). Among the soaked army recruits are Merton Tolliver (Carleton Carpenter, left) and Lobo Naglaski (Steve Forrest, crouching).*

recognized by the industry when the film's writing (by Millard Kaufman) was nominated for an Academy Award (the writing award went to *Titanic*). In terms of its other goals, however, the film is less successful.

While the conscripted recruits are an engaging bunch, it is also obvious that they are representative of the standard stereotypes of this formula. There is a drawling Texan who stubbornly refuses to follow rules (Carleton Carpenter), an energetic goofball who cannot stop talking (Russ Tamblyn), an aristocratic rich kid who is secretly a coward (Robert Arthur), a lumbering, good natured Swede from Kentucky (Steve Forrest), an enigmatic Indian trying to prove himself the equal of anybody (Maurice Jara) and a sensitive black man who reads poetry (William Hairston). And, of course, whipping them all into shape is the good sergeant/bad sergeant tandem of Holt and Ryan. The tough

sergeant, Ryan, helps each and every one of them become a soldier; no one is allowed to fail. Yet even this inevitability is comforting and satisfying in its simplicity.

More troublesome is the subplot dealing with Julie Mollison. In an effort to bring some romance to the story, the shady character of Julie is introduced, and both Holt and Ryan are attracted to her. A normal cinematic romance would find Julie attached to one but attracted to the other, and force the better man to prove himself. But here, Julie is a self-confessed tramp, a woman who left one husband in Korea to die and who has thrown herself at many soldiers since then just to assuage her guilt. Furthermore, Holt does not seem to care; he just wants Julie for himself, and Ryan is sickened by the waste of her life. This unholy triangle comes to no good end; it is a relief when Julie leaves these men behind and catches a train for her future.

This odd and ill-informed romance does not contribute to the film in any way. Nice guy Laverne Holt comes on to Julie like a hustler, casting doubts about his intellect and character. There is chemistry between Julie and Ryan, but when he makes his pass at her, lit by the flashing of a neon sign, the movie moves uncomfortably close to rape. The dialogue is hopelessly melodramatic (she sobs, "I'm just no good!" to Holt), and her backstory is needlessly sour. The movie loses its pace and tempo during Julie's scenes and lightens considerably once she boards that train.

Julie is portrayed by Elaine Stewart, a beautiful woman who flashed across many theater screens in the early 1950s, appearing in thirteen films in three years. Stewart does what she can in a thankless role, but the movie is better without her character. Richard Widmark is his usual tough-as-nails self, and impressive in the few moments when he lowers his character's guard to reveal his humanity. Likewise, Karl Malden is solid, though his scenes chasing Julie Mollison are creepy rather than fun or romantic. Of the recruits, Russ Tamblyn and William Hairston are the most impressive. Tamblyn, who had made *Retreat, Hell!* just the year before billed as "Rusty," is a born showoff, and energizes the film with his humor and acrobatics. Hairston plays the role of an educated, poetry-loving man with dignity and just the right sense of pride.

With its high production values and talented cast, *Take the High Ground!* was very successful for MGM during its release. Most critics liked and recommended it. Moira Walsh of *America* termed it "For the most part a remarkably lively and interesting movie on a subject about which a great many people could profitably know more." *Variety* called it "an absorbing study," while Edward F. Dolan agreed in his book *Hollywood Goes to War*, judging the film "a taut and interesting study of raw recruits being trained for Korean combat." Philip T. Hartung of *Commonweal* summarized it nicely: "In covering its main theme, the training of men, *Take the High Ground!* is most successful. It puts over well its point: a drill sergeant, as tough as he is, isn't as tough as the enemy."

Take the High Ground! actually does little with its opening segment set in Korea; it's aim is to train the future fighting men not to make the same mistake as the soldier who stops for a drink during battle. But the film comes full circle, sending soldiers who have spent sixteen weeks preparing for combat to battle in Korea, and the audience now knows that they will be better prepared than that ill-fated soldier in the first scene. This circle of training concept was repeated even more successfully some thirty years later in *An Officer and a Gentleman*, wherein Richard Gere and a group of other people discover themselves during basic training to become naval aviators. For its time, however, the most successful movie of this type is certainly *Take the High Ground!*

Tank Battalion
(aka *Korean Attack*; *The Valley of Death*)

Credits: 1958. Viscount Films. *Distributed by* American International Pictures. *Directed by* Sherman A. Rose. *Produced by* Richard Bernstein. *Executive Producer*: Richard B. Duckett. *Associate Producer*: George W. Waters. *Screenplay by* Richard Bernstein and George W. Waters. *Based on a Story by* George W. Waters. *Music Composed and Conducted by* Dick La Salle. *Director of Photography*: Frederick Gately, A.S.C. *Film Editor*: Sherman A. Rose. *Production Supervisor*: Herbert G. Luft. *Assistant to the Producer*: Gabriel de Caesar. *Makeup*: Harry Thomas. *Art Director*: Rudi Feld. *Assistant Directors*: Richard Dixon and C. M. Florance. *Set Decorator*: Lyle B. Reifsnider. *Property Master*: Charles E. Stokes. *Key Grip*: Charles W. Hanawalt. *Special Effects*: Herman E. Townsley. *Costumer*: Frank Delmar. *Wardrobe*: Sabine Manela. *Script Supervisor*: Helen Gailey. *Sound*: Herman Lewis. *Production Secretary*: D. Jane Williams. *Sound Facilities*: Ryder Sound. *Camera Operator*: Harry L. Underwood. *Technical Advisor*: Charles L. Brooks. Not Rated. Black and White. Flat (1.33:1). 80 minutes. Released in July, 1958. Not currently available on commercial home video.

Cast: Sergeant Brad Dunne, Don Kelly; *Lieutenant Alice Brent*, Marjorie Hellen (Leslie Parrish); *Corporal Corbett*, Edward G. Robinson, Jr.; *Skids Madigan*, Frank Gorshin; *Lieutenant Norma "Red" O'Brian*, Regina Gleason;

Nikko, Barbara Luna; *Danny Collins*, Bob Padget; *Captain Caswell*, Mark Sheeler; *Buck*, Baynes Barron; *Egg Charlie*, Tetsu Komai; *Lieutenant*, John Trigonis; *Soldiers*, Don Devlin, Troy Patterson, Warren Crosby.

Historical Accuracy Level: Low. The action and romance which occur in this story have little relation to the actual fighting in Korea.

Patriotic Propaganda Level: Medium. A motley tank crew must prove their worth under fire, and spend much screen time romancing nurses and native women.

Elements: Army, Behind Enemy Lines, Females in the Field, Musical Performance, Nurses, Romance.

American International Pictures jumped into the Korean War film genre in 1958 with two releases: the abysmal *Jet Attack* and the seemingly more ambitious yet similarly ludicrous *Tank Battalion*. With *Tank Battalion*'s inclusion of women in the battle area, it also — like the other AIP Korean War films *Jet Attack* and *Operation Dames* — contains elements of exploitation, designed to attract a young audience. Of this trio of Korean War films, two of which were produced independently and only distributed by AIP, *Tank Battalion* ranks in the middle in terms of general quality.

Tank Battalion is the story of a four-man American tank crew in Korea during 1951. While fighting during a battle — composed of stock footage seen through the tank's rectangular viewfinder — the tank is damaged by enemy fire and the crew guides it back to camp for repairs. The crew leader is Sergeant Brad Dunne (Don Kelly), and he is happily surprised to find his girlfriend, nurse Lieutenant Alice Brent (Marjorie Hellen [actually Leslie Parrish]) awaiting his return. They renew their romantic relationship despite the presence of Captain Caswell (Mark Sheeler), who would like to keep Alice for himself. Meanwhile, "Skids" Madigan (Frank Gorshin) avails himself of nurse Lieutenant Norma O'Brian's (Regina Gleason) attentions, whom he refers to as "Red."

While the tank is being repaired, the men and women enjoy the hospitality of a local bar called "Egg Charlie's" because the proprietor, Egg Charlie (Tetsu Komai), is able to regularly secure fresh eggs for the fighting men. Besides eggs and beer, the bar's other attraction is Nikko (Barbara Luna), a beautiful Eurasian woman who works as a waitress and sings for entertainment. The tank crew's youngest member, Danny Collins (Bob Padget), becomes entranced with Nikko, even after telling his buddies that he is married. Only Corporal Corbett (Edward G. Robinson, Jr.), who objected to going into battle during the film's opening scenes, is left without a date during their hiatus.

The three men and their women drive into an "out of bounds" area for a late night picnic, and each couple is viewed talking and spooning. Returning to their jeep, the trio of women spy an enemy guerilla hiding in the woods. Collins finds him but cannot kill him; Dunne finishes the job with a knife. Other guerillas follow the jeep back to the camp and raid the nurses' tent after everyone goes to sleep. Medical supplies are stolen and Alice is attacked, but Nikko stabs the enemy soldier in the back, killing him. Another guerilla attacks Nikko but is killed by Dunne. The men, led by Captain Caswell, spread out and search for more soldiers, finding and killing three more. Collins professes his love to Nikko and promises to take her back to America; she gives him a necklace to indicate that she now belongs to him.

After the tank is repaired, the crew is sent into action again as part of "Operation Spider." The tank's gearbox is damaged by an enemy grenade, leaving it in a precarious position between a steep hillside and an enemy machine gun nest. The men decide that one of them must make a dash through enemy fire to find and return a tie rod for the damaged gearbox. Corbett draws the long match, but refuses to leave the safety of the tank. Realizing that someone has to try, Collins attempts the run and is killed. Shamed by his own cowardice, Corbett leaves the tank through a hatch in the bottom, successfully evades enemy fire and returns with the tie rod by sliding down the steep hillside behind the tank. Dunne quickly repairs the tank and eliminates the enemy machine gun nest with a grenade.

Tank Battalion was made to appeal to younger viewers by mixing romance and the hint of sex with its war action and the inclusion of familiar comic actor Frank Gorshin, who had appeared in a number of youth-oriented, low-budget films, in the cast. Because the men's women are menaced by North Korean soldiers, the film seems to emphasize personal indignity and revenge as motivating factors for fighting the Reds more than basic patriotism, thus making its battle action easier for younger audiences to accept and appreciate. The enemy soldiers are referred to as "guerillas" throughout, except for one mention of "North Koreans" by Corbett. And the battle action is almost entirely comprised of stock footage from Korean battlefields, poorly matched with the film's own footage. The matching problem is especially evident in the scene when the nurses and Nikko watch the tank depart for battle. The women are on the small camp set, while the tank drives away on a street that could not possibly exist in that vicinity.

Equally embarrassing is the interior of the tank. Actual tank interiors are dark, loud and crowded with machinery. This tank seems to be made of sheetrock, and has handy signs on its walls indicating various pieces of equipment. It is roomy and quiet as well, providing the men with a comfortable, if somewhat greasy, home away from home. At least the exterior is the real thing. It is also somewhat strange that the crew never provides their tank with a name, a practice that became common in the tank corps. An evocative name would have given the nondescript tank a bit more personality.

The film's script is routine and occasionally contradictory. "Operation Spider" is supposed to be a large-scale offensive, yet only the one tank is to be viewed. Danny Collins claims that he is married, but he goes after Nikko without a second's hesitation. Dunne receives a briefing on the operation, yet attempts to call for instructions in the midst of battle. Collins runs away from the tank quickly but is killed. Corbett staggers, falls down and has trouble jogging away, but he makes it safely, with Skids commenting "Look at that crazy guy go!" Only one aspect of the script works, which is the grudging acceptance of Nikko by the nurses who initially resent her open sexuality. Nikko watches the nurses work and finally asks to help, saying "I want to do something good, too." Their acceptance of her saves their lives when the guerillas attack, and helps them deal with the death and tragedy of war.

Don Kelly is rugged as Brad Dunne, Frank Gorshin is his usual impressionistic self as Skids and Bob Padget is earnest as Collins, but Edward G. Robinson Jr. is stone-faced and unimpressive as Corbett. His hair is also longer than would be allowed in the army. Marjorie Hellen and Regina Gleason are adequate as the lonely nurses, but they are upstaged by Barbara Luna as Nikko. Luna is lithe and sexy as the hot-blooded Eurasian, who has been invited to America "by every G. I. in the army." Luna sings one song, "If You Should Fall in Love With Me," in Egg Charlie's bar and displays her figure to advantage in several scenes.

Variety termed *Tank Battalion* "a routine Korea war yarn with generally good production values and performances," while *Boxoffice* judged the picture a "well-paced, hard-hitting war drama." The British Film Institute's *Monthly Film Bulletin* was less positive, judging the effort a "not very credible or creditable production," and noting that the musical score "is mainly a succession of free variations from Debussy." Top-billed actress Marjorie Hellen subsequently changed her name to Leslie Parrish and became a minor star, appearing in such films as *Lil' Abner* and *The Manchurian Candidate*. *Tank Battalion* comprised half of an AIP double feature, with the other half being a World War II adventure by Burt Topper entitled *Hell Squad*.

Target Zero

Credits: 1955. Warner Bros. *Directed by* Harmon Jones. *Produced by* David Weisbart. *Screen Play by* Sam Rolfe. *Story by* James Warner Bellah. *Music by* David Buttolph. *Director of Photography*: Edwin DuPar, A.S.C. *Film Editor*: Clarence Kolster, A.C.E. *Art Director*: Leo K. Kuter. *Sound by* Leslie G. Hewitt. *Set Decorator*: G. W. Berntsen. *Wardrobe by* Moss Mabry. *Dialogue Supervisor*: Michael Audley. *Makeup Artist*: Gordon Bau, S.M.A. *Orchestrations by* Maurice De Packh. *Assistant Director*: Oren Haglund. *Technical Adviser*: Major John R. Rawlings. Not Rated. Black and White. Flat (1.33:1). 92 minutes. Released in November, 1955. Filmed at Fort Carson, Colorado. Not currently available on commercial home video.

Cast: *Lieutenant Tom Flagler,* Richard Conte; *Ann Galloway,* Peggie Castle; *Sergeant Vince Gaspari,* Charles Bronson; *Sergeant David Kensemmit,* Richard Stapley; *Private Felix O'Hara,* L. Q. Jones; *Private Moose,* Chuck Connors; *Corporal Devon Enoch,* John Alderson; *Private Harry Fontenoy,* Terence de Marney; *Private First Class George,* John Dennis; *Sue,* Angela Loo; *Private Geronimo,* Abel Fernandez; *Private Ma Koo Sung,* Richard Park; *Private Stacey Zorbados,* Don Oreck; *Dan O'Hirons,* Strother Martin; *Strangler,* Aaron Spelling; *Priest,* George Chan; *Soldier,* Joby Baker; *Colonel,* Leo K. Kuter; *Marine Officer,* Hal Sheiner.

Historical Accuracy Level: Medium. The film has an authentic feel, though the story which ties its incidents together is not totally convincing.

Patriotic Propaganda Level: Medium. These Army men are certainly heroic, but the film also depicts the bloody consequences of war quite vividly.

Elements: Air War, Army, Behind Enemy Lines, Females in the Field, Infighting, Romance, United Nations Forces.

Many Korean War films were produced in the same mold as standard World War II movies. This group, of which *Target Zero* is representative, is not concerned with the politics or philosophies of the Korean situation and avoids bringing such complications to the foreground of their stories. Instead, these movies concentrate on conventional battle action, easily recognizable character types and formulaic Hollywood heroics. *Target Zero* recruits a British tank crew and a pretty United Nations biochemist for a variety of personnel under fire, but it does not stray far from conventional war film formulas familiar to audiences since the midpoint of World War II.

Target Zero takes place in 1952, as the United Nations forces battle the Communist forces of North Korea and China for the same territory, over and over again. Two women constituting a United Nations civil assistance team are fired upon and one is killed. The other, Ann Galloway (Peggie Castle), remains unconscious until a British tank unit happens upon her. Now behind enemy lines, she joins the trio of British soldiers in their American tank (dubbed "Phyllis") as they attempt to drive to safety. When

the tankers stop to repair their vehicle, they are joined by a handful of American soldiers, led by Lieutenant Tom Flagler (Richard Conte), who promptly takes charge of the group and points it — and the tank — toward Hill 806. This hill, also known as "Sullivan's Muscle," was the last reported location of Flagler's outfit, Easy Company, and he means to rejoin them.

Two mortar men, or "plumbers," are added to the group, which survives an attack by Chinese Communists without a single casualty. The group then marches toward Hill 806. Ann is angered by Flagler's arrogant attitude, but his second in command, Sergeant Vince Gaspari (Charles Bronson), explains to her that Flagler's toughness keeps the men alive. They march straight into a minefield, and one of the mortar men is wounded. British tank officer Sergeant David Kensemmit (Richard Stapley) drives the tank forward through the minefield, exploding about fifteen of the mines, and the personnel walk in the tracks behind the tank in single file.

In a wooded area a Korean temple is found, and the unit's Korean soldier (Richard Park) stops to worship, allowing the others to rest. Sergeant Kensemmit tells Ann that he dislikes American soldiers because one of them drunkenly attacked his sister during World War II. Flagler interrupts their talk, taking the opportunity to become a bit more friendly while rubbing Ann's sore calves. The radio man, Private Moose (Chuck Connors), is still unable to contact Easy Company or any other friendly fighting force.

On the move again, the unit is approached by a Chinese convoy. The men use their knives to set an ambush, stopping the convoy's vehicles without firing a shot. They drain the Communists' vehicles of gas, using it to refill Phyllis' empty tank. One of the Reds grabs a knife and kills one of the mortar men; the other is killed during a brief and brutal massacre which cuts down the remaining Chinese. After burying the two "plumbers," Flagler and Kensemmit fight briefly over Ann.

Sullivan's Muscle is quiet. Flagler climbs to the top to find the remains of Easy Company, lying in the trenches. He is distraught and unable to direct the rest of his unit, which has followed him up the hill. That changes when Sergeant Felix O'Hara (L. Q. Jones) makes

"MISS IT AND YOU'RE A ZERO —
HIT IT AND YOU'RE A HERO!"

The hell-hill they held was called 'Sullivan's Muscle'...
The 'pick-up army' was Flagler's 'Irregulars'...
The behind-the-lines break out was 'Operation Hero'...
and the circle of fire that held the lone nurse was

TARGET ZERO

The Story of the Glory of the Fighting G.I.!

PRESENTED BY WARNER BROS. STARRING
RICHARD CONTE · PEGGIE CASTLE with CHARLES BRONSON · RICHARD STAPLEY · L.Q. JONES
CHUCK CONNORS · Screen Play by SAM ROLFE · Produced by DAVID WEISBART · Directed by HARMON JONES

The description of the dramatic action on the poster for Warner Bros.' drama Target Zero *(1955) is almost a riddle, but the design is excellent, especially with the use of the targeting circle. Nowhere, however, is the Korean War indicated; it could just as easily be a WWII adventure.*

contact with the main fighting force while playing around with a field phone. Flagler is told that the Chinese are being driven back toward the hill and that he must hold his strategic position. The dozen men under Flagler's command clear the trenches and prepare for battle.

The next day, hundreds of Chinese soldiers walk toward Sullivan's Muscle, which they believe is unoccupied. Air Force Shooting Star jets swoop into the valley and attack the enemy force with bombs and napalm. Pinpointed by Flagler, artillery from a Navy ship fifteen miles offshore bombards the Chinese. The artillery fire slowly moves closer to the hill as the enemy does, and then the telephone line is cut. Flagler scampers over the edge of the hill to repair it and stop the barrage before it reaches his men. The Chinese attack up the hill and are slaughtered by the American and British machine guns. One of the scouts, Private Geronimo (Abel Fernandez), is killed, but everyone else survives. While the soldiers await the arrival of the main U.N. forces, Flagler takes Ann's hand and leads her out of a bunker and into the sunshine.

From left to right, Lieutenant Flagler (Richard Conte), Private Moose (Chuck Connors), Private O'Hara (L.Q. Jones) and Sergeant Gaspari (Charles Bronson) examine field telephone lines in Target Zero *(1955).*

Target Zero is a routine war film. Its characters are the familiar stereotypes of many other war films and its linear plot does not test the conventions of the genre in any meaningful way. The dialogue is realistic, if not fresh and original. Though the setting is Korea and the enemy the Chinese, this could just as easily be World War II with Nazis. Filmed at Fort Carson, Colorado, *Target Zero* has a generic outdoor feel to it rather than the specific look and texture which actual location shooting in Korea would have contributed. Finally, the film has little to say, whether in dialogue or by example of action, about war in general or the Korean War in particular.

To its credit, the script is not bloated with self-important statements about war or the nature of heroism. Instead, it paints a picture of Flagler as a mother hen, learning some of the details of his men's lives so that he will know how to lead them. He genuinely cares for them, and they in turn, as shown by Gaspari's confidence

in him, appreciate his leadership. This is nothing new, of course, but it is competently executed by a cast that consists of familiar faces, including Richard Conte, Charles Bronson, Chuck Connors, L. Q. Jones and, as the injured man, Strother Martin.

The addition of Ann Galloway and the British tank crew adds an international flavor to the story, reminding the audience that the war's cast of participants was, indeed, cosmopolitan. Two of the Brits have little to do but take orders and pretend to be cheerful for Ann's sake. Sergeant Kensemmit's surliness derives from being outranked by Flagler and losing Ann's affections to the American, but his attitude towards Americans in general seems too harsh to be caused by the one past incident to which he refers.

The key character is Ann Galloway. Her presence amplifies the tough soldiers' protective natures and allows them to express sensitivity and vulnerability. They respond to her because she is attractive, smart, brave and personable, and yet, somewhat surprisingly, there is little sexual tension surrounding her character. The men understand that she is off-limits and leave her alone. She slowly develops an interest in Flagler, and the men do not begrudge their commander some female companionship. Ann coaxes a few of the men to reveal their pasts or their dreams. She is the key to getting to know these men; it is, however, a disappointment to find that the secrets, stories and personality traits locked inside of the soldiers are largely unoriginal.

Critics of the time felt the same way. Bosley Crowther of the *New York Times* was not impressed. "That sanguinary business in Korea was unquestionably grim and wearying. But it certainly was not wearying in the way that it is made to be in this film." He also disapproved of "the casual, wholesale slaughter" of enemy soldiers in the ambush scene. The British Film Institute's *Monthly Film Bulletin* judged, "After a few tentative attempts at individual characterization, the film soon deteriorates into routine battle exploits culminating in one of the most cold-blooded massacres yet seen in an American war film. The romance between the tough, ruthless commander and the highly unlikely U.S. biochemist appears peculiarly repellent against this background of carefully contrived bloodshed."

Unfortunately, the bloodshed was not confined to the screen. Two explosives handlers were killed during filming. Apart from this tragedy, the film is not particularly memorable in any respect. It is very representative of routine Korean War films, which often find ways to interject women into battles, and massacre the Communists with bullets and napalm. Ultimately, even its action sequences are familiar and unexciting, resulting in an equally desultory movie.

Three Wishes

Credits: 1995. Rysher Entertainment. *Distributed by* Savoy Pictures. *Directed by* Martha Coolidge. *Produced by* Clifford Green,

Ellen Green and Gary Lucchesi. *Executive Producers*: Keith Samples and Larry Y. Albucher. *Screenplay by* Elizabeth Anderson. *Story by* Clifford Green and Ellen Green. *Music by* Cynthia Millar. *Director of Photography*: Johnny E. Jensen, A.S.C. *Editor*: Steven Cohen, A.C.E. *Casting by* Aleta Chappelle, C.S.A. *Costume Designer*: Shelley Komarov. *Visual Effects Supervisor*: Phil Tippett. *Production Designer*: John Vallone. *Unit Production Manager*: Larry Y. Albucher. *First Assistant Director*: Randall Badger. *Second Assistant Director*: Rebecca Strickland. *Stunt Coordinator*: Lisa Cain. *Stunt Doubles*: Cliff McGloughlin, Kay Kimler, Laura Dash, Taylor Burgess and Joshua Haines. *Betty Jane's Stunt Doubles*: Tito and Nikki. *Stunt Performers*: Joey Box, Christopher Fletcher, Shane Dixon, Tracia Lofdahl and Lisa Dalton. *Art Director*: Gae Buckley. *Assistant Art Director*: Natalie Richards. *Art Department Coordinator*: Nancy King. *Storyboard Consultant*: Harold Michelson. *Illustrators*: Brent Boates, David Negron, Sr., George Jensen and Carl Aldana. *Set Designer*: Tom Reta. *Camera Operator*: P. Scott Sakamoto. *First Assistant Camera*: Jimmy Jensen, Michael Weldon and Ken W. Fisher. *Second Assistant Camera*: Don Duffield III. *"B" Camera Operator*: Billy Brao. *Film Loaders*: Jason Jensen and Alex Haapaniemi. *Script Supervisor*: Karen Wookey. *Chief Lighting Technician*: Robert E. Krattiger. *Assistant Chief Lighting Technician*: Walter Nichols. *Rigging Gaffer*: William Krattiger. *Operators*: Tom Cantrell, Don Nesmith, Frank Jiminez, Brennan Price, Jim Krattiger and Daryl Smith. *First Company Grip*: Richard Moran. *Second Company Grip*: Hugh Langtry. *Dolly Grip*: Thomas R. Miller. *Additional Grips*: Mark W. Elias, John P. Morris, Kris Guthrie, Steve Robertson, Joe Kraft and Hank Sheppherd. *Sound Mixer*: Lee Orloff, C.A.S. *Boom Operator*: Nicholas Allen. *Sound Utility*: Tom Payne. *Set Decorator*: Robert Gould. *Assistant Set Decorator*: Etta Leff. *Lead Person*: Joanna Gilliam. *Set Dressing Buyer*: Stephanie Ziemer. *On Set Dresser*: Mara Massey. *Swing Gang*: Roberto Malerba, Marco Del Campo and Scott Garrett. *Property Master*: William A. Petrotta. *Assistant Property Masters*: Michael R. Gannon and Kevin Gannon. *Betty Jane Trained by* Birds and Animals Unlimited. *Animal Trainers*: Gary Gero and Roger Schumacher. *First Assistant Ed-*

itor: Scot Scalise. *Avid Assistant Editor*: Alexis Seymour. *Apprentice Editor*: Lance Chapman. *Visual Effects Assistant*: Audrey Chang. *Sound Designer*: Leslie Shatz. *Men's Costume Supervisor*: Bruce Ericksen. *Women's Costume Designer*: Carlene Passman Little. *Costumers*: Alison Gail Bixby and Bryan Birge. *Key Make-Up Artist*: John Elliott. *Make-Up Artist*: Gary Liddiard. *Key Hairstylist*: Hazel Catmull. *Hairstylists*: Kathrine Gordon and Dale Miller. *Mr. Swayze's Hair Stylist*: Paul Abascal. *Mr. Swayze's Meke-Up*: Scott Eddo. *Additional Make-Up*: Larry Abbott. *Special Effects Supervisor*: David P. Kelsey. *Special Effects*: Curtis Decker, Jeffrey D. Knott, Scott Garcia and Ronald M. MacInnes. *Construction Coordinator*: John Samson. *Set Estimator*: Felicidad Contreras. *Lead Painter Foreperson*: Peter Allen. *Paint Forepersons*: Alan Jones and Michael R. Blaich. *Painters*: Jeffrey Cahill and Cary Conway. *Stand-by Painter*: Paul J. Campanella. *Sign Supervisor*: Joe Murton. *Sign Writer*: Wayne Kerner. *General Foreperson*: William C. Jones. *Propmaker Foreperson*: Ronald C. Cox. *Propmaker Bosses*: Scott Annand, Jeff McMahon, Bobby Bednar, Tony R. Medina and Steve Bouchard. *Propmakers*: Daniel Blaha, Steve Eustace, Tim O'Brien, Joe Braus, Michael Forster, Jeff Poe, Joe Henry Catmull, Paul Koppelman, Charles Valley, Doug Crawford, Hugh Hanna, Joe Villalobos, Lance Crawford, Damon Hight, Gary Wortman, Scott Danielle and Richard Yeager. *Labor Foreperson*: Jan H. Marino. *Labor Gangbosses*: Alex Aguilar, Tony Castagnola and George Ward. *Purchasing Foreperson*: Roger D. Mervett. *Tool Handler*: Gary Metzen. *Greens Coordinator*: Lee Runnels. *Greens Foreperson*: John McCarthy. *Additional Greens*: Stephen Peiraro, Jason Vanover and Dennis Wood. *Transportation Coordinator*: David Marder. *Transportation Captain*: Marlo Hellerstein. *Picture Car Coordinator*: John Feinblatt. *Drivers*: Tom Battaglia, George Matejka, Tom Winchester, Tom Battoe, Mickey McAteer, John Sullivan, Russ Buckens, Doug Miller, David Turner, Lonnie Craig, Michael Price, Michael Wacker, Wayne Johnson, Brett Round and Shawn Wilson. *Mr. Swayze's Driver*: Frank Whiteley. *Production Office Coordinator*: Paula Benson-Himes. *Assistant Production Coordinator*: Katharine Rager. *Production Accountant*: Cynthia Quan. *Assistant Accountants*: Lisa Knudson, Victoria A. Zamora and Christine Tidman. *Location Manager*: Christopher W. Trott. *Location Consultants*: Michael Pew and Paul Harrison. *Second Second Assistant Directors*: Jennifer Wilkinson and Julie Herrin. *D.G.A. Trainee*: Sharon Swab. *Assistants to Ms. Coolidge*: Mary Lee and Sarah Grossman. *Assistant to Mr. Samples*: Brad Rivers. *Assistant to Mr. Albucher*: Penny Juday. *Assistant to Mr. and Mrs. Green*: Jennifer Verchow. *Assistant to Mr. Lucchesi*: Arnold Rudnick. *Assistant to Mr. Swayze*: Rosie Hygate. *Research*: Lillian Michelson. *Additional Research*: Deborah Fine. *Unit Publicist*: Donald B. Levy. *Still Photographers*: Lorey Sebastian, Richard Foreman and Bruce McBroom. *Acting Coaches*: D. W. Brown and Anne B. Dremann. *Casting Assistant*: Shaunda Jones. *Extras Casting*: Steve Spiker / Central Casting. *Extras Set Coordinator*: Gregg Kovan. *Magic Advisor*: John Carney. *Studio Teachers*: Rhoda C. Fine, Thomas McEnery, Jim Hartz and Richard Wicklund. *Baseball Coach*: Larry Baca. *First Aid*: John A. Flannagan, David Krupnick, Marie Hoke and Mary Mahler. *Caterer*: Tony's Food Service. *Chef*: Mara Kerum. *Craft Service*: Ted Yonenaka and Jon Gardner. *Fireworks by* Pyro Spectacular. *Fireworks Supervisor*: Jean Starr. *Production Assistants*: Jonathan Drubner, Matt Luber, Janet E. Jensen, Val Keller, Dr. Randy Olson, Steve Battaglia, Michael Williams, Kim Pribanic, Larry White, James Hoffman and Steve Cowie. *Music Editor*: Kathy Durning. *Orchestrator*: Emilie A. Bernstein. *Additional Orchestrations*: Patrick Russ. *Music Scoring Mixer*: Keith Grant. *Orchestra Contractor*: George Hamer. *Music Consultant*: Tim Hauser. *Music Coordinator*: Robin Urdang. *Supervising Sound Editor*: Teresa Eckton. *Dialogue Editors*: Richard Quinn and Dianna Stirpe. *Sound Effects Editor*: Malcolm Fife. *ADR Editor*: David A. Cohen. *Foley Editor*: Kyrsten Mate Comoglio. *First Assitant Sound Editor*: Marilyn S. Zalkan. *Assistant Dialogue Editor*: Lisa Storer. *Assistant ADR Editor*: Nancy Jencks. *Assistant EFX Editors*: Karen Alane Rester and Christopher E. Bennett. *Apprentice Sound Editor*: Frederic Vautier. *Foley Mixer*: Michael Semanick. *Foley Recordist*: James Pasque. *Foley Artists*: Margie O'Malley and Jennifer Myers. *ADR Mixers*: Bob Baron and Paul Zydel. *Re-Recording Mixers*: Leslie Shatz and Michael Semanick. *Dubbing Recordist*: W.

Phillip Rogers. *Voice Casting*: L. A. Mad Dogs. *Visual Effects Producer and Post Production Supervisor*: Laura Buff. *Visual Effects Coordinator and Post Production Coordinator*: Lauren Alexandra Ritchie. *Visual Effects Technician*: Mary E. Walter. *Visual Effects by* Tippett Studio. *Visual Effects Producer*: Jules Roman. *Supervisor / Art Director*: Craig Hayes. *Technical Supervisors*: Julie Newdoll and Adam Valdez. *Animators*: Blair Clark, Darby Johnston, Elias D'Elia and Tanya Spence. *FX Animators*: Deanan DaSilva and Brian LaFrance. *CG Coordinator*: Alonzo Ruvalcaba. *Performance*: Leonard Pitt. *Performance Capture Operator*: Bart Trickel. *CG Model Making*: Peter Konig and Paula Lucchesi. *Computer Graphics Artists*: Brennan Doyle, Aaron Kohr, Charles Granich, Steve Reding, Barbara Hryniewicz and Belinda Van Valkenburg. *Editor*: Kevin Rose-Williams. *Editorial Assistant*: Lisa Chino. *Film Recording*: David Rosenthal. *Software Engineers*: Doug Epps and Josh Minor. *Systems Administrator*: Dave Liebreich. *Facility Manager*: Linda Landry-Nelson. *Shop Foreperson*: Paul Silva. *Production Accountant*: Suzanne Niki Yoshii. *Additional Digital and Computer Generated Imagery by* R/Greenberg Associates West, Inc., a division of R/GA Digital Studios. *Visutl Effects Supervisor*: John Farhat. *Executive Producer R/GA L.A.*: Chip Houghton. *Producer R/GA L.A.*: Saffron Kenny. *VFX Art Director*: Tim Clark. *Lead Animator*: Scott Harper. *Matte Painters*: Bob Seifo and Craig Mullen. *Systems Administrator*: Peter Underkoffler. *Digital Technology Supervisor*: George Joblove. *CG Supervisor*: Joel Merritt. *Second Unit: Director*: Dennis Michelson. *Unit Production Manager*: Clifford T. E. Roseman. *First Assistant Director*: Jerry Sobul. *Second Assistant Director*: Alan Brimfield. *Director of Photography*: Bill Neil. *Aerial Camera Operator*: Rex Metz. *Aerial Camera Assistant*: Andrea Moraz. *Additional Camera Operator*: Garry Waller. *Assistant Camera Operators*: Brett Harding, Brian Lynch and Pat Swovelin. *VFX Video Assist*: Shockwave Entertainment. *Operators*: Bill McDonald, Ed Scnetzinger and Curtis Shenton. *Gaffer*: Lee Heckler. *Assistant Chief Lighting Technician*: Bill Krattiger. *First Company Grips*: Mike Anderson and Bobby Rose. *Second Company Grip*: Erich Rose. *Pilot*: James W. Gavin. *Props*: Eric J. Bates. *Assistant Props*: Kevin M. Gannon. *Songs*: "Do You Believe in Magic" *written by* John Sebastian, *performed by* The Lovin' Spoonful; "Seventeen" *written by* John Young, Charles Gorman and Boyd Bennett, *performed by* Boyd Bennett and The Rockets; "Earth Angel (Will You Be Mine)" *written by* Gaynel Hodge, Curtis Williams and Jesse Belvin, *performed by* The Penguins; "A Kiss From Your Lips" *written by* Billy Davis and Russ Fratto, *performed by* The Flamingos; "Secret Love" *written by* Sammy Fain and Paul Francis Webster, *performed by* Doris Day; "Crazy Man Crazy" *written by* Bill Haley, *performed by* Bill Haley and The Comets; "The Glory of Love" *written by* Billy Hill, *performed by* The Five Keys; "A Blossom Fell" *written by* Howard Barnes, Harold Cornelius and Dominic John, *performed by* Nat "King" Cole. *Soundtrack Album available on* Magnatone Records. *Main Title Sequence Designed by* Deborah Ross Film Design. *Main Title Animation*: Steve Scott, The Post Group. *Titles and Opticals by* Pacific Title. *Negative Cutter*: Mo Henry. *Color Timer*: Phil Hetos. *Prints by* DeLuxe. *Post Production Facilities*: Saul Zaentz Company Film Center. *Firework Stock Footage courtesy of* Illusion Arts. *VistaVision Camera*: Beumonte Cine Systems. *Cranes by* Chapman Cranes and Akela Cranes / Fluid Images. *Camera Dollies provided by* J. L. Fisher. *Avid Editing Equipment supplied by* Encore Video. *Office Computers supplied by* Balboa Computers. *Visual Effects powered by* Silicon Graphics. *The filmmakers gratefully acknowledge the following people and organizations for their cooperation and unending support during the filming of* Three Wishes: David Kirkpatrick, Robert McMinn, Melinda Farrell, Michael Backes, Pacific Family Entertainment, Pepsi-Cola, Video Resources New York, Inc., Mac Tools, Cadbury Beverages, Skycam, Rick Breniser, Cablecam, Lyle Trachtenberg, Teamster Local #399, Keppler Entertainment, Hershey Chocolate USA, Tootsie Roll Industries, Peter J. McGovern, Little League Baseball Museum, Los Angeles County Film Office, Canandiagua Wine Company, The Oakbrook Park Chumash Interpretive Center. *We remember with love*: Paula Benson-Himes. Rated PG. Technicolor. Dolby Stereo and Sony Digital Dynamic Sound. VistaVision (1.85:1). 115 minutes. Released in October, 1995. Currently available on VHS home video. Previously available on laserdisc.

Cast: *Jack McCloud*, Patrick Swayze; *Jeanne Holman*, Mary Elizabeth Mastrantonio; *Tom Holman*, Joseph Mazzello; *Gunther "Gunny" Holman*, Seth Mumy; *Phil*, David Marshall Grant; *Coach Schramka*, Jay O. Sanders; *Adult Tom*, Michael O'Keefe; *Joyce*, Diane Venora; *Leland's Father*, John Diehl; *Little Leland*, David Zahorsky; *Brian*, Brian Flannery; *Scott*, Brock Pierce; *Sackin*, Davin Jacob Carey; *Brian's Father*, David Hart; *Scott's Father*, Scott Patterson; *Sackin's Father*, Michael Laskin; *Hank*, Robert Starr; *Brian's Mother*, Simone Study; *Scott's Mother*, Lauren Sinclair; *Leland's Mother*, Annabelle Gurwitch; *Katherine Holman*, Moira Harris; *Policeman*, Neal McDonough; *Passerby*, Brad Parker; *Tool and Die Coach*, Philip Levien; *Colony Drive-Inn Coach*, Laurence R. Baca; *Neighbor*, Bill Mumy; *Neighbor's Wife*, Colleen Camp; *Little Magician*, Brandon LaCroix; *Cindy*, Jamie Cronin; *Hide and Seek Boy*, Alexander Roos; *Neighborhood Teenager*, Garette Ratliff Hensen; *Doctor Pavlick*, Jay Gerber; *Doctor*, William G. Schilling; *Holman Daughters*, Tiffany Lubran and Kathryn Lubran; *X-Ray Technician*: Marc Shelton; *Bystanders*, Vivien Strauss and Loanne Bishop; *Teenagers on Roof*, John Devoe and Ethan Jensen; *Man with Rake*, Robb Turner; *Betty Jane*, Rosa; *Stand-ins*, Michael Ashby, June Jordan, Robert Bell, Steven D. Mainz and Cheryl Gilbert; *Northridge 1994 USA Little League Champs*, Nathanial Dunlap, Michael Nesbit, Scott Drake, Todd Delevie, Peter Tuber, Justine Gentile, Jonathan Higashi, John-Michael Baca, David Teroaka, Spencer Gordon, Matthew Castle and Gregg Wallis; *Additional Ball Players*, Bobby Paschal, Ryan Drobinski, Jonathan Selman, Cody Cipriano, Brett Emma, Jimmy Sharp, Gary Sonkur, Tom Farron, Casey Shaw, David Anderson, Cody Haerther, Brooks Tinsley, Alex Chavez, Spencer Kelly, Derek Williams, Jimmy Drake, Marshall Plouffe, Michael Wong and Jeffrey Selman; *Jeffrey Holman*, D. B. Sweeney (uncredited).

Historical Accuracy Level: Medium. The depiction of a fatherless family soon after the Korean War is genuine and authentic, but their visitors are entirely too whimsical.

Patriotic Propaganda Level: Low. The story dissects how single mothers were treated in America during the 1950s and is not at all patriotic until the Independence Day sequence near the film's conclusion.

Elements: Army, Dogs, Homefront, Lonely Wives, Mystery, Returning Home.

Three Wishes is a movie that has some cogent things to say about America in the years just after the Korean War. While it doesn't directly deal with the war, the major characters — a widow and her two young boys — and their relationships to each other are affected by the war, particularly as they try to accept the loss of their husband/father, and proceed with their lives. The film also features an element of magic which unfortunately undermines its serious side and which makes for a very uneven motion picture experience.

The story begins in the present day as an adult Tom Holman (Michael O'Keefe) has lost his business and is forced to sell his home. His wife Katherine (Moira Harris) has a positive attitude about the change, but Tom is devastated. Driving his family away from their lost home, he almost hits a man crossing the road near a cemetery. Tom stops, remembering the man from long ago …

It is Memorial Day, 1955, and Jeanne Holman (Mary Elizabeth Mastrantonio) is struggling to raise her two young sons, Tom (Joseph Mazzello) and Gunther, nicknamed Gunny (Seth Mumy). The boys are fighting while in the car, distracting Jeanne's driving, and she hits a dog in the road. She stops, and finds that she has hit a hitchhiker and injured his leg, but the dog is unhurt. A local policeman orders her away from the scene and blames the bohemian-looking hitchhiker for the accident. Jeanne and her boys continue to a cemetery, where Jeanne tries to explain why their father was killed during the Korean War. That night, Tom befriends the dog from the road and lets it stay with him in the Holman house.

The next day, the dog leads the Holmans to the park, where the hitchhiker, Jack McCloud (Patrick Swayze), has slept. He has a broken leg, and after some hesitation, Jeanne insists that he stay with the family until his leg heals. The dog, Betty Jane (Rosa), befriends Gunny, the youngest Holman boy who is afraid of everything and who suffers from stomach pains. Tom, the older boy, is teased by the neighborhood kids because he can't play baseball well and because

The otherworldly aspects of Savoy Pictures' whimsical drama Three Wishes *(1995) are emphasized in this poster artwork. Patrick Swayze and the dog, Betty Jane, are highlighted, while the family which comprises the core of the story is unjustly neglected.*

of Jack's strange habits, such as sunbathing nude. In this suburban subdivision in California where all the houses, streets and families look the same, the Holmans do not conform, and Jack's presence only accentuates their oddness. Jeanne has left a secretarial job and is trying to make a living as an accountant, but she wonders whether it would be better for her family for her to accept the advances of wealthy friend Phil (David Marshall Grant) and thus provide a father for her boys.

Jack slowly wins Tom's trust and teaches him to play baseball. This success spreads to the rest of the team after they ask Jack to help them improve their play. Jack, a loner who has wandered the highways for years, is also drawn to Jeanne. Gunny experiences more stomach pains, and is taken to the hospital for tests. Back home, Gunny realizes that Betty Jane is more than just a dog, and allows the magical dog to allay his fears about many things. Betty Jane transforms his room into a jungle where a frightening "shadow creature" lives, but the creature is actually gentle, despite its appearance. Later, Jeanne confides in Jack that Gunny has cancer, and she is terrified and angry at the prospect of losing another member of her family.

The baseball team wins under Jack's tutelage, and Jack and Tom are invited to camp with the other fathers and sons. In the forest, Jack is shunned when he denies being the person the fathers want him to be. Tom and Jack walk home. As Tom accepts Jack as a father figure, Jack pulls away, insisting that the boy should resist conformity. Jeanne's friend Phil arranges for Gunny to be treated at the Mayo Clinic (without her consent) and proposes to her. When Phil insists that he is doing what is best rather than what is easy, she refuses to marry him. Lonely, Jeanne finds physical solace with Jack.

Jack's cast is removed and he prepares to leave. Gunny asks Jack about the dog and Jack explains that Betty Jane is really a genie who is providing three wishes to the people she loves: one for Jeanne, one for Tom, one for Gunny. Jack had a wish but gave it to the genie, who wished for his company on her travels. Gunny wishes to fly and see the July 4th fireworks up close. Jack prods Jeanne for her most heartfelt desire, which is to have Gunny beat cancer. Tom refuses to make a wish, so Jack makes one for

him. Jack leaves with Betty Jane, hitchhiking away from people they have learned to love.

At the Independence Day fair, Jeanne searches for Tom, leaving Gunny alone. The young boy flies up to the exploding fireworks and zooms unseen around the rides and amusements at the fair. In mid-air, he is subjected to bright lights and pulsing sounds that hint at a deeper purpose. Gunny comes to ground and finds his mother in anguish over his disappearance. Tom arrives to find a large group of people surrounding his entire family: Jeanne, Gunny and father Jeffrey (D. B. Sweeney), who has returned home after being kept in a Chinese prisoner of war camp for three years. Jack has left, but his real father has returned.

Adult Tom walks into the graveyard following the man he almost hit with the car. It is Jack, accompanied by Betty Jane. Jack explains that his wish for Tom was not the return of his father, as Tom thought, but that Tom should find happiness in whatever he has. "What have I got?" a despondent Tom asks. Jack points to Tom's family, playing together in the grass. Tom finally realizes that he truly is a lucky man. He turns to thank the genie and her companion, but they are gone. Tom returns to his family a happy man.

Three Wishes blends fantasy, whimsy, sentiment and social commentary within a serious study of a family trying to remain together, with very uneven results. Its central story, the difficulty of raising a fatherless, non-conforming family, is unquestionably its most effective aspect. Both Mary Elizabeth Mastrantonio and Joseph Mazzello deliver strong yet vulnerable performances, believable enough to carry the film without the more fanciful elements that are also employed by director Martha Coolidge. Mastrantonio is particularly impressive as a woman whose sense of self is bold enough to tweak the conservative social conventions and sexist attitudes of the period. Her convincing domesticity grounds the story in reality, always returning its whimsical fairy tale elements back to earth.

The secondary story, the drifter who enhances the stolid, suburban existence of the family and shows that differences are more valuable than conformity, also works, but not to the extent that it should. Jack's emphasis on meditation seems out of place in the 1950s and the reactions of the baseball team's fathers is unpleasantly depicted. And while the relationship between Tom and Jack is properly developed, it is hard to believe that Tom would so quickly accept Jack as a substitute father figure. The feelings between Jack and Jeanne are actually underplayed, which helps the viewer accept Jack's necessary departure when his leg heals.

The story's whimsical elements are the most troublesome. Why interrupt what could be a profoundly moving family story with magic and a dog genie? The filmmakers have tried to fashion a hybrid with a serious story that appeals to adults and a fantastic element for youngsters to enjoy, but the result is disjointed and unsatisfying. The premise of "three wishes" should have been rejected in favor of a more straightforward morality tale about the dangers of conformity. The fantasy scenes — Gunny's room transformed into a jungle and Gunny's flight at the 4th of July festivities — are well produced, but they are so different from the fact-based, solid feel of the rest of the story that the effect is jarring rather than sweet.

The film's final scene falls flat. It is nice that the adult Tom finally realizes the importance of his own family, but it is so sudden that it is not believable. Tom seemed like a smart, likeable kid when he was a boy; how did he mess up his life to the extent that he lost his home and business? Why doesn't he think about his loving mother holding the family together? Where are his parents, anyway? Wouldn't they be helping him cope with the situation? The final scene ignores these questions and provides Tom with an easy, obvious answer, one which is meaningful, but which is unsupported.

Three Wishes does have an emotional payoff, however, that arrives before the climactic present-day finale. It comes at the 4th of July fair, when Tom arrives to find that his father has returned. In retrospect, Tom considers his father's return to be Jack's wish for him; however, Tom narrates the story during that sequence to note that in the summer of 1955, fifteen American fliers were released from Chinese prisoner of war camps and returned to the United States, one of whom was his father. This simple reunion, though it is understated by the director, brings to the viewer a fulfillment, a sense of relief that the Holman family will be all right. Alas, the final scene brings that sense into question, only to reestablish it with words of wisdom from Jack.

It is because of Jeffrey Holman's wholly unexpected return that *Three Wishes* is considered a Korean War film. Throughout the film, Jeanne and her boys struggle to survive because Jeffrey is missing and presumed dead. In the fabric of 1955 suburban California society, a widow with two boys doesn't comfortably mesh. Jeffrey's absence is felt throughout the story; the boys are ostracized because they don't have a father and Jeanne is not given much opportunity to control her own life. But they do make progress, and Jack helps each member of the family to become a better person. Then, two years after the war ends, Jeffrey is thrust back into the picture, presumably for the good of all involved. While there is little record of prisoner of war returns so late after the end of the war, it is a true aspect of the conflict that U.S. personnel did return home long after they were presumed to be dead. In this case, Jeffrey arrives home at just the right time.

It is somewhat surprising that Jeanne seems to be the only single mother in the community, considering the probability that other husbands beside her own would have been killed or captured during the war. As it is, the movie spotlights Jeanne's as the one family that is directly affected by a husband/father absence. Jeanne and her boys are obviously pitied for their loss, but they are also ostracized, perhaps unintentionally, because they do not fit into the perfect family mold which is so prevalent in the film. People in the subdivision community (which is strikingly congruent, absurdly beautiful and precisely manicured, just like the one featured in *Chattahoochee*) do not speak of the war, but seemingly have made a pretence of getting back to "normal life" and staying there following the war.

Three Wishes was not well received by critics or audiences. Alison Macor of the *Austin Chronicle* wrote, "The film's mix of drama and fantasy doesn't blend well. Just as McCloud (Jack) coaches Tom in baseball by explaining how 'pushing too hard' achieves the opposite reaction, so too does Martha Coolidge lose the power in her film by striving for too magical an

Three Wishes (1995) is set just after the Korean War as widow Jeanne Holman (Mary Elizabeth Mastrantonio) tries to provide for and protect her young sons Gunny (Seth Mumy, left) and Tom (Josephy Mazzello, right).

ending." Jay Robert Nash and Stanley Ralph Ross judge it in their *Motion Picture Guide*: "Ultimately, *Three Wishes* is a bit predictable and heavy-handed for adults and too glum and long-winded for young children. While the endeavor is not without merit, most will leave the film comparing it unfavorably to [director Steven] Spielberg at his peak."

On the other hand, Paul Wunder of WBAI Radio termed the film "Moving, magical and utterly charming," and Kevin Thomas of the *Los Angeles Times* loved it. "*Three Wishes* is a wonderful film, full of warmth, humor and charm, a family drama with the possibility of the supernatural. It is an uncommonly accurate period piece, the kind that goes beneath the surface, and its stars, Mary Elizabeth Mastrantonio and Patrick Swayze, are in peak form."

An altogether odd movie, *Three Wishes* could have been a dramatic exploration of American mores as affected by events such as the Korean War and the rise to power of Senator Joseph McCarthy, but it instead turns to fantasy and whimsy to make its moral points. As such, it loses a great deal of power and wastes a warm and engaging portrayal by Mary Elizabeth Mastrantonio of a modern woman being smothered in a restrictive society.

Time Limit

Credits: 1957. Heath Productions. *Distributed by* United Artists. *Directed by* Karl Malden. *Produced by* Richard Widmark and William H. Reynolds. *Screenplay by* Henry Denker. *Based on the Play by* Henry Denker and Ralph Berkey *as produced by* The Theatre Guild. *Music Composed and Conducted by* Fred Steiner. *Director of Photography*: Sam Leavitt, A.S.C. *Film Editor*: Aaron Stell, A.C.E. *Art Direction*: Serge Krizman, E.M.P.A.D. *Set Decorations*: Victor Gangelin. *Technical Advisor*: Victor D. Baughman, J.A.G.C., U.S. Army. *Sound*: Fred Lau and Roger Heman. *Sound Editor*: Robert G. Carlisle. *Makeup*: Harry Maret, Jr. *Hairstylist*: Lillian Ugrin, C.H.S. *Wardrobe*: Henry West. *Script Supervisor*: Kathleen Fagan. *Dialogue Director*: Peter Simon. *Assistant Director*: Emmett Emerson. *Production Manager*: James

T. Vaughn. *Music Editor*: William Lloyd Young. *Titles by* Pacific Title. Not Rated. Black and White. Flat (1.33:1). 96 minutes. Released in October, 1957. Not currently available on commercial home video.

Cast: *Colonel William Edwards*, Richard Widmark; *Major Harry Cargill*, Richard Basehart; *Corporal Jean Evans*, Dolores Michaels; *Mrs. Cargill*, June Lockhart; *General Connors*, Carl Benton Reid; *Sergeant Baker*, Martin Balsam; *Lieutenant George Miller*, Rip Torn; *Captain Joe Connors*, Yale Wexler; *Mike*, Alan Dexter; *Colonel Kim*, Kaie Deei (Khigh Dhiegh); *Lieutenant Harvey*, Manning Ross; *Gus*, Joe Di Reda; *Steve*, James Douglas; *Boxer*, Kenneth Alton; *Lieutenant Harper*, Jack Webster; *Poleska*, Skip (Edward) McNally.

Historical Accuracy Level: Medium. This prisoner of war drama is fictional, but is factually representative of conditions to which American prisoners were subjected.

Patriotic Propaganda Level: Low. Delving beneath veneers, this film exposes harsh realities surrounding seemingly honorable American soldiers.

Elements: Army, Brainwashing, Collaboration, Mystery, Prisoners of War, Returning Home.

In subject and theme, *Time Limit* is very similar to *The Rack*, released just one year previously. Both films investigate conditions in Korean War prisoner of war camps which lead American prisoners to collaborate with their captors. Neither film provides a simple answer to the question of why a few Americans seemingly cooperated with their enemies, yet these two films offer the most comprehensive perspectives on the complex issues that are involved. *Time Limit* is based on a play by Henry Denker and Ralph Berkey, and has been transferred to the screen with its potent drama intact. It is also, incidentally, the only feature film to be directed by actor Karl Malden, and it proves that he could have had a profitable second career, had he pursued directing full time.

The film opens at prison camp GeeGee in North Korea, as four Chinese soldiers force a dozen or so soldiers from one hut outside for a surprise inspection. As the soldiers shiver in the cold, one drops a knife and tries to cover it with his foot. A guard notices the knife and the soldier panics and runs toward a perimeter fence. He is shot and killed from behind by the Chinese guards and the credits begin to roll. Colonel William Edwards (Richard Widmark) of the U.S. Army's Judge Advocate General's office on Governor's Island in New York has been investigating the case of a soldier named Harry Cargill charged with collaboration. Edwards has one final witness to interview, Lieutenant George Miller (Rip Torn), and he questions Miller while Women's Army Corps officer Corporal Jean Evans (Dolores Michaels) takes notes. Miller recalls in a flashback that Cargill "went over" to the Reds suddenly one morning, nine months after his arrival at the camp.

One blustery morning, Colonel Kim (Khigh Dhiegh) begins a lecture to the men of Miller's hut equating Communism to peace, but they interrupt him with coughing. Kim welcomes Major Harry Cargill (Richard Basehart) to the group and allows him to continue the lecture. Satisfied with Cargill's sincerity after listening for a few minutes, Kim drives away. The men tell Cargill he can stop, but the major continues the propaganda lecture. Realizing that Cargill has accepted Communism, his American colleagues walk away from him. "Don't you understand?" Cargill begs. "Don't you understand?"

Miller does not understand and says so to Colonel Edwards. Miller testifies that Cargill did not previously show any sympathy for the Communists and was respected by the men for his education — he was known as "the Professor" for having instructed at a college before joining the army. General Connors (Carl Benton Reid) interrupts and takes Miller away, wishing to talk to him about Connors' son Joe, who died in that very prison camp within days of Cargill's change of allegiances. Edwards' talkative aide, Sergeant Baker (Martin Balsam), takes advantage of the break to once again ask Edwards to get rid of the Cargill case before it politically ruins his career.

Major Cargill arrives and admits that he signed a germ warfare confession, made propaganda broadcasts for the Reds and gave indoctrination lectures to his own men in the camp. He says that he is guilty and just wants to end the inquisition as quickly as possible. But Edwards wants to know why Cargill "broke." Cargill explains that he was placed in solitary confinement and tortured several times. Edwards does not accept Cargill's easy explanation and plays an audio tape of Cargill's propaganda broadcast. Cargill squirms and finally shouts, "Turn it off!" Cargill is excused for the day, and Edwards is certain that there is some secret behind Cargill's actions. He determines to uncover that secret.

The following morning, Edwards visits Mrs. Cargill (June Lockhart), who doesn't know that her husband is refusing to defend himself. Since his return from Korea five months before, he has not discussed his experiences with her in any way, nor has he been intimate with her. She begs Edwards to help him. Back on Governor's Island, Edwards is informed by Evans of a peculiar similarity in the witness descriptions of how two men died in the camp, involving the term "acute dysentery." Before he can follow this new lead, Edwards is taken to task by General Connors for delaying the completion of an obviously open-and-shut case. When Edwards insists that he will do a thorough job, Connors takes him into his office for a private tongue-lashing. Baker takes the opportunity to tell Cargill that his case is ruining Edwards' chances for advancement in the army, and even Corporal Evans begs Cargill to tell Edwards what really happened in Korea. "There aren't any answers!" he replies.

Edwards returns and asks Cargill about the two men who died just before he accepted Communism. Cargill claims that he does not remember how they died. Edwards places Cargill in an adjoining room and brings Miller in for more questioning. Edwards again asks how the two men died, and again Miller insists they died of acute dysentery. Cargill is brought in and Miller goes crazy, yells that it wasn't his fault, and tries to attack Cargill. Eventually Miller admits, over another flashback, that all of the men in the hut (except Cargill) decided to kill Joe Connors (Yale Wexler). Connors, the general's son, had informed Colonel Kim that the soldier at the beginning of the story, Lieutenant Harvey (Manning Ross), had a knife and was planning to escape. The soldiers are angry that Harvey was killed and are seeking retribution. Miller draws the lot to kill Connors and strangles him with a rope while Cargill is held down securely, unable to prevent it.

The poster for United Artists' Time Limit *(1957) promises war violence and brutality, but the film's violence is all psychological in nature and is not shown onscreen. Nevertheless, the ad's central Christ-like image and small reference (in the lower box) to a returning P.O.W.'s sexual problems are true indicators of the film's powerful subject.*

Miller is glad at first to be rid of his "rotten secret," but then becomes agitated, thinking he alone will be blamed for Connors' death, even though he witnessed Edwards rip the notes of his confession to shreds. General Connors enters and Miller tries to confess. Edwards knocks

Miller senseless, then tries to prevent the general from learning the truth, but he is finally forced to tell the general that his son was the traitor, not Cargill. When Connors refuses to forgive his son, Cargill explodes. "You can't ask a man to be a hero forever; there ought to be a time limit!" Cargill finally tells the rest of the story, that Colonel Kim was so angry at the death of his prized informant that he threatened to kill all of the men unless Cargill cooperated. "Sixteen men seemed important. They still seem important," Cargill exclaims. General Connors understands Cargill's motivations, but insists that he made the wrong choice. "The choice you had to make in that prison camp is no different than the choice that confronts every military leader — the decision involving the life and death of his men. You are a sensitive man, a humane man. I sympathize with that man. But you are also a soldier. And as a soldier, you have failed, just as my own son failed."

Edwards makes his final recommendation that the criminal charges against Cargill be dropped, but he also believes that a court-martial is inevitable for the major. He offers to defend Cargill when the time comes. Cargill asks if a court-martial will provide any real answers. Edwards replies, "Well, they'll know we asked the questions."

Time Limit is one of several Korean War films to explore treatment of American prisoners of war, but it is the only one which depicts the prisoners' behavior just as harshly as their captors'. The central mystery's surprise ending is similar to that of *Murder on the Orient Express* in that everyone is involved, but the prisoners have strong motivation for their drastic action. Whether his fellow prisoners know that Joe Connors is the son of a general is not disclosed. It is likely that he has told them, and that Colonel Kim has chosen him in particular to intimidate because of his father's rank, but those issues are not raised. If they had been, killing Connors would be viewed as even more dangerous. But the movie uses Connors' execution as a moral issue, and perhaps the filmmakers did not want to complicate it.

The story's strongest irony is that during the time that the American prisoners held Joe Connors in place while another garrotted him, Harry Cargill was powerless to prevent the execution, and yet it is he who is likely to be court-martialed for treason. The film (and the play which is its source) argues that even a case like Cargill's which seems perfectly obvious from one angle can reveal important and devastating secrets if viewed from another perspective, and that care must be taken before prejudging someone for a serious crime such as treason.

Harry Cargill is certainly a hero in this story, and it should be obvious that he suffers far more humiliation and disgrace from American military justice than he ever did at the hands of the Chinese Reds. His key line of dialogue, spoken to General Connors in defense of the general's son, is, "You can't ask a man to be a hero forever; there ought to be a time limit!" Cargill goes on to tell the general that his son was a hero for hundreds of days, and only failed on one day. "Every man has his limit, sir. There's no crime in being human," adds Edwards. Despite understanding and sympathizing with Cargill, the general ultimately rejects humanism, declaring that the military code of behavior is of greater importance. "The Code is our Bible, and thank God for it," he exclaims. Thus, Cargill is sure to be court-martialed despite his self-sacrifice to save sixteen other men. There is hope for him, however, because Colonel Edwards now knows the truth, supports Cargill's decisions and is determined to defend him if and when the court-martial convenes.

The film's origin as a play is evident in its limited number of locales. Most of the action takes place in Colonel Edwards' office and the adjoining offices; only Edwards' visit to Mrs. Cargill's apartment, the Korean War flashbacks and footage of Edwards traveling to and from work take place anywhere else. The sequence involving Joe Connors' execution also points to a theatrical origin; every character is involved and participates in the action in some dynamic way. The movie is driven by its dialogue, which is consistently sharp, incisive and dramatic. Even the story's resolution, which is somewhat incomplete, indicates that it was adapted from a play. There is no traditional Hollywood happy ending here, yet the film does provide a meaningful and hopeful conclusion.

The movie only addresses the issue of "brainwashing" indirectly. General Connors is convinced that Cargill has "gone over" to the

Major Harry Cargill (Richard Basehart) is one of the freezing U.S. prisoners in a North Korean prison camp in Time Limit *(1957).*

Communists completely and should be punished for treason. Edwards is unsure but doubts that Cargill has accepted Communism, despite repeated torture and time spent "in the hole." Cargill's fellow prisoners accept that he has turned without ever trying to think the matter through. Cargill maintains the charade to keep the other men alive, and continues it after the war to cover their execution of Connors, for whom nothing more can be done. Cargill believes that his own sacrifice to the army's system of justice will atone for the sins of his fellow prisoners. Once the truth about Connors' execution is revealed, the notion that Cargill was actually brainwashed becomes moot. In actuality, the entire brainwashing theme is simply misdirection employed by Cargill to keep his men alive and by the filmmakers to prevent audiences from guessing the actual events of the story.

Time Limit was the first film star Richard Widmark made as an independent producer.

His company, Heath Productions, purchased the film rights to the play and hired actor Karl Malden to helm its production. Malden shot the film in twenty-two days with a cast of theatrical veterans, including Rip Torn and Martin Balsam in their first truly substantial movie roles. Malden accepted the challenge to film *Time Limit* because of its emphasis on relationships and small scope, and because of his friendship with Richard Widmark. He coaxed excellent performances from virtually every cast member, despite occasional battles over various acting styles on the set, and kept the film from becoming talky by employing a swift dramatic pace. The slowest scene takes place when Edwards visits Mrs. Cargill — that scene is also the movie's most sensitive. Karl Malden is justly proud of his only foray into the arena of film directing; although he was offered other projects, he preferred to act rather than to direct.

The performances are first-rate. Richard

Widmark is solid as usual as Edwards, displaying perhaps more sensitivity than usual in the role. Richard Basehart adds Major Harry Cargill to his long list of intense, psychologically troubled characters. Basehart is appropriately obdurate early in the film and wonderfully earnest once General Connors refuses to forgive his own son. Also impressive are Carl Benton Reid as General Connors, June Lockhart as Mrs. Cargill, Rip Torn as Lieutenant Miller and Dolores Michaels as the stenographer, Corporal Evans. Michaels is superb in the role, supplying Edwards with key information, attempting to prevent both Baker and Cargill from undermining Edwards' authority and just hinting at the feelings she carries for her boss. A full-blown romantic subplot would have interfered with this story, but the tenderness that Evans expresses for Edwards in her care of him communicates the relationship beautifully.

A. H. Weiler of the *New York Times* loved the film. "No less than the shattering drama that gave Broadway playgoers pause last year, this screen dissection of men's minds under the stress of war, is both tense melodrama and incisive drama ... it meticulously arrives at terrible truths that are timeless and universal." *Time*'s critic judged *Time Limit* to be "the best picture made to date on the subject of brainwashing." *Variety* called it "a good professional job of picturemaking in all departments and the grim and gripping flashback sequences lend dramatic vigor to what is essentially a sobering study of a contemporary problem." And *Boxoffice* raved, "A powerful, intensely dramatic and emotionally harrowing tale dealing with the aftermath of Communist indoctrination on American soldiers in Korea, this explosive picture should interest all serious-minded moviegoers."

Time Limit is among the best of the prisoner of war sub-genre of Korean War movies. Its prison camp sequences are not as harsh or vivid as *Prisoner of War*'s or *Strange Intruder*'s, but they are certainly believable. Its depiction of Communist indoctrination isn't as convincing as *The Bamboo Prison*'s, but then, that isn't its point. *Time Limit* excels, as does *The Rack*, in exploring what forces a patriotic American soldier to willingly allow the Communists to take control of his life. *The Rack* addresses the larger issue of courage in greater detail, but *Time Limit*

focuses its view on one person's choice between two evils borne of war. The film provides no easy answers, but as Colonel Edwards notes, "they'll know we asked the questions."

Tokyo File 212

Credits: 1951. Breakston-McGowan Productions. *Distributed by* RKO Radio Pictures. *Directed by* Dorrell and Stuart McGowan. *Produced by* George Breakston and Dorrell McGowan. *Associate Producer:* C. Ray Stahl. *Executive Producer:* Melvin M. Belli. *Screen Play:* Dorrell and Stuart McGowan. *Original Story:* George Breakston. *Music Composed and Conducted by* Albert Glasser. *Director of Photography:* Herman Schopp. *Film Editor:* Martin G. Cohn. *Geisha number* "Oyedo Boogie," *performed by* Ichimaru; *written by* Yasuo Shimizu and Shizuo Yoshikawa; *played by* Tainosuke Mochizuki Band. *Imperial Theatre number performed by* Takarazuka Revue. *Production Manager:* B. C. Wylie. *Sound:* Charles L. King III. *Art Director:* Seigo Shindo. *Unit Manager:* Hiroji Oshiyama. *Casting Director:* Ichiro Yoda. *Assistant Director:* Tadashi Tanjo. *Makeup:* Shigeo Kobayashi. *Assistant to the Producer:* Irene Breakston. Not Rated. Black and White. Flat (1.33:1). 84 minutes. Released in May, 1951. Filmed entirely in Japan. Currently available on VHS home video.

Cast: *Steffi Novac,* Florence Marly; *Jim Carter,* Robert Peyton (Lee Frederick); *Taro Matsuto,* Katsuhiko Haida; *Namiko,* Reiko Otani; *Mr. Matsuto,* Tatsuo Saito; *Mr. Oyama,* Satoshi Nakamura (Tadao Nakamaru); *Joe,* Suisei Matsui; *Mr. Jeffrey,* Byron Michie; *with* Heihachiro Okawa, Jun Tazaki, Dekao Yokoo, Hideto Hayasusa and Gen Shimizu; *Themselves,* Major Richard W. N. Childs, U.S. Army Reserve, Lieutenant Richard Finiels, GHQ U.S. Army Far East Command, Corporal Stuart Zimmerley, U.S. Army, Private James Lyons, U.S. Army, and Ichimaru.

Historical Accuracy Level: Low. The espionage which occurs in this story has little relation to the actual fighting in Korea.

Patriotic Propaganda Level: Medium. An American agent in Tokyo cracks a spy ring that is supporting the North Korean Communists.

Elements: Espionage, Japan, Musical Performance, Mystery, Red Menace, Secret Missions.

Because of its proximity to the Korean peninsula, the country of Japan was instrumental to the United Nations effort to defend South Korea. U.S. air and naval bases in Japan were used as staging and deployment areas, and air missions were flown from Japan throughout the war. Several movies depict life in Japan during the Korean War, but the first to do so — and the first to be filmed entirely in Japan — is the espionage thriller *Tokyo File 212*. While the story does not include any combat action, the activities described in the plot take place solely because of the nearness of the war.

Tokyo File 212 involves an American agent named Jim Carter (Robert Peyton, also known as Lee Frederick, and with a voice suspiciously like Hugh Beaumont's) who is sent on a "spot job" to intercept Japanese Communist agents who are threatening to cut U.S. Army supply lines to the Korean front. Carter poses as a reporter for the "National Weekly Indicator," conducting a survey of conditions in Tokyo during the war. Carter discovers sexy Steffi Novac (Florence Marly) in his room; she introduces herself to him as a guide who knows everything that is going on in Tokyo. Carter hires Steffi as his secretary and guide, and their first collaboration is to sample Tokyo's nightlife.

Taxi driver (and undercover agent) Joe (Suisei Matsui) delivers Carter and Steffi to a bar Communists frequent and Carter glimpses but does not make contact with Taro Matsudo (Katsuhiko Haida), an old friend from college. Carter's task in Tokyo is to persuade his former friend to defect from the Reds, and to expose the Communist cell in Tokyo. Carter discovers that Steffi has a sister in North Korea and begins to suspect that she is also an enemy agent. Carter meets with Taro's father (Tatsuo Saito), who explains that after Taro returned to Japan from college, he trained to become a kamikaze pilot during World War II, but never realized his destiny because of Japan's sudden surrender. Since that time, Taro has worked for the Communist cause. Taro contacts Carter and warns him to leave him alone. Carter is interrogated and beaten by a group of thugs in his lodgings, who reiterate Taro's message.

Steffi introduces Carter to businessman Mr. Oyama (Satoshi Nakamura), who has black market interests. An innocent dinner with Oyama results in a questioning that will prove fatal (by poisoning) to Carter if he answers untruthfully or refuses to answer altogether. Carter sweats through the meal, but survives. Carter finds Taro's former girlfriend Namiko (Reiko Otani), who agrees to help convince Taro of the error of his ways. She is injured by Taro's comrades, but Taro refuses to believe their complicity in her assault. Faced with proof that Steffi's letters to her sister contain secret military information, Carter arrests her, but releases her when she convinces him that she is helping Oyama in return for his promise to safely deliver her sister from North Korea. Carter wins Steffi's cooperation when he shows her a picture of her dead sister and explains that Oyama has murdered her.

Oyama leads Tokyo's Communist cell, and has been informed that "the situation in Korea has reached a critical stage." The Communists attempt to cause a transportation strike in order to interfere with operational support for the war. At a railroad yard, Taro's rhetoric rouses a crowd into a frenzy, but then Taro's father calms them by speaking. The Communist thugs beat Mr. Matsudo until Taro jumps to his father's rescue. Taro remains unconvinced that Carter's warnings about the Communists are true until he visits Namiko in the hospital and finds that she has also been murdered. Taro is caught by the thugs and taken to Oyama's office, where he is to witness the death — by time bomb — of his father, Carter and Steffi. Taro spoils the plan by diving from Oyama's high office window to his death, thereby drawing his friends away from the bomb's hiding place. Carter and the police surround Oyama, who decides to cooperate. Oyama is then stabbed to death by a Communist comrade, who is then shot and killed. Carter returns to the U.S., leaving behind repentant Steffi and Taro's proud but grieving father.

Tokyo File 212 is notable as the first American film lensed completely on the soil of Japan. Producer George Breakston, who had been a child actor in the 1930s, spent the early 1950s in the Far East, making low-budget movies with American leads that he could tout in America as being exotic and mysterious. Two of those films,

Special agent Jim Carter (Robert Peyton) and espionage suspect Steffi Novac (Florence Marly) try to bluff each other in Tokyo File 212 *(1951).*

Tokyo File 212 and *Geisha Girl*, are fashioned around the Korean War, while a third, *Oriental Evil*, takes place in Hong Kong and was filmed just before the war began. Though the films are photographed on location — and feature a small number of U.S. servicemen portraying themselves in tiny roles — budgetary constraints and a general lack of imagination prevent them from becoming the travelogue triumphs envisioned by producer Breakston. It was not until the major studios began using Far Eastern locales in their glossy films, lensing them in color and various widescreen processes, that the exotic appeal of the Orient was fully accepted and appreciated by movie audiences. Thus, in the mid 1950s, films such as *Love Is a Many-Splendored Thing, Sayonara, The King and I* and *The Teahouse of the August Moon* fascinated audiences and made huge sums of money. A similar trend occurred at the same time with movies set in Europe.

As a travelogue of Japan, *Tokyo File 212* is definitely minor. It is surprising that George Breakston did not include more than a few shots of scenic Tokyo or try to exploit his opportunity more aggressively. There is one scenic sequence involving a Japanese parade and a shrine in the town of Inoshima, but the remaining references to Japanese culture are in Oyama's dinner scene and the nightlife tour which Steffi and Carter take together. And the highlight of the nightlife tour is the Communist bar, which is an unintentionally comical den of iniquity. This movie has a fair share of unintentionally comic moments, but the Communist bar and its patrons are a real hoot.

The central story of Communist interference with the supply routes to the Korean front might be engrossing if it were handled intelligently, but rarely do the enemy agents depicted in this film pose a serious threat to anyone. Their plan of a transportation strike seems not only pointless as interference but also impossible to execute. The script fails to provide the Reds with any real menace, and also dilutes the danger at the very beginning, when Carter's narration notes that the people in Tokyo hardly seem aware of "the war in Korea just six hundred short air miles away." Likewise, the espionage angles of the story make little sense and tend to contradict the logical progression of the plot.

The movie does benefit from good performances, however. Robert Peyton, who was formerly known as Lee Frederick, is solid as Jim Carter, although his voice sounds suspiciously like that of Hugh Beaumont of the television series *Leave It to Beaver*. Satoshi Nakamura is smooth and oily as the villain Oyama, who at heart is as much a capitalist as a Communist. But the best performance is delivered by Florence Marly as sultry Steffi Novac. Steffi not only speaks several languages, but also speaks of herself in the third person, making the film's conversations intriguing to hear. Marly pours on the sex appeal, lithely pulling nylons onto shapely legs, and flirting with Jim Carter in a mysterious, exotic accent. While the espionage plot and travelogue aspects of the film disappoint, Florence Marly makes *Tokyo File 212* worth watching.

Variety declared the film "an atmospheric melodrama, filmed entirely in Japan, with good exploitation values" but complained that "had scripters come up with a story equally as interesting [as its visuals], *Tokyo File 212* could have been sock." A. H. Weiler of the *New York Times* judged the film to be "fiction on a comic-strip level" and decreed that "This is one 'file' that should never have been plucked from the archives."

The film remains interesting as a time capsule of Tokyo in 1951, but has little to say about the Korean War or the international situation at the time. If not for Florence Marly's impressive, flamboyant performance, it would be rather dull. It does intrigue, however, as an espionage tale in which no one seems completely trustworthy and danger lurks around every corner. The Japanese locale adds to the film's mystery, although it certainly could have been better exploited. And of the trio of Breakston-produced motion pictures, *Tokyo File 212* is by far the best.

Top Secret Affair

(aka *Their Secret Affair*)

Credits: 1957. Warner Bros. *Directed by* H. C. Potter. *Produced by* Martin Rackin. *Su-*

pervising Producer: Milton Sperling. *Written by* Roland Kibbee and Allan Scott. *Based on Characters from* "Melville Goodwin, U.S.A." *by* John P. Marquand. *Music by* Roy Webb. *Director of Photography*: Stanley Cortez, A.S.C. *Film Editor*: Folmar Blangsted, A.C.E. *Art Director*: Malcolm Bert. *Sound by* Stanley Jones. *Set Decorator*: William Wallace. *Costumes Designed by* Charles LeMaire. *Technical Adviser*: Lieutenant Colonel Frederick J. Bremerman. *Makeup Supervisor*: Gordon Bau, S.M.A. *Orchestrations by* Gus Levene and Maurice De Packh. *Assistant Director*: Russell Saunders. Not Rated. Black and White. Flat (1.33:1). 100 minutes. Released in February, 1957. Not currently available on home video.

Cast: Dorothy "Dottie" Peale, Susan Hayward; *Major General Melville A. Goodwin*, Kirk Douglas; *Phil Bentley*, Paul Stewart; *Colonel Homer W. Gooch*, Jim Backus; *General Grimshaw*, John Cromwell; *Senator Burwick*, Roland Winters; *Butler*, A. E. Gould-Porter; *Lotzie*, Michael Fox; *Sergeant Kruger*, Frank Gerstle; *Bill Hadley*, Charles Lane; *Myrna Maynard*, Edna Holland; *German Field Marshal*, Ivan Triesault; *Korean Dignitary*, Lee Choon Wha; *Armande*, Franco Corsaro; *Stumpy*, Lyn Osborn; *Girl*, Patti Gallagher; *Drunk at Table*, Sid Chatton; *Mr. Jones*, Jonathan Hale; *Personage*, Charles Meredith; *Man*, James Flavin; *Reporters*, Hal Dawson, Hugh Lawrence, Richard Cutting.

Historical Accuracy Level: Low. This movie recounts a fictional episode during the Korean War which never would have happened.

Patriotic Propaganda Level: High. An Army general is lampooned, but he consistently wins his battles and eventually has the last laugh.

Elements: Army, Collaboration, Comedy, Espionage, Journalism, Multiple Wars, Musical Performance, Mystery, Romance, Secret Missions.

Characters from John P. Marquand's novel *Melville Goodwin, U.S.A.*, form the basis of this comedy that contrasts civilian ambiguity against military precision and which generally seems to favor the military side of things. Billed as a "battle between the sexes," the movie is rather a personal campaign initiated by an arrogant, power-mad publisher who cannot abide the same level of confidence in a two-star general whom she attempts to discredit. Most of the comedy hinges

The poses of publisher Dottie Peale (Susan Hayward) and Major General Melville A. Goodwin (Kirk Douglas, center), reveal a playful, if contentious, relationship in Warner Bros.' comedy Top Secret Affair *(1957). The stars are the entire show in this underrated comedy, though calling it "the biggest happiness-maker since* Mister Roberts*" is a bit hard to swallow.*

on the opposite approaches to various situations displayed by the civilian publisher and the military commander. Their volatile relationship sparks this amusing and occasionally incisive motion picture.

Media mogul Dorothy "Dottie" Peale (Susan Hayward) is taken aback when her nominee for the post of chairman of the Joint Atomic International Commission is passed over by the U.S. President in favor of Major General

Melville Goodwin (Kirk Douglas). Determined to get her way, Dottie decides to discredit the general, and offers to write a cover story on Goodwin for her magazine "News World." Goodwin is ordered by the Pentagon to cooperate, so he and Public Information Officer Homer Gooch (Jim Backus) move into the Peale mansion to submit to an in-depth interview.

After four days, Dottie and her tart-tongued editor Phil Bentley (Paul Stewart) have nothing incriminating whatsoever, so Dottie tries a different tack. She dresses up and takes the general out on the town, arranging for photographers to catch Goodwin in compromising situations. During the evening, she "accidentally" knocks him into a table while dancing, forces him to sing in a jazz nightclub and inadvertently falls in love with him. Goodwin is angry at the humiliation, but finds himself drawn to her as well.

Dottie changes her plans, cancels the story and considers a future with the general, but he doesn't want to be "tied down" and tells her so. Furious at being rejected, Dottie decides to go ahead with the story, including incriminating information about a woman to whom Goodwin divulged military secrets during the Korean War. The story's publication leads to a Senate investigation of Goodwin's conduct, which he cannot properly defend since the Korean War information is still classified as top secret. Dottie is subpoenaed to appear before the Senate committee, where she admits that her article is a fraud and that she published it for revenge. However, she cannot deny the story about the spy, which Goodwin told her himself.

As the Senate hearing is about to close, Goodwin's effort to declassify the top secret information is finally permitted by the president. Goodwin recounts how he fell in love with a woman whom Pentagon officials knew to be an enemy agent. He was ordered — against his own wishes — to continue the relationship and to feed false information to her in the days before the surprise landing at Inchon. Afterward, Goodwin had the woman arrested as a spy and executed by a firing squad. Once the full truth is known, Goodwin is celebrated as a hero and he is able to forgive Dottie, whom he wants to marry.

Top Secret Affair is a fluffy, bright comedy originally slated to star Humphrey Bogart and Lauren Bacall. The comedy roles were a change of pace for two highly dramatic actors, Kirk Douglas and Susan Hayward, but they work well in the formula — for different reasons. Douglas plays his tough-as-steel role straight, with no mugging or hijinks. He is effective precisely because he is so ramrod straight. In the film's most poignant moment, Goodwin is forced onstage at the jazz club to sing a song. He knows he is being humiliated and he doesn't like it, but he goes along with the gag anyway. He sings "The Caisson Song," and sings it as if he were in a military parade. The jazz club audience appreciates his effort and joins him in two refrains. Dottie watches from the bar, realizing that her joke has turned sour and that she has embarrassed him; she also realizes at that moment that she has sincere feelings for him because he is unwilling to compromise who he is.

Susan Hayward plays her role with flamboyant relish, enjoying the opportunity to insult or command virtually every other character. Accustomed to more dramatic parts, she takes the care to ground her own character, though at times she might have been better served letting Dottie seem even more malevolent than she is. Still, Hayward is fun to watch as she insults Goodwin as "Iron Pants," "Turtlehead" and "Blabbermouth," and plots his very public destruction. The supporting cast is strong, led by the impeccable Paul Stewart as Dottie's right-hand man, editor Phil Bentley. He is the voice of reason at News World, yet he is the most sarcastic character as well.

The comedy in *Top Secret Affair* is a nice mixture of sharp dialogue, broad insult and physical flair. Early in the film, Douglas plays most of a scene balancing precariously on a "bongo board," a slat perched on top of a rolling wooden cylinder. Douglas' deft balancing act adds enormously to Goodwin's reputation as a man who can handle anything and look good doing so. Hayward has a long comic drunk scene, culminating in her fully clothed dip into the pool, and she has an early comeuppance when Douglas attempts to teach her some self-defense moves. Perhaps the sharpest moment occurs as Dottie is wondering nervously how Goodwin will react to the negative article, and then he arrives with a gun in his hand.

Beneath the joviality, however, there is an undercurrent of seriousness — as there is in most good comedies. *Top Secret Affair* satirizes topics which, if taken seriously, might be melodramatic in nature. First is the military itself, as personified by eminently superior Melville Goodwin. The film pokes fun at his military precision and bearing while also respecting it and what it represents. Second is the battle between the sexes, particularly the depiction of the power plays between General Goodwin and media mogul Dottie Peale. Much of the film's playful sexual tension is based on the lead characters' distaste for the weakness of the opposite sex and slowly discovering that their perceptions are, at least in terms of each other, unfounded.

The third topic is the tawdry prosecution of Goodwin by News World — personal abuse of the First Amendment — which is played for laughs because the subject, Goodwin, is so supremely untouchable. This includes the Sen-

ate investigation of Goodwin's character. There is limited humor in this segment, which is obviously based on the McCarthy hearings of a few years earlier. What drama the film contains is in this area, which is also redundant in the way that the Senate investigator (Roland Winters, the only man on the committee to speak) manhandles Goodwin, though without the charm and tactfulness with which Dottie had handled him. The film raises the spectre of McCarthyism, threatening Goodwin's career with public humiliation at the hands of an egotistical senator, but then provides Goodwin with permission to speak and debunk the falsehoods which surround him. And the general provides a dramatic punctuation point for his testimony when he informs the court that the French spy with whom he dallied was summarily shot.

Goodwin is seen as "the perfect hero" because of his military action in World War II, when he was awarded the Distinguished Service

Publishing mogul Dottie Peale (Susan Hayward, right) discusses Major General Melville Goodwin (Kirk Douglas, center), a man she wants to publicly discredit, with her second in command, Phil Bentley (Paul Stewart, left) in the comedy Top Secret Affair *(1957).*

Cross, and Korea, where he was isolated behind enemy lines for twenty-two days before a heroic "return from the dead." Film footage of Goodwin on a tank during the Korean War is shown, causing Dottie to mutter, "Get back in your tank, Turtlehead!" And it is during the Korean War that Goodwin had his fateful encounter with Yvette DeFresney, the French woman found spying for the North Koreans.

Dottie's accusation that Goodwin was collaborating with the enemy, providing secret information to a civilian woman for sexual favors, is quite damning and is the main area of investigation by the Senate. Even four years after the conclusion of the Korean War, collaboration was still a sore subject, one that contributed a hard, sharp edge to an otherwise airy comedy. Adding yet another sharp edge to this sequence is the revelation that Goodwin eventually had the female spy arrested and executed! That act concludes one particular battle of the sexes, and should give Dottie fair warning about the man she intends to marry.

Top Secret Affair did not fare well in theatres, possibly because audiences were unwilling to accept dramatic stars Douglas and Hayward in a comedy. John McCarten of the *New Yorker* certainly could not: "What Mr. Douglas and Miss Hayward are primarily called upon to do is bicker. Neither of them reveals any particular flair for comedy, but under the circumstances who could?" Other weekly periodicals also dismissed the film, such as *Time*, which called the movie "a comedy of bad manners," and *Newsweek*, which complained that "The movie falls flat."

Boxoffice disagreed, judging the effort as "a hilarious comedy," and stating "Miss Hayward and Douglas make an excellent starring pair and prove that they are as effective in comical situations as they are in serious drama." *Boxoffice* was one of the few critical sources not to lambaste the film's producers for jettisoning the original storyline in Marquand's novel; the majority of critics seemed to be so angry that Marquand's plot was rejected that they automatically rejected the film's new story.

Top Secret Affair may not be a great movie, but it is certainly a lively and entertaining comedy. Its star performances and writing are first-rate, and the film contains a core of drama beneath its fluffy exterior. That it was a box office flop was a failure of audiences to abandon their preconceptions rather than any lack in quality of the film itself. It is gradually gaining in reputation as time passes, and one day will be recognized as the highly amusing spoof of leadership personalities that it is.

Torpedo Alley

Credits: 1952. Allied Artists. *Directed by* Lew Landers. *Produced by* Lindsley Parsons. *Associate Producer*: John H. Burrows. *Written by* Sam Roeca and Warren Douglas. *Musical Director*: Edward J. Kay. *Photographed by* William Sickner, A.S.C. *Supervising Film Editor*: Ace Herman, A.C.E. *Edited by* W. Donn Hayes, A.C.E. *Production Manager*: Rex Bailey. *Assistant Director*: Joe Wonder. *Art Director*: Dave Milton. *Set Continuity by* Gana Jones. *Makeup by* Ted Larsen. *Recorded by* Tom Lambert. *Naval Technical Advisor on Production*: Commander B. R. Van Buskirk (Retired). *Naval Technical Advisor on Screenplay*: Rear Admiral Thomas M. Dykers (Retired). Not Rated. Black and White. Flat (1.33:1). 84 minutes. Released in December, 1952. Partially filmed on location at the U.S. Submarine Bases in San Diego, California, and New London, Connecticut. Currently available on VHS videotape.

Cast: *Lieutenant Bob Bingham*, Mark Stevens; *Susan Peabody*, Dorothy Malone; *Peabody*, Charles Winninger; *Tom Graham*, Bill Williams; *Dory Gates*, Douglas Kennedy; *Heywood*, James Millican; *Instructor*, Bill Henry; *Skipper*, James Scay; *Anniston*, Robert Rose; *Professor*, John Alvin; *Psychiatrist*, Carleton Young; *Hedley*, Ralph Sanford; *Lookout*, Ralph Reed; *Happy*, Carl Christian; *Turk*, John Close; *Bit Parts*, Keith Larson, William Schallert, Ross Thompson, Richard Garland, Charles Bronson.

Historical Accuracy Level: Medium. The film spans two wars, yet the accurately portrayed years of submarine training and service between them are the heart of its story.

Patriotic Propaganda Level: High. This movie could certainly serve as a recruiting tool for prospective submariners, especially with its emphasis on expert training.

This ad for Allied Artists' adventure Torpedo Alley *(1952) is fairly representative of the film, mixing action, romance and submarine stealth. Note that Dorothy Malone, whose "lips moored fast the toughest torpedo-man afloat!" sports brunette hair rather than her trademark blonde.*

Elements: Behind Enemy Lines, Military Training, Multiple Wars, Navy (Sailors), Romantic Triangle, Secret Missions, Submarines.

The story told in *Torpedo Alley* spans seven years and two world wars, beginning at the very end of World War II and moving well into the Korean conflict. The film's linear narrative, however, is paralleled by its promotion of the U.S. submarine service. This is not as unfortunate as it may sound, since the technical details and daily workings of the submarine force are far more interesting than the pedestrian dramatic and romantic story arcs provided by the film's writers. This is also an excellent example of a story about military training because the training illustrated is so integral to the story in addition to being fascinating history on its own account.

In August of 1945 the submarine *Devilfish* picks up two downed fliers, one of whom soon dies. The survivor, ace pilot Bob Bingham (Mark Stevens), blames himself for the crash and the deaths of his two crewmen. The sub's executive officer, Dory Gates (Douglas Kennedy), tries to ease Bingham's guilt, but he has little luck. Nevertheless, even when immersed in dour self-pity, Bingham does learn to appreciate the workings of the *Devilfish* as it hunts and sinks a

German ship and safely escapes the depth charges sent to destroy it. Back at Pearl Harbor, Bingham takes a liking to brunette nurse Susan Peabody (Dorothy Malone) before discovering that she is Gates' girl, which once again sours his attitude toward life.

The war ends and Bingham tries civilian life as a businessman, but because he is unwilling to exploit his reputation as a war hero, is termed unsuccessful. He reenters the Navy, this time as a submariner, and is sent to the submarine training base in New London, Connecticut. There Bingham finds Gates as an instructor and Susan as a love interest, as she and Gates have continually postponed the idea of marriage. Bingham and fellow trainee Tom Graham (Bill Williams) quickly become best friends, and battle for the top ranking in their class. One day Graham surprises Bingham with news that South Korea has been invaded. Bingham frowns and replies, "How about that. Every time I join the Navy, somebody starts a war."

Training accelerates and Bingham's somewhat shady reputation comes into question, but he ends any action over it by reacting quickly and saving a submarine and its crew when a training mission is interrupted by fire. On the other hand, a Bingham error involving a runaway torpedo gives Graham the honor of top student in their sub class. Meanwhile, Susan is unable to make up her mind between the two men in her life and is transferred onto a hospital ship stationed near Korea, thus delaying any romantic decision.

After graduation, Gates recommends Bingham and Graham for service aboard the *Stingray*, on which he will serve as executive officer. The *Stingray* is sent into North Korean waters and assigned a secret mission: four men are to sneak onto a beach from the sub, work their way inland, demolish an important train tunnel and successfully escape. Naturally, Bingham and Gates volunteer for the dangerous assignment. The tunnel is successfully destroyed, but both men are wounded and two other volunteers are killed during the escape; however, the story ends happily as Bingham and Susan are reunited on the hospital ship while a bemused Gates watches from a nearby bed.

As a war film, *Torpedo Alley* is somewhat weak. The only action occurs during the beginning, where a German ship is hunted and destroyed, and at the ending, when the four Navy submariners sneak ashore, destroy a train tunnel and escape from North Korean forces. Though the film's publicity emphasizes its war action, the two sequences comprise only ten minutes or so of the film's running time. It is also obvious that submarine models are employed during the first battle scene.

As an exploration of the Korean War, *Torpedo Alley* is relatively insignificant. The one shore mission that is depicted is vague and could have occurred (or been filmed) at any time almost anywhere. This, however, was the nature of submarine warfare during the Korean conflict. With little opposition from an almost non-existent Communist navy, U.S. and U.N. naval forces, including submarines, were largely free to roam the China and Yellow Seas at will. Submarines were used to protect convoys, patrol shorelines and harbors, and for occasional bandit raids such as the one depicted in the film.

The film does deserve credit, however, for its detailed depiction of the submarine force — the men who sail below the seas. With scenes filmed on location at sub bases in New London, Connecticut, and San Diego, California, the film achieves an effective, documentary-like realism of a submariner's extensive and exhaustive training. The actors work with the actual mechanisms used to teach men to live and work under constant pressure from the sea. Various methods for controlling the underwater craft are seen and explained, and submarine operations are the subject of the movie's focus. The submarine sequences do tend to overwhelm the film's meager plot, but that is probably a benefit.

As a wartime romance, the film contains a formulaic triangle and rather obvious resolution, though a young, brunette Dorothy Malone is well worth watching. Susan's romantic options in the story seem rather limited considering her beauty and brains, but at least she has some choice. The film actually does a nice job of stressing the long friendship that Susan and Gates have cultivated, and while their friendship telegraphs Bingham's ultimate assurance of her affections, it also nicely balances her new love interest.

Released just after the end of the Korean War, *Torpedo Alley* (perhaps named to remind viewers of the more action-packed and familiar "MiG Alley") failed to find much of an audience and spent just a brief time on the nation's movie screens. *Boxoffice* called the film "engrossing entertainment," while Howard Thompson of the *New York Times* praised the submarine training sequences as "not only believable but absorbing as well," even though he felt the film as a whole was a "threadbare tribute to a far worthier subject." The British Film Institute's *Monthly Film Bulletin* commented, "A quite competent story of naval adventures also shows, in semi-documentary style, something of the training and inner workings of the U.S. submarine service. All parts are adequately played, with Dorothy Malone providing sufficient sex appeal as Susan."

Though the cast is peppered with familiar faces, only Dorothy Malone makes any lasting impression. She soon dyed her hair blonde, began playing more mature and manipulative women, and won an Oscar for *Written on the Wind* just five years later. Look fast for Charles Bronson early in the film — he appears in only one shot and has just one line.

Torpedo Alley contributes little knowledge or understanding of the Korean War, but does act as a reminder that the Navy used ships other

Submarine officer Dory Gates (Douglas Kennedy) practices command procedures in Torpedo Alley *(1953).*

than aircraft carriers in order to carry out its missions, and that patrolling the waters off of the Korean coastline was an occasionally dangerous job. In this regard, as in its multiple war structure, the film echoes *Submarine Command*, which was released the previous year. Both films attempt to profile heroism under pressure, but climaxes sabotage both films' premises with routine, formulaic action. In the case of *Torpedo Alley*, the story is entertaining as far as it goes, especially when it profiles the extensive training undertaken by prospective submariners, but it should have dived more deeply.

Toward the Unknown
(aka *Brink of Hell*)

Credits: 1956. Toluca Productions. *Distributed by* Warner Bros. *Directed and Produced by* Mervyn LeRoy. *Associate Producer:* Beirne Lay, Jr. *Written by* Beirne Lay, Jr. *Music by* Paul Baron. *Director of Photography:* Hal Rosson,

A.S.C. *Film Editor:* William Ziegler. *Art Director:* John Beckman. *Sound by* Stanley Jones. *Set Decorator:* Ralph Hurst. *Costumes Designed by* Moss Mabry. *Makeup Supervisor:* Gordon Bau, S.M.A. *Unit Manager:* Mel Dellar. *Assistant Director:* Russell Llewellyn. *Special Effects by* H. F. Koenekamp, A.S.C. *Special Effects Art Director:* Leo E. Kuter. *Second Unit Director:* Russ Saunders. *Second Unit Assistant Director:* Al Alleborn. *Second Unit Photography by* Harold E. Wellman, A.S.C. *Second Unit Film Editor:* Thomas Reilly, A.C.E. *Special Ariobatics by* The U.S.A.F. Thunderbirds. *Technical Advisors:* Lieutenant Colonel Ralph Martin, A.R.D.C.; Lieutenant Colonel Frank Everest, Jr., A.R.D.C.; and Major Price Henry, A.R.D.C. *Song:* "The U.S. Air Force" *by* Robert Crawford. *Aerial Director of Photography:* Paul Mantz (uncredited). Not Rated. WarnerColor. WarnerScope (2.35:1). 115 minutes. Released in September, 1956. Filmed at Edwards Air Force Base, California. Not currently available on commercial home video.

Cast: *Major Lincoln Bond,* William Holden; *General William "Bill" Banner,* Lloyd

Nolan; *Connie Mitchell*, Virginia Leith; *Colonel R. H. "Mickey" McKee*, Charles McGraw; *Major Bromo Lee*, Murray Hamilton; *General Bryan Shelby*, Paul Fix; *Major Joe Craven*, James Garner; *Lieutenant Sweeney*, L. Q. Jones; *Polly Craven*, Karen Steele; *Senator Black*, Bartlett Robinson; *Hank*, Malcolm Atterbury; *H. G. Gilbert*, Ralph Moody; *Sara McKee*, Maura Murphy; *Debby*, Carol Kelly.

Historical Accuracy Level: High. This depiction of the test flight program at Edwards Air Force Base is ambitious, authentic and intelligent — one of the best of its kind.

Patriotic Propaganda Level: High. After viewing this film, what adventurous soul would not wish to become a test pilot?

Elements: Air Force, Brainwashing, Collaboration, Disability, Military Training, Returning Home, Romantic Triangle.

Veterans returning home from Korea are characters in quite a few Hollywood movies, only some of which (due to their large quantity and minimal study of the Korean War) are counted in this book. Often, returning veteran characters find a way to employ some of the survival and combat skills learned during their time in Korea in their private lives. Sometimes, their military experience is simply character background. And sometimes, as in *Toward the Unknown*, war experience greatly affects that person, to the extent of altering his or her basic personality and outlook on life. *Toward the Unknown* is a story about heroic test pilots, but it is also an intelligent, probing exploration of the effects of captivity and torture on one man, and how other people perceive that man upon his return from the war.

Major Lincoln Bond (William Holden) arrives at Edwards Air Force Base in California late one night, just in time to witness a jet crash. Bond attempts to extricate the pilot, but cannot open the canopy by himself. Firemen push him away and rescue the pilot, who happens to be General William "Bill" Banner (Lloyd Nolan), commander of the test pilot program at Edwards. Bond asks old friend Colonel R. H. "Mickey" McKee (Charles McGraw) to help him regain his former status as a test pilot, and McKee recommends him to Banner. Because of Bond's prisoner of war experiences in Korea, which include signing a germ warfare confes-

sion and attempting suicide, Banner refuses on the grounds that he cannot be trusted. Bond also renews his acquaintance with Banner's secretary Connie Mitchell (Virginia Leith), whom he was seriously dating before the war.

General Banner eventually changes his mind and allows Bond to fly as a "chase and pace" pilot, supporting the primary flier, Major "Bromo" Lee (Murray Hamilton), a man who makes no attempt to hide his dislike for Bond. After two months, Bond has won the appreciation of Banner and McKee, though General Shelby (Paul Fix) still doesn't trust him. Bond is given the opportunity to test the new Gilbert A-120 jet, but during his test flight, the jet develops "aileron reverse" and wrinkles appear on the wing. Because this condition had not previously occurred — and with Bond's reputation from Korea — neither the Air Force brass nor the jet's chief designer believe Bond's story. Banner arranges a flight to simulate Bond's, but the negative reaction to his report makes Bond angry. Connie warns him not to tangle with Banner; Bond relents and they kiss, renewing their romantic relationship.

The Gilbert A-120 test flight is inconclusive, but Banner orders more tests to pinpoint exactly what happened to Bond's jet. Bromo Lee and Major Joe Craven (James Garner) are assigned to rerun the A-120's test program again from scratch, while Bond is to work directly with Banner. Bond sees Banner fall over from dizziness in a locker room, but Banner lies about the reason and carries on. During another flight, Banner's jet fails to release its braking parachute, so Bond flies his own jet in close, spears the chute with his own wingtip fuel pod and lands in close formation behind Banner in the desert. Impressed by Bond's nerve and ability, Banner asks him directly why he collaborated with the enemy in Korea, but Bond is unable to give him a satisfactory answer. Still, Banner is inspired enough to award Bond with a role in the X-2 project, which will test a rocket-powered aircraft.

At the officers' club, Bromo Lee drinks heavily and becomes boorish. He taunts, and then swings at Bond, missing and falling to the floor. Another man, thinking that Bond has slugged a drunk, pins Bond's arms behind him, and Lee punches Bond in the belly. When his arms are pinned behind him, as they had been

High-flying drama is the lure of Warner Bros.' drama Toward the Unknown *(1956), but the corny dialogue over the faces at right hints at pilot Lincoln Bond's (William Holden) troubles in Korea, which form the psychological angle of the picture.*

during torture in a Chinese prisoner of war camp, Bond loses control of himself. He flips the man holding him to the floor and then rushes Lee, punching him twice before Connie is able to get his attention and bring his mind back to the present. Afterward, Bond realizes he has just thrown away his only chance to fly, and prepares to resign. He tells Connie that the Reds broke his spirit in the camp; that he had put a temporary patch on the injury by flying; but now the fight has pulled off the patch, revealing that the old war wound is still there.

Banner reprimands both men, ordering Lee to totally refrain from drinking, but asks Bond to keep flying. He quotes William Faulkner: "Man will not only endure; he will prevail." Their meeting is interrupted with news that Joe Craven has experienced the same "aileron reverse" problem in the A-120. Craven's jet is badly damaged; both wings are visibly wrinkling. Craven waits while his wingman takes photographs of the damage, then ejects when one of the wings completely detaches. His parachute, however, fails to open in time and Craven is killed.

Fully supported by General Banner, Bond is granted the primary pilot's status for the X-2 project. Bond makes a flawless drop test, in which the aircraft is dropped from a bomber and glides to the ground with no power. McKee is the pilot for the next test, with one rocket engine operational. Bond is aboard the bomber as check officer and notices something wrong. He pulls McKee out of the rocket just as it drops and explodes, saving McKee's life. After further testing, Banner decides to make the final test himself, with both rocket engines powered. Bond protests, noting Banner's dizziness in the locker room, but Banner will not relinquish the responsibility. However, he agrees to one additional single-engine test, which Bond is to fly.

Bond has trouble sleeping before his test (as does Connie), but everything runs smoothly. Bond fires both engines, taking it upon himself to fully test the aircraft. Bond reaches an altitude of ninety-five thousand feet at a speed of mach three before losing control. Bond radios instructions to raise the tail fin higher on future flights for better stabilization before he ejects. He lands safely, suffering a hip injury and a mild brain concussion, but still has enough energy to leave the hospital a few days later to attend General Banner's farewell. Banner is transferring to Washington, leaving McKee in charge of the test flight program, and Connie in charge of Lincoln Bond. Banner is provided with a spectacular sendoff by the U.S. Thunderbird team, which performs acrobatic maneuvers over Banner and the onlooking crowd.

Toward the Unknown is an above average movie about test pilots which benefits from filming actual aircraft in flight at Edwards Air Force Base, as well as an interesting story and solid characterizations from a top-notch cast. From the mid 1950s through the early 1960s there were quite a few Hollywood movies about the development of faster-than-sound aircraft and the brave test pilots who risked life and limb to fly them. *Toward the Unknown*, which was the first film produced by William Holden's company, Toluca Productions, is better than most due to three key components: its basic premise is compelling, its characters and dialogue are very well-written and enacted, and its aerial scenes are impressive, utilizing a minimum of previously shot stock footage.

The danger facing test pilots and the bravado that they project in the face of that danger have long been movie clichés, but this film avoids (for the most part) such routine characters and situations. There is some discussion of General Banner's age and his ability to react in an emergency, but this is common sense and is an integral segment of the story. Banner leads by example, insisting on saving the most hazardous tests for himself. Yet he expects McKee, Bromo Lee and, eventually, Lincoln Bond to carry their own share of the workload and to do so professionally. McKee tells General Shelby that Banner's men would crawl on their bellies for him because he is such an inspirational leader, and that feeling is transmitted to the audience. Movie generals — including Shelby — often stand around, making judgments and ordering people about, seemingly because they have the power to do so. Banner is a full-fledged action character, fully capable of piloting an experimental aircraft, romancing his pretty secretary or ending the career of a junior officer who has disappointed him. The part is very well-written, and Lloyd Nolan plays it commandingly, yet evenly, and basically steals the picture from William Holden.

Believing that test pilot Lincoln Bond (William Holden, right) has just sucker-punched a drunk, another man holds him from behind, triggering Bond's memories of captivity during the Korean War, in Toward the Unknown *(1956).*

Holden's part, Major Lincoln Bond, is also a complex one. While many movie pilots have had to overcome adversity, Bond's is a special case. He is on the road to recovery after spend-

ing fourteen months in a Chinese prisoner of war camp, much of it in solitary confinement. Bond knows that he can still fly and pursues his dream, despite the obvious ostracism which his reputation and perceived disability attract. Although Bond cannot verbally express the hell he experienced in Korea, he is able to tell Connie that he needs someone's confidence in him in order to succeed, and this admission is an important key to understanding Bond's situation. He feels alone against the world, that he has fulfilled his capabilities as far as he can, and that it will take someone else's appreciation of him to prove that he still matters. When Banner, McKee and Connie place their faith in him, Bond is finally able to live and relax without fear.

The romantic relationship involving Connie (Virginia Leith) is also handled well. Connie seems to bounce between her former love, Bond, and her current beau, Banner, a man whom she greatly admires but may not love. She maintains a distance between both of them, allowing herself plenty of time to make up her mind, and yet supports each of them in his time of need. Connie's relationships with both men are adult and intimate, yet each has a distinct flavor and temperament. It is actually unclear to which man (if either) she will attach herself until the end of the movie, and that indicates strong writing. The credit for this writing goes to Beirne Lay, Jr., who specialized in military subjects (he wrote *Twelve O'Clock High, Flying Leathernecks, Above and Beyond, Strategic Air Command* and the Korean War film *The Young and the Brave*). The film's script is very good, much better than those of the majority of test pilot films or Korean War films.

Most impressive are the film's production values. Filmed at Edwards Air Force Base with full Air Force cooperation, *Toward the Unknown* features an authentic (if admittedly small-scaled) view of the test pilot program, its various aircraft and technology of the time, and the people who expand the frontiers of knowledge by testing the new equipment firsthand. General Shelby (Paul Fix) and Senator Black (Bartlett Robinson) are given a tour of some of Edwards' facilities, presented to them for their (and the audience's) perusal. The flying scenes are actually kept to a minimum, but the sequence during which Bond flies close to Banner's jet, spearing the half-open parachute with his own wingtip fuel pod and then landing in close formation behind Banner's jet, is magnificently staged.

Toward the Unknown is included in this book because of Lincoln Bond's recurring stress, which is directly related to his experiences in Korea. Several times during the film, Bond seems to hear sounds of battle or torture, as he flashes back to captivity in his mind. The audience never sees Bond's wartime horror except for what is present in his eyes, but the effects of Bond's captivity and torture are amply demonstrated by his humble bearing and the disgusted reactions of others who come in contact with him, due to his perceived disability and reputation as a collaborator.

Bond is reported to have cracked under fourteen months of brainwashing by the Chinese, finally signing a germ warfare confession, and later attempting suicide by slashing his right wrist. While Bond's brainwashing is never detailed, its ramifications are. Aircraft designer H. G. Gilbert (Ralph Moody) puts no stock in Bond's version of the "aileron reverse" event, suggesting that Bond was out of his head during the test flight and cannot be trusted. When Gilbert persists in his view that Bond exceeded the aircraft's design limit after Banner's follow-up test proves inconclusive, Bond responds, "Who knows what a limit really is?" His rhetorical question causes Banner to ponder the matter and to later admit that Bond has fulfilled all of Banner's expectations.

By avoiding easy answers and explanations regarding Bond's brainwashing, the character becomes more complex and challenging, both for the actor to play and the audience to watch. The film also demonstrates, without being sappy or overtly inspirational, that it is possible that veterans who return from Korea with psychological trauma can successfully adjust to civilian life and suggests that they should be helped along whenever possible. This message is present in the film, but is not at all overbearing.

The film's cast is excellent. William Holden, Charles McGraw, Virginia Leith, Murray Hamilton, Paul Fix and Malcolm Atterbury all deliver strong performances in roles ranging from major to minor. This was James Garner's first film appearance; he followed this test pilot role with one similar, as a fighter pilot in his fourth film, *Sayonara*, just a year later. The one actor who is undermined by the script is L.Q. Jones. His character of Lieutenant Sweeney is solely one of comic relief; unfortunately, Jones' nervous flailing is painful to observe.

Overall, critics liked the film, though many seemed to find its story routine. A. H. Weiler of the *New York Times* wrote, "If his [William Holden's] story of test pilots and other experimenters at Edwards Air Force Base in California is slowed now and again by standard romance and military misunderstandings, his dedicated airmen and their strange, sleek, superpowered machines take up the slack in highly interesting and often thrilling style." Weiler also noted the film's topicality, comparing Bond's adventures with the Bell X-2 aircraft with real-life Captain Iven C. Kincheloe's new altitude record in the same aircraft, completed just before the film's release. *Time* also referred to the real Bell X-2 in its review, but was less than thrilled with the movie.

Toward the Unknown avoids the pitfalls of patriotic jingoism and the clichés of its "test pilots in danger" plot to tell an absorbing story about truly interesting people working in an extremely hazardous profession. The film promotes its subject, but does not shy away from depicting its dangers and liabilities. Ultimately, its human stories and concerns override its embrace of technological progress, and that is what makes it an emotionally affecting motion picture.

Truman

Credits: 1995. Spring Creek Productions. *Broadcast by* Home Box Office (HBO) Pictures. *Directed by* Frank Pierson. *Produced by* Doro Bachrach. *Executive Producers*: Paula Weinstein and Anthea Sylbert. *Screenplay by* Tom Rickman. *Based on the book by* David McCullough. *Music by* David Mansfield. *Director of Photography*: Paul Elliott. *Editor*: Lisa Fruchtman. *Casting by* Mary Colquhoun. *Production Designer*: Stephen Marsh. *Stunt Coordinator*: Andy Armstrong. *Stunt Performers*: John Casino, Richard Drown, Dennis Fitzgerald and Raleigh Wilson. *Unit Production Manager*: Steven Brown. *First Assistant Director*: Nicholas Mastandrea. *Second Assistant Director*: Susan Pickett. *Costume Designer*: Jill Ohanneson. *Special*

Makeup Created by Gordon J. Smith. *Special Makeup*: FXSmith, Inc. *Key Sculptor*: Evan Penny. *Sculptor*: Joe Ventura. *Key Prosthetics*: Raymond Mackintosh. *Prosthetics*: Ann Clifford and Mike Makischuk. *Assistant Prosthetics*: Jay McClennen. *Coordinator*: Gionilda Stolee. *Key Makeup*: Russell Cate. *Makeup*: Louise Mackintosh and Heidi Seeholzer. *Key Hair*: Benjamin Robin. *Dental Technician*: Gary Archer. *Wig Maker*: Stuart Artingstall. *Production Supervisor / Accountant*: Steven Shareshian. *Production Associate*: Tina Difeliciantonio. *First Assistant Accountant*: Peter McManus. *Archival Film Research*: Deborah Ricketts. *Associate Film Editor*: Marta Evry. *Assistant Film Editor*: Kristine McPherson. *Location Manager*: Michael Williams. *Assistant Location Manager*: Deirdre Costa. *Art Director*: Gary Kosko. *Set Decorator*: Joyce Anne Gilstrap. *Property Master*: Bradly E. Breitbarth. *Art Department Coordinator*: Francine Byrne. *Location Casting*: Wright / Laird Casting. *Additional Local Casting*: Carrie Houk. *Extras Casting Coordinator*: Vicki Evans. *Extras Casting Assistant*: Eryn A. Wright. *Dialect Coach*: Jessica Drake. *Post Production Supervisor*: Michael Tinger. *Post Production Accounting*: Owen and DeSalvo Company. *Second Second Assistant Director*: Jim Weis. *Production Sound*: R. Stergar. *Boom Operator*: Robert Polich. *First Assistant Camera*: Sue Zwilling. *Second Assistant Camera*: Birgitte Estelle Rasine. *Second Unit Operators*: Richard Eliano and David Boyd. *Steadicam Operator*: Bruce A. Greene. *Still Photographer*: D Stevens. *Gaffer*: Louis DiCesare. *Best Boy Electric*: Cory Bibb. *Rigging Gaffer*: Darryl R. Cowherd, Jr. *Key Grip*: Michael Pizzuto. *Best Boy Grip*: Steven Pehl. *Dolly Grip*: Dennis K. Wilson. *Key Makeup Artist*: Ashlee Petersen. *Second Makeup*: Rebecca Alling. *Hair Designer*: Mona Orr. *Key Hair*: James S. Evanoff. *Assistant Costume Designer*: Bernie White. *Costume Supervisor*: Deborah Slate. *Set Costumer*: Cindy Evans. *Assistant Costumers*: Ele Johnson and Noelle Arens. *Dresser to Gary Sinise*: Linda Flake. *Assistant Set Decorator*: Lorrie Stieben. *Leadperson*: Scott A. Carruth. *Assistant Property Master*: Billy Campbell. *Assistant Property Master / On Set Dresser*: John Clark. *Script Supervisor*: Jill Gurr. *Production Coordinator*: Leigh Miller. *Assistant Office Coordinator*: Holly Edwards. *Production Secretary*: Melissa Willis. *Spe-*

cial *Effects Coordinator*: Larry Fioritto. *Special Effects / Kansas City:* Lillard and Stamps Special Effects. *Military Advisors*: Mike Stokey and Ruben Romo. *Assistant Film Researchers*: Horton and Associates and Raymond Smith. *Video Playback*: Pete Verrando. *Horse Wranglers*: Raleigh Wilson and Bob Wilson. *Animal Wrangler*: Shawn Patrick Nash. *Humane Society Representative*: Charlie Miller. *Assistant to Gary Sinise*: Michael Unger. *New York Casting Assistants*: Jean Osnos and Joseph Cerami. *Assistant to Mr. Pierson*: Nicole Panter. *DGA Trainee*: Sharon Swab. *Set Production Assistants*: John Niernberger, Michael T. Rozmarin and Jamie Richardson. *Office Production Assistant*: Walter Klammer. *Music Coordinator*: Russell Jones. *Construction Coordinator*: G. Lynn Maughan. *Construction Foreman*: Layne Robinson. *Head Scenic*: Chris Barnes. *Greensman*: S. Ford Jones. *Caterer*: Antonio Deleon and A&M Catering. *Sound Editorial by* Tape Effects, Inc. *Supervising Sound Editor*: Michael Le Mare, M.P.S.E. *Sound Editors*: Karola Storr, M.P.S.E., Ken Gladden, Jeff Kaplan, Tom Scurry, William Schleuter, Greg Conway, Solange S. Schwalbe, M.P.S.E. and Steve Livingston. *Assistant Sound Editor*: Joelle Taar. *Foley Artists*: Bess Hopper and Nancy Parker. *ADR Mixer / Foley Mixer*: Ronald Bedrosian. *Re-recording Mixers*: Wayne Heitman, Jim Bolt and Joel Fein. *Piano Solos Performed by* Michael Lang. *Music Contractor*: Patti Zimmitti. *Music Editors*: David Olson and Alan Rosen. *Recording Engineer*: Dan Wallin. *Voice Casting*: Barbara Harris. *Main Title Design*: Ernest Farino. *Titles / Opticals*: Title House. *Optical Effects*: OCS / Freeze Frame / Pixel Magic. *Camera Systems by* Clairmont. *Grip Equipment*: Bullet Proof Grips. *Grip and Electric Equipment*: Hollywood Rentals. *The Makers of this Film wish to thank*: Kansas City Film Office, Patti Watkins; Kansas Film Office, Vicki Henley; Park Hill High School Symphonic Band, Director John Bell; Sprint; Union Station Assistance Corporation, Andy Scott; Burlington Northern Railroad Company; Museum of Transportation, St. Louis, Missouri; St. Louis Steam Train Association; Transport Museum Association, St. Louis, Missouri; and the Harry S. Truman Library. *Stock Footage Provided by*: John E. Allen, Inc.; Columbia Pictures Television; Grinberg Film Libraries; MacDonald and

Associates; Marquette University; NBC News Archives; National Archives; Producers Library Service; Harry S. Truman Library; and the UCLA Film and Television Archive. *Audio of* "Charlie McCarthy Rides Again" *and* "V-E Day Coverage" *Courtesy of* Radio YesterYear. *Songs*: "Happy Days Are Here Again," *by* Milton Agar and Jack Yellen, *courtesy of* EMI, Robbins Catalog, Inc.; "It's a Long, Long Way to Tipperary," *by* Jack Judge and Harry Williams, *published by* Warner Bros., Inc.; "Missouri Waltz," *by* James R. Shannon and Frederick Knight Logan, *published by* Forster Music Publisher, Inc.; "Voi Che Sapete" *from* "Le Nozze Di Figaro," *by* W. A. Mozart, *performed by* Margaret Truman, *courtesy of* Edward Roche. Rated PG. Dolby Surround Stereo. Color by DeLuxe. Widescreen (1.85:1). 135 minutes. Broadcast on September 9, 1995. Currently available on VHS videotape and DVD. Previously available on laserdisc.

Cast: *Harry S Truman*, Gary Sinise; *Bess Truman*, Diana Scarwid; *Henry L. Stimson*, Richard Dysart; *Charlie Ross*, Colm Feore; *Sam Rayburn*, James Gammon; *Clark Clifford*, Tony Goldwyn; *Boss Tom Pendergast*, Pat Hingle; *General George Marshall*, Harris Yulin; *Frank Vassar*, Leo Burmester; *Margaret Truman*, Amelia Campbell; *Elizabeth Moore*, Virginia Capers; *Bob Hannegan*, John Finn; *Eddie Jacobson*, Zeljko Ivanek; *Lieutenant Jim Pendergast*, David Lansbury; *Dean Acheson*, Remak Ramsey; *Eleanor Roosevelt*, Marion Seldes; *Madge Wallace Gates*, Lois Smith; *J. Lester Perry*, Richard Venture; *General Douglas MacArthur*, Daniel Von Bargen; *Marine*, Craig Benton; *Engineer*, Jim Birdsall; *Alonzo*, Freeman Bosley, Sr.; *Black Delegate*, Walter Coppage; *Mama Truman*, Nora Denney; *Woman Reporter*, Jessica Drake; *Producer*, John Durbin; *Lazy Worker*, Joe Erker; *Newswoman*, Peggy Friesen; *MacArthur Reporter*, David Fritts; *Garner*, Harry Gibbs; *MacArthur's Officer*, Tim Gillin; *Ike Aide*, Larry Greer; *Senator #1*, Wiley Harker; *Convention Reporter #1*, Marlon Hoffman; *First Politician*, Harold S. Herd; *Senator #2*, Gary Holcombe; *Margaret (age 7)*, Rachel Holferty; *Jester*, Brad Holiday; *Judge Stone*, Chief Justice Richard Holmes; *Sergeant O'Hare*, Hollis Huston; *Woman Reporter #3*, Jeannine Hutchings; *Senator #3*, Joneal Joplin; *Vietta*, Lynn King; *Usher #2*, Jonathon Lamer; *Judge Vrooman*, Jerry Lange;

Third Politician, Robert R. Lynn; *Convention Reporter #2*, Michael T. McGraw; *Fred Wallace*, Joseph P. Moynihan; *Operator*, Addison Myers; *Dixicrat*, Holmes Osborne; *Woman Reporter #2*, Stellie Siteman; *Page*, Peter Slowey; *Pendergast Politician*, John Smith; *Reporter #2*, David Snell; *Usher #1*, Brian Stemmler; *Barnett*, Jerel Taylor; *Woman Reporter #1*, Donna Thomason; *Reporter #1*, Dean Vivian; *Woman Reporter*, Cheryl Weaver; *Judge Barr*, Charles Whitman; *Groom*, Robert Wilson; *Franklin Delano Roosevelt*, Lee Richardson (uncredited); *with* Mat Hostetler.

Historical Accuracy Level: High. Harry Truman's political career is covered in depth, though specific episodes, including those dealing with the Korean War, are superficially examined at best.

Patriotic Propaganda Level: High. Truman is elevated to the rank of the finest presidents and his actions are firmly supported in this engrossing biographical picture.

Elements: Army, Biography, Day of the Invasion, Homefront, Leaders, Multiple Wars, Red Menace.

The most important American connected with the Korean War was President Harry S. Truman. It was his decision to attempt to limit the war to the Korean peninsula without involving either of the Communist Asian superpowers, and when Red China joined the fight, it was Truman's adamance that prevented the war from escalating further, despite the vehement objections of military leaders such as General Douglas MacArthur. While the point is debatable, it is a widely held historical belief that Truman's refusal to broaden the scope of the war prevented the Korean conflict from becoming World War III. President Truman's views and policies are documented in three cinematic portaits of American leaders: *Truman*, *MacArthur* and *Collision Course: Truman vs. MacArthur*. *Truman* chronicles events from the president's perspective and details why he was so strongly opposed to widening the fight in Korea.

The film begins in 1948, as Harry S. Truman (Gary Sinise) campaigns across country by train to retain the office of President of the United States. Polls indicate that he will lose to New York governor Thomas Dewey, and upon reflection, Truman wonders why anyone (including himself) would want to be president …

The story flashes back to 1917 as Truman courts Bess Wallace (Diana Scarwid) and announces that at age thirty-three, he will join the army. Bess wants to marry, but Truman refuses until his return from Europe. His experiences during the war (two battle scenes are depicted) develop into a distaste for battle and suffering. After World War I, Truman marries Bess and moves into her family's mansion in Independence, Missouri. Truman and Eddie Jacobson (Zeljko Ivanek) open a haberdashery but run into financial difficulty when the Great Depression takes hold of the country. Truman is persuaded to run for election as a county judge for Boss Tom Pendergast (Pat Hingle), a powerful regional politician. He wins, gradually pays off the store's debt and resists becoming a political pawn of Pendergast's.

Truman serves two terms as county judge and oversees a $6 million roadway construction program while studying law at night. Following his second term, he returns to farming, but is not very successful. Pendergast suggests Truman run for the senate and supports him. Truman enters the U.S. Senate as "the man from Pendergast." World War II begins and Truman discovers that money earmarked for military bases is being stolen and squandered. He heads a senate committee, becomes a national political figure by pursuing "crookedness," and gradually develops a reputation for integrity. President Franklin D. Roosevelt (Lee Richardson) wants Truman for his running mate in 1944 and uses guilt over the Democratic Party's future to persuade Truman to accept the position over Bess' objections. After becoming Vice President, Truman travels to Missouri to attend Tom Pendergast's funeral, fueling speculation that Truman is not as honest as he seems. On April 12, 1945, President Roosevelt dies and Harry S. Truman assumes the office of President of the United States.

President Truman, frightened and humbled by the responsibilities of the office, names old friends and advisors Charlie Ross (Colm Feore) as his press secretary and Frank Vassar (Leo Burmester) as his personal secretary. He is informed by Henry L. Stimson (Richard Dysart) about the progress of atomic bomb development (about which he had inquired as a senator and been told to forget he had ever heard of the

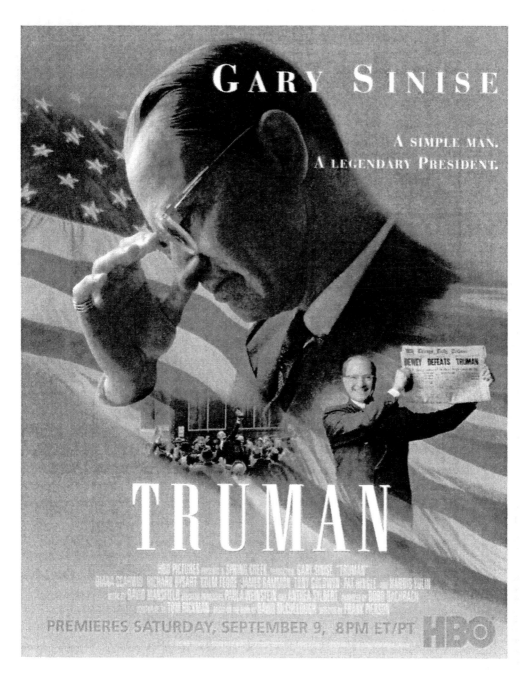

This classy advertisement for HBO's drama Truman *(1995) simply, elegantly and effectively conveys its subject's thoughtfulness and charisma.*

project). On his birthday, Truman learns that the war in Europe has ended, but unhappy in Washington, Bess and daughter Margaret (Amelia Campbell) return to Missouri. Thus, Truman alone makes the decision to use the atomic bomb against Japan. His reasoning is that using the bomb would prevent hundreds of thousands of American casualties if an invasion of Japan were attempted. Over footage of the bombs exploding and victims suffering, the voice of Truman threatens that Japan or any country which fights against America risks destruction from this ultimate weapon. Japan surrenders and World War II concludes.

Peace is hardly less difficult for the president, even with the return of Bess and Margaret to Washington. He negotiates with Britain and Russia over the fate of Europe, transfers the responsibility for atomic power away from the military to science, writes an executive order confirming civil rights, threatens to draft striking coal miners and railroad workers into the armed services, oversees the confirmation and recognition of Israel as a Jewish state and battles a Republican congress. He determines not to seek election in 1948, but Bess refuses to believe him. She realizes that he has to be president in his own right, elected by the people, to affirm his own worth and secure his place in world history. So Truman begins to campaign against heavy odds, and the film returns to the present.

Truman announces the Marshall plan to reconstruct Europe and calls Congress back into session to pass economic initiatives. He campaigns heavily while the favored Dewey relaxes and awaits election as a foregone conclusion. Election day brings a stunning upset, as Truman defeats Dewey and reclaims the presidency as his own.

In June of 1950, Truman learns that South Korea has been invaded, with no advance warning. "How in the hell did we let this happen?" he asks. Truman meets with General Douglas MacArthur (Daniel Von Bargen) at Wake Island and gives him full authority to invade Korea at Inchon to halt the Communist agression. MacArthur assures the president that China will not join the fight and that "the boys will be home by Christmas." The general is proven wrong when he pursues the North Korean army toward the Chinese border and the Chinese invade en masse in retaliation. Secretary of Defense George Marshall (Harris Yulin) advises that MacArthur should be fired for bringing China into the war, but Truman refuses, and orders his cabinet to "give him all the help you can."

Months later, as Senator Joseph McCarthy (shown in newsreel footage) is rabble-rousing, Charlie Ross warns of McCarthy's growing influence. Preparing for a news conference, Ross keels over, dead of a heart attack. Soon after-

ward, Margaret Truman makes her operatic debut and is widely panned. The president angrily responds to one particular music critic and threatens him. McCarthy gains more power as fear regarding the threat of Communism spreads. Then, MacArthur demands that the Chinese surrender personally to him, forcing Truman to fire him for creating foreign policy. Criticism for firing the popular general is heavy, especially from McCarthy and the Republican Congress.

Having had enough of politics, Truman declines to run for the presidency again. Following a snub by incoming president Dwight D. Eisenhower, Truman and Bess leave for Missouri for the final time and are greeted by an enthusiastic crowd of supporters at Union Station who send them home with fanfare.

Truman is a generally compelling overview of the public life of America's thirty-third president. Harry S. Truman is described as a blunt, honest, man of the people who was saddled with some of the most difficult situations any president ever had to face and who used common sense as a guide. Narration notes that when he left office, Truman had a mere 32% approval rating; since the late 1950s, however, historical revisionists have gradually given Truman greater credit for having ended one war, limited another and wisely guided the United States during the years in between.

The film chronicles Truman's rise in politics from a Missouri county judge through the U.S. Senate to the exalted office of the presidency. At each level of government, Truman is viewed as stubbornly honest and determined to use his power for the benefit of taxpayers rather than for himself. However, writer Tom Rickman and director Frank Pierson prevent Truman from becoming sanctimonious; care is taken to present Truman as irascible, overbearing, cynical and "stubborn as a Missouri mule" at various times. It is indicated, though not emphasized, that his personal life with Bess was strained during their years in the White House, but his private life is rarely examined with any depth. The film is a standard Hollywood biography which, because of the quantity and wide range of its subject's incredible experiences, is unable to truly delve into any of those experiences with any particular zeal. The result, as defined by Jay Robert Nash and Stanley Ralph Ross in their *Motion Picture Guide (1997 Annual)*, is "a checklist of Truman's greatest hits."

Much of the film's early 135 minute running time is spent developing Truman's character and penchant for battling special interest groups. This character development definitely helps establish Truman as an honest underdog, but also limits exploration of later, globally significant events. The Marshall plan is discussed in just a few sentences. Wrestling with the world-shaking decision to use atomic weapons to end World War II passes quickly, as do the years between World War II and Korea. The Korean War and the firing of General MacArthur take place during just ten minutes, and those ten minutes also encompass the rise of Senator Joe McCarthy's influence and the sudden death of Charlie Ross.

President Harry S Truman (Gary Sinise) faced more national and international crises during his presidency than anyone else, before or since, in Truman *(1995).*

Neither war is examined closely, but the Korean War is particularly neglected. There is a moment of utter surprise for Truman as it begins — "How in the hell did we let this happen?" — which is immediately followed by the Wake Island conference with MacArthur. This conference actually took place four months after the invasion and one month after the successful operation at Inchon, yet the film stages it mere moments after Truman learns about the incursion, and MacArthur's dialogue in the scene is ambiguous as to whether the Inchon operation has already occurred or not. MacArthur's explanation to the reporters at Wake Island contains the film's only mentions of Inchon or the struggle to hold the Pusan Perimeter until the Inchon invasion was launched.

More significant is the conversation in the back of a sedan between Truman and

MacArthur at Wake Island. Truman repeats that he does not want the Korean conflict to escalate into World War III. "We are already in a worldwide war against the Communists, sir," replies MacArthur. "I'm surprised you don't see it that way. Korea is the opening round." This dialogue establishes the difference in philosophy between the two leaders that eventually forces Truman to fire the brilliant general. But Truman has the common sense not to fire the general for underestimating the Chinese. He realizes that relieving MacArthur at that moment in time would undermine the morale of the fighting men and indicate to them that the war had already been lost with that single miscalculation. Instead, he orders his cabinet to provide MacArthur with whatever he needs to battle the new, expanded enemy force.

It is when General MacArthur takes foreign policy into his own hands months later and demands the Chinese surrender personally to him that Truman finally sacks the general. He does this despite MacArthur's huge popularity and heavy criticism from political enemies like Senator McCarthy. To Truman, the matter is simple, a question of "Who's the boss? The military, or the people?" Even Bess' mother objects to the firing of MacArthur, but Truman has become accustomed to dissension from the Wallace side of his family. President Truman leaves office in 1953 with the Korean conflict unresolved. In his farewell address to the nation, he urges support for Eisenhower. "The Cold War, and the hot war in Korea, will be great tests of his strength," he states.

These events were tests for Harry S. Truman, and he faced them unflinchingly. Having personally seen the effects of World War I, he became determined that as few Americans as possible should have to share that experience unnecessarily, and so ordered the atomic bomb to be dropped on Japan to speed the end of World War II. Yet, when Communist aggression threatened South Korea — and, by extension, Japan and the rest of southeast Asia — the president made a principled stand and ordered Americans into harm's way to halt it. Truman understood the global picture and overrode his own dislike of war to protect freedom in South Korea; this biography communicates that without overemphasizing Truman's beneficence.

Gary Sinise is superb as Truman, delivering a finely nuanced and occasionally flamboyant performance. Sinise allows the decency and integrity of the man to shine through his skin while not resorting to noble posturing or flattering mimicry. Sinise won a Golden Globe award, a Screen Actors Guild and a Cable Ace award for his characterization, and was also nominated for an Emmy. Diana Scarwid (also nominated for an Emmy) is properly pungent as Bess Truman and the supporting cast is filled with familiar and talented character actors. Daniel Von Bargen is a cold, analytical Douglas MacArthur, nicely balancing Truman's concerned humanism. The film itself won the Emmy for outstanding made for television movie in 1995 and an Emmy for its casting.

Truman is faithful to the facts regarding Harry S. Truman (as documented in David McCullough's Pulitzer Prize-winning biography)

and it is a distinguished movie, although despite Gary Sinise's magnificent performance, it rarely blazes with intensity. The film is probably most valuable to viewers unfamiliar with Truman and his times, but its scope and understanding of Truman's place in history make it a rewarding chronicle even to history buffs. It makes a great companion piece with either *MacArthur*, which similarly documents the public career of an exalted leader, or *Collision Course: Truman vs. MacArthur*, which examines their differences over Korean War policy in great detail.

Twenty Plus Two

Credits: 1961. Allied Artists. *Directed by* Joseph M. Newman. *Written and Produced by* Frank Gruber. *Executive Producer*: Scott R. Dunlap. *Based on the Novel by* Frank Gruber. *Music*: Gerald Fried. *Director of Photography*: Carl Guthrie, A.S.C. *Film Editor*: George White. *Art Director*: David Milton. *Production Manager*: Edward Morey, Jr. *Assistant Director*: Lindsley Parsons, Jr. *Music Editor*: Neil Brunnenkant. *Sound Editor*: Charles Schelling. *Airplane Photography Courtesy of* United Airlines. *Set Decorator*: Joseph Kish. *Set Continuity*: Eylla Jacobus. *Sound Mixer*: Ralph Butler. *Wardrobe*: Roger J. Weinberg and Norah Sharpe. *Makeup Artist*: Harry Maret. *Construction Supervisor*: James West. *Special Effects*: Milt Olsen. *Property Master*: Ted Mossman. Not Rated. Todd A-O Sound. Black and White. Flat (1.33:1). 102 minutes. Released in August, 1961. Not currently available on commercial home video.

Cast: *Tom Alder*, David Janssen; *Linda Foster*, Jeanne Crain; *Nikki Kovacs/Lily Brown*, Dina Merrill; *Jacques Pleschette*, Jacques Aubuchon; *Douglas Slocum*, William Demarest; *Mrs. Delaney*, Agnes Moorehead; *Leroy Dane*, Brad Dexter; *James Honsinger*, Robert Strauss; *Harris Toomey*, Fredd Wayne; *Walter Collinson*, George Neise; *Harbin*, Mort Mills; *Bellboy*, Robert Gruber; *Newspaper Morgue Attendant*, Will Wright; *Stewardess*, Teri Janssen; *Colonel*, Carleton Young; *Stanley*, Robert H. Harris; *Mark*, Billy Varga; *Blonde Woman*, Ellie Kent.

Historical Accuracy Level: Low. The film's Korean War flashback has little to do with the war, though servicemen certainly frequented establishments such as the one presented in this story.

Patriotic Propaganda Level: Low. Apart from the sentiment conveyed from one soldier to a dance hostess, this picture promotes neither soldiering nor war.

Elements: Army, Japan, Mystery, Romance.

David Janssen's first 1961 movie in which he plays a serviceman in Korea (the second is *Man-Trap*) is *Twenty Plus Two*, a murder mystery based on a popular novel by Frank Gruber. Like *Man-Trap*, this film utilizes the Korean War as a setting to establish a relationship, one which is crucial to the development of the story. *Twenty Plus Two* is an odd story which takes thirteen years to consolidate its various elements and then rapidly solves its mysterious puzzle within just a few days.

In 1961 Hollywood, a woman named Julia Joliet is murdered. Joliet operated the Hollywood Fan Mail Service and was a secretary for movie star Leroy Dane. Her murder interests Tom Alder (David Janssen), a Korean War veteran who makes his living finding missing heirs (for 10% of their inheritances), because the only item missing from Joliet's office is a file on Doris Delaney, a woman who mysteriously disappeared some thirteen years previously and has never been found. At a bar, Alder meets Leroy Dane (Brad Dexter), who boasts of heroism during World War II. He also sees Linda Foster (Jeanne Crain), whom Alder had planned to marry before going to Korea, but who found someone else and sent him a "Dear John" letter. Linda apologizes and wants to rekindle their relationship, and Alder seems willing to go along.

Alder flies to New York to further investigate the Doris Delaney disappearance. On the plane, he talks to Linda Foster's friend Nikki Kovacs (Dina Merrill). Nikki departs the flight in Chicago while Alder continues to New York. He discovers that when Doris disappeared in 1948, she may have been pregnant. Alder also discovers a large, erudite Frenchman named Jacques Pleschette (Jacques Aubuchon) in his hotel room. Pleschette, who followed Alder from Hollywood, offers to hire Alder to find his brother Auguste for $10,000. Pleschette also admits to spending twenty-six of his years in

prison, where he educated himself. Alder requests time to consider Pleschette's offer.

The following day, he visits Mrs. Delaney (Agnes Moorehead) and convinces her that he can find her missing daughter. He also learns that Julia Joliet had a criminal record for blackmail and that Leroy Dane never served in World War II. In fact, the Army service record which Dane claims as his own actually belongs to a man named Danny Koenig, who died in 1948. Linda calls from Chicago and tells Alder that Nikki is now missing. Alder flies to Chicago, meeting Linda and her fiancé, Harris Toomey (Fredd Wayne), and Nikki's fiancé, Walter Collinson (George Neise), at the Palmer House. Also present is Leroy Dane. When Toomey makes it clear he doesn't like having Alder around, Alder goes to his hotel room alone and recalls Korea …

In a flashback to Tokyo in 1951, Alder recalls meeting hostess Lily Brown in a dance hall bar. Alder is recovering from a war wound and Linda's "Dear John" letter, and Lily is kind to him. They fall in love, but Lily refuses to talk about her past. Their brief yet blossoming relationship ends when Alder reports back to the army.

Alder now knows that Nikki Kovacs, Lily Brown and Doris Delaney are the same person. He insinuates to Leroy Dane that he knows Dane is really Auguste Pleschette, and Dane threatens him. Alder tracks Nikki to North Dakota, and she tells him the truth: that she was Doris Delaney and was raped by Auguste Pleschette. When Pleschette discovered she was pregnant, he and a friend (Danny Koenig) raped her again. She shot Pleschette and ran away, thinking she had killed him. Doris had an abortion and travelled to Japan, where she became Lily Brown and met Tom Alder. Later, she returned to America as Nikki Kovacs.

Alder and Nikki drive to the nearby Pleschette family cabin. Jacques Pleschette is waiting, and confirms Nikki's story. Leroy Dane suddenly appears with a shotgun and threatens to kill everyone. He admits to being Auguste Pleschette and describes being only slightly injured by Nikki and killing Danny Koenig to steal Koenig's identity (because a newspaper photo had incorrectly identified him as Koenig). As Dane prepares to kill Nikki and Alder, he is

Women in provocative poses, including the unfortunate miss gagged at the top of the ad calling for secrecy, are the lure for Allied Artists' mystery Twenty Plus Two *(1961). David Janssen is caught in the middle, but his character's Korean War background is not revealed in the advertisement.*

shot and killed by his brother Jacques. Alder and Nikki leave together as Jacques awaits the police and a return to the comfortable surroundings and friends of prison.

Twenty Plus Two is an entertaining mystery, though its twists and turns lead to an eventually obvious conclusion. The film's first half is dense and confusing, as all good mysteries should be, as various characters and scenarios are introduced and viewers try to make sense of the incomplete puzzle. The Korean War flashback settles the biggest question when Dina Merrill appears as Lily Brown. Once she appears, it becomes obvious who Doris Delaney is and why Alder reacted with recognition when shown a photograph of Doris by her mother. The audience is never shown that photograph, because it would have indicated Nikki's identity immediately. If the film has one major flaw, it's that Alder does not recognize Nikki on the plane to Chicago, though she does seem familiar to him. It is difficult to believe that he would not know her after thirteen years — even with a new hair style and color — if she truly had meant that much to him in Japan.

Julia Joliet's murder is only an indication of the criminality within the story; in classic mystery fashion, her initial murder is relatively insignificant by the story's climax. Frank Gruber's intricate plot moves from Hollywood to New York City to Chicago and eventually settles in a decrepit little cabin in North Dakota, where the last pieces of the puzzle are finally put into place. Ultimately, *Twenty Plus Two* is the story of two brothers who rose from humble beginnings in North Dakota to positions of power, albeit through criminal acts. One of the brothers, Jacques, has used his time in prison to educate himself and to accept who he is. The other, Auguste, is living a public lie and will do anything to camouflage the truth about his past. It is inevitable that these brothers should eventually hunt each other and battle to the death.

It is stylish misdirection that the Pleschette brothers story is secondary to the efforts of Tom Alder to find Doris Delaney and reconcile his own past. By putting Alder at the center of the story, viewers naturally believe that the important events circle around him, though in fact he is merely the one character who ties everything together. Linda Foster makes a strong effort to recapture Alder's affection, but she is completely forgotten in the last quarter of the movie. As for Nikki, it is obvious early on that she has some relationship to Alder, and once the flashback reveals her as Lily Brown, her role becomes obvious.

As a mystery, the movie is entertaining, if not completely satisfying. The story seems full of coincidences, and the idea that a thirteen-year-old disappearance could so suddenly be solved by an amateur sleuth is hard to swallow. Yet the movie's flaws are compensated for by its intelligent structure, strong supporting characters, jazzy music score and quick pacing. Several small roles are filled by terrific character actors, including Agnes Moorehead as Mrs. Delaney, William Demarest as the boozy ex-reporter who provides Alder with a vital clue regarding Doris Delaney, Robert Strauss as James Honsinger, a detective who feeds information to Alder upon request, Brad Dexter as Leroy Dane, the movie star who makes only war pictures, and Jacques Aubuchon as Jacques Pleschette. Though all of the characters are well-rounded, it is "Big Frenchy" Pleschette who is the most inventive, and Aubuchon's performance steals the show. The star's sister, Teri Janssen, makes an appearance as a United Airlines stewardess.

David Janssen is unusually active in the lead role. The laconic actor who made his name as television investigators of one sort or another on *Richard Diamond Private Detective*, *The Fugitive*, *O'Hara U.S. Treasury* and *Harry O* seems spirited and energetic as Tom Alder, except in the Korean War scenes where he is recuperating. Jeanne Crain is strong as Linda Foster, while Dina Merrill has the trickiest role(s) of all. Merrill's acting is convincing throughout, but perhaps more care could have been taken to differentiate her appearance during the Korean War flashback. It is perfectly obvious who Lily Brown has become, and Alder seems stupid not to recognize her.

The Korean War scenes establish the rapport between Alder and Lily and depict how he overcomes a broken heart with Linda only to then return the favor to Lily. It also provides a place far away from America to which Doris Delaney can escape. The depiction of the Japanese dance hall bar seems authentic, with exotic women used as the bait to lure servicemen into

Dance hall hostess Nikki Kovacs (Dina Merrill) tries to interest soldier Tom Alder (David Janssen) in more than a dance during the Korean conflict in the mystery Twenty Plus Two *(1961).*

spending their money for booze and companionship. But that is the extent of the film's use of the war.

Twenty Plus Two is not very well known and was not successful in its theatrical run. Jay Robert Nash and Stanley Ralph Ross note its peculiarity in their *Motion Picture Guide* review: "At times the dialog borders on self-parody, though that's not always a fault. The film is slightly ridiculous as it is and good pulpy fun at its best moments." It is a sleeper film, one which surprises with its intelligence and vitality even while its plot goes to extremes. Although it is not a very good Korean War film, it is an engrossing mystery with fine performances, and it should be considered when movie mysteries are remembered and discussed.

Underwater Warrior

Credits: 1958. Underwater Productions. *Distributed by* Metro-Goldwyn-Mayer. *Directed*

by Andrew Marton. *Produced by* Ivan Tors. *Associate Producer*: John Florea. *Written by* Gene Levitt. "The unusual experiments in shark-infested waters were conducted in the Marshall Islands by Commander Francis D. Fane, U.S.N.R., Technical Advisor for this production, whose life and adventures inspired our picture." *Music Composed and Conducted by* Harry Sukman. *Director of Photography*: Joseph Biroc, A.S.C. *Director of Underwater Photography*: Lamar Boren. *Film Editor*: Charles Craft, A.C.E. *Production Supervisor*: Barry Cohon. *Assistant Director*: Frank Parmenter. *Special Underwater Effects*: Harry Redmond, Jr. Not Rated. Black and White. CinemaScope (2.35:1). 91 minutes. Released in March, 1958. Filmed at San Clemente Island, Coronado, and in the Hawaiian and Marshall Islands. Not currently available on commercial home video.

Cast: *Commander David Forest*, Dan Dailey; *Anne Winnmore*, Claire Kelly; *Doctor (Lieutenant) William Arnold*, James Gregory;

Sergeant Joe O'Brien, Ross Martin; *Admiral Ashton*, Raymond Bailey; *Captain of Battleship*, Alex Gerry; *Maria Theresa Valdez (Marie)*, Genie Coree (Virginia Core); *Submarine Captain*, Charles Keane; *Boat Officer*, Jon Lindbergh; *Girl Swimmer*, Zale Perry; *David Forest, Jr.*, Alex Fane; *Captain of Submarine Rescue Vessel*, Francis D. Fane (uncredited).

Historical Accuracy Level: High. The film links two wars and several underwater sequences through the experiences of a veteran Navy diver, whose exploits are faithfully fictionalized.

Patriotic Propaganda Level: High. This Navy diver fights in two wars, braves shark-infested waters and rescues important military secrets while he raises a family.

Elements: Biography, Lonely Wives, Military Training, Multiple Wars, Navy (Sailors), Romance, Submarines.

Hollywood's depictions of the Korean War usually center on the air war and the bloody ground fighting. Because of their close proximity to the Korean shore, the aircraft carriers and pilots of the Navy receive their share of cinematic attention, but other, more specialized sections of the armed forces do not. For instance, paratroopers, tank crews and bomber crews are largely ignored by filmmakers. One specialized service which is highlighted in a movie all its own is the Navy's Underwater Demolitions Team, conceived and led by Commander Francis D. Fane, who served as *Underwater Warrior*'s technical advisor and who can be seen in the film's scenes involving shark investigation. For reasons only clear to MGM, the studio opted to create a fictional lead character rather than use Fane, "whose life and adventures inspired our picture."

Underwater Warrior chronicles Commander David Forest's rise through the Navy, beginning with his most recent — and dangerous — dive. Narrated by Forest's protective friend, Dr. William Arnold (James Gregory), the story quickly jumps back twelve years to World War II, when Lieutenant Forest (Dan Dailey) applies for a position with the Navy's Underwater Demolitions Team (UDT). Arnold, then in charge of the program, is curious why Forest, an older officer, would be interested in the UDT. Forest explains that he has imagined "a different kind of navy—where a man underwater can sink a battleship, foul up an enemy landing or neutralize a minefield." Arnold is impressed by Forest's vision, but turns skeptical when he learns that Forest cannot swim. Forest is given thirty days to meet the UDT's advanced swimming requirements.

Forest slowly learns to swim and joins the UDT. Difficult training follows, and the team prepares for its assignment, clearing a path for landing ships on Japanese shores. The Hiroshima explosion changes the situation, however, and the mission is cancelled as Japan surrenders. Undaunted, Forest persuades Admiral Ashton (Raymond Bailey) to support his efforts to continue developing underwater equipment and training. Forest is given command of a fifteen-man unit, including perennial sidekick Sergeant Joe O'Brien (Ross Martin). For the next five years, they work to expand the definition of underwater activity, becoming the first men to exit and return to a submarine while underwater. The intrepid diving pair use their underwater acumen to meet a pair of sailboating lovelies, Anne (Claire Kelly) and Marie (Genie Coree [Virginia Core]), who become their constant companions, both on- and off-shore.

The submarine captain (Charles Keane) is not convinced that the undersea activity is worthwhile and submits a negative report on Forest's progress. In response, Forest and O'Brien conclude war game maneuvers by disembarking from the submarine, swimming to the lead enemy battleship and placing a phony explosive charge on its hull, thus proving the effectiveness of underwater espionage. Forest asks Anne to marry him, but she objects to the lack of family time that would be occasioned by a military marriage, and refuses. After two months of testing new diving equipment in the Caribbean, he is joined by Anne, who has changed her mind. They are married and enjoy a wet honeymoon sailing around the Caribbean before he must report for duty—in Korea.

Forest and his UDT men are assigned to clear a path through an underwater minefield for a massive troop landing. The UDT divers place explosives on the mines and return to safety, except for Forest, who ventures close to the coastline and is fired upon by a sentry with a machine gun. Enemy mortars are then used,

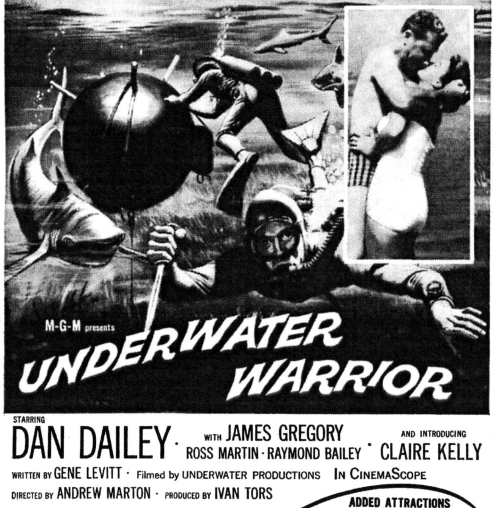

The men of the U.D.T. face dangerous sharks, unexploded mines and bathing beauties in MGM's multiple war adventure Underwater Warrior *(1958), starring Dan Dailey, Claire Kelly and Ross Martin.*

which knock Forest unconscious; he is saved by a rescue boat which has gathered the other divers. The mines explode and the landing progresses.

Home once more, Forest is chastised by his wife for spending too much time away from home and not enough with their son, David Jr. (Alex Fane). Admiral Ashton has other plans, however, and assigns Forest and a cameraman to make films showing man's interaction with sharks in the Marshall Islands. Forest does so, boldly venturing out of his shark cage, and proves that divers have far less to fear from sharks than has been previously believed. Anne discovers his assignment by seeing him on her local theater's newsreel and becomes quite angry. She is also pregnant again, so Forest promises to take things easy.

An experimental plane crashes near San Diego and the UDT men are assigned to make a 300-foot dive, fifty feet deeper than they've ever gone before, to destroy the plane (to keep its secrets out of enemy hands). Forest and O'Brien descend and find the plane, but O'Brien is ensnared on wires while planting the explosives and both men use their last air while surfacing. The film returns to its starting point, and after nearly two days in decompression chambers, both men are released. Forest admits that it's time for both of them to retire from active duty and joins Anne, who is anxiously waiting for him.

Underwater Warrior spends much of its time, as its title implies, underwater. Its producer, Ivan Tors, made a specialty of exotic location shoots featuring friendly human interaction with wild animals in their natural habitats, and particularly views of undersea life. Tors became famous producing the television series *Sea Hunt*, *Gentle Ben* and *Flipper*, and most of his film projects are similarly themed, although he also produced the Korean War film *Battle Taxi* three years earlier. For *Underwater Warrior*, Tors filmed predatory sharks in the Marshall Islands and frolicking humans in the Caribbean.

Although much of the underwater photography is clear and effective, such as the submarine scenes, the shark scenes, the sailboat anchor scene and the wedding proposal scene, not all of that photography matches the movie's action. The barracuda viewed outside of the sub-

marine are obviously not in the same area (they are insert shots) and the climactic sequence, supposedly three hundred feet below the surface of the sea, is far too light to be a believable portrayal of such a depth. Despite these occasional lapses, however, the underwater scenes do provide authenticity and are usually visually interesting. Director of Photography Joseph Biroc also makes good use of his widescreen CinemaScope lenses, providing a panoramic feel to the picture.

The story itself is low-key and realistic. Director Andrew Marton makes no attempt to exploit particular situations, such as the shark sequence, for cheap thrills; rather he is more interested in re-creating a few of the more adventurous moments of Francis Fane's adventurous life. That it is Fane's story is beyond doubt, in spite of the curious opening credit. Fane not only worked as the film's technical advisor but also appeared in one scene, unbilled, as the captain of the submarine rescue vessel. Over the same period of time as the movie takes place, Fane became renowned as the Navy's top frogman, and he published "Naked Warriors," an unofficial history of the UDT in 1956. Why then would the film not use Fane's own identity?

Probably money. Ivan Tors' studio, Underwater Productions, may not have had the cash to pay Fane for the use of his name. Instead, they used a fictional character and paid Fane for his technical consultations. Between World War II and Korea, Fane was the man who not only kept the UDT alive and kicking, but proved its intrinsic, lasting value. *Underwater Warrior* succeeds in chronicling that struggle, whether its protagonist is Fane or Forest. As an informal history of one man's vision brought to life, the movie works quite nicely, using its low-key approach, attractive performers and doses of humor to convey its surprisingly appealing story. There isn't a great deal of emotional drama or conflict, but this is intended as a story of pushing the limits of known science rather than as a turgid psychological drama.

The Korean War sequence is exciting, as Forest and the UDT are assigned to explode an underwater minefield in preparation for a massive troop landing. The mines are appropriately menacing and the sight of frogmen hanging further armament upon them is at least slightly

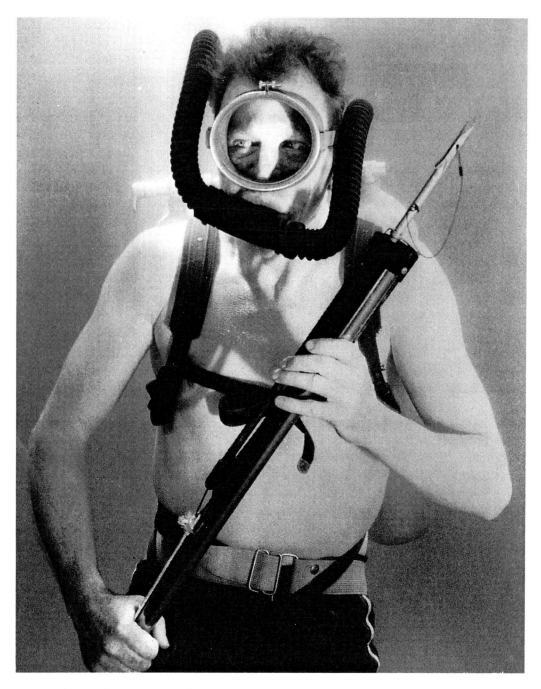

Commander David Forest (Dan Dailey) prepares to swim with dangerous sharks armed only with a spear gun in Underwater Warrior *(1958), based on the true-life exploits of Naval diver Commander Francis Douglas Fane.*

nerve-wracking. The sound of the activated bomb time fuses, a kind of squibby, burning noise, is also very cool.

However, the sequence loses credibility when Forest is seen close to shore and a North Korean sentry begins shooting at him with a machine gun. The North Korean shoreline looks an awful lot like Hawaii, and there's not a ship in sight, though the rescue boat is supposedly close by and the invasion force near as well.

Then a North Korean mortar nest begins to open fire on Forest. But would they shoot mortars into their own minefield? It doesn't make much sense. Forest is brought to the surface by the mortars, but the sentry doesn't shoot at him, though he does open fire when the rescue boat rushes toward shore to rescue the unconscious frogman. Suddenly, there are boats everywhere in stock war footage as the mines explode and the invasion takes place. The landing itself, seen at a great distance, is authentic but not impressive. The only amphibious landing of any real size which took place during the Korean War was at Inchon, when General MacArthur dared deep tidal fluctuations to slide in behind the North Korean lines.

As a tribute to one man's ingenuity, the film works rather well. As Forest, Dan Dailey is properly athletic and intelligent, personifying the best of the post-war breed of scientists who dare to venture into the new frontiers. Dailey is also personable enough to keep much of the film's tone light and enjoyable. Director Marton made the wise choice not to deify his naval hero, but rather to paint him as an engaging, industrious, fun-loving individual. The romance between Forest and Anne is realistic, and focuses on the happiness that they can provide for each other. And the friendship between Forest and O'Brien is both amusing and comforting. Also of note in the cast is Jon Lindbergh, son of famed flier Charles A. Lindbergh, in a tiny role as a diving officer. It was his only film appearance.

Despite its good story and excellent widescreen cinematography, *Underwater Warrior* was largely ignored by film critics. *Variety*'s critic termed the film a "routine programmer" and complained that "the land-bound stretches in between the watery sequences bog down so that it adds up to very mild entertainment." *Boxoffice* echoed those sentiments but was more positive, claiming that "Some interesting and authentic underwater sequences showing Navy frogmen in action, plus the marquee draw of Dan Dailey, make this fine fare for the action houses."

Although it never made waves commercially, *Underwater Warrior* is notable as the fictionalized but authentic career history of Commander Francis D. Fane. As directed by

Andrew Marton, it remains an enjoyable adventure when viewed today due to its bright approach to the material. Marton resists both melodrama and sentimental romance, maintaining a delicate balance between the true-life hazards and romantic commitment which populate Forest's story. The result is an enlightening and entertaining biographical study of a man whose importance to his chosen field is still felt today.

The Walking Major

(aka *Aru Heishi No Kake*)

Credits: 1970. Ishihara Productions. *Directed by* Keith Erik Burt (Keith Larsen). *Co-Directors*: Koji Chino and Nobuaki Shirai. *Produced by* Kikumaru Okuda. *Associate Producers*: Yoshio Yoda and Masanori Yamanoi. *Executive Producers*: Yujiro Ishihara and Akira Nakai. *Screenplay by* Vincent Fotre and Kengo Inomata. *Story Written by* James Miki. *Music by* Naozumi Yamamoto. *Photographed by* Mitsuji Kanau, Yuji Okumura and Haruo Nishiyama. *Film Editor*: Shiro Watanabe. *Art Director*: Toshiyuki Matsui. *Lighting*: Noboru Shiiba. *Sound*: Toru Sakata. *Department of Defense Project Officer*: Major William B. Bickwemert, U.S. Army. *Production Supervisor*: Masahiko Kobayashi. Not Rated. Color. Widescreen. 90 minutes. Released in 1970. Filmed on location in Japan. Previously available on VHS home video.

Cast: *Captain Clark J. Allen*, Dale Robertson; *Hiroshi Kitabayashi (Mr. Pentax)*, Yujiro Ishihara; *Specialist Jimmy Dickson*, Frank Sinatra, Jr.; *Mrs. Allen*, Dina Merrill; *Mother Yamada*, Michiyo Aratama; *Captain White*, Keith Larsen; *Setsuko Takiguchi*, Ruriko Asaoka; *Tadao Kinugasa*, Toshiro Mifune; *Frank Choe*, Arihiro Fujimura; *Kyoko*, Yuriko Ishihara; *Village Girl*, Mayumi Nagisa; *Rose Allen*, Linda Purl; *Danny Allen*, Keith Larsen, Jr.; *Carol White*, Marshie Patton.

Historical Accuracy Level: High. This story records the actual military career and philanthropic efforts of an Army officer whose name is inexplicably changed.

Patriotic Propaganda Level: High. An American Army officer walks over eight hundred miles to raise money for a Japanese orphanage, several times over several years.

Elements: Army, Biography, Combat Photography, Effects on Civilians, Japan, Lonely Wives, Multiple Wars, Orphans, Winter Fighting.

The most unfortunate by-product of war is its creation of orphans — children who lose their parents and their homes — many of whom are forced to become self-sufficient or die. Several Korean War films chronicle the assistance provided by American soldiers and sailors to Korea's orphans, with two of them spotlighting the good works of specific men, based on their true-life adventures during and after the Korean War. *Battle Hymn* depicts Air Force pilot and chaplain Dean Hess' efforts to save some four hundred orphans and establish an orphanage on the Korean island of Cheju, and *The Walking Major* follows an army captain who attempts to walk eight hundred twenty-six miles in two weeks to raise money to build a new orphanage in the Japanese city of Beppu.

On December 14, 1960, Captain Clark J. Allen (Dale Robertson) and Specialist Jimmy Dickson (Frank Sinatra, Jr.), leave the U.S. Army base at Camp Zama, near Tokyo, and begin walking to Beppu, some eight hundred miles away. Allen leaves behind his wife (Dina Merrill) and two children, but is willing to make the walk to collect $6,500 in pledges to be used to begin building a new orphanage in Beppu. Sleeping only three to five hours per night, Allen and Dickson (who barely know each other) average almost sixty miles a day. Dickson questions Allen about his motives for the walk, but the older man is reticent and does not reveal his thoughts.

Their departure is reported in local newspapers, prompting a writer-photographer named Kitabayashi (Yujiro Ishihara) to further investigate the army captain's motives. Kitabayashi remembers (in flashback) the Korean War, when he met Allen and followed his platoon for a story. Allen rescues Kitabayashi's camera during a skirmish and dubs him "Mr. Pentax." The U.N. platoon enters a village of straw huts and is targeted by a sniper. After the sniper is eliminated, Allen sees someone moving behind bundles of straw. Warnings are shouted in Korean and English, but no one replies.

Allen's men shoot, and kill a Korean couple that were hiding. A small child is unhurt next to them. Aghast at the killing of the parents, Kitabayashi slugs Allen and calls him a murderer.

Kitabayashi joins Allen and Dickson as they prepare to spend the night in a crematorium along the road. He reminds Allen of his past and threatens to publish a picture taken at the time of the parents' killing, but Allen doesn't answer. He's asleep.

Walking again, Allen asks Dickson why he came along. Dickson remembers how he was pushed into the situation in a bar, when he bragged that a young, strong man like himself could make the walk easily. Meanwhile, Kitabayashi travels to the orphanage in Beppu and interviews its administrator, known as Mother Yamada (Michiyo Aratama), about Allen's past. She tells him that after the Korean War, American soldiers came to paint and repair the orphanage, and that Allen was one of them. He continued to visit long after the others stopped and befriended a timid, angry boy named Takeshi. Since then, he has done everything possible to love the children and provide a good home for them. Yamada also tells Kitabayashi that Allen claims to be an orphan himself.

In a quick flashback to Korea, Allen picks up the young child whose parents were just killed and says, softly, while holding him tightly, "Forgive me. Forgive me."

Allen and Dickson traverse the final seventy-five miles of the journey without sleep. They limp into Beppu and find crowds of people waiting for them, including Allen's family. They are applauded as heroes, making the trip in thirteen days, nine hours.

Time passes, but Allen's devotion to the orphans does not. He walks again over the Christmas holidays of 1961 and 1962 to raise more money to continue the orphanage construction. In 1965, Allen is assigned to duty in Vietnam. On leave for two days, he visits the orphanage and plays harmonica for the kids. Upon seeing Takeshi, now a young teenager, he gives the boy his harmonica and departs once again.

In a letter, Allen relates to Yamada that he lied about being an orphan so that he would be accepted by the administrators as well as the children. He apologizes for the lie and wishes everyone well. On duty in Vietnam, Allen is visited again by Kitabayashi on Christmas Eve. They congratulate each other on their families and for continuing the charity work for the orphanage, which Kitabayashi's newspaper has assumed since Allen's departure from Japan. Allen finally talks about why it was important for him to walk, and remarks that the love of the children has repaid him tenfold. Jimmy Dickson arrives on the scene, now a sergeant, and takes the writer-photographer to a waiting helicopter.

Allen and Dickson take a jeep to one of the outposts, but are ambushed by enemy snipers and mortars. They hold until reinforcements arrive, but as Allen stands he is killed by a Vietcong sniper. Dickson kills the sniper and tries to help Allen, but it is too late. "Oh, God! Why him?" he cries. It is Kitabayashi who breaks the news of Allen's death to Yamada and the children, who have come to the airport to welcome Allen back to Japan. Kitabayashi is just as broken-hearted as the children, and he responds by walking Allen's route across Japan, taking up the challenge left by Allen to do something worthwhile with his life.

The Walking Major is a faithful recreation of the life of Captain John Arnn. It was Arnn who, in December of 1960 and at the age of 37, walked with Jimmie Dexter, a 19-year-old specialist, from Camp Zama to Beppu. The movie relates that Arnn made two additional walks, and this is also true. Because of Arnn's efforts, the orphanage was finally completed in 1964, and christened the Dormitory of the White Chrysanthemum. Omitted from the film was the fact that two Marines had made a similar trek more than a year earlier and raised $1,000 for Japanese orphans, and it was the Marines' journey that inspired John Arnn to make his own.

According to *Stars and Stripes*, in the early 1990s a sixth-grade student at Camp Zama named Janice Frew wrote a booklet about Arnn after interviewing several of his friends and family members. She was told that Arnn had, as the film purports, accidentally killed a Korean couple and rescued their young son. And it is also true that Arnn died in Vietnam on Christmas Eve. The film is remarkably faithful to the true story of one man who wanted to make the world a better place for a group of unlucky children.

The film benefits from location filming along the actual route of the trek and the use of widescreen lenses to make the journey more panoramic. And the casting of gentle but commanding Dale Robertson as Allen/Arnn is perfect. Robertson doesn't speak much but when he does, his melodious voice is filled with meaningful inflection.

Despite its veracity and the presence of Robertson, however, *The Walking Major* is a frustrating movie. Its Japanese filmmakers seem to be searching for a higher level of meaning or importance to the story, as personified by the character of Kitabayashi, but Allen/Arnn's personal journey remains enigmatic. Kitabayashi is told why it is so important for Allen/Arnn to return to the orphanage, and then to walk halfway across Japan to raise money for the orphans, yet he still remains unsatisfied by those answers. Ultimately, following Allen/Arnn's death, he decides to put himself in the captain's well-worn shoes and search for himself the meaning of the journey. Perhaps that is the message of the filmmakers: that everyone should undertake their own journey for self-fulfillment and the appreciation for others.

The key image in the film is Allen's quick second flashback in Korea, when he lifts the child his men have just orphaned and embraces the boy tightly. When Allen asks the uncomprehending child to forgive him, it explains everything about his endeavors. This simple, uncomplicated image expresses more emotion than any explanation Allen could hope to make to Kitabayashi.

The Korean War flashbacks are rather well done, showing the danger faced by the American soldiers in both winter and summer conditions. The locations seem authentic, rutted and muddy, and Allen's men behave like soldiers, not extras. The same is true later in Vietnam, which looks just like Korea, and is even more dangerous. Japanese locations were used for both sequences.

No proof was found for this book that the film ever played in the United States. Certainly, it never received a wide release. With a cast that includes Dale Robertson, Frank Sinatra Jr., Dina Merrill and Toshiro Mifune, and an English-language soundtrack, it is amazing that the film was never widely distributed. It was popular, however, in Japan, where Captain John Arnn is remembered with pride and respect. Today, *The Walking Major* is primarily remembered by the people who celebrate the legacy of John Arnn and the Beppu orphanage. A showing of the film accompanies the orphanage's annual fundraising drive and reminds its audiences of the difference that one person can make in the lives of other people.

War Hunt

Credits: 1962. T-D Enterprises. *Released by* United Artists. *Directed by* Denis Sanders. *Produced by* Terry Sanders. *Co-Producer*: Denis Sanders. *Written by* Stanford Whitmore. *Music by* Bud Shank. *Director of Photography*: Ted McCord, A.S.C. *Film Editor*: John Hoffman. *Pictorial Continuity*: Terry Sanders. *Art Direction*: Edgar Lansbury. *Titles Designed by* Vance Jonson. *Assistant Producer*: Noel Black. *Assistant Director*: Jack Bohier. *Production Assistant*: William J. Claxton. *Technical Advisor*: Jerry Preshaw. *Special Effects*: Joe Lombardi. *Script Supervisor*: Betty Crosby. *Gaffer*: Lloyd Garnell. *Sound*: Roy Meadows. *Wardrobe*: Frank Novak. *Property Master*: John Orlando. *Key Grip*: Chuck Hanawalt. *Camera Operator*: Bill Schurr. *Assistant Editor*: Edward Dutko. *Sound Effects Editor*: John Mick. *Music Editor*: Kenny Wilhoit. *Recording*: Ryder Sound Service. *Optical Effects*: Modern Film Effects. Not Rated. Black and White. Widescreen (1.66:1). 81 minutes. Released in August, 1962. Filmed in the Topanga Canyon area of Los Angeles, California. Not currently available on commercial home video.

Cast: *Private Raymond Endore*, John Saxon; *Private Roy Loomis*, Robert Redford; *Captain Wallace Pratt*, Charles Aidman; *Sergeant Owen Van Horn*, Sydney Pollack; *Charlie*, Tommy Matsuda; *Private Crotty*, Gavin MacLeod; *Private Joshua Fresno*, Anthony Ray; *Corporal Stan Showalter*, Tom Skerritt; *Lieutenant Colonel*, William Challee; *Mama San*, Nancy Hsueh.

Historical Accuracy Level: Medium. Though fictional, the story of a troubled soldier who does not want to stop fighting when the cease-fire commences is one with universal truth and meaning.

Patriotic Propaganda Level: Low. A fresh soldier watches several of his colleagues die and one lose his mind; this does not exactly extoll the virtues of war.

Elements: Army, Cease-Fire, Infighting, Orphans, Prisoners of War.

Made and released a decade after the Korean War, the independently made feature *War Hunt* remains one of the most interesting explorations of human nature and the psychology of warfare ever put on screen. Like *Platoon*, which followed a quarter of a century later, it features two characters, one representing good and one representing evil, who battle for the soul of a third, in this case a young Korean boy. Both films examine war's dehumanizing effects, both physically and psychologically, on the men who fight. Today, *War Hunt* is chiefly known as Robert Redford's debut film, and one which offers strong early career performances by John Saxon, Gavin MacLeod, Tom Skerritt and especially Sydney Pollack, who later established himself as an Oscar-winning director, but the film has far more to offer than its excellent performances.

War Hunt takes place along the MLR (the main line of resistance) in Korea in May of 1953. Private Roy Loomis (Robert Redford) narrates his journey as he is propelled toward the front lines by the army's pipeline, its systematic movement of men and materiel to and from the battle front. Loomis and his fellow replacement soldiers are briefed that the enemy, chiefly the Chinese at this point, must be hurt daily to speed along the peace talks at nearby Panmunjom. When he reaches an area near the front, Loomis meets other members of the First Squad, including soft-spoken Sergeant Van Horn (Sydney Pollack), southern Corporal Stan Showalter (Tom Skerritt), and slovenly Private Crotty (Gavin MacLeod).

The first night, Loomis glimpses a figure in blackface and black clothing leaving a tent. The figure returns the next morning, whistling, after a successful night patrol. He is Private Raymond Endore (John Saxon), a soldier who patrols alone, armed with only a knife, into the battle area and behind enemy lines. He kills, silently, and returns with information on enemy positions and intentions. Endore is accompanied in camp by Charlie (Tommy Matsuda), a young

This poster for United Artists' drama War Hunt *(1962) asks the rhetorical question, "Where does the hero end and the killer begin?" Judging from the images of John Saxon dressed in black and wielding a dagger and blond Robert Redford pointing a pistol at Saxon, the answer is simple.*

Korean boy who reluctantly stays behind while Endore conducts his patrols.

The men are transported to the front line. Fighting occurs only at night, except for occasional sniper shots at figures standing up too straight. On one horizon is the beacon of neutral area Panmunjom, brightly lit so that neither side will bomb the peace negotiators. The Chinese play music over loudspeakers constantly, except when they are about to attack. On his first night patrol, Loomis watches incredulously as Endore circles a freshly killed enemy, crouching around it in some weird ritual. He begins to think that something is deeply wrong with Private Raymond Endore.

Loomis befriends Charlie, but is told by several soldiers to "leave the kid alone." Nobody wants to antagonize Endore. Captain Pratt (Charles Aidman) recommends Endore for several battlefield commissions, but a visiting lieutenant colonel (William Challee) is not impressed with Endore's lack of military courtesy and orders that Endore receive some rest. At Endore's urging, Pratt ignores the colonel's order and continues to send Endore on night sorties, alone. One night, Endore returns with a wound on his arm and words of warning. "They're coming."

A few nights later, the First Squad is situated in an outpost in the battle area when the music stops and the Chinese begin shelling. The artillery barrage lasts two-and-a-half hours, numbing the men's senses. Suddenly the shelling stops and the Chinese soldiers attack. The Americans hold back the initial charge with rifles and grenades; Loomis' rifle jams and he stands by helplessly as Endore steps into his position and kills several enemy soldiers. Loomis is still stunned as Captain Pratt orders a retreat back to the trenches, and is left behind in the confusion. A Chinese soldier jumps into the outpost and lands on top of Loomis, knocking him unconscious. Loomis awakens after the battle is over to find another Chinese soldier raiding the valuables of the dead men. They fight and Loomis knocks him unconscious with a sandbag. With an injured leg, Loomis crawls back to the safety of the American trenches.

Loomis' sprained knee relegates him to duty as clerk for a supply sergeant. In his free time, Loomis talks to Charlie and gradually attempts to lessen Endore's hold on the boy's affections. Charlie tells Loomis that he and Endore will stay together in Korea after the war. Loomis tells Endore that the boy will have to go to an orphanage, and that he will see to it if Endore does not. Endore pulls his knife on Loomis and threatens to kill him if he doesn't leave them alone.

A cease-fire is declared to take effect at 10:00 p.m., but while celebrating, Private Fresno (Anthony Ray) is killed by a sniper. The cease-fire officially begins, but Endore blackens his face and leaves as usual, this time taking Charlie with him. Loomis informs Pratt of Endore's disappearance, and of his own opinion that Endore isn't coming back. Captain Pratt waits until morning, then organizes a graves detail of himself, Loomis and Van Horn to find Endore and bring him back before he threatens the armistice.

Meanwhile, Endore kills another North Korean and shows Charlie how it is done, actually putting his knife in the boy's hand and forcing him to stab the dead body. Endore tells Charlie his secret: he is invisible; he explains that "The truth can blind." After hours of searching, the trio of Americans finally locates Endore, who refuses to return, and warns the men away. Van Horn rushes Endore and is thrown aside; Loomis rushes and is cut on the arm. Before Endore can kill any of his men, Pratt shoots Endore to death. Charlie runs from the violence, having lost another father figure, and escapes into the no man's land of the Korean hills.

War Hunt was a low-budget production (it was shot in just three weeks in the Topanga Canyon area of Los Angeles for about $250,000) from two brothers who were angling to make their mark in the feature film business. The Sanders brothers, director Denis and producer Terry, had previously made short films and documentaries, one of which, *A Time Out of War*, had won the best short film (two-reel) Oscar in 1954. Their first feature film, *Crime and Punishment USA* in 1959, had introduced George Hamilton to the big screen; now they were trying again with a Korean War drama and a young discovery named Robert Redford.

Because of budgetary limitations, and a refusal of military assistance from the army, *War*

Hunt is largely devoid of routine battlefield dramatics. Instead, its drama is psychological in origin and symbolic in scope. It is a battle of wills over the soul of the innocent Korean boy, Charlie. Yet in this battle of good and evil, good is not wholly good nor is evil wholly evil. Endore may be a killing machine, but he takes good care of the boy and protects him fiercely. His fighting tactics might be bizarre, but he provides needed data to headquarters and, as one soldier remarks, "I'm glad he's on our side." Loomis most certainly has the welfare of the boy in mind, but his best solution is an orphanage. Loomis is naive in the ways of the world and when it comes time to fight, he panics.

Charlie needs a father figure to replace the father he lost in the war. He wants someone strong, someone who won't be killed, so it is natural that he would gravitate to Endore. Charlie's friendship gives Endore a human interest which is evidently lacking in his own personality and which humanizes him to a great degree. Their plan to live together in the Korean wilds would work, and might be right for them, if it weren't for Endore's association with the army. From Endore's admittedly insane perspective, it is the army, and specifically Loomis' obtrusive interest in Charlie's welfare, which spoils their plan for happiness.

The key to all this, of course, is Endore's insanity. There is something in his personality which finds killing not only attractive but necessary, and the Korean War provides an outlet for this behavior. When the cease-fire goes into effect, Endore is unable to stop the habit of killing. Proof of Endore's insanity comes once he has taken Charlie "over the hill" with him. When Endore puts his stiletto in the boy's hand and teaches him how to kill, it is obvious that Endore has crossed a moral line. Then he tells the boy his secret, that he is invisible. That statement is partly true, since Endore sports a blackened face and black clothes and is difficult to see, but he means it in a different sense. "The truth can blind," he says wonderingly. And when he is finally cornered by Captain Pratt, Endore rejects Pratt's command to return by mumbling, "You don't command—I command the commandments—"

It would be easy for the film to blame Endore's insanity on the dehumanizing effect of the war, but it does not. The war simply creates an opportunity for Endore's condition to prosper, while the cease-fire complicates the situation. The war affects Loomis to a greater degree; he eventually loses his naivete, and nearly his life. At the conclusion of the film, Pratt asks Loomis, "You all right, soldier?" and Loomis replies in a definitive tone, "No." It is one of the ironies of the story that when Loomis' gun jams at the outpost, it is Endore who steps into his position and prevents the Chinese from killing the greenhorn. At that time, Endore gives Loomis looks of disgust, as Loomis has just proven that he is, like everyone else but Endore, weak in the ways of killing.

Of course, the biggest effect of the war is on Charlie. The young Korean boy saw his family killed, ironically by Americans, yet had adopted the army, and specifically Private Raymond Endore, as a surrogate father. When Loomis calls Endore a liar, Charlie responds by killing a sick bird rather than giving it to Loomis for treatment. And when Endore is finally killed, again before his very eyes, Charlie runs into the Korean hills alone. Perhaps he will carry some of Loomis' nobility with him, but it is more likely that he will remember Endore's savagery; that savagery might just keep him alive.

Despite its low-budget and lack of military accoutrements, *War Hunt* succeeds in creating an eerie, atmospheric setting of war. The trenches and bunkers seem detailed and authentic, as does the lassitude of daytime soldiering in Korea. The only action during the day comes when Private Crotty balances a helmet on a stick above the trench to entice a sniper's shots. Otherwise, the action takes place at night, as patrols sneak across the no man's land between both sides, avoiding each other. It is this quiet, dangerous place in which Endore conducts his business.

The one battle sequence is nicely handled. An artillery barrage begins and Loomis glances at his watch to note the time. A little while later, Loomis looks again. Only two minutes have passed, and Loomis is astounded. The barrage continues for two-and-a-half hours, deafening and numbing the Americans into shock. Only then do the Chinese soldiers advance. This brief episode, which does perhaps suffer from a lack of extras and equipment on both sides, never-

Korean orphan Charlie (Tommy Matsuda, left) and Private Raymond Endore (John Saxon, right) enjoy a respite from the Korean War in the psychological drama War Hunt *(1962).*

theless imparts the realism of battle and the fear of the men fighting it. The fear which Loomis feels upon awakening, injured, alone and among the enemy, is palpable.

The script also details the cease-fire arrangements with care. The soldiers, who have been so careful in remaining out of sight from the Chinese snipers, forget about this precaution once the armistice has been announced, and as a result, one of them dies. It is with rage that Pratt reminds the men that the cease-fire doesn't go into effect for another twelve hours, and that wartime conditions still continue.

The film also touches on the issue of prisoners of war. When Loomis arrives at the First Squad's encampment, there is a fenced area containing Korean prisoners. Loomis is warned to keep away from the men and women behind the fence, but finds it difficult not to commiserate with them. Charlie threatens young boys like himself with a knife, safe in the knowledge that he is outside the fence and not a victim, like them. One young woman tries to interest

Loomis in a dalliance, but he wisely spurns the offer. These prisoners are not emphasized within the story, but remind Loomis (who cares) and the other soldiers (who do not care) that the ground over which they are fighting and dying is home to these displaced people.

It is because *War Hunt* eschews the common, routine action and sentiment found in Korean War films that it is superior to so many of them. While the actual story of the film is not revolutionary, the Sanders brothers and writer Stanford Whitmore have invested their scenario and characters with genuine feeling and meaning. In so many war films, war itself is the horror; here, the horror is in the ways that the war affects the men who fight it and the children who are orphaned by it. And although *War Hunt* makes no claim as a history of the war, its dramatic story, combined with Denis Sanders' sensitive direction and the strong performances, provides the film with more power and truthfulness than many generally accurate yet dull Korean War stories.

Critics were bowled over by the film's approach to its subject. Howard Thompson of the *New York Times* declared, "If you want to see one of the most original and haunting war movies in years, don't miss *War Hunt*" and remarked that "And most of this little picture is pure, unvarnished gold." *Times* colleague Bosley Crowther agreed, noting, "A happy instance of stunning achievement on the part of two young filmmakers is evident in *War Hunt*, a tightly-packed, tensely drawn war drama ... in which there is not one conspicuously conventional GI type. It reaches a rare emotional level — a kind of poetry — for this type of film."

Robert Salmaggi of the *New York Herald Tribune* praised the filmmakers. "The youthful team of Denis Sanders, 33, the director, and his brother Terry, 29, the producer, has come up with an arresting war drama ... rich in dramatic intensity. They have focused not so much on the physical scars of war — there is just one major battle scene — as on its traumatic effects on both the warrior and non-warrior." The laurels for *War Hunt* extended to the year-end top ten lists, when it was named as one of 1962's best English-language films by the National Board of Review. The film might have achieved more acclaim but for 1962's more lavish war-themed extravaganzas *Lawrence of Arabia* and *The Longest Day*.

Although it was critically applauded in its time, *War Hunt* was only moderately successful. It became notable for launching Robert Redford's acting career, and it introduced Redford to fellow thespian Sydney Pollack, who soon became a major film director, hiring actor Redford seven separate times. Assistant producer Noel Black, who held — and, according to Redford, continually dropped — a light reflector, moved on to a directing career beginning with *Pretty Poison*. Francis Ford Coppola worked on the film driving a truck. The Sanders brothers made a few more feature films together, then split, with Denis returning to documentary filmmaking, winning another Oscar in 1968 for *Czechoslovakia* and delivering a huge hit with *Elvis: That's the Way It Is*, in 1970.

Today, *War Hunt* remains among the most effective and meaningful Korean War films. It is a classic of its kind, a minor masterpiece, which measures the impact of war by its impact on its participants. It keeps the stated military goal of "hurting the enemy on a daily basis to help our side in the peace talks" firmly in mind, and yet highlights the steep price of that goal in terms of human life and sanity. Most impressively, it does not provide a happy ending for anyone, particularly Charlie, the Korean boy who represents those for whom the war is being fought. For Charlie, war is indeed hell.

War Is Hell
(aka *War Hero*; *War Madness*)

Credits: 1964. Allied Artists. *Directed, Produced and Written by* Burt Topper. *Produced by* Ross Hahn. *Associate Producer*: Sam Altonian. *Music by* Ronald Stein. *Director of Photography*: Jacques R. Marquette. *Film Editor*: Ace Herman, A.C.E. *Production Manager*: Willard Kirkham. *Key Grips*: Frank Lambers and Richard M. Rubin. *Properties*: Karl R. Brainard. *Sound*: Al Overton. *Special Effects*: Pat Dinga. *Wardrobe*: Marge Corso. *Script Supervisor*: Fred Applegate, Sr. *Camera Operator*: Nelson Cordes. *Gaffer*: Bill Kain. *Transportation*: Allee R. Reed. *Still Man*: Roger Mace. *Unit Manager*: Edward Knight. Not Rated. Black and White. Widescreen (1.85:1). 81 minutes. Released in January, 1964. *Note*: This Burt Topper film was originally shown in Britain in 1960 under the title *War Hero*, but remained unreleased in the United States until 1964. Not currently available on commercial home video.

Cast: Sergeant *Keefer*, Tony Russel; Sergeant *Garth*, Baynes Barron; *Yung Chi Thomas*, Judy Dan; *Lieutenant Hallen*, Burt Topper; *Miller*, Tony Rich; *Koller*, J. J. Dahner (J. J. Dana); *Laney*, Wally Campo; *Gresler*, Bobby Byles; *Seldon*, Michael Bell; *Bender*, Russ Prescott; *Conners*, Robert Howard; *Thurston*, Paul Sherriff; *Korean Lieutenant*, Kei Chung; *Narrator of Introduction*, Audie Murphy.

Historical Accuracy Level: Low. Fortunately, stories like this tale of cowardice and murder have little relation to the actual fighting in Korea.

Patriotic Propaganda Level: Low. None of the main American soldiers in this story seem to have any patriotic scruples.

Elements: Army, Cease-Fire, Females in the Field, Infighting.

Filmmaker Burt Topper made some low-budget war films in the late 1950s and early 1960s, such as the World War II programmer *Hell Squad*, which was paired on a double feature with the Korean War film *Tank Battalion* by American International Pictures. One of his independent productions is *War is Hell*, which was released in Britain as *War Hero* in 1960, four years before it premiered in the United States. The distribution rights to *War Hero* were evidently purchased by Allied Artists, which released the film as *War is Hell* in early 1964. The story centers around a cowardly, selfish soldier named Keefer (Tony Russel) who remains behind when his platoon storms a Communist bunker, but then takes credit for the assault in order to win a medal for himself. He is promoted by a lieutenant (Burt Topper), but when the lieutenant begins to question what really happened, Keefer kills the officer to keep his secret.

An armistice goes into effect, but Keefer assumes command of the lieutenant's men without telling them about the cease-fire. The Americans attack a group of Reds who are celebrating the cease-fire and slaughter them; most of the Americans are killed in turn by avenging Communists. Keefer is killed, leaving only another soldier and a young woman as survivors. The surviving soldier does not report Keefer's actions, reasoning that since he is dead, the truth is unimportant.

While this plot is somewhat similar to that of *War Hunt* in some respects, it sounds (no copy of the film could be found for review) purely exploitive and not at all credible. The idea that one soldier would place his own desire for a medal above the lives of his fellow soldiers, even killing the lieutenant who suspects the truth about him, is repugnant and fallacious.

Film Daily's critic wrote that "The film is a brisk, hard-hitting action drama." Allen M. Widem of the *Motion Picture Herald* praised Tony Russel's characterization as "incisiveness that's truly exciting to behold." *Boxoffice* was also impressed. "Triple-threat talent Burt Topper is to be congratulated for spiritedness and inventive touches with which he has discernibly infused this Allied Artists release." Adding to the appeal of the film is an introduction filmed by World War II's most decorated soldier, Audie Murphy, who discusses the impact of war upon the men who fight.

A Yank in Korea
(aka *Letter from Korea*)

Credits: 1951. Columbia. *Directed by* Lew Landers. *Produced by* Sam Katzman. *Screen Play by* William Sackheim. *From a Story by* Leo Lieberman. *Musical Director:* Ross DiMaggio. *Director of Photography:* William Whitley. *Film Editor:* Edwin Bryant. *Art Director:* Paul Palmentola. *Set Decorator:* Sidney Clifford. *Unit Manager:* Herbert Leonard. *Assistant Director:* Leonard Katzman. *Sound Engineer:* John Westmoreland. Not Rated. Black and White. Flat (1.33:1). 73 minutes. Released in February 1951. Not currently available on commercial home video.

Cast: Andy Smith, Lon McCallister; *Sergeant Mike Kirby*, William "Bill" Phillips; *Milo Pagano*, Brett King; *Sollie Kaplan*, Larry Stewart; *Lieutenant Lewis*, William Tannen; *Jinx Hamilton*, Tommy Farrell; *Stan Howser*, Norman Wayne; *Sergeant Hutton*, Rusty Wescoatt; *Corporal Jawolski*, William Haade; *Peggy Cole*, Sunny Vickers; *Powers*, Richard Paxton; *Randy Smith*, Ralph Hodges; *Junior*, Richard Gould.

Historical Accuracy Level: Medium. The episodes within this story are said to be based on actual Korean War events, although the story which ties them together is fictional.

Patriotic Propaganda Level: High. The letter on which the film is based is propaganda of the best and most effective kind.

Elements: Army, Behind Enemy Lines, Military Training, Returning Home, United Nations Security Council.

Publicized as "First on the Screen!" in terms of chronicling the Korean conflict, *A Yank in Korea* (titled *Letter from Korea* in Great Britain) was released almost simultaneously with *The Steel Helmet* and *Korea Patrol* as Hollywood's first celluloid versions of the fighting overseas. It was the first Korean War film from a major studio; the others had been independent productions. Based on a nationally publicized letter from Private John J. McCormick to his children back home in Collingsdale, Pennsylvania, *A Yank in Korea* has at least some basis in reality. The letter itself is, of course, better than the movie at conveying a lonely soldier's feelings, but the reading of the letter at the end of the movie provides one of the most touching moments in any Korean War film.

A Yank in Korea begins with a written prologue that declares that PFC John J. McCormick's letter "is destined to become an historic document," and notes that the film was inspired by McCormick and is dedicated to his memory. Then, actual footage of the United Nations Security Council meeting is shown where Warren Austin declares that the United States will furnish assistance to South Korea.

The scene switches to a small town, where a group of young men listen to the radio and hear that all men between the ages of nineteen and twenty-six must be screened for a possible military draft. A reporter overhears Randy Smith (Ralph Hodges) declare his intention to enlist in the Army and relates the story to his editor, inadvertently naming the young man Andy Smith. The story is carried on the front page of the newspaper, surprising Andy Smith (Lon McCallister), a self-employed fix-it man who has not considered volunteering for service. He is persuaded to do so by the thrilled reaction of his girlfriend Peggy (Sunny Vickers), who agrees to marry him before he leaves for war. Andy Smith passes his physical (Randy Smith does not), marries Peggy and immediately departs for training.

The army teaches the young men how to march, shoot and survive. Six men, including Andy, Milo Pagano (Brett King), Sollie Kaplan (Larry Stewart), Jinx Hamilton (Tommy Farrell), and Stan Howser (Norman Wayne) are selected to be sent to Korea. They are immediately put into the field, paired together and forced to sleep in foxholes. Sergeant Kirby (William "Bill" Phillips) leads one patrol to flush North Korean "spotters," while Sergeant Hutton (Rusty Wescoatt) leads another. A sudden enemy ambush anchored by a machine gun emplacement eliminates several of the soldiers, including Jinx Hamilton, before Andy destroys the pillbox with a handy bulldozer.

That night, a soldier named Powers (Richard Paxton) feels ill in his foxhole. Andy leaves his own post to talk to Powers, allowing two North Korean soldiers to sneak past. Sollie Kaplan is knifed to death and Powers is killed by a grenade; both North Koreans escape. Later, Andy tries to explain why he left his foxhole, but Lieutenant Lewis (William Tannen) refuses to listen. He blames Andy for the attack, and the other men begin to avoid contact with Andy. As the North Koreans break through the U.N. lines, the men are pulled south to the Pusan Perimeter before fighting their way north again. A montage illustrates this period, with the infantrymen reclaiming bombed-out cities, street by street. The ostracism of Andy continues, even after he saves lives by killing roof snipers with a grenade.

Sergeant Kirby takes Andy, Howser and Pagano on a mission to destroy an underground ammunition dump. They successfully complete the mission, and Kirby leads them into enemy territory to escape detection. By so doing, they discover that the North Koreans are constructing an underwater bridge to transport tanks and artillery across a river. Howser and Pagano attempt to return to the Army camp while Kirby and Andy try to create a diversion. Andy and Kirby are taken prisoner and beaten by the Communists while the others return to safety. Awaiting death, Kirby gives Andy a letter to give to his surviving family, just in case. The information provided by Hower and Pagano leads to an air raid which destroys the tanks crossing the river and frees the two prisoners, who also return to safety.

Howser is promoted to corporal and Andy is to be transferred back to the States. Kirby is assigned to guard a stranded train, loaded with wounded soldiers, until a railroad specialist can arrive to fix the damaged locomotive. Andy volunteers to try to fix the train and ignores his official transfer in order to do so. Just as he finishes the repairs, the train is attacked by enemy soldiers from another train. Kirby is killed, and Andy is shot in the leg, but he drives the train away from the danger. Following the battle, Andy is evacuated to a hospital, then flown back to the U.S. After recuperating, Andy takes Peggy with him to visit the Kirby family. Andy meets Kirby's children and reads them the letter which Kirby gave to him (the McCormick letter, with slight alterations).

The marketing for Columbia's drama A Yank in Korea *(1951) stresses romance, action and comedy, but most of all, its own timeliness. This film was one of the first trio of Korean War movies to reach audiences indicated by its reference to "the hottest spot on earth!"*

A Yank in Korea is intended to depict some of the challenges facing young men who devote themselves to the war effort. Andy Smith is an everyman, representing a host of young men, who are trained to remain calm and clear-headed in the line of fire. Perhaps the best of Andy's attributes is industriousness. Twice during the film — when he uses the bulldozer, and when he drives the locomotive — this soldier is able to use his mechanical talents to save his colleagues. Both of these episodes are reportedly based on actual events that took place early during the war.

But Andy also allows his concern for another soldier to interfere with his guard duty, with disastrous results. Despite his best intentions, his decision to leave his own foxhole to comfort a sick friend, Powers, leads directly to the deaths of two men, one of whom is Powers. Lieutenant Lewis correctly blames Andy for the infiltration, and this lesson is reinforced by the ostracism which surrounds Andy thereafter. Because this is a movie, Andy is provided with an opportunity to redeem himself, which he does by fixing and driving the locomotive, thereby saving dozens of wounded men. Nevertheless, it is an unusual mark of maturity that Lew Landers' film would so vividly demonstrate Andy's poor judgment and make it a central issue to the story.

Another moment, though trivial, also marks the film as adult. After Andy and Kirby escape from the North Koreans, there is a scene where a group of soldiers bathe and cavort in a river, in their swimsuits. It is a comic scene that finds Andy being pushed into the river, now being accepted by the men who previously turned their backs to him. In the background of a long shot showing the men splashing around, there is a nude figure with his back toward the camera. This is mentioned only because male nudity (even seen from behind) is virtually unheard of in American films of this period, yet it is visible here.

Although *A Yank in Korea* is timely, well-intentioned and does contain some worthwhile drama, it is also shallow and uninspired. The low budget works against the story, particularly during the sequence when Andy leaves his foxhole. The foxholes are so close together that the pair of North Korean soldiers can easily be seen creeping past, and it is unbelievable that neither Andy nor Powers sees them. The scale of the film is small, with Hollywood backlots serving rather poorly as Korean terrain. The air raid upon the underwater bridge found by the Americans is heard rather than seen, and no military hardware can be seen being hit at all, leaving the impression that the raid was a failure, though

the dialogue states otherwise. Even the climactic railroad firefight makes little visual sense, heroic though it may be. Director Lew Landers has far more success with the personal scenes than with the action scenes.

Most problematic is the sequence after the Communist ammunition dump is destroyed. Andy and Kirby are supposed to create a diversion in order for Howser and Pagano to escape detection, but they simply walk into the enemy's hands. Both men are beaten by the North Koreans, but no interrogation is depicted. One guard is placed to watch the prisoners, but he is stupidly killed by the strafing jets, allowing Andy and Kirby to escape. This whole sequence is very poorly executed and is never convincing. It even contains an insult to the air force, when Kirby remarks, "The air force couldn't hit the broad side of a barn."

The characters, except for Andy and the beneficent Sergeant Kirby, are skeletal and uninspired. Andy Smith is the entire show, and he is characterized by young-looking Lon McCallister. Twenty-eight when the film was released, McCallister had found success playing callow youths in 1940s dramas such as *Home in Indiana* and *Winged Victory*. McCallister is still youthful enough to accept as Andy, but he only made two more films (including *Combat Squad*, a Korean War film) before retiring.

Because of its timeliness, *A Yank in Korea* was moderately successful upon its release, more so than *Korea Patrol*, but it was not as popular as Samuel Fuller's *The Steel Helmet*. Critics were largely ambivalent about the film, but it made money for Columbia. *New York Times* reviewer A. H. Weiler judged it "a minor Hollywood item replete with simulated G.I.'s and their enemies," as well as "trite and unconvincing." The British Film Institute's *Monthly Film Bulletin* found it to be "a conventional story of military adventures," and *Variety* called it "an okay program feature."

The film's most compelling feature, and the inspiration for its creation, is Andy's recitation of Kirby's (actually McCormick's) letter to his children in the final scene. The filmmakers changed the gender of one of the children, and it is somewhat strange that Andy reads it to the children without their mother being present, but the letter remains otherwise intact. The original

American soldiers Andy Smith (Lon McCallister, left), Sergeant Mike Kirby (William "Bill" Phillips, center) and Milo Pagano (Brett King, right) search for a solution to the ambush in which they are trapped in A Yank in Korea *(1951).*

version of Private John J. McCormick's acclaimed letter is included here in its entirety:

Dear Joanie and Rose Marie:

This is Daddy. I want you to listen and pay attention while Mommie reads this to you. Just try and make believe I was there, talking to you.

Joanie, I don't think you'll remember me because you were a little baby when I had to go away, but I used to sit and hold you a lot, and when you were a bad little girl, I used to make you sit in a chair until you were good, but I always loved you a lot and I was very proud of you.

Rose Marie, you should remember me because I used to take you out with me a lot, and I used to buy you a lot of candy and sodas, and I used to feel so good when people used to say you had eyes like mine. Remember the little puppy I bought you? Your Mummie used to tie a little pink ribbon around its neck and you used to carry it in your arms. You looked awfully cute.

I want you both to know that I'd be with you if I could, but there are a lot of bad men in the world, and if they were allowed to do what they wanted to do, little girls like you wouldn't be allowed to do what they wanted to do; little girls like you wouldn't be allowed to go to church on Sunday or be able to go to the school you wanted to.

So I have to help fight these men and keep them from coming where you and Mummie live. It might take a long while, and maybe Daddy will have to go and help God up in Heaven, and if I do, I always want you both to be good for Mummie, because she is the best Mummie in the whole wide world.

She has always taken care of you while I have been away. You see, kids, I happened to be caught in two wars inside ten years, and the reason I am where I am today is because I am fighting for what I think is right.

That's one thing I always want both of you to

remember. If your conscience tells you something is right, always stand up for it. You might be ridiculed for doing so, but in the long run you'll always find out that people respect you more for doing so.

When you grow up to be young ladies, don't ever forget all that Mummie has done for you. She has often gone without clothes for herself so that both of you could have nice things. I want you to do as she says; go to church on Sundays and you can always pray for Daddy.

So remember, kids, when you grow up, save this letter in case I'm not there to talk to you, and try and remember all I am saying, for it's for your good, and because I love you and Mummie so much.

I'll be in a hole, fighting, in a few days, in a place called Korea, so I'm sending you all the love that's in my heart on this sheet of paper. I carry your picture, and Mummie's, next to my heart, and if I have to go help God, you'll know that the last thought I had on this earth was for the two of you and Mommie. All my love and kisses. Be good and God bless you. Daddy.

The Young and the Brave

Credits: 1963. Metro-Goldwyn-Mayer. *Directed by* Francis D. Lyon. *Produced by* A. C. Lyles. *Screen Play by* Beirne Lay, Jr. *Story by* Ronald Davidson and Harry M. Slott. *Music by* Ronald Stein. *Director of Photography:* Emmett Bergholz. *Film Editor:* Robert Leo. *Art Direction:* Paul Sylos, Jr. *Assistant Director and Assistant to the Producer:* Harry F. Hogan. *Recording Supervisor:* Al Overton, Sr. *Make-Up:* Ted Coodley. *Special Visual Effects:* Roger George. *Wardrobe:* James Taylor. Not Rated. Black and White. Widescreen (1.85:1). 84 minutes. Released in August, 1963. Not currently available on commercial home video.

Cast: *Sergeant Ed Brent,* Rory Calhoun; *Staff Sergeant Peter L. Kane,* William Bendix; *Corporal John Estway,* Richard Jaeckel; *Colonel Ralph Holbein,* Richard Arlen; *Intelligence Officer,* John Agar; *Han,* Manuel Padilla; *Private Kirk Wilson,* Robert Ivers; *Communist Soldier,* Weaver Levy; *Stretcher Bearer,* Dennis Richards; *Lieutenant Ulysses Nero,* Robert Goshen; *Han's Father,* Willard Lee; *Army Major,* Beirne Lay, Jr.; *Lobo,* Flame.

Historical Accuracy Level: Low. This story about escaped American prisoners, an orphan and a dog in Korea is strictly fantasy.

Patriotic Propaganda Level: High. The American soldiers save the orphan (and vice versa) and the dog (Lobo, "a good G.I. dog") saves everyone.

Elements: Army, Collaboration, Dogs, Effects on Civilians, Helicopters, Orphans, Rescues.

An old actors' credo is to avoid working with children and dogs, as they tend to steal the spotlight. This Korean War film features both a Korean youngster and a German shepherd, the young and the brave of the title. Both acquit themselves impressively, with as much or more screen time than stars Rory Calhoun and William Bendix. The script, though rather routine, does examine the immediate effects of the war on innocent Korean people more than most other films of this nature.

Set in Korea in 1951, *The Young and the Brave* finds three American soldiers on the run after escaping from a prison camp. As the movie begins, they are hiding in a friendly Korean farmer's home when a North Korean patrol arrives. The soldiers escape undetected but the Korean couple is locked inside the hut and it is set on fire while their young son watches, unable to prevent their deaths, on a nearby hill. Having just lost his family, the nine year old boy Han (Manuel Padilla) begins to wander the countryside to find a new home with no provisions — just the clothes on his back. Han finds a wrecked U.S. Army camp with a leashed German shepherd that will not let the boy near him. Han eventually befriends the dog by giving it water and letting it loose. The dog is a "good G. I. dog" named Lobo, and it devotes itself to Han, heart and soul. That night, they sleep together out of the rain under an overturned jeep. The next morning, after eating "K" rations which Han finds in the wreckage of the camp, the boy and his dog begin their search for food, shelter and a new life.

After much walking, Han meets the three American soldiers and instructs Lobo to attack them because they caused the death of his parents.

The young Korean boy Han (Manuel Padilla) and his faithful dog Lobo (Flame) share the spotlight in this ad for MGM's adventure They Young and the Brave (1963). *This ad displays three tanks and one jet, although none of them are seen in the actual film. and the tasteless tagline "The Battleground Was His Playground" could apply equally to Han or to the dog.*

Sergeant Brent (Rory Calhoun) explains to the boy that, since they had no weapons, they could not help Han's parents. Brent wants to take the boy with them, but the other two soldiers, Kane (William Bendix) and Wilson (Robert Ivers), vote to leave him behind. As the highest ranking officer, Brent insists, and the men agree to split up in the morning and go their own ways. During the night, Lobo attacks an intruder: a soldier named Estway (Richard Jaeckel) who carries a radio, but one which has dead batteries. Estway was a collaborator with the North Koreans, making anti-American broadcasts for

them. Nobody wants Estway around but everybody wants his radio. As a result the men decide to stick together until they can find fresh batteries and radio for help. Brent persuades Han to promise not to run away and gives him dogtags, making him an official soldier.

They move at night with the North Korean patrol close behind. In an open area, Wilson steps on a landmine and is killed. The men are too afraid to move until Han points out that Lobo has detected another mine. In single file, the group crosses the minefield, led by the brave German shepherd. The following day, the men march until they are exhausted, taking turns carrying Han. They decide to take an hour to forage for food, and Lobo locates a pig which becomes their dinner. Han still harbors resentment toward the men for not saving his parents, but Kane tries to explain their helplessness without weapons against the North Koreans. He tells Han about America, which results in the boy believing that Kane will take him to America after the end of the war. Brent and Estway tease Kane about becoming a father figure, but he is secretly pleased.

In a small valley near their lines, the men spy a cottage with an aerial antenna. Brent, Kane and Estway argue about how to approach the cottage until Han supplies the answer: he will march right up to the door. Brent reluctantly goes along with the idea, and Han is grabbed by six North Korean soldiers. Han leads four of his six captors away, leaving two guarding the cottage. The Americans ambush the two North Koreans, dress in the Communist uniforms and lead Brent down to the cottage as their prisoner, where they bushwhack the remaining soldiers who have returned after Han ran away. Estway makes contact with the American forces and a helicopter is dispatched to rescue them. When it arrives, Brent and Kane refuse to leave, as they have not found Han. Estway does go, leaving the two soldiers alone to search for Han.

Estway forces the helicopter pilot to search for the boy, and drops a note to Brent and Kane, telling them where to find him. Unfortunately, Han is injured and sleeping in an area close by North Korean troops. Brent, Kane and Lobo get as close as they can during the night, then go to Han when an artillery barrage begins the following morning. Amid all the shooting, Lobo is killed and Brent is shot in the knee, but American forces move in and chase away the North Koreans. Safe behind their own lines, the soldiers await their fate. Kane tells their story to Colonel Holbein (Richard Arlen), who agrees to give Estway a fair hearing. Kane also persuades Brent to take Han back with him to America, and Han gives Kane his dogtags by which to remember him. Kane rejoins the war effort.

The Young and the Brave is routine in many ways, with familiar characters, dialogue and situations, but it's also a compelling film if one can seriously accept the premise of a child and a dog not only helping the American soldiers to survive, but providing symbolic meaning to the war itself. Han and Lobo personify the civilian suffering of war and are forced to endure war's brutality despite having nothing to do with its causes. They are victims, for whom the American soldiers learn to take responsibility, albeit reluctantly. They also represent the fighting spirit of freedom better than their guardians; after all, they are young and brave.

The lessons of the film are told simply and effectively: that people carry a responsibility for children and their future; that war is being fought for those who cannot or are unable to fight; that innocent people are always the victims of war; and that heroism can and does appear in many places and forms, often where it's least expected. Though this movie is clichéd, it does support the view that people make a difference, that the acts of an individual (man, boy or dog) can positively affect another person's life, and that personal freedom is more important than just about anything else imaginable.

Although the film's simple premise and low budget are clearly evidenced, it is a serious drama and action picture. The film is quite earnest about its subject and takes care to dramatize the act of cruelty which leaves Han an orphan. It is also made clear that Han will truly be on his own if the U.S. soldiers do not protect the boy. Han is resourceful, but the soldiers realize that his chances of survival are slim if they do not safeguard him. Their choice is clear. Lobo, on the other hand, is another matter. The soldiers do not want to be bothered with a dog until Lobo proves that he can obey—and protect—the boy, alert the men of mines and enemy soldiers, and lead them when necessary. The men grow to love the dog and the boy, but are not overtly sentimental when Lobo is killed in action. They respect that Lobo sacrificed himself for Han, and they try to console the boy, who has lost yet another loved one in the Korean conflict.

Set in Korea, the film's action could be transferred to any war of the twentieth century. The enemy soldiers are mostly a faceless bunch, crisply uniformed in opposition to the sloppy and bedraggled Americans. Little time is used for philosophizing about the war or even the complaining that is so familiar to the genre. As

"Good G.I. dog" Lobo (Flame, who also portrayed Rin Tin Tin in several movies) leads Sergeant Ed Brent (Rory Calhoun, right) and Staff Sergeant Peter Kane (William Bendix, left) toward safety in The Young and the Brave *(1963).*

a result, the film has nothing specific to say about the Korean conflict. The fact that Estway collaborated with the Communists is revealed only for the purpose of distrusting the character. It is suggested that he might surrender the men, who escaped from a prisoner of war camp, in return for a reward from the Reds, but it is obvious that Estway has no intention of doing so. Estway admits his guilt but never truly explains why he collaborated. He redeems himself, at least in the eyes of Brent and Kane, by forcing the helicopter pilot to find Han, and at the story's conclusion is promised fair consideration by Colonel Holbein.

Han is played by a young Mexican boy named Manuel Padilla, who, for a time in 1963, had two movies playing simultaneously in theatres. The other, also for MGM, is titled *Dime With a Halo* and concerns a group of kids who bet on a horserace and win, though they are too young to collect the prize. Padilla continued to

act throughout the 1960s and 1970s, appearing in *American Graffiti* and its sequel and several of the Tarzan films of the '60s, as Jai. Though he does not look particularly Korean, Padilla does a nice job as the film's most important character. Han has learned to hold in his feelings, and Padilla is quite believable as an embittered survivor.

The American soldiers are portrayed by Rory Calhoun, William Bendix, Richard Jaeckel and Robert Ivers. Bendix stands out in his scenes with the boy, and Calhoun registers a steely resolve which Kane eventually comes to respect. The other actor of note is Flame, the German shepherd who portrays Lobo. Flame is as expressive as anybody else in the cast and seemingly braver. He is, indeed, "a good G. I. dog."

The film disappeared from public view very quickly. Arthur Knight of *Saturday Review* complained that "Whatever it is trying to say about courage in wartime and trust in the decency of people (except, of course, the Russians) is lost in a welter of flat dialogue and one-dimension people." It was also (in awkward English) panned in the *Motion Picture Guide*: "Though a good cast was assembled for this routine feature, it was virtually wasted with material laden with sappy cliches and overly talk."

The Young and the Brave takes a premise which could have been awfully silly or cloying and presents it as earnest drama. It certainly isn't a wild success — it is a talky film with stereotyped characters and obvious situations — but it deserves some respect for trying to add new elements to a tired formula and mixing those elements rather intriguingly. Its view of war is honest and unflinching, particularly in regard to the fate of a little orphan boy and his faithful companion.

APPENDIX A:
CHRONOLOGY OF FILMS

This appendix lists Korean War films in order of their theatrical release in the United States, as noted by film reviews, *Screen World* notations and miscellaneous information. Specific dates can be attributed to some titles, particularly post–1970 releases (when nationwide release dates were adopted by most studios), but for the sake of consistency, a monthly schedule is utilized here. Three releases do have specific dates: they are the initial broadcast dates for made-for-television and made-for-cable titles. A few titles only have the year of release noted; in these cases, no further information could be located as to when they actually played in theatres. Where two or more titles are listed in the same month, they are alphabetized.

Following the title and any acknowledged alternative title are the production and distribution companies (within parentheses) and the month of release.

Korea Patrol (Jack Schwarz Productions; Eagle-Lion) January, 1951

The Steel Helmet (Deputy Corporation Productions; Lippert) January, 1951

A Yank in Korea (aka *Letter from Korea*) (Columbia) February, 1951

Mask of the Dragon (Spartan Productions; Lippert) March, 1951

Tokyo File 212 (Breakston-McGowan Productions; RKO) May, 1951

Fixed Bayonets! (20th Century–Fox) November, 1951

Submarine Command (Paramount) November, 1951

I Want You (Samuel Goldwyn; RKO Radio Pictures) December, 1951

Starlift (Warner Bros.) December, 1951

Japanese War Bride (aka *East is East*) (Bernhard Productions; 20th Century–Fox) January, 1952

Retreat, Hell! (United States Pictures Productions; Warner Bros.) February, 1952

My Son John (Rainbow Productions; Paramount) April, 1952

Geisha Girl (Breakston-Stahl Productions; Realart) May, 1952

Glory Alley (MGM) June, 1952

One Minute to Zero (RKO Radio Pictures) August, 1952

Back at the Front (aka *Willie and Joe Back at the Front*; *Willie and Joe in Tokyo*) (Universal) October, 1952

Battle Zone (Allied Artists) October, 1952

Mr. Walkie Talkie (Rockingham Productions; Lippert) December, 1952

Torpedo Alley (Allied Artists) December, 1952

Battle Circus (MGM) March, 1953

The Glory Brigade (20th Century–Fox) August, 1953

Mission Over Korea (aka *Eyes in the Sky*) (Columbia) August, 1953

Sky Commando (Columbia) August, 1953

Combat Squad (Border Productions; Columbia) October, 1953

Cease Fire (Paramount) November, 1953

Flight Nurse (Republic) November, 1953

Sabre Jet (Carl Krueger Productions; United Artists) November, 1953

Take the High Ground! (MGM) November, 1953

Dragonfly Squadron (Allied Artists) March, 1954

Prisoner of War (MGM) April, 1954

Men of the Fighting Lady (aka *Jet Carrier; Panther Squadron*) (MGM) May, 1954

Return from the Sea (aka *Home from the Sea*) (Allied Artists) July, 1954

The Bamboo Prison (Columbia)   December, 1954

Battle Taxi (Ivan Tors Productions; United Artists) January, 1955

The Bridges at Toko-Ri (Perlberg-Seaton Productions; Paramount)   January, 1955

An Annapolis Story (aka *The Blue and the Gold; Navy Air Patrol*) (Allied Artists)   April, 1955

The Eternal Sea (aka *The Admiral Hoskins Story*) (Republic)   May, 1955

Air Strike (Cy Roth Productions; Lippert)   July, 1955

Love Is a Many-Splendored Thing (20th Century–Fox)   August, 1955

The McConnell Story (aka *Tiger in the Sky*) (Warner Bros.)   September, 1955

Target Zero (Warner Bros.)   November, 1955

Hell's Horizon (Wray Davis Productions; Columbia) December, 1955

Hold Back the Night (Allied Artists)   July, 1956

Strange Intruder (Allied Artists)   September, 1956

Toward the Unknown (aka *Brink of Hell*) (Toluca Productions; Warner Bros.)   September, 1956

A Hill in Korea (aka *Hell in Korea*) (Wessex Film Productions; British Lion)   October, 1956

The Rack (MGM)   November, 1956

Battle Hymn (Universal)   February, 1957

Men in War (Security Pictures; United Artists) February, 1957

Top Secret Affair (aka *Their Secret Affair*) (Warner Bros.)   February, 1957

Time Limit (Heath Productions; United Artists) October, 1957

Bombers B-52 (aka *No Sleep Till Dawn*) (Warner Bros.)   November, 1957

Sayonara (William Goetz Productions; Warner Bros.)   December, 1957

Jet Attack (aka *Jet Squad; Through Hell to Glory*) (American International Pictures)   March, 1958

Underwater Warrior (Underwater Productions; MGM)   March, 1958

Tank Battalion (aka *Korean Attack; The Valley of Death*) (American International Pictures)   July, 1958

The Hunters (20th Century–Fox)   August, 1958

The Fearmakers (Pacemaker Productions; United Artists)   September, 1958

A Stranger in My Arms (Universal)   February, 1959

Operation Dames (aka *Girls in Action*) (Camera Eye Pictures; American International Pictures) March, 1959

Pork Chop Hill (Melville Productions; United Artists)   May, 1959

Battle Flame (Allied Artists)   July, 1959

All the Young Men (Jaguar Productions; Columbia) August, 1960

The Great Impostor (Universal)   November, 1960

Cry for Happy (William Goetz Productions; Columbia)   March, 1961

Marines, Let's Go (20th Century–Fox)   August, 1961

Sniper's Ridge (Associated Producers; 20th Century–Fox)   August, 1961

Twenty Plus Two (Allied Artists)   August, 1961

Man-Trap (aka *Man in Hiding*) (Tiger Productions; Paramount)   September, 1961

The Nun and the Sergeant (Springfield Productions; Eastern Film Productions; United Artists)   January, 1962

War Hunt (T-D Enterprises; United Artists)   August, 1962

The Manchurian Candidate (M. C. Productions; United Artists)   October, 1962 (the film was re-released theatrically in February, 1988)

The Hook (Perlberg-Seaton Productions; MGM) February, 1963

The Young and the Brave (MGM)   August, 1963

War Is Hell (Allied Artists)   January, 1964

Iron Angel (Ken Kennedy Productions)   April, 1964

No Man's Land (Cinema-Video International) 1964

Not with My Wife, You Don't! (Fernwood-Reynard Productions; Warner Bros.)   November, 1966

Marine Battleground (Paul Mart Productions; Manson Distributing Corporation)   1966

Sergeant Ryker (aka *The Case Against Paul Ryker; The Case Against Sergeant Ryker; Torn Between Two Values*) (Roncom Films; Universal)   February, 1968

MASH (Aspen Productions; 20th Century–Fox) January, 1970
(the film was re-released theatrically in 1973, with a PG rating)

The Walking Major (Ishihara Productions)   1970

The Reluctant Heroes (aka *The Egghead on Hill 656*) (Aaron Spelling Productions; ABC-TV)   November 23, 1971

Collision Course: Truman vs. MacArthur (David L. Wolper Productions; ABC-TV)   January 4, 1976

MacArthur (aka *MacArthur, the Rebel General*) (Universal)   June, 1977

Inchon (One Way Productions; MGM; United Artists)   August, 1982 (the film was released on a limited basis in May, 1981, then pulled and re-edited into the shorter 1982 version)

Field of Honor (Oranda Films, The Cannon Group) June, 1986

Chattahoochee (Hemdale Film Corporation)   May, 1990

For the Boys (All Girl Productions; 20th Century–Fox)   November, 1991

Truman (Spring Creek Productions; HBO Pictures) September 9, 1995

Three Wishes (Rysher Entertainment; Savoy Pictures)   October, 1995

APPENDIX B: FILMS LISTED BY PRODUCTION COMPANY AND DISTRIBUTOR

This appendix lists Korean War films by the production companies and studios which made and distributed them. Some of these titles, particularly during the 1960s, were produced by small, independent production companies and were collected by the larger studios for distribution. In these cases, the production company and the distributor are both noted. Some of these independent companies may not be listed by exact title; for certain companies which are otherwise uncredited, the producer's name is used, followed by the word "Productions." Within each company listing, titles and any acknowledged alternative titles are both listed. As with Appendix A, the films are arranged in chronological order (month and year of release are included) for a concise snapshot of each company's Korean War film profile.

Aaron Spelling Productions
The Reluctant Heroes (aka *The Egghead on Hill 656*) (ABC-TV)   November 23, 1971

All Girl Productions
For the Boys (20th Century–Fox)   November, 1991

Allied Artists (AA)
Battle Zone   October, 1952
Torpedo Alley   December, 1952
Dragonfly Squadron   March, 1954
Return from the Sea (aka *Home from the Sea*)   July, 1954
An Annapolis Story (aka *The Blue and the Gold; Navy Air Patrol*)   April, 1955
Hold Back the Night   July, 1956
Strange Intruder   September, 1956
Battle Flame   July, 1959

Twenty Plus Two   August, 1961
War is Hell   January, 1964

American Broadcasting Company (ABC-TV)
The Reluctant Heroes (aka *The Egghead on Hill 656*) (Aaron Spelling Productions)   November 23, 1971
Collision Course: Truman vs. MacArthur (David L. Wolper Productions)   January 4, 1976

American International Pictures (AIP)
Jet Attack (aka *Jet Squad; Through Hell to Glory*)   March, 1958
Tank Battalion (aka *Korean Attack; The Valley of Death*)   July, 1958
Operation Dames (aka *Girls in Action*) (Camera Eye Pictures)   March, 1959

Aspen Productions
MASH (20th Century–Fox)   January, 1970

Associated Producers, Inc.
Sniper's Ridge (20th Century–Fox)   August, 1961

Bernhard Productions
Japanese War Bride (aka *East is East*) (20th Century–Fox)   January, 1952

Border Productions
Combat Squad (Columbia)   October, 1953

Breakston-McGowan Productions
Tokyo File 212 (RKO Radio Pictures)   May, 1951

Breakston-Stahl Productions
Geisha Girl (Realart)   May, 1952

427

British Lion Films

A Hill in Korea (aka *Hell in Korea*) (Wessex Film Productions)   October, 1956

Camera Eye Pictures

Operation Dames (aka *Girls in Action*) (AIP)   March, 1959

The Cannon Group

Field of Honor (Oranda Films)   June, 1986

Carl Krueger Productions

Sabre Jet (United Artists)   November, 1953

Cinema-Video International (CVI)

No Man's Land   1964

Columbia Pictures Corporation (CPC)

A Yank in Korea (aka *Letter from Korea*)   February, 1951
Mission Over Korea (aka *Eyes in the Sky*)   August, 1953
Sky Commando   August, 1953
Combat Squad (Border Productions)   October, 1953
The Bamboo Prison   December, 1954
Hell's Horizon (Wray Davis Productions)   December, 1955
All the Young Men (Jaguar Productions)   August, 1960
Cry For Happy (William Goetz Productions)   March, 1961

Cy Roth Productions

Air Strike (Lippert)   July, 1955

David L. Wolper Productions

Collision Course: Truman vs. MacArthur (ABC-TV)   January 4, 1976

Deputy Corporation Productions

The Steel Helmet (Lippert)   January, 1951

Eagle-Lion

Korea Patrol   (Jack Schwarz Productions)   January, 1951

Eastern Film Productions

The Nun and the Sergeant (Springfield Productions; United Artists)   January, 1962

Fernwood-Reynard Productions

Not with My Wife, You Don't! (Warner Bros.)   November, 1966

Heath Productions

Time Limit (United Artists)   October, 1957

Hemdale Film Corporation

Chattahoochee   May, 1990

Home Box Office Pictures (HBO)

Truman (Spring Creek Productions)   September 9, 1995

Ishihara International Productions

The Walking Major   1970

Ivan Tors Productions

Battle Taxi (United Artists)   January, 1955

Jack Schwarz Productions

Korea Patrol (Eagle-Lion)   January, 1951

Jaguar Productions

All the Young Men (United Artists)   August, 1960

Ken Kennedy Productions

Iron Angel   April, 1964

Lippert

The Steel Helmet (Deputy Productions)   January, 1951
Mask of the Dragon (Spartan Productions)   March, 1951
Mr. Walkie Talkie (Rockingham Productions)   December, 1952
Air Strike (Cy Roth Productions)   July, 1955

M. C. Productions

The Manchurian Candidate (United Artists)   October, 1962

Manson Distributing Corporation

Marine Battleground (Paul Mart Productions)   1966

Melville Productions

Pork Chop Hill (United Artists)   May, 1959

Metro-Goldwyn-Mayer (MGM)

Glory Alley   June, 1952
Battle Circus   March, 1953
Take the High Ground!   November, 1953
Prisoner of War   April, 1954
Men of the Fighting Lady (aka *Jet Carrier; Panther Squadron*)   May, 1954
The Rack   November, 1956
Underwater Warrior (Underwater Productions)   March, 1958
The Hook (Perlberg-Seaton Productions)   February, 1963
The Young and the Brave   August, 1963
Inchon (One Way Productions; United Artists)   August, 1982

One Way Productions

Inchon (MGM; United Artists)   August, 1982

Oranda Films

Field of Honor (The Cannon Group)   June, 1986

Pacemaker Productions

The Fearmakers (United Artists)   September, 1958

Paramount

Submarine Command   November, 1951
My Son John (Rainbow Productions)   April, 1952
Cease Fire   November, 1953
The Bridges at Toko-Ri (Perlberg-Seaton Productions)   January, 1955
Man-Trap (aka *Man in Hiding*) (Tiger Productions)   September, 1961

Paul Mart Productions

Marine Battleground (Manson Distributing Corporation)   1966

Perlberg-Seaton Productions

The Bridges at Toko-Ri (Paramount)   January, 1955
The Hook (MGM)   February, 1963

Rainbow Productions

My Son John (Paramount)   April, 1952

Realart

Geisha Girl (Breakston-Stahl Productions)   May, 1952

Republic Pictures

Flight Nurse   November, 1953
The Eternal Sea (aka *The Admiral Hoskins Story*)   May, 1955

RKO Radio Pictures (RKO)

Tokyo File 212 (Breakston-McGowan Productions)   May, 1951
I Want You (Samuel Goldwyn)   December, 1951
One Minute to Zero   August, 1952

Rockingham Productions

Mr. Walkie Talkie (Lippert)   December, 1952

Roncom Films

Sergeant Ryker (aka *The Case Against Paul Ryker*; *The Case Against Sergeant Ryker*; *Torn Between Two Values*) (Universal)   February, 1968

Rysher Entertainment

Three Wishes (Savoy Pictures)   October, 1995

Samuel Goldwyn

I Want You (RKO Radio Pictures)   December, 1951

Savoy Pictures

Three Wishes (Rysher Entertainment)   October, 1995

Security Pictures

Men in War (United Artists)   February, 1957

Spartan Productions

Mask of the Dragon (Lippert)   March, 1951

Spring Creek Productions

Truman (HBO Pictures)   September 9, 1995

Springfield Productions

The Nun and the Sergeant (Eastern Film Productions; United Artists)   January, 1962

T-D Enterprises

War Hunt (United Artists)   August, 1962

Tiger Productions

Man-Trap (aka *Man in Hiding*) (Paramount)   September, 1961

Toluca Productions

Toward the Unknown (aka *Brink of Hell*) (Warner Bros.)   September, 1956

20th Century–Fox

Fixed Bayonets!   November, 1951
Japanese War Bride (aka *East is East*) (Bernhard Productions)   January, 1952
The Glory Brigade   August, 1953
Love Is a Many-Splendored Thing   August, 1955
The Hunters   August, 1958
Marines, Let's Go   August, 1961
Sniper's Ridge (Associated Producers)   August, 1961
MASH (Aspen Productions)   January, 1970
For the Boys (All Girl Productions)   November, 1991

Underwater Productions

Underwater Warrior (MGM)   March, 1958

United Artists (UA)

Sabre Jet (Carl Krueger Productions)   November, 1953
Battle Taxi (Ivan Tors Productions)   January, 1955
Men in War (Security Pictures)   February, 1957
Time Limit (Heath Productions)   October, 1957
The Fearmakers (Pacemaker Productions)   September, 1958
Pork Chop Hill (Melville Productions)   May, 1959
War Hunt (T-D Enterprises)   August, 1962
The Manchurian Candidate (M.C. Productions)   October, 1962
The Nun and the Sergeant (Springfield Productions; Eastern Film Productions)   January, 1962
Inchon (One Way Productions; MGM)   August, 1982

United States Pictures Productions

Retreat, Hell! (Warner Bros.)   February, 1952

Universal

Back at the Front (aka *Willie and Joe Back at the Front; Willie and Joe in Tokyo*)   October, 1952
Battle Hymn   February, 1957
A Stranger in My Arms   February, 1959
The Great Impostor   November, 1960
Sergeant Ryker (aka *The Case Against Paul Ryker*; *The Case Against Sergeant Ryker*; *Torn Between Two Values*) (Roncom Films)   February, 1968
MacArthur (aka *MacArthur, the Rebel General*)   June, 1977

Warner Bros.

Starlift   December, 1951
Retreat, Hell! (United States Pictures Productions)   February, 1952
The McConnell Story (aka *Tiger in the Sky*)   September, 1955
Target Zero   November, 1955
Toward the Unknown (aka *Brink of Hell*) (Toluca Productions)   September, 1956
Top Secret Affair (aka *Their Secret Affair*)   February, 1957
Sayonara (William Goetz Productions)   December, 1957
Bombers B-52 (aka *No Sleep Till Dawn*)   November, 1957
Not With My Wife, You Don't! (Fernwood-Reynard Productions)   November, 1966

Wessex Film Productions

A Hill in Korea (aka *Hell in Korea*) (British Lion)   October, 1956

William Goetz Productions

Sayonara (Warner Bros.)   December, 1957
Cry for Happy (Columbia)   March, 1961

Wray Davis Productions

Hell's Horizon (Columbia)   December, 1955

APPENDIX C: FILMS LISTED BY LEVELS OF ACCURACY AND PROPAGANDA

This appendix lists Korean War films according to the author's judgment of the levels of historical accuracy regarding their storylines and patriotic propaganda which is incorporated within each title. These can be viewed as rather vague classifications, so some definitions are in order.

Both listings are divided by three general rankings: High, Medium and Low. These are generalized levels which, in direct relation to each other, help determine how "historically accurate" a film is, and how much of its effort is devoted to "patriotic propaganda." Every film is rated as High, Medium or Low in both categories.

Historical Accuracy Level

The term "historical accuracy" refers mostly to whether action depicted in each film reflects circumstances which could have or would have occurred during the time of the war. As a general rule, stories which follow the general historical path of the war are considered to be more "historically accurate" than those which are vague and non-specific regarding the time and place of their settings. Thus, *Retreat, Hell!* is judged to be more accurate than *Combat Squad*, and *The Bridges at Toko-Ri* is judged to be more accurate than *The Hunters*. The intent of ranking films by level in this manner is purely to provide a framework which might allow viewers searching for films considered to be the most authentic and legitimate studies and histories of the war to find them without having to watch fluff such as *Jet Attack*.

It is also unavoidable that certain plots and storylines are judged by the author to be contrived, which might then prevent the film from attaining a "High" accuracy rating. Within each level, films are listed in alphabetical order.

Historical Accuracy Level: **High** **(18)**

Battle Hymn (1957)
The Bridges at Toko-Ri (1955)
Cease Fire (1953)
Chattahoochee (1990)
Collision Course: Truman vs. MacArthur (1976, TV Movie)
The Eternal Sea (1955) (aka *The Admiral Hoskins Story*)
The Great Impostor (1960)
Hold Back the Night (1956)
MacArthur (1977) (aka *MacArthur, the Rebel General*)
The McConnell Story (1955) (aka *Tiger in the Sky*)
Men of the Fighting Lady (1954) (aka *Jet Carrier; Panther Squadron*)
Pork Chop Hill (1959)
Retreat, Hell! (1952)
Take the High Ground! (1953)
Toward the Unknown (1956) (aka *Brink of Hell*)
Truman (1995, Cable TV Movie)

Underwater Warrior (1958)

The Walking Major (1970) (aka *Aru heishi no kake*)

Historical Accuracy Level: Medium   (41)

All the Young Men (1960)

An Annapolis Story (1955) (aka *The Blue and the Gold; Navy Air Patrol*)

The Bamboo Prison (1954)

Battle Circus (1953)

Battle Flame (1959)

Battle Taxi (1955)

Battle Zone (1952)

Bombers B-52 (1957) (aka *No Sleep Till Dawn*)

Dragonfly Squadron (1954)

Field of Honor (1986, Dutch)

Fixed Bayonets! (1951)

Flight Nurse (1953)

For the Boys (1991)

The Glory Brigade (1953)

A Hill in Korea (1956) (aka *Hell in Korea*)

The Hunters (1958)

I Want You (1951)

Inchon (1982)

Japanese War Bride (1952) (aka *East is East*)

Korea Patrol (1951)

Love Is a Many-Splendored Thing (1955)

Marine Battleground (1966)

MASH (1970)

Men in War (1957)

Mission Over Korea (1953) (aka *Eyes in the Sky*)

My Son John (1952)

One Minute to Zero (1952)

Prisoner of War (1954)

The Rack (1956)

Sabre Jet (1953)

Sayonara (1957)

Starlift (1951)

The Steel Helmet (1951)

Strange Intruder (1956)

Submarine Command (1951)

Target Zero (1955)

Three Wishes (1995)

Time Limit (1957)

Torpedo Alley (1952)

War Hunt (1962)

A Yank in Korea (1951) (aka *Letter From Korea*)

Historical Accuracy Level: Low   (32)

Air Strike (1955)

Back at the Front (1952) (aka *Willie and Joe Back at the Front; Willie and Joe in Tokyo*)

Combat Squad (1953)

Cry for Happy (1961)

The Fearmakers (1958)

Geisha Girl (1952)

Glory Alley (1952)

Hell's Horizon (1955)

The Hook (1963)

Iron Angel (1964)

Jet Attack (1958) (aka *Jet Squad; Through Hell to Glory*)

The Manchurian Candidate (1962)

Man-Trap (1961) (aka *Man in Hiding*)

Marines, Let's Go (1961)

Mask of the Dragon (1951)

Mr. Walkie Talkie (1952)

No Man's Land (1964)

Not with My Wife, You Don't! (1966)

The Nun and the Sergeant (1962)

Operation Dames (1959) (aka *Girls in Action*)

The Reluctant Heroes (1971, TV Movie) (aka *The Egghead on Hill 656*)

Return from the Sea (1954) (aka *Home from the Sea*)

Sergeant Ryker (1968) (aka *The Case Against Paul Ryker; The Case Against Sergeant Ryker; Torn Between Two Values*)

Sky Commando (1953)

Sniper's Ridge (1961)

A Stranger in My Arms (1959)

Tank Battalion (1958)

Tokyo File 212 (1951)

Top Secret Affair (1957) (aka *Their Secret Affair*)

Twenty Plus Two (1961)

War Is Hell (1964)

The Young and the Brave (1963)

It has long been perceived that, as a rule, Korean War films do not found their war on the same factual basis and verisimilitude as do movies of other wars, and this listing does tend to agree with that assessment. There are certainly films which chronicle actual stories and personalities of the war, but they are outnumbered, if not overshadowed, by films which use the Korean War setting to indict war in general or merely employ the wartime period as background for other stories. This particular listing should convince anyone that Hollywood filmmakers generally have not attempted to tell genuine and important Korean War stories.

Patriotic Propaganda Level

"Patriotic propaganda" is an even trickier description. The word "propaganda" has gradually gained a negative connotation, so that many people now automatically dismiss anything associated with the word. But "propaganda" means an effort to spread or promote an idea, cause, opinion or feeling. In and of itself, propaganda is a neutral term. This book, for instance, is propaganda to promote the viewing of movies, Korean War films specifically.

The term "patriotic propaganda" then refers to efforts in Korean War movies to promote patriotic ideals, which at that time were largely in favor of halting the spread of communism by engaging "the enemy" in North Korea. Over time these ideals changed, so that during the Vietnam War, a public majority did not agree with the same expressed ideals because the cost in human life seemed exorbitant for Vietnam's illusory fight for freedom. But early in Korea, the majority of Americans believed that communism had to be stopped. Movies which reflect this attitude are considered to be "High" in patriotic propaganda.

However, the term also refers to the way in which military subjects are treated in movies. Films like *An Annapolis Story* and *Submarine Command* are propaganda for the U.S. Navy, displaying that particular armed force's technological might and promoting the Navy as an essential, responsible and heroic defender of freedom during the Korean War. The Air Force, Marine Corps and Army also have their propaganda films, as do such specialized services as the Navy's Underwater Demolitions Team, the Marine Corps' Photographic Division and the Air Force's Air Rescue Service. Films which promote these varied military organizations always boast full cooperation with their subject service and are often dedicated to those organizations. It should be noted that ranking a film such as *An Annapolis Story* as "High" in terms of patriotic propaganda is not a judgment of its political stance or quality of entertainment. It merely means that *An Annapolis Story* is primarily intended to promote its subject, which is the training and resulting adventures of naval aviators.

In this book, propaganda should not be considered a negative term, even when it applies to political rhetoric such as *My Son John*. Even there, where the filmmaker's intent is clearly to rouse audiences against the specter of communism, the definition of the word is being fulfilled without bias. *MASH* is just as clearly filled with anti-war sentiment, and indicates a similar level of propaganda. The difference is that *My Son John* promoted ideals of patriotism (at that time, anyway) to extremes, and therefore is considered "High" in terms of patriotic propaganda. *MASH* receives a "Low" rating because its propaganda takes the opposite approach, arguing against the patriotic ideal of fighting war in the name of freedom. Both films are equally propagandistic; the operative word which divides them is "patriotic," and that word denotes the film's approach to its subject. Patriotic films of the time promoted military might and public support to stop Communist aggression in Korea.

Again, these judgments are the author's viewpoint, and are intended as guidelines to lead viewers through the maze of films about the Korean War. These levels are not indicative of a film's quality in any way — merely its political stance regarding the war or the continued development of American military power.

Patriotic Propaganda Level   High   (40)

Air Strike (1955)

An Annapolis Story (1955) (aka *The Blue and the Gold; Navy Air Patrol*)

The Bamboo Prison (1954)

Battle Flame (1959)

Battle Hymn (1957)

Battle Taxi (1955)

Bombers B-52 (1957) (aka *No Sleep Till Dawn*)

The Bridges at Toko-Ri (1955)

The Eternal Sea (1955) (aka *The Admiral Hoskins Story*)

The Fearmakers (1958)

Flight Nurse (1953)

For the Boys (1991)

Geisha Girl (1952)

The Glory Brigade (1953)

A Hill in Korea (1956) (aka *Hell in Korea*)

Hold Back the Night (1956)

The Hunters (1958)

I Want You (1951)

Inchon (1982)

MacArthur (1977) (aka *MacArthur, the Rebel General*)

The McConnell Story (1955) (aka *Tiger in the Sky*)

Marine Battleground (1966)

Men of the Fighting Lady (1954) (aka *Jet Carrier; Panther Squadron*)

Mission Over Korea (1953) (aka *Eyes in the Sky*)

My Son John (1952)

Pork Chop Hill (1959)

Prisoner of War (1954)

Retreat, Hell! (1952)

Return from the Sea (1954) (aka *Home from the Sea*)

Sabre Jet (1953)

Starlift (1951)

Take the High Ground! (1953)

Top Secret Affair (1957) (aka *Their Secret Affair*)

Torpedo Alley (1952)

Toward the Unknown (1956) (aka *Brink of Hell*)

Truman (1995, Cable TV Movie)

Underwater Warrior (1958)

The Walking Major (1970) (aka *Aru heishi no kake*)

A Yank in Korea (1951) (aka *Letter From Korea*)

The Young and the Brave (1963)

Patriotic Propaganda Level: Medium   (27)

Back at the Front (1952) (aka *Willie and Joe Back at the Front; Willie and Joe in Tokyo*)

Battle Circus (1953)

Battle Zone (1952)

Cease Fire (1953)

Cry for Happy (1961)

Dragonfly Squadron (1954)

Fixed Bayonets! (1951)

The Great Impostor (1960)

Hell's Horizon (1955)

Iron Angel (1964)

Jet Attack (1958) (aka *Jet Squad; Through Hell to Glory*)

Korea Patrol (1951)

Marines, Let's Go (1961)

Mr. Walkie Talkie (1952)

No Man's Land (1964)

The Nun and the Sergeant (1962)

One Minute to Zero (1952)

Operation Dames (1959) (aka *Girls in Action*)

The Rack (1956)

The Reluctant Heroes (1971, TV Movie) (aka *The Egghead on Hill 656*)

Sergeant Ryker (1968) (aka *The Case Against Paul Ryker; The Case Against Sergeant Ryker; Torn Between Two Values*)

Sky Commando (1953)

A Stranger in My Arms (1959)

Submarine Command (1951)

Tank Battalion (1958)

Target Zero (1955)

Tokyo File 212 (1951)

Patriotic Propaganda Level: Low   (24)

All the Young Men (1960)

Chattahoochee (1990)

Collision Course: Truman vs. MacArthur (1976, TV Movie)

Combat Squad (1953)

Field of Honor (1986, Dutch)

Glory Alley (1952)

The Hook (1963)

Japanese War Bride (1952) (aka *East is East*)

Love is a Many-Splendored Thing (1955)

The Manchurian Candidate (1962)

Man-Trap (1961) (aka *Man in Hiding*)

MASH (1970)

Mask of the Dragon (1951)

Men in War (1957)

Not with My Wife, You Don't! (1966)

Sayonara (1957)

Sniper's Ridge (1961)

The Steel Helmet (1951)

Strange Intruder (1956)

Three Wishes (1995)

Time Limit (1957)

Twenty Plus Two (1961)

War Hunt (1962)

War Is Hell (1964)

This listing proves that the wide majority of Korean War movies contain at least some "patriotic propaganda," and that nearly half, in the author's opinion, contain a high degree. Simply put, most Korean War films are intended to spur public support for the fighting troops as well as the military machinery and organization needed for the fight. This was certainly true of World War II films, and it is only slightly less so for movies about the Korean conflict.

It is important to note, however, that there is a minority of films which do not approve of the fight; most of these films do not approve of war in general. And it should be understood that nineteen of these twenty-four anti-war statements were produced and released *after* the war. As society changed in the 1960s, so did Hollywood's approach to war, and very few Korean War films made after 1960 contain a pro-war message. Later films which focus on the actual fighting, such as *MacArthur* and *The Reluctant Heroes*, do support their soldiers overseas, but most of the others reflect society's growing discontent with the expense and suffering increasingly associated with waging war.

APPENDIX D: FILMS LISTED BY ELEMENTS OF SUBJECT AND THEME

Throughout the book, Korean War movies have been annotated with specific "elements." These elements usually refer to specific subjects and plot conventions used within the stories, such as "submarines," "courts-martial," "medicine" and "collaboration." Themes and genres are also included as elements, as exemplified by "comedy," "racism" "biography" and "homefront." Each one of the U.S. armed forces has its own element, as do very specific military machines and situations which appear in more than one Korean War film.

The purpose of elements is to point viewers in the direction of movies which have specific, desired subjects, themes or conditions which they might wish to view. For example, someone could research "prisoners of war," "courts-martial," "repatriation," "brainwashing" and "collaboration," cross-referencing between those elements to receive the fullest picture of the Korean War films which depicted the conditions of American prisoners of war. Similarly, a person looking for Korean War films which feature aircraft carriers, submarines or helicopters would simply refer to those element listings. A brief description of each element and its importance to the Korean War film genre is included. Within each element listing, films are listed in alphabetical order, just as in the main text.

Aircraft Carriers

Because Korea is a large peninsula, surrounded on three sides by seas, and also due to its close proximity to American forces and supplies in Japan, U.S. aircraft carriers were extensively used during the Korean War, and some Korean War films went to great lengths to present the power and capability of these city-sized behemoths. *The Bridges at Toko-Ri* and *Men of the Fighting Lady* are particularly devoted to the big carriers and each movie features multiple take-offs and landings, including shots from the jet pilots' point of view, while *The Eternal Sea* chronicles the efforts of Admiral John Hoskins to bring the big carriers into the jet age. Interestingly, all five movies which spotlight aircraft carrier operations were released within a two year period just after the war's conclusion.

Air Strike (1955)
An Annapolis Story (1955) (aka *The Blue and the Gold; Navy Air Patrol*)
The Bridges at Toko-Ri (1955)
The Eternal Sea (1955) (aka *The Admiral Hoskins Story*)
Men of the Fighting Lady (1954)

Air Force

The U.S. Air Force was vitally important during the Korean War, controlling the skies over the battle areas, bombing and strafing the enemy with reliable propeller-driven planes and, later, the newest, streamlined jets. The Air Force also delivered manpower and supplies in their big C-4 transports and evacuated areas threatened by the Communists. Korean War films stressed these activities and more, such as training Republic of Korea pilots in *Dragonfly Squadron* and *Battle Hymn*, artillery spotting in *Mis-*

sion Over Korea, helicopter rescue missions in *Battle Taxi* and an overtaxed ground crew in *Bombers B-52*.

Any film which depicted Air Force activity is included here. Many of them focus on training methods and procedures as much as or more than actual combat. Two tell the stories of real-life pilots: *The McConnell Story* chronicles the exploits of the Korean War's top jet ace, Joseph J. McConnell, Jr., who scored sixteen kills, while *Battle Hymn* depicts Colonel Dean Hess' efforts to save Korean orphans. Hess was a chaplain as well as a pilot, and later served as technical advisor for *Dragonfly Squadron*, which is loosely based on his experiences training South Korean pilots.

Air Strike (1955)
Battle Hymn (1957)
Battle Taxi (1955)
Bombers B-52 (1957) (aka *No Sleep Till Dawn*)
Dragonfly Squadron (1954)
Flight Nurse (1953)
Hell's Horizon (1955)
The Hunters (1958)
Jet Attack (1958) (aka *Jet Squad; Through Hell to Glory*)
The McConnell Story (1955) (aka *Tiger in the Sky*)
Mission Over Korea (1953) (aka *Eyes in the Sky*)
Not with My Wife, You Don't! (1966)
One Minute to Zero (1952)
Sabre Jet (1953)
Sayonara (1957)
Sky Commando (1953)
Starlift (1951)
A Stranger in My Arms (1959)
Toward the Unknown (1956) (aka *Brink of Hell*)

Air War

This element refers to actual combat—bombings, dogfights or raids—irrespective of the armed forces taking part. Films which specifically dramatize aspects of the air war, usually from the perspective of the pilots, are included. Also included are films in which ground forces are supported or saved by their comrades in the air.

Hollywood filmmakers devoted attention to this aspect of the war, while others were ignored or neglected. Korea's air war featured the newest jet technology, dramatic dogfights and impressive bombing runs, and bases on aircraft carriers at sea and in Japan, all of which appealed to Hollywood producers. From 1953 through the conclusion of the decade, films about the air war attained a higher public profile than movies portraying any other aspect of the war, and received the most publicity.

The introduction of sleek jets such as the F-80 Shooting Star, the F-84 Thunderjet and the F-86 Sabre jet provided Korean War films with a visible difference from the technology displayed in studies of World War II. Filmmakers embraced the jets and produced movies to feature them as prominently as possible.

An Annapolis Story (1955) (aka *The Blue and the Gold; Navy Air Patrol*)
Battle Hymn (1957)
Battle Taxi (1955)
The Bridges at Toko-Ri (1955)
Dragonfly Squadron (1954)
The Eternal Sea (1955) (aka *The Admiral Hoskins Story*)
Hell's Horizon (1955)
A Hill in Korea (1956) (aka *Hell in Korea*)
The Hunters (1958)
Jet Attack (1958) (aka *Jet Squad; Through Hell to Glory*)
Love Is a Many-Splendored Thing (1955)
The McConnell Story (1955) (aka *Tiger in the Sky*)
Men of the Fighting Lady (1954) (aka *Jet Carrier; Panther Squadron*)
Mission Over Korea (1953) (aka *Eyes in the Sky*)
Not with My Wife, You Don't! (1966)
One Minute to Zero (1952)
Retreat, Hell! (1952)
Return from the Sea (1954) (aka *Home from the Sea*)
Sabre Jet (1953)
Sky Commando (1953)
Target Zero (1955)

Ambulances

One Korean War film, *Iron Angel*, has as its centerpiece an ambulance; in this story, the ambulance and its driver, a pretty nurse, are caught behind enemy lines. Other films refer to Red Cross ambulances, with the big red crosses on their sides, as ideal targets for the enemy. A character in one film suggests that an ambulance be used for love trysts. Mostly, however, ambulances are viewed as vital, life-sustaining transportation, whether the ambulance happens to be a transport truck, light plane or helicopter pressed into service.

Battle Taxi (1955)
Battle Zone (1952)
Iron Angel (1964)

Army

This branch of service, more than any other, is featured in Korean War movies. Army infantrymen, occasionally referred to as "G.I.s" and "grunts," marched and drove the length and breadth of Korea for the first year of the war, before battle lines stabilized near the 38th parallel close to the area where the fighting had begun. The majority of Korean War films, fifty in all, include some aspect of the Army in their dramatizations.

Army films also comprise most of the comedies, medical movies, musical movies, biographies and political diatribes about the war, as well as films about prisoners of war. Because the majority of American ground forces in Korea were Army soldiers, it is only natural that they should figure in so many disparate types of stories.

Back at the Front (1952) (aka Willie and Joe Back at the Front; Willie and Joe in Tokyo)
The Bamboo Prison (1954)
Battle Circus (1953)
Cease Fire (1953)
Chattahoochee (1990)
Collision Course: Truman vs. MacArthur (1976, TV Movie)
Combat Squad (1953)
Dragonfly Squadron (1954)
The Fearmakers (1958)
Fixed Bayonets! (1951)
For the Boys (1991)
Geisha Girl (1952)
Glory Alley (1952)
The Glory Brigade (1953)
The Hook (1963)
I Want You (1951)
Inchon (1982)
Iron Angel (1964)
Japanese War Bride (1952) (aka East is East)
Korea Patrol (1951)
MacArthur (1977) (aka MacArthur, the Rebel General)
The Manchurian Candidate (1962)
MASH (1970)
Mask of the Dragon (1951)
The McConnell Story (1955) (aka Tiger in the Sky)
Men in War (1957)
Mr. Walkie Talkie (1952)
My Son John (1952)
No Man's Land (1964)
One Minute to Zero (1952)
Operation Dames (1959) (aka Girls in Action)
Pork Chop Hill (1959)
Prisoner of War (1954)
The Rack (1956)
The Reluctant Heroes (1971, TV Movie) (aka The Egghead on Hill 656)
Sergeant Ryker (1968) (aka The Case Against Paul Ryker; The Case Against Sergeant Ryker; Torn Between Two Values)
Sniper's Ridge (1961)
Starlift (1951)
The Steel Helmet (1951)
Strange Intruder (1956)
Take the High Ground! (1953)
Tank Battalion (1958)
Target Zero (1955)
Three Wishes (1995)
Time Limit (1957)
Top Secret Affair (1957) (aka Their Secret Affair)
Truman (1995, Cable TV Movie)
Twenty Plus Two (1961)
The Walking Major (1970) (aka Aru heishi no kake)
War Hunt (1962)
War Is Hell (1964)
A Yank in Korea (1951) (aka Letter from Korea)
The Young and the Brave (1963)

Behind Enemy Lines

These films comprise stories where American or U.N. troops are caught away from their own ground, behind enemy lines. Sometimes the soldiers become lost or are trapped by sudden enemy maneuvers; sometimes pilots crash-land or bail out. Often these stories chronicle the efforts of individual soldiers or pilots just to stay alive. *The Bridges at Toko-Ri* is a memorable example of the fate awaiting unlucky fliers who happened to land behind enemy lines.

Battle Zone (1952)
The Bridges at Toko-Ri (1955)
The Glory Brigade (1953)
The Hunters (1958)
Jet Attack (1958) (aka Jet Squad; Through Hell to Glory)
Man-Trap (1961) (aka Man in Hiding)
Mr. Walkie Talkie (1952)
The Nun and the Sergeant (1962)
One Minute to Zero (1952)
Operation Dames (1959) (aka Girls in Action)
The Reluctant Heroes (1971, TV Movie) (aka The Egghead on Hill 656)
Submarine Command (1951)
Tank Battalion (1958)
Target Zero (1955)
Torpedo Alley (1952)
A Yank in Korea (1951) (aka Letter from Korea)

Biography

Several prominent military officers have been profiled in Korean War films, particularly General Douglas MacArthur and President Harry S. Truman, whose conflict over the parameters of the war is one of the most fascinating, complex and often-told cinematic war stories. Pilots whose deeds have been dramatized include triple jet ace Joseph McConnell, who shot down sixteen enemy aircraft over Korea, and Dean Hess, a chaplain and fighter pilot who saved hundreds of Korean orphans from slaughter. On the high seas, John Hoskins lost one leg yet stayed in active service, became an admiral and was the driving force behind bringing jets to America's aircraft carriers.

Only a handful of regular soldiers have had movies made about their adventures. Lieutenant Joe Clemons was instrumental in holding a piece of crucial, yet unimportant ground in *Pork Chop Hill*, while Ferdinand Demara impersonated a ship's doctor (and successfully operated!), among other disguises, in *The Great Impostor*. And Emmett Foley's true test of character came not on the battlefields of Korea, but back home in the U.S., trying to adjust to civilian life.

Two stories feature pseudonyms for their subjects. Clark J. Allen subs for Captain John Arnn in *The Walking Major*, while David Forest's exploits in *Underwater Warrior* are based on Commander Francis Douglas Fane's adventures in the Navy. It is to be supposed that money (rights fees) is the rationale for not using the subjects' actual names.

Battle Hymn (1957) (Colonel Dean Hess)

Chattahoochee (1990) (Emmett Foley)

Collision Course: Truman vs. MacArthur (1976, TV Movie) (President Harry S. Truman and General Douglas MacArthur)

The Eternal Sea (1955) (aka *The Admiral Hoskins Story*) (Admiral John Hoskins)

The Great Impostor (1960) (Ferdinand Demara, Jr.)

Inchon (1982) (General Douglas MacArthur)

MacArthur (1977) (aka *MacArthur, the Rebel General*) (General Douglas MacArthur)

The McConnell Story (1955) (aka *Tiger in the Sky*) (Captain Joseph McConnell, Jr.)

Pork Chop Hill (1959) (Lieutenant Joe Clemons)

Starlift (1951) (Hollywood stars entertain soldiers traveling to and returning from Korea)

Truman (1995, Cable TV Movie) (President Harry S. Truman)

Underwater Warrior (1958) (Commander Francis Douglas Fane; called David Forest)

The Walking Major (1970) (aka *Aru heishi no kake*) (Captain John Arnn; called Clark J. Allen)

Brainwashing

Perhaps the most troubling topic of the war was Communist "brainwashing" of U.S. and U.N. troops in prisoner of war camps. The prospect of American personnel adopting Communist ideals, and the possibility of bringing their newfound political beliefs home with them, shocked and bewildered the public. As information concerning the Reds' methods of indoctrination became known (they included solitary confinement and physical torture for men unwilling to listen to Communist rhetoric), that bewilderment evolved into anger. International protests were made, but the Communists continued to alter their captives' political beliefs until the armistice was signed.

It is worth noting that no "brainwashing" film appeared while the war was still being fought, and then all but one were released within five years of the war's conclusion. All of these movies earnestly attempt to depict brainwashing in various ways, and *The Manchurian Candidate* takes the practice to its obvious extreme, positing that the Reds can control "sleeper agents" long after their indoctrination has ended.

The Bamboo Prison (1954)

The Fearmakers (1958)

The Manchurian Candidate (1962)

Prisoner of War (1954)

The Rack (1956)

Time Limit (1957)

Toward the Unknown (1956) (aka *Brink of Hell*)

Bridge Bombing

The object of warfare is to destroy the enemy, but the object of many Korean War films is to destroy the enemy's bridges. The strategic importance of bridges is explored in many war films, but the subject seemingly has a special place in Korean War film annals. More time is spent trying to dynamite or drop bombs onto bridges (and a few tunnels) in Korea than on almost any other aspect of the war depicted on celluloid. Hollywood has always loved to create explosions; perhaps that explains the focus on bridge bombing.

In addition to these depictions, the subject of bridge bombing is important in *MacArthur*, when the General is denied permission to destroy the spans linking China to North Korea. Instead, he is allowed to bomb only the bridge halves that are connected to the North Korean side of the river!

The Bridges at Toko-Ri (1955)

Glory Alley (1952)

The Glory Brigade (1953)

Hell's Horizon (1955)

Korea Patrol (1951)

Men of the Fighting Lady (1954)

The Reluctant Heroes (1971, TV Movie) (aka *The Egghead on Hill 656*)

Return from the Sea (1954) (aka *Home from the Sea*)

Bugles

When the Chinese joined the fight in Korea, they introduced a new element of communication to battle — bugling. Chinese orders were transmitted to troops by bugles and whistles, which also had the effect of terrifying opposing forces with a cacophony of sound. Surprisingly, very few Korean War films (only six of ninety-one) depict this practice in any detail; this fact is one which seems to prove that Hollywood had little interest in authenticating their movies about the conflict. One of the films which features bugling also gives North Koreans credit for the practice.

Battle Flame (1959)

Fixed Bayonets! (1951)

A Hill in Korea (1956) (aka *Hell in Korea*)

Hold Back the Night (1956)

Pork Chop Hill (1959)

Retreat, Hell! (1952)

Cease-Fire

The conclusion of the Korean War is only depicted in these few films, one of which (*The Hook*) takes place on a ship at the time of the cease-fire announcement. The other four are set during the days leading to the armistice and strikingly depict the silence that sweeps over Korea when the agreement takes effect. The appropriately titled *Cease Fire* utilizes actual Army personnel for its characters.

Cease Fire (1953)

The Hook (1963)

Sniper's Ridge (1961)

War Hunt (1962)
War Is Hell (1964)

Clergy

Religion is sometimes used as symbolism in war films, but in these four examples, ministers, clerics and nuns are incorporated into their movies' storylines, and not always in positive ways. Father Mulcahy in *MASH*, who is also known as "Dago Red," is a naive buffoon, well-intentioned though he may be, and Father Dolan in *The Bamboo Prison* is actually a Communist spy! Balancing these negative portrayals is Rock Hudson's earnest portrayal of Colonel Dean Hess in *Battle Hymn*, a man who saves the lives of hundreds of Korean orphans.

The Bamboo Prison (1954)
Battle Hymn (1957)
MASH (1970)
The Nun and the Sergeant (1962)

Collaboration

Almost as upsetting as brainwashing to the American public was the idea that some of their countrymen collaborated with the enemy during the Korean conflict. Several films explore this area and offer various reasons for this behavior. It should be noted that in very few films do American citizens actually collaborate willingly; most of the time, they are coerced into giving "aid and comfort" to the Communists. In fact, some of the movie collaborators are revealed to be double agents, reporting brutality and atrocities viewed in prisoner of war camps back to U.N. officials.

The Bamboo Prison (1954)
My Son John (1952)
Prisoner of War (1954)
The Rack (1956)
Sergeant Ryker (1968) (aka *The Case Against Paul Ryker; The Case Against Sergeant Ryker; Torn Between Two Values*)
Time Limit (1957)
Top Secret Affair (1957) (aka *Their Secret Affair*)
Toward the Unknown (1956) (aka *Brink of Hell*)
The Young and the Brave (1963)

Combat Photography

This seldom-seen topic of war is emphasized in a handful of Korean War films. It is given a great deal of credibility in *Battle Zone*, the most serious observance of the subject. Combat photographers are used for comedic purposes in *Cry for Happy*.

Battle Zone (1952)
The Bridges at Toko-Ri (1955)
Cry for Happy (1961)
Mission Over Korea (1953) (aka *Eyes in the Sky*)
Sky Commando (1953)
The Walking Major (1970) (aka *Aru heishi no kake*)

Comedy

These dozen comedies prove that humor can be found — or manufactured — in any war movie. The majority of war films contain comedy of one form or another, but these are dedicated to making people laugh by lampooning the military establishment, silly soldiers or social conventions of some sort. It is unfortunate that the comedies set in Japan ridicule Japanese customs and culture rather than appreciating its differences, but constructive messages in comedy are simply not taken very seriously. This is proven by *MASH*, which savages all things military but was a huge commercial and critical hit.

Back at the Front (1952) (aka *Willie and Joe Back at the Front; Willie and Joe in Tokyo*)
Cry for Happy (1961)
Geisha Girl (1952)
The Great Impostor (1960)
Marines, Let's Go (1961)
MASH (1970)
Mask of the Dragon (1951)
Mr. Walkie Talkie (1952)
Not with My Wife, You Don't! (1966)
The Reluctant Heroes (1971, TV Movie) (aka *The Egghead on Hill 656*)
Starlift (1951)
Top Secret Affair (1957) (aka *Their Secret Affair*)

Congressional Medal of Honor

Four films include references to the Congressional Medal of Honor, the highest citation that U.S. service personnel can obtain. It is discussed earnestly in *A Stranger in My Arms*, used symbolically in *The Manchurian Candidate* and disgraced in *Glory Alley*.

Glory Alley (1952)
The Manchurian Candidate (1962)
Mr. Walkie Talkie (1952)
A Stranger in My Arms (1959)

Courts-Martial

Only three Korean War films include courts-martial, though many others use the threat of the proceeding to keep rascally personnel in line. *The Rack*'s court-martial is serious and dramatic, *Sergeant Ryker*'s is serious and artificial, and Ferdinand Demara talks his way out of one in *The Great Impostor*.

The Great Impostor (1960)
The Rack (1956)
Sergeant Ryker (1968) (aka *The Case Against Paul Ryker; The Case Against Sergeant Ryker; Torn Between Two Values*)

Day of the Invasion

Relatively few films dramatize the initial day on which South Korea was initially invaded: June 25,

1950. Few American personnel were on hand, which probably explains this fact. Only *Korea Patrol* puts its troops into immediate action; others simply have their officer characters react to the news. American officers are on hand in *Dragonfly Squadron* and *One Minute to Zero*, but all they can do is to get out of the way and regroup further south.

Collision Course: Truman vs. MacArthur (1976, TV Movie)
Dragonfly Squadron (1954)
Inchon (1982)
Korea Patrol (1951)
One Minute to Zero (1952)
Truman (1995, Cable TV Movie)

Disability

Physical and mental disabilities encountered during wartime are depicted in this group of stories. Characters in *Strange Intruder* and *Toward the Unknown* display mental effects suffered in prisoner of war camps; a pilot is blinded in *Men of the Fighting Lady* and must land his jet on the aircraft carrier anyway; Captain John Hoskins loses his lower right leg in battle but refuses to retire; and a colonel is shell-shocked in *Men in War*. All of these men are forced to face and overcome the restrictions of their disabilities.

The Eternal Sea (1955) (aka *The Admiral Hoskins Story*)
Men in War (1957)
Men of the Fighting Lady (1954)
Strange Intruder (1956)
Toward the Unknown (1956) (aka *Brink of Hell*)

Dogs

Occasionally dogs are interjected into Korean War stories. "Chippy" befriends a Dutch infantryman in *Field of Honor*, "Eloise" is adopted by an American prisoner in *Prisoner of War*, and German shepherd "Lobo" leads an orphan and three U.S. soldiers to safety in *The Young and the Brave*. These films cannot be labeled as overly sentimental, however, as all three dogs are killed in action. "Betty Jane," the dog in *Three Wishes*, is revealed to be a genie! Other pertinent animals in Korean War films include snakes (*The Nun and the Sergeant*), ducks (*Mr. Walkie Talkie*), sharks (*Underwater Warrior*) and chickens (*Pork Chop Hill*).

Field of Honor (1986, Dutch)
No Man's Land (1964)
Prisoner of War (1954)
Three Wishes (1995)
The Young and the Brave (1963)

Effects on Civilians

The most dramatic points that movies can make about war should be the deadly and devastating effects that war has on civilians. Some Korean War films take the time or make the attempt to include civilian suffering within their structures, but the majority do not. Movies intended to promote the machinery of war would be foolish to show that machinery's devastating effects on the lives of innocent bystanders. Films released after the war have little compunction about depicting civilian anguish and grief. While these films explore the area of what the Korean War did to native Koreans, most do so very superficially. Orphans are a big concern, but most films simply depict long lines of struggling refugees burdened with livestock and their worldly possessions searching for a new place to live. By far the most realistic and explicit view of the subject is in the Dutch film *Field of Honor*, where civilian women adapt to the war by selling themselves to lonely U.N. soldiers.

All the Young Men (1960)
Battle Hymn (1957)
Field of Honor (1986, Dutch)
Inchon (1982)
Marine Battleground (1966)
Marines, Let's Go (1961)
The Nun and the Sergeant (1962)
One Minute to Zero (1952)
Operation Dames (1959) (aka *Girls in Action*)
The Walking Major (1970) (aka *Aru heishi no kake*)
The Young and the Brave (1963)

Espionage

These films have espionage plots at their centers and utilize the Korean War as a background for their stories. Some deal with smuggling, others with spying, but all take place within the Korean War milieu and are somehow affected by the war.

Back at the Front (1952) (aka *Willie and Joe Back at the Front; Willie and Joe in Tokyo*)
The Bamboo Prison (1954)
Dragonfly Squadron (1954)
Geisha Girl (1952)
Jet Attack (1958) (aka *Jet Squad; Through Hell to Glory*)
The Manchurian Candidate (1962)
Mask of the Dragon (1951)
Sergeant Ryker (1968) (aka *The Case Against Paul Ryker; The Case Against Sergeant Ryker; Torn Between Two Values*)
Tokyo File 212 (1951)
Top Secret Affair (1957) (aka *Their Secret Affair*)

Females in the Field

A surprising number of Korean War films (almost one-fifth) manage to place comely females in harm's way on the battlefields of Korea. For a war in which women did not serve near the front lines except as nurses, this percentage is indeed large. Hollywood has always attempted to mix romance and war, and several of these films include wartime dalliances. Half of the titles in this group feature nurses or U.N. health workers in peril. The other half is mainly comprised of U.S.O. performers and native women caught in the web of war. *Jet Attack* actually has a woman as a Russian officer, while Jacqueline Bisset evacuates Seoul at the beginning of *Inchon*, interrupting her shopping. Perhaps more to the point, the Korean women of *Field of Honor* prostitute themselves to stay alive.

Battle Circus (1953)
Battle Flame (1959)
Dragonfly Squadron (1954)
Field of Honor (1986, Dutch)
Flight Nurse (1953)
For the Boys (1991)
Inchon (1982)
Iron Angel (1964)
Jet Attack (1958) (aka *Jet Squad; Through Hell to Glory*)
Korea Patrol (1951)
Marine Battleground (1966)
MASH (1970)
Mr. Walkie Talkie (1952)
No Man's Land (1964)
The Nun and the Sergeant (1962)
One Minute to Zero (1952)
Operation Dames (1959) (aka *Girls in Action*)
Tank Battalion (1958)
Target Zero (1955)
War Is Hell (1964)

Helicopters

These are movies which feature helicopters as an important element of the Korean War. The Korean conflict was the first war where helicopters were vital for American transport and rescue operations, and these films reflect the versatility and reliability of whirlybirds in battle. For the most part, rescue operations are dramatized — over both land and sea — but even basic transport of personnel is depicted. The most unusual view of chopper activity must be the staged duel between a tank and a helicopter in *Battle Zone*. Helicopter operations were vital in Korea and became even more important, and offensive in nature, during the Vietnam War.

An Annapolis Story (1955) (aka *The Blue and the Gold; Navy Air Patrol*)
Battle Circus (1953)
Battle Taxi (1955)
The Bridges at Toko-Ri (1955)
The Glory Brigade (1953)
Hold Back the Night (1956)
MASH (1970)
Men of the Fighting Lady (1954)
The Nun and the Sergeant (1962)
The Young and the Brave (1963)

Home Front

A minority of Korean War films try to encompass feeling regarding the Korean War back home in the United States. Other than letters from home, which several films document, this group of films actually attempts to gauge and reflect public sentiment, whether it is for or against the war. Mostly, they try to capture the feeling of the time without philosophizing about the conflict. *Chattahoochee* and *Three Wishes* in particular demonstrate that the sunny exterior of suburban American life is a thin veneer for a society which is confused about the current state of the world. Two conservative viewpoints are displayed in *I Want You*, which exhibits strong support for the war, and *My Son John*, which dramatizes the threat of Communist activity at home.

Chattahoochee (1990)
Collision Course: Truman vs. MacArthur (1976, TV Movie)
I Want You (1951)
Japanese War Bride (1952) (aka *East is East*)
My Son John (1952)
Starlift (1951)
Three Wishes (1995)
Truman (1995, Cable TV Movie)

Infighting

Despite the presence of enemy soldiers and armament, many servicemen in Korea seemed to fight among themselves; at least, these movies present that perspective. Often the disputes among men revolve around race; these titles are also included in "racism." Whatever the reason, a large number of titles seem to fixate on the concept that soldiers would rather fight among themselves than fight their stated enemy. This could indicate a basic confusion about or rejection of the reasoning behind America's presence in Korea, or it could just be lazy scriptwriting.

All the Young Men (1960)
Fixed Bayonets! (1951)
The Glory Brigade (1953)
Hell's Horizon (1955)
A Hill in Korea (1956) (aka *Hell in Korea*)
The Hook (1963)
The Hunters (1958)
Iron Angel (1964)
The Manchurian Candidate (1962)
MASH (1970)
Mr. Walkie Talkie (1952)
Not with My Wife, You Don't! (1966)
The Nun and the Sergeant (1962)
The Reluctant Heroes (1971, TV Movie) (aka *The Egghead on Hill 656*)
Sky Commando (1953)
Sniper's Ridge (1961)
A Stranger in My Arms (1959)
Take the High Ground! (1953)
Target Zero (1955)
War Hunt (1962)
War Is Hell (1964)

Integration

Only one title dares to explore the ramifications of race relations in combat. While other films include black, Hispanic, or foreign-born soldiers among their ranks, only *All the Young Men* makes a dramatic issue of the situation.

All the Young Men (1960)

Japan

Japan became a staging and support area for U.N. interests in Korea, and a rest and recreation stop for weary soldiers from the front lines. Almost one-sixth of all Korean War films feature scenes in Japan, which indicates Japan's importance to the war, as well as Hollywood's ever-increasing interest in Japan. George Breakston produced the first films to be entirely filmed in Japan and added Korean War elements for timeliness. Comedies about cultural differences became popular and continued into the 1960s; they used the war as an excuse for Americans to visit (and often mock) Japan. A tiny minority showcase Japanese culture without resorting to ridicule — *Sayonara* is undoubtedly the best of these titles.

Back at the Front (1952) (aka *Willie and Joe Back at the Front; Willie and Joe in Tokyo*)
The Bridges at Toko-Ri (1955)
Cry for Happy (1961)
Geisha Girl (1952)
The Hunters (1958)
Inchon (1982)
Japanese War Bride (1952)
MacArthur (1977) (aka *MacArthur, the Rebel General*)
Marines, Let's Go (1961)
One Minute to Zero (1952)
Sayonara (1957)
Tokyo File 212 (1951)
Twenty Plus Two (1961)
The Walking Major (1970) (aka *Aru heishi no kake*)

Journalism

The subject of journalism should have been a popular theme for filmmakers, but that is not the case. The most famous journalist depicted among these titles is writer James Michener, who is a character collecting war stories in *Men of the Fighting Lady*. Two films (*Battle Zone, The Walking Major*) depict photojournalists, while William Holden portrays an ill-fated war correspondent in *Love Is a Many-Splendored Thing*. It is amazing, however, that no Hollywood movie features the most famous of all Korean War journalists: Marguerite Higgins. Her story begs for a movie treatment.

Battle Zone (1952)
Collision Course: Truman vs. MacArthur (1976, TV Movie)
Cry for Happy (1961)

Love Is a Many-Splendored Thing (1955)
Marine Battleground (1966)
Men of the Fighting Lady (1954)
Sabre Jet (1953)
Top Secret Affair (1957) (aka *Their Secret Affair*)

Leaders

President Harry S. Truman and General Douglas MacArthur are spotlighted in four films which explore their conflicts from various perspectives, but no other Korean War leader (including renegade South Korean President Syngman Rhee) has been profiled by Hollywood's image makers.

Collision Course: Truman vs. MacArthur (1976, TV Movie)
Inchon (1982)
MacArthur (1977) (aka *MacArthur, the Rebel General*)
Truman (1995, Cable TV Movie)

Lonely Wives

Besides placing women in peril, the only other way for Hollywood filmmakers to inject a feminine aspect into their Korean War stories is to spotlight the lonely wives of the men serving overseas. These films, in varying degrees, examine women who stay at home and raise families while their husbands are fighting thousands of miles away. The best shed some light on the emotional trauma which some wives face; the worst use the stereotype as an excuse for histrionics.

The Bridges at Toko-Ri (1955)
The Eternal Sea (1955) (aka *The Admiral Hoskins Story*)
Hell's Horizon (1955)
Hold Back the Night (1956)
The Hunters (1958)
The McConnell Story (1955) (aka *Tiger in the Sky*)
Not with My Wife, You Don't! (1966)
One Minute to Zero (1952)
Return from the Sea (1954) (aka *Home from the Sea*)
Sabre Jet (1953)
Submarine Command (1951)
Three Wishes (1995)
Underwater Warrior (1958)
The Walking Major (1970) (aka *Aru heishi no kake*)

Marine Corps

There are fewer Marine Corps studies than Army movies regarding the Korean War, but those which involve the Marines are generally more dramatic than their Army counterparts. Approximately half of them recount the Marines' hellish trek from the Chosin Reservoir to the port city of Hungnam, made necessary by the unexpected Chinese entry into combat. The best of these are *Hold Back the Night* and *Retreat, Hell!*, with *Battle Flame* an interesting variation. Unfortunately, two of the worst of all Korean War tales — *Inchon* and *Marines, Let's Go* — are also featured within this group.

All the Young Men (1960)
Battle Flame (1959)
Battle Zone (1952)
For the Boys (1991)
Hold Back the Night (1956)
Inchon (1982)
Man-Trap (1961) (aka *Man in Hiding*)
Marine Battleground (1966)
Marines, Let's Go (1961)
The Nun and the Sergeant (1962)
Retreat, Hell! (1952)
Sayonara (1957)

Medicine

The art of saving lives is presented in several Korean War films, most of which focus on battlefield hospitals of one sort or another. *MASH* is the most famous of these, but *Battle Circus* and *The Great Impostor* both display hospital operations, while blood transfusions are important in others. Nurses are prominent in *MASH* and *Flight Nurse*, and appear in a few other films. *Chattahoochee* is an exposé of mental health institutions in Florida, to which a veteran is committed after the war.

All the Young Men (1960)
Battle Circus (1953)
Chattahoochee (1990)
Flight Nurse (1953)
The Great Impostor (1960)
Marine Battleground (1966)
MASH (1970)
Prisoner of War (1954)
The Steel Helmet (1951)

Military Training

A large minority of Korean War films focus not so much on battles, but on the training which servicemen in all branches must undergo before being sent to war. The films of this group are perhaps the most vocal concerning the need for continued military strength, and attempt to win viewer support by depicting in detail the rigors and demands to which trainees are subjected. All armed services are represented, and all contributed time, facilities and even personnel to the making of these films. There is no denying the propagandistic intent of building public support for military might of the films contained within this group, but it must also be noted that they are usually of greater production quality and entertainment value than routine battle action flicks.

Air Strike (1955)
An Annapolis Story (1955) (aka *The Blue and the Gold; Navy Air Patrol*)
Battle Hymn (1957)
Battle Zone (1952)

Bombers B-52 (1957) (aka *No Sleep Till Dawn*)
Dragonfly Squadron (1954)
The McConnell Story (1955) (aka *Tiger in the Sky*)
Men of the Fighting Lady (1954)
Mission Over Korea (1953) (aka *Eyes in the Sky*)
Retreat, Hell! (1952)
Return from the Sea (1954) (aka *Home from the Sea*)
Take the High Ground! (1953)
Torpedo Alley (1952)
Toward the Unknown (1956) (aka *Brink of Hell*)
Underwater Warrior (1958)
A Yank in Korea (1951) (aka *Letter from Korea*)

Multiple Wars

Several Korean War stories actually begin during World War II and usually feature a soldier, sailor or pilot who has some unfinished business (and/or intense psychological problem) from action in World War II which he can put to rights in Korea. Two of these titles, *For the Boys* and *The Walking Major*, actually present sequences from three wars, as they also include action in Vietnam.

Air Strike (1955)
Back at the Front (1952) (aka *Willie and Joe Back at the Front; Willie and Joe in Tokyo*)
Battle Hymn (1957)
The Eternal Sea (1955) (aka *The Admiral Hoskins Story*)
For the Boys (1991)
Hold Back the Night (1956)
I Want You (1951)
MacArthur (1977) (aka *MacArthur, the Rebel General*)
The McConnell Story (1955) (aka *Tiger in the Sky*)
Marine Battleground (1966)
Sky Commando (1953)
Submarine Command (1951)
Top Secret Affair (1957) (aka *Their Secret Affair*)
Torpedo Alley (1952)
Truman (1995, Cable TV Movie)
Underwater Warrior (1958)
The Walking Major (1970) (aka *Aru heishi no kake*)

Musical Performance

Along with romance, Hollywood filmmakers were encouraged to include musical interludes in as many war films as possible. It was thought that female viewers especially enjoyed story threads involving romance and music in virtually any movie, and would not attend shows which did not include these elements. Thus, many war films made during the 1940s and 1950s contain musical moments that today seem intrusive.

The musical performances noted in these movies are mostly songs sung by cast members, ranging from Gloria Jean and Margia Dean to Ken Berry and Ingemar Johansson. There are also revue numbers, most of which are presented in stories set in Japan, such as *Geisha Girl* and *Sayonara*, and a few choral numbers spread throughout the listing. Perhaps the most inspired is William Chun's rendition of the Korean national anthem in *The Steel Helmet,* sung to the music of "Auld Lang Syne"!

Air Strike (1955) (Gloria Jean sings two songs)
All the Young Men (1960) (James Darren and Ingemar Johansson each sing a song)
An Annapolis Story (1955) (aka *The Blue and the Gold; Navy Air Patrol*) (Choral)
Cease Fire (1953) (Choral)
Collision Course: Truman vs. MacArthur (1976, TV Movie) (Margaret Truman's operatic debut is excerpted)
For the Boys (1991) (Bette Midler sings several songs; James Caan accompanies)
Geisha Girl (1952) (Japanese revues)
Glory Alley (1952) (Leslie Caron sings two songs)
Marines, Let's Go (1961) (Japanese revues)
MASH (1970) (Ken Prymus sings "Suicide is Painless")
Mask of the Dragon (1951) (Curt Barrett and the Trailsmen sing two songs)
Mr. Walkie Talkie (1952) (Margia Dean sings a song)
One Minute to Zero (1952) (Robert Mitchum and Ann Blyth sing a duet)
Operation Dames (1959) (aka *Girls in Action*) (Eve Meyer and the cast sing a song; Cindy Girard sings another)
The Reluctant Heroes (1971, TV Movie) (aka *The Egghead on Hill 656*) (Ken Berry leads local children in singing "Old MacDonald Had a Farm")
Sayonara (1957) (Japanese revues)
Starlift (1951) (Songs abound, from Doris Day, Jane Wyman, Janice Rule, et al.)
The Steel Helmet (1951) (William Chun sings the Korean national anthem)
Tokyo File 212 (1951) (Japanese revues)
Top Secret Affair (1957) (aka *Their Secret Affair*) (Kirk Douglas sings "The Caisson Song")

Mystery

One-eighth of all Korean War movies are mysteries, in which some secret is held until the final few minutes. About half of the secrets involve the Korean War in some way. Some of the films merely use the wartime setting as background for their mystery stories. It should be noted that the film reviews in this book reveal plot descriptions and surprises; it is recommended that readers view the films before reading about them.

Glory Alley (1952)
The Manchurian Candidate (1962)
Mask of the Dragon (1951)
My Son John (1952)
Sergeant Ryker (1968) (aka *The Case Against Paul Ryker; The Case Against Sergeant Ryker; Torn Between Two Values*)
A Stranger in My Arms (1959)

Three Wishes (1995)
Time Limit (1957)
Tokyo File 212 (1951)
Top Secret Affair (1957) (aka *Their Secret Affair*)
Twenty Plus Two (1961)

Navy (Aviators)

These are the same five titles which are listed in "aircraft carriers." These films spotlight the men who fly the fighter jets as well as the floating cities on the high seas that they take off from and land on. Other Navy personnel are presented in these films, but it is the flyboys, the naval aviators, who are the focus.

Air Strike (1955)
An Annapolis Story (1955) (aka *The Blue and the Gold; Navy Air Patrol*)
The Bridges at Toko-Ri (1955)
The Eternal Sea (1955) (aka *The Admiral Hoskins Story*)
Men of the Fighting Lady (1954)

Navy (Sailors)

This group highlights naval personnel other than the fighter pilots who served in the Korean War. Submariners, sailors, combat photographers and admirals are included here. Two of these stories depict genuine Navy mavericks: Admiral John Hoskins in *The Eternal Sea* and Commander Francis Douglas Fane (called David Forest) in *Underwater Warrior.*

Cry for Happy (1961)
The Eternal Sea (1955) (aka *The Admiral Hoskins Story*)
Inchon (1982)
MacArthur (1977) (aka *MacArthur, the Rebel General*)
Return from the Sea (1954) (aka *Home from the Sea*)
Submarine Command (1951)
Torpedo Alley (1952)
Underwater Warrior (1958)

Nurses

Nurses are a primary focus in only two of these films—*Flight Nurse* and *Iron Angel.* They appear and are important in the others, but are not the central characters. They are romantic interests for soldiers in *Battle Flame* and *Not with My Wife, You Don't!,* and for doctors in *Battle Circus* and *MASH.* The one film which explores the importance of field nurses is *Flight Nurse,* but it is as much a romance as a war drama.

Battle Circus (1953)
Battle Flame (1959)
Flight Nurse (1953)
Iron Angel (1964)
Marine Battleground (1966)
MASH (1970)

Not with My Wife, You Don't! (1966)
Tank Battalion (1958)

Orphans

The most heart-rending aspect of war is its creation of orphans. The majority of these titles display how U.S. and U.N. personnel come to the aid of Korean children and try to improve their chances for survival. The bleakest picture is painted in the Dutch film *Field of Honor*, in which orphan teenagers are forced to prostitute themselves for survival. Orphans are usually presented as a group; individual orphans of note include Short Round in *The Steel Helmet* and Clancy in *Mission Over Korea* (both played by William Chun), Takeshi in *The Walking Major*, Charlie in *War Hunt* and Han in *The Young and the Brave*.

Battle Hymn (1957)
Cry for Happy (1961)
Field of Honor (1986, Dutch)
Inchon (1982)
Marine Battleground (1966)
Mission Over Korea (1953) (aka *Eyes in the Sky*)
The Steel Helmet (1951)
The Walking Major (1970) (aka *Aru heishi no kake*)
War Hunt (1962)
The Young and the Brave (1963)

Peace Negotiations

These three titles include drama concerning the peace negotiations being held at Panmunjom, though only one, *Pork Chop Hill*, actually dramatizes the process. The long-awaited prospect of peace is mentioned in many war dramas, but only these make that process an active part of their storylines.

The Bamboo Prison (1954)
Cease Fire (1953)
Pork Chop Hill (1959)

Politics

American political activity is chronicled in these films, which feature a widespread fear of communism. *The Bamboo Prison* is an exception, in that its political view is more global, as represented by the Russian advisor to the Chinese prisoner of war camp, and *Dragonfly Squadron*'s politics are confined to the question of whether the U.S. has committed itself to the war in the first few days after the invasion.

The Bamboo Prison (1954)
Collision Course: Truman vs. MacArthur (1976, TV Movie)
Dragonfly Squadron (1954)
The Fearmakers (1958)
MacArthur (1977) (aka *MacArthur, the Rebel General*)
The Manchurian Candidate (1962)
My Son John (1952)

Post-traumatic Stress Syndrome

These four titles feature characters who seem to be suffering from what is now known as post-traumatic stress syndrome. The lead characters of these stories are each stressed from battle or captivity and find it very difficult to adjust to civilian life. William Holden's character in *Toward the Unknown* may be another, but he does not suffer from the general symptoms of the syndrome that the men in these stories suffer from.

Chattahoochee (1990)
The Fearmakers (1958)
The Manchurian Candidate (1962)
Strange Intruder (1956)

Prisoners of War

Perhaps the most dynamic subgenre of Korean War films involves prisoners of war. These movies are mostly high-profile examinations of Communist treatment of U.S. and U.N. prisoners, although *The Hook*, *The Nun and the Sergeant* and *War Hunt* reverse that trend. The only North Korean prisoners are only to be found in *The Hook* and *War Hunt*. *The Nun and the Sergeant* is a *Dirty Dozen*-like adventure in which American prisoners are sent on a suicide mission into North Korea.

The others dramatize captivity, physical abuse, solitary confinement and even torture of U.S. and U.N. prisoners at the hands of Communist captors. Though the films' views of such treatment are varied, they are all based on stories and evidence from former prisoners that such barbaric treatment was common. As a group, these titles examine how prisoners withstand Communist indoctrination and torture — how they endeavor to survive in hostile environments where they are underfed and maltreated. Issues of brainwashing, collaboration and repatriation are all linked to prisoners of war.

The Bamboo Prison (1954)
The Fearmakers (1958)
The Hook (1963)
The Manchurian Candidate (1962)
The Nun and the Sergeant (1962)
Prisoner of War (1954)
The Rack (1956)
Strange Intruder (1956)
Time Limit (1957)
War Hunt (1962)

Racism

In Korean War films, racism usually involves conflict between white and black soldiers on the same side. The most dramatic example is *All the Young Men*, where a black sergeant assumes command over jittery white soldiers, but *Iron Angel*, *MASH*, *The Reluctant Heroes* and *The Steel Helmet* also examine racial conflicts in some detail.

Japanese, Eurasians and Greeks also face discrimination in the other titles of this listing. The majority of these films end with white people accepting their foreign-born counterparts as equals, although *Japanese War Bride* and *Sayonara* are clear indictments of American society's reluctance to recognize the validity of other cultures.

All the Young Men (1960)
The Glory Brigade (1953)
The Hook (1963)
Iron Angel (1964)
Japanese War Bride (1952) (aka *East is East*)
Love Is a Many-Splendored Thing (1955)
MASH (1970)
The Reluctant Heroes (1971, TV Movie) (aka *The Egghead on Hill 656*)
Sayonara (1957)
The Steel Helmet (1951)

The Red Menace

"The Red Menace" is the global threat of Communism to democratic ideals and is included in stories which take the perspective of the "Big Picture." At the time of Korea's invasion, people viewed the act as a possible first step of Communist Russia and China in an attempt at global domination — thus, the Red menace to the American way of life. The movies which scrutinize the Red threat try to contextualize it in global terms, hoping that audiences will be convinced that a larger enemy is more dramatic than the localized conflict in Korea.

The Bamboo Prison (1954)
Collision Course: Truman vs. MacArthur (1976, TV Movie)
The Fearmakers (1958)
Geisha Girl (1952)
I Want You (1951)
Love Is a Many-Splendored Thing (1955)
MacArthur (1977) (aka *MacArthur, the Rebel General*)
The Manchurian Candidate (1962)
The McConnell Story (1955) (aka *Tiger in the Sky*)
My Son John (1952)
Tokyo File 212 (1951)
Truman (1995, Cable TV Movie)

Repatriation

Two films show repatriation. In *The Fearmakers*, it is thrust upon Dana Andrews without warning. Only *The Bamboo Prison* displays the actual ritual, where prisoners are asked to choose where they would prefer to be sent after the war. This was an issue for prisoners in U.N. prison camps, many of whom were South Koreans conscripted into military service as the North Koreans marched southward. In *The Bamboo Prison*, an American soldier is given the opportunity to return to America, but he instead chooses, as twenty-one American soldiers did, to travel to communist North Korea or China.

The Bamboo Prison (1954)
The Fearmakers (1958)

Rescues

War films often include scenes of rescue against seemingly insurmountable odds; these are the Korean War films which follow that tradition. Some rescues are made by helicopter, others by airplane or submarine. All are meant to display American heroism at its finest.

An Annapolis Story (1955) (aka *The Blue and the Gold; Navy Air Patrol*)
Battle Circus (1953)
Battle Flame (1959)
Battle Hymn (1957)
Battle Taxi (1955)
The Bridges at Toko-Ri (1955)
Flight Nurse (1953)
The Glory Brigade (1953)
Jet Attack (1958) (aka *Jet Squad; Through Hell to Glory*)
Man-Trap (1961) (aka *Man in Hiding*)
Men of the Fighting Lady (1954)
Submarine Command (1951)
The Young and the Brave (1963)

Returning Home

Veterans returning to America from overseas are highlighted in this listing. Unlike some later Vietnam War films, most of these veterans are not depicted as bloodthirsty or deranged, though some of them suffer from mental disturbances. Some of these veterans return home injured, either mentally or physically, and must make adjustments to cope with the specter of civilian life. Others return as heroes, joyfully rejoining a society which they wondered if they would ever see again. Either way, returning home is almost always viewed as better than remaining to fight (although *War Hunt* features a character who would rather remain at war).

Chattahoochee (1990)
Collision Course: Truman vs. MacArthur (1976, TV Movie)
The Fearmakers (1958)
Glory Alley (1952)
Japanese War Bride (1952) (aka *East is East*)
MacArthur (1977) (aka *MacArthur, the Rebel General*)
The Manchurian Candidate (1962)
The McConnell Story (1955) (aka *Tiger in the Sky*)
The Rack (1956)
Return from the Sea (1954) (aka *Home from the Sea*)
Starlift (1951)
Strange Intruder (1956)
Three Wishes (1995)
Time Limit (1957)
Toward the Unknown (1956) (aka *Brink of Hell*)
A Yank in Korea (1951) (aka *Letter from Korea*)

Romance

Fully one-third of Korean War films include romance as an element, and if "romantic triangle" is included, almost half feature romantic interests in and between battles. Considering that women were not given combat roles in the war, that percentage is very high. Hollywood has traditionally tried to "soften" its hard-edged war films by featuring romance in one form or another. Flashbacks are often used, for then filmmakers are able to picture women back home, where they can be seen at their most romantic.

Battlefield romances involve liaisons with nurses, U.N. health inspectors, U.S.O. entertainers, native women and even one female Russian officer. Romances are intended to remind the fighting men (and the audience) for what they are fighting, and to give them the moral strength to continue the fight. Perhaps more important, these interludes are designed to placate female members of the audience who grow tired of watching men kill each other.

Battle Circus (1953)
Battle Flame (1959)
Bombers B-52 (1957) (aka *No Sleep Till Dawn*)
Cry for Happy (1961)
Geisha Girl (1952)
Glory Alley (1952)
The Great Impostor (1960)
Hold Back the Night (1956)
I Want You (1951)
Japanese War Bride (1952) (aka *East Is East*)
Love Is a Many-Splendored Thing (1955)
The Manchurian Candidate (1962)
Marines, Let's Go (1961)
The McConnell Story (1955) (aka *Tiger in the Sky*)
Mission Over Korea (1953) (aka *Eyes in the Sky*)
No Man's Land (1964)
Not with My Wife, You Don't! (1966)
One Minute to Zero (1952)
Operation Dames (1959) (aka *Girls in Action*)
Return from the Sea (1954) (aka *Home from the Sea*)
Sabre Jet (1953)
Sayonara (1957)
Sergeant Ryker (1968) (aka *The Case Against Paul Ryker; The Case Against Sergeant Ryker; Torn Between Two Values*)
Sky Commando (1953)
Starlift (1951)
A Stranger in My Arms (1959)
Tank Battalion (1958)
Target Zero (1955)
Top Secret Affair (1957) (aka *Their Secret Affair*)
Twenty Plus Two (1961)
Underwater Warrior (1958)

Romantic Triangle

This variation of romance involves two men competing for the same woman, a touch which adds inherent drama to the wartime situation. Sometimes, the two men are brothers. Sometimes they are of varying ranks, and the lower ranking man occasionally wins the woman's heart. Sometimes one of the men dies, leaving an easy path for his rival. And sometimes, neither man wins the girl's affections. All is fair in love and war.

An Annapolis Story (1955) (aka *The Blue and the Gold; Navy Air Patrol*)
Battle Zone (1952)
Dragonfly Squadron (1954)
Flight Nurse (1953)
Hell's Horizon (1955)
The Hunters (1958)
Not with My Wife, You Don't! (1966)
Submarine Command (1951)
Take the High Ground! (1953)
Torpedo Alley (1952)
Toward the Unknown (1956) (aka *Brink of Hell*)

Secret Missions

Most Korean War films feature straightforward battle sequences, but some offer what are best described as "secret missions." Two submarine movies, for instance, feature bandit raids on North Korean targets which are executed quietly in the dark of night. Commando raids are presented in *Inchon, Jet Attack* and *Return From the Sea*. Some characters are given secret missions to perform, such as the protagonists of *Sergeant Ryker, Strange Intruder, Top Secret Affair* and, most frighteningly, *The Manchurian Candidate*. In general terms, "secret missions" covers any action which is not considered a normal, routine function in war.

The Bamboo Prison (1954)
Battle Zone (1952)
Inchon (1982)
Jet Attack (1958) (aka *Jet Squad; Through Hell to Glory*)
The Manchurian Candidate (1962)
Marines, Let's Go (1961)
Prisoner of War (1954)
Return from the Sea (1954) (aka *Home from the Sea*)
Sergeant Ryker (1968) (aka *The Case Against Paul Ryker; The Case Against Sergeant Ryker; Torn Between Two Values*)
Strange Intruder (1956)
Submarine Command (1951)
Tokyo File 212 (1951)
Top Secret Affair (1957) (aka *Their Secret Affair*)
Torpedo Alley (1952)

Sibling Rivalry

Five Korean War films feature brother acts. The most entertaining is the rivalry between the Scott brothers in *An Annapolis Story*, but the most meaningful relationship exists between the Korean brothers Kim and Ching in *Korea Patrol*. Brothers are noted but disappear early in *Mission Over Korea* and *My Son John*, while Ed Hall's brother remains an unseen but powerful influence in *The Rack*.

An Annapolis Story (1955) (aka *The Blue and the Gold; Navy Air Patrol*)
Korea Patrol (1951)
Mission Over Korea (1953) (aka *Eyes in the Sky*)
My Son John (1952)
The Rack (1956)

"Somewhere in Korea"

Three titles begin "Somewhere in Korea," which seems to indicate that the writers responsible for their stories could not be bothered to assign actual settings to them. To be fair, *Return From the Sea* begins "Somewhere off the coast of Korea" on a ship, so it may be forgiven. But the other two are among the most ludicrous of Korean War movies, and their faults begin with the first image seen on the screen, "Somewhere in Korea…"

Geisha Girl (1952)
Jet Attack (1958) (aka *Jet Squad; Through Hell to Glory*)
Return from the Sea (1954) (aka *Home from the Sea*)

Submarines

The U.S. Navy played a limited role in the Korean War, as evidenced by the small number of films involving submarine activity. Submarines were used to patrol shorelines and support convoys, with occasional duties as chauffeurs for commando raids. One film, *Underwater Warrior*, does detail the eventual use of frogmen from subs, as demonstrated by its inspiration, Commander Francis Douglas Fane. The others take care to display sub training methodology, but conclude with commando raids on the Korean shore.

Submarine Command (1951)
Torpedo Alley (1952)
Underwater Warrior (1958)

United Nations Forces

That the allies in Korea were an international coalition is demonstrated in these titles, which range from spotlighting Greek infantrymen in *The Glory Brigade* to Dutch infantrymen in *Field of Honor*. British and Australian combatants are introduced in several films, and the South Korean armed forces, such as they were, are included in more. Only *A Hill in Korea* and *Field of Honor*, however, utilize perspectives of the war other than American.

Field of Honor (1986, Dutch)
Flight Nurse (1953)
The Glory Brigade (1953)
The Great Impostor (1960)
A Hill in Korea (1956) (aka *Hell in Korea*)
The Hunters (1958)
Inchon (1982)

One Minute to Zero (1952)
Retreat, Hell! (1952)
Strange Intruder (1956)
Target Zero (1955)

United Nations Security Council

Two of the initial Korean War offerings include actual footage of the United Nations Security Council. Both include footage of the Security Council adopting resolutions against communist aggression in Korea for the basis of their drama, and begin their stories once the resolutions have passed.

Korea Patrol (1951)
A Yank in Korea (1951) (aka *Letter from Korea*)

U.S.O. (United Service Organizations, Inc.)

The U.S.O. is a consolidation of welfare organizations which formed during World War II in order to provide recreational facilities and entertainment to members of the armed services. Disbanded in 1947, it was reactivated in 1951 for the troops stationed in Korea and Japan. The U.S.O. features prominently in a few Korean War films, mostly to put lovely females in peril and to provide musical interludes during dramatic war stories. *For the Boys* and *Starlift* are the prime titles in this group; both endeavor to provide at least some authenticity for their stories.

Combat Squad (1953)
For the Boys (1991)
Mr. Walkie Talkie (1952)
Operation Dames (1959) (aka *Girls in Action*)
Starlift (1951)

Winter Fighting

The vast majority of Korean War films take place in summer, when the invasion was first launched. The first four months of the war encompassed the initial invasion, the Pusan Perimeter fighting and the counteroffensive launched at Inchon. But the war continued into the winter, culminating in the "advance in another direction" from the Chosin Reservoir under bitter winter conditions. Only a handful of Korean War films occur in winter, but they are among the genre's most dramatic. In these films, the fighting forces must battle the frosty weather as much as an enemy which, with the entry of the Chinese into the war, greatly outnumbers them.

All the Young Men (1960)
Battle Flame (1959)
Chattahoochee (1990)
Fixed Bayonets! (1951)
For the Boys (1991)
Hold Back the Night (1956)
Retreat, Hell! (1952)
The Walking Major (1970) (aka *Aru heishi no kake*)

APPENDIX E: FILMS WITH INCIDENTAL KOREAN WAR REFERENCES

There are other films which refer to the Korean War in passing, but which do not feature extensive combat action or enough of a connection to the war to be included in the main text of this book. These various movies do not focus on the Korean War or its consequences, but rather feature a character who is going to or has already served in the war, or who is somehow affected by the war. Others are about completely different subjects but have a specific scene which somehow relates to the war.

The Canon Operation (1983)
Video City Prod. D: Unknown. This Japanese-made action film was dubbed in English and released on videotape in 1983 by Video City Productions. An American intelligence officer is hidden among prisoners of war, but the North Koreans are torturing all of their prisoners until they find him. Meanwhile, a rescue operation is being mounted. Despite some rigorous action scenes, this is bottom-of-the-barrel drama, particularly when scenes of the chief American spy reveal cars and buildings of 1960s and later vintage.

Child Bride of Short Creek (1985, TV Movie)
(Company uknown) D: Robert Michael Lewis. A young man (Christopher Atkins) returns from Korea to his home town in Arizona to find that his fundamentalist father (Conrad Bain) is planning to take a fourth wife (young Diane Lane). This true-life polygamy drama also features Dee Wallace-Stone and a young Helen Hunt.

The Crimson Kimono (1959)
Globe Ent./Columbia. D: Samuel Fuller. Two Los Angeles detectives (Glenn Corbett and James Shigeta) investigate the murder of a showgirl on a downtown street. During their investigation, the detectives — who were best buddies and survived the Korean War together — both fall for the same girl (Victoria Shaw), a material witness to the murder. When she chooses one of them over the other, the men's relationship sours. There is also reference to another friend, killed during the war, and his father, who still grieves his loss.

Danielle Steele's "Family Album"
(1994, TV Miniseries)
NBC D: Jack Bender. An army lieutenant (Michael Ontkean) falls for a U.S.O. actress (Jaclyn Smith) during the Korean War. She becomes a famous film director as his career slumps. They are finally brought back together before tragedy strikes. No copy of the film could be found to review for this book.

Flying Leathernecks (1951)
RKO. D: Nicholas Ray. During World War II in the South Pacific, two Marine officers (John Wayne and Robert Ryan) butt heads over the best way to handle their squadron, which always seems to be in imminent danger of attack. This is reputed to have originally been planned as a Korean War film, and is — allegedly — the first Hollywood film to feature battle footage from the Korean War edited into its action sequences.

The Front (1976)
Columbia. D: Martin Ritt. In 1952, a black-

listed writer (Michael Murphy) asks a nebbishy friend (Woody Allen) to pretend to write in order to sell television scripts. Soon, the "front" has added two more blacklisted clients and is touted as the hottest, most prolific writer in television. Ultimately, investigation into the phony's success forces him to make a dramatic decision regarding honor and loyalty. The film's prologue, which visually describes the tenor of the time, shows footage of soldiers in and returning home from Korea, as well as the return of General MacArthur and his parade through New York.

Going All the Way (1997)

Gramercy. D: Mark Pellington. Two young Korean War veterans (Jeremy Davies and Ben Affleck) return home to Indianapolis and try to pick up their lives where they left off before serving overseas. Their friendship, forged in Korea, is challenged by the women to whom they return (Amy Locane, Rachel Weisz and Rose McGowan) and by their own mothers (Jill Clayburgh and Lesley Ann Warren). The screenplay is by Dan Wakefield, based upon his popular novel.

Heartbreak Ridge (1986)

Warner Bros. D: Clint Eastwood. U.S. Marines train for combat under the command of a battle-hardened veteran of Korea and Vietnam (Clint Eastwood). He finds it increasingly difficult to relate to the younger generation, while trying to reconnect with his estranged wife (Marsha Mason). His troops are given a taste of real combat when America invades Grenada. Real footage from the Korean War is run during the opening credits.

Hell's Outpost (1955)

Republic. D: Joe Kane. A Korean War veteran (Rod Cameron) pretends to be a friend of a soldier killed in action in order to gain an interest in a silver mine. Despite the deception, he is an honest fellow who works hard to make the mine a success while falling for the girlfriend (Joan Leslie) of the town's wealthiest landowner (John Russell), who wants the mine for himself. Based upon the novel *Silver Rock* by Luke Short.

Here Come the Jets (1959)

20th Century–Fox. D: Gene Fowler, Jr. An alcoholic Korean War veteran (Steve Brodie) is hired as a test pilot to fly a new commercial airliner, despite repeated personal setbacks and problems with the aircraft prototype. No copy of the film could be found to review for this book.

I Was a Communist for the F.B.I. (1951)

Warner Bros. D: Gordon Douglas. This true story of Matt Cvetic (Frank Lovejoy), an F.B.I. undercover agent who infiltrated several Communist groups in America and reported their activities, focuses on the turmoil surrounding Cvetic's personal life, as his immediate family remain unaware of his true beliefs. At one point, a Communist official who visits the Pittsburgh area tells his comrades that North Korea is poised to invade South Korea and that the job of the U.S. Communists is to complain about the war and American leadership, thereby "softening up" the populace for a change in government.

Jet Over the Atlantic (1959)

Inter-Continent. D: Byron Haskin. A plane (not a jet) flying to New York is threatened by a fire bomb placed in its luggage hold by a suicidal man (George Macready). Among the other passengers is a Korean War vet (Guy Madison) who has been convicted of murder and is being extradited to the U.S. for execution, and the woman who loves him (Virginia Mayo). Guarding both, and arranging for an in-flight wedding of the two, is a gruff but sensitive detective (George Raft). When the pilots are killed by poison gas from the bomb, it is up to the Korean War veteran to safely land the plane in New York.

Killing of a Chinese Bookie (1976)

Faces. D: John Cassavetes. A Korean War veteran who operates an urban strip-club (Ben Gazzara) is forced by debt to undertake a murder for the local underworld. He survives the dangerous hit due in part to his military training. Cassavetes' empathy for urban lowlifes is compelling, but the strip-club is without doubt the sorriest ever seen in a major movie.

The Last Picture Show (1971)

Columbia. D: Peter Bogdanovich. Life in the dusty Texas town of Anarene is unexciting and dull for the town's young people (Timothy Bottoms, Jeff Bridges and Cybill Shepherd) who have just graduated high school and must now enter adulthood. The passing of the town's leading citizen (Ben Johnson) signals an end to an era; one of the young men (Bridges) leaves Anarene behind for the battlefields of Korea.

The Lieutenant Wore Skirts (1956)

20th Century–Fox. D: Frank Tashlin. A U.S. Air Force reservist (Tom Ewell) is recalled to duty during the Korean War era, but excused due to his bad leg. His wife (Sheree North), a WAF, re-enlists at the same time. His efforts to get her mustered out of service provide the film's slapstick comedy.

Mission Inferno (1984)

Video City Prod. D: Unknown. This straight-to-video release is listed in older VideoHound Golden Movie Retriever volumes as "The ups and downs of a hot-blooded Korean War commando taking revenge, escaping prison, fighting and just plain making war," but no copy of the film could be found to review for this book.

The Prophecy (1995)

Dimension. D: Gregory Widen. The archangel Gabriel (Christopher Walken) attempts to incite a war among angels and destroy the humans who have "an elevated place" in God's domain. He is opposed by a New York priest-turned-detective (Elias Koteas) and a good angel (Eric Stoltz) who destroys the body of the perfect human evil soul, a Korean War general disgraced for committing cannibalism. Good and evil battle in the desert of the American southwest.

Ride the High Iron (1956)

Columbia. D: Don Weis. An ambitious Korean War veteran (Don Taylor) disguises his humble origins and is hired as a public relations man. He falls in love with a society girl (Sally Forrest) and eventually must confess who he really is. No copy of the film could be found to review for this book.

Shock Corridor (1963)

Allied Artists. D: Samuel Fuller. A journalist (Peter Breck) is admitted to a mental institution as a patient to unmask the identity of a killer. Of course, after a few months with the insane, the reporter goes a bit nutty himself. One of the patients (James Best) is a Korean War veteran who became a Communist sympathizer during the war and who encountered nothing but hate upon returning to America. When his own father spit on him for accepting Communism, he retreated into a fantasy world and assumed the identity of Confederate general Jeb Stuart. A powerful, challenging film, arguably Samuel Fuller's best.

A Step Out of Line (1971, TVM)

Cinema Center 100. D: Bernard McEveety. Three middle-aged friends and Korean War veterans (Peter Falk, Vic Morrow and Peter Lawford) are having a tough time keeping financially afloat in 1970 and decide to pool their dormant military skills in order to rob a bank. The action rejuvenates them and reminds the men that life is still worth living.

They Still Call Me Bruce (1987)

New World. D: James Orr, Johnny Yune. A mild comedy in which a Korean man (Johnny Yune) travels to Houston, Texas, searching for the American G.I. who saved his life when he was a youngster during the Korean War. Along the way, he becomes embroiled with gangsters, involved in a martial arts contest and befriends a young American orphan (David Mendenhall).

A Thousand Men and a Baby (1997, TV Movie) (aka Narrow Escape)

Finnegan-Pichuk Prod. D. Marcus Cole. This true story chronicles the rescue of a Korean/American baby near the end of the war by the crew of the U.S.S. Point Cruz, and their efforts to find a home for the tot in America. Richard Thomas, Gerald McRaney and Jonathon Banks star. No copy of the film could be found to review for this book.

Thunderbolt and Lightfoot (1974)

Warner Bros. D. Michael Cimino. A Korean War veteran (Clint Eastwood) uses skills learned in the army to rob a bank in the northwest U.S. He is aided by his former co-horts in crime (George Kennedy and Geoffrey Lewis) as well as a necomer to thievery (Jeff Bridges, who received an Oscar nomination for his performance).

Welcome to Arrow Beach (1974)

Warner Bros. D: Laurence Harvey. A hitchhiking teenager (Meg Foster) is given a place to stay by a murderous, cannibalistic Korean War veteran (Laurence Harvey) and his sister (Joanna Pettet). She discovers his madness and escapes, but when the police (John Ireland and Stuart Whitman) don't believe her story, she returns to the house for evidence. This is the first film to feature Korean War cannibalism; it was followed by The Prophecy.

We're Not Married (1952)

20th Century–Fox. D: Edmund Goulding. In the fifth of five stories concerning marriages that technically never took place, a soldier on his way to Korea (Eddie Bracken) goes AWOL in order to remarry his wife (Mitzi Gaynor), who is pregnant. He is eventually caught and sent to Korea before fixing the problem, but the couple is married by radio as he sails to Korea. This is the most serious of the five comic episodes, the liveliest of which features a swimsuited Marilyn Monroe.

The Wonsan Operation (1978)

Toho/Video Action. D: Terrence Sul. This Japanese-made espionage thriller posits that rumors of bubonic plague during the Korean War might persuade General MacArthur to withdraw U.N. troops from combat. A commando party raids a field hospital in Wonsan to determine whether the plague rumors are true. This film is dubbed in English, but like The Canon Operation, it was only released in America on videotape. Both are awful.

A Yank in Indo-China (1952)

Columbia. D: Wallace A. Grissell. Two American pilots (John Archer, Douglas Dick) operate an air freight service in Indo-China during the time of the Korean War, but find themselves battling Communist agents more often than flying. Backed by United Nations forces, the two pilots rescue two women and destroy an enemy base before escaping from what would later become Vietnam. No copy of the film could be found to review for this book.

APPENDIX F: DOCUMENTARY AND COMPILATION FILMS

Anyone who wants to see what really happened in Korea (as opposed to the Hollywood versions) is encouraged to view some of the documentary and compilation films about the war, which have steadily multiplied over the past half-century. These films are comprised of footage photographed on the spot, while the conflict was occurring. There is no better way to get an authentic feel for the war than to watch a range of these short non-fiction films. The bulk of the titles on this non-comprehensive list are provided by Paul M. Edwards in his book *A Guide to Films on the Korean War.*

Air Power (1960) B&W. 30 minutes.
Another Ann Arbor: An Interview with Robert Fletcher (1990) C. 30 minutes.
Battle for Korea (2001) C/B&W. Malin Film and TV. 110 minutes.
Bloody Korea: The Real Story (1996) C/B&W. Dane Hansen Productions. 60 minutes.
Can India Bring Peace to Korea? (1952) B&W. Junior Press. 30 minutes.
Carrier Action Off Korea (1954) B&W. International History Films. 14 minutes.
Cassino to Korea (1950) B&W. Paramount News. 60 minutes. Narrated by Quentin Reynolds and Jackson Beck.
The Chopper War (1991) C. Star Home Video. 50 minutes.
Chosin to Sanhi (1988) C/B&W. U.S. Marine Corps. 60 minutes.
Combat Pilots: The Air Force Story (No year listed) C/B&W. Ferde Grofe Films. 450 minutes. Four video cassette series of pilots in action.
Dateline-1950: Korea (1989) B&W. MTI Films. 23 minutes.

Douglas MacArthur—Supreme Commander Pacific Theater (1961) C. Time-Life. 62 minutes.
Eighth Army in Korea (1963) B&W. 57 minutes.
Eighth Army—Shield of the Free World (1960) B&W. 30 minutes.
Eighth U.S. Army (1980) B&W. International Historical Video. 56 minutes.
A Fighting Lady Speaks (1950) B&W. 9 minutes.
Fighting Sabre Jets (1988) C/B&W. Aviation Library. 48 minutes.
Fire—Artillery Action in Korea (1952) B&W. 14 minutes.
The First Forty Days (1950) B&W. U.S. Army. 26 minutes.
Floating Fortress (1952/1982) B&W. 14 minutes.
Forgotten Heroes: The U.S. Marines in Korea (1994) Dane Hansen Productions. 60 minutes.
The Forgotten War: Korea 1950-1953 (1996) Marathon Music and Video. 7 cassettes. Seven separate documentaries in a box set. 294 minutes.
Go for Broke: Men in War (1987) C/B&W. 2 video cassettes. 197 minutes.
Heartbreak Ridge (1955) C. Tudor Pictures. In French with English subtitles. 86 minutes. Nominee for a best documentary feature Academy Award.
Hell for Leathernecks (1980/1987) C. Ferde Grofe Films. 60 minutes.
Hell Over Korea (1984) C. Ferde Grofe Films. 100 minutes.
Ike Goes to Korea (1960/1969) C/B&W. Pathé News. 5 minutes.
Korea (1959) B&W. D: John Ford. No time listed.
Korea (1991) C. Time-Life. *War in Peace* series. 41 minutes.

Korea, After the War (1954) National Film Board of Canada. 15 minutes.

Korea — Battleground for Liberty (1961) C. 48 minutes.

Korea: MacArthur's War (1988) C/B&W. MPI Home Video. 54 minutes.

Korea: Medal of Honor (1993) B&W. Cabin Fever. 30 minutes.

Korea: The Air Force Story (1980/1989) B&W. Boomerang. 42 minutes.

Korea: The Chosin Reservoir (1991) C/B&W. Cabin Fever. 46 minutes.

Korea: The Coldest War, 1950–1953 (1991) C. 60 minutes.

Korea: The Final Phase, 1950–1953 (1960) B&W. U.S. Air Force. 15 minutes.

Korea: The Forgotten War (1987) C/B&W. Fox Hills Video. 92 minutes. Narrated by Robert Stack.

Korea: The Unknown War (1988) C/B&W. Thames Television. 53 minutes. This was originally a six hour telecast; later condensed to a single videotape.

Korea: The Untold Story (1988) C/B&W. Pyramid Films. 34 minutes.

Korea: Tribute to the Forgotten Heroes (1993) C/B&W. TSM Productions. 97 minutes.

Korea: U.S. News and World Report (1991) C. 48 minutes.

Korea: War at the 38th Parallel (1989) C/B&W. Sterling Group. 140 minutes. A two cassette set.

Korean Armistice (1959) B&W. 27 minutes.

The Korean Conflict (1980) C/B&W. Viking Video Classics. 54 minutes.

Korean Jet Aces (1989) C/B&W. Simitar. 30 minutes.

The Korean War (1988) C/B&W. Coronet Films. 46 minutes.

The Korean War (1993) B&W. Films for the Humanities. 30 minutes.

The Korean War: A Motion Picture History of the Korean War (1986) C/B&W. 45 minutes.

Korean War Combat Bulletins (1950–1951) B&W. U.S. Army

    #101"Korea Battles for Time" (1950) 7/10–8/10, 1950. 22 minutes.

    #102"Korea Turning the Tide" (1950) 8/10–9/20, 1950. 22 minutes.

    #103"Korea U.N. Offensive" (1950) 9/20–10/20, 1950. 22 minutes.

    #104"Chinese Reds Enter the War" (1951) 10/20–11/20, 1950. 21 minutes.

    #105"U.N. Forces Escape Trap" (1951) 11/20–12/10, 1950. 16 minutes.

    #106"U.N. Forces Consolidate Below the 38th Parallel" (1951) 12/20, 1950 –1/20, 1951. 20 minutes.

    #107"U.N. Forces Move North" (1951) 1/20–2/20, 1951. 17 minutes.

    #108"Operation Killer" (1951) 2/20–3/20, 1951. 18 minutes.

    #109"U.N. Forces Cross the 38th Parallel" (1951) 3/20–4/20, 1951. 19 minutes.

    #110"Reds Launch Spring Offensive" (1951) 4/20–5/20, 1951. 15 minutes.

    #111"U.N. Counterattack" (1951) 5/20–6/20, 1951. 16 minutes.

    #112"Korean Cease-Fire Talks" (1951) 6/20–7/20, 1951. 18 minutes.

    #113"Stalemate in Korea" (1951) 7/20–8/20, 1951. 18 minutes.

Korean War: Fire and Ice (1999) C/B&W. History Channel. 4 parts. No time listed.

Korean War: Stalemate of Truce; Truce; To the North; The Omens of War (1992) C/B&W. White Star. 95 minutes.

Korean War Stories (2001) C/B&W. 56 minutes. Narrated by Walter Cronkite.

Korean War — The Big Picture (1959) B&W. 3 parts. 29 minutes each.

    Part 1. The military buildup for the war, narrated by Jim Lucas.

    Part 2. The history of the war, narrated by William H. Lawrence.

    Part 3. The final phase of the war, narrated by General S. L. A. Marshall.

MacArthur (1999) C/B&W. WGBH Boston. No time listed. Narrated by David Ogden Stiers.

The MacArthur Story (1951) B&W. No time listed.

The MacArthur Story (1964) B&W. 20 minutes.

MacArthur's War With Truman (1990) C. Zenger Video. No time listed.

Meeting the Red Challenge (1950) B&W. U.S. Air Force. 15 minutes.

Memory/All Echo (1991) C/B&W. Women Make Movies. 28 minutes.

Men of the Fighting Lady (1991) C. MGM. Production notes. No time listed.

Men with a Mission (1968) C/B&W. U.S. Army. 28 minutes.

MiG Alley (1989) C/B&W. Parade. 30 minutes.

MiG Alley (1990) C/B&W. MPI Video. 60 minutes.

A Motion Picture History of the Korean War (1958) B&W. 58/45/60 minutes.

National Air and Space Museum (1988) C/B&W. Smithsonian Institution. Laserdisc set of some fifty thousand photographs of wartime and peacetime.

Navy Log (1956) Forum Home. 50 minutes. Martin Milner, James Lyndon and George Conrad star.

One Who Came Back (1951) B&W. Disabled American Veterans. 21 minutes.

On to the Yalu, June 1950 (1959) B&W. U.S. Air Force. 15 minutes.

Operation Inchon (1952) B&W. 18/20 minutes.

P.O.W. (1961) B&W. CBS News. 27 minutes. Narrated by Walter Cronkite.

P.O.W. Americans in Enemy Hands (1987) C. Arnold Shapiro Productions. 93 minutes.

Proudly We Hail (1990) C. Bridgestone Group. 55 minutes. Narrated by Robert Stack.

Reunion (1973) C. 30 minutes.

Sabre Jet Pilot (1986) C. Combat Video. English subtitles. 90 minutes.

Sea Power: The Story of the U.S. Navy (No year listed) C/B&W. No time listed.

See It Now (1952) B&W. CBS News. 60 minutes.

Seventh Infantry Division (1949) B&W. 22 minutes.

That War in Korea (1966) B&W. NBC Films. 77 minutes.

The Third Infantry Division (1971) C. 29 minutes.

The 38th Parallel Korean Conflict (1988) C. Simitar Video. 30 minutes.

This is Korea! (1951) B&W. U.S. Navy. 50 minutes. Directed by John Ford. Released theatrically by Republic Pictures.

Thunder Out of Asia (1966) B&W. Screen News Digest. 14 minutes.

To Help Peace Survive (1974) C. 27 minutes.

Truman and the Korean War (1969) B&W. TVT. 18 minutes.

Truman and the Policy of Containment (1975) B&W. Chelsea House Productions. 2 video tapes. 9 minutes each.

The Truman Era Through the Korean War (1984) B&W. Chelsea House Productions. 72 minutes.

Truman vs. Korea: Clash Over Korea (1964) B&W. Films, Inc. 25 minutes.

The Twenty-Fourth Infantry Division (1971) C. 28 minutes.

U.N.: Korea 1950 (1994) Granada TV. C/B&W. 20 minutes.

U.S. Navy SEALs: Evolution of the Teams (1990) C. 90 minutes.

U.S.A. Wars: Korea (1991) Quanta Press. Laserdisc of 1071 photographs, oral interviews and narratives about the war.

Uneasy Peace and the Cold War, 1946-1956 (1965) 2 Filmstrips. 49 Frames each.

United Nations Campaign in Northeast Korea (1952) B&W. 25 minutes.

The Universal Video Yearbook Korean War (1988) C/B&W. 60 minutes.

War and Peace in the Nuclear Age (1988) C. Annenberg. 60 minutes.

War in Korea: The Dawn of the Fifties (1984) Thomas S. Klise Co. Filmstrip.

The War Remembered (1995) Courage Productions. 34 minutes.

Wars in Peace: Korea, Vietnam (1995) Central Park Media. 80 minutes.

The Weapon of Choice (1988) C. 60 minutes.

Why Korea? (1950) B&W. 20th Century–Fox. 30 minutes. Winner of an Academy Award for best documentary short subject.

With the Canadians in Korea (1952) B&W. 16 minutes.

With the Marines: Chosin to Hungnam (1951) B&W. TVT. 43 minutes.

This is an admittedly incomplete list, but should provide interested viewers with a solid starting point. In addition to the listed documentaries and compilations, a great many short films have been produced by the armed services regarding their operations. The films listed here are, or have been, publicly available. Contact your local library for more details.

APPENDIX G: SOUTH KOREAN FILMS ABOUT THE KOREAN WAR

Compiled by Darcy Paquet, Institute of Foreign Language Studies, Korea University, Seoul
www.Koreanfilm.org

Fifty years after the start of hostilities, the Korean War remains far from being forgotten by those who live on the Korean peninsula. With millions of people killed and separated from their families and the country reduced to rubble, the war left a permanent scar on Korea's culture. Indeed, North and South are still technically at war, as a peace treaty has never been signed. Over the years, the medium of film has acted as a key weapon in efforts to interpret and preserve in memory the events of the war, for both the South Korean military government and individual filmmakers with differing agendas. For an overview of the qualities and scope of Korean War films, this list has been compiled as a reference.

A quick introduction to the evolution of Korean War films:

The 1950s

The Korean War began on June 25, 1950, and continued until 1953. During the war itself there were very few feature films produced; those that were tended to focus on raising morale for the war effort. By 1954 the industry began its recovery with the help of American-donated equipment, and by the late 1950s the film industry was booming. A large number of war films were produced at this time, primarily action films. *Piagol* (1956) is considered to be the most famous war film of the decade, and one of the classics of Korean film.

The 1960s

The 1960s witnessed both the golden age of Korean film as well as increased interference in the film industry by the military government. A number of films from this period take a more humanistic approach, focusing on the tragedies of war. Nonetheless filmmakers were constrained in how far they could go: popular filmmaker Lee Man-hee was arrested in 1965 and his film *Seven Women Prisoners* was banned for portraying Communists in too positive a light. The government utilized film as a tool for propagating its own views of the war and preventing alternative viewpoints from reaching the screen. An award was even established as part of the government-sponsored Grand Bell Awards to reward the most strongly anti-Communist film of each year.

The 1970s

The 1970s ushered in an age of much stricter government censorship, and in this environment, film censors indicated a clear preference for certain genres of films, namely: traditional costume dramas, films about adolescence, soft porn, and war films. These war films generally feature a simpler moral framework than the works of the previous decade, and they were crafted chiefly for entertainment purposes.

The 1980s and 1990s

Most consider the 1980s to be a period of artistic renewal for the Korean film industry. Although censorship remained an issue, several complex and thought-provoking films opened up new, personal perspectives on the war, in particular Bae Chang-ho's *Warm Winter Was Gone*, Im Kwon-taek's *Gilsottom*, and Lee Jang-ho's *The Man with Three Coffins*. A gradual loosening of government censorship starting in 1988 allowed filmmakers to cover topics that were previously off-limits, in particular: the fate of leftist partisans from the South who fought for the Communist army (*Partisans of South Korea; The Taebaek Mountains*); critical portrayals of U.S. troop presence in Korea (*Silver Stallion; Spring in My Hometown*); and sympathetic portrayals of North Korean soldiers (*Shiri; Joint Security Area*). Although financial pressures have replaced government interference as a key constraint on the filmmaking process, the past two decades have allowed for a more detailed and somewhat more balanced portrait of the war to emerge.

The following is not an exhaustive list, as there were a staggering number of movies made from the 1950s to the 1970s that utilized the war as a backdrop. Instead, the most famous and respected of the Korean War movies are included, as well as a few of the more conventional films which are largely forgotten today. Unfortunately, access to films from the North is limited, and so they are not included in this reference. Films are listed in reverse chronological order, with the most recent listed first.

Address Unknown (2001)

["Su-chui-in-bul-myung"] Director: Kim Ki-duk. Starring Yang Dong-keun, Ban Min-jung, Kim Young-min, Jo Je-hyun and Pang Eun-jin. 117 min.

A group of adolescents growing up adjacent to a U.S. military base struggle with the continuing legacy of the war. A young girl becomes romantically involved with an American soldier who promises to pay for an operation on her eye. A wounded veteran regrets never having received his rightful medal. A half-Korean man is despised for his racial background, while his mother continues to write letters to her son's father in the U.S., despite the fact that they all come back stamped "Address Unknown."

Joint Security Area (2000)

["Kong-dong-gyung-bi-gu-yeok JSA"] Director: Park Chan-wook. Starring Lee Young-ae, Song Kang-ho, Lee Byung-hun and Shin Ha-kyun. 107 min. Awards: Best Film, Best Actor, and Audience Prize at the 2001 Deauville Asian Film Festival; 1st Runner Up for Best Film at the 2001 Seattle International Film Festival. World distribution: Japan (2001).

Set in the present day. Shooting breaks out at the truce village of Panmunjom, leaving two North Korean soldiers dead. With North and South holding widely diverging views of what happened, the two countries agree to have a neutral Swiss officer conduct an inquiry. Her investigation leads her past a string of false testimony to uncover a secret friendship that existed across the border.

Shiri (1999)

["Shi-ri"] Director: Kang Jae-gyu. Starring Han Suk-kyu, Choi Min-shik, Kim Yoon-jin and Song Kang-ho. 124 min. World distribution: U.S. (2001), Hong Kong (1999), Japan (2000), Spain (2000), etc. Available on DVD and VCD with English subtitles.

The best-selling Korean movie of all time. Set in the present day, a team of North Korean commandos intercept a high-tech weapon from the South Korean military and make plans to ignite a war. This film has been praised for putting a more human face onto soldiers from the North.

Spring in My Hometown (1998)

["A-reum-da-un Shi-jeol"] Director: Lee Kwangmo. Starring Ahn Sung-ki, Lee In, Bae Yoo-jung and Yoo Oh-sung. 113 min. Awards: Gold Prize at the 11th Tokyo Film Festival; best film, best director and best cinematography at the 36th Grand Bell Awards. Available on DVD and VCD with English subtitles.

Lee Kwangmo's debut feature about life in a small village during the war. Seen mostly through the eyes of a young boy, the film portrays the changes wrought by the war and by the presence of a nearby U.S. military base. The fighting itself remains offscreen throughout the film. In 1998, this became the first Korean film to screen in the Director's Fortnight section at the Cannes Film Festival.

The Taebaek Mountains (1994)

["T'ae-baek-san-maek"] Director: Im Kwon-taek. Starring Ahn Sung-ki, Kim Myung-gon, Kim Kap-soo, Shin Hyun-june, Oh Jung-hye and Bang Eun-jin. 168 min. Awards: Special Jury Prize and best actor (Kim Kap-soo) at the 33rd Grand Bell Awards.

Based on a famous and controversial Korean novel by Cho Jeong-rae, this 168-minute epic chronicles a guerilla campaign waged by pro-leftist forces both before and during the war. Based on real events, the film centers around Mt. Jiri in southwestern Korea, which provided a natural refuge for the leftist rebels. Veteran director Im Kwon-taek interweaves the experiences of a wide variety of characters to give a more balanced portrait of the conflict than earlier films made under the military government can provide.

Two Flags (Manmubang) (1994)

["Man-mu-bang"] Director: Aum Jong Sun. Starring Chang Dong-hwi, Yoon Jung-hee and Kim Hyung-il. 101 min. Awards: best actress (Yoon Jung-hee) and editing at the 32nd Grand Bell Awards; best film at the Miami Film Festival.

A remote mountain cottage near the 38th parallel is caught in the midst of battle. The owner, a woman who lives alone, flies either the flag of the North or the South, depending on which army advances closer. At this time, two men arrive at the cottage and the woman agrees to give them refuge. Her home, however, then becomes the scene of a new kind of struggle.

To the Starry Island (1993)

["Keu Som-ae Ka-go-ship-ta"] Director: Park

Kwang-soo. Starring Moon Sung-keun, Ahn Sung-ki and Shim Hye-jin. 101 min.

When a man attempts to bring the body of his father to his native island for burial, the local inhabitants protest angrily and prevent the coffin from coming ashore. Gradually we learn the events that took place on the island during the war, which implicate the recently deceased father in a crime against the community. Director Park Kwang-soo has called this work a study of the potential for Korea to heal from its past wounds and achieve reconciliation.

Silver Stallion (1991)

["Eun-ma-neun O-ji An-neun-da"] Director: Jang Kil-soo. Starring Lee Hye-sook, Kim Bo-yeon, Jun Mu-song and Son Chang-min. 123 min. Awards: best actress and screenplay at the 15th Montreal Film Festival; presented at the 44th Cannes Film Festival.

A young widow in a rural village is raped by a U.S. soldier from a nearby base. Shunned by the narrowly traditional inhabitants of her village, she and her two young children are driven into poverty. Finally she decides to work at "Texas Town," a prostitution district that caters to U.S. soldiers, bringing her into direct conflict with her fellow townspeople.

Partisans of South Korea (1990)

["Nam-bu-gun"] Director: Chung Ji-young. Alternative title: *North Korea's Southern Army*. Starring Ahn Sung-ki, Choi Min-soo, Choi Jin-shil and Lee Hye-young. 157 min. Awards: best director, best actor (Ahn Sung-ki) and best supporting actor (Choi Min-soo) at the 11th Blue Dragon (Chungryong) Awards.

Lee Tae, a leftist reporter living in South Korea at the outbreak of hostilities, joins a partisan army and participates in guerilla warfare against U.N. and South Korean troops. In the course of fighting he befriends a young poet and falls in love with a former nurse who treats his injury. As the fortunes of the partisans turn for the worse, Lee is forced to struggle for his very survival. Screenplay by director Jang Sun-woo (*Lies*).

The Man with Three Coffins (1987)

["Na-geu-ne-neun Kil-e-seo-do Sui-ji An-neun-da"] Director: Lee Jang-ho. Literal title: "Travelers Don't Rest, Even on the Road." Starring Kim Myong-gon and Lee Bo-hee. 104 min. World distribution: Japan (1988). Presented at the 38th Berlin International Film Festival and the 2nd Tokyo International Film Festival.

A challenging and beautiful film that weaves together historical traces of the war with native shamanist imagery to portray the experiences of a divided nation. The nurse of a dying company chairman agrees to undertake a journey to the old man's hometown, which is now located just to the north or south of the DMZ. Pursued by henchmen of the old man's son, a politician who does not want word of this leaked to the press, they encounter a man carrying the ashes of his wife. This man seems to bring death upon any women to whom he becomes close. The war is never in the foreground of this film; however, it is a key aspect of its themes.

Gilsottom (1986)

["Gil-so-tteum"] Director: Im Kwon-taek. Starring Kim Ji-mi, Shin Sung-il, Han So-ryong and Choi Bul-am. 105 min. World distribution: West Germany (1986), U.S. (1987), Japan (1991). Presented at the 36th Berlin Film Festival. Awards: best film and actress (Kim Ji-mi) at the 24th Grand Bell Awards.

Many families were separated during the war. These separated family members are often unaware if their loved ones are living on the opposite side of the DMZ, or if they live somewhere in the same country. In the mid-1980's, a television-sponsored drive to locate lost family members reunited many families in the South. This film takes place amidst this setting, where a woman travels to Seoul and is reunited with her old lover. The two have since remarried, but they undertake a search together to locate their lost son. Eventually they contact a man who may or may not be their son. They decide to undergo DNA testing to determine their relation, but in the course of their acquaintance, wide gaps in their social status and backgrounds cause tension among the three.

Warm Winter Was Gone (1984)

["Keu Hae Kyeo-ur-eun Dda-ddeut-haet-ne"] Director: Bae Chang-ho. Literal title: "That Year's Winter Was Warm." Starring Ahn Sung-ki, Lee Mi-sook, Yoo Ji-in and Han Jin-hee. 120 min. Awards: Special Prize at the 6th Three Continents Film Festival; best actress (Lee Mi-sook) at the 23rd Grand Bell Awards.

The story of two sisters who are separated as children during the war. Their various experiences lead them to encounter sharply contrasting fates in the years hence. As their lives intertwine they become acquainted with each other, without realizing their familial ties.

North and South (1984)

["Nam-gwa Buk"] Director: Kim Gi. Starring Yoo Young-guk, Kim Man and Won Mi-kyung. 110 min.

A Communist general named Jang surrenders to the South at the front line of war. A captain named Lee interrogates Jang, but the general will only agree to talk if efforts are made to locate his wife. Lee investigates and discovers that Jang's lost wife is his own wife, Eun-ah. A remake of the 1965 classic film of the same name.

Rainy Days (1979)

["Jang-ma"] Director: Yu Hyun-mok. Starring Lee Dae-geun, Hwang Jung-soon, Kim Seok-hoon and Kim Shin-jae. 114 min. World distribution: Japan (1991). Presented at the 4th Saõ Paulo International Film Festival.

During the war, a small village is caught in the midst of fighting. A family is torn apart when a son from one side of the family chooses to fight for the North, while one from the other side enlists with the South. Tensions grow between relatives until death causes a rupture in the family. This film, told mostly through the eyes of a young boy, is best remembered for the figure of the grandmother, who achieves a sort of reconciliation at the end by means of a shamanist act. Based on a famous novel by Yoon Heung-gil.

Jun-Woo's Last Words (1979)

["Jonu-ga Nam-gin Han-madi"] Director: Lee Won-se. Starring Jin Bong-jin, Jang Hyuk and Jun Young-sun. 105 min. World distribution: Asia, Africa (1980).

Peak 598, an important strategic point, is lost 39 times and recaptured 40 times in the course of the war. The North Korean army builds a natural fortress into the mountain, and a special suicide squad from the South is given the task of infiltrating and detonating the base. After numerous difficulties they enter a cave with a 60 degree downward slope, where they leave a time bomb and attempt to escape.

Last Day at Mt. Dosol (1977)

["Dosolsan Ch'oe-hu-ui Nal"] Director: Sol Tae-ho. Starring Hwang Hae, Jang Hyuk and Jin Bong-jin. 118 min. World distribution: Various countries (1979).

Lieutenant Kang's platoon is surrounded by the enemy, but he is saved by the platoon led by his friend Lieutenant Han. Together the two men come across a warehouse and rescue Su-Hyang, who is about to be raped by the enemy. Han falls in love with her, but shortly thereafter his plane crashes and he is taken prisoner by the enemy. Kang, believing his friend to be dead, asks Su-Hyang to marry him. A great battle follows at Mt. Dosol, where Han escapes but is killed by the enemy. Stricken with grief, Su-Hyang enters a convent with the tacit consent of Lt. Kang.

13-Year-Old Boy (1974)

["Ship-sam-sae So-nyun"] Director: Shin Sang-ok. Starring Shin Sung-il, Kim Jung-hoon and Na Ha-young. 85 min.

Second Lieutenant Kang, leading a mobile unit during the war, attacks a village to the rear of enemy territory. While there he comes into contact with a 13-year old boy who resists him at first, but eventually becomes his friend. One day Kang's unit comes under serious attack from the enemy, and the boy is hit by enemy fire. Screaming, Kang takes the boy in his arms...

Testimony (1973)

["Jeung On"] Director: Im Kwon-taek. Starring Shin Il-ryung, Kim Chang-sook and Kim Hee-ra. 125 min. World distribution: Hong Kong (1987). Awards: best actress (Kim Chang-sook) at the 20th Asian Film Festival.

A feature film shot on a grand scale and given a large release. Second Lieutenant Jang has a date with his girlfriend Sun-ah, when suddenly North Korean bombers attack Seoul on the first day of the war. This film recounts the progression of the war from Sun-ah's perspective.

Private First Class Kim (1969)

["Yuk-gun Kim-il-byung"] Director: Shin Sang-ok. Starring Shin Young-kyun, Choi Eun-hee and Nam Jung-im. Awarded the Editing Prize at the 15th Asia-Pacific Film Festival.

Nonsan Training Center receives a new batch of recruits. Among them are Sung-chil from a rural area; a university student Nam-chun; and prospective singer Du-seop. They finish their difficult training and are stationed in the same corps. The film goes on to show the various things they experience in their time together.

Mountain Fire (1967)

["San-bul"] Director: Kim Su-yong. Starring Shin Young-kyun and Do Geum-bong. 80 min. Presented at the 17th Berlin Film Festival.

An affair develops between a fugitive Communist soldier and a woman in a remote mountain village. This film is renowned for its erotic tension and fine cinematography, especially in the bamboo groves. From a key figure in 1960s Korean cinema.

Major Kang Jae-Gu (1966)

["So-ryung Kang Jae-gu"] Director: Go Yong-nam. Starring Shin Sung-il and Ko Eun-ah. 111 min. World distribution: U.S. (1967). Presented at the 5th San Francisco Film Festival.

About a heroic graduate of the military academy who saves the lives of his fellow soldiers when a practice drill involving hand grenades goes fatally wrong.

A Brave Soldier Without Serial Number (1966)

["Kun-bon-eom-neun Yong-sa"] Director: Lee Man-hee. Starring Shin Sung-il and Moon Jeong-suk. 121 min. World distribution: Japan (1967). Awards: Winner of the Anti-Communism Award at 5th Grand Bell Awards, and the Freedom Award at the 13th Asia-Pacific Film Festival.

A tale of two brothers—the older, who commands a flying corps in the Ma Shik Lyeong Mountains; and the younger, an official in the Department of Defense. After denouncing his father as a reactionary, the younger is tormented by guilt, and eventually volunteers to serve in the Air Force under his brother.

A Soldier Speaks After Death (1966)

["Byung-sa-neun Juk-eo-seo Mal-han-da"] Director: Kim Ki-young. Starring Shin Young-kyun. World distribution: Vietnam (1966).

From Kim Ki-young ("Mr. Monster"), the story of a general's son who works as a biologist. Upon being drafted, he gives his collection of flower seeds to his mother. At the front he joins a special attack unit which is ordered to destroy a bridge in enemy territory. After a heroic but costly mission, a cease-fire is called. Back at home, the colorful flowers bloom in his garden.

War and the Woman Teacher (1966)

["Jeon-jeng-gwa Yeo-gyo-sa"] Director: Im Kwon-taek. Starring Kim Jin-kyu and Eom Aeng-ran. 100 min. World distribution: Southeast Asia (1967).

A documentary based on the story of an elementary school teacher who is left behind enemy lines, unable to retreat. After learning of the movements of the Northern Army, she escapes to the South and informs the army of what she has learned. With this information it becomes possible to repel a Northern attack.

8240 KLO (1966)

["P'al-yi-sa-gong K.L.O"] Director: Chong Jin-woo. Starring Park Am and Nam Gung-won. 113 min. World distribution: Southeast Asia (1966). Awarded the Anti-Communism Prize at the 5th Grand Bell Awards.

During the war, the South Korean military receives word that the North is building a massive underground power plant. A special assignment is given to the 8240 K.L.O. military unit to destroy this plant. The members of the unit drop into North Korea, ready to sacrifice their lives to complete the mission.

Martyr (1965)

["Sun-gyo-ja"] Director: Yu Hyun-mok. Starring Kim Jin-kyu, Nam Gung-won and Chang Dong-hee.

Based on a novel by Korean-American writer Richard Kim (Kim Eun-Kuk), this film centers around both the war and the issue of religion. Fourteen ministers are taken away by Communist troops, and of them only two survive. The film presents the experiences of one of the survivors.

Seven Women Prisoners (1965)

["Ch'il-in-ui Yeo-p'o-ro"] Director: Lee Man-hee. Alternative title: The Returned Woman Soldier. Starring Moon Jung-sook, Ryu Kyu-sun and Lee Min-ja. After shooting this film, director Lee Man-hee was arrested and his film was banned for portraying Communists in a too positive light.

A North Korean army officer is placed in charge of seven medical officers who were captured in battle. When Chinese soldiers attempt to rape the women, he feels angry and kills the soldiers. He then leads the nurses to the border and defects to the South along with his men.

Inchon Landing Operation (1965)

["In-ch'on-sang-ryuk-jak-jun"] Director: Cho Gung-ha. Starring Shin Young-kyun, Kim Hye-jung and Yoon Il-bong. World distribution: Southeast Asia (1967).

In the midst of the Korean War, a female espionage agent sneaks into a South Korean military unit to obtain information about the U.N. army. While there she befriends an information officer named Captain Shin, and eventually she falls in love with him. At this point she tells him everything, and provides the military in the North with false information, allowing the U.N. army to conduct the Inchon landing operation successfully.

When That Day Comes (1965)

["Eon-je-na Keu-nal-i-myun"] Director: Cho Gung-ha. Starring Kim Hye-jung and Park Am. 100 min. World distribution: Japan, U.S. (1967).

The love between a young man and woman is complicated by their social background: she is the daughter of a devoted communist party member, while the other is the son of a feudal landowner. When war begins they are separated without any means of communication. The woman eventually crosses into the South and marries another man. Then one day, her old lover returns to her.

North and South (1965)

["Nam-gwa Buk"] Director: Kim Ki-duk. Starring Shin Young-kyun, Choi Moo-ryong and Eom Aeng-ran. 114 min. World distribution: Southeast Asia (1965). Awards: best tragedy at the 12th Asia-Pacific Film Festival. Screened at the 26th Venice Film Festival and the 9th San Francisco Film Festival.

A North Korean captain surrenders to a Southern division in hopes that he can locate his wife, who was separated from him in the midst of war. The commander of the Southern division realizes that the captain's lost wife is now married to him. He agonizes over the situation and finally decides to yield to the captain, volunteering for an assignment in a suicide squad.

Demilitarized Zone (1965)

["Bi-mu-jang-ji-dae"] Director: Park Sang-ho. Starring Cho Mi-ryung and Nam Gung-won. World distribution: Hong Kong, India, USA (1970). Awards: best film at the 13th Asia-Pacific Film Festival.

A young girl and boy are separated from their mother by the demilitarized zone. They decide to cross the border into South Korea, where they face many dangers in their quest to be reunited.

Red Muffler (1964)

["Bbal-gan Ma-hu-ra"] Director: Shin Sang-ok. Starring Shin Young-kyun, Choi Eun-hee and

Choi Mu-ryong. 100 min. World distribution: various countries (1964). Awards: best actor (Shin Young-kyun), best director, and best editing at the 11th Asia-Pacific Film Festival.

A story of the various air force pilots stationed at Kangneung Air Force Base during the war. Captain Na is a brave pilot with over 100 sorties on his record. A fellow soldier, who has married a bar hostess, dies in the war. A third soldier comforts the widow and begins to fall in love with her.

The Marines Who Never Returned (1963)

["Tor-a-o-ji An-neun Hae-byung"] Director: Lee Man-hee. Starring Jang Dong-hee, Choi Mu-ryung, Koo Bong-suh and Lee Dae-yeop. 110 min. World distribution: Malaysia, Taipei, USA (1964).

Follows a group of marines as they adopt an orphaned girl and eventually move to the front for a heroic but costly battle. Focuses on the brutality of war. Considered to be a classic of Korean film.

Five Marines (1961)

["O-in-ui Hae-byung"] Director: Kim Ki-duk. Starring Choi Mu-ryong, Shin Young-kyun and Hwang Hae. 118 min. World distribution: Taiwan (1962).

A commanding officer chooses five marines to form a special attack unit that will infiltrate enemy territory and detonate a powder magazine. The soldiers are successful in their objective, but are discovered by the enemy during their retreat. The debut film of Kim Ki-duk (not to be confused with the contemporary director).

The Defeat (1956)

["Gyuk-t'oe"] Director: Lee Kang-cheon. Starring Hwang Nam and Choi Bong. 80 min.

Recounts the real-life adventures of a Major Kim Man-Sul.

Piagol (1955)

["Pi-a-gol"] Director: Lee Kang-cheon. Starring Kim Jin-gyu and No Kyung-hee. 110 min.

An anti-Communist film which portrays the barbarity of the leftist guerillas who hid themselves on Mt. Jiri during the war. Conflicts arise among the guerillas due to the presence of a female soldier, while another soldier seeks to escape to find his freedom.

The Attack Order (1954)

["Ch'ul-gyuk-myung-ryung"] Director: Hong

Song-ki. Starring Yeom Mae-ri, Lee Jib-kil and Kim Il-hae.

Produced by the Korean Air Force. The first film to portray air combat in the Korean War. Two pilots fall in love with the same woman, and a rivalry develops. When one pilot is shot down by the enemy, however, the other risks his life to save him. Praised for its dynamic, realistic battle scenes.

Arirang (1954)

["A-ri-rang"] Director: Lee Gang-chon. Starring Heo Jang Kang and Kim Jae Seon. World distribution: Hong Kong (1957).

Borrows narrative elements from Na Un-gyu's classic Arirang (1926), but adapts the film to reflect the situation during the war and the division of Korea into North and South. A family conceals two American soldiers from the occupying forces of the North. A local Communist sympathizer discovers the soldiers and threatens to expose them unless the daughter, whom he has always admired, submits to his desire.

The Song of My Hometown (1954)

["Ko-hyang-ui No-rae"] Director: Yun Bong-chun. Starring Lee Sun-kyung, Kim Shin-jae. Awards: recipient of 4th Seoul City Cultural Award.

A young couple is separated by the war, the boy joining the army and the girl, an army nursing unit. They come to love each other more deeply through the hardships of war. After losing his leg in battle, the boy returns to his hometown to help with reconstruction. Director Yun made this film at the end of a long and distinguished career.

Songbul Temple (1952)

["Song-bul-sa"] Director: Yun Bong-chun. Starring Yoon Sang-hwa and Lee Bin-hwa in her debut role.

A young man wishes to avoid serving in the army, so he takes refuge in a Buddhist temple, claiming to be sick. The chief monk of the temple then persuades him to go back and enter the military. Shot during the war and used to rally support for the war effort.

NOTE: Readers wishing to find more information about Korean films before 1990 may consult *The History of Korean Cinema*, a work by Lee Young-il and Choe Young-chol which has been translated (quite badly) into English and published by Jimoondang Publishing Company.

BIBLIOGRAPHY

This bibliography is designed to help readers locate sources pertaining to the individual films discussed in the main text. Films are listed alphabetically, with relevant sources listed alphabetically following each film title.

Books are identified — in their initial listings only — by the publishing date and company, which are noted in parentheses. Book authors are listed after each title, where known, but again, only in their initial listings. Thus, later references to a book which has already been listed will be succinct, featuring only title and page number.

Magazines are identified by volume and issue, page number and author when known. Full information is provided for each magazine listing.

The final notation of each entry is the type of source: *review* indicates that an evaluation of the film is made, even if that evaluation is a simple star rating; *synopsis* indicates a description of the film, which might include background information; *listing* indicates capsulized facts about the film within the context of others, usually from the same studio; *profile* indicates biographical information about one of the film's participants; *remembrance* indicates a participant's recollection of the film's making or of its original source; *interview* indicates an interview with one or more participants in the film; *pictorial* indicates a photographic preview of the film, usually accompanied by brief text; *article* indicates a wider range of subjects to which the film is related in some way; *history* indicates information regarding the film's production and contextual place within the war film genre; *mention* indicates that the film is briefly mentioned or referred to in some way; *advertisement* indicates publicity for the film; and *source* indicates a published origination of the film, usually a novel, play or short story.

Some sources were used for almost all of the films. These include the Internet Movie Database, Leonard Maltin's *Movie and Video Guide*, *The Motion Picture Guide* by Jay Robert Nash and Stanley Ralph Ross, *Encyclopedia of American War Films* by Larry Langman and Ed Borg, *War Movies* by Brock Garland, *A Guide to Films on the Korean War* by Paul M. Edwards and the annual *Screen World* series, overseen by Daniel Blum and John Willis. The author appreciates these sources and recommends them. Besides this book, these are the most comprehensive sources for data about Korean War films.

The Korean Conflict: 1950–1953

Battle for Korea (1993, Combined) Robert J. Dvorchak history

Battle Hymn (1956, McGraw-Hill) Dean E. Hess remembrance

The Best Years of Their Lives: The National Service Experience 1945–1963 (1997, John Murray) Trevor Royle history

The Bridge at No Gun Ri (2001, Henry Holt) Charles J. Hanley, Sang-Hun Choe and Martha Mendoza history

Chosin: Heroic Ordeal of the Korean War (1994, Presidio) Eric Hammel history

The Coldest War (1990, Orion) James Brady remembrance

Decision in Korea (1954, McBride) Rutherford M. Poats history

Fighting Jets (1983, Time-Life) Bryce Walker history

Fire and Ice: The Korean War 1950–1953 (2000, Savas) Michael J. Varhola history

The Korean War (1967, Doubleday) Matthew B. Ridgway remembrance and history

The Korean War (1987, Touchstone) Max Hastings history

The Korean War (1999, Overlook) Michael Hickey history

Korean War Aces (Osprey Aircraft of the Aces 4) (1995, Osprey) Robert F. Dorr, Jon Lake and Warren Thompson history

MacArthur's War (2000, Free Press) Stanley Weintraub history

MASH: An Army Surgeon in Korea (1998, University Press of Kentucky) Otto F. Apel, Jr., M.D. remembrance with Pat Apel

The River and the Gauntlet (1982, Time Life) S. L. A. Marshall remembrance and history

The Three Day Promise: A Korean Soldier's Memoir (1989, Father and Son) Donald K. Chung, M.D. remembrance and history

Thunder in the Morning Calm (1992, Vanwell) Edward C. Meyers remembrance and history

Toy Soldiers (1991, McFarland) John A. Sullivan remembrance

21 Stayed (1955, Farrar, Straus and Cudahy) Virginia Pasley history

U.S. Army Uniforms of the Korean War (1992, Stackpole) Shelby Stanton history

War in Korea (1951, Doubleday) Marguerite Higgins remembrance and history

Air Strike (1955)

BFI Monthly Film Bulletin June, 1957 24:281 page 68 review

The Motion Picture Guide A-B (1985, Cinebooks) page 33 Jay Robert Nash and Stanley Ralph Ross review

Screen World 1956 Annual (1956, Biblo and Tannen) page 181 Daniel Blum listing

Variety July 13, 1955 Whit. review

All the Young Men (1960)

America September 10, 1960 103:24 pages 632–633 Moira Walsh review

BFI Monthly Film Bulletin October, 1960 27:321 page 141 review

Blacks in American Films and Television (1988, Garland) page 12 Donald Bogle article

The Cinema of Sidney Poitier (1980, A.S. Barnes) pages 58–59 Lester J. Keyser and Andre H. Ruszkowski review

The Columbia Checklist (1991, McFarland) page 8 #45 Len D. Martin listing

The Columbia Story (1989, Crown) page 236 Clive Hirschhorn synopsis

Encyclopedia of American War Films (1989, Garland) page 15 Larry Langman and Ed Borg synopsis

The Films of Alan Ladd (1981, Citadel) pages 237–238 Marilyn Henry and Ron De Sourdis review

The Great Combat Pictures (1990, Scarecrow) pages 16–17 James Robert Parish synopsis

A Guide to Films on the Korean War (1997, Greenwood) pages 54–55 Paul M. Edwards review

Hollywood Goes to War (1985, Gallery) page 109 Edward F. Dolan, Jr. mention

Ladd (1979, Berkley) pages 233–234 Beverly Linet profile

The Motion Picture Guide A-B page 48 review

New York Times March 4, 1959 34:5 Thomas M. Pryor article

New York Times August 27, 1960 8:6 Bosley Crowther review

New Yorker September 10, 1960 36:30 pages 78, 80 Whitney Balliett review

Newsweek September 5, 1960 56:10 page 72 review

Once Was Enough (1997, Citadel) pages 29–30 Douglas Brode profile

The Player (1984, Limelight) pages 109–110 Lillian Ross and Helen Ross profile

Saturday Review August 20, 1960 43:34 page 32 Arthur Knight review

Screen World 1961 Annual pages 92–93 listing

Sidney Poitier: The Long Journey (1981, Signet) pages 93–94 Carolyn H. Ewers profile

Strength for the Fight (1986, Free Press) pages 255–269, 390–391, 242 Bernard C. Nalty article and notes

This Life (1980, Ballantine) page 234 Sidney Poitier remembrance

Time August 29, 1960 76:9 page 45 review

VideoHound's War Movies (1999, Visible Ink) pages 458–459 Mike Mayo review

War Movies (1987, Facts on File) page 22 Brock Garland review

An Annapolis Story (1955)

The Allied Artists Checklist (1993, McFarland) pages 4–5 #8 Len D. Martin listing

BFI Monthly Film Bulletin October, 1955 22:261 page 152 review

Boxoffice March 26, 1955 66:22 page 1737 review

Encyclopedia of American War Films pages 24–25 synopsis

The Motion Picture Guide A-B page 76 review

New York Times April 9, 1955 8:2 Howard H. Thompson review

Screen World 1956 Annual page 52 listing

A Siegel Film (1993, Faber and Faber) pages 174–177 Don Siegel remembrance

Variety March 23, 1955 Whit. review

Back at the Front (1952)

BFI Monthly Film Bulletin April, 1953 20:231 page 57 review

Boxoffice October 4, 1952 61:23 page 1413 review

Film Daily review

A Guide to Films on the Korean War page 56 review

The Motion Picture Guide A-B page 119 review

Motion Picture Herald William R. Weaver review

Screen World 1953 Annual page 100 listing

Time October 20, 1952 60:16 pages 112, 114 review

Universal Pictures (1977, Arlington House) page 583 Michael G. Fitzgerald listing

The Universal Story (1983, Octopus) page 209 Clive Hirschhorn synopsis

Variety November 5, 1952 Brog. review

The Bamboo Prison (1954)

BFI Monthly Film Bulletin March, 1955 22:254 page 37 review

Boxoffice December 18, 1954 66:8 page 1672 review

The Columbia Checklist page 18 #105 listing
The Columbia Story page 200 synopsis
Encyclopedia of American War Films page 43 synopsis
Film Daily review
A Guide to Films on the Korean War pages 56–57 review
The Motion Picture Guide A-B page 133 review
Screen World 1956 Annual page 16 listing
Variety December 15, 1954 Brog. review

Battle Circus (1953)

America April 18, 1953 89:3 pages 87–88 Moira Walsh review
BFI Monthly Film Bulletin May, 1953 20:232 page 64 review
Bogart (1997, William Morrow) pages 461–464 A. M. Sperber and Eric Lax profile
Bogey: The Films of Humphrey Bogart (1979, Citadel) pages 168–169 Clifford McCarty review
Boxoffice January 31, 1953 62:14 page 1445 review
Christian Century April 22, 1953 70:16 page 495 review
Commonweal April 17, 1953 58:2 page 53 Philip T. Hartung review
Encyclopedia of American War Films page 47 synopsis
Film Daily March 2, 1953 review
The Great Combat Pictures pages 35–36 synopsis
The Great War Films (1994, Citadel) pages 125–127 Lawrence J. Quirk review
A Guide to Films on the Korean War pages 57–58 review
Hollywood Goes to War pages 104, 106 mention
The MGM Story (1977, Crown) page 250 John Douglas Eames synopsis
The Motion Picture Guide A-B page 147 review
New York Times May 28, 1953 27:5 Howard H. Thompson review
Newsweek June 8, 1953 41:23 pages 101–102 review
Saturday Review March 7, 1953 36:10 page 36 Arthur Knight review
Screen World 1954 Annual page 28 listing
Time March 16, 1953 61:11 pages 108, 110 review
Variety February 4, 1953 Brog. review
VideoHound's War Movies pages 460–461 review
War Movies page 34 review

Battle Flame (1959)

The Allied Artists Checklist page 10 #24 listing
BFI Monthly Film Bulletin July, 1959 26:306 pages 86–87 review
Boxoffice May 11, 1959 75:3 page 2331 review
Encyclopedia of American War Films page 49 synopsis
A Guide to Films on the Korean War page 58 review
The Motion Picture Guide A-B page 147 review
Screen World 1960 Annual page 45 listing

Battle Hymn (1957)

America March 16, 1957 96:24 page 686 Moira Walsh review
Aviation in the Cinema (1985, Scarecrow) pages 235–237 Stephen Pendo synopsis and history
Battle Hymn Dean E. Hess remembrance
BFI Monthly Film Bulletin March, 1957 24:278 pages 27–28 review
Boxoffice December 29, 1956 70:10 page 2043 review

Encyclopedia of American War Films page 49 synopsis
Film Daily March 13, 1957 review
The Great Combat Pictures pages 38–39 synopsis
The Great War Films pages 148–151 review
A Guide to Films on the Korean War pages 58–59 review
Library Journal February 1, 1957 82:3 page 349 Alice G. Owen review
The Motion Picture Guide A-B page 148 review
New York Times February 16, 1957 14:1 Bosley Crowther review
New Yorker February 23, 1957 33:1 pages 75–76 John McCarten review
Newsweek August 1, 1955 46:5 page 28 profile
Newsweek February 25, 1957 49:8 page 119 review
Rock Hudson: A Bio-Bibliography (1995, Greenwood) pages 86–88 Brenda Scott Royce synopsis
Saturday Review February 16, 1957 40:7 page 28 Hollis Alpert review
Screen World 1958 Annual page 24 listing
Sirk on Sirk (1997, Faber and Faber) pages 122–127 Douglas Sirk remembrance with Jon Halliday
Time March 11, 1957 69:10 page 98 review
Universal Pictures page 625 listing
The Universal Story page 240 synopsis
Variety December 19, 1956 Brog. review
War Movies page 35 review

Battle Taxi (1955)

Aviation in the Cinema pages 234–235 synopsis
BFI Monthly Film Bulletin July, 1955 22:258 pages 104–105 review
Boxoffice January 15, 1955 66:12 page 1692 review
Encyclopedia of American War Films page 53 synopsis
Farm Journal March, 1955 79:3 page 103 Charles F. Stevens review
Film Daily January 12, 1955? review
The Great Combat Pictures pages 45–46 synopsis
A Guide to Films on the Korean War pages 59–60 review
The Motion Picture Guide A-B page 150 review
Screen World 1956 Annual page 18 listing
The United Artists Story (1986, Crown) page 157 Ronald Bergan synopsis
Variety January 12, 1955 Gene. review

Battle Zone (1952)

The Allied Artists Checklist page 11 #26 listing
BFI Monthly Film Bulletin August, 1953 20:235 page 120 review
Boxoffice October 18, 1952 61:25 page 1418 review
Encyclopedia of American War Films pages 53–54 synopsis
The Great Combat Pictures pages 46–47 synopsis
A Guide to Films on the Korean War page 60 review
The Motion Picture Guide A-B page 150 review
New York Times November 1, 1952 17:2 Bosley Crowther review
Variety October 15, 1952 Brog. review

Bombers B-52 (1957)

America December 7, 1957 98:10 page 328 Moira Walsh review
BFI Monthly Film Bulletin October, 1957 24:285 page 129 review

Boxoffice November 2, 1957 72:2 page 2155 review
Library Journal December 1, 1957 82:21 page 3096 Charlotte Bilkey Speicher review
The Motion Picture Guide A-B page 258 review
New York Times November 23, 1957 11:2 Howard H. Thompson review
New Yorker December 7, 1957 33:42 page 100 John McCarten review
Screen World 1958 Annual page 124 listing
Seeing is Believing (1983, Henry Holt) pages 58, 69 Peter Biskind mentions
Time December 9, 1957 70:24 page 108 review
The Warner Bros. Story (1979, Crown) page 332 Clive Hirschhorn synopsis
When Do I Start? (1997, Simon and Schuster) page 262 Karl Malden remembrance with Carla Malden

The Bridges at Toko-Ri (1955)

America January 29, 1955 92:18 page 463 Moira Walsh review
Aviation in the Cinema pages 233–234 synopsis
BFI Monthly Film Bulletin February, 1955 22:253 page 18 review
Boxoffice January 1, 1955 66:10 page 1682 review
The Bridges at Toko-Ri (1953, Random House) James Michener source novel
Commonweal February 4, 1955 61:18 pages 477–478 Philip T. Hartung review
The Complete Films of William Holden (1986, Citadel) pages 161–163 Lawrence J. Quirk review
Encyclopedia of American War Films page 78 synopsis
Farm Journal February, 1955 79:2 page 149 Charles F. Stevens review
Film Daily review
The Films of Fredric March (1971, Citadel) pages 211–212 Lawrence J. Quirk review
The Films of the Fifties (1976, Citadel) pages 158–159 Douglas Brode review
Golden Boy: The Untold Story of William Holden (1983, Berkley) pages 110–111 Bob Thomas profile
Grace (1994, G.P. Putnam) pages 156–161 Robert Lacey profile
Grace: The Secret Lives of a Princess (1987, Doubleday) pages 84–86 James Spada profile
The Great Combat Pictures pages 76–78 synopsis
The Great War Films pages 136–139 review
A Guide to Films on the Korean War pages 61–62 review
History Goes to the Movies (1999, Main Street) pages 231–232 Joseph Roquemore review
Hollywood Goes to War pages 111, 113 mention
Library Journal January 15, 1955 80:2 page 150 Earle F. Walbridge review
Life February 7, 1955 38:6 pages 91–92, 94 pictorial
Look February 8, 1955 19:3 pages 92, 94 pictorial
The Motion Picture Guide A-B page 296 review
New Republic March 14, 1955 132:11 pages 28–29 Delmore Schwartz review
New York Times January 21, 1955 20:2 Bosley Crowther review
New Yorker January 29, 1955 30:50 page 79 John McCarten review
Newsweek January 17, 1955 45:3 page 86 review
Oscar A to Z (1995, Doubleday) page 118 #288 Charles Matthews synopsis
The Paramount Story (1985, Crown) page 212 John Douglas Eames synopsis
Princess Grace pages 85–87 (1984, Stein and Day) Sarah Bradford profile
Saturday Review January 22, 1955 38:4 page 43 Lee Rogow review
Time January 24, 1955 65:4 page 75 review
Variety December 29, 1954 Whit. review
VideoHound's War Movies pages 463–464 review
War Movies pages 49–50 review

Cease Fire (1953)

America December 12, 1953 90:11 pages 304–305 Moira Walsh review
BFI Monthly Film Bulletin April, 1954 21:243 pages 51–52 review
Boxoffice November 28, 1953 64:5 page 1535 review
Camp Gordon Rambler February 5, 1954 Sergeant Bill Russell article
Commonweal December 4, 1953 59:9 page 226 Philip T. Hartung review
Encyclopedia of American War Films page 100 synopsis
A Guide to Films on the Korean War page 62 review
Look December 29, 1953 17:26 page 38 pictorial
The Lost Films of the Fifties (1988, Citadel) pages 83–85 Douglas Brode review
New York Times November 25, 1953 17:1 Bosley Crowther review
New Yorker December 5, 1953 29:42 pages 141–142 John McCarten review
Newsweek December 14, 1953 42:24 pages 90–91 review
Reader's Digest November, 1959 75:451 pages 122–124 Hal Wallis remembrance
Saturday Review December 5, 1953 36:49 pages 52–53 Arthur Knight review
Screen World 1954 Annual page 136 listing
3-D Movies (1989, McFarland) pages 37–38 R. M. Hayes mention
Time December 14, 1953 62:24 page 114 review
Variety November 25, 1953 review
War Movies page 56 review

Chattahoochee (1990)

Chicago Sun-Times May 4, 1990 Roger Ebert review
Deseret News May 17, 1990 Chris Hicks review
The Motion Picture Guide 1991 Annual page 27 review
New York Times April 20, 1990 C11 Janet Maslin review
Sight and Sound ? page 44 Nigel Floyd review
Stedman's Medical Dictionary 25th Edition (1990, Williams & Wilkins) pages 457, 1535 article
Washington Post May 4, 1990 Hal Hinson review
Washington Post May 4, 1990 Desson Howe review

Collision Course: Truman vs. MacArthur (1976, TVM)

A Guide to Films on the Korean War page 63 review
TV Guide January 3–9, 1976 24:1 #1188 pages A-42, A-45 review and advertisement

Combat Squad (1953)

BFI Monthly Film Bulletin March, 1954 21:242 page 39 review

Boxoffice October 3, 1953 63:23 page 1519 review
The Columbia Checklist page 59 #373 listing
The Columbia Story page 194 synopsis
Encyclopedia of American War Films page 119 synopsis
Film Daily review
A Guide to Films on the Korean War page 63 review
Hollywood Reporter September 25, 1953 review
The Motion Picture Guide C–D page 531 review
Screen World 1954 Annual page 172 listing
Variety September 30, 1953 Brog. review

Cry for Happy (1961)

America March 18, 1961 104:24 page 800 Moira Walsh
    review
BFI Monthly Film Bulletin June, 1961 28:329 page 80 review
The Columbia Checklist page 70 #439 listing
The Columbia Story page 242 synopsis
A Guide to Films on the Korean War pages 63–64 review
The Motion Picture Guide C–D page 531 review
New York Times March 4, 1961 16:1 Bosley Crowther review
Screen World 1962 Annual page 29 listing
Time March 17, 1961 77:12 page 70 review

Dragonfly Squadron (1954)

The Allied Artists Checklist page 42 #114 listing
Aviation in the Cinema page 232 synopsis
BFI Monthly Film Bulletin September, 1954 21:248 page 132 review
Boxoffice February 6, 1954 64:15 page 1556 review
Chuck Connors: The Man Behind the Rifle (1997, Artist's) pages 92–93 David Fury profile
Encyclopedia of American War Films page 169 synopsis
Film Daily review
A Guide to Films on the Korean War pages 64–65 review
The Motion Picture Guide C–D page 711 review
Screen World 1954 Annual page 154 listing
Variety February 3, 1954 Brog. review

The Eternal Sea (1955)

BFI Monthly Film Bulletin May, 1955 22:256 page 74 review
Boxoffice April 9, 1955 66:24 page 1747 review
Encyclopedia of American War Films page 183 review
Film Daily review
A Guide to Films on the Korean War page 65 review
The Motion Picture Guide E–G page 779 review
New York Times June 10, 1955 16:2 Howard H. Thompson review
Newsweek May 2, 1955 45:18 page 91 review
The Republic Pictures Checklist (1998, McFarland) pages 51–52 #211 Len D. Martin listing
Saturday Review May 14, 1955 38:20 pages 26–27 Lee Rogow review
Screen World 1956 Annual page 60 listing
Variety April 6, 1955 Brog. review

The Fearmakers (1958)

It Wasn't All Velvet (1988, Zebra) pages 222–223 Mel Torme remembrance
Jacques Tourneur: The Cinema of Nightfall (1998, Johns Hopkins University) pages 256–261 Chris Fujiwara review

The Motion Picture Guide E–G page 828 review
The United Artists Story page 188 synopsis

Field of Honor (1986)

Dutch Film 1986–1987 (1987, Government Publishing House, Netherlands) synopsis
A Guide to Films on the Korean War pages 65–66 review
The Motion Picture Guide 1987 Annual page 93 Ross review
Variety May 28, 1986 Silv. review

Fixed Bayonets! (1951)

BFI Monthly Film Bulletin April, 1954 21:243 page 56 review
Boxoffice December 1, 1951 60:5 page 1323 review
Christian Century January 2, 1952 69:1 page 31 review
Commonweal December 14, 1951 55:10 page 255 Philip T. Hartung review
Encyclopedia of American War Films pages 198–199 synopsis
Film Daily review
The Films of 20th Century–Fox (1985, Citadel) pages 220–221 Tony Thomas and Aubrey Solomon synopsis
The Great Combat Pictures pages 155–157 synopsis
Guide for the Film Fanatic (1986, Fireside) page 153 Danny Peary review
A Guide to Films on the Korean War page 66 review
History Goes to the Movies page 239 review
Hollywood Goes to War pages 102–104 review
Library Journal January 1, 1952 77:1 page 44 Earle F. Walbridge review
The Motion Picture Guide E–G pages 866–867 review
Nation January 5, 1952 174:1 page 18 Manny Farber review
New York Times November 21, 1951 20:2 Bosley Crowther review
Newsweek December 3, 1951 38:23 pages 94–95 review
Rebel (1996, Harper) page 107 Donald Spoto mention
Sam Fuller: Life Is a Battleground (1994, McFarland) pages 30–31, 66–68, 105–107 Lee Server review and interviews
Samuel Fuller (1971, Viking) Nicholas Garnham review
Samuel Fuller (1970, Praeger) pages 73–75 Phil Hardy review
Screen World 1952 Annual page 114 listing
Variety November 21, 1951 Gilb. review
War Movies pages 93–94 review

Flight Nurse (1953)

Aviation in the Cinema pages 230–231 synopsis
BFI Monthly Film Bulletin February, 1954 21:241 page 24 review
Boxoffice November 14, 1953 64:3 page 1531 review
Call Bureau Cast Service October 1, 1953 listing
Encyclopedia of American War Films page 202 synopsis
Film Daily review
A Guide to Films on the Korean War page 67 review
MASH: An Army Surgeon in Korea pages 113–116 history
The Motion Picture Guide E–G page 876 review
New York Times January 30, 1954 9:6 Oscar A. Godbout review
The Republic Pictures Checklist page 59 #241 listing
Screen World 1954 Annual page 173 listing
Variety November 4, 1953 Gilb. review

For the Boys (1991)

Austin Chronicle December 6, 1991 Kathleen Maher review

Bette (1995, Birch Lane) pages 229–235 George Mair profile

The Bette Midler Scrapbook (1997, Citadel) pages 121–125, 39, 40, 43 Allison J. Waldman profile and review

Chicago Sun-Times November 27, 1991 Roger Ebert review

Christopher Street January, 1992 pages 8–9 Quentin Crisp review

Deseret News November 27, 1991 Chris Hicks review

Good Housekeeping March, 1991 212:3 pages 64, 27, 70–71 Vernon Scott profile

A Guide to Films on the Korean War pages 67–68 review

Macleans December 2, 1991 104:48 page 86 Brian D. Johnson review

The Motion Picture Guide 1992 Annual pages 116–117 review

National Review January 20, 1992 44:1 pages 64–65 John Simon review

New York Times June 30, 1991 pages ?, 14 Aljean Harmetz article

New York Times November 22, 1991 C12 Janet Maslin review

New York Times December 5, 1991 Bernard Weintraub article

New Yorker December 16, 1991 67:43 pages 117–118 Terrence Rafferty review

Newsweek November 25, 1991 118:22 pages 54–55 David Ansen profile

Oscar A to Z page 290 #700 synopsis

People Weekly December 2, 1991 36:21 page 30 Leah Rozen review

People Weekly December 23, 1991 36:24 pages 79–80 Michael A. Lipton and John Griffiths profile

Roman Soldiers Don't Wear Watches (1999, Citadel) page 46 Bill Givens mention

Time December 2, 1991 138:22 page 86 Richard Schickel review

Variety November 18, 1991 Amy Dawes review

Vogue December, 1991 181:12 pages 202–207, 309–310 Jonathan Van Meter profile

Washington Post November 27, 1991 Hal Hinson review

Washington Post November 29, 1991 Joe Brown review

Geisha Girl (1952)

BFI Monthly Film Bulletin September, 1954 21:248 pages 132–133 review

Los Angeles Daily News January 29, 1954 profile

Los Angeles Times May 6, 1951 article

Los Angeles Times July 3, 1955 profile

The Motion Picture Guide E-G page 986 review

Variety May 21, 1952 Gilb. review

Glory Alley (1952)

BFI Monthly Film Bulletin December, 1952 19:227 pages 171–172 review

Boxoffice May 24, 1952 61:4 page 1375 review

Film Daily review

The MGM Story page 250 synopsis

The Motion Picture Guide E-G page 1038 review

New York Times July 30, 1952 20:8 Bosley Crowther review

Newsweek June 16, 1952 39:24 pages 110–111 review

Screen World 1953 Annual page 55 listing

Time June 9, 1952 59:23 page 106 review

The Glory Brigade (1953)

America August 29, 1953 89:22 page 526 Moira Walsh review

BFI Monthly Film Bulletin July, 1953 20:234 page 107 review

Boxoffice May 23, 1953 63:4 page 1477 review

Call Bureau Cast Service March 1, 1953 listing

Encyclopedia of American War Films pages 230–231 synopsis

The Films of 20th Century-Fox pages 246–247 synopsis

A Guide to Films on the Korean War page 68 review

Hollywood Citizen News September 26, 1952 article

Hollywood Goes to War page 107 mention

Lee Marvin: His Films and Career (2000, McFarland) pages 28–30 Robert J. Lentz review

Los Angeles Daily News August 1, 1953 Roy Ringer review

Los Angeles Times August 1, 1953 John L. Scott review

The Motion Picture Guide E-G page 1038 review

Motion Picture Herald May 16, 1953 V.C. review

New York Times August 15, 1953 8:4 Howard H. Thompson review

Screen World 1954 Annual page 169 listing

Swashbucklers (1976, Rainbow) page 458 James Robert Parish and Don E. Stanke mention

Variety May 13, 1953 Brog. review

War Movies page 105 review

The Great Impostor (1960)

America April 1, 1961 105:1 page 26 Moira Walsh review

BFI Monthly Film Bulletin February, 1961 28:325 page 19 review

A Guide to Films on the Korean War pages 68–69 review

The Motion Picture Guide E-G page 1097 review

New York Times March 30, 1961 24:1 A. H. Weiler review

Newsweek February 27, 1961 57:9 page 92 review

Ottawa Citizen date unknown Pat MacAdam profile

Saturday Review March 4, 1961 44:9 page 36 Arthur Knight review

Screen World 1962 Annual page 17 listing

Thunder in the Morning Calm pages 167–176 history

Tony Curtis: The Autobiography (1993, William Morrow) pages 188–189, 322–323 Barry Paris review

Universal Pictures pages 661–662 listing

The Universal Story page 265 synopsis

Hell's Horizon (1955)

Aviation in the Cinema page 235 synopsis

Boxoffice November 26, 1955 68:5 page 1882 review

The Columbia Checklist page 139 #857 listing

Encyclopedia of American War Films page 260 synopsis

A Guide to Films on the Korean War page 70 review

The Motion Picture Guide H-K page 1199 review

Screen World 1956 Annual page 186 listing

Variety November 23, 1955 Whit. review

A Hill in Korea (1956)

BFI Monthly Film Bulletin October, 1956 23:273 page 125 review

Candidly Caine (1990, Pan) pages 38–39 Elaine Gallagher profile
The Great Combat Pictures pages 210–212 synopsis
A Guide to Films on the Korean War pages 71–72 review
Hollywood Goes to War page 109 mention
The Motion Picture Guide H-K page 1191 review
The Player page 146 profile
Raising Caine (1981, Prentice-Hall) pages 53–54 William Hall profile
Robert Shaw: More Than a Life (1994, Madison) page 64 Karen Carmean and Georg Gaston profile
Variety October 10, 1956 Clem. review
What's It All About? (1992, Ballantine) pages 101–106 Michael Caine remembrance

Hold Back the Night (1956)

The Allied Artists Checklist page 63 #173 listing
BFI Monthly Film Bulletin April, 1957 24:279 page 47 review
Boxoffice July 28, 1956 69:14 page 1995 review
Chuck Connors: The Man Behind the Rifle pages 98–100 profile
Encyclopedia of American War Films page 270 synopsis
Film Daily review
The Film Encyclopedia (Third Edition) (1994, Harper Collins) pages 399–400 Ephraim Katz profile
A Guide to Films on the Korean War page 72 review
The Motion Picture Guide H-K page 1248 review
Variety July 25, 1956 Brog. review

The Hook (1963)

America February 23, 1963 108:8 page 275 Moira Walsh review
BFI Monthly Film Bulletin April, 1963 30:351 pages 42–43 review
Encyclopedia of American War Films pages 275–276 synopsis
The Films of Kirk Douglas (1972, Citadel) pages 188–190 Tony Thomas review
A Guide to Films on the Korean War pages 72–73 review
The MGM Story page 309 synopsis
The Motion Picture Guide H-K page 1270 review
New York Times February 16, 1963 5:6 Bosley Crowther review
New Yorker March 9, 1963 39:3 pages 145–146 Brendan Gill review
Newsweek March 4, 1963 61:9 page 85 review
The Ragman's Son (1988, Pocket Books) page 316 Kirk Douglas remembrance
Saturday Review February 16, 1963 46:7 page 26 Arthur Knight review
Screen World 1964 Annual page 15 listing
Time March 1, 1963 81:9 page 79 review
The Tough Guys (1976, Arlington House) pages 141–142 James Robert Parish profile

The Hunters (1958)

America September 20, 1958 99:25 page 650 Moira Walsh review
Aviation in the Cinema pages 237–238 synopsis
BFI Monthly Film Bulletin October, 1958 25:297 page 128 review
Boxoffice August 25, 1958 73:18 page 2262 review
Encyclopedia of American War Films page 282 synopsis

The Films of 20th Century-Fox page 300 synopsis
The Great Combat Pictures pages 222–223 synopsis
A Guide to Films on the Korean War pages 73–74 review
Library Journal November 1, 1958 83:19 page 3098 Alice G. Owen review
The Motion Picture Guide H-K page 1315 review
New York Times August 27, 1958 33:1 Howard H. Thompson review
Newsweek September 15, 1958 52:11 page 106 review
Robert Mitchum: "Baby, I Don't Care" (2001, St. Martin's) pages 319–320 Lee Server profile
Robert Mitchum on the Screen (1978, A.S. Barnes) pages 158–159 Alvin H. Marill review
Screen World 1959 Annual page 87 listing
The Sunday Press 1978 Roderick Mann profile
Time August 25, 1958 72:8 page 78 review
Variety August 6, 1958 Holl. review
VideoHound's War Movies pages 465–466 review
War Movies pages 119–120 review

I Want You (1951)

BFI Monthly Film Bulletin January, 1952 19:216 pages 2–3 review
Boxoffice November 3, 1951 60:1 page 1313 review
Christian Century February 13, 1952 69:7 page 207 review
Commentary March, 1952 13:3 pages 275–281 Robert Warshow article
Commonweal December 28, 1951 55:12 page 301 Philip T. Hartung review
Encyclopedia of American War Films page 285 synopsis
Goldwyn (1989, Alfred A. Knopf) pages 456–459 A. Scott Berg profile
A Guide to Films on the Korean War page 74 review
Library Journal December 15, 1951 76:22 page 2110 Marilla Waite Freeman review
The Motion Picture Guide H-K pages 1341–1342 review
Nation January 19, 1952 174:3 page 66 Manny Farber review
New Republic December 31, 1951 125:27 page 22 Robert Hatch review
New York Times December 24, 1951 9:1 Bosley Crowther review
New Yorker January 5, 1952 27:47 pages 65–66 John McCarten review
Newsweek January 7, 1952 39:1 page 59 review
Oscar A to Z page 414 #974 synopsis
The RKO Story (1982, Arlington House) page 261 Richard B. Jewell and Vernon Harbin synopsis
Samuel Goldwyn Presents (1976, A.S. Barnes) pages 279–282 Alvin H. Marill review
Saturday Review December 22, 1951 34:51 pages 34–35 Hollis Alpert review
Screen World 1952 Annual page 113 listing
Time January 28, 1952 59:4 page 96 review
Variety October 31, 1951 Gene. review
War Movies pages 123–124 review

Inchon (1982)

Christianity Today October 22, 1982 26:17 page 63 Rodney Clapp history
The Great Combat Pictures pages 232–233 synopsis
Encyclopedia of American War Films page 290 synopsis
A Guide to Films on the Korean War pages 74–75 review

The Hollywood Hall of Shame (1984, Perigee) pages 186–199 Harry Medved and Michael Medved review
The Motion Picture Guide H-K page 1379 review
Nation October 16, 1982 235:12 page 380 Robert Hatch review
New York Times September 17, 1982 C9 Vincent Canby review
Newsweek September 27, 1982 100:13 page 76 Jack Kroll review
Screen World 1982 Annual (1982, Crown) page 115 John Willis listing
Variety May 6, 1981 Paul. review
Washington Post September 17, 1982 D1-D2 Gary Arnold review
The Worst Movies of All Time (1995, Citadel) pages 196–199 Michael Sauter review

Iron Angel (1964)

A Guide to Films on the Korean War page 75 review
The Motion Picture Guide H-K page 1407 review

Japanese War Bride (1952)

BFI Monthly Film Bulletin April, 1952 19:219 page 51 review
Boxoffice January 12, 1952 60:11 page 1334 review
Film Daily review
The Films of 20th Century-Fox page 233 synopsis
A Guide to Films on the Korean War page 76 review
King Vidor, American (1988, University of California) pages 280–285 Raymond Durgnat and Scott Simmon review
The Motion Picture Guide H-K page 1446 review
New York Times January 30, 1952 22:6 A.H. Weiler review
Newsweek February 11, 1952 39:6 page 90 review
Screen World 1953 Annual page 12 listing
Time February 4, 1952 59:5 page 74 review
Variety January 9, 1952 Brog. review

Jet Attack (1958)

Aviation in the Cinema page 237 synopsis
Boxoffice April 7, 1958 72:24 page 2214 review
Encyclopedia of American War Films page 304 synopsis
The Fifty Worst Films of All Time (1978, Popular Library) pages 121–125 Harry Medved and Randy Dreyfuss review
A Guide to Films on the Korean War pages 76–77 review
The Motion Picture Guide H-K page 1456 review
Screen World 1959 Annual page 140 listing
Variety March 26, 1958 Powe. review

Korea Patrol (1951)

BFI Monthly Film Bulletin March, 1951 18:206 pages 233–234 review
Boxoffice January 13, 1951 58:11 page 1222 review
Encyclopedia of American War Films pages 321–322 synopsis
Film Daily review
A Guide to Films on the Korean War page 77 review
Hollywood Reporter December 27, 1950 review
The Motion Picture Guide H-K page 1560 review
Variety January 3, 1951 Brog. review

Love Is a Many-Splendored Thing (1955)

America August 27, 1955 93:22 page 519 Moira Walsh review
BFI Monthly Film Bulletin November, 1955 22:262 page 164 review
Boxoffice August 13, 1955 67:16 page 1822 review
The Complete Films of William Holden pages 164–166 review
Film Daily review
The Films of Jennifer Jones (1979, W. Franklin Moshier) pages 122–129 W. Franklin Moshier review
The Films of 20th Century-Fox pages 265–266 synopsis
Golden Boy: The Untold Story of William Holden page 114 profile
A Guide to Films on the Korean War pages 77–78 review
Library Journal October 1, 1955 80:17 page 2080 Charlotte Bilkey Speicher review
The Motion Picture Guide L-M page 1752 review
New York Times August 19, 1955 10:1 Bosley Crowther review
New Yorker August 27, 1955 31:28 page 101 Philip Hamburger review
Newsweek August 29, 1955 46:9 page 77 review
Oscar A to Z page 512 #1213 synopsis
Portrait of Jennifer (1995, Simon and Schuster) pages 317–324 Edward Z. Epstein profile
Screen World 1956 Annual pages 107–109 listing
Time September 12, 1955 66:11 pages 116, 118 review
Variety August 10, 1955 Hift. review
Washington Post June 29, 1980 Parade page 2 history

MacArthur (1977)

Encyclopedia of American War Films pages 350–351 synopsis
The Films of Gregory Peck (1984, Citadel) pages 226–232 John Griggs review
The Great Combat Pictures pages 263–266 synopsis
Gregory Peck (1980, William Morrow) pages 231–241 Michael Freedland profile
A Guide to Films on the Korean War pages 78–79 review
Guts and Glory (1978, Addison-Wesley) pages 295–297 Lawrence H. Suid article
The Motion Picture Guide L-M page 1785 review
New York Times July 1, 1977 C8:1 Vincent Canby review
Screen World 1978 Annual pages 66–67 listing
The Universal Story page 333 synopsis
War Movies page 133 review

The Manchurian Candidate (1962)

America November 24, 1962 107:34 pages 1158–1159 Moira Walsh review
Balancing Act (1999, Little, Brown) pages 127–131 Martin Gottfried profile
BFI Monthly Film Bulletin December, 1962 29:347 page 168 review
Captured on Film (1989, B.T. Batsford) pages 136–137 Bruce Crowther review
Chicago Sun-Times March 11, 1988 Roger Ebert review
Cult Movies (2000, Billboard) pages 139–141 Karl French and Philip French synopsis

Encyclopedia of American War Films pages 358–359 synopsis

Fifty Grand Movies of the 1960s and 1970s (1986, Crown) pages 144–147 David Zinman review

The Films of Frank Sinatra (1993, Citadel) pages 184–187 Gene Ringgold and Clifford McCarty synopsis

The Films of John Frankenheimer (1988, Lehigh University) pages 35–41 Gerald Pratley review

The 500 Best American Films to Buy, Rent or Videotape (1985, Pocket) page 240 review

The Great Movies (1973, Ridge) pages 204–205 William Bayer review

The Great Spy Pictures (1974, Scarecrow) pages 288–290 James Robert Parish and Michael R. Pitts synopsis

A Guide to Films on the Korean War pages 79–80 review

The Historical Journal of Film, Radio and Television March, 1998 18:1 pages 75–94 Susan L. Carruthers article

History Goes to the Movies pages 232–234 review

John Frankenheimer: A Conversation (1995, Riverwood) pages 67–73 John Frankenheimer remembrance with Charles Champlin

The Manchurian Candidate laserdisc (1997, MGM) commentary and history

The Motion Picture Guide L–M pages 1865–1866 review

New Republic December 1, 1962 147:22 page 26 Stanley Kauffmann review

New York Times October 25, 1962 48:3 Bosley Crowther review

New Yorker November 3, 1962 38:37 pages 115–116 Brendan Gill review

Newsweek October 29, 1962 60:18 page 88 review

Oscar A to Z page 532 #1265 synopsis

Retakes (1989, Ballantine) pages 204–205 John Eastman history

Saturday Review October 27, 1962 45:43 page 65 Arthur Knight review

Screen World 1963 Annual page 83 listing

Time November 2, 1962 80:18 page 101 review

The United Artists Story page 208 synopsis

VideoHound's War Movies pages 467–469 review

War Movies page 135 review

Washington Post February 12, 1988 Desson Howe review

Washington Post February 13, 1988 Hal Hinson review

Man-Trap (1961)

Call Bureau Cast Service October 1, 1961 listing

The Motion Picture Guide L–M page 1850 review

Screen World 1962 Annual page 80 listing

Marine Battleground (1966)

A Guide to Films on the Korean War page 80 review

The Motion Picture Guide L–M page 1879 review

Marines, Let's Go (1961)

America August 26, 1961 105:22 pages 669, 671 Moira Walsh review

BFI Monthly Film Bulletin October, 1961 28:333 page 143 review

Encyclopedia of American War Films page 362 synopsis

The Films of 20th Century–Fox page 330 synopsis

The Great Combat Pictures pages 272–273 synopsis

A Guide to Films on the Korean War pages 80–81 review

Hollywood Goes to War page 111 mention

The Motion Picture Guide L–M page 1880 review

New York Times August 16, 1961 37:2 Howard H. Thompson review

Screen World 1961 Annual page 73 listing

War Movies page 136 review

MASH (1970)

The Complete Book of M*A*S*H (2000, Abradale) page 26 Suzy Kalter history

Doctors in the Movies (2000, Medi-Ed) pages 199–202 Peter E. Dans review

Encyclopedia of American War Films pages 364–365 synopsis

Entertainment Weekly 1996 Academy Awards Issue March, 1996 pages 104–106 Steve Wulf history

Fifty Grand Movies of the 1960s and 1970s pages 80–83 review

The Films of Robert Altman (1981, Scarecrow) pages 17–29 Alan Karp review

The 500 Best American Films to Buy, Rent or Videotape page 244 review

The Great Combat Pictures pages 273–276 synopsis

The Great Movies pages 117–118 review

The Great War Films pages 208–211 review

Guide for the Film Fanatic page 267 review

A Guide to Films on the Korean War pages 81–82 review

Guts and Glory pages 267–269 article

Hollywood Goes to War pages 113–114 review

Hollywood in the Seventies (1981, A.S. Barnes) pages 57, 60–61 Les Keyser review

Legendary War Movies (1996, Metro) pages 114–115 Peter Guttmacher review

The MASH DVD (2002, 20th Century–Fox) commentary and history

The Motion Picture Guide L–M page 1782 review

New York Times January 26, 1970 26:1 Roger Greenspun review

New York Times February 1, 1970 II:1:5 Vincent Canby article "Blood, Blasphemy and Laughs"

New York Times March 22, 1970 II:19:1 Richard Corliss article "I Admit It, I Didn't Like *M*A*S*H*"

New Yorker January 24, 1970 Pauline Kael review

Oscar A to Z pages 540–541 #1286 synopsis

Retakes pages 207–208 history

Robert Altman (1985, Twayne) pages 10–21, 147–148 Gerald Plecki review

Robert Altman: Jumping Off the Cliff (1989, St. Martin's) pages 295–324 Patrick McGilligan review and history

Roger Ebert's Video Companion (1994 Edition) (1993, Andrews and McMeel) pages 415–416 Roger Ebert review

Roman Soldiers Don't Wear Watches pages 36–37 mention

Second Sight (1972, Simon & Schuster) pages 283–285 Richard Schickel review

Talking Pictures (1974, Penguin) pages 336–346 Richard Corliss profile

VideoHound's War Movies pages 470–471 review

The War Film (1974, A.S. Barnes) page 141 Ivan Butler review

War Movies pages 136–138 review

Mask of the Dragon (1951)

Film Daily March 19, 1951 review

Hollywood Reporter March 19, 1951 review

Los Angeles Times review
The Motion Picture Guide L-M page 1897 review
Variety May 2, 1951 review

The McConnell Story (1955)

Aviation in the Cinema page 235 synopsis
BFI Monthly Film Bulletin December, 1955 22:263 pages
178–179 review
Boxoffice August 13, 1955 67:16 page 1823 review
Encyclopedia of American War Films page 367 synopsis
The Films of Alan Ladd pages 204–207 review
A Guide to Films on the Korean War page 83 review
June Allyson (1983, Berkley) pages 169–190 June Allyson
remembrance with Frances Spatz Leighton
Ladd pages 187–196 profile
The Motion Picture Guide L-M page 1910 review
New York Times September 30, 1955 23:1 A. H. Weiler
review
Newsweek October 10, 1955 46:15 pages 116–117 review
Screen World 1956 Annual page 131 listing
Time October 17, 1955 66:16 pages 115–116 review
Variety August 17, 1955 Brog. review
The Warner Bros. Story page 321 synopsis

Men in War (1957)

Anthony Mann (1979, Twayne) pages 185, 189–199 Jea-
nine Basinger review
BFI Monthly Film Bulletin November, 1957 24:286 pages
135–136 review
Boxoffice January 26, 1957 70:14 page 2052 review
Encyclopedia of American War Films pages 370–371 syn-
opsis
The Great Combat Pictures pages 276–277 synopsis
A Guide to Films on the Korean War pages 83–84 review
History Goes to the Movies pages 234–235 review
Hollywood Goes to War page 110 mention
Library Journal February 15, 1957 82:4 page 528 Earle
F. Walbridge review
New York Times March 20, 1957 32:4 Bosley Crowther
review
New Yorker April 6, 1957 33:7 pages 76, 78 John Mc-
Carten review
Newsweek March 4, 1957 49:9 page 101 review
Saturday Review February 16, 1957 40:7 page 28 Hollis
Alpert review
Screen World 1958 Annual page 15 listing
Time April 8, 1957 69:14 pages 92, 94 review
The Tough Guys page 564 profile
The United Artists Story page 179 synopsis
Variety January 23, 1957 Brog. review
VideoHound's War Movies pages 473–474 review
War Movies page 139 review

Men of the Fighting Lady (1954)

America May 22, 1954 91:8 pages 229, 231 Moira Walsh
review
Andrew Marton (1991, Scarecrow) pages 242–254 Joanne
D'Antonio interview with Andrew Marton
Aviation in the Cinema page 232 Stephen Pendo synop-
sis
BFI Monthly Film Bulletin November, 1954 21:250 page
163 review
Boxoffice May 15, 1954 65:3 page 1582 review
Encyclopedia of American War Films pages 371–372 syn-
opsis

The Great Combat Pictures pages 277–278 synopsis
A Guide to Films on the Korean War page 84 review
History Goes to the Movies page 232 review
Hollywood Goes to War page 110 mention
Library Journal June 15, 1954 79:12 page 1168 Earle F.
Walbridge review
The MGM Story page 263 synopsis
The Motion Picture Guide L-M page 1930 review
New York Times May 8, 1954 15:2 Bosley Crowther re-
view
New Yorker May 15, 1954 30:13 page 74 John McCarten
review
Newsweek June 7, 1954 43:23 page 56 review
Saturday Evening Post May 10, 1952 224:45 pages 19–21,
124, 126, 128 James Michener source article "The For-
gotten Heroes of Korea"
Saturday Evening Post November 29, 1952 225:22 pages
41, 66–67, 69 Commander Harry A. Burns source ar-
ticle "The Case of the Blind Pilot"
Screen World 1955 Annual page 71 listing
Time May 31, 1954 63:22 page 72 review
Variety May 12, 1954 Brog. review
War Movies pages 139–140 review

Mission Over Korea (1953)

Aviation in the Cinema page 230 synopsis
Boxoffice July 25, 1953 63:13 page 1498 review
The Columbia Checklist page 220 #1319 listing
The Columbia Story page 197 synopsis
A Guide to Films on the Korean War pages 84–85 review
The Motion Picture Guide L-M page 1975 review
New York Times September 19, 1953 7:2 Howard H.
Thompson review
Screen World 1954 Annual page 104 listing

Mr. Walkie Talkie (1952)

BFI Monthly Film Bulletin May, 1954 21:244 page 76 re-
view
Boxoffice December 6, 1952 62:6 page 1432 review
A Guide to Films on the Korean War page 85 review
The Motion Picture Guide L-M page 1993 review
Quinlan's Illustrated Directory of Film Comedy Actors
(1992, Henry Holt) pages 279–280 David Quinlan
profile
Screen World 1953 Annual page 145 listing
Variety December 3, 1952 Brog. review

My Son John (1952)

BFI Monthly Film Bulletin May, 1953 20:232 pages
69–70 review
Boxoffice March 22, 1952 60:21 page 1355 review
The Great Spy Pictures pages 322–324 review
A Guide to Films on the Korean War pages 85–86 review
The Motion Picture Guide L-M page 2086 review
New York Times April 9, 1952 27:1 Bosley Crowther re-
view
New Yorker April 19, 1952 28:9 pages 93–94 John Mc-
Carten review
Newsweek April 14, 1952 39:15 page 96 review
Oscar A to Z page 587 #1404 synopsis
The Paramount Story page 204 synopsis
Running Time: Films of the Cold War (1982, Dial) pages
94–99 Nora Sayre review
Saturday Review April 19, 1952 35:16 page 46 Gilbert
Seldes review

Screen World 1953 Annual pages 32–33 listing
Time April 7, 1952 59:14 page 104 review

No Man's Land (1964)

A Guide to Films on the Korean War page 80 review
The Motion Picture Guide N–R page 2177 review

Not with My Wife, You Don't! (1966)

The Motion Picture Guide N–R pages 2200–2201 review
New York Times November 3, 1966 45:2 Vincent Canby review
Screen World 1967 Annual page 83 listing
Time November 11, 1966 88:20 pages 107–108 review
Tony Curtis: The Autobiography page 227 remembrance
The Warner Bros. Story page 371 synopsis

The Nun and the Sergeant (1962)

BFI Monthly Film Bulletin March, 1963 30:350 page 37 review
Encyclopedia of American War Films page 404 synopsis
The Great Combat Pictures pages 295–296 synopsis
A Guide to Films on the Korean War pages 87–88 review
The Motion Picture Guide N–R page 2209 review
Screen World 1963 Annual page 125 listing

One Minute to Zero (1952)

ABP News (ABPnews.com) October 26, 1999 "Pentagon Sought to Censor Korean War Movie" Jim Krane article
BFI Monthly Film Bulletin February, 1953 20:229 page 25 review
Boxoffice July 19, 1952 page 61:12 page 1391 review
Encyclopedia of American War Films page 411 synopsis
The Great Combat Pictures pages 301–302 synopsis
A Guide to Films on the Korean War pages 88–89 review
Hollywood Goes to War page 106 mention
Howard Hughes in Hollywood (1985, Citadel) page 132 Tony Thomas synopsis
Light Your Torches and Pull Up Your Tights (1973, Arlington House) pages 280–285 Tay Garnett remembrance with Fredda Dudley Balling
The Motion Picture Guide N–R page 2268 review
New York Times September 20, 1952 13:2 Bosley Crowther review
Newsweek October 6, 1952 40:14 pages 114–115 review
The RKO Story page 262 synopsis
Robert Mitchum: "Baby, I Don't Care" pages 223–225 profile
Robert Mitchum on the Screen pages 122–123 review
Saturday Review September 20, 1952 35:38 page 35 Arthur Knight review
Screen World 1953 Annual page 88 listing
Time August 25, 1952 60:8 page 72 review
The Tough Guys pages 300–302 profile
Variety July 16, 1952 Brog. review
War Movies page 153 review

Operation Dames (1959)

Boxoffice March 9, 1959 74:20 page 2315 review
Encyclopedia of American War Films page 412 synopsis
A Guide to Films on the Korean War page 89 review
The Motion Picture Guide N–R page 2282 review

Pork Chop Hill (1959)

America May 30, 1959 101:9 page 397 Moira Walsh review
BFI Monthly Film Bulletin July, 1959 26:306 page 84 review
Boxoffice May 11, 1959 75:3 page 2332 review
Encyclopedia of American War Films pages 435–436 synopsis
The Films of Gregory Peck pages 146–160 review
The Great Combat Pictures pages 320–323 synopsis
The Great War Films pages 167–170 review
Gregory Peck page 161 profile
A Guide to Films on the Korean War pages 89–90 review
History Goes to the Movies pages 236–237 review
Hollywood Goes to War page 113 review
Legendary War Movies pages 47–48 review
Library Journal June 1, 1959 84:11 page 1801 Gerald D. MacDonald review
The Motion Picture Guide N–R page 2432 review
New Republic June 15, 1959 140:24 page 22 Stanley Kauffmann review
New York Times May 30, 1959 9:2 Bosley Crowther review
New Yorker June 13, 1959 35:17 pages 117–118 John McCarten review
Newsweek September 15, 1958 52:11 page 106 profile
Newsweek June 1, 1959 53:22 pages 94–95 review
Saturday Review May 16, 1959 42:20 page 60 Hollis Alpert review
Screen World 1960 Annual page 45 listing
Time June 8, 1959 73:23 page 91 review
The United Artists Story page 192 synopsis
VideoHound's War Movies pages 475–476 review
War Movies page 161 review

Prisoner of War (1954)

America May 22, 1954 91:8 pages 229, 231 Moira Walsh review
Andrew Marton pages 239–242 interview
BFI Monthly Film Bulletin April, 1955 22:255 page 53 review
Boxoffice March 27, 1954 64:22 page 1469 review
Captured on Film page 137 review
Commonweal April 9, 1954 60:1 page 15 Philip T. Hartung review
Encyclopedia of American War Films page 440 synopsis
The Films of Ronald Reagan (1980, Citadel) pages 206–209 Tony Thomas review
The Great Combat Pictures pages 324–326 synopsis
A Guide to Films on the Korean War pages 90–91 review
Hollywood Goes to War page 110 mention
The MGM Story page 263 synopsis
The Motion Picture Guide N–R pages 2462–2463 review
New York Times May 10, 1954 20:2 A. H. Weiler review
Newsweek May 17, 1954 43:20 page 101 review
Ronald Reagan (1982, Optimum) page 39 Janice Anderson synopsis
Saturday Review April 17, 1954 37:16 page 24 Arthur Knight review
Screen World 1955 Annual page 55 listing
Variety March 24, 1954 Brog. review
War Movies page 162 review

The Rack (1956)

BFI Monthly Film Bulletin June, 1956 23:269 page 74 review

Boxoffice April 21, 1956 68:26 page 1964 review
Catholic World May, 1956 183:? pages 145–146 Robert Kass review
Commonweal May 18, 1956 64:? page 179 Philip T. Hartung review
Encyclopedia of American War Films page 453 synopsis
The Films of Paul Newman (1981, Citadel) pages 48–52 Lawrence J. Quirk review
The Films of the Fifties pages 185–186 review
A Guide to Films on the Korean War pages 91–92 review
History Goes to the Movies page 234 review
Hollywood Goes to War page 110 mention
Lee Marvin: His Films and Career pages 77–79 review
Library Journal November 15, 1956 81:20 pages 2676–2677 Herbert Cahoon review
The MGM Story page 275 synopsis
The Motion Picture Guide N-R page 2521 review
Nation November 24, 1956 183:? page 467 Robert Hatch review
New York Times November 6, 1956 30:1 Bosley Crowther review
New Yorker November 17, 1956 32:39 page 102 John McCarten review
Newman (1996, Turner) pages 41–43 Eric Lax profile
Newsweek June 4, 1956 47:23 page 99 review
Paul Newman (1997, Taylor) page 65 Lawrence J. Quirk profile
Paul Newman: Superstar (1978, St. Martin's) page 46–50 Lionel Godfrey profile
The Player page 245 profile
Saturday Review May 19, 1956 39:20 page 47 Arthur Knight review
Screen World 1957 Annual page 56 listing
Serling (1992, E. P. Dutton) pages 108–110 Gordon F. Sander profile
Variety April 18, 1956 Brog. review
Variety Television Reviews 1954–1956 April 20, 1955 Hift. review
War Movies page 165 review

The Reluctant Heroes (1971, TVM)

The Great Combat Pictures page 338 synopsis
A Guide to Films on the Korean War page 92 review
Movies Made for Television (1980, Da Capo) pages 76–77 #0173 Alvin H. Marill listing
TV Guide November 20–26, 1971 19:47 #973 page A-57 synopsis and advertisement

Retreat, Hell! (1952)

BFI Monthly Film Bulletin January, 1953 20:228 pages 5–6 review
Boxoffice February 16, 1952 60:16 page 1343 review
Christian Century April 9, 1952 69:15 page 447 review
Encyclopedia of American War Films page 469 synopsis
The Great Combat Pictures pages 338–339 synopsis
The Great War Films pages 122–125 review
A Guide to Films on the Korean War pages 93–94 review
History Goes to the Movies pages 238–239 review
Hollywood Goes to War page 104 mention
New York Times February 20, 1952 26:2 Bosley Crowther review
Newsweek March 3, 1952 39:9 pages 88, 90 review
Screen World 1953 Annual page 13 listing
Time March 24, 1952 59:12 pages 100, 102 review
Variety February 13, 1952 Brog. review

War Movies page 171 review
The Warner Bros. Story page 298 synopsis

Return from the Sea (1954)

The Allied Artists Checklist page 111 #325 listing
BFI Monthly Film Bulletin April, 1955 22:255 page 59 review
Boxoffice July 17, 1954 65:12 page 1598 review
Encyclopedia of American War Films page 469 synopsis
A Guide to Films on the Korean War page 94 review
The Motion Picture Guide N-R page 2587 review
New York Times July 10, 1954 7:3 Oscar A. Godbout review
Screen World 1955 Annual page 178 listing
Variety July 14, 1954 Brog. review

Sabre Jet (1953)

Aviation in the Cinema pages 231–232 synopsis
BFI Monthly Film Bulletin January, 1954 21:240 page 12 review
Boxoffice September 12, 1953 63:20 page 1513 review
Encyclopedia of American War Films page 486 synopsis
A Guide to Films on the Korean War page 94–95 review
The Motion Picture Guide S page 2697 review
New York Times November 3, 1953 34:1 Bosley Crowther review
Newsweek November 16, 1953 42:20 page 104 review
Screen World 1954 Annual page 114 listing
Time December 14, 1953 62:24 page 114 review
The United Artists Story page 145 synopsis
Variety September 9, 1953 Brog. review

Sayonara (1957)

America December 21, 1957 98:12 page 384 Moira Walsh review
The Best Supporting Actor and Actress Oscar Winners (1974, ESE California) Robert Osborne profiles
BFI Monthly Film Bulletin February, 1958 25:289 page 17 review
Boxoffice November 23, 1957 72:5 page 2165 review
Brando (1973, Henry Regnery) pages 109–115 Ron Offen profile
Brando (1994, Studio Vista) pages 74–77 Robert Tanitch review
Brando: The Biography (1994, Hyperion) pages 420–441 Peter Manso profile and history
Coronet December 1957 43:2 page 10 Mark Nichols review
Encyclopedia of American War Films page 495 review
The Films of Marlon Brando (1973, Citadel) pages 102–107 Tony Thomas review
The 500 Best American Films to Buy, Rent or Videotape page 371 review
A Guide to Films on the Korean War page 95 review
Library Journal December 15, 1957 82:22 pages 3199, 3198 Charlotte Bilkey Speicher review
Marlon Brando (1973, Pyramid) pages 74–80 Rene Jordan profile
Marlon Brando: The Only Contender (1985, St. Martin's) pages 124–129 Gary Carey profile
The Motion Picture Guide S page 2753 review
The Movie Makers: Brando (1974, Doubleday) pages 58–60 David Shipman review

Movie Stars, Real People and Me (1978, Delacorte) pages 93–121 Joshua Logan remembrance
New York Times December 6, 1957 39:4 Bosley Crowther review
New Yorker December 14, 1957 33:43 pages 89–90 John McCarten review
Newsweek December 9, 1957 50:24 page 96 review
Oscar A to Z pages 744–745 #1763 synopsis
Retakes pages 302–303 history
Screen World 1958 Annual pages 137–139 listing
Time December 16, 1957 70:25 pages 94–95 review
Variety November 13, 1957 Hift. review
War Movies page 177 review
The Warner Bros. Story page 333 synopsis

Sergeant Ryker (1968)

Are You Anybody? (1997, Fithian) pages 70–71 Bradford Dillman remembrance
A Guide to Films on the Korean War pages 95–96 review
Harry and Wally's Favorite TV Shows (1989, Prentice-Hall) page 106 Harry Castleman and Walter Podrazik synopsis
History Goes to the Movies page 234 review
Lee Marvin: His Films and Career pages 119–122 review
The Motion Picture Guide S page 2826 review
New York Times March 21, 1968 56:2 Howard H. Thompson review
Screen World 1969 Annual page 12 listing
Total Television (1996, Penguin) page 183 Alex McNeil synopsis
Universal Pictures page 712 listing
Variety Television Reviews 1963–1965 October 16, 1963 Bill. review
War Movies page 180 review

Sky Commando (1953)

BFI Monthly Film Bulletin January, 1954 21:240 page 12 review
Boxoffice August 22, 1953 63:17 page 1507 review
The Columbia Checklist page 313 #1847 listing
Encyclopedia of American War Films page 530 synopsis
A Guide to Films on the Korean War pages 96–97 review
The Motion Picture Guide S page 2960 review
Screen World 1954 Annual page 171 listing
Variety August 26, 1953 Gilb. review

Sniper's Ridge (1961)

BFI Monthly Film Bulletin April, 1963 30:351 page 50 review
Encyclopedia of American War Films page 532 synopsis
The Films of 20th Century-Fox pages 332–333 synopsis
A Guide to Films of the Korean War page 97 review
The Motion Picture Guide S page 2991 review
New York Times August 24, 1961 25:3 Eugene Archer review
Screen World 1961 Annual page 126 listing

Starlift (1951)

BFI Monthly Film Bulletin April, 1952 19:219 page 54 review
Boxoffice November 3, 1951 60:1 page 1313 review
Call Bureau Cast Service November 1, 1951 listing
Christian Century January 9, 1952 69:? page 55 review

The Films of Doris Day (1977, Citadel) pages 116–119 Christopher Young review
The Films of James Cagney (1972, Citadel) pages 199–200 Homer Dickens review
A Guide to Films on the Korean War pages 97–98 review
The Hollywood Musical (1981, Crown) page 324 Clive Hirschhorn synopsis
Hollywood Reporter November 1, 1951 review
Los Angeles Daily News November 17, 1951 Howard McClay review
Los Angeles Examiner November 17, 1951 Kay Proctor review
Los Angeles Times November 17, 1951 Philip K. Scheuer review
The Motion Picture Guide S pages 3113–3114 review
New York Times December 15, 1951 11:2 Bosley Crowther review
Newsweek December 10, 1951 38:24 page 98
Screen World 1952 Annual page 122 listing
Time December 3, 1951 58:23 page 108 review
Variety November 7, 1951 Brog. review
The Warner Bros. Story page 296 synopsis

The Steel Helmet (1951)

BFI Monthly Film Bulletin April, 1951 18:207 page 253 review
Boxoffice January 13, 1951 58:11 page 1222 review
Encyclopedia of American War Films pages 554–555 synopsis
The Films of the Fifties pages 45–46 review
The Great Combat Pictures pages 375–377 synopsis
Guide for the Film Fanatic pages 404–405 review
A Guide to Films on the Korean War pages 98–99 review
History Goes to the Movies pages 235–236 review
Hollywood Goes to War pages 102–104 review
The Motion Picture Guide S pages 3123–3124 review
New Republic February 12, 1951 124:7 pages 22–23 Robert Hatch review
New York Times January 25, 1951 21:5 Bosley Crowther review
New Yorker February 3, 1951 26:50 page 89 John McCarten review
Newsweek January 29, 1951 37:5 pages 90–91 review
Running Time: Films of the Cold War pages 182–185 review
Sam Fuller: Life is a Battleground pages 26–30, 62–66, 102–105 review and interviews
Samuel Fuller pages 30, 100–104 review
Saturday Review February 3, 1951 34:5 page 25 Arthur Knight review
Screen World 1952 Annual page 20 listing
Variety January 3, 1951 Brog. review
VideoHound's War Movies pages 478–479 review
War Movies page 187 review

Strange Intruder (1956)

The Allied Artists Checklist page 124 #371 listing
BFI Monthly Film Bulletin November, 1957 24:286 page 141 review
Boxoffice September 8, 1956 69:20 page 2010 review
A Guide to Films on the Korean War page 99 review
The Motion Picture Guide S page 3158 review
Screen World 1957 Annual page 108 listing
Variety September 5, 1956 Brog. review

A Stranger in My Arms (1959)

America February 14, 1959 100:19 page 587 Moira Walsh review
Boxoffice January 19, 1959 74:13 page 2301 review
Library Journal March 1, 1959 84:5 page 734 Mary C. Hatch review
New York Times March 4, 1959 34:2 Bosley Crowther review
Screen World 1960 Annual page 15 listing
Universal Pictures page 656 listing
The Universal Story page 255 synopsis

Submarine Command (1951)

BFI Monthly Film Bulletin October, 1951 18:213 page 350 review
Boxoffice September 1, 1951 59:18 page 1294 review
Christian Century March 26, 1952 69:? page 383 review
The Complete Films of William Holden pages 122–124 review
Encyclopedia of American War Films page 558 synopsis
The Great Combat Pictures pages 383–384 synopsis
A Guide to Films on the Korean War pages 99–100 review
The Motion Picture Guide S page 3187 review
New York Times January 19, 1952 13:2 Bosley Crowther review
Newsweek November 12, 1951 38:20 page 102 review
The Paramount Story page 198 synopsis
Screen World 1952 Annual page 104 listing
Time February 18, 1952 59:7 page 88 review
Variety August 29, 1951 Gene. review

Take the High Ground! (1953)

America November 28, 1953 90:9 page 249 Moira Walsh review
BFI Monthly Film Bulletin July, 1954 21:246 pages 102–103 review
Boxoffice September 26, 1953 63:22 page 1517 review
Commonweal December 11, 1953 59:10 pages 257–258 Philip T. Hartung review
A Guide to Films on the Korean War pages 100–101 review
Hollywood Goes to War page 107 mention
Life December 7, 1953 35:23 pages 185–186, 188 pictorial
The MGM Story page 257 synopsis
The Motion Picture Guide T–V page 3264 review
New York Times November 20, 1953 19:2 Bosley Crowther review
Newsweek November 16, 1953 42:20 pages 106–107 review
Oscar A to Z pages 851–852 #1995 synopsis
Richard Widmark: A Bio-Bibliography (1990, Greenwood) pages 51–52 Kim Holston synopsis
Saturday Review October 31, 1953 36:44 page 32 Hollis Alpert review
Screen World 1954 Annual page 122 listing
Time November 9, 1953 62:19 page 108 review
Variety September 23, 1953 Brog. review
War Movies page 190 review

Tank Battalion (1958)

BFI Monthly Film Bulletin December, 1958 25:299 page 159 review
Boxoffice November 3, 1958. 74:2 page 2282 review
Encyclopedia of American War Films page 567 synopsis
A Guide to Films on the Korean War page 101 review

The Motion Picture Guide T–V page 3277 review
Screen World 1959 Annual page 149 listing
Variety Oct. 29, 1958 review

Target Zero (1955)

BFI Monthly Film Bulletin February, 1956 23:265 page 21 review
Boxoffice November 19, 1955 68:4 page 1879 review
Charles Bronson (1983, St. Martin's) page 26 David Downing mention
Charles Bronson: The 95 Films and the 156 Television Appearances (1999, McFarland) pages 216–218 Michael R. Pitts synopsis
Chuck Connors: The Man Behind the Rifle page 98 profile
Encyclopedia of American War Films page 571 synopsis
The Films of Charles Bronson (1980, Citadel) pages 63–64 Jerry Vermilye synopsis
The Great Combat Pictures pages 388–390 synopsis
A Guide to Films on the Korean War pages 101–102 review
Hollywood Goes to War page 109 review
The Motion Picture Guide T–V page 3280 review
New York Times November 16, 1955 43:2 Bosley Crowther review
Screen World 1956 Annual page 159 listing
Variety November 23, 1955 Brog. review
The Warner Bros. Story page 321 synopsis

Three Wishes (1995)

Austin Chronicle October 27, 1995 Alison Macor review
Boxoffice Jon Silberg review
Chicago Sun-Times October 27, 1995 Roger Ebert review
Deseret News October 27, 1995 Chris Hicks review
Knoxville News-Sentinel Betsy Pickle review
Los Angeles Times October 27, 1995 Kevin Thomas review
Magill's Cinema Annual 1996 (1996, Gale) page 515 listing
The Motion Picture Guide 1996 Annual pages 299–300 review
San Francisco Chronicle October 27, 1995 Nick LaSalle review
San Francisco Examiner October 27, 1995 Barbara Shulgasser review
Syracuse New Times Bill DeLapp review
USA Today October 27, 1995 Susan Wloszczyna review
Washington Post October 27, 1995 Hal Hinson review

Time Limit (1957)

America October 26, 1957 98:4 page 120 Moira Walsh review
BFI Monthly Film Bulletin December, 1957 24:287 page 149 review
Boxoffice September 28, 1957 71:23 page 2142 review
Coronet October, 1957 42:6 page 10 Mark Nichols review
Encyclopedia of American War Films page 588 synopsis
A Guide to Films on the Korean War pages 102–103 review
The Lost Films of the Fifties pages 215–217 review
The Motion Picture Guide T–V page 3455 review
New York Times October 24, 1957 37:2 A. H. Weiler review
New Yorker November 2, 1957 33:36 pages 165–166 John McCarten review
Newsweek October 28, 1957 50:18 page 104 review
Richard Widmark: A Bio-Bibliography pages 61–62 synopsis

Saturday Review October 19, 1957 40:42 page 54 Arthur Knight review
Screen World 1958 Annual page 115 listing
Time October 28, 1957 70:18 pages 98, 100, 102 review
The United Artists Story page 176 synopsis
Variety September 18, 1957 Kap. review
War Movies page 194 review
When Do I Start? pages 263–269 remembrance

Tokyo File 212 (1951)

Boxoffice May 5, 1951 59:1 page 1255 review
A Guide to Films on the Korean War page 103 review
The Motion Picture Guide T-V page 3478 review
New York Times June 1, 1951 20:7 A. H. Weiler review
The RKO Story page 257 synopsis
Screen World 1952 Annual page 133 listing
Variety April 25, 1951 Brog. review

Top Secret Affair (1957)

America February 16, 1957 96:20 page 568 Moira Walsh review
Boxoffice January 19, 1957 70:13 page 2050 review
The Films of Kirk Douglas pages 141–143 review
A Guide to Films on the Korean War pages 103–104 review
Kirk Douglas (1985, St. Martin's) page 67 Michael Munn profile
Library Journal February 15, 1957 82:4 page 528 Alice G. Owen review
The Motion Picture Guide T-V page 3498 review
New York Times January 31, 1957 21:1 Bosley Crowther review
New Yorker February 9, 1957 32:51 page 108 John McCarten review
Newsweek February 18, 1957 49:7 page 110 review
Saturday Review February 2, 1957 40:5 page 25 Hollis Alpert review
Susan Hayward: Portrait of a Survivor (1981, Berkley) pages 205–206 Beverly Linet profile
Time February 4, 1957 69:5 page 92 review
The Warner Bros. Story page 328 synopsis

Torpedo Alley (1952)

The Allied Artists Checklist page 135 #401 listing
BFI Monthly Film Bulletin May, 1953 20:232 pages 76–77 review
Boxoffice December 20, 1952 62:8 page 1436 review
Charles Bronson: The 95 Films and the 156 Television Appearances pages 233–234 synopsis
Encyclopedia of American War Films pages 595–596 synopsis
The Great Combat Pictures pages 412–413 synopsis
A Guide to Films on the Korean War pages 104–105 review
The Motion Picture Guide T-V page 3504 review
New York Times December 20, 1953 15:3 Howard H. Thompson review
Screen World 1954 Annual page 91 listing
Variety December 17, 1952 Brog. review

Toward the Unknown (1956)

Boxoffice September 29, 1956 69:23 page 2016 review
The Complete Films of William Holden pages 177–179 review
The Motion Picture Guide T-V page 3513 review
New York Times September 28, 1956 24:4 A. H. Weiler review

Screen World 1957 Annual page 124 Daniel Blum listing
Time October 8, 1956 68:15 page 104 review
Variety September 26, 1956 Brog. review
The Warner Bros. Story page 325 synopsis

Truman (1995, Made for Cable)

Entertainment Weekly September 8, 1995 #291 page 68 Ken Tucker review
The Motion Picture Guide 1997 Annual pages 385–386 review

Twenty Plus Two (1961)

The Motion Picture Guide T-V page 3573 review
Screen World 1962 Annual pages 72, 129 listing

Underwater Warrior (1958)

BFI Monthly Film Bulletin June, 1958 25:293 page 79 review
Boxoffice March 10, 1958 72:20 page 2201
Library Journal April 15, 1958 83:8 page 1179 Herbert Cahoon review
The MGM Story page 289 synopsis
The Motion Picture Guide T-V page 3627 review
Screen World 1959 Annual page 139 listing
Variety February 26, 1958 Powe. review

The Walking Major (1970)

Stars and Stripes December 28, 1960 Staff Sergeant Frank Ermence profile
Stars and Stripes September 30, 2000 Richard Roesler profile

War Hunt (1962)

BFI Monthly Film Bulletin October, 1963 30:357 page 144 review
Encyclopedia of American War Films pages 636–637 synopsis
The Films of Robert Redford (1984, Citadel) pages 66–72 James Spada review
The Great Combat Pictures pages 436–437 synopsis
A Guide to Films on the Korean War pages 105–106 review
Guts and Glory pages 184–185 history
Hollywood Goes to War pages 110–111 mention
The Motion Picture Guide W-Z page 3733 review
Nation August 25, 1962 195:4 page 80 Robert Hatch review
New York Times August 8, 1962 35:2 Howard H. Thompson review
New Yorker August 18, 1962 38:26 pages 68–69 Whitney Balliett review
Newsweek August 20, 1962 60:8 page 86 review
Robert Redford: A Photographic Portrayal of the Man and His Films (1975, Popular Library) pages 10–15 Dr. Donald A. Reed review
Screen World 1962 Annual page 130 listing
Screen World 1963 Annual page 42 listing
Time August 3, 1962 80:5 page 36 review
The United Artists Story page 207 synopsis
War Movies page 205 review

War Is Hell

The Allied Artists Checklist page 140 #418 listing

BFI Monthly Film Bulletin March, 1962 29:338 page 42 review
Boxoffice Feb. 27, 1964 review
Film Daily Jan. 20, 1964 review
A Guide to Films on the Korean War pages 106–107 review
The Motion Picture Guide W–Z page 3734 review
Motion Picture Herald Feb. 5, 1964 Allen M. Widem review
New York Times Jan. 23, 1964 26:1 Bosley Crowther review
Screen World 1964 Annual page 105 listing

A Yank in Korea (1951)

BFI Monthly Film Bulletin April, 1951 18:207 page 251 review
The Columbia Checklist page 399 #2344 listing

The Columbia Story page 185 synopsis
Encyclopedia of American War Films page 672 synopsis
The Great Combat Pictures pages 454–455 synopsis
A Guide to Films on the Korean War pages 107–108 review
The Motion Picture Guide W-Z page 3943 review
New York Times April 2, 1951 29:2 A. H. Weiler review
Variety February 14, 1951 Brog. review

The Young and the Brave (1963)

Encyclopedia of American War Films page 676 synopsis
A Guide to Films on the Korean War page 108 review
The MGM Story page 313 synopsis
The Motion Picture Guide W-Z page 3968 review
Saturday Review July 27, 1963 46:30 page 34 Arthur Knight review
Screen World 1964 Annual page 63 listing

INDEX

Films in **bold** have individual entries. Page numbers in **bold** have photographs.